The Great Republic

A HISTORY OF THE AMERICAN PEOPLE

Volume II

A HISTORY OF THE AMERICAN PEOPLE

Volume II

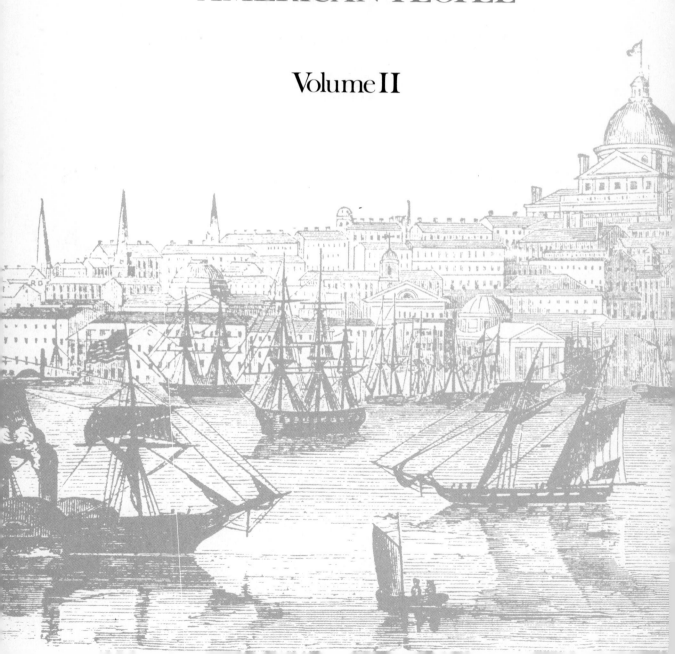

The Great Republic

BERNARD BAILYN
Harvard University

DAVID BRION DAVIS
Yale University

DAVID HERBERT DONALD
Harvard University

JOHN L. THOMAS
Brown University

ROBERT H. WIEBE
Northwestern University

GORDON S. WOOD
Brown University

D. C. HEATH AND COMPANY
Lexington, Massachusetts   Toronto

Acknowledgements

In the course of writing this book each of the authors has incurred debts to many individuals and institutions, but it would be inappropriate to list here six sets of personal acknowledgements. All the authors, however, owe a debt of gratitude to one individual, Ann Knight, history editor of D. C. Heath, for her diligence and skill in editing the manuscript, her assistance on a hundred details, and above all her wonderfully sensitive diplomacy.

B.B. J.L.T.
D.B.D. R.H.W.
D.H.D. G.S.W.

Cover illustration from a membership certificate of the Massachusetts Mechanics Association, 1800. *(Library of Congress.)*

Cartography by NORMAN CLARK ADAMS

Design and layout by ROBERT AND MARILYN DUSTIN

Photo research by JUDY POE

Contents

PART FOUR
UNITING THE REPUBLIC
1860–1890

PART FIVE
NATIONALIZING THE REPUBLIC
1890–1920

PART SIX
MODERNIZING THE REPUBLIC
1920 to the Present

Maps and Charts

Introduction

This book is a history of the American people, from the earliest settlements in the New World to the 200th anniversary of the birth of the United States as a nation. We call our book "The Great Republic," adopting a phrase Winston Churchill used to describe the United States. No one can doubt the greatness of the American republic if it is measured in terms of the size of our national domain, the vastness of our economic productivity, or the stability of our government and basic institutions. Whether that greatness has been equaled in the realm of culture, in the uses of power, or in the distribution of social justice is more debatable; on these matters readers will make up their own minds. Our task has been to present the story of America as we have understood it—a story of great achievement, of enormous material success and of soaring idealism, but a story too of conflict, of tumultuous factionalism, of injustice, rootlessness, and grinding disorder.

Each of the six sections of the book contains its own thematic emphasis, set out in a separate introduction. But there are two general themes that unify the book as a whole. The first theme is the development and constant testing of free political institutions in America. To understand the United States today, one must analyze the conditions of life in the colonial period that made popular self-government at first possible, then likely, in the end necessary. One must see how the American Revolution expressed the longings of provincial Britons for a total reform of political culture and projected this idealism onto a nation of continental scale. One must discover how democratic institutions and practices expanded during the nineteenth century and received their crucial testing in the American Civil War. One must understand how urbanization and industrialization produced a new political culture in the United States by the beginning of the twentieth century. And one must ask how free, democratic institutions have sustained themselves through decades of international crises and world wars. Without an understanding of popular self-government, from eighteenth-century republicanism to modern political democracy, no sense at all can be made of the history of the American people.

A second theme, which has persisted from the very earliest days, is the tension between majority rule and minority rights in America. From the beginning the New World provided a feast for the ambitious, for the discontented, for the individualistic. Its vast resources, open for exploitation by the talented, the shrewd, the enterprising, and the energetic, have produced a society constantly in danger of fragmentation. The huge geographical extent of the country has nourished divisive interests of all kinds, and the admixture of peoples from every quarter of the world has led to ethnic and cultural pluralism, at times so strong as to threaten the disintegration of the social fabric. At the same time, however, there have been, from the founding of the Puritan colonies to the present, powerful forces working toward social stability and agreement.

The Founding Fathers correctly recognized that this constant struggle between the general interest and the special interests posed the most severe threat to the continuance of a self-governing democratic nation. They knew there would be no automatic harmonizing of regional, economic, and social group ambitions, no easy reconciliation of competing needs and desires. The divisive forces, they knew, would be powerful; the inevitable clashes of opinion and the conflicts of interest and ambition would be bitter and intense. At the same time they feared centralizing tendencies that might threaten despotism, and worried that minorities might become subject to the tyranny of majorities. Could public institutions sensitive to popular pressures successfully reconcile these conflicts? Could they provide the instruments of compromise that would make and remake a stable, nation-wide agreement from a tumult of clashing ambitions?

The two hundred years of our national history clearly show that the Founding Fathers did not resolve this tension between the interest of the society as a whole and the special interests of its parts, but the federal system they devised provided mechanisms for the mediation of the struggles. With the one horrendous exception of the Civil War, the institutions set up by the Founders have succeeded in harnessing the explosive energies of the American people. Often the balance has been precarious between the interest of society as a whole and that of its parts, between the needs of the nation and the rights of regions and states, between the power of majorities and the desires of minorities. From time to time the balance has tipped, first in the one direction, then in the other, yet the eighteenth-century republican design remains viable—still hopeful, still workable as a result of constant adjustment, despite the tremendous pressure that constantly threatens to overwhelm it.

The tracing of these two themes—the development of free political institutions in America and the maintaining of a balance between majority rule and minority rights—links together the six sections written by six separate authors and gives an overarching unity to the book. The sections are further unified by the authors' shared view of the nature of history. We all believe that historical knowledge is not simply the accumulation of information about the past. It is a mode of understanding. The historian is obliged not merely to describe what happened but to explain it, to make clear why things developed as they did. We share, too, an aversion to any simply deterministic interpretation of historical change. At certain junctures economic and demographic forces are dominant, but they are themselves shaped by cultural forces. Great political events are at times triggered by economic drives, but at other times they are responses to beliefs and to aspirations that are not a direct reflection of economic needs. Political decisions alter economic life, social organization, and even the way people think— yet economic, social, and intellectual forces change politics too.

History, we believe, is a complex intermingling of forces, whose relations fall into no predetermined pattern. We have sought to explore this complexity as well as to narrate the succession of important events. The book is therefore self-contained, in that it supplies the basic factual information and the essential narratives that readers will need, but it presents that information within a framework of analysis and explanation. We hope that *The Great Republic* will help readers understand why and how America developed as it did, and where, as a result of this historical evolution, we have arrived after more than three centuries of growth and two centuries of nationhood.

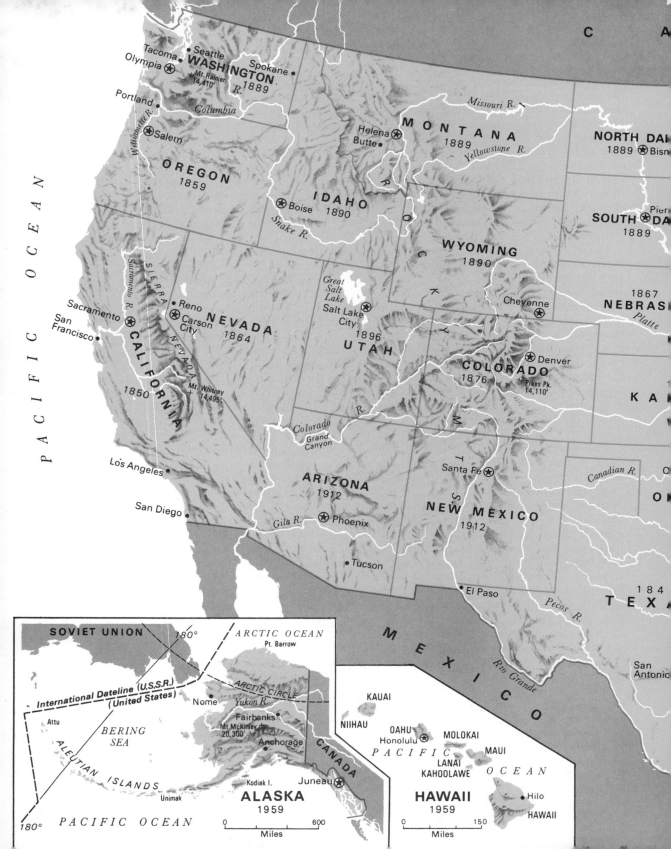

The United States of America

★ ★ ★ ★ ★ ★ ★ ★ ★ ★ ★ ★ ★ ★ ★

⊛ National Capital ⊛ State Capital • Other Major Cities
1845 Date of Admission to the Union

0   100   200   300   400   500
Scale of Miles

CARVED IVORY AMERICAN EAGLE
(MID-NINETEENTH CENTURY)

The Eagle, the ancient Roman
symbol of Jove, was adopted in
1782 as part of the Great Seal of
the United States. By the mid-
nineteenth century, the eagle had
become an increasingly popular
symbol of power and grandeur
and was used everywhere from
figure heads and military insignia
to the fine and decorative arts.
(*The Museum of Fine Arts, Boston*).

PART FOUR

Uniting the Republic

1860-1890

DAVID HERBERT DONALD

These [Northern] people hate us, annoy us, and would have us assassinated by our slaves if they dared," a Southern leader wrote when he learned that a "Black Republican," Abraham Lincoln, would certainly be elected President in 1860. "They are a *different* people from us, whether better or worse and *there is no love* between us. Why then continue together?" The sectional contests of the previous decades suggested that Americans had become members of two distinct, and conflicting, nationalities. By 1860, Northerners and Southerners appeared not to speak the same language, to share the same moral code, or to obey the same law. Compromise could no longer cobble together a union between two such fundamentally different peoples. "I do not see how a barbarous and a civilized community can constitute one state," Ralph Waldo Emerson gravely concluded for many Northerners. "The North and the South are heterogeneous and are better apart," agreed the New Orleans *Bee*. "We [Southerners] are doomed if we proclaim not our political independence."

On first thought, the four-year civil war that broke out in 1861 seems powerfully to confirm this idea that the Union and the Confederacy were two distinct nations. Yet the conduct of the war suggested that Northerners and Southerners were not so different as their political and intellectual leaders had maintained.

At the beginning of the conflict both governments tried in much the same ways to mobilize for battle their invertebrate, unorganized societies. As the war progressed, both Union and Confederacy adopted much the same diplomatic, military, and economic policies. By the end of the war both governments were committed to abolishing slavery, the one institution that had most clearly divided the sections in 1860.

The events of the postwar period gave further evidence that the inhabitants of the North and the South were—what they had always been—part of the same nationality. Though some Republicans wanted a radical revolution in the social and economic system of the conquered Confederacy, there were relatively few, and only limited, social experiments or political innovations during Reconstruction. In both the North and the South, shared beliefs in limited government, in economic laissez-faire, and in the superiority of the white race blocked drastic change, while shared economic interests and national political parties pulled the sections back into a common pattern of cooperation.

In the backward glance of history, then, the conflicts and the quarrels of the Civil War era take on a significance different from their meaning to participants and contemporaries. In retrospect it is clear that the Civil War was not so much a contest between two separate nations as a struggle within the American nation to define a boundary between the centralizing, nationalizing tendencies in American life and the opposing tendencies toward localism, parochialism, and fragmentation. The issue, then, was the familiar one of majority rule and minority rights: How could a society follow the dictates of the majority of its members without infringing on the essential interests of those who were in the minority? For Americans in the 1860s, this was no new question; it had been the central concern of American political philosophers from James Madison to John C. Calhoun. Even today, when the balance of power has shifted so markedly toward a national, centralized society, the rights of regional and ethnic minorities remain a topic for hot dispute.

Perhaps there can be no final resolution to the problem of reconciling, in a single nation, the interests of the whole and those of the parts. Certainly the Civil War generation did not find one. But the painful experience of war and its aftermath led them to work out a series of informal agreements and understandings that, on the one hand, guaranteed to the national government sufficient strength to sustain the interests of the country as a whole. On the other hand, this loose set of compromises secured some degree of autonomy to many—but not all—local and parochial groups adversely affected by centralization. After decades of strife and years of bloodshed, Americans, both in the North and the South, came to accept this pragmatic compromise. It was a solution that was neither completely satisfactory nor wholly logical. It rested less upon reason than upon emotion. It reflected the hard-learned lesson of the Civil War that Americans were, after all, one people.

21

The Limits of Innovation, 1865-1869

"A house divided against itself cannot stand," Abraham Lincoln prophesied in 1858. The Civil War proved that the United States would stand, not as a loose confederation of sovereign states but as one nation, indivisible. Never again would there be talk of secession. The war also ended slavery, the most divisive institution in antebellum America. Weakened by the advances of the Union armies and undermined by Lincoln's Emancipation Proclamation, slavery received its death blow in February 1865, when the Congress adopted the Thirteenth Amendment, outlawing slavery and involuntary servitude. Ratified by three-fourths of the states, the amendment became a part of the Constitution in December 1865.

But the Civil War did not settle the terms and conditions on which the several states, sections, races, and classes would live in the firmly united "house." Those problems formed the agenda of the Reconstruction era, one of the most complex and controversial periods in American history. During these postwar years some basic questions had to be answered: What, if any, punishment should be imposed on Southern whites who had supported the Confederate attempt to disrupt the Union? How were the recently emancipated slaves to be guaranteed their freedom, and what civil and political rights did freedmen have? When and on what conditions were the Southern states so recently in rebellion to be readmitted to the Union—that is, entitled to vote in national elections, to have Senators and Representatives seated in the United States Congress, and, in general, to become once more full-fledged, equal members in the national body politic?

The initial moves to answer these questions came from the President, whose powers had been greatly expanded during the war years. President Lincoln in December 1863 announced a generous program of amnesty to repentant rebels and inaugurated a plan for reorganizing loyal governments in the South when as few as 10 percent of the voters in 1860 were willing to support them. After the assassination of Lincoln in April 1865, President Andrew Johnson, his successor, continued the process of Reconstruction under a similar plan. Although Johnson required former Confederate leaders and Southerners with estates worth more than $20,000 to make individual applications for pardon—applications that were for the most part promptly granted—he, like Lincoln, expected Southern whites to take the lead in establishing new state governments loyal to the Union. To initiate the process he appointed a provisional governor for each of the former Confederate states (except those where Lincoln had already initiated Reconstruction) and directed them to convene constitutional conventions. These were expected to adopt the Thirteenth Amendment ending slavery, nullify or repeal the ordinances of secession, and repudiate state debts incurred for the prosecution of the war. By early 1866 each of the states that had once formed the Confederacy completed these required steps, and the President viewed the process of Reconstruction as concluded. He recommended that the senators and representatives chosen by these reorganized governments be promptly given their rightful seats in Congress.

From the outset presidential Reconstruction had its critics. If Lincoln's plan met opposition, Johnson's program was certain to be fiercely attacked. For one reason, Congress, which had jealously watched the executive branch augment its power during the war, was ready to reassert its equality, if not its hegemony. For another, Andrew Johnson, a Tennessee Democrat and former slaveholder, had no popular mandate, as had President Lincoln, nor did the taciturn, inflexible, and pugnacious new occupant of the White House understand that politics is the art of compromise.

After an initial attempt to cooperate with the new President, Republican leaders in 1866 began to devise their own plans for Reconstruction. The first congressional plan was embodied in the Fourteenth Amendment to the Constitution, which made it clear that blacks were citizens of the United States and tried to define the rights and privileges of American citizens. When the Southern states refused to ratify this amendment, congressional Republicans moved in 1867 to a more stringent program of reorganizing the South by requiring Negro suffrage. Under this second plan of congressional Reconstruction, every Southern state (except for Tennessee, which had been readmitted to the Union in 1866) received a new constitution that guaranteed to men of all races equal protection of the laws, and between 1868 and 1871 all were readmitted to the Union. Republican governments, which depended heavily on Negro votes, controlled these states for a period ranging from a few months in the case of Virginia to nine years in the case of Louisiana.

Paths Not Taken

Contemporaries called this the period of Radical Reconstruction or, very often, Black Reconstruction, and it is easy to understand why many Americans of the 1860s and '70s viewed these changes as little short of revolutionary. To their Constitution, which had not been altered since 1804, were added during the five years after the Civil War the Thirteenth Amendment, ending slavery, the Fourteenth Amendment, defining the rights of citizens, and the Fifteenth Amendment (1870), prohibiting discrimination in voting on account of race or color. The national government, so recently tottering on the edge of defeat, was now more powerful than in any previous point in American history. The Southern ruling class of whites, lately in charge of their own independent government, were petitioners for pardon. More than 3 million blacks, slaves only a few months earlier, were free men, entitled to the same privileges as all other citizens. Americans fairly gasped at the extent and the speed of the transformation wrought in their society, and it is hardly surprising that most subsequent historians accepted this contemporary view of the Reconstruction era as one of turbulent disorder.

Without denying that real and important changes did occur during the Reconstruction period, it might help to put these into perspective by inventing a little conterfactual history, a recital of conceivable historical scenarios that were never acted out. For instance, it would be easy to imagine how the victorious North might have turned angrily on the prostrate South. In 1865, Northerners had just finished four years of war that cost the Union army more than 360,000 casualties. To destroy the Confederacy required Americans of that and subsequent generations to pay in taxes at least $10 billion. Northerners had reason to believe, moreover, that their Confederate opponents had prosecuted the war with fiendish barbarity. Sober Union congressmen informed their constituents that the Confederates employed "Indian savages" to scalp and mutilate the Union dead. Reliable Northern newspapers told how in April 1864 General Nathan Bedford Forrest and his Confederates overran the defenses of Fort Pillow, Tennessee, manned by a Negro regiment, and, refusing to accept surrender, deliberately beat, shot, and burned their prisoners. The influential *Harper's Weekly Magazine* carried apparently authentic drawings of a goblet that a Southerner had made from a Yankee soldier's skull and of necklaces made of Yankee teeth that Southern ladies wore. When Union armies liberated Northern prisoners from such hell-holes as Andersonville, Georgia, pictures of these half-starved skeletons of men, clad in grimy tatters of their Union uniforms, convinced Northerners that Jefferson Davis's policy had been "to starve and freeze and kill off by inches the prisoners he dares not butcher outright."

When the murder of Abraham Lincoln by the Southern sympathizer, John Wilkes Booth, added to this hyperemotionalism, an outraged North could easily have turned on the conquered Confederacy in vengeance. The victorious Northerners might have executed Jefferson Davis, Alexander H. Stephens, and a score of other leading Confederates and might have sent thousands more into permanent exile. The triumphant Union might have erased the boundaries of the Southern states and divided the whole region into new, conquered territories. They might have enforced the confiscation acts already on the statute books and have seized the plantations of rebels, for distribution to the freedmen. In short, the North could very easily have adopted the policy advocated by the generally cautious, middle-of-the-road Senator from Ohio, John Sherman: "We should not only brand the leading rebels with infamy, but the whole rebellion should wear the badge of the penitentiary, so that for this generation at least, no man who has taken part in it would dare to justify or palliate it."

No such drastic course was followed. With the exception of Major Henry Wirtz, commandant of the infamous Andersonville prison, who was hanged, no Confederate was executed for "war crimes." A few Southern political leaders were imprisoned for their part in the "rebellion," but in most cases their release was prompt. To be sure, Jefferson Davis was kept in shackles for two years at Fortress Monroe, and he was under indictment for treason until 1869, when all charges were dropped. His case was, however, as unusual as it was extreme, and one reason for the long delay in bringing him to trial was the certainty that no jury,

Northern or Southern, would find him guilty. There was no general confiscation of the property of Confederates, no dividing up on plantations.

Equally conceivable is another scenario—another version of history that did not happen—this time featuring the Southern whites. For four years Confederate citizens, like their counterparts in the Union, had been subjected to a barrage of propaganda designed to prove that the enemy was little less than infernal in his purposes. Many believed the Southern editor who claimed that Lincoln's program was "Emancipation, Confiscation, Conflagration, and Extermination." According to the North Carolina educator Calvin H. Wiley, the North had "summoned to its aid every fierce and cruel and licentious passion of the human heart"; to defeat the Confederacy it was ready to use "the assassin's dagger, the midnight torch, . . . poison, famine and pestilence." Such charges were easy to credit in the many Southern families that had relatives in Northern prison camps, such as the one at Elmira, New York, where 775 of 8347 Confederate prisoners died within three months for want of proper food, water, and medicine. The behavior of Union troops in the South, especially of Sherman's "bummers" in Georgia and the Carolinas, gave Southerners every reason to fear the worst if the Confederate government failed.

RUINS OF RICHMOND

When the Confederate government evacuated Richmond on April 3, 1865, orders were given to burn supplies that might fall into the enemy's hands. There were heavy explosions as ironclads, armories, and arsenals were blown up. The next morning, as the fires spread, a mob of men and women, whites and blacks, began to plunder the city. (*Library of Congress.*)

It would therefore have been perfectly reasonable for Confederate armies in 1865, overwhelmed by Union numbers, to disband quietly, disappear into the countryside, and carry on guerrilla operations against the Northern invaders. Indeed, on the morning of the day when Lee surrendered at Appomattox, Confederate General E. P. Alexander advocated just such a plan. He argued that if Lee's soldiers took to the woods with their rifles, perhaps two-thirds of the Army of Northern Virginia could escape capture. "We would be like rabbits and partridges in the bushes," he claimed, "and they could not scatter to follow us." The history of more recent wars of national liberation suggests that Alexander's judgment was absolutely correct. But even had his strategy not proved practicable, it would have given time for thousands of leading Southern politicians and planters, together with their families, to go safely into exile, as the Tories did during the American Revolution.

But, once again, no such events occurred. Lee firmly put down talk of guerrilla warfare and reminded his subordinates that they must henceforth think of "the country as a whole." To Virginia soldiers who pressed around him after the surrender, he gave the advice: "Go home, all you boys who fought with me, and help to build up the shattered fortunes of our old state." Following Lee's example, commanders of the other Southern armies also quietly surrendered, and Confederate soldiers promptly became civilians. Some few Confederate leaders did go into exile. For instance, General Jubal A. Early fled to Mexico and thence to Canada, where he tried to organize a Southern exodus to New Zealand; but finding that nobody wanted to follow him, he returned to his home and his law practice in Virginia. A few hundred Confederates did migrate to Mexico and to Brazil. But most followed the advice of General Wade Hampton of South Carolina, who urged his fellow Southerners to "devote their whole energies to the restoration of law and order, the reestablishment of agriculture and commerce, the promotion of education and the rebuilding of our cities and dwellings which have been laid in ashes."

Still a third counterfactual historical scenario comes readily to mind. Southern blacks, who had been for generations oppressed in slavery, now for the first time had disciplined leaders in the thousands of Negro soldiers who had served in the Union army. They also had arms. Very easily they could have turned in revenge on their former masters. Seizing the plantations and other property of the whites, the freedmen might have made of the former Confederacy a black nation. If the whites had dared to resist, the South might have been the scene of massacres as bloody as those in Haiti at the beginning of the nineteenth century, when Toussaint L'Ouverture and Dessalines drove the French out of that island.

Many Southern whites feared, or even expected, that the Confederacy would become another Santo Domingo. For more than a year after the war, Northern reporters in the South noted "a general feeling of insecurity on the part of the whites," derived from their "vague and terrible fears of a servile insurrection." Whites were much troubled by reports that blacks were joining the Union League, an organization that had originated in the North during the war to stimulate patriotism but during the Reconstruction era became the bulwark of the Republican party in the South. The secrecy imposed by the League on its members and its frequent nocturnal meetings alarmed whites, and they readily believed reports that the blacks were collecting arms and ammunition for a general uprising. Fearfully, Southern whites read newspaper accounts of minor racial clashes. Indeed, whites were told, racial tension was so great that blacks "might break into open insurrection at any time."

But no such insurrection occurred. Though the freedmen unquestionably coveted the lands of their former masters, they did not seize them. Indeed, black leaders consistently discouraged talk of extralegal confiscation of plantations. Nor did freedmen threaten the lives or the rights of whites. One of the earliest black political conventions held in Alabama urged a policy of "peace, friendship, and good will toward all men — especially toward our white fellow-citizens among whom our lot is cast." That tone was the dominant one throughout the Reconstruction period, and in many states blacks took the lead in repealing laws that disfranchised former Confederates or disqualified them from holding office.

The point of these three exercises in counterfactual history is to suggest the inadequacy of traditional accounts of the Reconstruction era as a period of revolutionary change. To those who lived through these years change did seem to come swiftly and drastically, but in retrospect it is clear that Southern society was transformed only to a quite limited degree. The unprecedented conditions of the Reconstruction era required innovation, but the shared beliefs and institutions of the American people, North and South, black and white, restricted the amount of change that would be tolerated.

Constitutionalism as a Limit to Change

One set of ideas that sharply curbed social experimentation and political innovation during the Reconstruction period can be labeled constitutionalism. It is hard for twentieth-century Americans to understand the reverence with which their nineteenth-century ancestors viewed the Constitution. In a country that lacked a ruling family, a hereditary aristocracy, and an established church, that document, next to the flag, was the most powerful symbol of American nationhood. Tested in the trial of civil war, the Constitution continued to command respect approaching veneration during the Reconstruction era.

Among the most sacrosanct provisions of the Constitution were those that separated the powers of the state and the national governments. Although the national government greatly expanded its role during the war years, Americans still tended to think of it as performing only the specific functions enumerated in the Constitution, which granted it virtually no authority to act directly on any individual citizen. The national government could not, for instance, prevent or punish crime; it had no control over public education; it could not outlaw discrimination against racial minorities; and it could not even intervene to maintain public order unless requested to do so by the state government. Virtually everybody agreed, therefore, that if any laws regulating social and economic life were required, they must be the work of state and local, not of national, government.

Nobody, consequently, even contemplated the possibility that some federal agency might be needed to supervise the demobilization after Appomattox. Everybody simply assumed that after some 200,000 of the Union army volunteers bravely paraded down Pennsylvania Avenue on May 23–24, 1865, and received applause from President Johnson, the cabinet, the generals, and the members of the diplomatic corps, the soldiers would disband and go back to their peaceful homes. This is precisely what they did. Of the more than one million volunteers in the Union army on May 1, 1865, two-thirds were mustered out by August, four-fifths by November. Of the 68,000 sailors, artisans, and laborers in the Union navy at the beginning of 1865, only 12,000 remained in active service by December. To the demobilized soldiers and sailors, the United States government offered no assistance in finding jobs, in purchasing housing, or in securing further education. It paid pensions to those injured in the war and to the families of those who had been killed, but beyond that it assumed no responsibility. Nor did anybody think of asking the national government to oversee the transition from a wartime economy to an era of peace. Without notice the various bureaus of the army and navy departments by the end of April 1865 simply suspended requisitions and purchases, government arsenals slowed down their production, and surplus supplies were sold off.

Hardly anybody had the thought that the national government might play a role in rebuilding the wartorn South. Everybody recognized that the devastation in the South was immense and ominous. The Confederate dead totaled more than a quarter of a million. In Mississippi, for instance, one-third of the white men of military age had been killed or disabled for life. Most Southern cities were in ruins. Two-thirds of the Southern railroads were totally destroyed; the rest barely creaked along on worn-out rails with broken-down engines. But none of this was thought to be the concern of the United States government.

The failure of the national government to come to the rescue was not caused by vindictiveness. To the contrary, Union officials often behaved with marked generosity toward Confederates. After Lee's hungry battalions surrendered at Appomattox, Grant's soldiers freely shared with them their rations. All over the South, Federal military officials drew on the full Union army storehouses to feed the hungry. In distributing these necessities, the Union army made no discrimination; newly freed slaves stood in line with former Confederate soldiers, all with bags to be filled. But beyond these attempts to avert starvation the Federal government did not go, and very few thought that it should. Not until the twentieth century did the United States make it a policy to pour vast sums of money into the rehabilitation of enemies it had defeated in war.

Rebuilding had, therefore, to be the work of the Southern state and local authorities, and this task imposed a heavy tax on their meager resources. In Mississippi, one-fifth of the entire state revenue in 1866 was needed to provide artificial limbs for soldiers maimed in the war. For the larger tasks of physical restoration, the resources of the South were obviously inadequate. Borrowing a leaf from antebellum experience, Southern governments did the only thing they knew how to do—namely, they lent the credit of the state to back up the bonds of private companies that promised to rebuild railroads and other necessary facilities. Since these companies were underfinanced and since the credit of the Southern state governments after Appomattox was, to say the least, questionable, these bonds had to be sold at disadvantageous prices and at exorbitant rates of interest. In later years, when many of these companies defaulted on their obligations and Southern state governments had to make good on their guarantees, these expenditures would be condemned as excessive and extravagant, and Democrats blamed them on the Republican regimes established in the South after 1868. In fact, however, the need for physical restoration immediately after the war was so obvious and so pressing that nearly every government, whether controlled by Democrats or Republicans, underwrote corporations that promised to rebuild the region.

Even in dealing with the freedmen—the some 3 million slaves emancipated as a result of the war—the United States government tried to pursue a hands-off policy. Few influential leaders, either in the North or in the South, thought that it was the function of the national government to supervise the blacks' transition from slavery to freedom. Politicians did not foresee that freedmen would require guidance, counseling, and, most of all, education in order to become free and equal citizens. Even abolitionists, genuinely devoted to the welfare of blacks, were so accustomed to thinking of the Negro as "God's image in ebony"—in other words, a white man in a black skin—that they had no plans for assisting him after emancipation. In 1865, William Lloyd Garrison urged the American Anti-Slavery Society to disband, since it had fulfilled its function, and he suspended the publication of *The Liberator*. Sharing the same point of view, the American Freedmen's Inquiry Commission, set up by the Union war department in 1863, unanimously opposed further governmental actions to protect the blacks. "The negro does best when let alone," argued one member of the commission, Samuel Gridley Howe, noted alike for his work with the deaf, dumb, and blind and for his hostility to slavery; "we must beware of all attempts to prolong his servitude, under pretext of taking care of him. The white man has tried taking care of the negro, by slavery, by apprenticeship, by colonization, and has failed disastrously in all; now let the negro try to take care of himself."

But the problem of the care of the freedmen could not be dismissed so easily. Wherever Union armies advanced into the South, they were "greeted by an irruption of negroes of all ages, complexions and sizes, men, women, boys and girls . . . waving hats and bonnets with the most ludicrous caperings and ejaculations of joy." "The poor delighted creatures thronged upon us," a Yankee soldier reported, and they insisted: "We'se gwin wid you all." "What shall be done with them?" commanders in the field plaintively wired Washington.

The administration in Washington had no comprehensive answer. Initially it looked to private philanthropic organizations to rush food, clothing, and medicine to the thousands of blacks that thronged in unsanitary camps around the headquarters of each Union army. The New England Freedmen's Aid Society, the American Missionary Association, and the Philadelphia Society of Friends promptly responded, but it was soon clear that the problem was too great for private charity.

Slowly, and without much guidance from Washington, Union commanders in the field began to improvise plans to assist the blacks clustered about their camps. In Louisiana, General N. P. Banks told freedmen that they had to support themselves, either by working on the levees or at other public employment or by returning to labor on the plantations, where, Banks said, "they belong." Farther north, Grant named Chaplain John Eaton general superintendent of all freedmen in his military department, which consisted mostly of Mississippi and Tennessee, and directed him to supervise the freedmen's camps, to provide for their education and health, and to set them to work picking cotton on abandoned plantations.

As such piecemeal and often inconsistent programs for dealing with the freedmen got under way, sentiment grew in the North for the creation of a general "Emancipation Bureau" in the federal government—only to conflict directly with the even stronger sentiment that the national government had limited powers. Out of this conflict emerged the Freedmen's Bureau Act of March 3, 1865. Congress established, under the jurisdiction of the war department, the Bureau of Refugees, Freedmen, and Abandoned Lands and entrusted to the new agency, for one year after the end of the war, "control of all subjects relating to refugees and freedmen." To head the new organization, Lincoln named Oliver O. Howard, a Union general less conspicuous for military skill than for devotion to Christianity and for paternalistic views toward blacks.

At first glance, the Freedmen's Bureau seems to have been a notable exception to the rule that the national government should take only a minor, passive role in the restoration of the South. Howard had a vision of a compassionate network of "teachers, ministers, farmers, superintendents" working together to aid and elevate the freedmen, and, under his enthusiastic impetus, the bureau appointed agents in each of the former Confederate states. The most urgent task of the bureau was issuing food and clothing, mostly from surplus army stores, to destitute freedmen and other Southern refugees. This action unquestionably prevented mass starvation in the South. The bureau also took the initiative in getting work for freedmen. Fearful on the one hand that Southern planters would attempt to overwork and underpay the freedmen, troubled on the other by the widespread belief that blacks, once emancipated, were not willing to work, the bureau agents brought laborers and landlords together and insisted that workers sign labor contracts.

No part of the bureau's work was more successful than its efforts in the field of education. The slow work of educating the illiterate Southern blacks had already begun under the auspices of army chaplains and Northern benevolent societies before the creation of the bureau, and Howard's bureau continued to cooperate with these agencies, providing housing for black schools, paying teachers, and helping to establish normal schools and colleges for the training of black teachers. All these educational efforts received an enthusiastic welcome from the freedmen. During the day, classrooms were thronged with black children learning the rudiments of language and arithmetic; in the evenings they were filled with adults who were "fighting with their letters," learning to read so that they would not be "made ashamed" by their children. "The progress of the scholars is in all cases creditable and in some remarkable," reported one of the teachers. "How richly God has endowed them, and how beautifully their natures would have expanded under a tender and gentle culture."

Even more innovative was the work of the bureau in allocating lands to the freedmen. During the war many plantations in the path of Union armies had been deserted by their owners, and army commanders like Grant arranged to have these tilled by the blacks who flocked to his camp. The largest tract of such abandoned land was in the Sea Islands of South Carolina, which were overrun by Federal troops in the fall of 1861. Though speculators bought up large

PRIMARY SCHOOL IN CHARGE OF MRS. GREEN — VICKSBURG, MISSISSIPPI

Freedmen were avid for learning. In schools sponsored by the Freedmen's Bureau, grandparents sat alongside toddlers, as all sought knowledge.

amounts of this land during the war, sizable numbers of black residents were able to secure small holdings. When General W. T. Sherman marched through South Carolina he ordered that the Sea Islands and the abandoned plantations along the river banks for thirty miles from the coast be reserved for Negro settlement and directed that black settlers be given "possessory titles" to tracts of this land not larger than forty acres. The act creating the Freedmen's Bureau clearly contemplated the continuation of these policies, for it authorized the new bureau to lease confiscated lands to freedmen and to "loyal refugees." The bureau could also sell the land to these tenants and give them "such title thereto as the United States can convey."

But if the Freedmen's Bureau was an exception to the policy of limited federal involvement in the reconstruction process, it was at best a partial exception. Though the agency did invaluable work, it was a feeble protector of the freedmen. Authorized to recruit only a minimal staff, Howard was obliged to rely heavily on Union army officers stationed in the South—at just the time when the Union army was being demobilized. Consequently the bureau never had enough manpower to look after the rights of some 3 million freedmen; toward the end of its first year of operation it employed only 799 men, 424 of whom were soldiers on temporary, assigned duty. Important as the work of the bureau was in Negro education, its chief function was to stimulate private philanthropy in this field. In providing land for the freedmen, the bureau was handicapped because it

CELEBRATION FOR NEWLY MARRIED BLACK COUPLES

Legally slaves could not marry. When blacks became free, they sought to regularize their marital arrangements and to legitimatize their children. Many Southern states passed blanket laws for this purpose, but thousands of Negroes desired formal wedding ceremonies. *(Frank Leslie's Illustrated Newspaper, August 19, 1871.)*

controlled only about 800,000 acres of arable land in the entire South, enough at best for perhaps one black family in forty. Moreover, its efforts to distribute lands to the Negroes were repeatedly undercut both by the Congress and the President. The very wording of the act creating the bureau suggested congressional uncertainty about who actually owned deserted and confiscated lands in the South. General Sherman announced that the "possessory titles" he had issued were valid only so long as the war lasted; and President Johnson issued pardons to Southerners that explicitly included "restoration of all rights of property." In October 1865, the President directed Howard to go in person to the Sea Islands to notify blacks there that they did not hold legal title to the land and to advise them "to make the best terms they could" with the white owners. When blacks bitterly resisted what they considered the bureau's betrayal, Union soldiers descended on the islands and forced blacks who would not sign labor contracts with the restored white owners to leave. Elsewhere in the South the record of the bureau was equally dismal.

In short, belief in the limited role to be played by the national government affected the rehabilitation of the freedmen, just as it did the physical restoration of the South and the demobilization in the North. In all these matters, the United States government was supposed to play the smallest possible part, and its minimal activities were to be of the briefest duration.

It is certain that most whites in the North and in the South fully approved these stringent limitations on the activities of the national government. What the masses of freedmen thought is harder to determine. On the one hand stands the protest of Sea Island blacks when they learned they were about to be dispossessed: "Why, General Howard, why do you take away our lands? You take them from us who have always been true, always true to the Government! You give them to our all-time enemies! That is not right!" On the other is Frederick Douglass's reply to the question, "What shall we do with the Negroes?" The greatest black spokesman of the era answered: "Do nothing with them; mind your business, and let them mind theirs. Your *doing* with them is their greatest misfortune. They have been undone by your doings, and all they now ask and really have need of at your hands, is just to let them alone."

Laissez-Faire as a Limit to Change

Along with the idea of limited government went the doctrine of laissez-faire ("let things alone"), which sharply limited what the government could do to solve economic problems that arose after the Civil War. Except for a handful of Radical Republicans, such as Charles Sumner and Thaddeus Stevens, most congressmen, like most academic economists, were unquestioning believers in an American version of laissez-faire. Though they were willing to promote economic growth through protective tariffs and land grants to railroads, they abhorred governmental inspection, regulation, and control of economic activities. These

A GROUP OF FREEDMEN IN RICHMOND, VIRGINIA, 1865

A central problem of the Reconstruction years was the future of the freedmen. Nobody had made any plans for a smooth transition from slavery to freedom. Consequently, when emancipation came, as one former slave recalled, "We didn't know where to go. Momma and them didn't know where to go, you see, after freedom broke. Just like you turned something out, you know. They didn't know where to go." *(Library of Congress.)*

matters were ruled by the inexorable laws of economics. "You need not think it necessary to have Washington exercise a political providence over the country," William Graham Sumner, the brilliant professor of political and social science, told his students at Yale. "God has done that a great deal better by the laws of political economy."

No violation of economic laws was deemed more heinous than interference with the right of private property—the right of an individual or group to purchase, own, use, and dispose of property without any interference from governmental authorities. There was consequently never a chance that congressmen would support Thaddeus Stevens's radical program to confiscate all Southern farms larger than 200 acres and to divide the seized land into 40-acre tracts among the freedmen. "No man in America," announced the *Nation,* a journal that spoke for educated Republicans, "has any right to anything which he has not honestly earned, or which the lawful owner has not thought proper to give him." Stevens's plan could lead only to socialism, or worse. "An attempt to justify the confiscation of Southern land under the pretense of doing justice to the freedmen," declared the New York *Times,* "strikes at the root of all property rights in both sections. It concerns Massachusetts quite as much as Mississippi."

Informed opinion in the North held that the best program of Reconstruction was to allow the laws of economics to rule in the South with the least possible interference by the government. Behind this theory lay the judgment, accepted by Republicans long before the Civil War, that the South was a land on which slavery had brought "the calamity of premature and consumptive decline, in the midst of free, vigorous and expanding states." The war served as drastic surgery to remove the cancer of slavery. Now it was reasonable to expect that, though there might be some soreness and subsequent healing, Southerners, white and black, should, without further governmental meddling, set about making money and acquiring property just like the free men in the northern and western states.*

Obsessed by laissez-faire, Northern theorists left out of their calculations the physical devastation wrought in the South by the war, and they did not recognize how feeble were the section's resources to rebuild its economy. Even excluding the loss of property in slaves, the total assessed property evaluation of the Southern states shrank by 43 percent between 1860 and 1865.

Northern pundits also failed to take into account the psychological dimensions of economic readjustment in the South. For generations Southern whites had persuaded themselves that slavery was the natural condition of the black race, and they truly believed that their slaves were devoted to them. But as Union armies approached and slaves defected, they were compelled to recognize that they had been living in a world of misconceptions and deceits.

So shattering was the idea that slaves were free that some Southern whites simply refused to accept it. Even after the Confederate surrender, some owners would not inform their slaves of their new status. As late as July 1865, according to officials of the Freedmen's Bureau, planters in Mississippi were resorting to "whipping and the most severe modes of punishment . . . to compel the Freedmen to remain at the old plantations and the negro [was] kept in ignorance of his real condition." A few planters angrily announced they were so disillusioned that they would never again have anything to do with blacks, and they sought, vainly, to persuade European immigrants and Chinese coolies to work their fields.

*Discussion of economic changes and problems in the North is reserved for the following chapter.

Even those whites who overtly accepted the reality of emancipation betrayed the fact that, on a deeper emotional level, they still could only think of blacks as performing forced labor. "The general interest both of the white man and of the negroes requires that he should be kept as near to the condition of slavery as possible, and as far from the condition of the white man as is practicable," explained Edmund Rhett of South Carolina. "Negroes must be made to work, or else cotton and rice must cease to be raised for export." The contracts that planters in 1865, under pressure from the Freedmen's Bureau, entered into with their former slaves were further indications of the same attitude. Even the most generous of these contracts provided that blacks were "not to leave the premises during work hours without the consent of the Proprietor," that they would conduct "themselves faithfully, honestly and civilly," and that they would behave with "perfect obedience" toward the land owner.

Blacks, too, had difficulties in adjusting to their new status that were never anticipated by the devotees of laissez-faire. *Freedom*—that word so often whispered in the slave quarters—went to the heads of some blacks. A few took the coming of "Jubilee," with the promise to put the bottom rail on top, quite literally. Nearly all blacks had an initial impulse to test their freedom, to make sure it was real. As Patience Johnson, a former slave in the Laurens District of South Carolina explained when her mistress asked her to continue working for wages: "No, Miss, I must go, if I stay here I'll never know I am free." During the first months after the war there was, then, much movement among Southern blacks. "They are just like a swarm of bees," one observer noted, "all buzzing about and not knowing where to settle."

Much of this black mobility was, however, purposeful. Thousands of former slaves flocked to Southern towns and cities where the Freedmen's Bureau was issuing rations, for they knew that food was unavailable on the plantations. Many blacks set out to find husbands, wives, or children, from whom they had been forcibly separated during the slave days. A good many freedmen joined the general movement of Southern population away from the seaboard states, devastated by war, and migrated to the Southwestern frontier in Texas. Most blacks, however, did not move so far but remained in the immediate vicinity of the plantations where they had labored as slaves.

The reluctance of freedmen in 1865 to enter into labor contracts, either with their former masters or with other white landowners, was also generally misunderstood. Most blacks wanted to work—but they wanted to work on their own land. Freedmen knew that the United States government had divided up some abandoned plantations among former slaves, and many believed that on January 1, 1866—the anniversary of their freedom under Lincoln's Emancipation Proclamation—all would receive forty acres and a mule. With this prospect of having their own farms, they were unwilling to sign contracts to work on somebody else's plantation.

Even when the hope of free land disappeared, freedmen were averse to sign-ing labor contracts because, as has been noted, so many white landowners ex-pected to continue to treat them like slaves. Especially repugnant was the idea of being again herded together in the plantation slave quarters, with their com-munal facilities for cooking and washing and infant care, and their lack of pri-vacy. Emancipation did much to strengthen the black family. Families divided by slave sales could now be reunited. Marital arrangements between blacks, which had had no legal validity during slavery, could be regularized. Freed-men's Bureau officials performed thousands of marriage ceremonies, and some states passed general ordinances declaring that blacks who had been living to-gether were legally man and wife and that their children were legitimate. This precious new security of family life was not something blacks were willing to jeopardize by returning to slave quarters. Before contracting to work on the plantations, they insisted on having separate cabins, scattered across the farm, each usually having its own patch for vegetables and perhaps a pen for hogs or a cow.

When these conditions were met, freedmen in the early months of 1866 en-tered into labor contracts, most of which followed the same general pattern. Rarely did these arrangements call for the payment of wages, for landowners were desperately short of cash and freedmen felt that a wage system gave plant-ers too much control over their labor. The most common system was share-cropping. Although there were many regional and individual variations, the system usually called for the dividing of the crop into three equal shares. One of these went to the landowner; another went to the laborer—usually black, though there were also many white sharecroppers in the South; and the third went to whichever party provided the seeds, fertilizer, mules, and other farming equip-ment.

For the planter this system had several advantages. At a time when money was scarce, he was not obliged to pay out cash to his employees until the crop was harvested. He retained general supervision over what was planted and how the crop was cultivated, and he felt he was more likely to secure a good harvest be-cause the freedmen themselves stood to gain by a large yield. Blacks, too, found the sharecropping system suited to their needs. They had control over how their crops were planted and when they were cultivated and harvested. They could earn more money by working harder in the fields. And, best of all, they could live in individual family units scattered over the plantation, each cabin having some privacy.

To some observers the disappearance of the slave quarters and the resettling of families in individual, scattered cabins seemed to mark a revolution in the character of Southern agriculture. According to the United States census, the number of Southern landholdings doubled between 1860 and 1880 and their average size dropped from 365 acres to 157 acres. In fact, the census figures

were misleading, because the census takers failed to ask farmers whether they
owned their land or were sharecroppers. An examination of tax records, which
show land ownership, in the representative state of Louisiana helps correct the
distortion of the census. Between 1860 and 1880 in Louisiana the number of
independently owned farms of less than 100 acres actually dropped by 14 percent, while during the same period the number of plantations increased by 287
percent. By 1900, plantations of 100 acres or more encompassed half the cultivated land in the state, and more than half the farmers were not proprietors.

If the postwar period did not see the breakup of large plantations, it did bring
some significant changes in ownership and control of the land. Hard hit by debt,
by rising taxes, and by increasing labor costs, many Southern planters had to sell
their holdings, and there was an infusion of Northern capital into the region after

THE SAME GEORGIA PLANTATION IN 1860 AND IN 1880

Before the Civil War slave quarters were located close
together, all near the white master's house, so that he could
impose order and prevent secret meetings of the blacks.
After emancipation freedmen insisted upon scattering out
over the plantation, so that each family could have its own
house and some privacy.

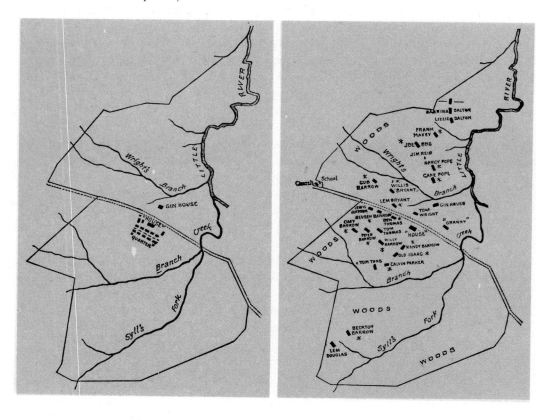

the war. More tried to cling to their acres by going heavily into debt. Since the banking system of the postwar South was inadequate, the principal source of credit was the local merchant, who could supply both the landowner and his sharecroppers with clothing, shoes, some food, and other necessities to tide them over the lean months between the planting of the tobacco or cotton crop and its harvest. On each sale the merchant charged interest, to be paid when the crop was sold, and he also charged prices ranging from 40 percent to 110 percent higher for all goods sold on credit. It is hardly surprising that those planters who could afford to do so set up their own stores and extended credit to their own sharecroppers, and quite soon they discovered they were making more profits on their mercantile enterprises than from farming. Planters who could not make such arrangements frequently had to sell their lands to the neighborhood merchant. It is not accidental that in William Faulkner's fictional saga of Southern history the power of planter families like the Compsons and the Sutpens diminished during the postwar years, while the Snopes family of storekeepers, hard-trading, penny-pinching, and utterly unscrupulous, emerged prosperous and successful.

It would be a mistake, however, to accept the novelist's hostile characterization of the Southern merchant without reservation. If the storekeeper insisted on a crop-lien system, which required the farmer legally to pledge that the proceeds from his crop must go first to pay off his obligation to the merchant, it was because he was aware that, as in both 1866 and 1867, crops throughout the South could fail. And if the merchant urged farmers to forget about soil conservation, diversification, and experimentation with new crops, it was because he knew that the only way to pay his own debts was to insist that his debtors must raise cotton and tobacco, for which there was a ready cash market.

Thus merchants, landowners, and sharecroppers, thus white Southerners and black Southerners, became locked into an economic system that, at best, promised them little more than survival. At worst, it offered bankruptcy, sale of lands, and hurried nocturnal migrations in an attempt to escape from a set of debts in one state but with little more than the hope of starting a new set in another.

By the 1880s, then, the South had become what it remained for the next half-century, the economic backwater of the nation. In 1880 the per capita wealth of the South was $376, that in the states outside the South $1,086. Yet it was this impoverished region that had to deal with some of the most difficult political and racial problems that ever have confronted Americans. In attacking these problems, Southerners, black and white, could expect no assistance from the government, since such intervention would violate the immutable laws of laissez-faire economics. Even the most humane national leaders could discover no way to help this backward region. They could only agree with Whitelaw Reid, editor of the influential New York *Tribune*, who concluded after his tour of the South in 1879, "Manifestly something is wrong," and gave as his diagnosis: "Economic laws are violated in some way."

Political Parties as a Limit to Change

Of the institutions that checked radical change during Reconstruction, none were more influential than the national political parties. The fact that both parties were conglomerates of disparate and often competing sectional and class interests meant that party policy had to be arrived at through compromise and concession. In that process extreme and drastic measures were nearly always screened out.

Nationally the Democratic party during the postwar years was torn by two conflicting interests. On the one hand Democrats sought the immediate readmission of the Southern states under the governments President Johnson had set up. Controlled by whites hostile to the Republican party, these states would surely send Democrats to Congress and support Democratic candidates in a national election. Even during the 1850s, the South had increasingly become a one-party region; now the goal of a solidly Democratic South appeared within reach. On the other hand, too enthusiastic advocacy of the Southern cause could hurt Democrats in the North by reviving talk of disloyalty and the Copperhead movement during the war. Throughout the Reconstruction era, Democrats remained vulnerable to charges like those brought by Governor O. P. Morton of Indiana during the 1868 campaign: "Every unregenerate rebel . . . every deserter, every sneak who ran away from the draft calls himself a Democrat. . . . Every man who labored for the rebellion . . ., who murdered Union prisoners by cruelty and starvation . . . calls himself a Democrat. . . . In short, the Democratic party may be described as a common sewer and loathsome receptacle, into which is emptied every element of treason North and South, every element of inhumanity and barbarism which has dishonored the age." To minimize the effectiveness of such attacks, Democrats had no choice but to mute their defense of the South and to urge restraint on their colleagues in the former Confederacy.

Among Republicans, similar constraints operated to dampen any ideas of taking vengeance on the South or of encouraging blacks to seize control of that region. From its inception the Republican party had been an uneasy admixture of antislavery men, former Whigs, disgruntled Democrats, and Know Nothings. How tenuous were the ties that bound these groups together became evident in the factional disputes that racked Lincoln's administration, and for the party it was a bad omen that the sharpest area of disagreement between Radical and Conservative Republicans concerned Lincoln's plan to reorganize the Southern states.

During the first year after Lincoln's death, quarrels between the Radicals and the Conservatives were somewhat muted because practically all Republicans could join in opposing President Johnson's program of Reconstruction. Followed only by Secretary of State Seward, Navy Secretary Gideon Welles, and a handful of other very cautious Republicans, Johnson began to work closely with the Democrats of the North and South. He announced that the Southern states had

never been out of the Union, and he insisted that, under the provisional governments he had set up, they were ready to reclaim their right to be represented in
Congress.

It is easy to understand why almost all Radical and Conservative Republicans
rejected the President's argument. Regardless of faction, they were outraged
when the Southern elections in 1865, held at the direction of the President,
resulted in the choice of a Confederate brigadier-general as governor of Mississippi, and they were furious when the new Georgia legislature named Alexander
H. Stephens, the Vice President of the Confederacy, to represent that state in
the United States Senate.

What made these newly elected Southern officials more threatening to Republicans was the fact that (though many had been Whigs before the war) they
clearly contemplated allying themselves with the Democratic party. However
much Republicans disagreed among themselves, they all agreed that their party
had saved the Union. They believed, with Thaddeus Stevens, "that upon the continued ascendency of that party depends the safety of this great nation." Now
that ascendency was threatened. What made the threat so grave, and so ironic,
was the fact that when the Southern states were readmitted to the Union they
would receive increased representation in Congress. Prior to the ratification of
the Thirteenth Amendment, only three-fifths of the slave population of the South
had been counted in apportioning representation in the House of Representatives;
but now that the slaves were free men, all would be counted. In short, the Southern states, after having been defeated in the most costly war in the nation's history, would have about fifteen more representatives in Congress than they had
had before the war. And under the President's plan, all of the Southern Congress
unquestionably would be Democrats.

Equally troubling to Republicans of all factions was the fear of what white
Southerners, once restored to authority, would do to the freedmen. The laws
that the Southern provisional legislatures adopted during the winter of 1865–66
gave reason for anxiety on this score. Not one of these governments considered
treating black citizens just as they treated white citizens. Instead, the legislatures
adopted special laws, known as the Black Codes, to regulate the conduct of
freedmen. On the positive side, these laws recognized the right of freedmen to
make civil contracts, to sue and be sued, and to acquire and hold most kinds of
property. But with these rights went restrictions. The laws varied from state to
state, but in general they specified that blacks might not purchase or carry fire-
arms, that they might not assemble after sunset, and that those who were idle
or unemployed should "be liable to imprisonment, and to hard labor, one or
both, . . . not exceeding twelve months." The Mississippi code prohibited blacks
from renting or leasing "any lands or tenements except in incorporated cities or
towns." That of South Carolina forbade blacks from practicing "the art, trade or
business of an artisan, mechanic or shopkeeper, or any other trade, employment
or business (besides that of husbandry, or that of a servant)." So clearly did these

measures seem designed to keep the freedmen in quasi-slavery that the Chicago *Tribune* spoke for a united, outraged Republican party in denouncing the first of these Black Codes, that adopted by the Mississippi legislature: "We tell the white men of Mississippi that the men of the North will convert the state of Mississippi into a frog-pond before they will allow any such laws to disgrace one foot of soil over which the flag of freedom waves."

Unwilling, for all these reasons, to recognize the regimes Johnson had set up in the South, all Republicans easily rallied in December 1865, when Congress reassembled, to block seating of their senators and representatives. All agreed to the creation of a special joint committee on Reconstruction to handle questions concerning the readmission of the Southern states and their further reorganization. In setting up this committee, congressional Republicans carefully balanced its membership with Radicals and Moderates. If its most conspicuous member was the Radical Stevens, its powerful chairman was Senator William Pitt Fessenden, a Moderate.

Congressional Republicans found it easier to unite in opposing Johnson's plan of Reconstruction than to unite in devising one of their own. Throughout the winter of 1865–66, the joint committee met to consider various plans for reorganizing the South. With its evenly balanced membership, the committee dismissed, on the one side, the President's theory that the Southern states were, in reality, already reconstructed and back in the Union. On the other side, it discarded the theory of Thaddeus Stevens that the Confederacy was conquered territory over which Congress could rule at its own discretion, and it rejected Charles Sumner's more elaborate argument that the Southern state governments had committed suicide when they seceded, so that their land and inhabitants now fell "under the exclusive jurisdiction of Congress." More acceptable to the majority of Republicans was the "grasp of war" theory advanced by Richard Henry Dana, Jr., the noted Massachusetts constitutional lawyer, who was also the author of *Two Years before the Mast*. Dana argued that the federal government held the defeated Confederacy in the grasp of war for a brief and limited time, during which it must act swiftly to revive state governments in the region and to restore promptly the constitutional balance between national and state authority. Dana's theory was an essentially conservative one, in that it called for only a short period of federal hegemony and looked toward the speedy restoration of the Southern states on terms of absolute equality with the loyal states.

Finding in Dana's theory a constitutional source of power, the Joint Committee after much travail produced the first comprehensive congressional plan of Reconstruction in a proposed Fourteenth Amendment to the Constitution, which was endorsed by Congress in June 1866 and submitted to the states for ratification. Some parts of the amendment were noncontroversial. All Republicans recognized the need authoritatively to overturn the Supreme Court decision in the Dred Scott case (1857), which had declared Negroes were not citizens of the United States, and consequently accepted the opening statement of

RECONSTRUCTION.

Uncle Sam—"WELL, ANDY, DO YOU THINK THAT YOU CAN GET MY COAT TOGETHER BEFORE YOU CLOSE SHOP?"
Andy—"WELL, IT'S BEEN TORN PRETTY BADLY, BUT I GUESS ME AND MUM SEWARD CAN GET IT TOGETHER BEFORE WE CLOSE SHOP."

RECONSTRUCTION: A DIALOGUE BETWEEN
UNCLE SAM AND A. JOHNSON, TAILOR

Taking off from Andrew Johnson's
frequent bragging about his humble
origins as a tailor, this cartoon shows
the President and Secretary of State
Seward busily mending Uncle Sam's
coat, badly torn by the recently ended
Civil War. (*American Antiquarian Society.*)

the amendment: "All persons born or naturalized in the United States, and subject to the jurisdiction thereof, are citizens of the United States and the State
wherein they reside." There was also no disagreement about the provision declaring the Confederate debt invalid.

All the other provisions, however, represented a compromise between Radical
and Moderate Republicans. For instance, Radicals wanted to keep all Southerners who had voluntarily supported the Confederacy from voting until 1870, and
the arch-Radical Stevens urged: "Not only to 1870 but 18070, every rebel who
shed the blood of loyal men should be prevented from exercising any power in
this Government." Moderates favored a speedy restoration of all political rights
to former Confederates. As a compromise the Fourteenth Amendment included
a provision to exclude high-ranking Confederates from office but one that did
not deny them the vote.

Similarly, the Fourteenth Amendment's provisions to protect the freedmen
represented a compromise. Radicals like Sumner (who was considered too radical
to be given a seat on the joint committee) wanted an unequivocal declaration of
the right and duty of the national government to protect the civil liberties of the
former slaves. But Moderates drew back in alarm from entrusting additional
authority to Washington. The joint committee came up with a provision that
granted no power to the national government but restricted that of the states:

RETURN OF THE PRODIGAL SON—NEW VERSION.

KIND-HEARTED DEMOCRAT. "THERE, MOTHER, THERE'S YOUR BOY COME HOME AGAIN; MAKE HIM WELCOME."
PENITENT SOUTH. "YES, BY THUNDER, I'VE COME BACK; AND D'YE HEAR? HURRY UP THEM CAKES AND HOT WHISKY, AND DON'T LET US SEE
ANY DARN'D NIGGERS AROUND."

"RETURN OF THE PRODIGAL SON — NEW VERSION"

This Republican view of Reconstruction depicts the
unregenerate South — still bullying, whiskey-loving, and
Negro-hating — welcomed as the prodigal son by Northern
Democrats. (*American Antiquarian Society.*)

"No State shall make or enforce any law which shall abridge the privileges and immunities of citizens of the United States; nor shall any State deprive any person of life, liberty, or property, without due process of law; nor deny to any person within its jurisdiction the equal protection of the laws."

Finally, another compromise between Radicals and Moderates resulted in the provision of the amendment concerning voting. Though Sumner and other Radicals called Negro suffrage "the essence, the great essential," of a proper Reconstruction policy, Conservatives refused to give to the national government power to interfere with state requirements for suffrage. The joint committee thereupon devised a complex and, as it proved, unworkable plan to persuade the Southern states voluntarily to enfranchise blacks, under threat of having reduced representation in Congress if they refused.

The efficacy of the Fourteenth Amendment as a program of Reconstruction was never tested because of the deterioration of relations between Congress and the President. While the joint committee was deliberating, Johnson further alienated the Republicans, who were already distrustful of his policy. Recognizing that a constitutional amendment would take time for ratification, congressional leaders early in 1866 tried to pass interim legislation to protect the freedmen.

One bill extended the life and expanded the functions of the Freedmen's Bureau, and a second guaranteed minimal civil rights to all citizens. Contrary to expectations, Johnson vetoed both these measures. Incorrectly terming these bills the work of Radical Republicans who wanted "to destroy our institutions and change the character of the Government," the President publicly announced that he intended to fight these enemies of the Union just as he had once fought secessionists and traitors in the South. Congress sustained Johnson's veto of the Freedmen's Bureau bill (a later, less sweeping measure extended the life of that agency for two years), but it passed the Civil Rights Act over his disapproval.

From this point, open warfare existed between the President and the majority of the Republican party that had elected him Vice-President in 1864. During the summer of 1866, Johnson and his friends tried to create a new political party, which would rally behind the President's policies Conservative Republicans, Northern Democrats, and Southern whites. With the President's hearty approval, a National Union Convention held in Philadelphia in August stressed the theme of harmony among the sections. The entry into the convention hall of delegates from Massachusetts and South Carolina, arm in arm, seemed to symbolize the end of sectional strife. The President himself went on a "swing around the circle" of leading Northern cities, ostensibly on his way to dedicate a monument to the memory of another Democrat, Stephen A. Douglas. In his frequent public speeches he defended the constitutionality of his own Reconstruction program and berated the Congress, and particularly the Radical Republicans, for attempting to subvert the Constitution. In a final effort to consolidate sentiment against the Congress, he urged the Southern states not to ratify the proposed Fourteenth Amendment. With the exception of Tennessee, which was controlled by one of Johnson's bitterest personal and political enemies, all the former Confederate states rejected the congressional plan. In ten Southern legislatures not a single vote was cast in favor of it.

When Congress reassembled in December 1866, the Republican majority had therefore to devise a second program of Reconstruction. Cheered by overwhelming victories in the fall congressional elections, Republicans were even less inclined than previously to cooperate with the President, who had gone into political opposition, or to encourage the provisional regimes in the South, which had unanimously rejected their first program. Republican suspicion that Southern whites were fundamentally hostile toward the freedmen was strengthened by reports of a race riot in Memphis during May 1866, when a mob of whites joined in a two-day indiscriminate attack on blacks in that city, and of a more serious affair in New Orleans four months later, when a white mob, aided by the local police, attacked a black political gathering with what was described as "a cowardly ferocity unsurpassed in the annals of crime." In New Orleans, 45 or 50 blacks were killed, and 150 more were wounded.

Once again, however, the Republican majority in Congress found it easier to agree on what to oppose than what to favor in the way of Reconstruction legis-

lation. Stevens urged that the South be placed under military rule for a generation and that Southern plantations be sold to pay the national debt. Sumner
wanted to disfranchise large numbers of Southern whites, to require Negro
suffrage, and to create racially integrated schools in the South. Moderate Republicans, on the other hand, were willing to retain the Fourteenth Amendment
as the basic framework of congressional Reconstruction and to insist on little
else but ratification by the Southern states.

The second congressional program of Reconstruction, embodied in the Military Reconstruction Act of March 2, 1867, represented a compromise between
the demands of Radical and Moderate Republican factions. It divided the ten
former Confederate states that had not ratified the Fourteenth Amendment into
five military districts. In each of these states, there were to be new constitutional
conventions, for which black men were allowed to vote. These conventions must
draft new constitutions that had to provide for Negro suffrage, and they were
required to ratify the Fourteenth Amendment. When thus reorganized, the
Southern states could apply to Congress for readmission to the Union.

The radical aspects of this measure, which were pointed out by Democrats
during the congressional debates and were denounced by President Johnson in
his unsuccessful veto of the act, were easy to recognize. In particular, the requirement of Negro suffrage, which Sumner sponsored, seemed to Radicals "a pro-
digious triumph."

In fact, however, most provisions of the Military Reconstruction Act were more
acceptable to Moderate than to Radical Republicans. The measure did nothing
to give land to the freedmen, to provide education at national expense, or to
end racial segregation in the South. It did not erase the boundaries of the Southern states, and it did not even sweep away the provisional governments Johnson
had established there, though it did make them responsible to the commanders of
the new military districts. So conservative was the act in all these respects that
Sumner branded it as "horribly defective."

Intent on striking some kind of balance between the Radical and Conservative
wings of the Republican party, the framers of the Military Reconstruction Act
drafted the measure carelessly, and it promptly proved, as Sumner had predicted,
"Reconstruction without machinery or motive power." Facing the acceptance of
military rule or Negro suffrage, the provisional governments in the South chose
the former, correctly believing that army officers were generally in sympathy with
white supremacy. To get the Reconstruction process under way, Congress had
therefore to enact a supplementary law (March 23, 1867), requiring the federal
commanders in the South to take the initiative, when the local governments did
not, in announcing elections, registering voters, and convening constitutional
conventions. During the summer of 1867, as the President, the attorney general,
and Southern state officials tried by legalistic interpretations to delay the Reconstruction program, Congress had to pass two further supplementary acts, explaining the "true intent and meaning" of the previous legislation.

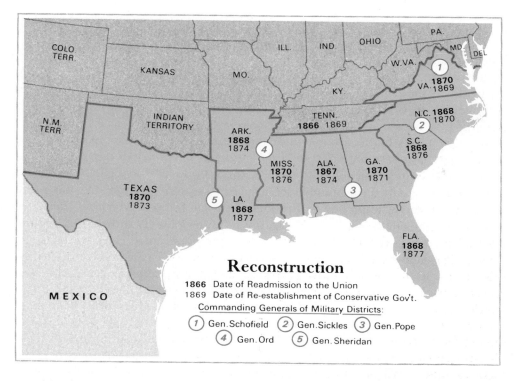

Reconstruction

1866 Date of Readmission to the Union
1869 Date of Re-establishment of Conservative Gov't.
Commanding Generals of Military Districts:
(1) Gen. Schofield (2) Gen. Sickles (3) Gen. Pope
(4) Gen. Ord (5) Gen. Sheridan

With these measures, the fabric of congressional Reconstruction legislation as it affected the South was substantially completed. Both the first and the second congressional plans of Reconstruction were compromises between the Radical and the Moderate factions in the Republican party. The Radicals' insistence on change was essential in securing the adoption of this legislation, but the Moderates blocked all measures that would have revolutionary social or economic consequences in the South.

The same need to compromise between the factions of the Republican party shaped the relation between Congress and the other two branches of the national government during the Reconstruction era. Many Republicans in both factions were profoundly suspicious of the Supreme Court, because of its decision in the Dred Scott case before the war. Not even Lincoln's appointment of Salmon P. Chase in 1864, to succeed Roger B. Taney as Chief Justice, removed their doubts about the judiciary. They grew alarmed when the Court in 1866 handed down its decision in *ex parte Milligan,* a landmark case in the history of American civil liberties, which denied the power of a Civil War military tribunal to try the Indiana Copperhead conspirator Lambdin P. Milligan, and held that he should have been brought before a civil tribunal. Some Republicans in Congress feared—quite incorrectly—that the Court was getting ready to invalidate military rule in the South and thus destroy the main protection for the freedmen's rights.

Timorous Republicans watched in something approaching panic as the provisional governments in both Georgia and Mississippi brought suit to test the constitutionality of the Military Reconstruction Act, and they were relieved when the Supreme Court refused to hear these cases. When, however, one McCardle, a Mississippi editor arrested and tried by military commission for publishing criticism of the congressional Reconstruction policy, succeeded in bringing his case before the Court, Republicans in Congress acted swiftly to deprive the Court of jurisdiction in such cases.

This step was highly exceptional, and Republican fulminations against the Court were largely a matter of Radicals' letting off steam. Moderate Republicans were always numerous enough to block Radical proposals to hobble the judiciary. Congress did reduce the number of justices from ten to seven, but this was a nonpartisan move, approved by President Johnson himself, which was designed to increase the efficiency of the Court, not to undermine its authority. Even the Radical success in the McCardle case was of little significance, since, as the Court promptly demonstrated in *ex parte Yerger* (1869), another case involving a Mississippian, that its jurisdiction derived not from an act of Congress but from the Constitution itself, and it freed Yerger from the prison to which a military court had sentenced him. Radicals stewed impotently, while Moderates prevented them from taking further measures against the Court.

The same balance between Radical and Moderate Republican factions dictated the policy of Congress toward the President during the Reconstruction years. Almost all Republicans were suspicious of the President and were fearful that he intended turning the South over to Confederate rule. Most were angered by Johnson's repeated veto messages, assailing carefully balanced compromise legislation as the work of Radicals and attacking the Congress itself as an unconstitutional body, since it refused to seat congressmen from all the states. Republicans of both factions were, therefore, desirous of keeping a close eye on the President and were willing to curb executive powers that had grown during the war. In 1867, fearing that Johnson would use his power as commander in chief to subvert their Reconstruction legislation, Republican factions joined to pass an army appropriations bill that required all military orders to the army, including those of the President himself, to go through the hands of General Grant. Suspecting that Johnson wanted to use the federal patronage to build up a political machine of his own, they adopted at the same time the Tenure of Office Act, which required the President to secure the consent of the Senate not merely when he appointed officials but when he removed them.

Up to this point the Republicans in Congress were prepared to go in striking unanimity—but no further. When Radical Republican James M. Ashley in January 1867 moved to impeach the President, he was permitted to conduct a serio-comic investigation of Johnson's alleged involvement in Lincoln's assassination, his purported sale of pardons, and other trumped-up charges; but when Ashley's motion reached the floor of the House of Representatives Moderate Republicans saw that it was soundly defeated.

A subsequent attempt at impeachment fared better, but it also revealed how the Radical and Moderate factions checked each other. In August 1867, President Johnson suspended from office Secretary of War Edwin M. Stanton, whom he correctly suspected of having collaborated closely with the Radicals in Congress, and, as required by the Tenure of Office Act, he asked the Senate to consent to the removal. When the Senate refused, the President removed Stanton and ordered him to surrender his office. News of this seemingly open defiance of the law caused Republicans in the House of Representatives to rush through a resolution impeaching the President, without waiting for specific charges against him to be drawn up.

The trial of President Johnson (who was not present in court but was represented by his lawyers) was not merely a test of strength between Congress and the chief executive, but between the Radical and the Moderate Republicans. Impeachment managers from the House of Representatives presented eleven charges against the President, mostly accusing him of violating the Tenure of Office Act but also censuring his repeated attacks upon the Congress. With fierce joy Radical Thaddeus Stevens, who was one of the managers, denounced the President: "Unfortunate man! thus surrounded, hampered, tangled in the meshes of his own wickedness—unfortunate, unhappy man, behold your doom!"

But Radical oratory could not persuade Moderate Republicans and Democrats in the Senate to vote for conviction. Though Sumner, like a handful of other Radicals, was prepared from the outset of the trial to pronounce that Johnson was "guilty of all, and infinitely more," most senators were open-minded. They listened as Johnson's lawyers challenged the constitutionality of the Tenure of

AWKWARD COLLISION ON THE GRAND TRUNK COLUMBIA R. R.
A. J. (Driver of Engine "President")—"LOOK HERE! ONE OF US HAS GOT TO BACK."
THADDEUS (Driver of Engine "Congress")—"WELL, IT AIN'T ME, THAT'S GOING TO DO IT. YOU BET!"

"AWKWARD COLLISION ON THE GRAND TRUNK COLUMBIA RAILROAD"

In this cartoon "A. J[ohnson]." personifies presidential Reconstruction and "Thaddeus [Stevens]" congressional Reconstruction. The two plans are obviously on a collision course. which led ultimately to the impeachment of the President. (*Library of Congress.*)

Office Act, showed that it had not been intended to apply to cabinet members, and proved that, in any case, it did not cover Stanton, who had been appointed by Lincoln, not Johnson. When the critical vote came, Moderate Republicans like Fessenden voted to acquit the President, and Johnson's Radical foes lacked one vote of the two-thirds majority required to convict him. Several other Republican Senators who for political expediency voted against the President were prepared to change their votes and favor acquittal if their ballots were needed.

Nothing more clearly shows how the institutional needs of a political party prevented drastic change than did this decision not to remove a President whom a majority in Congress despised, hated, and feared. The desire to maintain the unity of the national Republican party, despite frequent quarrels and incessant bickering, overrode the wishes of individual congressmen. Moderate Republicans felt that throughout the Reconstruction period they were constantly being rushed from one advanced position to another in order to placate the insatiable Radicals. With more accuracy, Radical Republicans perceived that the need of retaining Moderate support prevented the adoption of any really revolutionary Reconstruction program.

Racism as a Limit to Change

A final set of beliefs that limited the nature of the changes imposed upon, and accepted by, the South during the Reconstruction period can be labeled racism. In all parts of the country, white Americans looked with suspicion and fear on those whose skin was of a different color. For example, in California white hatred built up against the Chinese, who had begun coming to that state in great numbers after the discovery of gold and who were later imported by the thousands to help construct the Central Pacific Railroad. White workers resented the willingness of the Chinese to work long hours for "coolies'" wages; they distrusted the unfamiliar attire, diet, and habits of the Chinese; and they disliked all these things more because the Chinese were a yellow-skinned people. Under the leadership of a newly arrived Irish immigrant, Dennis Kearney, white laborers organized a workingman's party, with the slogan, "The Chinese must go."

The depression of 1873 gave impetus to the movement, for day after day thousands of the unemployed gathered in the sand lots of San Francisco to hear Kearney's slashing attacks on the Chinese and on the wealthy corporations that employed them. In the summer of 1877 San Francisco hoodlums, inspired by Kearney, burned 25 Chinese laundries and destroyed dozens of Chinese houses. Politically the movement was strong enough to force both major parties in California to adopt anti-Chinese platforms, and California congressmen succeeded in persuading their colleagues to pass a bill limiting the number of Chinese who could be brought into the United States each year. Since the measure clearly conflicted with treaty arrangements with China, President Rutherford B. Hayes vetoed it, but he had his secretary of state initiate negotiations leading to a new treaty that permitted the restriction of immigration. Congress in 1882 passed the Chinese Exclusion Act, which suspended all Chinese immigration for ten years and forbade the naturalization of Chinese already in the country.

If white Americans became so agitated over a small number of Chinese, who were unquestionably hard-working and thrifty and who belonged to one of the most ancient of civilizations, it is easy to see how they could consider blacks an even greater danger. There were more than 3 million Negroes, most of them recently emancipated from slavery. The exploits of black soldiers during the war—their very discipline and courage—proved that Negroes could be formidable opponents. The fact that blacks were no longer portrayed as invisible men but now, in photographs and caricatures, had sharply etched identities exacerbated, rather than allayed, white apprehensions. More clearly than ever before Negroes seemed distinctive, alien, and vaguely menacing. After all, according to the defective ethnology of the day, they were lazy and improvident by nature, the descendants of barbarous African tribes that had never shown a trace of civilization.

THE MARTYRDOM OF ST. CRISPIN.

"THE MARTYRDOM OF ST. CRISPIN"

Racism in postwar America took many forms. Here the artist Thomas Nast shows the obviously 100 percent American "St. Crispin," the patron saint of shoemakers, threatened by the cheap labor of Chinese immigrants. (*American Antiquarian Society.*)

Most American intellectuals of the Civil War generation accepted unquestioningly the dogma that blacks belonged to an inferior race. Though a few reformers like Charles Sumner vigorously attacked this notion, a majority of even philanthropic Northerners accepted the judgment of the distinguished Harvard scientist Louis Agassiz that while whites during antiquity were developing high civilizations "the negro race groped in barbarism and never originated a regular organization among themselves." Many accepted Agassiz's conjecture that Negroes, once free, would inevitably die out in the United States. Others reached the same conclusion by studying the recently published work of Charles Darwin, *Origin of Species* (1859), and they accepted the Darwinian argument that in the inevitable struggle for survival "higher civilized races" must inevitably eliminate "an endless number of lower races." Consequently the influential and tender-hearted Congregational minister Horace Bushnell could prophesy the approaching end of the black race in the United States with something approaching equanimity. "Since we must all die," he asked rhetorically, "why should it grieve us, that a stock thousands of years behind, in the scale of culture, should die with few and still fewer children to succeed, till finally the whole succession remains in the more cultivated race?"

When even the leaders of Northern society held such views, it is hardly surprising that most whites in the region were overtly anti-Negro. In state after state whites fiercely resisted efforts to extend the political and civil rights of blacks, partly because they feared that any improvement of the condition of Negroes in the North would lead to a huge exodus of blacks from the South. At the end of the Civil War only Maine, New Hampshire, Vermont, Massachusetts, and Rhode Island allowed Negroes to have full voting rights, and in New York blacks who met certain property-holding qualifications could have the ballot. During the next three years in referenda held in Connecticut, Wisconsin, Kansas, Ohio, Michigan, and Missouri, constitutional amendments authorizing Negro suffrage were defeated, and New York voters rejected a proposal to eliminate the property-holding qualifications for black voters. Only in Iowa, a state where there were very few blacks, did a Negro suffrage amendment carry in 1868, and that same year Minnesota adopted an ambiguously worded amendment. Thus at the end of the 1860s most Northern states—and all of the Northern states that had substantial numbers of Negro residents—refused to give black men the ballot.

In words as well as in votes, the majority of Northerners made their deeply racist feelings evident. The Democratic press constantly preyed on the racial fears of its readers, and they regularly portrayed the Republicans as planning a "new era of miscegenation, amalgamation, and promiscuous intercourse between the races." From the White House, denouncing Republican attempts "to Africanize the [Southern] half of our country," President Andrew Johnson announced: "In the progress of nations negroes have shown less capacity for self-government than any other race of people. . . . Whenever they have been left to their own devices they have shown an instant tendency to relapse into barbarism." Even Northern Republicans opposed to Johnson shared many of his racist views. Radical Senator Timothy O. Howe of Wisconsin declared that he regarded "the freedmen, in the main . . . as so much animal life," and Senator Benjamin F. Wade of Ohio, whom the Radical Republicans would have elevated to the presidency had they removed Johnson, had, along with a genuine devotion to the principle of equal rights, an incurable aversion to blacks. Representative George W. Julian of Indiana, one of the few Northern congressmen who had no racial prejudice, bluntly told his colleagues in 1866: "The real trouble is that *we hate the negro*. It is not his ignorance that offends us, but his color. . . . Of this fact I entertain no doubt whatsoever."

Both personal preferences and the wishes of constituents inhibited Northern Republicans from supporting measures that might alter race relations. When Sumner sought to expunge federal laws that recognized slavery or to prohibit racial discrimination on the public transportation in the District of Columbia, his

From Eden to Babylon

Just as the Civil War required Americans to reconsider the meaning of national loyalty, so it compelled them to rethink the bases of a good society. Before the war their vision of America was primarily agrarian. Most of the inhabitants of the United States lived on farms, plantations, and ranches. Of course there were bustling cities, but most city dwellers had been born in the countryside, whether in the United States, Ireland, Germany, or England. It was natural, then, that when mid-century Americans portrayed themselves, it was as farmers, herdsmen, trappers, and explorers—not as businessmen, factory laborers, or clerks.

Just before the outbreak of the war Emanuel Leutze accurately recaptured the Americans' definition of themselves in *Westward the Course of Empire Takes Its Way*, which filled a six-hundred-square-foot panel in the rotunda of the national Capitol. It was not a great painting, not even a good painting; in it, as one contemporary remarked, "confusion reigns paramount." But it did serve to perpetuate the myth that Americans were a people close to the land, who drew their strength from nature.

Courtesy of National Collection of Fine Arts, Smithsonian Institution.

Nature had a special place in the thought of antebellum Americans. The most influential American philosophical work published in the first half of the nineteenth century was Ralph Waldo Emerson's essay on that topic. "Nature," to Emerson and the thousands who read his essays and heard him lecture, included those "essences unchanged by man: space, the air, the river, the leaf." It was to be distinguished from "art," the imposition of man's will upon nature that resulted in "a house, a canal, a statue, a picture." "Nature," then, had emotional and moral primacy over "art," and most Americans believed, with Emerson himself, that by shedding all artifice man could again become part and parcel of nature itself.

A self-taught Massachusetts painter, Erastus Salisbury Field, perfectly recaptured the spirit behind Emerson's ideas. With only three months of informal training as an artist, Field personified the spirit of spontaneity and improvisation that Emerson extolled. More important, his early paintings showed an attachment to, and a meticulous interest in, nature. The land he portrayed was a tidied-up, New England version of Leutze's sprawling continent. Field's *The Garden of Eden* did not have a specifically American setting, though his neatly paired animals of peculiar anatomy and his trees with their improbable fruit might have flourished in America, if anywhere. There is, however, a distinctively American note in Field's treatment of nudity in the Garden of Eden: a clump of strategically placed lilies preserves Adam's modesty, and Eve lurks behind some unlikely blossoms. Clearly for Field, as for Emerson, man is at his best when most closely linked to nature, in a scene unmarred by human artifice or ingenuity.

Yale University Art Gallery, Mabel Brady Garvan Collection.

During the Civil War years Americans' perception of the good society dramatically changed. The war may not have stimulated economic growth, but it did promote mechanization. Steam power largely replaced horse power and water power. Machines of ever increasing complexity, with fascinating gears and gauges, replaced men. The vast foundries and rolling mills that had turned out cannons during the war were diverted to the production of structural iron girders, and later steel beams, which made possible a new American architecture. No longer was it necessary to erect buildings out of huge piles of masonry, and no longer was it dangerous to build them too high. Using steel beams, innovative architects like Louis Sullivan invented the skyscraper, a triumphant fusing of form and function. The skyscraper, Sullivan proclaimed, "must be every inch a proud and soaring thing, rising in sheer exultation that from bottom to top it is a unit without a single dissenting line." Imaginative engineers, like Samuel B. B. Nowlan of New York, foresaw the day when whole cities would be made of steel, and Nowlan's sketch, *Proposed Arcade Railroad under Broadway,* looked ahead to a new era in urban design.

Magnum.

3

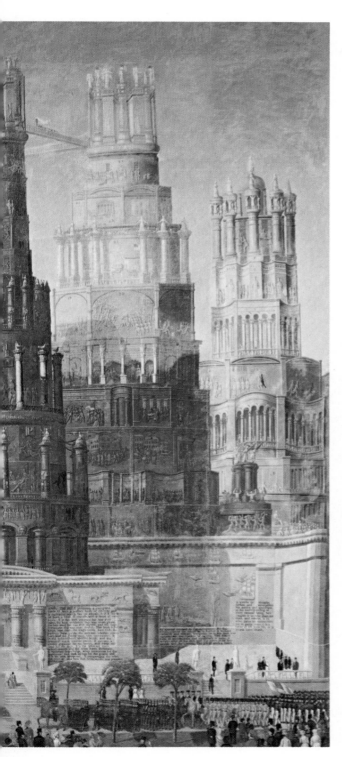

Postwar Americans found the new technology exhilarating to the point of intoxication. Gone now was the day when Erastus Field portrayed man in the bosom of nature. Instead, looking forward to the Centennial Exposition in Philadelphia, the aging Field painted his *Historical Monument of the American Republic*. Field's picture showed America as wholly urban, entirely built over with huge towers, with round or octagonal sides, rising in diminishing stages. The central and tallest tower commemorated Abraham Lincoln and the Constitution. Near the top, several of these towers were joined together with vaulting steel bridges, along which steam railroad trains puffed. As a significant reminder of Civil War days, soldiers paraded the avenue in front of Field's monumental vision of America as Babylon.

By 1876, then, Field's ideas, like those of most Americans, had completely shifted. Rural peace paled beside the attractions of mechanized urban life. The machine was now the magnet of the American mind. When the novelist William Dean Howells visited the Centennial Exposition, he, like thousands of other Americans, was most impressed by the gigantic Corliss engine, which gave power to the 8000 other machines, large and small, that sewed cloth, printed newspapers, made shoes, and pumped water on the thirteen-acre Exposition grounds. After comparing the displays of painting and sculpture with the Corliss engine, Howells concluded: "It is in these things of iron and steel that the national genius most freely speaks."

The greatest painter of the postwar period, Thomas Eakins of Philadelphia, shared Howells's admiration of the machine and his respect for the scientific knowledge that it represented. Just as the Corliss engine was "an athlete of steel and iron, without a superfluous ounce of metal on it," so a painting, thought Eakins, should be lean and objective. In order to portray the human figure scientifically, he studied anatomy at Jefferson Medical College. Eakins also linked painting with mathematics, because both were disciplines in which "the complicated things are reduced to simple things." Eakins's portrait, *Max Schmitt in a Single Skull,* shows how perfectly he fused art, anatomy, and the mathematics of perspective. More subtly it also speaks of the changed values of postwar American society. In decisive contrast to the absence of all man-made artifacts in Leutze's painting and in Field's *The Garden of Eden,* a superb steel bridge is a vital part of Eakins's portrait. More emphatically than any number of words, the presence of that bridge shows that, by the end of the Civil War era, Americans had come to think of nature as something to be spanned, conquered, and controlled.

Metropolitan Museum of Art, Alfred N. Punnett Fund and Gift of George D. Pratt, 1934.

Black Population, 1880

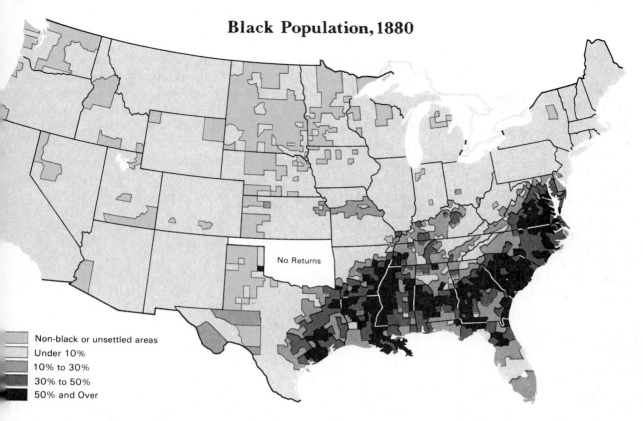

No Returns

Non-black or unsettled areas
Under 10%
10% to 30%
30% to 50%
50% and Over

colleagues replied: "God has made the negro inferior, and . . . laws cannot make him equal." Such congressmen were hardly in a position to scold the South for racial discrimination or to insist on drastic social change in that region.

If racism limited the innovation that Northerners were willing to propose during the Reconstruction period, it even more drastically reduced the amount of change that white Southerners were prepared to accept. The note of racial bigotry runs through both the private correspondence and the public pronouncements of Southern whites during the postwar era. "Equality does not exist between blacks and whites," announced Alexander H. Stephens. "The one race is by nature inferior in many respects, physically and mentally, to the other. This should be received as a fixed invincible fact in all dealings with the subject." A North Carolina diarist agreed: "The Anglo-Saxon and the African can never be equal . . . one or the other must fall." Or, as the Democratic party of Louisiana resolved in its 1865 platform: "We hold this to be a Government of white people, made and to be perpetuated for the exclusive benefit of the white race; and . . . that people of African descent cannot be considered as citizens of the United States, and that there can, in no event, nor under any circumstances, be any equality between the white and other races." The Black Codes were the legal embodiment of these attitudes.

These racist views shaped the attitude of most Southern whites toward the whole process of Reconstruction. They approved of President Johnson's plan of

Reconstruction because it placed government in the Southern states entirely in the hands of whites. They rejected the Fourteenth Amendment primarily because it made blacks legally equal to whites. They watched with incredulity bordering on stupefaction as Congress passed the 1867 Military Reconstruction Act, for they simply could not believe that the freedmen were to vote. Stunned, they watched army officers supervise the process of voter registration, a process that excluded many prominent whites who had participated in the Confederate government but included more than 700,000 blacks, who formed a majority of eligible voters in South Carolina, Florida, Alabama, Mississippi, and Louisiana. Knowing that these Negro voters were well organized by the Union League, often with the assistance of agents of the Freedmen's Bureau, whites were more apathetic than surprised when the fall elections showed heavy majorities in favor of convening new constitutional conventions.*

With hostile and unbelieving eyes, most Southern whites observed the work of these conventions, which between November 1867 and May 1868 drafted new constitutions for the former Confederate states. To Southern whites unaccustomed to seeing blacks in any positions of public prominence, the presence of freedmen in these conventions meant that they were Negro-dominated. In fact, except in the South Carolina convention, in which blacks did form a majority, only between one-fourth and one-ninth of the delegates were Negroes. Whites ridiculed the Negro members' ignorance of parliamentary procedures, and they laughed sardonically when they read how the "coal black" temporary chairman of the Louisiana convention put a question by asking those who favored a motion "to rise an stan on der feet" and then directing "all you contrairy men to rise."

The reactions of Southern whites to the constitutions these conventions produced were also determined by their racial prejudice. Generally they denounced these new charters as "totally incompatible with the prosperity and liberty of the people." In fact the constitutions, often copied from Northern models, were generally improvements over the ones they superseded. In addition to requiring Negro suffrage (as Congress had directed), they promised all citizens of the state equality before the law. They reformed financial and revenue systems, reorganized the judiciary, improved the organization of local government, and, most important of all, instituted a state-supported system of public education, hitherto notably lacking in most Southern states.

Because these constitutions guaranteed racial equality, Southern whites tried, without great success, to block their ratification. In Alabama, whites boycotted the ratification election; in Mississippi, they cast a majority of votes against the new constitution. In Virginia, ratification was delayed because the conservative army commander of that district discovered that there was no money to hold an

---

*The Texas election was not held until February 1868. Tennessee had no election, because it had already been readmitted to the Union.

election, and in Texas all moves toward the creation of a new government lagged several months behind those in the Eastern states. Despite all the foot-dragging, new governments were set up, and in June 1868 Congress readmitted representatives and senators from Alabama, Arkansas, Florida, Georgia, Louisiana, North Carolina, and South Carolina. Two years later the reconstruction of Virginia, Mississippi, and Texas was completed, and in early 1870 these states were also readmitted. Meanwhile Georgia underwent one further reorganization after the legislature of that state attempted to exclude Negroes who had been elected to that body. But by 1871, when Georgia senators and representatives again took their seats in Congress, all the states of the former Confederacy had undergone the process of Reconstruction and had been readmitted to the Union.

With bitter hostility, most Southern whites witnessed this reorganization of their state governments, and the name "Black Reconstruction," which they gave to the ensuing period of Republican ascendency in the South, reveals the racial bias behind their opposition. In fact, these Southern state governments were not dominated by Negroes, and blacks generally held fewer offices than their numbers entitled them to. Only in South Carolina did the legislature have a black majority. No Negro was elected governor, though there were black lieutenant governors in South Carolina, Louisiana, and Mississippi. Only in South Carolina was there a black state supreme court justice. During the entire Reconstruction period only two blacks, Hiram R. Revels and Blanche K. Bruce, both from Mississippi and both men of exceptional ability and integrity, served in the United States Senate, and only fifteen blacks were elected to the House of Representatives.

Even to the most racist Southern whites it was obvious that most of the leaders of the Republican party in that section, and a large part of the Republican following as well, were themselves white. To those white Republicans born in the North, racists gave the label Carpetbaggers, because they allegedly came South with no more worldly possessions than could be packed into a carpetbag, or small suitcase, ready to live on and to exploit the prostrate region. The term, with its implication of corruption, was applied indiscriminately to men of Northern birth who had lived in the South long before the war as well as to newly arrived fortune hunters, many of them recently discharged Union army officers.

Southern-born white Republicans were called Scalawags, a term that cattle drovers applied to "the mean, lousy and filthy kine that are not fit for butchers or dogs." Again the term was used indiscriminately. Southern racists applied it to poor hill-country whites, who had long been at odds with the planters in states like North Carolina and Alabama and now joined the Republican party as a way of getting back at their old enemies. But other "Scalawags" were members of the planter, mercantile, and industrial classes of the South; many of these were former Whigs who distrusted the Democrats, and they felt at home in a Republican party that favored protective tariffs, subsidies for railroads, and appropriations for rebuilding the levees along the Mississippi River. A surprising number of Southern-born white Republicans were former high-ranking officers in the

COLORED RULE IN A RECONSTRUCTED (?) STATE

As postwar racism mounted, cartoonists no longer depicted
Negroes as handsome, intelligent fighters for freedom but
painted them as grotesque and animal-like. In addition to
perpetuating racial stereotypes, this drawing of Thomas
Nast's exaggerates the number and influence of blacks in the
Southern legislatures. *(American Antiquarian Society.)*

Confederate army, like General P. G. T. Beauregard and General James Long-
street, who knew at first hand the extent of the damage wrought by the war and
were willing to accept the victor's terms without procrastination.

Bitterly as they attacked these white Republicans, Southern Democrats reserved their worst abuse for Negroes, and they saw in every measure adopted by
the new reconstructed state governments evidence of black incompetence, extravagance, or even barbarism. In truth, much that these state governments did
supplied the Democrats with ammunition. The postwar period was one of low
political morality, and there was no reason to expect that newly enfranchised
blacks would prove any less attracted by the profits of politics than anybody
else. Petty corruption prevailed in all the Southern state governments. Louisiana legislators voted themselves an allowance for stationery—which covered

purchases of hams and bottles of champagne. The South Carolina legislature ran up a bill of more than $50,000 in refurbishing the statehouse with such costly items as a $750 mirror, $480 clocks, and 200 porcelain spittoons at $8 apiece. The same legislature voted $1,000 to the speaker of the House of Representatives to repay his losses on a horse race.

Bad as these excesses were, Southern Democrats were angered less by them than by the legitimate work performed by the new state governments. Unwilling to recognize that Negroes were now equal members of the body politic, they objected to expenditures for hospitals, jails, orphanages, and asylums to care for blacks. Most of all they objected to the creation of a public school system. Throughout the South there was considerable hostility to the idea of educating any children at the cost of the taxpayer, and the thought of paying taxes in order to reach black children seemed wild and foolish extravagance. The fact that black schools were mostly conducted by Northern whites, usually women, who came South with a reforming mission, did nothing to increase popular support; too many of the teachers stated plainly and publicly their intention to use "every endeavor to throw a ray of light here and there, among this benighted race of ruffians, rebels by nature." Adding to all these hostilities was a fear that a system of public education might some day lead to a racially integrated system of education. These apprehensions had little basis in fact, for during the entire period of Reconstruction in the whole South there were significant numbers of children in racially mixed schools only in New Orleans between 1870 and 1874.

Not content with criticizing Republican rule, Southern Democrats organized to put an end to it. Theirs was a two-pronged attack. On the one hand they sought to intimidate or to drive from the South whites who cooperated politically with the Republican regimes; on the other, they tried to terrorize and silence blacks, especially those active in politics. Much of this pressure was informal and sporadic, but much was the work of racist organizations that sprang up all over the South during these years. The most famous of these was the Ku Klux Klan, which originated in 1866 as a social club for young white men in Pulaski, Tennessee. As the Military Reconstruction Act went into effect and the possibility of black participation in Southern political life became increasingly real, racists saw new potential in this secret organization with its cabalistic name and its mysterious uniforms of long flowing robes, high conical hats that made the wearers seem preternaturally tall, and white face masks. In 1867 the Klan was reorganized under a new constitution that provided for local dens, each headed by a Grand Cyclops, linked together into provinces (counties), each under a Grand Titan, and in turn into realms (states), each under a Grand Dragon. At the head of the whole organization was the Grand Wizard, who, according to most reports, was former Confederate General Forrest. Probably this elaborate table of organization was never completely filled out, and certainly there was an almost total lack of central control of the Klan's activities. Indeed, at some point in early 1869 the Klan was officially disbanded. But even without central direction its members, like those of the Order of the White Camellia and other racist vigilante groups, continued in their plan of disrupting the new Republican regimes in the South and terrorizing their black supporters.

Along with other vigilante organizations, the Klan was an expression of the traditional racism of Southern whites. They were willing to accept the defeat of the Confederacy, and they were prepared to admit that slavery was dead; but they could not bring themselves to contemplate a society that would treat blacks and whites as equals. As a group of South Carolina whites protested to Congress in 1868: "The white people of our State will never quietly submit to negro rule. . . . We will keep up this contest until we have regained the heritage of political control handed down to us by honored ancestry. That is a duty we owe to the land that is ours, to the graves that it contains, and to the race of which you and we alike are members—the proud Caucasian race, whose sovereignty on earth God has ordained."

The appeal was shrewdly pitched, for the Southern racist knew how to reach his Northern counterpart. Joined together, their fears of men with darker skins helped to undercut the Reconstruction regimes in the South and to halt any congressional efforts at further innovative Reconstruction legislation.

Suggested Readings

The Civil War and Reconstruction (1969), by J. G. Randall and David Donald, continues to be useful, especially for its full bibliography. Three modern treatments of the postwar period are John H. Franklin, *Reconstruction after the Civil War* (1961), Kenneth M. Stampp, *The Era of Reconstruction* (1965), and Rembert W. Patrick, *The Reconstruction of the Nation* (1967).

The best account of steps taken during the Civil War to reorganize the Southern states is Herman Belz, *Reconstructing the Union* (1969). William B. Hesseltine, *Lincoln's Plan of Reconstruction* (1960), argues that Lincoln had not one but many approaches to Reconstruction, all of them unsuccessful.

Robert W. Winston, *Andrew Johnson, Plebeian and Patriot* (1928), is the best of several unsatisfactory biographies of that President. More valuable are the markedly favorable estimates of Johnson's program in George F. Milton, *The Age of Hate* (1930), and Howard K. Beale, *The Critical Year* (1930), and the strongly critical analyses in Eric L. McKitrick, *Andrew Johnson and Reconstruction* (1960), LaWanda Cox and John H. Cox, *Politics, Principle, and Prejudice* (1963), and W. R. Brock, *An American Crisis* (1963).

Four major studies of postwar constitutional changes are Harold M. Hyman, *A More Perfect Union* (1973), Stanley I. Kutler, *Judicial Power and Reconstruction Politics* (1968), William Gillette, *The Right to Vote* (1965), and Charles Fairman, *Reconstruction and Reunion* (1971).

George R. Bentley, *A History of the Freedmen's Bureau* (1955), is a standard work, but it should be supplemented by William S. McFeely, *Yankee Stepfather: General O. O. Howard and the Freedmen* (1968), and Louis S. Gerteis, *From Contraband to Freedman* (1973).

Four perceptive and sympathetic analyses of blacks' responses to emancipation are Willie Lee Rose, *Rehearsal for Reconstruction* (1964), Joel Williamson, *After Slavery* (1965), Peter Kolchin, *First Freedom* (1972), and Vernon L. Wharton, *The Negro in Mississippi* (1947).

Fred A. Shannon, *The Farmer's Last Frontier* (1945), is an excellent discussion of postwar Southern agricultural problems. There is much information on Southern economic life in E. Merton Coulter, *The South during Reconstruction* (1947), and in C. Vann Woodward, *Origins of the New South* (1951). On the alleged breakup of the plantation system, see Roger W. Shugg, *Origins of Class Struggle in Louisiana* (1939).

Two articles provide the best brief introduction to the modern interpretation of Reconstruction politics: Larry G. Kincaid, "Victims of Circumstance: An Interpretation of Changing Attitudes toward Republican Policy Makers and Reconstruction," *Journal of American History* 57 (1970), 48–66, and Michael L. Benedict, "Preserving the Constitution: The Conservative Basis of Radical Reconstruction," ibid., *61* (1974), 65–90. See also Hans L. Trefousse, *The Radical Republicans* (1969), David Donald, *The Politics of Reconstruction* (1965), and Michael L. Benedict, *A Compromise of Principle* (1974). Among the fullest biographies of Radical leaders are Fawn M. Brodie, *Thaddeus Stevens* (1959), David Donald, *Charles Sumner and the Rights of Man* (1970), and Benjamin P. Thomas and Harold M. Hyman, *Stanton* (1962).

David M. DeWitt, *Impeachment and Trial of Andrew Johnson* (1903), is the standard account, strongly pro-Johnson in tone. Michael L. Benedict's book of the same title (1973) is a useful, anti-Johnson corrective. The best explanation of why impeachment occurred when it did is to be found in Hans L. Trefousse, *Impeachment of a President* (1975).

On American racial attitudes, George M. Fredrickson, *The Black Image in the White Mind* (1971), is excellent. On Northern racism, see V. Jacque Voegeli, *Free but Not Equal* (1967), and Forrest G. Wood, *Black Scare* (1968). A thoughtful and provocative essay is C. Vann Woodward, "Seeds of Failure in Radical Race Policy," *American Philosophical Society Proceedings 110* (1966), 1–9.

On the work of the Reconstruction governments in the South. see W. E. B. DuBois, "Reconstruction and Its Benefits," *American Historical Review* (1910), 781-99, and DuBois, *Black Reconstruction* (1935). The best accounts of Reconstruction in individual states are Francis B. Simkins and Robert H. Woody, *South Carolina during Reconstruction* (1932), Jerrell H. Shofner, *Nor Is It Over Yet: Florida in the Era of Reconstruction* (1974), Thomas B. Alexander, *Political Reconstruction in Tennessee* (1950), James W. Garner, *Reconstruction in Mississippi* (1901), and Joe G. Taylor, *Louisiana Reconstructed* (1974).

On the education of blacks after the war, see Henry A. Bullock, *A History of Negro Education in the South* (1967), William P. Vaughn, *Schools for All* (1974), and Roger A. Fischer, *The Segregation Struggle in Louisiana* (1974).

Southern white resistance to the Reconstruction process is the theme of Michael Perman, *Reunion without Compromise* (1973). Allen W. Trelease, *White Terror* (1971), is a harrowing account of white vigilantism, as carried on by the Ku Klux Klan and less formally organized groups.

22

The American Compromise, 1865-1880

An exclusive focus on the Southern states during the postwar years obscures the fact that Reconstruction was a national, not just a sectional, process. In both sections the nationalistic impulses unleashed by the war portended revolutionary consequences. Just as some Radical Republicans sought to overturn the entire Southern social system, so other postwar nationalists yearned to expand the role of the federal government and to integrate the hitherto inverterbrate American economy. Many Northerners considered the changes introduced into their section during the Civil War and Reconstruction period as offensive and unacceptable as most white Southerners found the program of the Radical Republicans. In the South, plans for drastic social and economic change ran headlong into long-established institutions and values, so that the amount of innovation tolerated was limited. A similar fate met schemes to transform the ideas, the society, and the economy of the North and the West. Here, too, deeply rooted local and parochial interests resisted the forces of nationalism.

The resolution of this conflict was what can be called — for lack of a better phrase — "The American Compromise." The term does not refer to formal agreements or legislative enactments embossed on parchment. Instead, it embraces a whole series of loose, informal, and frequently tacit understandings that by the 1880s legitimated the broader role played by the national government and the national economy but also protected the states and local or regional economic interests. To an observer from Bismarck's recently reunited Germany, these arrangements would doubtless have seemed chaotic and incomprehensible, for, like most American solutions to difficult problems, they were entirely pragmatic and not alway logical or consistent. But, like many other such informal American agreements, the American Compromise rested upon a broad popular consensus, and it worked. This uneasy equilibrium between national and local interests, achieved by the 1880s, served for a generation as the basis for the country's social and political order.

American Nationalism

The Civil War strongly encouraged the sentiment of nationalism among Northerners. The primary Northern war aim was not to guarantee equal rights to all men nor even to end slavery; it was to preserve the Union. By that often repeated phrase, men and women of the war years meant something more than merely maintaining the country as a territorial unit. Attached to the idea of union was an almost mystical sense of the wholeness of the American people. Americans viewed themselves as a chosen people, selected to conduct an experiment in self-government, to be a test case as to the viability of democratic institutions. As Lincoln declared, the United States was nothing less than "the last, best hope of earth."

That faith in the special destiny of the United States gave courage and hope to Northerners during the darkest hours of the war. Defeats on the battlefield, properly understood, were the fire that served to burn away the dross and impurities in American life. As the Reverend Marvin R. Vincent of Troy, New York, announced: "God has been striking, and trying to make us strike at elements unfavorable to the growth of a pure democracy; and . . . he is at work, preparing in this broad land a fit stage for a last act of the mighty drama, the consummation of human civilization." A similar inspiration moved Julia Ward Howe to draw on the imagery of the Book of Revelations in composing the most powerful and popular battle hymn ever written:

> Mine eyes have seen the glory of the coming of the Lord:
> He is trampling out the vintage where the grapes of wrath are stored;
> He has loosed the fateful lightning of his terrible swift sword:
> His truth is marching on.

Northerners believed that the Union would emerge from the war more powerful, more cohesive than ever before. They expected that the United States would no longer be a confederation or a union of states but, in the fullest sense a nation. A small shift in grammar tells the whole story. Before the Civil War many politicians and writers referred to the United States in the plural, but after 1865 only a pedant or the most unreconstructed Southerner would have dreamed of saying "the United States *are*."

The word *nation* came easily now to American lips. Unlike his predecessors who generally avoided the term, Lincoln regularly referred to the United States as a nation. For example, he used the word no fewer than five times in his brief Gettysburg Address, most eloquently in the concluding pledge: ". . . that this nation, under God, shall have a new birth of freedom." In 1865 when Republicans agreed to establish a weekly journal that would reflect their views, they called it, as a matter of course, *The Nation,* and it became, as it has remained, one of the most influential periodicals in the country. In 1867 when Sumner took to the lecture circuit to supplement his senatorial salary, he chose for his topic, "Are We a Nation?" The answer, he believed, was obvious. Americans were "one people, throbbing with a common life, occupying a common territory, rejoicing in a common history, sharing in common trials." Never again should any "local claim of self-government" be permitted "for a moment [to] interfere with the supremacy of the Nation." He concluded: "Such centralization is the highest civilization, for it approaches the nearest to the heavenly example."

Political theorists as well as public men in the postwar generation exalted American nationalism. In 1865 Orestes Brownson, the former Jacksonian spokesman, published the first book-length contribution to the bibliography of American nationalism, *The American Republic: Its Constitution, Tendencies, and Destiny.* "Nations are only individuals on a larger scale," Brownson argued, and his treatise was designed to resolve the identity crisis of the Civil War by persuading the American nation to "reflect on its own constitution, its own separate existence, individuality, tendencies, and end." Even more soaring were the claims of the Reverend Elisha Mulford's *The Nation: The Foundations of Civil Order and Political Life in the United States* (1870). The nation, Mulford argued in terms of Hegelian philosophy, was a mystic body, endowed with a spirit and a majesty of its own. "The Nation," he concluded, "is a work of God in history. . . . Its vocation is from God, and its obligation is only to God."

It would be easy to believe from such statements that Americans of the post–Civil War generation, rejoicing in the newly restored unity of their country, were swept up into an ultranationalistic frenzy comparable to that of the Germans, who almost simultaneously achieved national unity under Bismarck, or of the Italians, who were being reunited under Cavour. But a moment's reflection shows the weakness of these historical parallels. After all, the federal structure of the American government survived the Civil War. The national government continued to consist of three separate centers of power, which often checked each other. If there was no further talk of secession, there was frequent invocation of state rights, and regionalism and localism did not disappear from American life. The very fact that the Reconstruction policies imposed on the conquered South were so limited in scope and so brief in duration is the best evidence that the high priests of American nationalism did not have things their own way.

Indeed, if the works of these nationalistic writers are read carefully, they convey an ambivalent message. While rejoicing in the growth of American na-

MENDING THE MAPS OF THE WORLD.
King of Prussia—"Aha! Mad'moiselle! What you think of my needle-gun work?"
Columbia—"Well I think I can produce a better thing with my Union Sewing-Machine."

"MENDING THE MAPS OF THE WORLD"

Conveniently forgetting the bloodshed of the Civil War, an American cartoonist contrasts the restoration of the American Union with Bismarck's unification of Germany. *(American Antiquarian Society.)*

tionality, Brownson warned that this could lead to "consolidation," which might result in "socialism, or centralized democracy." Nationalism, then, needed to be checked, not, as in the past, by state sovereignty, which led toward disintegration, but by state rights. One of Brownson's admirers, the able lawyer J. C. Hurd, warned even more vigorously against the dangers from a despotic national government. In *The Theory of Our National Existence* (1881), Hurd strongly endorsed national sovereignty, but he also sought liberty, under the national aegis, for the growth of localism and particularism. Too much concentration of power in Washington, he feared, might lead to another civil war; and the next time it would be truly internecine, not a contest between sections but a war of interest groups and classes that would divide the American people "as the constituent members of States, cities, towns, communes, families, and even households."

The most successful attempt to work out a political theory that would at once safeguard the gains made by American nationalism during the Civil War and also recognize the wide diversity of regional, class, and ethnic interests in American society was that of Professor Francis Lieber, whose career, appropriately enough, was a kind of epitome of the American national experience. As a lad this Prussian-born savant had wept when he saw the troops of Napoleon overrun his native land, and he had been old enough to fight against the French at Waterloo. But he had also experienced the repressive side of nationalism when the Prussian government arrested him for harboring dangerous, liberal ideas. After a disillusioning experience in the war for Greek independence, Lieber came to the United States, where he founded and edited the *Encyclopaedia Americana* (13 volumes, 1829–33). Unable to find an academic or literary position in New England, he accepted a professorship at South Carolina College (now the University of South Carolina), where he taught history and political economy. Suspected by Southerners because of his friendship for Charles Sumner and other abolitionists and distrusted by Northerners because he did not speak out against the South's peculiar institution—indeed, he even owned slaves—Lieber felt caught in the middle, and he found no escape until 1857, when he was appointed professor at Columbia College (later Columbia University) in New York. When war broke out, one of Lieber's sons joined the Confederate army and was killed in action; the other two fought for the Union, and one lost an arm at Fort Donelson.

A passionate American nationalist, Lieber did all he could to sustain the Union government during the war. Highly respected in Washington, he became an adviser to the war department, and he drafted for the guidance of the Union army General Orders No. 100, the first codification of military law ever published. Alarmed at the lack of popular support for the national government, he helped found the Union League; he was also instrumental in setting up the Loyal Publication Society, for which he and other nationalists prepared pamphlets to promote the Union cause. Lieber's wartime message was consistent: "The people are conscious that they constitute and ought to constitute a nation, with a God appointed country, the integrity of which they will not, and must not, give up, cost what it may."

But along with Lieber's exaltation of nationalism went warnings against excess. He opposed efforts of the Radical Republicans, like his friend Sumner, to permit the national government to supervise the daily activities of citizens in the South. These attempts would "run the [national] cart into such a mire that we shall be able to extricate it only by sacrificing a good deal of our best baggage." Lieber's concern became greater when he observed how Bismarck's triumphant reuniting of Germany was followed by curbs on civil liberty. The United States, he feared, might face a similar danger.

To forestall this threat, Lieber reverted to arguments that he had earlier developed in his influential book *On Civil Liberty and Self-Government*, which had gone through two editions before the war. Without disavowing his nationalism, he sought to distinguish it from centralism. "Centralism is the convergence of all the rays of power into one central point," Lieber wrote; "nationalization is the diffusion of the same life-blood through a system of arteries, throughout a body politic. . . . " Nationalism was to be encouraged, centralism to be avoided. The most effective restraint on despotism, toward which centralism tended, lay in what Lieber called Institutional Liberty. Seeing that mechanical checks and balances between the various branches of government had already proved themselves ineffectual limits on power, Lieber looked instead to organically related institutions—the family, the churches, the scientific community, the business community, the literary world, and the like—to provide "a union of harmonizing systems of laws instinct with self-government." Such "self-evolving," "interlimiting," and "inter-guaranteeing" institutions could supply "the negation of absolutism" and thus lead to "the only self-government, or self-government carried out in the realities of life."

Lieber's theory of Institutional Liberty was thus a compromise, one particularly congenial to the postwar generation. So popular was it that when Lieber died in 1872, President Theodore Dwight Woolsey of Yale willingly undertook the preparation of a new edition of *On Civil Liberty,* for he enthusiastically endorsed both Lieber's high nationalism and his fear of "a more centralized government." That ambivalence, indeed, was the special attraction of Lieber's theory. He exalted American nationalism—but encouraged autonomy for local and particularistic interests. He upheld the Union—but sought to prevent its powers from becoming despotic. His solution for the theoretically unresolvable antagonism between liberty and authority was pragmatic; he allowed Americans to eat their cake and have it.

Postwar Diplomacy

American diplomacy during the post–Civil War generation followed a pattern that Lieber undoubtedly would have approved. On the one hand, it was vigorously nationalistic, even at times bellicose; on the other, it drew back from conflict with foreign powers, and it refrained from pursuing goals strongly opposed by influential interest groups. In short, American foreign policy showed how Lieber's Institutional Liberty worked. It showed the American Compromise in action.

During the decade after Appomattox, hardly a year passed without some significant American diplomatic initiative. With President Johnson's willing acquiescence, Secretary of State Seward maneuvered skillfully to force the withdrawal of French troops from Mexico, and he tried unsuccessfully to persuade Queen Victoria's government to pay for the damages British-built Confederate cruisers inflicted on Union shipping during the war. Seward also promoted the construction of a canal across the isthmus of Panama, the annexation of all or part of Santo Domingo, the acquisition of the Danish West Indies, and the purchase of Russian North America. There was no diminution of America's outward thrust during the first five years of President Grant's administration. His able secretary of state, Hamilton Fish, succeeded in settling the Alabama claims (as the whole groups of shippers claims against Great Britain came to be called), in adjudicating the long-standing controversy between Canadians and Americans over fisheries in the North Atlantic, and in demarcating the disputed boundary between British Columbia and the state of Washington. The President himself took a deep interest in the efforts of Cuban insurgents to oust their Spanish rulers, and at one point Spain and the United States came close to war. Grant also took the lead in seeking the annexation of the Dominican Republic.

These foreign policy initiatives received considerable popular support. After Appomattox there was a general feeling that the United States, with a million seasoned veterans under arms, was in a position to humiliate the French Emperor Napoleon III, to have a showdown with John Bull, and to pick up any adjacent territory that it pleased. The old spirit of Manifest Destiny, quiescent during the war, sprang to life again. Even those who feared it anticipated its triumph. The more optimistic rejoiced in the prospect. Advocating the annexation of both Haiti and the Dominican Republic and hoping for the future acquisition of the Kingdom of Hawaii, President Johnson's 1868 annual message to Congress concluded: "The conviction is rapidly gaining ground in the American mind that with the increased facilities for intercommunication between all portions of the earth the principles of free government, as embraced in our Constitution, if faithfully maintained and carried out, would prove of sufficient strength and breadth to comprehend within their sphere and influence the civilized nations of the world."

Despite both fears and hopes, the accomplishments of American foreign policy during the Reconstruction years were few. From the point of view of national security the most important feat was Seward's success in getting French troops

THE LAST ACT OF THE MONROE DOCTRINE

Reflecting exuberant postwar American nationalism, this artist in 1866 predicts the simultaneous expulsion of the French (personified by an effete Emperor Maximilian) from Mexico and of the British (represented by a corpulent John Bull) from Canada. *(American Antiquarian Society.)*

removed from Mexico. Introduced into Mexico during the Civil War, ostensibly to compel the bankrupt Mexican government of President Benito Juarez to pay its debts, French troops in 1864 provided the support for the installation of the Archduke Maximilian of Austria as emperor of Mexico. Unable to do more than protest against this violation of the Monroe Doctrine while the war was going on, Seward adopted a more vigorous tone after Appomattox. Yet, knowing the French emperor was a proud and volatile man, he refrained from direct threats and allowed Napoleon to discover for himself how expensive, unpopular, and unsuccessful his Mexican adventure was proving. By 1867 Napoleon finally decided to cut off further financial support for Maximilian's shaky regime and, under steady American pressure, withdrew his troops. Captured by Juarez's troops, Maximilian was shot by a firing squad on June 19, 1867. Never again would a European power so openly challenge the Monroe Doctrine.

A second diplomatic achievement of the Reconstruction years was the settlement of the Alabama claims. Immediately after the war it probably would have been possible to clear up this controversy speedily and inexpensively, had not the British government haughtily denied that it had violated international law in permitting Confederate raiders to be built in its shipyards. With delay, American grievances festered. Sumner, the powerful chairman of the Senate Committee on Foreign Relations, began to argue that the British owed not merely repayment for actual damages done by the *Alabama* and other vessels; they were also responsible for protracting the war, for the "immense and infinite" cost of the entire last two years of the conflict. The failure of Reverdy Johnson, Seward's special envoy to Great Britain, to secure an apology or expression of regret from the stubborn British government further exacerbated American feelings. Not until after Hamilton Fish took charge of the American State Department and not until after there was a change of government in Great Britain could a settlement be worked out. In the Treaty of Washington of 1871 Great Britain admitted negligence in permitting the Confederate cruisers to escape and expressed regret for the damages they had caused; and the United States tacitly abandoned the extravagant claims put forward by Sumner and agreed that the amount of damages should be assessed by a commission of arbitration representing five nations. Ultimately damages to American shipping were estimated at $15.5 million and the British government paid this amount. More important than any monetary settlement was the precedent set for arbitrating international disputes, and the Treaty of Washington paved the way for the rapprochement of the two greatest English-speaking nations. Not until the two world wars of the twentieth century would the full consequences of this development emerge.

Apart from the almost unnoticed American occupation of the Midway Islands in August 1867, the sole territorial acquisition of the United States during the Reconstruction era—and it was a very considerable addition—was the purchase of Alaska. There was little public enthusiasm for Seward's 1867 treaty to buy Russian America for $7.2 million. Newspapers called the territory "a national

RUSSIAN AMERICA — CANVASSING
THE STATE TICKET

Critics of the purchase of Alaska in
1867 called the Russian territory
"Seward's Icebox" or Andrew Johnson's
"Polar Bear Garden." (*American
Antiquarian Society.*)

icehouse" consisting of nothing but "walrus-covered icebergs." Congressmen were
equally unenthusiastic. Yet after much grumbling the Senate finally ratified the
treaty and the House reluctantly appropriated the money for the purchase.
Seward's success was due in part to his ability to convince senators that Alaska
had vast hidden natural resources; in part it was due to the judicious payments of
money to American congressmen by the Russian minister in Washington. More
influential than either of these factors, however, was the general feeling that
rejecting the treaty would alienate Czar Alexander II, who alone of the important European rulers had been sympathetic to the Union cause during the
Civil War.

Nothing came of the other postwar plans for expansion. Each of them ran into
snags that made American diplomats draw back. For instance, the desire of many
United States politicians, including Grant, Fish, and Sumner, to annex Canada
had to be abandoned when it became clear that the British would not withdraw
a fight. Grant's plan to acquire the Dominican Republic aroused the opposition
of Sumner, who considered himself the senatorial voice of the blacks and wanted
the island of Santo Domingo to become not an American possession but the center
of "a free confederacy [of the West Indies], in which the black race should predominate." Seward's treaty for the purchase of the Danish West Indies was
pigeonholed by the Senate when those unfortunate islands were visited by a
hurricane, a tidal wave, and a series of earthquake shocks.

It would, however, be a mistake to put too much stress on these idiosyncratic
factors that stopped American expansion, for there were broader forces at work.
The American people, exhausted by four years of fighting, were not prepared to
support a vigorously nationalistic foreign policy if it threatened another war.

Northern businessmen felt that it was more important to reduce taxes and to return to a sound monetary policy than to engage in foreign adventures. Because of the difficulties of racial adjustment in the South, increasing numbers of politicians hesitated before agreeing to annex additional populations of dark-skinned inhabitants. During Johnson's administration, many Republicans opposed all Seward's plans for expansion because they might bring credit to that unpopular President. During Grant's tenure, disaffected Republicans, who by 1872 joined the Liberal Republican party and opposed Grant's reelection, had similar motives for blocking his diplomatic schemes. So powerful were these combined elements of opposition that after 1874 there was little further talk of a vigorous nationalistic foreign policy or of American expansionism.

American foreign policy during the Reconstruction generation, then, illustrates the operation of Lieber's principle of Institutional Liberty. On issues that clearly touched the national security, those that affected the existence of the nation itself —such as the presence of French troops in Mexico and the difficulties with Great Britain that might have resulted in war—there was a consensus sufficiently strong to permit the national government to act. Even the purchase of Alaska, which seemed to involve the friendship between the United States and the powerful Russian empire, fell into this category. But where there was no clear, overriding national interest, local, sectional, racial, and class objections to expansion prevailed. Though Presidents and secretaries of state might fume, there was a tacit agreement that the wishes of these minorities must be respected. To use Lieber's phraseology, American foreign policy during the postwar years was an expression of nationalism but a rejection of centralism.

Toward a National Economy

The years immediately following the Civil War witnessed an enormous boom in the American economy. Except for the South, still recovering from the ravages of war, every region of the country prospered during the eight years after Appomattox. Except for the merchant marine, which never recovered from the damages inflicted by Confederate raiders, every branch of commerce, industry, and agriculture flourished.

The age was an expansive one, and Americans rushed to settle vast tracts of hitherto uninhabited land in the West. In 1860 the western frontier of settlement lay near the Missouri River, and between eastern Kansas and California there were hardly any white inhabitants except in the Mormon settlement in Utah and in the Spanish-speaking community at Santa Fe. Thirty years later, immigrants pushing west into the Great Plains and Rocky Mountain region and pushing east from California formed a virtually uninterrupted pattern of settlement across the continent. In 1890 the superintendent of the United States census announced— a bit prematurely—that the frontier was gone: "Up to and including 1880 the country had a frontier settlement, but at present the unsettled area has been so broken into by isolated bodies of settlement that there can hardly be said to be a frontier line."

To some extent the peopling of the West was triggered by the passage in 1862 of the Homestead Act, which offered free of charge to any citizen who was over 21 or the head of a family 160 acres of public lands if he resided on them for five continuous years. As an alternative, a homesteader could purchase his land from the government for $1.25 an acre after six months' residence. Between 1862 and 1900 about 400,000 families received free homesteads under this program, but the dream that free public land would siphon off industrial workers from the overcrowded cities of the East was not realized. Very few urban artisans could afford to transport themselves and their families to the frontier, pay the necessary fees at the land office, to construct a cabin, to purchase the necessary tools and seeds, and buy food during the long growing season before the wheat or corn was harvested. Even fewer knew how to farm. Consequently the great majority of homesteaders were men and women who had spent all their earlier years on the land. Even experience was no guarantee of success, for fully two-thirds of all homestead claimants before 1890 failed at the venture.

Most settlers in the West did not stake claims under the Homestead Act but continued, as they had always done, to purchase land directly from the government. Thousands more bought land from the railroad companies, which received from state and national governments enormous tracts of land, equal to more than twice the acreage made available to homesteaders. For instance, Congress gave the Union Pacific and the Central Pacific lines ten square miles of public land for every mile of track completed in the states, twenty square miles for every mile built in the territories.

However Western settlers secured their land titles, they looked to the national government to protect their farms from the Indians, about 225,000 of whom roamed the Great Plains and Rocky Mountains. In the north the Sioux, Arapaho, Cheyenne, and Nez Percé were the most powerful tribes; to the south the most warlike were the Comanches, Apaches, and Utes. Intrepid and hardy, the braves of all these tribes were fine horsemen and superb marksmen; they were exceedingly dangerous foes of the whites who penetrated their territory to build railroad lines, to mine for gold, or to farm. Hostilities between white settlers and Plains Indians, which broke out during the Civil War, continued almost without interruption for a quarter of a century, with the most barbarous atrocities committed by both sides. After the war, the army slowly but ineluctably forced the tribes into ever smaller reservations. Some desperately resisted, as did the Sioux led by Sitting Bull and Crazy Horse, who tried to keep the Black Hills, their tribal holy grounds, from spoliation by gold miners. In 1876, when the army attempted to disperse the Sioux, the Indians succeeded in massacring the whole force of 264 officers and men commanded by the dashing, golden-haired Civil War hero, George A. Custer, at Little Big Horn. Such Indian successes were, however, at best temporary, for the army ultimately subdued such great tribal leaders as Chief Red Cloud of the Sioux, Chief Joseph of the Nez Percé, and Geronimo of the Apaches. The final victory of the white settlers was symbolized in the Dawes Act of 1887, which allotted the lands within the still further restricted Indian reservations in 160-acre parcels to Indian residents and thus anticipated an end of the traditional Indian tribal relationship. The West, it was clear, would belong to the white settlers, whose numbers were mounting astronomically.

Indeed, the whole country was growing at a fantastic pace. During the decade

WAGON TRAIN CROSSING THE PLAINS DURING THE 1870S

For able-bodied single men a pack train was the most efficient way of moving West. But for families, undertaking a trip that might last from three to five months, a wagon train was more practicable. The covered wagon, or prairie schooner, usually pulled by oxen, had iron tires four inches wide and held up to 7,000 pounds. Such a wagon allowed a family to bring along its cherished possessions, and it also offered a place where the pregnant mother could rest, the children could sleep, or a sick member of the family could recuperate. (*University of Washington.*)

CHIEF JOSEPH OF THE NEZ PERCÉ

After white squatters committed
repeated outrages upon the Nez
Percé Indians, Chief Joseph was
reluctantly drawn into hostilities
with the United States army.
Realizing that he could not cope
with the whites' superior manpower and firepower, he led his
people in a brilliantly executed
retreat toward the safety of the
Canadian border. In October 1877,
only thirty miles from his
destination, he was cornered,
besieged, and defeated.
(Smithsonian Institute.)

from the end of the Civil War to 1876, when the Republic celebrated its centennial
year, the population of the United States jumped by 30 percent, from 35.7 million to 46.1 million. During these same years more than 3 million immigrants,
mostly from Europe, poured into the country. Railroad mileage increased by 111
percent during the decade, the number of bushels of corn by 100 percent, and
production of bituminous coal by 163 percent. Almost no American steel was
manufactured at the end of the war; 390,000 tons were made ten years later.

This phenomenal rate of growth fostered a tendency to consolidate the American economy into one huge functional unit. This had been the dream of some
businessmen long before the war, but after 1865 for the first time the necessary
preconditions for economic integration existed. Never before had the United
States had a national currency, and earlier businessmen had been obliged to
settle their obligations with an assortment of state bank notes, local script, and
coin; but passage of the National Banking Act of 1864 created a uniform circulat-
ing medium. Banks chartered by the national government were allowed, in return for purchasing government bonds, to issue the new national bank notes
supplied by the federal comptroller of the currency. A tax placed on state bank

notes in 1865 ensured that these national bank notes would thereafter have no competition.

For the first time, too, the United States after 1865 was bound together by a modern communications network. Before the Civil War, a number of rival telegraph companies had been constructing lines but their efforts had been sporadic and uncoordinated. Thanks in part to the extensive military use of the telegraph during the war, the Western Union Telegraph Company grew strong enough to absorb smaller rivals, extended a line across the continent to San Francisco, and secured a virtual monopoly in the field. Western Union made it possible for a citizen in almost any part of the country to communicate almost instantaneously with his fellows in any other part of the reunited nation. After Alexander Graham Bell invented the telephone in the 1870s, and particularly after he demonstrated the miraculous ability to transmit the human voice by electrical current at the great Centennial Exhibition at Philadelphia in 1876, a second communications network appeared. By the 1880s most city physicians

SIOUX INDIAN ENCAMPMENT, DAKOTA TERRITORY, 1891

The Sioux, led by such chiefs as Crazy Horse and Sitting Bull, fiercely resisted white settlement of the northern Great Plains. *(Library of Congress.)*

A BRIGHT, HEALTHFUL SKIN AND COMPLEXION ENSURED BY USING PEARS' SOAP. Recommended as "A BALM FOR THE SKIN" by the greatest English Authorities on the Skin, Prof. Sir ERASMUS WILSON, F. R. S., L. L. D., Pres. of the Royal Col. of Surgeons, England, and other eminent men. COUNTLESS BEAUTEOUS LADIES, INCLUDING Mrs. LILLIE LANGTRY, M'lle ADELINA PATTI, Miss MAY FORTESCUE, and others praise its virtues and prefer Pears' Soap to any other, which is the purest and best for the skin and the most economical in use. This Soap has been established in London nearly 100 years and has received 15 International Awards. The Proprietors, Messrs. A. & F. Pears, are Soapmakers by sealed appointment to H.R.H., The Prince of Wales.

PEARS SOAP ADVERTISEMENT, 1887

The completion of a national system of transportation and communication encouraged the sale of nationally known, brand-name products. One of the first of these was Pears Soap, the nationally circulated advertisements for which managed simultaneously to titillate and to convey the impression of purity and cleanliness. *(Culver Pictures.)*

had telephones, and during President Hayes's administration an instrument was installed in the White House. The telephone was still such a novelty that, when it rang, the President himself was likely to pick up the receiver.

An improved transportation network also cemented the nation together. A transcontinental railroad, long advocated but repeatedly postponed because of sectional controversies, received the support of Congress in 1862, when it incorporated the Union Pacific Railroad Company. Financed by vast tracts of public lands, the Union Pacific began constructing a line from western Iowa to join the Central Pacific Railroad, which was pushing eastward from San Francisco. In 1869 the two roads met at Promontory Point, Utah, and it became possible to move passengers and freight by rail from the Atlantic Ocean to the Pacific. Less dramatic but more economically significant was the simultaneous coordination and consolidation of rail lines in more settled areas. Before the Civil War, there had been eleven different rail gauges in use on northern roads; President Lincoln's choice of the 4-foot 8½-inch gauge for the Union Pacific led to the standardization of all roads at this width. Before the war, rail travel from New York to Chicago had been barely possible by using eight or ten independent lines, with repeated transfers. In 1869, Commodore Vanderbilt consolidated the New York Central and the Hudson River railroads to give continuous service from New York to Buffalo, and five years later he completed arrangements with western railroads to offer through service to Chicago. At about the same time the Pennsylvania Railroad, the Erie Railroad, and the Baltimore and Ohio Railroad also completed connections with Chicago.

A national communications and transportation network encouraged businessmen to seek national markets for their products. Business consolidation, already under way before the war, proceeded rapidly, and a striking number of new entrepreneurs—"robber barons," as later critics called them—were men whose wartime experience had taught them the advantages of technological innovation and large-scale management. For instance, Andrew Carnegie, who came to the United States as a poor Scottish immigrant and trained himself to become a skilled telegraph operator, served during the war as aide to Thomas A. Scott, the assistant secretary of war in charge of all government railroads and transportation lines. From this vantage point, Carnegie shrewdly foresaw the postwar expansion and reorganization of the railway system, and he invested his early savings in the company that owned the patents for Pullman sleeping cars. When these cars became standard equipment on railroads, Carnegie was on his way to acquiring his huge fortune, with which he subsequently helped build the steel industry in the United States.

John D. Rockefeller, the pious young Baptist from Cleveland, Ohio, got his start through handling wartime government contracts for hay, grain, meat, and other commodities. Quickly he learned how a company that was managed with order and enterprise could drive inefficient competitors out of business, and he decided to apply this lesson to the new petroleum industry. Astutely recognizing that the way to dominate the industry was to control the refining process, Rockefeller in 1863 constructed the largest refinery in Cleveland, and two years later he built a second one. His brother, William, developed the Eastern and the export market for their products. Enlisting Harry M. Flagler as a partner in 1867, Rockefeller worked systematically to cut costs and to rationalize an industry hitherto unstandardized and intensely competitive. By 1870, Rockefeller's company, Standard Oil of Ohio, made its own barrels, built its own warehouses, and owned its own fleet of tankers. Because of the volume of his business, Rockefeller was able to force the railroads to give his firm lower rates, or rebates, on all his shipments. Then, as his power grew, he compelled the railroads to turn over to Standard Oil "draw-backs," or a portion of what other oil companies had to pay in the way of freight. As a consequence of these business practices, which were at once shrewd and unscrupulous, Standard Oil by 1880 controlled 95 percent of the refining business of the country and practically all the transportation of oil in the United States, whether by pipeline or railroad.

While businesses that operated on a nationwide scale were emerging, so was a national labor movement. There were several attempts to organize labor on a national scale. One of the earliest was the eight-hour movement, led by Ira Steward, a Boston machinist, who sought legislation to limit the work day to eight hours without reduction of wages. Under this pressure the United States established an eight-hour day for its employees in 1868, and legislatures in six states passed acts to make eight hours a legal day's work. In private industry these laws proved ineffectual because they instituted the eight-hour restriction only "where there is no special contract or agreement to the contrary." Consequently most businessmen required employees to agree to work longer hours as a condition of employment.

The National Labor Union, created in 1866 at a Baltimore conference of delegates from various unions, proved little more successful. It was headed by William H. Sylvis, a dedicated propagandist and a superb speaker, whose interests, however, were not in conventional labor issues like hours and wages but in cooperatives and currency reform. Sylvis recruited many members for the National Labor Union—it claimed 640,000 in 1868—but whether these were

SPECIMEN DIAL FOR MECHANICSVILLE TOWN HALL — HANDS EMPLOYED TO WORK EIGHT HOURS ONLY

The eight-hour movement was the most popular of the early postwar labor reform drives. Its slogan was: "Eight hours work a day leaves eight for sleep and eight for play." *(American Antiquarian Society.)*

actual workingmen is questionable. A scornful observer remarked that the National Labor Union was made up of "labor leaders without organizations, politicians without parties, women without husbands, and cranks, visionaries, and agitators without jobs." After Sylvis's death in 1869, the organization began to decline, and it disappeared during the depression of 1873.

A more successful labor movement was the Knights of Labor, founded in 1869 by Uriah Stevens and other garment workers of Philadelphia. It grew slowly at first and, like the National Labor Union, received a serious setback in the depression. By the 1880s, however, its membership increased in a spectacular fashion as it attempted to create a broad union of all workingmen, skilled and unskilled. But its leadership, like that of the National Labor Union, was averse to discussing hours, wages, and working conditions and was reluctant to call strikes. After 1879, the General Master Workman of the Knights of Labor was the idealistic, eloquent, and neurasthenic Irishman Terence V. Powderly, who preferred to think of himself as the head of a national educational institution rather than of a labor union. Indeed, Powderly never behaved like a labor leader but, as an analyst has said, "acted more like Queen Victoria at a national Democratic convention." Consequently, size failed to bring strength to the Knights of Labor, and until the organization of the American Federation of Labor in 1886 there was no national organization that could rightfully claim to speak for the labor movement.

While industry was expanding to reach a national market, other segments of the economy were becoming integrated into the national system. In the post-Civil War years a huge Western range-cattle industry became the prime supplier of beef for the East, and also for Europe. Even before the Civil War, cattle raising had become a major occupation in the Great Plains area, stretching from Texas to Canada. There hardy cattle, descendants of Mexican longhorns, fed on open ranges. At yearly roundups calves were branded so that their owners could identify them, and cowboys selected the strongest steers for the long drive east. Since the war cut off markets for Texas cattle, herds became uncomfortably large, and as soon as peace was restored Texas cattlemen renewed their annual drive of cattle at an unprecedented scale. Initially these vast herds headed for the railhead at Sedalia, Missouri, where they could be transported to Chicago, Saint Louis, and other Eastern markets, but when the Kansas Pacific Railroad reached Abilene, Kansas, in 1867, cattlemen found a shorter, safer route to market. From Texas alone, 35,000 head of cattle came to the new railhead in its first year of operation; 350,000 in 1869; and 700,000 in 1871. Thereafter, as the national rail network extended farther west, Wichita and Dodge City came to rival, if not to replace, Abilene. These were rowdy frontier towns, where the cowboys, black as well as white, lonely after long months on the range, could let off steam in the dance halls, the saloons, and the red-light districts. But these cattle towns also served a basic economic function by tying the range cattle industry into the national economy.

TRANSPORT OF TEXAS BEEF ON THE KANSAS-PACIFIC RAILWAY, ABILENE

Beginning in 1867 Abilene, Kansas, became the principal railhead to which Texas ranchers brought their long-horn cattle, after the long drive, for shipment to the East. By 1871 1,460,000 head of cattle were shipped out of Abilene. *(Library of Congress.)*

Farmers, too, became part of that national network in the postwar era. The first few years after the war were boom times for Northern and Western farmers. With the growth of American cities, the domestic demand for grain constantly increased, and at the same time Great Britain was becoming more dependent on American harvests. By 1880, for the first time, the value of American wheat and flour exports nearly equaled that of exported cotton.

Heartened by rising prices, Northern and Western farmers expanded their operations. Using new and improved farm machinery, such as Cyrus Hall McCormick's reaping machine, they were able to cultivate and harvest large crops with fewer workers. Since this machinery was expensive and since it operated best on large, level tracts of land, small, self-sufficient farmers, chronically short of cash, were at a disadvantage. The future seemed to belong to large producers, and confident Western farmers went heavily into debt to buy more land and better machines. More than in any previous era they were now tied into a national market economy. Their fortunes depended not alone on the land, the weather, and their efforts, but on the grain elevators, the railroads, and the national and international markets.

Tariff and Currency Controversies

The movement toward a national economy in the post-Civil War decades encountered opposition. It rapidly became evident that complete integation could be achieved only at enormous economic, social, and psychological costs. Not even the business interests of the Northeast, which tended to be the primary beneficiaries of a national economic system, were unanimously in favor of integration. If New York City grew because of the increasingly centralized financial and transportation networks, that growth was at the expense of such former rivals as Boston and Philadelphia. If Standard Oil benefited by Rockefeller's rationalization of the refining industry, hundreds of less successful oil men were forced into failure. If mass production of nails at Andrew Carnegie's massive J. Edgar Thompson steel mill made building construction cheaper and safer, it also cost local blacksmiths and ironmongers their markets.

These tensions within the business community rarely surfaced as issues of public policy to be settled in the political arena. During the Gilded Age—so called from the novel by Mark Twain and Charles Dudley Warner depicting the boom-and-bust speculative mentality of businessmen of the post–Civil War era and the willing complaisance of the politicos who served their interests—almost everyone agreed that the role of government, and especially of the national government, in economic life should be minimal. In only two principal fields was it considered proper for the national government to act in a way that affected the economy: the tariff and the currency. Disagreements among business interests were therefore usually voiced in connection with these two endlessly troublesome, highly technical questions, so complex that only a handful of congressmen fully understood them.

The tariff was rarely debated in terms of free trade versus protection. Except for a few doctrinaire economic theorists, virtually everybody recognized that some tariff barrier was needed to protect some American industries. The debates in Congress revolved about which industries and how much protection. At the end of the Civil War the high tariffs of the war period, enacted in part to protect heavily taxed American industry from untaxed foreign competition, were clearly out of date.

Seeking some reasonable compromise, the New England economist David A. Wells, who was appointed Special Commissioner of the Revenue in 1866, drafted a bill to reduce duties upon imported raw materials such as scrap iron, coal, and lumber, to eliminate arbitrary and unnecessary duties on items like chemicals and spices, and to lower slightly duties on most manufactured articles. Virtually all lawmakers admitted the theoretical excellence of Wells's bill—and virtually all opposed the provisions that lessened or removed protection for their own constitutents' businesses. Consequently Wells's bill was defeated, and during the next fifteen years there was no general revision of the tariff legislation.

The absence of general tariffs acts did not mean that discussion of tariff rates

PIONEER RUN, 1865

The discovery of petroleum in western Pennsylvania led to
its rapid and wasteful exploitation. Not more than one well
out of twenty was properly sunk and carefully managed.
(*American Petroleum Institute.*)

was at an end. To the contrary, there was throughout the period an endless pulling and hauling between economic interests that stood to gain or lose from
changes in duties on specific imported items. For example, during the war a considerable copper industry had grown up in Boston and Baltimore that smelted
and refined Chilean ore, which paid a very low tariff duty. But in the late 1860s,
the great copper mines around Lake Superior began to be worked on a large
scale, and their owners asked Congress to protect their product by raising duties
on imported ore. After sharp disagreement, in which President Johnson took the
side of the refiners and most congressional Republicans the side of the ore producers, the tariff on copper ore was increased in 1869 to a point at which most of
the Eastern smelting firms had to go out of business.

Other tariff changes were the consequence of combined efforts by the producers and processors of raw materials. An 1867 act revising the duties on raw
wool and on woolen cloth was drafted at a convention of wool producers and
manufacturers at Syracuse, and it was lobbied through Congress by the indefatigable and effective secretary of the Wool Manufacturers' Association, John
L. Hayes.

Some of the minor adjustments made in the tariff during the postwar years
reflected political pressures. In a general way Republicans, with some notable
exceptions, tended to favor high protective tariffs, and Democrats, especially

PETROLEUM GALLOP

Petroleum seized the American imagination. Poets waxed rhapsodic about the soft kerosene light that was weaving a "golden web" over all America. The refrain of a popular song was "Oil on the Brain." The cover of this sheet music, by the pseudonymous "Oily Gammon"—i.e., bacon—captures the frenetic spirit of the oil fields. *(American Antiquarian Society.)*

those in the South who needed foreign markets for their cotton, wanted to reduce duties. But the issue was rarely clear-cut, for Democrats in manufacturing states like Pennsylvania were high-tariff men. Moreover, both parties tinkered with the tariff issue at election time. In 1872, for instance, the Republican party faced a split, when many tariff reformers in the Liberal Republican movement were preparing to join the Democrats. Attempting to check the bolt, the Republican-dominated Congress rushed through a bill reducing all duties by 10 percent. Once Grant was triumphantly reelected, the Congress promptly repealed the reduction. Again in 1883, when it seemed likely that in the next election Democrats would elect Grover Cleveland President and would win majorities in both houses of Congress, Republicans hurriedly enacted the first general tariff act since the Civil War. They claimed that it reduced duties by an average of 5 percent, but in fact the measure was so complex and so contradictory that nobody could predict its impact. John L. Hayes, now president of the United States Tariff Commission, gave the secret away when he explained, shortly after the passage of the 1883 act: "In a word, the object was *protection through reduction.* . . . We wanted the tariff to be made by our friends."

The whole complex history of tariff legislation during the Gilded Age, then, demonstrates the continuing strength of the highly nationalistic impulse toward protectionism. At the same time it shows how powerful regional and economic

interests adversely affected by excessively high duties were able to secure concessions that gave relief without compromising the general protective framework.

The debate over currency during the post–Civil War generation was more
complex, but in general it illustrates the same point. Unless a historian is prepared to write a book about these monetary issues, perhaps he ought to confine
his account to two sentences: During the generation after the Civil War there
was constant controversy between those who wished to continue, or even to
expand, the inflated wartime money supply and those who wanted to contract
the currency. Most debtors favored inflation, since it would allow them to pay
debts in money less valuable than when they borrowed it; and creditors favored
contraction, so that the money they received in payment of debts would be more
valuable than when it was loaned.

But those two sentences, accurate enough in a general way, fail to convey the
full dimensions of the controversy. They make the whole argument seem a
purely economic question of profit and loss. In fact, for many people the resumption of specie payments—that is, the redemption of the paper money issued by
the United States government in gold, at face value—involved the sanctity of
contracts, the reliability of the government's pledges, and the rights of private
property. Indeed, the return to the gold standard seemed to have almost a religious significance. Probably most economists of the period shared the conviction of Hugh McCulloch, Johnson's secretary of the treasury, that "gold and silver
are the only true measure of value. . . . I have myself no more doubt that these
metals were prepared by the Almighty for this very purpose, than I have that
iron and coal were prepared for the purposes for which they are being used."
On the other hand, the advocates of so-called soft money argued that it was down-
right un-American to drive greenbacks out of circulation and return to the gold
standard. "Why," asked the promoter Jay Cooke, "should this Grand and Glorious Country be stunted and dwarfed—its activities chilled and its very life blood
curdled—by these miserable 'hard coin' theories, the musty theories of a bygone
age?"

That two-sentence summary also ignores the fact that the currency controversy
involved economic interests falling into more sophisticated categories than
debtors and creditors. Merchants in foreign trade were ardent supporters of
resumption because fluctuations in the gold value of United States paper money
made the business of these importers and exporters a game of chance. On the
other hand, many American manufacturers, especially iron makers, were stanch
foes of resumption because they needed an inflated currency to keep their national markets expanding.

Finally, that two-sentence summary does not indicate that attitudes toward
these monetary policies changed over time. Throughout the postwar period
farmers were mostly debtors, but they were primarily concerned with such issues
as railroad regulation and until 1870 showed little interest in the currency.
Creditor interests of the Northeast were indeed mostly supporters of resumption,

but when the depression began, they unsuccessfully urged President Grant to sign a so-called Inflation Bill of 1874, which would have slightly increased the amount of paper money in circulation. In other words, they preferred mild inflation to economic collapse. Moreover, by the late 1870s, inflationists were no longer calling for additional greenbacks; instead, they joined forces with Western mining interests to demand that the government expand the currency by coining silver dollars. When they discovered that, partly by oversight, partly by plan, the Coinage Act of 1873 had discontinued the minting of silver, they were outraged. Protesting the "Crime of '73," they demanded a return to bimetallism (both gold and silver being accepted in lawful payment of all debts) and the free and unlimited coinage of silver dollars.

With so many opposing forces at work, it is scarcely surprising that the history of currency policy and financial legislation in the postwar years is one of sudden fits and starts. Right after the war, Secretary McCulloch assumed that everybody wanted to return to specie payments promptly, and, as a means of raising the value of the paper currency, he quietly sequestered greenbacks paid into the United States treasury for taxes and for public lands. His mild contraction of the currency checked business expansion, and Congress forced him to desist. Subsequently the sequestered greenbacks were reissued, and in the total amount of $382 million they remained in circulation for the next decade.

In an indirect fashion, the currency became an issue in the presidential election of 1868. During the previous year, what became known as the Ohio Idea gained popularity in the Middle West. Critics of hard money objected to the government's practice of paying interest on the national debt in gold—which was, of course, much more valuable than greenbacks. Since the bonds had been purchased with greenbacks, they argued, it would be entirely legal and proper to pay their interest in the same depreciated currency. In this way the crushing burden of the national debt on the taxpayer would be reduced. So attractive was this argument that the Democratic national convention incorporated a version of the Ohio Idea in its 1868 platform, but it negated this move by nominating Governor Horatio Seymour of New York, an earnest hard-money man, for President. The Republican national convention, against the wishes of many Western delegates, sternly rejected the Ohio Idea, and Grant was nominated with a pledge to reject "all forms of repudiation as a national crime.'

Despite this commitment, Grant's administrations witnessed the completion of a series of compromises on currency. The new President announced that he favored a return to the gold standard; but at the same time he warned: "Immediate resumption, if practicable, would not be desirable. It would compel the debtor class to pay, beyond their contracts, the premium on gold . . . and would bring bankruptcy and ruin to thousands.' But, lest anyone think that this last statement meant he desired further issues of paper money, Grant vetoed the Inflation Bill of 1874, against the advice of many of his advisers.

It was within this broad policy of affirmation checked by negation that John

Sherman, the Senate expert on finance, persuaded Congress in 1875 to pass the Resumption Act, announcing the intention of the United States government to redeem its paper money at face value in gold on or after January 1, 1879. Ostensibly a victory for hard-money interests, the act was, in fact, a brilliant compromise. It did commit the United States to resumption—but only after a delay of four years. Sherman sweetened this pill for the silver mining interests by providing that "as rapidly as practicable" silver coins would be minted to replace the "fractional currency"—notes of postage-stamp size in 3, 5, 10, 15, 25, and 50-cent denominations—issued during the war. To placate the greenback interests in the South and West, Sherman's measure made it easier to incorporate national banks, which had the right to issue treasury notes, in those regions.

Though attempts were made after 1875 to repeal the Resumption Act, it was such a carefully constructed compromise that they all failed. Sherman, who became Secretary of the Treasury in President Hayes s cabinet, skillfully managed the transition in 1879 so that resumption took place without fanfare and without economic disturbance. The whole controversy over currency during the Gilded Age was thus another illustration of the kind of compromises Americans of this generation worked out. The national policy of resumption, desired by most businessmen and needed if the United States was to play a part in world trade, was sustained; but local business interests were able to delay and modify implementation of the policy so that it did not impose too sudden or heavy a burden on groups adversely affected by hard money.

Discontent among Farmers and Laborers

If the emergence of a national economy produced strains within the business community, it created severe problems for farmers and laborers, who felt that they were not fairly sharing its rewards. Discontent became vocal first among farmers. Even in the buoyant years immediately after the Civil War, the life of the Northern and Western farmer was often lonely and dull. On the western plains, where farmers lived miles from stores, schools, and churches, where there were often no near neighbors, and where there was no regular mail service, even the prosperous lived stunted lives. Perhaps farm women felt the isolation even more deeply than the men.

In an effort to remedy these problems, Oliver Hudson Kelley, a clerk in the United States Department of Agriculture, in 1867 founded a secret society called the Patrons of Husbandry. Kelley, who had lived in Massachusetts, Iowa, and Minnesota and who had traveled extensively in the South after the war, knew at first hand the bleakness and the deprivation of rural living, and he wanted to give farmers all over the country a broader vision and a livelier social and intellectual life. The Patrons of Husbandry was intended to stimulate farmers thinking through lectures, debates, and discussions, and it was designed to promote a sense of social solidarity through group singing, picnics, and other family entertainment. Each local unit of Kelley's society was called a Grange, and women as well as men belonged as equal members. So new was the whole idea to American farmers that the organization got off to a slow start, and at the end of 1868 only ten Granges had been established.

In the following year, when the price of farm commodities dropped sharply, agrarian discontent mounted, and by the mid-1870s about 800,000 farmers, mostly in the Middle West and South, joined the Granger movement. Though the Granges never abandoned their social and intellectual objectives, the meetings came increasingly to focus on economic issues important to farmers, such as the declining price of wheat and the mounting costs of railroad transportation. Forbidden by the constitution of the Patrons of Husbandry to engage in politics, the Grangers found it easy after the recital of the Grange litany and the standard literary or musical program to move that the meeting be adjourned; then, technically no longer Grangers but simply farmers gathered together, they discussed politics and endorsed candidates who favored the farmers' cause.

That cause embraced a variety of discontents with the operations of the national economy. Farmers in Iowa, Nebraska, and Kansas complained that it took

The Patrons of Husbandry (the Grange) had a double function. Officially the organization was designed to promote better methods of agriculture and to improve the social and intellectual life of farmers. Unofficially Grangers often supported independent political candidates pledged to regulate rates charged by railroads and grain elevators. (*American Antiquarian Society.*)

The Granger at Home.   The Granger abroad.

the value of one bushel of corn to pay the freight charges for shipping another bushel to Eastern markets; farmers in Minnesota and Dakota said the same of wheat. Middle Western farmers protested the policy of the grain elevators, used to store their wheat and corn until it could be picked up for rail shipment. Elevator operators frequently misgraded grain, offering the farmer with superior produce only the price for a lower grade, and the farmer usually had to accept, for he could not dump his grain on the ground. Southern and Western farmers also objected to the limited bank credit available in their regions. When the national banking system was set up, the war was still going on, and no provision was made for establishing national banks in the South. In the West there were few national banks because Congress required a minimum capital of $50,000, which few Western towns could raise. Consequently, the circulation of national bank notes, and hence the availability of loans, were grossly inequitable. Connecticut alone had more national bank notes in circulation than Michigan, Wisconsin, Iowa, Minnesota, Kansas, Missouri, Kentucky, and Tennessee.

Farmers dissatisfaction with the national economy blended into a more general pattern of Middle Western discontent. It was not farmers alone who objected to high and discriminatory railroad rates; businessmen in Middle Western cities and towns, especially those served by only one rail line, also protested. Because the railroads set rates that favored large grain terminals, wheat produced twenty miles from Milwaukee might be diverted to Chicago. Because railroads gave special preference to long-distance shippers, lumber merchants in Clinton, Iowa, found that Chicago lumber dealers could undersell them; trainloads of lumber rumbled in from Chicago on the way to central and western Iowa without even slowing down at Clinton. The inequities in the national banking system affected Western businessmen at least as much as they did farmers, for the absence of credit crippled business expansion in the South and West.

Out of these general Western grievances emerged what came to be known, somewhat inaccurately, as the Granger laws. Between 1869 and 1874, legislatures in Illinois, Iowa, Wisconsin, and Minnesota set maximum charges for grain elevators and railroads, and some of these states established regulatory commissions with broad powers. Though farmers supported this legislation, it was actually framed by Western lawyers and pushed by Western businessmen; only in Wisconsin were the Grangers the principal advocates of regulation. Promptly the railroad and grain elevator companies challenged the constitutionality of these acts, but the United States Supreme Court in *Munn* v. *Illinois* (1877) upheld the right of states to regulate railroads, even to the point of setting maximum rates.

In the long run, state regulation of railroads and grain elevators proved ineffectual, and the Granger laws were repealed or seriously modified. Nevertheless, their temporary success marked a victory for the forces of localism injured by a national economy. The Supreme Court's decision, in effect, endorsed Lieber s theory of Institutional Liberty: Middle Western farmers and businessmen made no attempt to dismantle the national system of transportation, communications, and marketing, but that system was required to concede some autonomy to localities and interests harmed by economic consolidation.

Far different was the outcome of labor protests against a national economic system during these same years. Labor discontent became articulate and forceful when the panic of 1873, precipitated by the failure of Jay Cooke and Company, led into the longest and most severe depression Americans had yet experienced. As business activity declined about one-third between 1873 and 1879 and the number of bankruptcies doubled during the same period, workers were laid off. During the winter of 1873–74 about one-fourth of all laborers in New York City were unemployed, and during the following winter the number increased to one-third.

While private charities did what they could to relieve distress, nobody seemed to know how to end the depression. Informed opinion tended to view the panic and the subsequent unemployment and suffering as part of the natural workings of the national economic order, necessary to purge unsound businesses and speculative practices. Economists warned that "coddling" laborers would only retard this inevitable and necessary process. Blaming the depression on the wartime habit of looking to the federal government for leadership, Democratic Governor Samuel J. Tilden of New York called for a return to "government institutions, simple, frugal, meddling little with the private concerns of individuals . . . and trusting to the people to work out their own prosperity and happiness."

Labor leaders were not much more helpful. For one reason, the national labor movement collapsed during the depression, and many local unions disappeared as well. In New York City, for example, membership in all unions dropped from 45,000 in 1873 to 5000 in 1877. Those labor spokesmen who remained active tended to advocate panaceas. A writer in the *Radical Review* found the cause of the depression in the private ownership of land, which in his words, "begets . . . ground rent, an inexorable, perpetual claim for the use of land, which, like air and light, is the gift of Nature." In 1879, Henry George made that proposition the basis for the economic system proposed in *Progress and Poverty* Other labor voices supported the Socialist Labor movement, founded in 1874, which foresaw the ultimate overthrow of the capitalist system through a socialist revolution; it advocated, as interim measures to combat the depression, federal aid for education, industrial accident compensation, and women's suffrage. The movement attracted a minuscule following.

Some labor spokesmen sought the way out of the depression by supporting independent political parties pledged to protect labor's position in the national economy. There was considerable labor support for the Greenback, or National Independent, party, which was organized in 1874 at Indianapolis. The party's national platform opposed the resumption of specie payments, recently voted by Congress, and advocated further issues of paper money to furnish relief to the depressed industries of the country. That the Greenback party was not a labor movement exclusively is attested by the fact that its presidential candidate in 1876 was the 85-year-old New York iron manufacturer, Peter Cooper. The 80,000 votes Cooper received came mostly from Middle Western farm states. In the congressional elections two years later, however, more laborers supported the National Independent party as it campaigned for government regulation of the hours of labor and for the exclusion of Chinese immigrants. Like other advocates of inflation, the party by this time had moved beyond favoring greenbacks and urged expansion of the currency through silver coinage. Candidates endorsed by the National Independent party received more than a million votes in the 1878 congressional elections.

Other laborers during the depression rejected politics in favor of direct action. With the collapse of the trade union movement, the "Molly Maguires," a secret ring that controlled the popular fraternal society, the Ancient Order of Hibernians, gained power in the anthracite coal region of Pennsylvania. Soon mine owners reported a "crime wave" in collieries, as the Mollies allegedly intimidated

THE GREAT RAILROAD STRIKE

Labor unrest mounted during the severe depression that began in 1873. The most severe outbreak of violence was in Pittsburgh, to which federal troops were dispatched after rioters set fire to the Pennsylvania Railroad roundhouse. (*New York Public Library.*)

and even murdered bosses and superintendents they considered unfair. Eventually, on the dubious testimony of a paid infiltrator, a number of the ringleaders were arrested, and when twenty-four of them were convicted in late 1876, the disturbances ended.

Labor unrest reached its peak in 1877, the worst year of the long depression. Railroad managers precipitated a crisis when, without warning, they cut wages on most railroads east of the Mississippi River by 10 percent. On July 17, the day after the cut became effective, workers on the Baltimore and Ohio Railroad went on strike, took possession of the railyards at various points, and refused to let any freight trains depart. Promptly employees of other Eastern railroads also went on strike, and traffic on the four trunk lines connecting the Atlantic coast and the Middle West was paralyzed. Shortly afterward, the strike spread to some of the roads beyond the Mississippi and in Canada.

Local and state governments proved unable or unwilling to cope with the crisis. The governor of Maryland called out the state militia, but these civilian soldiers fraternized with their friends and relatives among the strikers. In Pittsburgh, the strikers had the sympathy of the local government, for the city fathers had long felt that the Pennsylvania Railroad was discriminating against their city. Employees of nearby iron works joined the railroad men in blocking all traffic on the Pennsylvania. When the governor sent in state militia companies from Philadelphia to clear the tracks, they succeeded in dispersing a large mob by killing twenty-six persons, but their action roused so much additional hostility that the troops were obliged to retreat into the roundhouse, which the mob promptly surrounded and set on fire. The next morning the Philadelphia soldiers fought their way out of the roundhouse and retreated from the city, leaving it in control of a mob of strikers, sympathizers, and looters, who proceeded to destroy railroad property worth some $5 million.

To protect the national system of transportation so essential to the national economy, President Hayes sent in regular army troops. This was the first time in American history that the army had been used on any extensive scale to crush a labor disturbance. Promptly the army restored order, and the strike collapsed. Deeply disturbed members of the business community took steps to prevent any recurrence of such labor violence. State legislatures began passing conspiracy laws directed against labor organizations, and the courts began to invoke the doctrine of malicious conspiracy to break strikes and boycotts. Throughout the North the state militia, which had so often proved untrustworthy during the 1877 crisis, was reorganized and given stricter training. Cyrus Hall McCormick personally purchased equipment for the Second Regiment of Illinois militia because it had "won great credit for its action during . . . disturbances and can be equally relied on in the future."

Thus labor protests against the national economy failed at just the time that farm protest movements largely succeeded. This different outcome is attributable, in part, to the fact that there was a long history of agrarian discontent in the

United States, and the Granger movement seemed as American as apple pie. Urban labor, labor unions, and massive strikes were, on the other hand, something novel to most Americans, and no doubt all three seemed the more dangerous since so many industrial laborers were immigrants with strange-sounding names and alien ways of behavior. In part, too, the differences stemmed from the fact that farmers and their allies lived in a distinct region of the United States, where they were strong enough to control local and state governments in the South and Middle West; industrial laborers were scattered geographically and the labor movement nowhere had political power commensurate with its numbers.

More important than either of these differences was the fact that agrarian discontent did not pose a basic threat to the structure of the national economy. The imposition of limits on the power of railroads and a few other monopolies was an idea that many businessmen also thought desirable. Labor unrest, on the other hand, appeared to strike at the heart of the national economic system. A popular Boston minister declared that the rioting of "the lawless classes at the

THE EMANCIPATOR OF LABOR AND
THE HONEST-WORKING PEOPLE

To terrified conservatives, like
the cartoonist Thomas Nast, labor
organizers were "Communists,"
with "foreign" ideologies, intent
upon leading honest American
working people to death and
destruction. (*Harper's Weekly*,
February 7, 1874.)

bottom of our cities" had been instigated by "secret socialistic societies." The prominent financial editor, W. M. Grosvenor, spoke for much of the business community when he announced that "the light of the flames at Pittsburgh" portended "a terrible trial for free institutions in this country." He warned: "The Communist is here."

In short, Lieber's theory of Institutional Liberty worked only within limits. Advocates of a national economy could accept compromise when various segments of the business community differed over particular legislative issues, such as the tariff or the currency. They could coexist with the local autonomy demanded by the Granger movement. But they could not tolerate the fundamental threat that insurrectionary labor seemed to pose to the capitalist system.

Suggested Readings

The best general treatment of social and economic change during the post–Civil War period is Allan Nevins, *The Emergence of Modern America, 1865–1878* (1927). There is an enormous amount of unassimilated data in Ellis P. Oberholtzer's *History of the United States Since the Civil War,* Vols. 1–4 (1926–31).

On the growth of American national sentiment, see Hans Kohn's *American Nationalism* (1957) and Herbert W. Schneider, *A History of American Philosophy* (1946). George M. Fredrickson, *The Inner Civil War* (1965) is indispensable on intellectual developments. Frank Freidel's *Francis Lieber* (1947) is authoritative, but there is also an important discussion of Lieber in Philip S. Paludan, *A Covenant with Death* (1975).

Foreign affairs during the Reconstruction era are treated in Glyndon G. Van Deusen, *William Henry Seward* (1967), Allan Nevins, *Hamilton Fish* (1936), and David Donald, *Charles Sumner and the Rights of Man* (1970). Ernest N. Paolino, *The Foundations of the American Empire: William Henry Seward and U.S. Foreign Policy* (1973), and Milton Plesur, *America's Outward Reach* (1971), are both valuable. Adrian Cook's *The Alabama Claims* (1975), is authoritative. On expansionism, the standard work is A. K. Weinberg, *Manifest Destiny* (1935). For opposition to Manifest Destiny, see Donald M. Dozer, "Anti-Expansionism during the Johnson Administration," *Pacific Historical Review 12* (1943), 253–76.

Fred A. Shannon, *The Farmer's Last Frontier* (1945), and Edward C. Kirkland, *Industry Comes of Age* (1961), are admirable studies of postwar economic change. Joseph F. Wall, *Andrew Carnegie* (1970), and Allan Nevins, *Study in Power, John D. Rockefeller* (2 vols., 1953), are excellent biographies. The classic account of unionization during this period is Norman J. Ware, *The Labor Movement in the United States, 1860–1890* (1929). Walter P. Webb, *The Great Plains* (1931), contains a brilliant account of the range cattle industry; also see Robert R. Dykstra, *The Cattle Towns* (1968).

Three modern, sophisticated accounts of the currency controversy are Robert P. Sharkey, *Money, Class, and Party* (1959), Irwin Unger, *The Greenback Era* (1964), and Walter T. K. Nugent, *The Money Question during Reconstruction* (1967).

Solon J. Buck, *The Granger Movement* (1913), continues to be a standard work; but George H. Miller, *Railroads and the Granger Laws* (1971), shows the influence of Western businessmen on the so-called Granger legislation. Samuel Rezneck, "Distress, Relief, and Discontent in the United States during the Depression of 1873–78," *Journal of Political Economy 58* (1950), 494–513, is exceptionally helpful, and there is much information about labor unrest in John R. Commons et al., *History of Labor in the United States,* Vol. 2 (1918).

23

Reconciliation
1865-1890

It is evident, then, that the nationalistic impulse stimulated during the Civil War lost much of its momentum during the Reconstruction years. In both the North and the South, long-established institutions, deeply rooted interests, and ingrained American values limited innovation and slowed down the tendency toward centralization. By the 1870s the forces of nationalism and localism reached equilibrium. The American Compromise between these forces guaranteed, within a sphere much broader than before the war, the supremacy of the national government and the primacy of the nationally integrated economy. It also protected, though within limits more constricted than in 1860, the rights of regions and states and localities.

So long as this American Compromise was simply the result of a balance between opposing forces, it was a fragile arrangement. Any change in the business cycle, any significant shift of voters, could easily upset it and again set North against South, East against West, hard-money advocate against inflationist, businessman against farmer. In order to endure, the American Compromise had to be legitimated. Politicians of both national parties had to agree not to consider these informal arrangements as issues in elections. Equally important, these agreements had to find a place in the minds and hearts of the American people. A lasting compromise had to rest not on calculation but on consensus. The times called for reconciliation.

Politics of the Gilded Age

In this process of reconciliation, the politicians during the final years of the Reconstruction era played a vital part. On first thought this may seem an odd idea to advance, since the 1870s and '80s are generally considered a singularly uninteresting period in American political history, when the holders of public office appeared as interchangeable as Tweedledum and Tweedledee. Many historians have written of the Gilded Age as a time of mediocre Presidents, uninspired congressmen, and unimportant legislation.

That verdict fails to take into account the fact that these politicians most effectively gave legitimacy to the American Compromise by not upsetting the balance. Their most useful role was the one W. S. Gilbert attributed to the British peers:

> The House of Lords throughout the war
>   Did nothing in particular,
> And did it very well.

It must be conceded that the success of the politicos of the Gilded Age was in large measure inadvertent. Many of them professed to have policies they wished to pursue, but fortunately they failed to receive any popular mandate for action. Most of the Presidents of the period barely squeaked into office. Grant's success in 1868 was a popular tribute to a great military leader, not an endorsement of the policies of the Republican party that nominated him. Even so, he received only 53 percent of the popular vote. Grant's reelection by a huge popular margin in 1872 was due chiefly to the fact that his opponents committed political suicide. Dissatisfied members of Grant's own party joined the Liberal Republican movement, which agitated for lower tariffs and for reconciliation with the South—and then proceeded to nominate for President the erratic New York *Tribune* editor, Horace Greeley, famed as a protectionist and noted for his prewar denunciations of slaveholders. Holding its nose, the Democratic party also endorsed Greeley, but thousands of Democrats and Liberal Republicans stayed away from the polls. In 1876, Rutherford B. Hayes received a minority of the popular vote and, after prolonged controversy, was elected by a majority of only one vote in the electoral college. Hayes's successor, James A. Garfield, had a plurality of 9000 votes over his Democratic rival in the 1880 presidential election, when over 9 million votes were cast. Chester A. Arthur, who became President in 1881 after Garfield's assassination, clearly had no mandate from anybody. In 1884 Grover Cleveland, the first Democrat elected President after the Civil War, received less than a majority of the total popular vote and only 70,000 votes more than his Republican rival. Four years later, in 1888, that rival, Benjamin Harrison, defeated Cleveland by winning a majority in the electoral college, although the Democratic candidate had a plurality of the popular votes.

Even had these Presidents been elected by overwhelming majorities in order to carry out ambitious programs, they would have been frustrated by the fact that

THE PHILOSOPHER'S STONE.

A Republican cartoon shows the difficulties Horace Greeley
had in uniting the anti-Grant forces in 1872. Sitting on the
political fence are the laboring man, hostile because of
Greeley's opposition to strikes, and the Negro, distrustful
because Greeley favo., amnesty for the Confederates. The
German voter, beer in hand, sits the election out because
Greeley supports prohibition. (*American Antiquarian Society.*)

control of Congress was usually in the hands of their political enemies. To be
sure, Grant started with safely Republican majorities in both houses of Congress,
but Carl Schurz, Charles Sumner, and other leading Republicans soon joined the
Liberal Republican movement, voted with the Democrats, and blocked the administration's favorite measures. In the congressional elections of 1874, Democrats for the first time since the Civil War won a majority in the House of Representatives, and, except for two years (1881–83), they retained control of the
House until 1889. It was not, therefore, until the inauguration of the Democratic
President Grover Cleveland in 1885 that the executive and the legislative branches
of the national government represented the same political party. Given these
facts, it is easy to understand why the politicians of the Gilded Age accomplished
so little and why the few measures they succeeded in adopting had to be compromises.

Though untutored in politics, Grant seems to have sized up the political situation at once. The same strategic sense that dictated his offensive campaign against Vicksburg suggested his defensive, compromising role as President. "Let us have peace," the President urged in his inaugural address—but it was not clear whether he was addressing the white Ku Kluxers who were trying to overthrow the Reconstruction governments in the South or the Northern Radicals who wanted to impose further conditions on the Southern states. As it proved, Grant had both extremes in mind. On the one hand, the President warmly supported the immediate and unconditional readmission of Virginia to the Union, even though Radicals like Sumner warned that the Virginia legislature was "composed of recent Rebels still filled and seething with that old Rebel fire." On the other, Grant was outraged by the terrorism rampant in the South, and he insisted that Congress pass a series of Enforcement Acts (1870–71) enabling him to crush the Ku Klux Klan. Under this legislation, the President proclaimed martial law in nine South Carolina counties where white terrorists were most active, and federal marshals arrested large numbers of suspected Klansmen in North Carolina, Mississippi, and other Southern states. In brief, then, Grant's policy was to warn Southern whites that the national government would not tolerate overt violence and organized military activity—but to let them understand that at the same time they would not be harassed if they regained control of their state governments through less revolutionary tactics.

. Though a few old Radicals like Sumner attacked Grant's Southern policy and blamed him for shedding the blood of innocent white and black Unionists in the South, most Northerners accepted the President's program without difficulty. They were growing tired of the whole question of Reconstruction. Other issues claimed their attention, as debates over the resumption of specie payments and the annexation of Santo Domingo pushed stories about the South off the front pages of the newspapers.

Especially diverting were the revelations that newspapers began to make about corruption at all levels of government. The Civil War inaugurated a period of low public morality in the United States, and wartime patterns of favoritism, fraud, and bribery continued into the Reconstruction era. Then, about 1870, reformers and crusading newspaper editors started to expose the scandals. The earliest revelations concerned New York City, which had fallen under the control of "Boss" William Marcy Tweed, who proceeded joyfully to loot the taxpayers. Tweed's ring began construction of a new county courthouse, on which $11 million was spent. Nearly $3 million went to a man named Garvey for plastering; after the amount of his fees leaked out, he became known as the "Prince of Plasterers." Tweed approved the purchase of so many chairs, at $5 each, that if placed in line they would have extended seventeen miles. In 1871 when the New York *Times* began to expose the ring's padded bills, faked leases, false vouchers, and other frauds, the attention of the whole nation was attracted, and when

Harper's Weekly started carrying Thomas Nast's devastating caricatures of the Boss, Tweed's face became more familiar to Americans than that of any other man except Grant. As readers followed the stories of Tweed's arrest, trial, escape from detention, flight to Spain, and return to a New York prison, they had little time or interest in the customary tales of terrorism in the South.

Soon revelations about the national government began to make equally fascinating reading. Shortly before the 1872 election, the New York *Sun,* a Democratic paper, exposed the workings of the Credit Mobilier, the construction company that the Union Pacific Railroad Company paid to build its transcontinental route. Investigation proved that members of the Credit Mobilier were also members of the board of directors of the Union Pacific, who were thus paying themselves huge profits. What was even more damaging was the revelation that, in

"BOSS TWEED" BY THOMAS NAST

Thomas Nast's caricatures of the corrupt William M. Tweed of New York were devastatingly effective. When the "Boss" fled the United States to escape prosecution, a Spanish immigration official identified him on the basis of Nast's drawings, and he was sent back to New York to serve his prison sentence. *(American Antiquarian Society.)*

order to avert public inquiry, the Credit Mobilier offered stock to Vice-President Schuyler Colfax, Representative (and future President) James A. Garfield, and other prominent politicians. They were allowed to "purchase" the stock on credit, the down payment being "earned" by the high dividends that the stock began to pay.

Though Republicans found it advisable to drop Colfax from their ticket in 1872, scandal did not seriously touch the Grant administration until after the election. Then, in short order, stories of fraud began to appear about practically every branch of the executive offices. In the Treasury Department unscrupulous customhouse officers, especially in New York, preyed on importers. Merchants who failed to pay off the brigands had their shipments delayed, their imported goods subjected to minute, time-consuming inspection, and their crates and boxes that were not immediately removed from the docks stored at exorbitant rates. Corruption was rampant in the Navy Department, where political favoritism dictated everything from the employment of workers in the shipyards to the contracts for the construction of new vessels. Secretary of War William W. Belknap was proved to have accepted bribes from Indian traders, who had the exclusive and remunerative franchise to sell goods to Indians and soldiers at frontier posts.

Of all these scandals, the closest to the White House was the Whiskey Ring. In order to avoid heavy excise taxes, first levied during the war, whiskey distillers, especially those at St. Louis, had for years been conspiring with officials of the internal revenue service. During Grant's administration they secured the cooperation of none other than Orville E. Babcock, the President's private secretary, who warned the swindlers whenever an inspection team was sent out from Washington. In return for his assistance, Babcock received such favors as a $2,400 diamond shirt stud, which he found defective and asked to have replaced with another, more expensive one, and from time to time the ministrations of a "sylph." When Grant first learned of the scandal, he urged, "Let no guilty man escape." But as it became clear that his close friends and his personal staff were involved, he did everything possible to block further investigation. When Babcock went on trial, the President of the United States offered a deposition expressing "great confidence in his integrity and efficiency." Babcock was acquitted, and Grant retained him on the White House staff.

As news of these shabby scandals—and there were scores of others, on all levels of government—spread, large numbers of Northerners came to think it was more important to set their own house in order than to tell Southerners how to behave. As early as 1867, *The Nation* announced: "The diminution of political corruption is the great question of our time. It is greater than the [question of Negro] suffrage, greater than reconstruction. . . ."

The desire to reduce political corruption led to the emergence of the civil service reform movement during the Gilded Age. Though voices had been raised against the spoils system long before the Civil War, it was not until after Appomattox that an organized reform drive appeared. Knowledge of widespread corruption among government officials, fear that President Johnson might convert the government bureaucracy into a tool to promote his renomination, and the example of the British system of appointing civil servants after competitive examinations gave strength to the movement. Early efforts to require federal appointees to pass competitive examinations failed in Congress, but the reformers, led by the politically ambitious George William Curtis, editor of *Harper's Weekly*, and by E. L. Godkin of *The Nation*, hoped for success under Grant's administration.

They were doomed to disappointment, for on this, as on all other controversial topics, Grant perfectly understood that compromise was the mood of the age, and he straddled. He made no mention of civil service reform in his first message to Congress, and Henry Adams—the son of Lincoln's minister to Great Britain and the grandson and great-grandson of American Presidents—remarked in his supercilious way that Grant was inaugurating "a reign of western mediocrity." But when disgruntled civil service reformers began to talk loudly about joining the Liberal Republican movement, Grant moved swiftly to head them off. In 1871 he pressured Congress into creating the Civil Service Reform Commission, and he neatly co-opted his chief critic by naming Curtis chairman. Though the commission had little power and achieved less success, the move kept Curtis and a sizable number of reformers as supporters of Grant's reelection. Once the election was over, Grant lost interest in the commission and so blatantly violated its rules that Curtis had to resign.

Strengthened by the news of the scandals that rocked Grant's second administration, civil service reformers claimed some of the credit for the nomination of Hayes in 1876, but they found him as difficult to manage as Grant. On the one hand, the new President did take on the powerful political machine of New York's Senator Roscoe Conkling, and he succeeded in ousting some of Conkling's supporters, including future President Chester A. Arthur, from the New York customshouse. On the other hand, at election time the President wanted his own appointees to contribute to Republican campaign funds and to help organize Republican state conventions, much as their predecessors had done. "I have little or no patience with Mr. Hayes," exclaimed the reforming editor of the New York *Times*. "He is a victim of . . . good intentions and his contributions to the pavement of the road to the infernal regions are vast and various."

Hayes's successor, Garfield, gave civil service reformers little more satisfaction. With cruel accuracy one Massachusetts reformer characterized the new President as "a grand, noble fellow, but fickle, unstable, . . . timid and hesitating." Civil service reform advocates noted suspiciously that Garfield's Vice-President was Arthur, named by the Republican national convention in a vain attempt to placate Conkling. Consequently reformers felt no special sense of victory when

IN MEMORIAM — OUR CIVIL SERVICE AS IT WAS

Thomas Nast proposes a substitute for Clark Mills's famous equestrian statue of Andrew Jackson, in Lafayette Square across from the White House. Nast incorrectly attributes to Jackson the phrase, "To the Victors belong the Spoils," which was a remark of William L. Marcy, a New York Democrat. (*Harper's Weekly, April 28, 1877.*)

Garfield began to oust more of Conkling's "Stalwarts" from the New York customshouse. Conceited and imperious, Conkling resigned in a huff from the Senate and rushed to Albany seeking vindication through reelection. To his surprise, the removal of his friends from federal office undercut his support, and the New York legislature failed to send him back to the Senate. Shortly afterward, a crazed office seeker named Charles Guiteau assassinated Garfield, shouting that he was a Stalwart and rejoicing that Arthur was now President. Shocked by Garfield's assassination, Congress in 1883 passed the Pendleton Act, which required competitive examinations of applicants for many federal jobs. Though the measure covered only a fraction of all government employees, it was a genuine measure of civil service reform and permitted the emergence of a professional government bureaucracy.

The Restoration of "Home Rule"

While Northern opinion was focused on corruption and civil service reform, and while it was further diverted by the depression, unemployment, and strikes, state after state in the former Confederacy was restored to what was euphemistically called home rule—which meant the rule of native white Democrats. The Redeemers, as they called themselves, gained power first in Virginia, North Carolina, Tennessee, and Georgia. In 1875 they won control of Alabama, Mississippi, Arkansas, and Texas, and early in 1877 they ended Republican rule in Florida.

To the relatively few Northerners who were concerned about these developments, the new rulers of the South seemed much like the antebellum slavocracy. All stanch Democrats, the Redeemers sported the traditional Southern mustacios and goatees, they bragged about their records in the Confederate army, and they erupted in florid Southern oratory. In fact, however, they represented a very different interest from the plantation oligarchs of the prewar era; they allied themselves instead with the factory owners, railroad men, and city merchants of the New South. In public stance, the Redeemers identified themselves with the romantic cult of the Confederacy and yearned over "the dignifying memories of the war," but they were really in favor, as a Vicksburg, Mississippi, editor admitted, "of the South, from the Potomac to the Rio Grande, being thoroughly and permanently Yankeeized."

But the process of creating a Yankee South, the Redeemers made very clear, had to be directed by Southerners like themselves. Their experience during the Reconstruction years taught them to distrust Northerners, even Northerners of their own economic backgrounds and viewpoints. Consequently, in state after state, the Redeemers systematically went about overthrowing Republican rule. The tactics varied according to the locality, but the strategy was everywhere the same. White Republicans were subjected to social pressure, economic boycott, and outright violence; many fled the South. Redeemers exercised economic pressure on blacks by threatening not to hire or extend credit to those who were politically active. In several states whites organized rifle clubs, which practiced marksmanship on the outskirts of Republican political rallies. When the blacks attempted to defend themselves, whites overpowered them and slaughtered their leaders. In state after state Republican governors appealed to Washington for additional federal troops, but Grant, convinced that the public was tired of "these annual autumnal outbreaks" in the South, refused. In consequence, by the end of Grant's second administration, South Carolina and Louisiana were the only Southern states with Republican governments.

The fate of these two remaining Republican regimes in the South became intricately connected with the outcome of the 1876 presidential election. The Democratic nominee, Samuel J. Tilden, undoubtedly received a majority of the popular votes cast—though, equally undoubtedly, thousands of blacks who would have voted for his Republican rival, Hayes, were kept from the polls. But Tilden lacked one vote of having a majority in the electoral college unless he received some of the votes from South Carolina, Florida, and Louisiana, all of which submitted to Congress competing sets of Democratic and Republican ballots. (There was also a technical question of the eligibility of one Republican elector from Oregon.)

Consequently when Congress assembled in December 1876 it confronted a crisis. If it decided to accept the disputed Democratic electoral votes, Republican control of the White House would be broken for the first time in a quarter of a century and the Reconstruction in the South would be ended. If Congress accepted the Republican electoral votes, that decision would run counter to the will of a majority of the voters in the country.

To resolve the impasse required a compromise—not a single compromise, but a complicated, interlocking set of bargains. After intricate and secret negotiations, several agreements were reached. First, Congress decided that the disputed electoral votes should be referred to a special electoral commission, which should consist of five members from the House of Representatives, five members from the Senate, and five associate justices from the Supreme Court. This body was composed of eight Republicans and seven Democrats, and on every disputed ballot the commission ruled in favor of Hayes by that same vote. In consequence of these decisions, Tilden's electoral vote remained at 184, while Hayes's slowly mounted to 185. In March 1877, for the fifth time in succession, a Republican President was inaugurated.

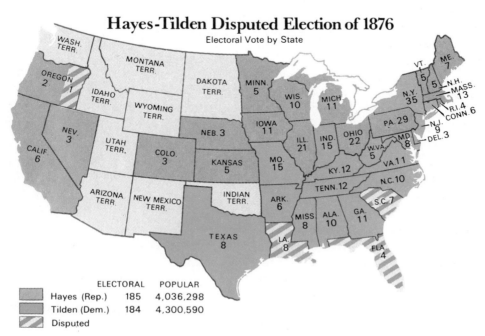

Hayes-Tilden Disputed Election of 1876

Electoral Vote by State

	ELECTORAL	POPULAR
Hayes (Rep.)	185	4,036,298
Tilden (Dem.)	184	4,300,590
Disputed		

Democrats reluctantly accepted the election of Hayes because of some other bargaining that took place while the electoral votes were being counted. One set of compromises came to be known as the Wormley agreement, because it was negotiated in the luxurious Washington hotel owned by the Negro restaurateur, James Wormley. Representing Hayes at these sessions were Senator Sherman, Representative Garfield, and other prominent Republicans. Across the table sat Southern Democratic leaders, including Senator John B. Gordon, the former Confederate general who now represented Georgia in Congress, and L. Q. C. Lamar, once Confederate minister to Russia, who was senator from Mississippi. The Republicans promised the Southerners that, if allowed to be inaugurated, Hayes "would deal justly and generously with the south." Translated, that meant that Hayes would withdraw the remaining federal troops from the South and acquiesce in the overthrow of the Republican regimes in South Carolina and Louisiana. The Southerners found the terms acceptable, and they promptly leaked the news of the agreement, so as to protect themselves from charges that they had betrayed their section.

Behind the Wormley agreement lay other, less formal, compromises. Hayes's backers promised that the new President would not use federal patronage in the South to defeat the Democrats. They further pledged that he would support congressional appropriations for rebuilding levees along the flood-ridden Mis-

"WE'LL SHOW YOU WHEN WE COME TO VOTE"

The attitude of Northern women contributed to the declining interest in the problems of the South. Many women who had loyally supported the war and emancipation felt that they, as well as the freedmen, should have been enfranchised under the Reconstruction amendments to the Constitution. In 1869 Elizabeth Cady Stanton, Susan B. Anthony, and others organized the National Woman Suffrage Association to promote a sixteenth amendment to the Constitution, enfranchising women. *(American Antiquarian Society.)*

sissippi River and for constructing a transcontinental railroad along a Southern route. In return, Southerners agreed to allow the Republicans to elect Garfield speaker of the new House of Representatives, with the power to determine the membership of congressional committees. More important, they promised to protect the basic rights of blacks, as guaranteed in the Thirteenth, Fourteenth, and Fifteenth Amendments to the Constitution.

Once Hayes was inaugurated, virtually all these informal agreements were flouted by both sides. Hayes, for his part, ordered the removal of federal troops from the South and did appoint a Southerner, former Confederate David M. Key, to his cabinet as postmaster general. But two-thirds of the federal office-holders in the South remained Republicans. Hayes changed his mind about supporting a Southern transcontinental railroad. To "make possible any more Credit Mobilier operations," he said piously, "would be a serious mistake."

Southern Democrats for their part reneged on their promise to support Garfield for speaker, and, once the House was organized under Democratic leadership, they eagerly joined in an investigation of alleged fraud in Hayes's election. Only a very few Southern Democratic politicians, like Governor Wade Hampton of South Carolina, remembered their promises to respect the rights of blacks. Instead, almost all took the final withdrawal of federal troops from the South as a signal that the Negro, already relegated to a position of economic inferiority, could be excluded from Southern political life. Southern whites had to act cautiously, so as not to offend public opinion in the North or to invite renewed federal intervention, but they moved steadily and successfully to reduce Negro voting. One of the simplest devices was the poll tax, adopted by Georgia in 1877 and quickly copied by other Southern states. To Northerners the requirement that a voter had to pay $1 or $2 a year did not seem unreasonable, yet in fact, since three-fourths of the entire Southern population had an average income of only $55.16 in 1880, the poll tax was a considerable financial drain, especially to poverty-stricken blacks. More imaginative was the "eight box" law, adopted by South Carolina in 1882 and imitated by North Carolina and Florida. Under this system ballots for each contested race had to be deposited in separate boxes. Thus a voter must cast in one box his ballot for governor, in another box his ballot for sheriff, and so forth. The system frustrated the illiterate Negro voter, who could no longer bring to the polls a single ballot, marked for him in advance by a Republican friend. To make the task of semiliterate voters more difficult, election officials periodically rearranged the order of the boxes. Still another device, which did not become popular until the late 1880s, was the secret, or Australian, ballot. Ostensibly introduced in the South, as in the North, in order to prevent fraud, the secret ballot actually discriminated heavily against blacks, for as late as 1900 the number of illiterate adult Negro males ranged from 39 percent in Florida to 61 percent in Louisiana.

Despite all these devices, Southern blacks continued to vote in surprising numbers. In the 1880 presidential election, for example, more than 70 percent of the eligible Negroes voted in Arkansas, Florida, North Carolina, Tennessee, and Virginia, and between 50 percent and 70 percent voted in Alabama, Louisiana, South Carolina, and Texas. To the Redeemers these black voters posed a double threat. They were numerous enough that ambitious Northern Republicans might be tempted again to try federal intervention in state elections, with the hope of breaking the now solidly Democratic South. Even more dangerous was the possibility that poor whites in the South, whose needs for public education and welfare the business-oriented Redeemers consistently neglected, might find common cause with their black peers.

The Redeemers saw both these dangers materialize after 1890. Shortly after the Republicans gained control of the House of Representatives in 1889, Representative Henry Cabot Lodge of Massachusetts introduced a strong bill for federal control of elections, which was promptly christened the Force Bill. Though Democrats in the Senate defeated Lodge's bill in January 1891, Redeemers saw in it a threat to renew "all the horrors of reconstruction days.' Their fear was doubtless the greater because the almost simultaneous rise of the Populist movement threatened, as never before, to split the white voters of the region. Appealing to farmers and small planters, the Populist party was the enemy of lawyers and bankers and of the rising commercial and industrial spokesmen of the "New South.' Some of the Populist leaders, like Thomas Watson of Georgia, were openly critical of the Redeemers' policy of repressing the blacks and seemed to be flirting with the Negro voters.

Faced with this double threat, Southern states moved swiftly to exclude the Negro completely and permanently from politics. Mississippi led the way with a constitutional convention in 1890 that required voters to be able to read and interpret the Constitution to the satisfaction of the white registration officials. It is not hard to imagine how difficult even a graduate of Howard University Law School would have found the task of satisfactory constitutional exegesis. In 1898 a Louisiana constitutional convention improved on the Mississippi example by requiring a literacy test of all voters except the sons and grandsons of persons who had voted in state elections before 1867. Since no Louisiana Negroes had been permitted to vote before that date, this provision allowed illiterate whites to vote, while the literacy test excluded most Negro voters.

State after state across the South followed, or elaborated on, these requirements. South Carolina held a disfranchising convention in 1895. North Carolina amended its constitution to limit suffrage in 1900. Alabama and Virginia acted in 1901–02, and Georgia adopted a restrictive constitutional amendment in 1908. The remaining Southern states continued to rely on the poll tax and other varieties of legislative disfranchisement. When opponents of these measures accused their advocates of discriminating against the Negroes, Carter Glass of Virginia replied for his entire generation: "Discrimination! Why that is precisely what we propose; that exactly is what this convention was elected for.'

It took time, then, for the complete working out of the political compromises of the Reconstruction era. Not until the end of the nineteenth century did white Southerners receive the full price they had exacted in permitting the election of Rutherford B. Hayes. But by 1900 that payment had been made in full. The Negro was no longer a political force in the South, and the Republican party was no longer the defender of Negro rights.

Literary Reconciliation

These political arrangements, which, in effect, ratified the American Compromise and excluded the Negro question from national politics for more than a generation, were probably less important in bringing the Civil War era to a close than the changes that were simultaneously occurring in the minds of Americans. If the American Compromise was to hold, it had to rest on a fundamental consensus, a desire to forget or ignore the differences that had hitherto divided sections, interests, and races. In short, the theme of reconciliation had to dominate the world of ideas as it did the world of economics and politics.

During the first few years after the Civil War, it was not at all clear that such an intellectual reconciliation could occur. Northern writers and intellectuals during the war had been intensely patriotic and highly nationalistic. Even the best of their productions were suffused with a tone of Northern superiority. Although he was compassionate toward the fallen soldiers of the South, Walt Whitman never concealed his belief in the righteousness of the Union cause, and his greatest war poems, "O Captain! My Captain!" and "When Lilacs Last in the Dooryard Bloom'd," were tributes to Lincoln, the fallen leader of the national cause. Similarly Herman Melville's *Battle Pieces and Aspects of the War* (1866), spare, gnomic verses whose greatness was not to be recognized until a later generation, exulted in Union victory even while expressing sympathy for individual Rebels. James Russell Lowell also turned literary nationalist. His second series of *Biglow Papers* used Yankee dialect to explain why Southerners had to give up their sectional identity:

> Make 'em Amerikin, an' they'll begin
> To love their country ez they loved their sin;
> Let 'em stay Southun, an' you've kep' a sore
> Ready to fester ez it done afore.

In fiction as in verse Northern writers during and immediately after the war insisted that Southerners must repent and accept Northern values. That was the central theme of *Miss Ravenel's Conversion from Secession to Loyalty*, John W. DeForest's 1867 novel, which remains perhaps the best novel ever written about the Civil War. A native of Connecticut, DeForest had spent some time in the South before the war, commanded a company of Union volunteers in Louisiana and in the Shenandoah Valley, and after Appomattox served with the

BLUE AND GRAY MEET AT SEVEN PINES BATTLEFIELD AFTER
THE WAR

As the bitterness of the Civil War years faded, Union
soldiers and Confederate veterans began to hold joint
reunions on the battlefields, where they engaged in
reminiscences about a struggle they increasingly
romanticized. Note that each of the veterans here shown
has lost an arm. *(Valentine Museum, Richmond.)*

Freedmen's Bureau in South Carolina. He was not, therefore, ignorant of the
South, and some aspects of Southern life seem to have had sensuous charm for
this straitlaced New Englander. The most credible characters in his novel are
the corrupt, whiskey-drinking Virginian, Captain Carter, whose animal mag-
netism is so strong that Lillie Ravenel marries him against her own better judgment, and the lurid Creole, Mrs. Larue, with whom Carter continues to carry on a
torrid affair even after his marriage. But in the end it is not these Southern-born
characters who have the strength to win victory. After Carter's fortunate death in
battle, Lillie weds her patiently waiting Northern lover, Captain Colbourne—as

stiff and as formal as DeForest himself. Sententiously, Colbourne and Miss
Ravenel's father discuss the significance of the romances that have occurred, and
of the war itself. "The right always conquers because it always becomes the
strongest," Dr. Ravenel suggests. "In that sense 'the hand of God' is identical with
'the heaviest battalions.'" Agreeing, Colbourne summarizes in a sentence the
theme of Northern superiority: "The Southern character will be sweetened by
adversity as their persimmons are by frost."

Like DeForest, Whitman initially assumed that the national sentiment aroused
by the Civil War would erase sectional feelings and ultimately would produce a
national literature, which could provide for America's democratic society "that
glowing, blood-throbbing, religious, social, emotional, artistic, indefinable, in-
describably beautiful charm and hold which fused the separate parts of the old
feudal societies together." But by the time Whitman got around to elaborating
his theory in his strange, rambling essays, *Democratic Vistas*, published in 1871, his
confidence had begun to wane. "Society, in these States, is cankered, crude, su-
perstitious and rotten," he judged, and he feared that America might be suffering from "the lack of a common skeleton, knitting all close." On all levels government was "saturated in corruption, bribery, falsehood, maladministration," and
the cities reeked "with respectable as much as non-respectable robbery and
scoundrelism." Despite obvious signs of material progress, he was tempted to
conclude that the United States was "so far, an almost complete failure in its social aspects, and in really grand religious, moral, literary, and aesthetic results."
But that "so far" suggested that there was a possible remedy. It was the emergence of a powerful national literature, and Whitman longed for the appearance
of "a single great literatus," who could issue a clarion call for American culture.

Whitman's hopes were not to be fulfilled. The giants of American literature
belonged to a previous generation. Whitman himself was too exhausted, too old,
to serve as "literatus" of the new age; in 1873 he suffered a stroke of paralysis
and retired to Camden, New Jersey. Melville after the war sank into decades of
silence, only to complete the manuscript of *Billy Budd* just before his death in
1891. Ralph Waldo Emerson, who during the pre–Civil War period had come
nearest to fulfilling Whitman's specifications for an American "literatus," was
now slowly slipping into senility.

The new generation of Northeastern writers offered little more hope for literary leadership. Once the intellectual capital of the country, New England was
now stagnant. Its ablest poet, Emily Dickinson, lived a recluse in her house in
Amherst, Massachusetts, her verse unseen by the public until after her death.
Its ablest novelist, the transplanted New Yorker Henry James, found the American scene uncongenial and fled to Europe. Its supply of local talent was so bankrupt that in 1871 the editorship of the *Atlantic Monthly* went to a Middle Westerner,
William Dean Howells. The New York publishing scene was, as always, bustling,
but Whitman correctly dismissed the now deservedly forgotten poets and essay-
ists of the era as "a parcel of dandies and ennuyees, dapper little gentlemen from

"WALT WHITMAN" BY THOMAS EAKINS

Old and ill, Whitman longed for the appearance of a "literatus," who could write the story of "the actual Soldier of 1862–'65, North and South, with all his ways, his incredible dauntlessness, habits, practices, tastes, language, his appetite, rankness, his superb strength and animality, lawless gait, and a hundred unnamed lights and shades of camp." But, he feared, this history "will never be written—perhaps must not and should not be." *(Pennsylvania Academy of the Fine Arts.)*

abroad who flood us with their thin sentiments of parlors, parasols, piano songs, [and] tinkling rhymes. '

Instead of the national literature for which Whitman hoped, there emerged between 1865 and 1890 strong regional schools of literature—"local colorists," as they have somewhat condescendingly been called. It was in the Far West, where a motley group of Indians, Mexicans, Chinese, Yankees, and Southerners were engaged in the experiment of constructing an instant society, that the first of these regional writers appeared. The center of the group was the dapper, elegant New Yorker Bret Harte, who had moved to California in the 1850s and, with the support of a lucrative but undemanding job in the United States mint at San Francisco during the 1860s, wrote prolific verse and fiction. Not until Harte became editor of the *Overland Monthly* in 1868, however, did he turn his imagination to the local area, and the publication of "The Luck of Roaring Camp" and "The Outcasts of Poker Flat" proved that he had struck a literary pay dirt in the garish, tawdry, but deeply romantic adventurers in the California mining country. Immediately lionized by both English and Eastern literary circles, Harte generously assisted his fellow Western local colorists. It was with Harte's encouragement that Mark Twain (Samuel L. Clemens) published *The Celebrated Jumping Frog of Calaveras County and Other Stories* (1867), a transposition of the traditional American tall tale to a Far Western setting, and became a world celebrity. Less enduring was the fame of another Harte protégé, Joaquim Miller, who compensated for his limited literary talents by self-dramatization; appearing at London dinner parties in his sealskin coat, his red plaid shirt, and his hip boots, Miller seemed so completely the personification of the Wild Westerner that the English forgot his limping rhymes.

A second regional school of writers emerged in the Middle West in the 1870s. Stimulated by reading Bret Harte, Constance Fenimore Woolson—the grandniece of James Fenimore Cooper—sought in her stories of French voyageurs, of fur trappers and traders, and of rough lumbermen to recapture the traditions and the color of the Great Lakes region where she was brought up. In 1871 John Hay, who had served as Lincoln's private secretary, succumbed to the regional impulse and published his *Pike County Ballads,* which reproduced in frontier dialect both the crudeness and the humor of early Illinois. More prolific was Edward Eggleston, a Methodist minister who made a systematic study of life and language in his native southern Indiana before writing *The Hoosier Schoolmaster* (1871), *The Circuit Rider* (1874), and other novels that attempted to re-create life on a frontier that was beginning to slip from memory. Soon that frontier would be romanticized and subdued in the ever popular verse of the Hoosier poet James Whitcomb Riley, who wrote his jingles about "just plain folks.'

Regional writing emerged in the South more slowly than that in other sections. Some older Southern writers could not break themselves of the habit of writing polemics in defense of slavery. Others were too embittered by the war to appeal to a national audience. Younger writers were for the most part less sore, but they were too exhausted to write the kind of regional romance that a national audience sought. Paul Hamilton Hayne, the Charleston poet who saw his house and library burned in the bombardment of his city and had his silver stolen by Sherman's "bummers," lived out his days in north Georgia, in a rough "shanty of uncouth ugliness," so dilapidated that he tried to paper over the holes in the walls with pictures his wife cut from magazines. Henry Timrod, the South Carolina poet who died of tuberculosis at the age of thirty-nine, summarized his life after the war as "beggary, starvation, death, bitter grief, utter want of hope." The ablest of Southern poets, Sidney Lanier, whose health had been broken during service in the Confederate army and who was also destined for a premature death from tuberculosis, epitomized in a sentence the experience of Southern writers in the 1860s: "Pretty much the whole of life has been merely not dying."

Thanks largely to the enterprise of Northern magazine editors, Southern writers fared very differently during the 1870s and '80s. The warm reception readers gave Western local color fiction and verse led the editors of *Scribner's Monthly Magazine* (after 1881, *The Century Magazine*) and of *Lippincott's Magazine* actively to solicit contributions from Southern authors. Early successes in these journals brought offers to Southern writers from *Harper's Monthly Magazine* and finally even from the formerly antislavery journal *The Atlantic Monthly*. Publication of stories or serialization of novels in these prestigious monthlies usually led to successful book publication by a major Northern firm, so that for the first time writing became a remunerative occupation in the South.

The successful Southern writer had first to meet terms and conditions of his Northern editors. *Scribner's,* which set the standard, sought to promote "a sane and earnest Americanism" and constantly "to increase the sentiment of union throughout our diverse sisterhood of States." Southern writers were tacitly barred from any expression of the old hostility between the sections. Northern editors wanted no polemics defending slavery or justifying secession, no jeremiads about what the North had done during the war, no objective reporting on the

workings of Reconstruction. Instead, they sought stories set in the South, long on local color, heavy in Southern dialect, ingenious in plot, and romantic in tone.

These were terms that Southern writers of the new generation found easy to accept. Most young Southerners were prepared to admit that they were glad the Confederacy had failed; nearly all felt that their section had a brighter future in the Union. Many consciously sought in their writing to bring about sectional reconciliation. The Virginia novelist Thomas Nelson Page declared that he had "never wittingly written a line which he did not hope might tend to bring about a better understanding between the North and the South, and finally lead to a more perfect Union." They agreed that regional literature must be part of a broad national literature. Joel Chandler Harris, author of the Uncle Remus stories, spoke for his generation in asserting "that whatever in our literature is distinctly Southern must . . . be distinctly American."

In return for accepting American nationality, Southern writers were allowed great freedom in their choice of subjects. George Washington Cable's fiction explored the mysteries of that least American of cities, New Orleans, where Creoles and Yankees, 'Cajuns, quadroons, and slaves mixed together in a cosmopolitan and fascinatingly decadent society. Mary Noailles Murfree wrote of Southern Appalachian folk, so isolated from the American mainstream that their dialect, which she laboriously attempted to reproduce, was full of Elizabethan idioms. Harris wrote scores of conventional novels and stories about Southern life, but his readers identified him as author of the Uncle Remus tales, about Br'er Rabbit, that defenseless yet preternaturally clever animal, who was able—perhaps like the slaves who had originally told Harris the tales—to outwit his more powerful enemies like Br'er Fox and Br'er Bear. Page's stories had a courtly Virginia setting, and the lush bluegrass country of Kentucky was the scene of James Lane Allen's impressionistic tales.

In all this postwar Southern writing, the Negro played a surprisingly small part. As in the Uncle Remus stories, a black was often allowed to be the narrator, a gentle, aged former slave, full of folk wisdom and glowing with happy memories about "dose times befoah de wah." "Dem wuz good ole times, marster," said Sam, the former slave who narrated Page's most popular story, *Marse Chan* (1884), "de bes' Sam uver see! Niggers didn' hed nothin' 'tall to do. . . . Dyar warn' no trouble nor nuthin'." Though the point was never made explicitly, the implica-

UNCLE REMUS

In the Southern literature of reconciliation, the Negro played a surprisingly small role. Often he appeared as the narrator of tales, like Joel Chandler Harris's Uncle Remus. Even more frequently he reminisced happily about "dose times befoah de wah." (*American Antiquarian Society.*)

tion was that race relations in the South had been exemplary until disrupted by Northern invaders. Though the recommendation was never given overtly, the promise was that if white Southerners were left alone there would be a return to the good old days.

If slaves and slavery were peripheral in this Southern literature, the theme of reconciliation was central. Again and again the stories dealt with the Civil War as the result of misunderstanding, of a failure of Northerners and Southerners to recognize how much they had in common. In one of Harris s stories, a wounded Union officer, captured by a black "mammy" and nursed back to health by her white mistress, proved to have such a noble character as to shatter the Southerners' stereotypes about Yankees. "He gave . . . a practical illustration of the fact that one may be a Yankee and a Southerner too, simply by being a large-hearted, whole-souled American." Typically in these romances, understanding leads to marriage. Time and again the Union officer, befriended by a Southern planter's family during the conflict, returns South after Appomattox to claim the hand of the planter's daughter and to save the plantation from foreclosure for debts.

The product of changing sectional sentiment after the Civil War, Southern fiction also helped to produce that change. Both sides in the recent conflict had been right. Both sides shared equally in the glory and the gallantry. To Northern readers, as well as to Southern, these were ideas immensely appealing, immensely consoling. They permitted the Civil War generation to gloss over the brutal past, and they allowed the postwar generation of Northerners to shed any guilt it felt at abandoning the Negro. Indicative of the power of Southern romance was the response of Thomas Wentworth Higginson to Page's *Marse Chan*, a tale about a political quarrel that kept two Southerners from marrying before the young man rode away to the war. By the time the girl's father relented, the hero had bravely died on the battlefield, and shortly after, the girl too expired of grief. Sitting in his study in Cambridge, Massachusetts, Higginson—who had once organized an attempt to free a fugitive slave, who had been a confidant of John Brown, who had heroically commanded a regiment of Negro soldiers during the Civil War—let the tears trickle down his face as he grieved over the death of a fictional Southern slaveholder.

Thus Americans of the postwar generation became emotionally reconciled to a series of compromises that ended decades of conflict between national interests and local concerns. In foreign policy and in economic organization, in race relations and in politics, informal agreements were hammered out that served to guarantee the primacy of the nation but also to protect local and regional rights. These compromises made no provision to protect the Indians, who were being ruthlessly pushed into barren reservations. They systematically relegated blacks to the category of second-class citizens. They took little account of the needs of labor. But, especially when veiled by literary sentimentality, the compromises seemed to most white middle-class Americans to provide a tolerable way of life that preserved both the national Union and their own individual freedom.

Suggested Readings

Volumes 6–8 of James Ford Rhodes's *History of the United States* (1906–19) chronicle political history from Grant to McKinley. H. Wayne Morgan, *From Hayes to McKinley* (1969), is a modern treatment. The best account of Grant's presidency remains William B. Hesseltine's unsatisfactory *Ulysses S. Grant, Politician* (1935). Ari A. Hoogenboom, *Outlawing the Spoils* (1961), is a superior account of the civil service reform movement. Earl D. Ross, *The Liberal Republican Movement* (1919), remains a standard account. Harry Barnard, *Rutherford B Hayes and His America* (1954), is the best biography of that President, and Thomas C. Reeves, *Gentleman Boss* (1975) is a fine life of Chester A. Arthur.

C. Vann Woodward, *Reunion and Reaction* (1951), is a highly original account of the compromises of 1876–77. On the Redeemer regimes, see Woodward's authoritative *Origins of the New South* (1951). The best account of the disfranchisement of the Negro is J. Morgan Kousser, *The Shaping of Southern Politics* (1974).

Robert E. Spiller et al., *Literary History of the United States,* Vol. 2 (1948), is a good introduction to its subject. Edmund Wilson, *Patriotic Gore* (1962), and Robert A. Lively, *Fiction Fights the Civil War* (1957), are thoughtful studies. On the local colorists, there is much in Van Wyck Brooks, *New England: Indian Summer* (1940) and *The Times of Melville and Whitman* (1947). The best account of the literary reconciliation between North and South is Paul H. Buck's *The Road to Reunion* (1937).

1860
Democratic party deadlocked at Charleston convention finally divides along sectional lines at Baltimore. Constitutional Union party nominates John Bell for President. Republicans nominate Abraham Lincoln, who wins. Senator John J. Crittenden unsuccessfully offers series of constitutional amendments to settle the sectional controversy.

South Carolina secedes from the Union.

1861
Secession of remaining states of deep South (Mississippi, Florida, Alabama, Georgia, Louisiana, and Texas).

Jefferson Davis inaugurated provisional president of the Confederate States of America. Morrill Tariff Act, first of a series of highly protective tariff acts.

Firing on Fort Sumter precipitates war.

Secession of Virginia, North Carolina, Tennessee, and Arkansas.

Union army routed at first battle of Bull Run (Manassas).

George B. McClellan becomes Union commander in chief.

Captain Charles Wilkes (USN) stops British steamer *Trent* on high seas and removes Confederate envoys, James M. Mason and John Slidell. War with England avoided when Lincoln's government releases envoys.

1862
General U. S. Grant captures Fort Henry and Fort Donelson, breaking Confederate line in the West. Further Union advance halted by Confederates at Shiloh.

Union forces capture New Orleans.

Confederacy adopts its first conscription act.

Union Congress passes Homestead Act, Internal Revenue Act, Morrill Act creating land-grant colleges, and Pacific Railroad Act, authorizing transcontinental railroad.

First battle of ironclads, *Merrimack v. Monitor.* McClellan's Peninsula campaign brings Union army to outskirts of Richmond.

Robert E. Lee becomes commander of Army of Northern Virginia. T. J. ("Stonewall") Jackson's raid in Shenandoah Valley prevents

Bragg's army defeats Union forces under Rosecrans at Chickamauga: General George H. Thomas saves Union army from rout. Reinforced by Grant and W. T. Sherman, Union army defeats Confederates in battle of Chatanooga (Lookout Mountain and Missionary Ridge).

1864
Lincoln announces lenient program of amnesty and pardon and introduces 10 percent plan for reconstructing Southern states.

Grant named Union general in chief.

Union Congress passes Wade-Davis bill, a more stringent reconstruction plan. When Lincoln pocket vetoes it, Radical Republicans angrily denounce him.

Grant's direct advance on Richmond checked in the battles of the Wilderness, Spotsylvania, and Cold Harbor. Grant moves south of James River to begin "siege" of Petersburg.

Sherman pushes back Confederates under Joseph E. Johnston and captures Atlanta.

Farragut captures Mobile.

Lincoln reelected President over Democratic candidate McClellan.

Sherman marches from Atlanta to the sea, devastating Georgia.

1865
Sherman pushes northward through South Carolina and North Carolina.

Cut off from supplies and nearly surrounded, Lee gives up Petersburg and Richmond, and Confederate government flees.

Lee surrenders at Appomattox. Johnston surrenders to Sherman. Kirby-Smith surrenders Confederate forces west of the Mississippi. Lincoln assassinated; Andrew Johnson becomes President.

Walt Whitman publishes *Drum Taps.*
Johnson moves for speedy, lenient restoration of Southern states to Union.

Congress creates Joint Committee of Fifteen to supervise reconstruction process.

Thirteenth Amendment ratified.

1866
Johnson breaks with Republican majority in Congress by vetoing Freedmen's Bureau bill and Civil Rights bill. Latter is passed over his veto.

Congress passes Fifteenth Amendment and submits it to states for ratification.
Transcontinental railroad completed.
Public Credit Act affirms government's obligation to pay its debts in gold, not in depreciated paper money.

1870
First Ku Klux Klan (or Enforcement) Act gives Grant power to move against white terrorists in South. A second act in 1871 further strengthens President's hand.

Grant's proposal to annex the Dominican Republic leads to feud with Senator Charles Sumner and break in Republican party.

Incorporation of Standard Oil Company of Ohio.

Grant names G. W. Curtis to head Civil Service Commission.

1871
Treaty of Washington, settling differences between United States and Great Britain, signed.

Knights of Labor formed.

Tweed Ring in New York City exposed.

Whitman publishes *Democratic Vistas.*
Edward Eggleston publishes *The Hoosier Schoolmaster.*

1872
Liberal Republicans and Democrats nominate Horace Greeley for President; Republicans renominate Grant, who is elected.

Exposure of Credit Mobilier scandal shows prominent Republican politicians tainted by graft.

1873
Coinage Act demonetizes silver in so-called Crime of '73.

Panic of 1873 begins long economic depression.

In Slaughterhouse Cases, Supreme Court begins narrow interpretation of Fourteenth Amendment.

1874
Grant vetoes Inflation Act.
Greenback party founded.
Democrats, for first time since 1860, secure majority in House of Representatives.

1875
Specie Resumption Act provides for return to gold standard by 1879.

1876
Exposure of Whiskey Ring reveals further corruption in Republican administration.

rebellion.

C. S. S. *Alabama*, built in British shipyards, begins its career of devastating United States merchant marine.

Lee and Jackson defeat Union General John Pope at second battle of Bull Run (Manassas).

Lee's invasion of Maryland halted at Antietam (Sharpsburg), the bloodiest day of the war.

Lincoln issues his preliminary Emancipation Proclamation, promising to free slaves in rebellious region on January 1.

Gravest threat of Anglo-French intervention in American Civil War averted because of dissension in British cabinet.

1863 Confederate invasion of Kentucky, led by Braxton Bragg and Edmund Kirby-Smith, halted at Perryville. Union General William S. Rosecrans forces Bragg to withdraw from central Tennessee in battle of Murfreesboro (Stones River).

Lee defeats Union commander Ambrose P. Burnside at Fredericksburg.

Cabinet crisis in Union government as Radical Republicans attempt to oust Seward; Lincoln remains in control.

Napoleon III offers to mediate American quarrel; rebuffed by Seward.

Union Congress adopts first real conscription act.

Confederate Congress passes broad internal revenue taxes.

Lee defeats new Union commander, Joseph Hooker, at Chancellorsville.

Grant captures Vicksburg.

Lee invades the North but is checked by General George G. Meade at Gettysburg.

Draft riots throughout the North, especially in New York City.

Union Congress passes National Banking Act (strengthened in 1864).

Union minister Charles Francis Adams persuades British government to prevent sailing of Laird rams.

In the Prize Cases, the United States Supreme Court upholds legality of the war and of Lincoln's actions to subdue the Confederates.

Herman Melville publishes *Battle-Pieces*.

National Labor Union organized at Baltimore.

Johnson tries to form new Union party of conservative Republicans, Democrats, and white Southerners. Despite "arm-in-arm" convention at Philadelphia and Johnson's speeches on his "Swing around the Circle," Republicans win fall congressional elections.

In *ex parte* Milligan, Supreme Court forbids military trials in areas where civil courts are functioning.

Southern whites in Pulaski, Tennessee, organize Ku Klux Klan, which rapidly spreads over the South.

1867 Congress passes Military Reconstruction Act over Johnson's veto. (Two supplementary acts in 1867 and a third in 1868 passed to put this measure into effect.)

Congress passes Tenure of Office Act and Command of Army Act to reduce Johnson's power.

Annexation of Alaska.

Execution of Emperor Maximilian marks end of French adventure in Mexico.

John W. DeForest publishes *Miss Ravenel's Conversion*.

Samuel L. Clemens (Mark Twain) publishes *The Celebrated Jumping Frog of Calaveras County*.

O. H. Kelley founds Patrons of Husbandry (Granger movement).

1868 Former Confederate states hold constitutional conventions, for which former slaves are allowed to vote, and adopt new constitutions guaranteeing universal suffrage.

Arkansas, Alabama, Florida, Georgia, Louisiana, North Carolina, and South Carolina readmitted to representation in Congress. Because of discrimination against Negro officeholders, Georgia representatives are expelled. (State is again admitted in 1870.)

President Johnson impeached. Escapes conviction by one vote.

Republicans nominate Grant for President; Democrats select Governor Horatio Seymour of New York. Grant elected President.

Middle Western states begin passing Granger laws, regulating railroads and grain elevators.

In *Texas v. White*, Supreme Court declares Union indissoluble and affirms authority of Congress to reconstruct Southern states.

President, Democrats nominate Samuel J. Tilden. Tilden secures majority of popular vote but electoral vote in doubt because of disputed returns from three Southern states.

1877 After elaborate political and economic bargaining, Congress creates an electoral commission, which rules that all disputed ballots belong to Hayes, who is inaugurated President.

In *Munn v. Illinois*, Supreme Court upholds Granger legislation.

Nationwide railroad strike and ensuing violence lead to first significant use of federal troops to suppress labor disorders.

1878 Bland-Allison Act requires United States Treasury to purchase $2 to 4 million of silver each month and coin it, thus slightly inflating the currency but not assuring unlimited coinage as silver interests demanded.

Hayes ousts Chester A. Arthur and Alonzo B. Cornell from New York customshouse and precipitates break with "Stalwart" Republican faction of Roscoe Conkling.

Timber and Stone Act permits inexpensive sale of public lands considered unfit for cultivation. Miners, lumbermen, and speculators reap huge profits.

1879 As authorized by the 1875 act, Secretary of the Treasury John Sherman begins resumption of specie payments.

Terence V. Powderly elected head of the Knights of Labor, which enters a period of great expansion until by 1886 it has more than 700,000 members.

The First Church of Christ, Scientist, opened in Boston. This is the mother church of the Christian Science faith established by Mary Baker Eddy.

Henry George publishes *Progress and Poverty*.

1880 In the presidential contest, Republicans nominate James A. Garfield and Chester A. Arthur; Democrats choose Winfield Scott Hancock and William H. English; Greenback Labor party selects James B. Weaver and B. J. Chambers. Garfield elected President.

Joel Chandler Harris publishes *Uncle Remus*.

1881 Charles J. Guiteau assassinates Garfield.
Chester A. Arthur succeeds Garfield as
President.
Publication of Helen Hunt Jackson's *A Century
of Dishonor* calls attention to serious defects in
United States Indian policy.
Publication of *The Portrait of a Lady* inaugurates
Henry James's major phase as a novelist.

1882 Chinese Exclusion Act restricts immigration of
Chinese laborers for ten years.
In *San Mateo County v. Southern Pacific Railroad
Company*, Supreme Court accepts Roscoe Conkling's argument that word *persons* in the Fourteenth Amendment was deliberately chosen to
extend protection of due process clause to
corporations.

1883 In the Civil Rights Cases Supreme Court declares unconstitutional 1875 Civil Rights Act,
because it protected social rather than political
rights.
Anticipating Democratic control of Congress,
Republicans pass the Tariff of 1883, which
nominally makes some reductions in rates but
firmly keeps protectionist principle.
In reaction to assassination of Garfield by a
disappointed office-seeker, Congress passes
Pendleton Act, setting up Civil Service Commission and requiring many future federal
appointees to take competitive examinations.
Congressional authorization to build three steel
cruisers begins renovation of the United States
navy.
James Whitcomb Riley publishes *The Old
Swimming Hole.*
Mark Twain publishes *Life on the Mississippi.*

1884 In the presidential campaign Republicans
nominate James G. Blaine, Democrats Grover
Cleveland, Prohibitionists John P. St. John, and
National Greenback Labor party Benjamin F.
Butler. Cleveland narrowly wins, becoming the
first Democrat to be elected President since
Buchanan.

1885 Founding of Leland Stanford, Junior, University (now Stanford University).
Mark Twain publishes *Huckleberry Finn.*

1886 After police break up an anarcho-communist
rally in Haymarket Square, Chicago, a bomb
explodes among the police, who then open fire.
In ensuing trials, August Spies, Albert Parsons,
and other radical agitators sentenced to death.
Petitions circulated by William Dean Howells
and other intellectuals convince Governor John
Peter Altgeld of Illinois that the trial was
unfair, since the identity of the bomb thrower
was never established, and in 1893 he frees the
surviving prisoners.
American Federation of Labor organized;
Samuel Gompers, first president.
In *Wabash, St. Louis & Pacific Railroad Company
v. Illinois*, the Supreme Court invalidates state
regulation of railroads when it affects interstate
commerce, thus weakening Court's previous
ruling in *Munn v. Illinois* (the Granger Cases,
1877).

1887 To fill gap in railroad regulation left by
Wabash decision, Congress creates Interstate
Commerce Commission, first federal regulatory
commission in United States history.
Cleveland vetoes Dependent Pension Bill and
numerous individual pension bills, declaring
that they would make the pension roll a refuge
for frauds rather than a "roll of honor."
Congress repeals 1867 Tenure of Office Act.
Looking toward the dissolution of the Indian
tribes, Congress passes the Dawes Severalty Act
providing for the division of tribal lands among
individual members.

1888 In the presidential campaign, Democrats renominate Grover Cleveland and Republicans
nominate Benjamin Harrison. Harrison elected
President by a majority in the electoral college
but receives fewer popular votes than Cleveland.
Edward Bellamy publishes *Looking Backward.*

1889 Department of Agriculture raised to cabinet
status.
Omnibus Act admits North Dakota, South
Dakota, Montana, and Washington as states.
Germany, Great Britain, and United States
agree to set up a tripartite protectorate over
Samoa.

1890 Sherman Anti-Trust Act passed in attempt to
regulate monopolies in restraint of trade.
Sherman Silver Purchase Act passed, resulting
in depleted gold reserves.
McKinley Tariff raises duties to average
49.5 percent.

Descended from "Uncle Sam"
Wilson, a real-life butcher
from Troy, New York, who
provisioned the militia in the
War of 1812, the symbolic
Uncle Sam was born during the
Age of Jackson and was raised
by politicos in the Whig and
Democratic parties. During the
Gilded Age the pictorial Uncle
Sam spent most of his time
enforcing the law, punishing
political miscreants, and
lecturing the rest of the world
on the blessings of democracy.
Even his recreation was grimly
purposeful: in this piece of
folk sculpture he is seen on his
bicycle riding hell-bent for
prosperity. (Courtesy Mr. & Mrs.
Leo Rabkin.)

PART FIVE

Nationalizing the Republic

1890 - 1920

JOHN L. THOMAS

A s the American people completed their industrial revolution in the half-century following the Civil War, they continued to celebrate unprecedented growth even as they were driven to experiment with new ways of regulating it. In 1900 as in 1850 most Americans saw cause for national self-congratulation in the numerous signs of prosperity all around them: an improved standard of living; rapid population growth; the rise of great cities; and an ever-growing stock of consumer goods. More thoughtful observers, however, noted that all of these achievements had come at a high social price: the sudden uprooting of a rural people and the disruption of their communities; the forced mobility of new masses of underprivileged; deplorable working conditions for too many Americans; and the persistence of a conspicuously unequal distribution of wealth. Still, for most people caught up in America's industrial transformation the benefits of rapid material growth clearly outweighed its costs.

For economic growth continued to verify earlier predictions of illimitable progress, and most Americans, whether they consulted population statistics or production charts, still sought confirmation of their cherished ideal of progress. The key concept in this doctrine of progress—freedom from external restraints on individual ambitions and energies—had survived the Civil War, if not unscathed at least intact. A simple faith in the individual continued to claim the allegiance of a majority of Americans in 1900 just as it had an earlier generation.

Yet in spite of the optimum mood of the country, reform-minded citizens in all walks of life by 1880 were beginning to note the signs of mounting social disorder. Under the triple impact of industrialization, modernization, and urbanization a growing number of leaders in all parts of the national community came to recognize the need for controls and system as new means of acquiring efficiency and stability. Businessmen sought consolidated power within their firms with which to improve their operations and increase their profits. Farmers quickly discovered an urgent need for better credit facilities and marketing mechanisms. Social theorists and urban reformers began to adjust their vision to the requirements of systematic planning. By 1890 what had once been considered a self-regulating device for producing happiness automatically had come to be seen as a machine badly in need of repair if not a complete overhaul.

Not all these would-be reformers of American society after 1890 agreed either on priorities or means. But the thrust of their ideas and programs pointed unmistakably toward the construction of a new national order. The historical meaning of this new vision declared itself in a repudiation of the permissive philosophy of Thomas Jefferson and the refurbishing of the original nationalist model of Alexander Hamilton. In the fields of law and constitutional theory the change brought replacement of outworn formal definitions of rights and duties with more flexible concepts of social utility requiring new roles for lawyers and legislators alike. In social reform the steady drift away from midcentury absolutes was accompanied by a new emphasis on training, expertise, and the predictive functions of science. To politics, the organizational revolution brought new styles of leadership and new approaches to the workings of government.

The distance the nation had traveled by 1920 could be measured in two widely different assessments of American politics and society, the first by the individualist prophet Ralph Waldo Emerson in the salad days of moral reform before the Civil War. Emerson located the national genius in the "wise man" with whose appearance "the state expires." "The tendencies of the times," Emerson predicted, "favor the idea of self-government, and leave the individual . . . to the rewards and penalties of his own constitution; which works with more energy than we believe whilst we depend on artificial restraints." Three-quarters of a century later the progressive sociologist Charles Horton Cooley took the measure of Emerson's prophecy only to discard it. Cooley dismissed Emerson's self-enclosed individual as a moral abstraction unknown to history. "In a truly organic life the individual is self-conscious and devoted to his work, but feels himself and that work as part of a large joyous whole. He is self-assertive, just because he is conscious of being a thread in the great web of events." The story of the years separating the sage of Concord from the progressive social scientist is the account of the American discovery of the great social web and the multitude of connecting threads that composed it.

24

Stabilizing the American Economy

The American people greeted the arrival of the twentieth century by consulting the facts and figures they hoped would explain the abundance heaped upon them by their industrial revolution. Looking back across the previous decade, they could trace the rise of their country's wealth from $65 billion to $90 billion and the growth of their national income from $12 billion to $18 billion. If progress could be measured in dollars and cents, then who could quarrel with the obvious?

Nowhere was the American faith in the quantitative more evident than in the popular account of the recent economic growth of the nation. From a new breed of economic experts, from professional economists and financial commentators, from statistical compilations and industrial reports came reams of data, which, Americans reasoned, could tell them not simply where they had been but where they were headed. The mass of statistics distinguished two phases of growth in American industry and agriculture in the sixty years before 1900. The first phase had begun well before the Civil War, gathered momentum in the decades following it, and culminated in the year of the Republican presidential triumph of William McKinley, 1896. In business this first stage of economic growth was typified by the startling success of John D. Rockefeller's Standard Oil Company in gaining control over the oil industry; in agriculture, by the appearance of mammoth ten-thousand-acre "bonanza" farms run with new mechanical seeders and harvesters. The second and still developing phase of economic consolidation was marked by the growth of industrial and financial mergers that, beginning in 1898 demolished the brownstone order of Gilded Age capitalism and cleared the ground for twentieth-century skyscrapers housing new corporate giants.

By 1900, most Americans looked to the merger movement for the clues to their recently acquired munificence. From one angle, the great merger movement appeared to be a towering peak of corporate consolidations. The number of mergers traced a sharp trajectory from 69 in 1897 to 303 a year later to 1,208 in 1899, before leveling off in the next three years at between 350 and 425. By 1900, there were already 73 so-called trusts, with capitalizations of over $10 million, and two-thirds of them had been established within the previous three years.

Viewed negatively, the merger movement looked like nothing so much as a gigantic hole into which some 300 businesses tumbled each year, swallowed by huge new combinations like United States Steel and General Electric. United States Steel absorbed over 200 manufacturing and transportation companies and quickly won control over two-thirds of the steel market. American Tobacco combined 162 independent companies and ruled all but 10 percent of the tobacco market. By 1904, the approximately 2000 largest firms in the United States composed less than 1 percent of the total number of the nation's businesses yet produced 40 percent of the annual value of the nation's industrial goods. By 1910, monopoly (domination of an industry by a single firm) and oligopoly (control established by a few large firms) had secured the commanding positions from which they would continue to dominate twentieth-century American life.

The merger movement that ended a half-century's search for economic order was both the logical outgrowth of rapid industrial development and at the same time an unsettling departure from remembered ways, the forerunner of massive changes in the way Americans lived and worked. The reorganization of the national economy after 1900 generated hopes and fears, made promises and raised doubts as it worked a revolution in the habits and values of the American people. How did it happen? What forces accounted for it?

The Foundations of the American Industrial Revolution

The key factor in the earlier phase of the economic transformation of the United States in the thirty years following the Civil War was the unprecedented growth of American cities. An enormous demographic shift had piled native-born citizens and recently arrived immigrants into metropolitan areas where they furnished vast new markets for consumer goods of all kinds, both basic necessities like food and clothing and newly developed products like sewing-machines, typewriters, and cigarettes. In the four decades surrounding the Civil

CITY TRAFFIC IN THE NINETIES

Trolleys, horse-drawn cabs, delivery wagons, and wary
pedestrians compete for space on Chicago's Clark Street.
(*Library of Congress.*)

War, the population of American cities rose at the rate of 4 percent per decade;
by 1880 over a quarter of the nation's people lived in urban areas. In the remaining years of the century, the urban population grew even faster—at the phenomenal rate of 6 percent per decade, until by 1900 a full 40 percent of the American
people lived in cities. Even more important, they tended to concentrate in giant
metropolitan centers like New York, Chicago, Philadelphia, and Detroit. "We
cannot all live in cities," Horace Greeley complained to a younger generation
headed toward the metropolis, "yet nearly all seem determined to do so. . . . 'Hot
and cold water,' baker's bread, the theatre, and the streetcars . . . indicate the
tendency of modern taste."

As cities grew at a pell-mell pace, pushing the boundaries of old commercial centers into surrounding suburbs along elevated railroads and trolley lines, they themselves became consumers of heavy industrial goods—electric dynamos, telephone wire, lead pipe and copper tubing, streetcars and the motors to run them. Cities, whether underwriting large public constructions like John and Washington Roebling's magnificent Brooklyn Bridge or encouraging private ventures like Louis Sullivan's steel-framed Wainwright Building in Saint Louis, supplied an insatiable appetite for all the products turned out by the American industrial machine. And with huge concentrations of "new immigrants" from southern and eastern Europe, cities also became producers as well as consumers of industrial abundance.

It was not only the mushroom growth of cities that made an economic revolution, but also the continuing expansion of a transcontinental railroad network. Railroads fed growing heavy industry with orders for equipment, triggered a process of large-scale formation of investment capital, and linked the cities of the nation, first in a loose network of commercial centers and then in the outlines of a national market system. Total railroad mileage rose from 35,000 miles of track in 1865 to 166,000 a quarter-century later. Transcontinental lines became primary arteries for distributing consumer goods. By 1890 railroad transporta-

Principal Railroads, 1890

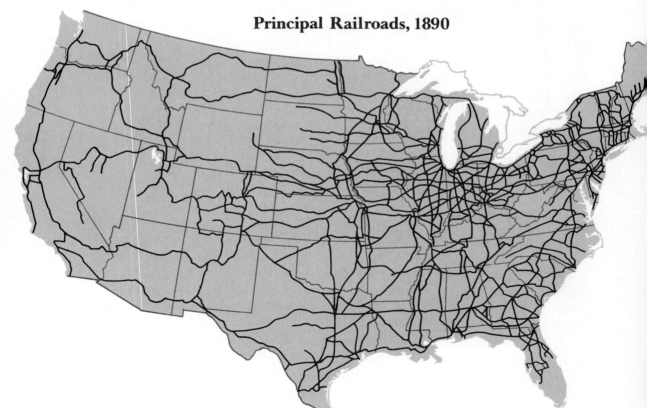

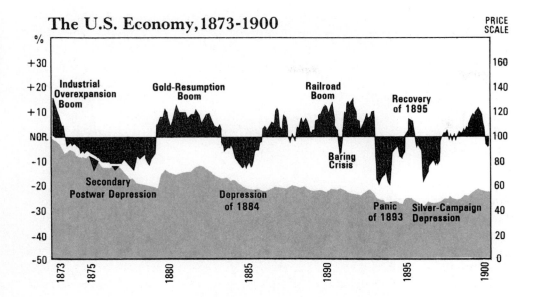

The U.S. Economy, 1873-1900

tion was dominated by a small group of integrated lines like the New York Central and the Pennsylvania roads in the East, the Burlington system in the Midwest, and the Union Pacific, Northern Pacific, and Great Northern routes to the West Coast. Once an efficient distributing system complete with telegraph network had been built, American businessmen were able to envision for the first time a national complex of large integrated firms, practicing economies of scale and passing these savings along to consumers in all parts of the country in lower prices for their goods they sent rolling along the nation's railroad tracks. Both as fact and as organizational idea, the railroad played a major role in the economic transformation of the country.

Still another component of economic growth was the steady increase in labor-saving machinery that eventually and often unintentionally led to better working conditions and a growing investment in education. Technological development and managerial innovation worked together to improve the quality and performance of American labor. Throughout the nineteenth century, a huge reservoir of unskilled labor was considered essential to economic expansion, and as late as the First World War the national economy continued to depend on the unskilled labor of women and children. But propelled by technology, the long-term trend pointed in another direction. Despite the willingness of native-born youths fresh from the farm and young immigrants just off the boat to feed the furnaces and sweep the floors, it was machines that sent American productivity soaring after the turn of the century. And it was machines that accounted for the annual increase of 1 percent in the physical output per man-hour between 1889 and 1919.

Equally important in quickening the rate of national economic growth was the increasing availability of large amounts of investment capital. By the 1880s the

EDGAR THOMSON STEEL WORKS,
BRADDOCK, PENNSYLVANIA, 1908

Rapid industrialization was not
gained without high ecological
costs. (*Library of Congress.*)

rate of savings of Americans, which had doubled in thirty years, was helping to
form a huge pool of investment funds that began to flow into industry in increasing volume. Technology bred great expectations and with them a mounting demand for capital. In the early years of the oil business just after the Civil War,
John D. Rockefeller was able to acquire a small refinery for $10,000 and a large
one for $50,000. Twenty-five years later, it took over $200 million to incorporate
Federal Steel. In steel production, the expensive Bessemer process turned brittle
iron into flexible steel and transformed the industry. In oil, the development of
refining techniques accompanied the discovery of new uses for petroleum. In
nearly every industry—meat-packing with the refrigerated car, the electric industry with alternating current, the railroads with the air brake—technology
brought ever greater efficiency as it created ever greater demands for capital. On
the eve of the Civil War a total of $1 billion was invested in the nation's manu-
facturing plants, which turned out a collective product worth $1.8 billion and
employed 4.3 million workers. By 1900 the size of the work force had grown
fivefold and the total value of products nearly tenfold; at the same time, the
amount of invested capital had multiplied twelvefold.

Thus the merger movement at the end of the century seemed to have a logic
all its own. Mergers, with their vast concentration of power and control, appeared
to mark the emergence of a stable corporate society from the chaos of small-
scale competitive capitalism. Big businessmen and the new investment bankers
presumably held the answers to the pressing problems of economic disorder,
which was no longer seen as the price of progress.

The continuing instability of the American economy between 1870 and 1900—itself the most persuasive argument for economic concentration—was no mere figment of the business imagination but a hard-edged reality. For every year of upswing and expansion in this thirty-year period there was another of downturn and contraction. The American economy moved like a pendulum from flush to hard times and back again. The Panic of 1873 plunged the country into six years of depression, with mass unemployment, wage cuts, and price decline. Following a short season of recovery, a second recession buffeted the economy in 1884 and again sent prices skidding and workers into the ranks of the unemployed. Once more, after a brief respite, the Panic of 1893 brought four years of economic paralysis, from which the country had just recovered at the end of the century.

All three depressions were triggered by financial panics—the collapse of the investment houses of Jay Cooke in 1873 and of Grant and Ward in 1884, and of nearly the entire railroad empire in 1893. But satisfactory explanations of the causes of depressions were hard to come by. Whether they compared them to the swing of a pendulum, the breaking of a wave, or the onset of a fever, most American observers despaired of controlling the business cycle or easing the effects of periodic slumps. Despite the lessons in the need for economic planning that the Civil War had taught, the great majority of Americans still held fast to a Jacksonian faith in the self-regulating market, with which, conventional wisdom declared, government interfered at its peril.

The result of this popular belief in untrammeled business opportunity was a national government in the Gilded Age that frequently subsidized but seldom regulated. Politicians vied with businessmen in predicting marvelous achievements for a new industrial statesmanship left to its own devices. Corporations, Abram S. Hewitt, the wealthy iron-master told the Chicago Board of Trade in 1885, were the "best friends" the American people had. Farseeing industrialists were now "doing the work which was done by Jefferson and Madison in the early years of the Republic."

Politicians deferred to such business leadership, and the directive force of government at all levels tended to disappear in misty hopes for ever growing prosperity. The great steel manufacturer Andrew Carnegie explained the terms of the new social contract in language that a business civilization readily understood. It would be a mistake, Carnegie insisted, for the American community to shoot its millionaires, since after all they were the "bees that [made] the most honey. "Under our present conditions the millionaire who toils on is the cheapest article which the community secures at the price it pays for him, namely, his shelter, clothing and food." Carnegie need not have worried; there would never be an open season on American millionaires.

Business Fills a Vacuum

The renunciation of public authority over industrial growth cast the burden of creating economic stability on American businessmen themselves. Blessed with innovative talent, abundant material resources, and the nearly total freedom to use them, American businessmen were the first to respond to the challenge of disorder with new devices for securing stability and increasing profits. But businessmen after the Civil War tended to direct the diagnostic skills they possessed to specific problems only. In their view, the troubles besetting the American economy required, not a public policy designed to regulate growth, but short-term survival strategies to protect the individual firm against fate.

Chief among the most obvious threats to American prosperity was a long-term drop in prices in the last three decades of the nineteenth century. In these years the wholesale price index fell from a high of 174 in 1866 to 135 four years later and then to 100 by 1880 and 82 in 1890. Although scarcely continuous—as consumers knew full well—this general downward trend of prices clearly showed the effects of two new factors in the national economy. Production costs were declining, and competiton for markets was increasing dramatically. Threatened with recurrent panics, intense competition, collapsing prices and the prospect of shrinking profits, the more innovative of the nation's business leaders began to experiment with a variety of techniques for gaining greater control over their industries. Their inventions were the structural improvisations of a business community confronted with severe problems but left to find its own solutions. In deciding to replace a small business economy with its free market system, Amer-

ON THE PROMENADE, BROOKLYN BRIDGE, 1897

In this stereopticon view New Yorkers enjoy a Sunday afternoon stroll. (*Library of Congress.*)

ican business leaders quickly came to play, however reluctantly, a revolutionary role.

Attaining stability in major industries required increasingly sophisticated techniques. The earliest and most primitive forms of organization, necessitating the least amount of change, were *cartels,* loose trade associations (pools) of independent business firms joined together to dominate an industry. The organizer of the Wire Nail Association explained the case for cartels with disarming candor:

There is nail machinery enough in this country to produce four times as many nails as can be sold. When there is no pool the makers simply cut each other's throats. Some people think there is something wicked about pools. When we were trying to get up the nail pool, I talked with directors of companies who held up their hands against going into any sort of combination. I said to them, "How much did you make last year?" "Not a cent." "Are you making anything now?" "No." "Well, what do you propose to do? Sit here and lose what capital you have got in the business . . . ?" There is only one way to make any money in a business like the nail business, and that is to have a pool.

Cartels met the problem of overproduction and falling prices through gentlemen's agreements; independent competitors agreed among themselves to accept quotas and refrain from price cutting. In organizing a pool in 1881 the whiskey distillers, for example, agreed that "only 28 percent of the full capacity [of member firms] shall be operated, and no stocking up beyond this amount under any circumstances." To tighten sagging steel prices, the steel rail manufacturers in 1887 formed the Steel Rail Association, one of the few genuinely successful pools, which established a strict quota system and instituted a series of stiff fines for uncooperative members. Although the Steel Rail Association continued to deny charges of price fixing, it nevertheless enjoyed a period of remarkable price stability thereafter.

Yet cartelization had distinct liabilities. Pools and trade associations flourished in good times but fell apart during recessions. Their agreements were unenforceable in the courts, and in general they tended to assume the community of interests they were in fact designed to create. American consumers, moreover, regarded such combinations an undue restraint of trade and scrutinized their operations with an ever more jaundiced eye.

Recognizing the limitations of pools, and confronted with aroused public opposition to secret agreements, pioneer reorganizers like John D. Rockefeller turned to "horizontal" combinations in the form of the trust. The trust was the brainchild of a member of Standard Oil's legal staff, the affable and shrewd Samuel C. T. Dodd, who patiently explained its advantages to his hesitant colleagues. Since state laws prohibited outright ownership by one company of the stock of another, Dodd admitted, there was no foolproof way of consolidating, holding and managing a string of separate companies.

But you could have a common name, a common office, and a common management by means of a common executive committee. . . . If the Directors of one of the companies and their successors shall be made Trustees of all such stock, you thus procure a practical unification of all the companies.

The idea worked. In 1882, forty-one stockholders in the Standard Oil Company of Ohio signed an agreement creating a board of nine trustees to whom they transferred all the properties and assets of their own companies in exchange for trust certificates. The trust agreement declared that "it shall be the duty of said Trustees to exercise general supervision over the affairs of said Standard Oil Companies, and as far as practicable over the other Companies or Partnerships, any portion of whose stock is held in said trust." The visible signs of this financial feat were 700,000 hundred-dollar certificates, the price of consolidated control over the oil industry. The corporate spirit had wrought its first miracle.

Many trusts and holding companies (integrated firms allowed to hold the stocks of other corporations), having won formal control over production and prices, were content to operate as loose cartels, simply parceling out shares of the market to their newly acquired properties without trying to impose a centralized management and authority. But soon the largest and most powerful businesses began to follow the examples of the Carnegie Steel Company, and of Gustavus Swift in meatpacking, by achieving "vertical" integration of their industries. They sought to combine under a single management all the processes of production and distribution—from sources of raw material to new marketing mechanisms. Increasingly after 1890, big business sought control that extended "backward" to resources and transportation as well as "forward" towards market control maintained by research departments and the development schemes of central business offices.

Financing this corporate revolution required immense sums of money, much of it recently made available in new forms. For the first seventy-five years of the nineteenth century, most of the capital for industrial investment had come out of the savings of the firms that used it. By 1900, however, the stock market had established itself as the main mechanism for exchanging securities and mobilizing the vast funds large-scale integrated businesses demanded. By the time the United States entered the First World War, Wall Street had succeeded in creating a genuine national capital market. Part of this growing supply of capital was derived from foreign investment, which increased from $1.5 to $3.5 billion between 1870 and 1900. Even more important was the dramatic rise in the personal savings of Americans, which peaked in the 1870s and 1880s and provided large reserves of investment capital eventually flowing into the new "industrials."

The increase in personal savings was accompanied by the rapid growth of financial institutions—commercial banks, savings banks, and life insurance companies—that served as intermediaries between the investor and the business firm. Above all, the stock market facilitated the work of promoters and investment bankers by mobilizing buyers of stock and stimulating demand through overcapitalization. Growing numbers of investors, responding to the lure of profits, became buyers of more and more securities. "Probably four-fifths of the companies that are organized," Roger Babson reported, "whether in the transportation, electric power, or industrial field, are organized primarily not to transport passengers or generate power or manufacture goods, but to get securities to sell." Between 1896 and 1900 the number of new industrials listed on the board of the New York Stock Exchange more than doubled—from 20 to 46—with the securities of integrated corporations leading the way.

It was natural for a new generation of promoters and investment bankers to discern in industrial combination, if not the hand of God, at least an inexorable law of nature at work ordering the business affairs of the world. Samuel C. T. Dodd, Rockefeller's counsel, warned of the futility of tinkering with the celestial machinery. "You might as well endeavor to stay the formation of the clouds, the falling of the rains, or the flowing of the streams as to attempt by any means or in any manner to prevent organization of industry, association of persons, and the aggregation of capital to any extent that the ever growing trade of the world may demand."

And indeed, the success of mergers was difficult to deny. The facts of industrial and financial combination seemed to emphasize several practical advantages of monopoly and oligopoly. By 1895, the remarkable growth and swelling profits of Standard Oil, American Sugar Refining, and American Tobacco had marked out what appeared to be a sure route to salvation through combination. John W. "Betcha-Million" Gates, the flamboyant president of the newly fashioned American Steel and Wire Company, boasted of the blessings conferred on his trust by integration. "We are the owners of iron mines, miners of ore, owners of coal mines, burners of coke." Judge Elbert Gary explained Federal Steel's sudden success in similar terms: "It takes the ore from the ground, transports it, manufactures it into pig iron, manufactures pig iron into steel, and steel into finished products, and delivers those products." Even more impressive was the formation of United States Steel (1901), into which went some 200 manufacturing plants and transportation companies, 1000 miles of railroad, 112 blast furnaces, and 78 ore boats. Soon U.S. Steel was employing 170,000 workers as it gathered control over 60 percent of the country's steel capacities. Its initial capitalization at $1.4 billion was three times the annual expenditure of the federal government.

Increased efficiency, elimination of waste, bigger shares of the market, and anticipated though not always actual economies of scale—all were factors that ensured larger profits and convinced adventurous businessmen of the need to pursue mergers. By 1910, mergers had spread to all the principal sectors of the economy, and many of the twentieth century's most powerful corporations had been formed: Swift and Armour, Standard Oil and Texaco, General Electric and Westinghouse, International Harvester and DuPont. When the first great wave of mergers receded, it left standing the institutional forms of a new corporate

capitalism; they were the mammoth integrated enterprises with interlocking structures, managed by professionals with newly acquired expertise, selling their increasing variety of products in shared markets at administered prices. The great merger movement declared the bankruptcy of laissez-faire competition and announced the imminent arrival of a modern corporate society in need of new definitions to replace the outworn pieties of pluck and luck. In place of a host of small- and medium-sized business firms scrambling for a share of the market and justifying their rivalry with clichés drawn from classical economy, there stood an increasing number of huge unified structures based on the bureau-cratic values of efficiency and predictability. The corporate revolution was by no means over by 1914, and the nation in the Progressive years continued to support a dual economy of big and little business. But the meaning of the merger movement was unmistakable: most Americans believed that bigger was better.

Organizing the mergers and raising the capital to launch them quickly became the specialty of investment bankers like J. P. Morgan and Jacob Schiff, who dom-inated the American economy in the first years of the twentieth century as they never would again. While taking a handsome slice of stock in the consolidations they created, they became powerful middlemen between an eager investing pub-lic and an expansive business community. They arranged the mergers and floated the stock, stabilizing the workings of their new creations, and manufacturing favorable publicity. Their success could be read in the achievements of the House of Morgan, which by 1912, together with the Morgan-controlled First National

TWO AMERICAN HEROES

Edward Steichen's portrait of J. Pierpont Morgan as the awesome financial wizard (left) contrasts sharply with Thomas A. Edison in his laboratory in the legendary pose of the native American genius (right). (*Left, The Museum of Modern Art; right, Courtesy of National Park Service.*)

Bank of New York and the Rockefeller-managed National City Bank, held 341 directorships in 112 national corporations worth $22.2 billion.

In the public imagination the entire merger movement became personified in the investment banker, part savior of a threatened economy, part devil in disguise. For their everyday heroes, Americans might prefer the inventor and the engineer—Thomas Edison, Alexander Graham Bell, George Westinghouse; but they also admired, feared, envied, and puzzled over the new industrial and financial moguls who now presumably managed the economy of the country. The awesome J. P. Morgan, the circumspect Jacob Schiff, and their clients and lesser breeds of big businessmen seemed to embody the combination of inventive energy and financial shrewdness, the drive for power and the pursuit of profits, an alternating boldness and extreme caution that mirrored an American public's ambivalence towards industrial plenty and the concentrated power needed to produce it.

The heroes of the new corporate age, like their many admirers, were never entirely clear about their aims. The president of the newly formed International Silver Company, an amalgam of 16 former independents, as he testified before the Industrial Commission in 1899, betrayed the confusion of motives underlying the merger movement. To his persistent questioners, he unwittingly confessed the difficulty of distinguishing between scale economies and the desire for monopoly control as the primary incentive for combination.

Q. What was the purpose of your combination—to repress this competition, or to make economies of manufacturing?
A. That was what we were trying to do; both.
Q. Both?
A. To make economies and put the thing under one administration, just as I said before. That was all there was to it.

None of the new men of business—corporate executive, financial mogul, professional manager—was very explicit about the ultimate meaning of his vision of an industrial heaven on earth. Heavy capital investment, rapid plant expansion, increased production and reduced overhead, economies of scale, market control—all to what greater good? For profits, surely, and for rising quantities of consumer goods for more and more people. But beyond that? What did the manufacture and constant manipulation of consumer demand mean for individual freedom of choice? Was standardization of products and prices really so desirable? How were Americans to equate rising standards of living with loss of control over production? How could big business be called to account and made to deliver on its promise of economic security for all citizens? Were huge industrial and financial combinations compatible with political democracy and social responsibility? These were questions that neither the corporate revolutionists nor their uneasy admirers equipped with production statistics could quite answer. Such fundamental questions posed a continuing twentieth-century dilemma.

The Counterrevolution Fails

The same questions troubled the opponents of big business, whose numbers and influence also grew rapidly after the Civil War. Ultimately the antimonopolists failed, but not for lack of numbers. The antimonopoly army in the last quarter of the nineteenth century included at one time or another farmers and working-men clinging to a belief in equal opportunity; small businessmen with their dreams of sudden fortune; and liberal publicists, country lawyers, clergymen, and academicians who enjoyed a traditional and honorable status and feared losing it to new big businessmen. Antimonopoly found a congenial home in the major protest parties of the period, from the Grangers and the Greenbackers of the 1870s to the Populists of the 1890s. According to their sharpest antagonists, trusts held the people's hands while they picked their pockets. Other critics pointed to the political depredations of monopolies, "these unnatural and unnecessary monsters" roaming the American terrain. A Populist editor in 1891 summed up the frustration of discovering that monopoly was the "logical result of the individual freedom which we have always considered the pride of our system." Americans, he added, had always subscribed to the "very greatest degree of liberty" and the "very least legal restraint," a creed which, paradoxically, had encouraged a predatory big business to preempt the powers of the community and defy the public will.

Most of the opposition to bigness was based on apprehension rather than solid evidence. The antimonopoly indictment tended to dissolve into charges of conspiracy and denunciations of greed precisely because the facts of economic concentration seemed so inconclusive. Monopolies, it was widely held, misallocated and underused resources and thus kept the nation's total output lower than it might have been. If pools, trusts, and all the other instruments of business collusion did not actually raise prices, they at least had the power to do so at will. Their power, moreover, had been acquired by driving out the small competitor, another good reason for demanding their dissolution.

Trusts, according to still another group of critics, were socially inefficient. They protected the weak at the expense of the strong. They sheltered inefficient producers within vast integrated structures where their inefficiencies went unnoticed. Not all the opponents of monopoly agreed that the business world should be ruled by the law of the survival of the fittest, but the word *unnatural* struck a universal chord of response on whose notes hung the real meaning of the case against big business.

Beneath the antimonopolist account of the recent past lay the presumption of a "natural development" that trusts were violating. For social prophets like Henry George and Edward Bellamy, whose bestsellers *Progress and Poverty* (1879) and *Looking Backward* (1888) commanded national attention, for countless other publicists and popularizers of the case against monopoly, "natural" economic growth meant a steady rate of development accompanied by full employment and

LOUIS SULLIVAN BUILDINGS

By 1880 Chicago had become the center of a new "commercial style" of city architecture, the home of the steel-framed tall office building that frankly combined the commercial and the functional. The city boasted Henry H. Richardson's mammoth Marshall Field Warehouse, the pioneer William L. Jenney's Home Insurance Company, and impressive commercial structures by Daniel Burnham, William Holabird, John W. Root, and, the greatest of the Chicago school, Louis Sullivan. Three of Sullivan's most famous buildings are shown here. On the opposite page, the Guaranty Building, Buffalo, New York. (*Chicago Architectural Photo Co.*) On this page right, the Carson, Pirie, Scott Department Store, Chicago. (*Chicago Architectural Photo Co.*) On this page below, the "Golden Door" entrance to the Transportation Building, Chicago World's Fair. (*Brown Brothers.*)

widespread consumption. According to this reasoning, healthy societies like the United States enjoyed a "normal" pace of growth with which monopolies played havoc by accelerating the growth rate and stimulating speculation. If trusts, pools, and all other artificial contrivances could simply be dismantled and their privileges annulled, the American economy would return to a steadier rate of "real growth" that would spread the benefits of industrialism evenly throughout society.

This fiction of the "natural economy," which Americans had inherited from midcentury, tended to direct attention away from the central problem of stabilizing the economy and towards peripheral matters of morality. Monopolies, the indictment went, choked off inventions and bottled up technological improvement. They fixed prices, rigged markets, and hoodwinked consumers. They gave to selfish men the power to direct and dispose of the wealth of an entire society. They corrupted the political process. Total moral collapse would surely follow the arrival of corporate consolidation. Not all these charges were wide of the mark, but they offered little in the way of useful strategy. Stability, in the view of the antimonopolists, was generally assumed to be an automatic by-product of a free market. Because the opponents of monopoly refused to consider controls on the business cycle or a consistent policy of business regulation, they let the initiative fall into the hands of the nation's industrial and financial leaders.

Before 1890 opposition to monopoly proved largely ineffective. In the 1870s, the Patrons of Husbandry, or the Grange, as the national farmers' organization was called, turned to politics in states like Illinois and Wisconsin and passed laws regulating the rates charged by railroads for hauling freight and storing grain. Although the Supreme Court had originally upheld these so-called Granger laws, in 1885 the Court made it painfully clear that individual states were forbidden to regulate rates for interstate carriers.

Nor on the federal level was the Interstate Commerce Act (1887) much more successful in bringing the railroads to heel. The act prohibited pools, rebates, and rate discrimination and set up a commission to investigate violations, but the commission's findings could be enforced only in the courts, a costly and cumbersome procedure. Although the Interstate Commerce Act marked the beginning of the public's acceptance of federal government intervention, it did not establish an effective policy of rate regulation.

By the time Congress responded to the public clamor to "do something about the trusts" by passing the Sherman Antitrust Act in 1890, more than a dozen states had already attempted some kind of antitrust legislation aimed at making restraint of trade "illegal, actionable and indictable." Big business, however, countered these attempts by moving into more permissive states like New Jersey, where they secured generous enabling laws. Henry Demarest Lloyd, perhaps the severest critic of monopoly, complained that Standard Oil, in its bid for preferential treatment, had done everything to the Pennsylvania legislature except refine it.

The Sherman Act brought no antimonopoly millennium. The bill, which John Sherman of Ohio introduced in the Senate, quickly found its way to the Judiciary Committee, which rewrote it before sending it to the full Senate where it passed by a vote of 52 to 1. The House, in turn, passed the measure unanimously. The Sherman Act was an honest if confused effort to create legislation that was more than symbolic. Yet big business could take heart from the long list of unanswered questions concerning enforcement. Article I declared "every contract, combination in the form of trust or otherwise, or conspiracy in restraint of trade or commerce among the several States . . . illegal." But what was "unreasonable restraint"? What constituted monopoly? How much directive power over an industry spelled "control"? More difficult still, how was the government to proceed in breaking up monopolies?

These questions the Sherman Act left to the government attorneys and the judges, who at least during Cleveland's and McKinley's administrations in the 1890s were not disposed to halt the merger movement. Richard Olney, Cleveland's waspish attorney general, spoke the collective mind of business when he approved the Supreme Court's refusal to break up the sugar trust in the E. C. Knight case. "You will observe that the government has been defeated in the Supreme Court on the trust question. I always supposed it would be, and have taken responsibility of not prosecuting under a law I believed to be no good."

MADISON SQUARE PARK CAB STAND, 1900

New York shows its best face along a fashionable boulevard. (*Museum of the City of New York.*)

Labor unions, on the other hand, seemed to Olney and his masters thoroughly objectionable conspiracies against trade. When Eugene Debs' American Railway Union in its epochal battle with the Pullman Company in Chicago in 1894 refused to move the mails, Olney drew up an injunction declaring the union in restraint of trade and successfully prosecuted Debs for contempt of court in violating the injunction. On appeal, the Supreme Court upheld the application of the Sherman Act to labor unions.

The Sherman Act was applied adversely in two railroad cases in 1897 and 1898 and again, more notably, in the Northern Securities case in 1903, which put an end to J. P. Morgan's dream of merging the Northern Pacific, Union Pacific, and Burlington railroads. Yet only eighteen cases were initiated in the first ten years following the passage of the Act, and in the crucial Knight case a poorly drafted brief allowed a conservative Court to declare the American Sugar Refining Company—a trust controlling 98 percent of the industry—not technically in restraint of trade.

When Theodore Roosevelt arrived in office as the new century began, the fortunes of the antimonopolists appeared to improve. Moreover, Roosevelt's successor, William Howard Taft, continued to initiate suits against monopolies. The Sherman Act, besides breaking up the Northern Securities Company, was applied successfully in 1911 against the Standard Oil and American Tobacco companies. Still, by that time it was all too evident that the Act, far from achieving the results its framers intended, was strengthening rather than checking the forces behind the merger movement. By making it clear that not every restraint of trade was unreasonable, and further, by ruling cartel behavior unacceptable but full-blown mergers legitimate, the courts invited big business to abandon looser forms of organization for tighter and more controlling ones.

Battered but durable, the spirit of antimonopoly survived down to the First World War, kept alive by various reform enthusiasms like those of Wisconsin's Governor Robert LaFollette and by new energies generated in the Democratic South during the first administration of Woodrow Wilson. Gathering coherence from the economic analysis and social theory of several of Wilson's advisors, in particular Louis Brandeis, antimonopoly sentiment supplied the impetus for the passage in 1914 of the Clayton Antitrust Act. Yet while the Clayton Act duly defined certain unfair practices like interlocking directorates and price discrimination, and a supplementary Federal Trade Commission act provided for publicity and prosecution of violators, the momentum of business combination was scarcely broken. The advantages of bigness now appeared compelling, a fact attested to by the incorporation of the giant General Motors soon after the Clayton Act was passed. With these meager accomplishments to show for forty years of continual agitation, the opponents of monopoly quit the field to await another call to battle in the waning years of the New Deal. The counterattack against big business had failed.

The Farmers' Fight Against Disorder

Although American farmers were loath to admit it, their problems from 1870 to 1900 were not very different from the problems that industry confronted—enormously increased production, falling prices, and inefficient and generally inequitable marketing processes. Just as technology revolutionized industrial production after 1870, so mechanical reapers, harrowers, spreaders, and harvesters dramatically expanded agricultural productivity. With a cradle scythe, a wheat farmer could cut two to three acres a day; with a self-raking reaper he could cut twelve. By 1880 a full 80 percent of American wheat was being harvested by machine. Farm machinery, valued at $42 million in 1870, surpassed the $100 million mark thirty years later.

Another important cause of increased productivity was regional crop specialization—wheat and hogs in the trans-Mississippi West, dairy products in the Old Northwest, and cotton in the South—encouraged by the railroads and new machinery. Beyond these two factors, however, lay a startling increase in world demand for staples after 1870 which acted much like growing American cities in

POPULIST COUNTRY

Beyond the 100th meridian rain was scarce, trees nonexistent, neighbors few, and life bleak. (*National Archives.*)

providing markets for industrial goods. The two developments were related. As American staples flooded Europe, prices for foodstuffs fell sharply there, an event quickly followed by collapsing land prices. The agricultural depression in Europe drove millions of peasants and small farmers out of the countryside and into seaports, the first stopping point en route to American cities. Both in Europe and in America, cheaper food hastened industrial transformation, but in the United States the farmers also paid a large part of the bill for modernization by ensuring a favorable balance of trade with massive exports of staple crops at declining prices.

From one vantage point, the American farmer's shift from subsistence farming to specialized commercial farming meant progress toward a higher standard of living. But this advantage was soon offset by the commercial farmer's suspicions that he had become a prisoner of the market, locked into a price structure from which there was no ready means of escape. With the onset of the world agricultural depression in the 1870s, the price curve for staple crops dropped precipitously and the income of the farmer slid down it. Wheat plummeted from $1.19 a bushel in 1881 to a low of 49¢ in the depression year 1894. Corn fell in the same period from 63¢ a bushel to 18¢. Buying in a protected market and selling in an unprotected one, the staple-crop farmer saw himself as the victim of a logical absurdity: he was forced to overproduce while someone else walked off with his dwindling profits. Why, he asked, as the producer of the largest share of the nation's abundance, should his burdens grow heavier every year? Why, while the rest of the country advanced towards prosperity, was he going backwards? A Kansas farmer in 1891 summarized these feelings of betrayal.

At the age of 52 years, after a long life of toil, economy, and self-denial, I find myself and family virtually paupers. With hundreds of hogs, scores of good horses, and a farm that rewarded the toil of our hands with 16,000 bushels of golden corn we are poorer by many dollars than we were years ago. What once seemed a neat little fortune and a house of refuge for our declining years, by a few turns of the monopolistic crank has been rendered valueless.

As God's chosen, the American farmers were being sorely tried.

To increase output and cut costs, many staple-crop farmers, like their counterparts in business, borrowed heavily to buy mechanized equipment only to find themselves faced with high interest rates and tight money. Currency contraction, they reasoned, lay at the root of their troubles; it cut consumption, and so prices fell. Economists and eastern financial experts might assure the American public that price decline was a natural result of overproduction, but farmers in the trans-Mississippi West and the South explained their difficulties in terms of "underconsumption" and blamed hard-money "gold bugs" and the bankers.

As staple-crop farmers singled out the gold standard as their chief enemy, and identified their own distress with the plight of debtors everywhere, they dreamed of forging a common cause of "true producers" on which to build a new national economy. When prices decline, so their reasoning went, all little people, the urban as well as the rural, find themselves in exactly the same predicament, squeezed between the fixed costs of borrowing capital and the slumping prices resulting from the tight money policies of an unresponsive federal government. Though this reasoning was accurate in a way, the hopes for a national coalition of farmers and industrial workers foundered on the rocks of cultural and religious as well as regional and economic differences. American farmers never would succeed in converting city workers to their cause.

Meanwhile tight money and sharp price drops combined, first in the 1870s and then again in the 1890s, to drive the farmer into protest politics and third parties. Reform politics came first to the farmers of the Old Northwest in the aftermath of the Panic of 1873, as the Grangers began to experiment with cooperative storage and marketing schemes. At the same time these Western farmers together with businessmen of the region conducted forays into state politics to force passage of railroad regulation. Yet significant rate regulation would be late in coming to the rescue of farmers; when it did, it was more a result than a cause of their improved bargaining power.

The 1880s saw the growth of regional farm organizations like the Agricultural Wheel and the National Farmers Alliance, which joined in 1888 to form the Southern Alliance boasting more than a million members. In the Great Plains states the Northern Alliance became the mouthpiece of staple-crop producers. Even though the South and West agreed on diagnosis and prescription—antimonopoly, producers' and marketing cooperatives, and cheap money—only with reluctance did they enter the political arena together as a third party. Out of their agreement at Omaha in 1891 came the Populist crusade, which rallied agrarian discontent around the symbols of conspiracy and decline while advancing specific interest-group demands. This coupling of rhetorical excess and hardnosed analysis had scarcely altered in twenty years even though farmers' attitudes had swung from an initial nonpartisanship to intense political involvement. Until the defeat of William Jennings Bryan by McKinley in 1896 shattered the farmer's dream of national redemption, recurrent apocalyptic fantasies and millennial hopes continued to characterize his discontent Populism when it arrived drew on profound convictions of betrayal.

The basic insight of American farmers throughout the nineteenth century was the moral primacy of agriculture. This view was stated most eloquently by William Jennings Bryan in his famous "Cross of Gold Speech," at the Democratic convention in 1896. "You come to us and tell us that the great cities are in favor of the gold standard," the Great Commoner declaimed. "We reply that the great cities rest upon our broad and fertile prairies. Burn down your cities and leave our farms, and your cities will spring up again as if by magic; but destroy our farms and grass will grow in the streets of every city in the country." Bryan confirmed the farmer's own belief, borne out by the record, that he had indeed built America. He had cleared and cultivated the land, raised the foodstuffs, supplied

Passing of the Frontier, 1870 - 1890

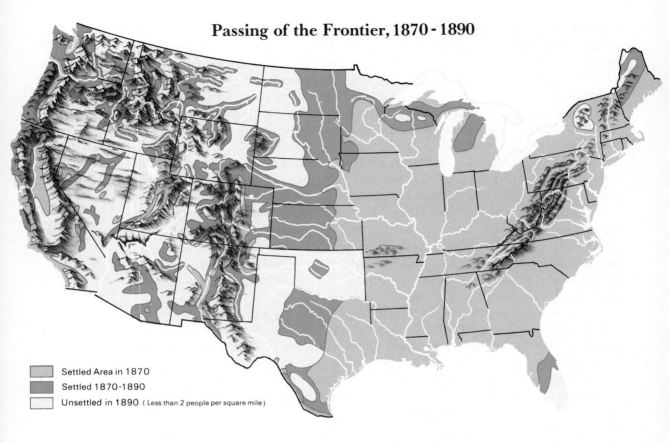

Settled Area in 1870

Settled 1870-1890

Unsettled in 1890 (Less than 2 people per square mile)

the foreign trade, and constructed the material base on which a modern industrial society rested. The land, in spite of the violence methodically visited upon it, remained foremost in the American moral imagination. "On the land we are born, from it we live, to it we return again—children of the soil as truly as is the blade of grass or the flower of the field," Henry George wrote in *Progress and Poverty* in celebrating the redemptive power of the American land. George's message reached millions of already converted farmers who sought only endorsement of their faith.

In more measurable terms the American land produced the agricultural abundance with which the United States paid for the European goods and capital needed to modernize. Farmers, who still considered themselves the owners of the Garden of the World, lashed out with mounting frustration as an ungrateful urban society denied their achievements, neglected their interests, ridiculed their proposals for reform, and mocked their provincial ways and narrow lives. Out of this massive loss of confidence came a compensatory politics of alienation in Populism. The Populists gathered their forces for the presidential election of 1892 determined to rescue the nation from moral and material ruin. "A vast conspiracy against mankind has been organized on two continents and is taking possession of the world," their Saint Louis platform declared. "If not met and overthrown at once it forbodes terrible social convulsions, the destruction of civilization, or the establishment of an absolute despotism." With the advent of Populism, the American farmer's twenty-year crusade became a holy war.

By 1900, however, the predicted end of the world had failed to materialize. In the sharp upturn of the economy that opened the twentieth century, American farmers appeared willing to relinquish their millennial expectations for the more immediate gains that rising farm incomes furnished. The advantages of organization, consolidation and integration, which were the lessons being taught by big business, had now become too obvious for the farmer to ignore. He too could learn to read the statistics that told him what to do. The cheering figures on production and price that he began to consult were being compiled by the Division of Statistics of the Department of Agriculture whose other departmental divisions—soils, chemistry, pomology, and animal industry—attested to the effects of the continuing bureaucratic revolution in American agriculture. These figures, whether for soaring staple prices, or declining shipping costs, or estimates of rising production, continued to assure the farmer down to the First World War of the reality of his new-found prosperity. Between 1900 and 1910, the price of corn shot up from 35¢ to 52¢ a bushel, wheat from 62¢ to 91¢, as the wholesale farm price index jumped 50 percent and the average price of farm land doubled from $20 to $40 an acre. As staple-crop farmers remembered with chagrin, if it had not been a frantic third-party politics that had accomplished all this, nevertheless the national economy was at last responding to their needs and demands. Just as American business opened the twentieth century by applying the lessons of consolidation with a will, so American farmers were beginning to follow the seemingly simple directives for finding safety in system and security in organization.

The most durable of the early twentieth-century farm organizations were producers' cooperatives that concentrated on solving the problems of price stability and marketing procedures. Except for their official nonprofitmaking status and their democratic voting procedures, cooperatives were modern corporations that became as streamlined and efficient as their counterparts in business. They also came to rely on experts and specialists, trained managers and accountants, legal advisers, lobbyists, and public relations men. Like the integrated industrial enterprise, they also achieved the equivalent of forward integration and market control by building their own facilities at railroad terminals and by writing iron-clad contracts with their members compelling them to withhold their crops until the price was right. By 1910 the antimonopoly scruples of big farmers were already disappearing.

Prosperous farmers, like the big businessmen they were fast becoming, designed and built cooperatives as interest-group devices for solving particular problems. The Grangers, Knights of Labor, and Populists, who pioneered with

IN THE FIELDS OF WESTERN CALIFORNIA, 1902

Bonanza farms brought an end to the day of the self-
sufficient yeoman but also the beginning of agricultural
abundance. (*Library of Congress.*)

commodity cooperatives, envisioned the preservation of earlier conditions of independence and equality. The new farm organizations that accompanied the rise of Progressivism professed no such grandiose social aims but were content, with the return of flush times, to perfect the means the bureaucratic revolution had assigned to them. Why replace an economic system capable of producing the abundance that, however belatedly and unaccountably, was now being showered upon Jefferson's chosen people?

The leading advocates of the organizational revolution in American agriculture were not the staple-crop farmers in the trans-Mississippi West but the dairy, poultry, and fruit and vegetable farmers in the older sections of the East and Northwest and their competitors on the Pacific Coast, whose fortunes had risen steadily with the growth of metropolitan markets. With the return of prosperity, these groups put aside their interest in protest politics, never very strong, in favor of scientific methods and interest-group associations. By 1914 the cooperative marketing movement was in full swing, and dozens of livestock unions, dairymen's leagues, grain exchanges, cotton cooperatives, and tobacco pools were being founded each year. Cooperatives in turn spawned new pressure groups—the Farmers' Equity Union, the Farmers' Mutual Benefit Association, the Farmers' Social and Economic Union, the Farmers' Relief Association—all of them proclaiming as their own the slogan of the American Society of Equity: "What the farmer wants to produce is not crops, but money." In 1912, cooperatives secured the blessing of the Department of Agriculture, which provided them with their own fact-finding agency, the Bureau of Markets. Eight years later the formation of the American Farm Bureau Federation announced the arrival of modern agriculture as a national political force. Although the chief gains in numbers and influence were not to come until the 1920s, the commercialization of the American farmer had begun in earnest.

The dramatic shift in agrarian perceptions that accompanied the return of prosperity could be read in the changed outlook of one of the farmers' most impassioned spokesmen. Returning home to the Middle Border in 1889 at the height of the agrarian distress, Hamlin Garland, still an unknown but aspiring young writer, found his old neighbors caught up in social crisis and engaged "in a sullen rebellion against government and against God."

Every house I visited had its individual message of sordid struggle and half-hidden despair. . . . All the gilding of farm life melted away. The hard and bitter realities came back upon me in a flood. Nature was as bountiful as ever . . . but no splendor of cloud, no grace of sunset, could conceal the poverty of these people; on the contrary, they brought out, with a more intolerable poignancy, the gracelessness of these homes, and the sordid quality of the mechanical routine of these lives. I perceived beautiful youth becoming bowed and bent.

Convinced that "men's laws" rather than God's were responsible for "industrial slavery" as well as the degradation of the farmer, Garland brought to the Populist cause an enthusiasm for root-and-branch reform and an aesthetic theory to match. Yet fifteen years later with the Populist years behind him, Garland left the main traveled thoroughfares of agrarian protest for nostalgic excursions into the romantic high country of the Far Northwest, abandoning reform to settle in the bureaucratic environs staked out by Theodore Roosevelt's Country Life Commission. The commission, itself proof of the revival of the farmers' influence, was appointed in 1908 and charged with the task of improving rural life in the United States. The commissioners concluded, after taking the pulse of rural America and listening to a recital of its ailments, that what the farmer needed was simply to catch up with his city cousin, to "even up" the distribution of amenities between town and country. This recovery, according to the commission's diagnosis, involved agricultural credits, a highway program, rural free delivery, better schools, a country church movement to rescue "lost sheep," and very little else. Prosperity had soothed old discontents. By 1910, Hamlin Garland's outraged cry for justice "for the toiling poor wherever found" had receded into memory as American farmers settled in to enjoy their golden age, which statistics, government recognition, and their own pocketbooks told them had come at last.

Workers and the Challenge of Organization

Of all the groups enmeshed in the American economic revolution, the industrial workers depended the least on statistics to confirm what they already knew. And what they knew was that their rewards for tending the American industrial machine hardly matched their services. From assembled data at the end of the century, workers could have verified their impressions that the workweek for the "average" worker in industry was little less than 60 hours and that the "average" wage for skilled workers was about 20¢ an hour and for unskilled workers just half that amount. Annual wages for the factory worker in 1900 came to an average of $400 to $500, from which a working family saved an average $30 after spending nearly half the remainder for food, another quarter on rent, and the balance on fuel, light, and clothing. Earnings for workers engaged in manufacturing went up 37 percent between 1890 and 1914, but the cost of living between 1897 and 1914 rose 39 percent.

If there was a certain grim satisfaction in the knowledge that others shared their straitened circumstances, there was considerably less in the daily reminder that in spite of growing national abundance American workers and their families managed on very narrow margins. Their share of the pie, though larger than it had been a half-century earlier, was still comparatively small. A statistical breakdown of national income, had they consulted it, would have strengthened their conviction that workers, too, must organize for bargaining power. The richest tenth of the population received 33.9 percent of the nation's income, the poorest, 3.4 percent. The wealthier half of the country's income recipients accounted for over 70 percent of all income. The rich were certainly getting richer in 1900 while the American workers, if not absolutely poorer, were still not enjoying much of the wealth they were helping to create. Nor had they yet found the organizational power with which to counter the growing strength of big business. In 1900 a full 95 percent of the labor force in the United States remained unorganized, captive still of public opinion dead set against unions.

Prospects for the American worker had not always seemed so dim. As late as the 1880s, the goal of industrial unionism had remained within sight. The tradition of the solidarity of true producers, like the American farmers' myth of the chosen people, had originally been assembled by the Jacksonians and had survived the Civil War. This utopian ideal, foreshadowed in the National Labor Union in the early 1870s, was most eloquently stated in the platform of the Knights of Labor. There was no good reason, Terence V. Powderly, the mercurial president of the Knights insisted, why American workers building unions and cooperatives, owning and operating mines, factories, and railroads, should not usher in a new age of harmony and cooperation. This was the dream he held before his membership, which reached a peak of 700,000 in 1886.

In fact there were excellent reasons why the Knights of Labor failed to sustain its reform crusade. The attempt to organize workers by industry rather than craft put the organization in direct competition with skilled workers who resented its efforts. Powderly's antistrike policy seriously impaired the leaders' control

A HOT-WEATHER NIGHT ON NEW YORK'S LOWER EAST SIDE

For this father and his children, the sidewalk provided cooler sleeping quarters than the tenement apartment above. (*Brown Brothers.*)

over an increasingly militant rank and file. Cooperatives, overly ambitious and badly underfinanced, collapsed one after another, and the general executive board of the union could not meet the demands for support thrust upon it by hard-pressed locals determined to strike. "The number of appeals for assistance," Powderly complained in 1883, "now being showered on the board is frightful, and nothing but a treasury of millions could stand it. My advice to the board is to shut down on all appeals and stick to the original plan of the order, that of educating the members as to the folly of strikes."

Education converted neither businessmen, who were inclined to equate union leaders with secessionists in the late War of the Rebellion, nor local members, who were anxious to test their strength in encounters with railroad management. A series of strikes culminated in the disastrous contest with Jay Gould's Texas Pacific Railroad in 1886, and thereafter the Knights entered a period of sharp decline, a victim of business antagonism, craft union fears, and not least, its own illusions of grandeur. With the retreat of the Knights of Labor before the steady advance of the American Federation of Labor, the torch of industrial unionism and radical reform after 1900 passed to militant but marginal organizations like the Western Federation of Miners and its stepchild, the Industrial Workers of the World. The narrowed field of craft unionism was left to the country's skilled workers, who were not averse to a labor caste system, as it soon became apparent.

The American Federation of Labor (AFL), a flexible organization of craft unions formed in 1886, represented a new generation's capitulation to the corporate revolution. Labor too could learn the lessons of consolidation. "It is our purpose and a large part of our work has been devoted to gathering and concentrating the forces of labor into compact National Unions, and that work has been crowned with a success never before equalled," Samuel Gompers, the founder and longtime president of the AFL, reported in 1892. Gompers and his lieutenant, Adolph Strasser, readily confessed that their sole concern was for the skilled trades they represented and the immediate welfare of their members. Asked to define the "ultimate ends" of "pure and simple unionism," Strasser replied at once that the two terms were contradictory. "We have no ultimate ends. We are going on from day to day. We are fighting for immediate objects— objects that can be realized in a few years."

The new union leaders reminded businessmen that they too were "practical men," neither theorists nor reformers but pragmatists and opportunists, like their employers, organizers with their eyes on the main chance. The distance separating the AFL from its now moribund rival, the Knights of Labor, was best measured in Gompers's reply to the Socialist Morris Hillquit, who was bent on discrediting his rival. Hillquit demanded to know whether the president of the AFL really believed that American workers received the "full product" of their labor. Gompers brushed aside the question as meaningless in terms of the new industrial instrumentalism. "I will say," he replied, sidestepping the rusty ethical trap his interrogator had set, "that it is impossible for anyone to definitely say what proportion the workers receive as a result of their labor, but it is the fact that due to the organized-labor movement they have received and are receiving a larger share of the product of their labor than they ever did in the history of modern society." Accused by irate socialists and labor radicals of having betrayed the labor movement by refusing to develop a genuine social philosophy, Gompers and his craft unionists cheerfully admitted to a belief in half a loaf and a willingness to follow "the lines of least resistance."

"Least resistance" for organized labor as the twentieth century opened meant accepting the merger movement and closing a bargain with big business. The trusts, Gompers announced, "are our employers, and the employer who is fair to us, whether as an individual, or a collection of individuals in the form of a corporation or a trust, matters little to us so long as we obtain fair wages." As for the wage system on which capitalism rested, there was little, he thought, to be gained by quarreling with it or dreaming up half-baked substitutes. Trade unionists should rest content with the argument that the right to strike was itself the greatest preventive of strikes.

The American Federation of Labor, modest in its aims and moderate in its counsels, overcame employer resistance only with difficulty and gained the leverage it sought at great cost. Although membership grew from 140,000 at its founding in 1886 to over 2 million in 1914, less than a third of the country's skilled workers could be found in its ranks by 1900. When war broke out in Europe in 1914, only 15 percent of the nonagricultural workers in the United States were members of any union.

With the banner of industrial unionism in tatters and the craft unions besieged by business opponents armed with new weapons like the injunction and the yellow-dog contract, American workers faced the prospect of increased control. Small businessmen sought to curtail their organizational freedom. This strategy promised a vigorous campaign of union-busting as the National Association of Manufacturers (NAM) in 1903 formed and funded the Citizens Industrial Association to spread the gospel of the open shop under the brand name "The American Plan." The success of their American Plan, conservative businessmen promised, would spell the doom of labor unions.

Big business hoped to control labor through the concepts of guided democracy. It offered a paternal concern for the American worker along with the concepts of arbitration and "responsible" leadership. The response of big business, unlike the NAM's unwieldy counteroffensive, recognized that labor's grievances were real and its demands for redress legitimate—an acknowledgment that workers' needs for security and stability were not so very different from the needs of management. In 1900, the agents of big business, led by progressive industrialists like George E. Perkins and financiers like J. P. Morgan, struck a bargain with

Gompers and founded the National Civic Federation on the proposition that labor, like business, must be encouraged to organize its interests and rally its forces for participation in the new corporate society.

The strategy of enlightened business interests required, first of all, vastly improved working conditions. Factory work was still alarmingly dangerous. A survey of industrial accidents for the year 1913 showed that some 25,000 workers had been killed on the job and another three-quarters of a million seriously injured. Then there were the problems of incentive, alienation, and the loss of community resulting from increased scale of business and the impersonality of the assembly line. These were eloquently described to the Industrial Commission in 1899 by a veteran shoe worker, who recalled the day of a rough shop-floor socialism before the advent of the giant mechanized factory. "In these old shops, years ago," he told the commissioners, "one man owned the shop; and he and three, four, five or six others, neighbors, came in there and sat down and made shoes right in their laps, and there was no machinery. Everybody was at liberty to talk. . . ."

But could this idyll be recovered or recreated? "We do not want to go back to the time when we could do without the sewing machine, or the machinery for manufacturing purposes, or the large aggregations of capital," a shoemaker replied, "but we want capital controlled in such a way that it will not result in the

SLUM INTERIOR

New Americans experienced various kinds of exploitation, among them unhealthy and expensive living quarters.

displacement of three-fourths of the population for the increased wealth of one-fourth of the population." In grudging admissions like this lay the secret of big business's success.

Workers packed in slums and ghettos of center cities in the opening years of the twentieth century knew precisely how far they stood from the margins of plenty. The quality of life in the working-class districts of most American cities was appalling. In 1915, President Wilson's Industrial Commission, still another investigatory body appointed to examine the causes of continuing industrial unrest, concluded: "A large part of the industrial population are . . . living in actual poverty." Exactly what proportion of the nation's working class lived below the subsistence level the commissioners did not care to estimate; they added, however, "It is certain at least one-third and possibly one-half of the families of wage earners employed in manufacturing and mining earn in the course of the year less than enough to support them in anything like a comfortable and decent condition." Urban housing for the new arrivals from Europe and the American countryside—whether three-story wooden firetraps in Boston's South End or

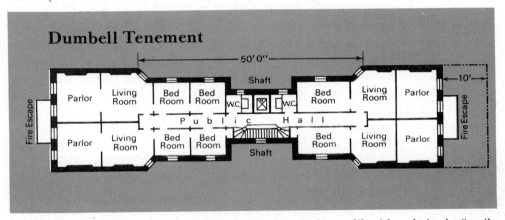

Dumbell Tenement

dumbbell tenements on New York's lower East Side or dilapidated single-family shanties in Cincinnati, St. Louis or Chicago—was generally deplorable and, worse still, expensive. Gas, water, electricity, sanitation, and transportation—all of the services needed to make the life of the city worker tolerable—were in short supply and of poor quality as late as 1900. These inadequacies, in fact, were the basis of the original reform challenge for urban coalitions of dissatisfied consumers.

The main surge in urban improvement began with the new century, and within a decade had succeeded in providing improved municipal services, better sanitation and health care, parks and recreational facilities, libraries and museums, giving cities a public face-lifting and genuine rejuvenation. But housing and personal standards of living improved much more slowly. The public life of American cities responded to the work of urban reformers with their vision of a renovated democratic purpose; yet blighted neighborhoods, fractured communities, crumbling apartments, and stunted lives continued to pose a stark reality for too many American workers. The environmental exploitation of American labor was not a major factor included in the pragmatic assessments of union organizers, but it was real nonetheless.

For recently arrived immigrants who endured these conditions and who comprised the major portion of the industrial labor force by 1900, there was yet another and more subtle kind of exploitation in the cultural drive to "Americanize" them as quickly as possible. All the ethnic groups arriving in such great numbers after 1880 — Italians, Greeks, Poles, Russian Jews — were viewed at one time or another as dissidents and potential bomb throwers in need of the ministrations of cultural counterrevolutionaries teaching a kind of "Americanism" indistinguishable from conformity. Status anxieties, religious fears, a distrust of cultural pluralism, and nostalgia for a largely imaginary age of stability — all the yearnings of older American groups — combined with recurrent malfunctionings of the economy to intensify the desires of native-born Americans for unity and homogeneity.

Where the previous generation had singled out the political party as the chief agent of acculturation, reformers emphasized the school. As one observer explained to the readers of *World's Work* in 1903, "The results shown by the public schools seem little short of marvellous. There are many things in which, as a rule, the public consider that the public schools fail, but the one thing that cannot be denied — and it is the greatest — is that these boys and girls of foreign parentage catch readily the simple American ideas of independence and individual work and, with them, social progress." "Social progress," in the half-century after 1880, meant social equilibrium through Americanization: widespread literacy, technological education, elimination of child labor, cultural conformity, and last but not least, cultivation in an aspiring working class of a hearty appetite for all the consumer goods produced by the huge American industrial machine.

Thus the stabilization of big business in patterns of monopoly and oligopoly and the organizational revolution in American agriculture had their equivalent for industrial workers after 1900 in an effort to adjust them both as producers and consumers to necessary but subordinate roles in a corporate capitalistic society. In largely ignoring the alternatives posed by socialism, and in seemingly accepting their assignments, American workers added their share to the impression of inevitability created by production statistics.

The Fruits of Revolution

The glowing statistics of a materialistic society seemed to establish beyond question the reality of American progress and unity. For at least the first half of the nineteenth century Americans had been intoxicated with a sense of boundlessness of time and space, of individual opportunity and the national future. They had ritualized freedom as providential and pointed proudly to the absence of social and geographical fixity. By midcentury, however, the nation's physical boundaries had been virtually settled, and the Civil War overturned the last barriers to rapid modernization. By 1870 American energies at last could be fully devoted to mining the country's vast material treasures. At first, no price seemed too great for sustained economic growth. But then, by 1880, the costs began to seem excessive, first to businessmen and then to farmers and workers, who eventually became uneasy partners in completing the organizational revolution.

Like all revolutions, the economic transformation of the United States had unintended consequences. Used as an index of national prosperity, the statistics of growth seemed a simple instrument for measuring the accomplishments of a whole people. The national wealth, $16 billion in 1860 according to the estimate of government statisticians, had grown by 1900 to $88 billion, a per capita increase from $500 to $1,110. But these figures effectively masked differences of class, region, occupation, and the persistence of a grossly uneven distribution of income. Americans were being affected by the organizational revolution in drastically different ways. Yet the American dream of 1900 remained what it had been a half-century earlier, a vision of a people uniquely equipped to create and enjoy abundance. Economic integration itself seemed convincing proof of the near approach of "the promise of American life." A national market had been built and the nation's shelves stocked with an incredible variety of goods. In this sense the economic well-being of the nation appeared to be exactly what a new generation of American businessmen pronounced it, that is, a single economic system binding citizen and nation in a network of mutual benefits.

But beneath the surface, as the new century opened, lay not unity but multiplicity; not a single national purpose but competing and even warring interests; not pressures unifying American society but forces that threatened to fling it apart; not the conservation of national energies but their diffusion in politically volatile forms. Americans in the opening years of the twentieth century thus confronted a paradox capping a half-century of growth: the economic integration that had seemingly rescued them from chaos had set in motion cultural and political counterforces that threatened fragmentation, dispersion, diffusion, and isolation. To cope with these threats to national order the American people would require new and more sophisticated conceptions of social and political organization, and the capacity somehow to use them.

Suggested Readings

There are two outstanding accounts of the organizational revolution in American society in the half-century after 1870. Brief but still the model for more recent interpretive work is Samuel P. Hays, *The Response to Industrialism* (1957). Robert Wiebe, *The Search for Order* (1968) traces the shift from small-town America to modern bureaucratic society in terms of political institutions and social values as well as economic reorganization. John A. Garraty, *The New Commonwealth, 1877–1890* (1968) focuses on the crucial decade of the

1880s. Ray Ginger, *The Age of Excess* (1965) is a lively and impressionistic survey, and so is Howard Mumford Jones, *The Age of Energy: Varieties of American Experience, 1865–1915* (1970).

The technical literature on the developing economy in this period is extensive. Among the most useful studies of aspects of American economic growth discussed here are Clarence D. Long, *Wages and Earnings in the United States, 1860–1900* (1960); Albert Rees, *Real Wages in Manufacturing, 1890–1914* (1961); Rendig Fels, *American Business Cycles* (1959); and Milton Friedman and Anna J. Schwartz, *A Monetary History of the United States, 1867–1960* (1963). The early chapters in Alfred D. Chandler, Jr., *Strategy and Structure: Chapters in the History of American Industrial Enterprise* (1966) provide a compact summary of the first phase of business concentration. Ralph L. Nelson, *Merger Movements in American Industry* (1959) gives a detailed account of the great merger movement at the end of the nineteenth century, and Hans B. Thorelli, *Federal Antitrust Policy: The Origination of an American Tradition* (1955) traces the origins and development of the countermovement against monopoly. These and other recent findings are ably synthesized in Stuart Bruchey's brief but perceptive essay, *Growth of the Modern Economy* (1975) and in greater detail in W. Elliot Brownlee, *Dynamics of Ascent: A History of the American Economy* (1974).

The industrial transformation of the United States is characterized as a success story in Edward C. Kirkland's survey, *Industry Comes of Age: Business, Labor, and Public Policy, 1860–1897* (1961), which should be supplemented with Thomas Cochran, *The Inner Revolution* (1964). The development of the oil industry is exhaustively treated in Harold F. Williamson and associates, *The American Petroleum Industry* (2 vols., 1959–63), and Ralph W. Hidy and Muriel E. Hidy, *Pioneering in Big Business, 1882–1911: History of Standard Oil (New Jersey)* (1955). For changes in American banking practices in this period, see Fritz Redlich, *Molding of American Banking: Men and Ideas: Part II: 1840–1910* (1951), and for railroads, George R. Taylor and Irene Neu, *The American Railroad Network, 1861–1890* (1956), and Oscar O. Winther, *The Transportation Frontier: Trans–Mississippi West 1865–1890* (1964). Julius Grodinsky, *Transcontinental Railway Strategy, 1869–1893* (1962), analyzes the ideas and plans of the railroad builders and organizers; Lee Benson, *Merchants, Farmers, and Railroads* (1955), explores the movement for increased regulation; and Robert Fogel, *Railroads and American Economic Growth* (1964), offers an econometric revision of the role of the railroads in stimulating American economic growth. For an account of iron and steel, see Peter Temin, *Iron and Steel in Nineteenth-Century America: An Economic Inquiry* (1964).

The connections between economic theory and social policy are explored in Sidney Fine, *Laissez-Faire and the General Welfare State* (1956). Richard Hofstadter, *Social Darwinism in American Thought* (1945), and Robert McCloskey, *Conservatism in the Age of Enterprise* (1951), are highly readable accounts of economic and social conservatism in the Gilded Age. James Weinstein, *The Corporate Ideal in the Liberal State, 1900–1918* (1960), is a carefully documented study of a central organizational concept and its wide social and political meanings. Irvin G. Wyllie's *The Self-Made Man in America* (1954), scrutinizes a resilient American myth, and Edward C. Kirkland's lively essays in *Dream and Thought in the Business Community, 1860–1900* (1956), describe the utopian musings of American businessmen.

Biographies of the leading figures in the American industrial transformation are legion. Among the best are three monumental studies: Joseph Wall, *Andrew Carnegie* (1970); Alan Nevins, *Study in Power: John D. Rockefeller, Industrialist and Philanthropist* (2 vols., 1953); and Matthew Josephson, *Edison* (1959). Frederick Lewis Allen, *The Great Pierpont Morgan* (1940), takes the measure of the great financier in a colorful portrait, and Edward C. Kirkland, *Charles Francis Adams, Jr., 1835–1915* (1965), gives sympathetic treatment to a frustrated planner and organizer. Keith Sward, *The Legend of Henry Ford* (1948), and Frank E. Hill, *Ford: The Times, the Man, the Company* (1954), provide useful estimates of the aut014mative pioneer.

The recent literature on American urbanization is admirably synthesized in two recent studies: Howard Chudacoff, *Evolution of American Urban Society* (1975), and Zane Miller, *Urbanization of America* (1973). Constance Green, *The Rise of Urban America* (1965), and A. T. Brown, *A History of Urban America* (1967), are also helpful surveys. For a model study of urban spread in this period see Sam Bass Warner, *Streetcar Suburbs: The Process of Growth in Boston, 1870–1900* (1971). The pervasive antiurbanism of American intellectuals is documented in Morton and Lucia White, *The Intellectuals vs. the City* (1962). Charles N. Glab, ed., *The American City: A Documentary History* (1963), offers a wide range of source materials. David Ward, *Cities and Immigrants: A Geography of Change in Nineteenth-Century America* (1971), traces the patterns made by the new arrivals from Europe, and Stephen Thernstrom, *The Other Bostonians* (1973), and Howard Chudacoff, *Mobile Americans: Residential and Social Mobility in Omaha, 1880–1920* (1972), are two important studies of urban mobility.

The story of agrarian developments after the Civil War is told in Fred A. Shannon, *The Farmer's Last Frontier* (1963). Two older works—Solon J. Buck, *The Granger Movement* (1913), and John D. Hicks, *The Populist Revolt* (1931)—are still useful surveys of their subjects. Irwin Unger, *The Greenback Era* (1964), and Walter T. K. Nugent, *Money and American Society, 1865–1880* (1968), examine monetary policy as it affected the farmer. For an illuminating discussion of agrarian politics in the South, see Theodore Saloutos, *Farmer Movements in the South, 1865–1933* (1960). Eric E. Lampard, *The Rise of the Dairy Industry in Wisconsin: A Study in Agricultural Change, 1860–1920* (1963), studies developments in a single industry, and Joseph C. Bailey, *Seaman A. Knapp* (1945), presents a profile of a "new" farmer. Harold Barger and H. H. Landsberg, *American Agriculture, 1899–1939: A Study of Output Employment and Productivity* (1942), traces the continuing rise of agricultural productivity in the early twentieth century. Allen G. Bogue, *Money at Interest: The Farm Mortgage on the Middle Border* (1955), offers a revisionist account of agrarian distress in that region. Grant McConnell, *The Decline of Agrarian Democracy* (1953), describes the growth of commercial farming, and Reynold M. Wik, *Steam Power on the American Farm* (1953), treats early technological change and its effect on American agriculture. The elimination of the Indian in the trans-Mississippi West is chronicled in two readable studies: Ralph K. Andrist, *The Long Death: The Last Days of the Plains Indians* (1964), and Dee A. Brown, *Bury My Heart at Wounded Knee* (1971).

Two brief surveys of American labor, Joseph G. Rayback, *A History of American Labor* (1959), and Henry Pelling, *American Labor* (1959), should be supplemented with the older but still valuable Norman J. Ware, *The Labor Movement in the United States, 1860–1896: A Study in Democracy* (1929). The conflict between the Knights of Labor and the new trade unions is explored in Gerald N. Grob, *Workers and Utopia* (1961). Philip Taft, *The A.F. of L. in the Time of Gompers* (1957), is an authoritative study of the organization in its formative years. Bernard Mandel, *Samuel Gompers, A Biography* (1963), and Stuart Bruce Kaufman, *Samuel Gompers and the Origins of the American Federation of Labor* (1973), focus on the problems of leadership. The role of the immigrant in the American industrial revolution is explored in Charlotte Erickson, *American Industry and the European Immigrant* (1957), and Rowland Berthoff, *British Immigrants in Industrial America, 1790–1950* (1953). A brilliant article that points towards a new synthesis of cultural and labor history is Herbert G. Gutman, "Work, Culture, and Society in Industrializing America, 1815–1919," *American Historical Review 78* (June 1973), 531–88.

25

The Politics
of Reform

Politics in the quarter-century following the Civil War gave Americans the sense of equilibrium that their economic system lacked. The Jacksonian generation had discovered in the idea of party a way of controlling the disruptive forces of modern democracy. Now their sons, the professional managers of the Republican and Democratic parties after 1865, perfected the machinery of party, which they proceeded to run with skill and zest until the very end of the century.

Political equilibrium depended, first of all, upon restoring a regional balance of power within both parties. A stable party system rested on regional interests as well as state machines. Republicans throughout the Gilded Age confronted the task of including the urban working classes in the Northeast and the farmers of the Midwest in their plans for industrial development and business enterprise. Democrats were busy repairing the broad Jacksonian coalition of Southern planters and Northern city bosses that had been smashed by the war. The primary unit in this renovated political system remained the state party machine, and both national parties continued to operate as loose assemblages of largely autonomous state organizations. But states also comprised regions, each with its own cultural identity and economic concerns that demanded attention. Increasingly after 1870 national tickets were arranged and party slates balanced with regional preferences as well as state claims in mind.

The smooth operation of American politics in the Gilded Age also depended on the mastery of a few basic rules. Chief among these was the assumption shared by political managers in both parties that their organizations differed, not so much in class or economic interests, which were often quite similar, as in religious, ethnic, and cultural values. Both parties, in fact, were supported by wealthy citizens whose opinions the party leaders duly acknowledged while maintaining an egalitarian posture before the rest of the country. Both parties operated as broad-based, nonideological coalitions that appealed to businessmen, farmers, professionals, and workers. What separated them at a deeper level was neither wealth nor status but differing clusters of values.

The Republican party was dominated until late in the century by values that could be called "pietistic." Democrats, except in the South where questions of race and economic recovery took precedence, were generally ruled by values that have been called "ritualistic" or "liturgical." Pietism pointed towards a politics of strict morality; ritualism, towards a politics of traditionalism and toleration. The original Whig party and its stepchild, the Republican party before the Civil War, had been governed by the forces of pietism. Party members were primarily Protestant, predominantly of native stock or Anglo-Saxon descent, aggressively evangelical and reformist, equipped with a keen sense of morality, and eager to use government at all levels to enforce their behavioral standards on the rest of the American community. Republicans assembled all of these cultural ingredients in their attack on slavery. Despite the steady infiltration of the party by business interests after the Civil War, Republicans continued to attract and hold in uneasy alliance a broad range of social moralists—prohibitionists, sabbatarians, blue law advocates, and moral reformers of all persuasions. Only at the very end of the century had such groups become marginal enough in the party as a whole for the managers to cast them aside as liabilities.

The Democratic party in respect to these values often seemed the precise opposite of the Republican. It embraced Catholics as well as Protestants, and professed a tolerance of immigrants who lacked the compulsive morality of the native-born. The party preached a "personal liberty" deemed safest when government was kept local and minimal and practiced a cultural as well as an economic laissez-faire. While Republicans expected government to be generous and active, Democrats hoped to keep it grudging and stingy, if only to check the cultural imperialism of its pietist foes. Thus the differences between the two parties in 1880 were real, but they concerned cultural outlook even more than economic interest or crude social differences, a distinction professional politicians in both camps fully appreciated.

Party managers also realized that the voters seldom approached political questions like the tariff or the currency as simple issues having scientific solutions, but instead responded to them as symbols that could be mobilized for the support of the party and its candidates. The skilled practitioners of Gilded Age politics

knew that the electoral behavior of most American voters was ultimately determined by images and impressions, prejudices and predilections. Voters
might consider themselves both rational and fully informed, but woe to any
office-seeker who really believed them such!

This configuration of a balanced and highly competitive politics lasted until the
last decade of the nineteenth century when the very idea of party rule came
under concerted attack by a younger generation of political reformers. By 1890,
the old pattern of political stability was breaking up, old loyalties were being discarded and traditional assumptions reversed as new political leaders in all sections of the country began to experiment with new techniques and devices for
modernizing government and making it more accountable and efficient.

UNVEILING A STATUE

Patriotism and purity combined readily in the Gilded Age
imagination. (*Pennell Collection, University of Kansas.*)

On the national level, the Republican party, casting off its pietistic garb, stepped forth as the champion of the workingman in the nation's cities. The Democrats, abandoning their urban base, embarked on an ill-fated alliance with agrarian reformers and Populists marching to battle beneath the symbolic banner of free silver. Their defeat under William Jennings Bryan at the hands of William McKinley in the election of 1896 left them stranded in the wilderness from which they would not emerge until the election of Woodrow Wilson sixteen years later.

Meanwhile in states like Wisconsin, California, and New York younger reformers like Robert LaFollette, Hiram Johnson, Charles Evans Hughes, and Theodore Roosevelt were clashing with railroad, lumber, oil and traction "interests" in their attempts to seize the political control of their states needed to launch experiments in economic and social legislation. And in the nation's cities, social reformers and charity organizers, urban planners and settlement-house workers, public health officials, university professors, and new business leaders were busy assembling urban coalitions for an assault on the citadel of Gilded Age politics, the "machine" presided over by the sinister figure of the "boss."

By 1890, rural Populists and urban progressives, in their separate attacks on the politics of equilibrium, were challenging the code of the old professionals and forcing them to respond to new pressures for change. Out of this revolt against the Gilded Age came a transformation of politics that paralleled the revolution in the American economy and brought new assessments of the American political process and new ways of ordering it.

The Politics of Equilibrium

The Civil War shaped the thinking and molded the political behavior of Americans for a generation. The success of Gilded Age politics in tapping the emotional reserves once monopolized by the war could be read, first of all, in the remarkably high levels of voter participation. In the six presidential elections between 1876 and 1896 an average 78.5 percent of the eligible voters of the country actually voted, and an equally impressive 62.8 percent turned out for off-year elections. If political democracy implies a high rate of voter participation, then the Gilded Age, despite its confused responses to industrialization, remained flamboyantly, defiantly democratic.

Americans in exercising their right to vote also remained stubbornly consistent. Whether they marched to the polls behind the "bloody shirt" of wartime Unionist fervor or stirred to the memories of the Lost Cause, voters in all sections of the country kept alive the spirit of the War between the States. Joining enthusiastically in campaigns complete with military mounted troopers and fancy drill teams, they made national elections extremely close. Sixteen states could always be counted on to go Republican; fourteen just as regularly voted Democratic. Elections usually hung on the disposition of voters in five key states—Connecticut,

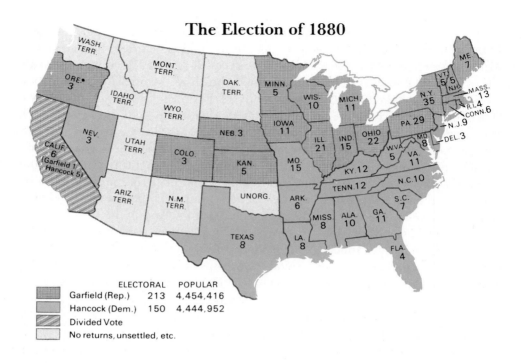

The Election of 1880

	ELECTORAL	POPULAR
Garfield (Rep.)	213	4,454,416
Hancock (Dem.)	150	4,444,952
Divided Vote		
No returns, unsettled, etc.		

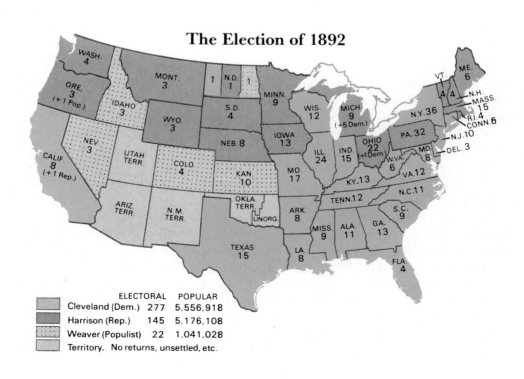

The Election of 1892

	ELECTORAL	POPULAR
Cleveland (Dem.)	277	5,556,918
Harrison (Rep.)	145	5,176,108
Weaver (Populist)	22	1,041,028
Territory. No returns, unsettled, etc.		

New York, Indiana, Nevada, and California. Although the Republicans' control of the presidency from 1872 to 1912, broken only by Cleveland's two victories in 1884 and 1892, seemingly established them as the majority party, in fact the Democrats, who controlled the House of Representatives with sizable majorities in seven out of ten congressional elections, secured their claims to dominance at the grass roots of politics. Pluralities in pivotal states were perilously slim, in New York and Indiana particularly. With intense competition and close elections the rule, winners were not only lucky but frequently surprised. In the presidential elections of 1880 and 1884, for example, fewer than fifty thousand votes separated the candidates. In the Hayes-Tilden contest of 1876 and again in the first Harrison-Cleveland election in 1888, the winners received fewer popular votes than the losers.

The two parties were drawn up against each other across the political terrain like equally matched armies, their battles resembling the engagements of a too familiar war. Even the language of politics was borrowed from recent martial exploits:

From the *opening gun* of the *campaign* the *standard bearer*, along with other *war-horses fielded* by the party, *rallied* the *rank and file* around the party *standard*, the *bloody shirt*, and other *slogans*. Precinct *captains aligned* their *phalanxes shoulder to shoulder* to mobilize votes for the *Old Guard*. Meanwhile the *Mugwumps* warned that the *palace troops* sought to *plunder* the treasury; their *strategy* was to *crusade* against the *myrmidons* of corruption. Even a *man on horseback* could not have saved the *lost cause* with his *jingoism*. But party *headquarters* changed *tactics* and emptied its *war chest* to buy *mercenaries* and *Hessians*. Finally the *well-drilled fugelmen* [sic] in the *last ditch* closed *ranks*, overwhelmed the enemy *camp*, and divided the *spoils* of victory.

Military figures invaded the campaign ceremony with songs, war whoops, and hours of speechifying from bewhiskered colonels "late of the Confederate Army" or beribboned commissary generals of the GAR (Grand Army of the Republic). The median age of voters in the Gilded Age was thirty-seven, and so they had generally arrived at political maturity under the tutelage of fathers who had fought to preserve the "glorious Union" or to rescue a "prostrate nation." In circumstances reminiscent of battlefield conditions, ticket splitting suggested a lack of patriotism, and the ingrate who switched parties was regarded as little better than a bounty jumper.

Yet politics in this era, stripped of its gaudy regalia, was a business in the same stage of early development as small-scale entrepreneurial capitalism. Recently arrived immigrants may have performed like well-drilled foot soldiers on election day, but they were also urban consumers needing jobs, favors, and services. Such voters created a vast human market in which a judicious investment of limited political capital could pay off handsomely. The business of politics, unlike the more established concerns, stayed open at the bottom to new talent and offered unlimited opportunity to get ahead and make good. Caught in the posture of go-getter, the professional politician—ward heeler, precinct captain, county chairman, state assemblyman, or senatorial aspirant—resembled a salesman with a territory to cover that was filled with prospective customers whose buying habits he had better know thoroughly.

In this sense the professional politician's motto had scarcely changed in the half-century or more separating Martin Van Buren's Albany Regency and George Washington Plunkitt's Tammany Hall. "I seen my opportunities and I took 'em," Plunkitt recalled for a progressive generation fully prepared to be outraged. "Ain't it perfectly honest to charge a good price and make a profit on my investment? Of course, it is. Well, that's honest graft." Plunkitt and his colleagues described the political district in terms familiar to every drummer out of New York or Chicago with a territory to cover, and concluded: "If he holds his district and Tammany is in power, he is amply rewarded by a good office and the opportunities that go with it." The Gilded Age politician's true American was Horatio Alger in ward heeler's attire and sporting a campaign button. "Yes, many of our men have grown rich in politics," Plunkitt admitted. "I have myself. I've made a big fortune out of the game, and I'm gettin' richer every day." The shortest route to success in the business of politics lay through the upstairs rooms at party headquarters, where the sign over the door read "Never Closed."

IMMIGRANTS ARRIVING AT ELLIS ISLAND, NEW YORK CITY

New recruits for the American political army. (*Culver Pictures, Inc.*)

Politics in the Gilded Age, from the city to the Senate, constituted a revitalized patronage society bearing some of the marks of its eighteenth-century ancestor. Under the guiding hand and sharp eye of the boss, power was organized vertically within the machine in a hierarchical system of patrons and clients. The style of the Gilded Age boss was innovative, coarse, and raw, at once more personalized, direct, and cynical than the style of his predecessors. To his critics, like Moisei Ostrogorski, whose *Democracy and the Organization of Political Parties* summarized the reformers' indictment of machine politics, the political boss was Machiavelli's prince come to life, an all-powerful leader, unsleeping, devious, and ruthless, who commanded through his "strength of will, his cleverness, his audacity and his luck."

To this one he lends a dollar; for another he obtains a railroad ticket without payment; he has coal distributed in the depth of winter; he makes gifts of other kinds; he sometimes sends poultry at Christmas time; he buys medicine for a sick person; he helps bury the dead by procuring a coffin on credit or half-price. He has a kind heart in virtue of his position and his position gives him the means of satisfying his need for kindness: the money which he distributes comes from the chest of the Machine; the latter has obtained it by the most reprehensible methods . . . but no matter. With this money he can also dispense an ample hospitality in the drinking-saloons. As soon as he comes in, friends known and unknown gather round him, and he treats everybody, he orders one drink after another for the company; he is the only one who does not drink; he is on duty.

The party machine's stock in trade was supplied by jobs and appointments in increasing numbers, transit franchises, paving contracts, public construction bids, licenses, permits and a hundred other salable items needed to conduct the business of the nation's cities.

Urban machines formed the base of the political pyramid on which state party bosses built organizations that dutifully sent their men to Washington to fill seats in the Senate. The new ruling heads of state politics—Tom Platt in New York, Nelson Aldrich in Rhode Island, and Justin Morrill in Vermont—conducted national business in Washington while they kept an eye on the statehouse gang back home, mediating patronage quarrels, settling factional disputes, and smoothing discontents. For all this continuing process, system and organization provided the answers. The Michigan boss, James McMillan, explained that his rise to the United States Senate only proved "what quiet work and an active continuance of party organization can accomplish." Running the state machine was half the battle. "When party organization is perfect, campaigns are more easily conducted and victory more certain." Democratic party bosses—Maryland's Arthur Pue Gorman, New York's David Hill, Virginia's Thomas Martin—perfected their control over their states more slowly than Republicans, and, particularly in the one-party South, kept a looser grip on the party reins. But in both parties, as in the business world after 1880, consolidation and concentration of power became the order of the day.

This recognition of the need for order and control led the boss to consider himself both a professional and a practical reformer. "Politics," Plunkitt reminded his enemies, "is as much a regular business as the grocery or dry goods or the drug business. You've got to be trained up to it or you're sure to fail." The besetting sins of the do-gooder, Plunkitt insisted, were amateurism and innocence. "He hasn't been brought up in the difficult business of politics and he makes a mess of it every time." From at least midcentury, bosses like New York City's William Marcy Tweed and Philadelphia's James McManes had watched the aimless spreading of their cities and understood the growing problem of managing them. Tweed frankly admitted that New York's population was "too hopelessly split into races and factions to govern it under universal suffrage, except by bribery of patronage and corruption." Their cities, the bosses realized, were fragmented like giant jigsaw puzzles. The boss alone could provide the liberal application of patronage to glue them together, though his workmanship might be both slipshod and expensive.

Tweed's reign in New York City immediately after the Civil War saw authority centralized in the city government, a new county courthouse built, Central Park in the planning stage, and a transit system begun. All this had been achieved at the cost of widespread corruption and an astronomical increase in the city's bonded debt. In Washington, D.C., Alexander Shepherd, real estate speculator-turned-boss, supervised the building of a new drainage system for the capital, constructed miles of paved streets, installed a new lighting system, and leveled and landscaped the center city. Bosses seldom achieved the efficiency and system they sought; at best, they acquired an oligarchy for managing loose federations of their constituents. Their failings in efficiency and accountability would subsequently provide progressive reformers with most of their ammunition in their attacks on the urban machines in the 1890s. In the absence of a genuine science of administration and a corps of professional managers, the bosses, improvising lavishly and corruptly with materials at hand, at least gave their cities a minimum of order and necessary services.

The politics of equilibrium pressed the strenuous life into service in behalf of spoilsmen preaching a joyful acceptance of the facts of political life, whether a bit of bribery or orders from above to stuff the ballot box. The cult of moral strenuosity, once the mark of the lone observer situated on the outskirts of society, was now enlisted on the side of political expediency—the need to win at any cost. The world of the professionals was a masculine one though it also appeared at times to be grossly sentimental. For the professionals, politics could not be cut and trimmed by the moral shears of women or patched together with the tiny needles of the men-milliners of reform. Gilded Age politicians, in claiming the political arena as an aggressive male preserve, repudiated the original alliance of women and reformers that had precipitated the very war the professionals now sought to mythologize. Dismissing feminine activism and moral reform as contrary to human nature, and ridiculing their champions as long-haired men and short-haired women, the politicians added their testimony to the

THE WOMAN'S SPHERE

For the Gilded Age politician the woman's proper
occupations were domesticity and motherhood.
(*Culver Pictures, Inc.*)

conservative meaning of the Civil War. The exquisite moral sensibilities of a
William Lloyd Garrison appeared unaffordable luxuries in a materialistic age,
the reformer a biological sport in a society that considered politics masculine,
culture feminine, and the gulf between them permanent. So orders came down
from party headquarters: Let the women and their carpet knights remain in
their well-appointed parlors where they could exchange rumors of political misbehavior while sipping lemonade. The real world, the Blaines and Conklings,
Aldriches and Hannas insisted, was their own world of cigar smoke and fifteen-
dollar votes, rolling logs, and brimming pork barrels.

But there were still deeper worlds stirring by the 1890s. In agrarian revolts
in the provinces and civic campaigns in the metropolis, reformers were beginning
to draw on the resources provided by two alternative traditions of American
politics that had survived the spoilsmen. The Populist movement in the trans-
Mississippi West and the South renewed a millennial vision promising the triumph

of political righteousness. And by 1895, in the nation's cities progressive reformers were drawing on patrician fears, business notions of efficiency, and the
scientific hopes of new professionals and academics. Working in tandem in the
midst of industrial unrest and agrarian discontent, these two groups of reformers,
Populists and urban progressives, shattered the confidence of party professionals
by confronting them with different interpretations of the American dream.

"Conditions Without Precedent" —
The Populist Revolt

The first reform tradition to challenge the politics of equilibrium as the nineteenth century drew to a close stemmed from a millennial outlook that had long
flourished in a Protestant frontier democracy. This reform model was constructed according to utopian blueprints for a world beyond politics in which
power and strife were finally relinquished for the righteous rule of "good men."
Those who envisioned this utopia, the political pietists, tended to personalize
evil and corruption and to define their task as essentially a religious undertaking
aimed at conversion and regeneration. The language of political pietism, unlike
the vocabulary of the professionals, was openly evangelical: A new heaven on
earth awaits the coming of the new dispensation; social salvation requires men of
Old Testament vision who will lead true believers through the political wilderness
into the promised land where they will need none but the Lord to rule over them.
Secular politics as practiced by the ungodly is an abomination, and party leaders
the willing instruments of the devil. Good politics is "no politics," as simple and
direct as the Golden Rule.

Part metaphor, part literal reading of religious promise, the millennial reform
tradition had continued to tantalize Americans throughout the nineteenth century. Translated into action, it had spawned a variety of third-party movements
before the Civil War, beginning with the anti-Masonic outbreak in the 1820s,
gathering force with the abolitionist campaigns and communitarian experiments
in the following decades, and fixing on the issue of slavery in the Free Soil and
Republican parties soon thereafter.

Pietists demanded a complete change in the rule of conventional political behavior. Instead of the easy tolerance of broker politics they advocated cultural
and political uniformity. In place of competing interest groups they proposed a
national congregation of the right-minded. No more minor skirmishes between
equally corrupt contestants, but the last mighty battle for the Lord: Armageddon.
Pietism invited total participation at the grass roots, chiefly in the form of camp
meetings of the faithful to support the few correctives considered necessary for
defeating corruption. Pietists promised to restore a lost community, a pre-
industrial solidarity that depended on the recovery of abandoned values. In its
purest form, pietism promoted counterrevolution—the overthrow of the modern,
secular, boss-run, or bureaucratic state and a return to the Golden Age.

Pietism's moral rejection of modernity, however, was not matched by its economic program, which remained solidly *petit bourgeois*, bearing all the marks of small-scale capitalism with its hopes for the independent producer, regional markets, and steady growth rate. These wish-pictures once had sustained the North in its war against slavery. Instead of the millennium, however, the Civil War brought business consolidation and the rule of the Spoilsmen, and the original vision dimmed until it guided only such marginal groups as the prohibitionists and the Greenbackers. It was from the margins, therefore, that the first calls for a "new politics" were heard—from Henry George's legion of single-taxers, the Nationalist recruits in Bellamy's industrial army, and converts to the "New Conscience" of the Social Gospelists. Pietist grievances in the 1880s continued to center on issues with social and cultural as well as economic meaning: cheap money, the power of monopoly, and Wall Street conspiracies, which all underscored the isolation and marginality of the little man in a rapidly industrializing society. Here, then, in the mounting frustrations of staple-crop farmers who were certain they had been victimized lay the deepest seedbed of Populism.

Populist grievances were real enough. In the trans-Mississippi West they were chargeable mainly to the hectic pace of economic development; in the South they resulted from the workings of a quasi-feudalized agricultural system complete

THE SOD-HOUSE FRONTIER

Picknicking in the front yard, Custer County, Nebraska, 1886. (*Solomon D. Butcher Collection, Nebraska State Historical Society.*)

with tenancy, a crop lien system, and a large submerged class of dirt-poor farmers, both black and white. In the West, exorbitant shipping charges and extortionate mortgage rates were compounded after 1887 by a series of crop failures that sent land prices and farm income skidding downhill. Years of retrenchment followed, and destitute farmers trekked back eastward from the sod-house frontier, leaving behind ghost towns with gilded opera houses and empty storefronts. Western Kansas lost half its population between 1882 and 1892, South Dakota some 30,000 people, while the number of prairie wagons lumbering back to Iowa from the Nebraska frontier in 1891 was estimated at 18,000. A sign on an abandoned farmhouse in Blanco County, Texas, in the drought year 1886 read: "200 miles to the nearest post office; 100 miles to wood; 20 miles to water; 6 inches to hell. God bless our home! Gone to live with the wife's folks."

The ebbing human tide left dark pools of discontent in isolated bypassed communities, where bitter men and women were determined to stick it out, blindly, uncomprehendingly. From the beginning, Populism required terms and symbols sufficiently stark to explain to the disinherited the cause of their affliction. Kansas Populist Mary E. Lease put it this way:

We were told two years ago to go to work and raise a big crop, that was all we needed. We went to work and plowed and planted; the rains fell, the sun shone, nature smiled, and we raised the big crop they told us to; and what came of it? Eight-cent corn, ten-cent oats, two-cent beef, and no price at all for butter and eggs—that's what came of it. Then the politicians said that we suffered from over-production.

Populism in the South, while plagued by many of the same problems, displayed regional features that had characterized the nonslaveholding farmer's struggle for survival before the Civil War. Tenancy and crop liens continued to exploit an underclass of blacks and whites, whose awareness of their plight was matched by their fears of challenging a Bourbon dynasty based on white supremacy. Western Populists risked little more than failure in organizing a third party. Southern farmers, in attacking the political establishment, put their personal security and sometimes their lives on the color line.

In both regions, Populism emerged rapidly from a nonpartisan background in 1890 and drew into protest politics groups that had previously been inarticulate if not inert. Some of the new recruits were women: Mary Lease, who harangued country audiences on their subservience to monopoly; Annie L. Diggs, a strict prohibitionist bent on saving the West from alcohol as well as Wall Street; Sarah Emery, whose tract *Seven Financial Conspiracies* traced the national decline along a descending curve of democratic participation. For every seasoned veteran of third-party politics like Minnesota's Ignatius Donnelly, the Sage of Nininger, there were three new converts like Georgia's Tom Watson fired by Populist speeches for campaigns "hot as Nebuchadnezzar's furnace."

The atmosphere at Populist meetings was heavy with the spirit of revivalism— "a pentecost of politics," according to observers, "in which a tongue of flame sat upon every man." Recruits, like converts, came from everywhere: farmers, hard-pressed local merchants, cattlemen, miners, small-town editors; men with chin whiskers, broad-brimmed hats and muddy boots, accompanied by wives "with skin tanned to parchment by the hot winds, with bony hands of toil, and clad in faded calico." Quickly they became stereotypes—comic hayseeds to the political opposition, heroic figures in the folklore of Populism with nicknames to match: "The Kansas Pythoness," "Bloody Bridles," "Sockless Socrates." Behind the mask frequently appeared the original types, biblical figures like Senator William A. Peffer, for example, a Topeka editor elected to the Senate who reminded Hamlin Garland of Isaiah. "His general appearance is that of a clergyman," full beard, steel-rimmed glasses and frock coat, with the "habitual expression" of gravity on an otherwise inscrutable countenance. "He made a peculiar impression upon me, something Hebraic," Garland recalled, "something intense, fanatical."

The People's party yoked political opposites to the vehicle of reform. Southern Populists listened to the saving word not only from "Stump" Ashby, the Texas cowpuncher, and "Cyclone" Davis toting his volumes of Jefferson, but also from Virginia patricians bearing the names of Page, Beverly, and Harrison. In Minnesota, Ignatius Donnelly's mercurial style was offset by the sensible advice of Charles H. Van Wyck, the party's candidate for governor in Nebraska, who singled out solid issues like railroad regulation for his campaign. For the most part, however, Populists were political innocents, and innocence was widely deemed a virtue. To Eastern professionals in the major parties, Populism, under banners urging the steadfast to vote as they prayed, presented the strange spectacle of an embittered interest group talking in tongues.

New to the work of organizing a national party, the Populists encountered formidable obstacles to building a platform designed to advance farmers' interests and at the same time attract the worker in the city. They discovered that appeal for votes could be made in two distinct ways: first, by explaining their problems as staple-crop farmers and calling on the federal government to help, and second, by avoiding interest-group tactics and waging a campaign against modernity in the name of the "true producers" all over the country. It was the peculiar mark of Populism that it sought to undertake both of these assignments simultaneously.

The interest-group program of the Populists grew out of the reasoning of political leaders like Governor Lorenzo D. Lewelling of Kansas, who demanded a federal government responsive to the needs of all its citizens. "If the Government fails in these things, it fails of its mission. ' Several of the party's planks rested on this construction: a graduated income tax to lift the financial burden from the shoulders of farmers and workers; postal savings banks and a flexible currency; and a subtreasury system to stabilize prices and provide agricultural credits. All of these demands, calling the federal government to the rescue, could be defended as protective measures for producers who lacked the privileges already accorded more favored industrial interests. Another and different set of demands

—for immigration restriction, antimonopoly legislation, and farmer-labor cooperation—suggested eternal brotherhood for those who lived by the sweat of their brows. Party delegates to the convention in Omaha in 1892 cheered lustily as their leaders denounced the "governmental injustice," which was dividing the nation into two great classes, "tramps and millionaires." To postpone the day of wrath, the Omaha platform called for the people to seize power in a new constituent act:

Assembled on the anniversary of the birthday of the nation, and filled with the spirit of the grand general and chieftain who established our independence, we seek to restore the government of the Republic to the hands of the plain people with whose class it originated. . . . We declare we must be in fact, as we are in name, one united brotherhood of freemen.

In the society envisioned by the Populists righteousness would infuse God's chosen with high purpose. In the recesses of the Populist imagination lay hopes for a transpolitical realm of permanent harmony, where peace and virtue reigned supreme over a vast fee-simple empire of rejuvenated yeomen. However differently they were heard, the millennialist strains in Populism sounded the call for a counterrevolutionary crusade. The triumph of American justice would come only when the people themselves had purified national life at its wellsprings. Only a small part of such a gigantic task required the passage of "wise and reasonable legislation." A much larger part involved a moral crusade "to bring the power of the social mass to bear upon the rebellious individuals who thus menace the peace and safety of the state."

Populism transcended conventional politics in declaring itself "not a passing cloud on the political sky" nor a "transient gust of political discontent" but "the hope of realizing and incarnating in the lives of common people the fulness of the divinity of humanity." With this shift in political perception came glimpses of catastrophe should the people's courage fail—the swift approach of the "last days, nightmares of "men made beastlike by want, and women shorn of the nobility of their sex" pouring through city streets past plutocrats who stand "grabbing and grinning" as the mob rushes to its destruction.

In this realm of the apocalyptic, the ordinary political rules of the road no longer applied. If the crisis facing the nation could be reduced to a simple choice between justice and injustice, liberty and slavery, what was the need for reasoned proofs and analysis? "The very fact of widespread suffering," a Nebraska Populist insisted, "is sufficient evidence that the whole system under they have lived is a lie and an imposture." Once allow the people to destroy the Money-Power, and politics as a selfish pursuit of wealth and power would disappear.

The Populist call for an evangelical politics violated a cardinal rule of the professionals, which Ohio's John Sherman once invoked in reminding his Republican colleagues that "questions based upon temperance, religion, morality, in all their multiplied forms, ought not to be the basis of politics." Populists flatly disagreed, and like the abolitionists before the Civil War, rested their case on symbolic issues—the Money Question and Free Silver—as explanations of their plight.

For Western Populists and silver interests, fusion with the Democrats offered the only alternative to continued failure. In 1892, the Populist party won over a million popular votes and 22 electoral votes and sent a dozen congressmen to Washington while securing the governor's chair in Kansas, North Dakota, and Colorado. As the Panic of 1893 tipped the country into the deepest depression it had ever known, the Populists sought to reach into the industrial masses for support. But underfinanced, lacking a roster of attractive candidates, and beset with severe organizational and financial problems, the party had made few electoral gains in 1894 even though it increased its total vote by nearly 50 percent.

As the election of 1896 approached, Populists split into two camps, one led by fusionists ready to join the Democrats on a platform of free silver, the other headed by diehard reformers who agreed with Ignatius Donnelly that while the Democratic party had learned at least some of its lessons, Populists ought not to "abandon the post of teacher and turn it over to [a] slow and stupid scholar." For Southern Populists fusion seemed an invitation to a suicide since it meant rejoining the establishment whose ranks they had so recently deserted. But for a majority of the delegates to the convention in Saint Louis in 1896, a "Demopop" ticket headed by William Jennings Bryan seemed to offer the only sure passage out of the political wilderness. Following a rancorous debate, in which it was charged that the People's party had become "more boss-ridden, gang-ruled, gang-gangrened than the two old parties of monopoly," the convention agreed to unite with their former rival under the banner of free silver.

The Great Reversal: The Election of 1896

By 1896 the Democratic party, bitterly divided between agrarians and Eastern business interests, needed all the support it could get. Cleveland's return to office four years earlier had been greeted with a series of industrial strikes that seemed to many Americans the opening shots of a class war. The first of these upheavals came at Homestead, outside of Pittsburgh, in 1892, when Andrew Carnegie sailed for Europe and left Henry Clay Frick, his hard-driving manager and an implacable enemy of labor unions, in charge of his steel company. Frick took advantage of his chief's absence by attempting to break the Amalgamated Iron and Steel Workers Union, which two years earlier had won a favorable wage settlement from the company. Frick decided on a wage cut as the best weapon for destroying the union; when the Amalgamated refused his terms, he cut off negotiations and hired a private police force to take over the plant at Homestead. The union retaliated by calling a strike and preparing to repel the Pinkertons who had been dispatched by barge up the Monongahela with orders to seize the plant. The invaders, numbering some three hundred, were met with a hail of

bullets from the workers lining the shore, and in the pitched battle that followed
they were routed by the angry mob and their barges burned to the waterline.
But final victory, as Frick had foreseen, lay with the company, which prevailed
on the governor of Pennsylvania to send in the militia to open the plant. Frick
nearly paid for his union-busting with his life when a young anarchist, Alexander
Berkman, attempted to assassinate him but bungled the job. Frick's principle of
the open shop, however, emerged triumphant. After five months out on strike
the Homestead workers were forced to accept the harsh new terms of the settlement, suffering a defeat that ended effective organizing in the industry for nearly
half a century.

In the Pullman strike in 1894, Grover Cleveland threw his considerable weight
on the side of management against the forces of organized labor. Like Homestead,
the Pullman strike grew out of the antiquated notions of a business paternalist
whose sense of duty to his employees included building them a model company
town but did not extend to their right to negotiate their wages. When workers
in the car shops went on strike, George Pullman, president of the Pullman Palace
Car Company and chief planner of the company town named after him, sent
instructions to his managers to refuse to bargain and to evict the strikers from
their homes. Then in the late spring of 1894, Eugene V. Debs and his newly
organized American Railway Union, fresh from a victory over the Great Northern
Railroad, came to the rescue of the Pullman strikers with funds and an offer to
help settle their grievances. When the company once again declined arbitration,
the ARU voted to boycott all Pullman cars by refusing to couple them to any
trains, even those carrying the mail. Here was the issue that the Pullman Company, now supported by the railroads' General Managers Association, seized on
in seeking an injunction and the dispatch of federal troops to Chicago. Over the
vehement protests of Governor John P. Altgeld, Cleveland obliged. Faced with
a choice between the rights of labor and the rights of property, Cleveland un-
hesitatingly elected to uphold the latter.

In 1894 the American economy hit bottom. Five hundred banks closed their
doors, sixteen thousand business firms collapsed, and unemployment stood at
nearly 20 percent. New issues on the New York Stock Exchange plummeted from
$100 million to $37 million as 2.5 million jobless men tramped winter streets in
the nation's cities looking for work. Neither municipal governments nor private
charity organizations could cope with such numbers of desperate men who wan-
dered aimlessly from city to city in search of a job. Everywhere the migrants found
factory gates closed and crowds of unemployed workers whom they joined in
long lines in front of soup kitchens. Not since the dark days of the Civil War
had the country seemed so threatened.

DEPRESSION LANDSCAPE

Pennsylvania coal miners' housing with outhouses
and railroad tracks. (*Carnegie Library, Pittsburg.*)

Workers met the depression with the only weapon at their disposal, the strike. In 1894 alone there were over thirteen hundred strikes, of which the confrontation at Pullman was only the most publicized. The mining industry, for example, was hit by a wave of strikes rolling across the country from the coalfields in the East to Coeur d'Alene in Idaho, where besieged miners fought back with sticks of dynamite, and Cripple Creek, Colorado, where armed deputies broke up demonstrations. For such economic distress, Cleveland prescribed heroic remedies of self-denial, and dispensed terse reminders that while it was the clear duty of citizens to support their government, the obligation was by no means reciprocal.

The spectre of masses of starving men marching on the nation's cities to plunder and pillage in an uprising of the dispossessed assumed the shape of farce in the spring of 1894 with the arrival in Washington of Coxey's Army, a "petition in boots", come to the capital to ask for work. The leader of the few hundred jobless men who straggled into the city was the self-appointed "General" Jacob Coxey, a small-town businessman from Massillon, Ohio, who simply wanted

to present his plan for solving unemployment with a "good roads bill," which would finance public improvement with $500 million worth of government bonds. The Cleveland administration's response to this "living petition" mirrored its fear of mass upheaval; Coxey's followers were dispersed and their leader jailed on a technicality, while rumors of revolution swept through the city.

For Coxey's futile gesture and also for the state of the economy Cleveland blamed the nostrums of the free silver forces. In 1890 Congress, responding to the clamor of bimetallists and inflationists, had passed the Sherman Silver Purchase Act, which required the government to buy 4.5 million ounces of silver each month and to pay for it with treasury notes redeemable in gold. The Sherman Act precipitated a sudden rush on the gold reserves of the United States, which declined from $190 million in 1890 to just over $100 million three years later. Confronted with an unfavorable balance of trade, depleted gold reserves, and industrial stagnation, Cleveland moved quickly to persuade Congress to repeal the Silver Purchase Act, a decision that seriously weakened his control over his own party. He succeeded in shutting off the flow of silver from the mines in the West but in doing so lost the support of the agrarian half of the Democratic party. By 1895 the President was complaining that there was "not a man in the Senate with whom I can be on terms of absolute confidence."

In calling on the banking syndicates of J. P. Morgan and August Belmont to help check the outflow of American gold, Cleveland only compounded his political problems. The administration and the bankers, working together, arranged a sale of government bonds for gold on terms that allowed the banking houses to manipulate exchange rates in their own favor. To Populists and irate Democrats in the South and West, Cleveland's deal was proof that their suspicions of a Wall Street conspiracy to rig the economy against them were firmly grounded in fact.

The issues of sound money and free silver involved choosing between a deflationist monetary policy and an inflationist one for economic recovery. Silver and gold quickly became the organizing symbols for diametrically opposed strategies for solving the depression. Cleveland chose "sound money,' the gold standard and currency restriction as the safest course. For bankrupt farmers and Western miners, on the other hand, gold was a "crown of thorns" pressed on the brow of the honest laborer who was being crucified by the money lenders. In fact, Cleveland's monetary policy did aggravate the effects of the depression by widening the gap between fixed costs and income and accentuating the long-term price decline. More important, it provided farmers with a highly visible target for their grievances. The South Carolina demagogue, Ben Tillman, denounced the President to his back-country constituents as a Judas who had thrice betrayed the Democracy. "He is an old bag of beef, and I am going to Washington with a pitchfork and prod him in his fat ribs."

Democrats gathered in Chicago for the convention in 1896 with similar intentions. Southern and Western Democrats saw that by repudiating Cleveland's policies and by advocating the free and unlimited coinage of silver they had an opportunity to win the support of the Populist movement. Bryan quickly emerged as the choice of the agrarian wing of the party, which rode roughshod over the defenders of "sound money" and drove them out of the convention to form their own splinter organization. Bryan spoke the mood of his followers in sounding a new note of resistance:

We have petitioned, and our petitions have been scorned; we have entreated, and our entreaties have been disregarded; we have begged and they have mocked when our calamity came. We beg no longer; we entreat no more; we petition no more. *We defy them!*

The Eastern press, both Republican and Democratic, replied with charges of anarchy and treason. "The Jacobins are in full control at Chicago," an editor announced. "No large political movement in America has ever before spawned such hideous and repulsive vipers." Both the promise and the danger of a Bryan victory seemed to increase after the Populists' convention in Saint Louis endorsed the Democrats' choice for President. Not since 1860 had the fate of the nation appeared to hang in the balance of a single election. In 1896, as in 1860, the differences were sectional and economic, but they were also social and cultural, as two fundamentally opposed views of politics competed for the allegiance of the American voter.

Bryan and McKinley between them gave over nine hundred speeches in the campaign of 1896, the Republican from his front porch in Canton, Ohio, to throngs of admiring visitors shipped in by party managers, and the "Boy Orator of the Platte" at every whistlestop in the West where local leaders could collect a crowd. Their speeches riveted national attention on the money question, which quickly brought into focus cultural and social disagreements between urban and rural America. Behind the façade of monetary policy a "new politics" of pietism competed against an equally new political coalition of pragmatists and pluralists. Bryan was soon forced to expand his economic indictment to a plea for moral revival. Republicans, capitalizing on an upturn in the economy late in the summer, continued to denounce the Democratic platform as "revolutionary and anarchistic . . . subversive of national honor and threatening to the very life of the Republic."

A powerful orator and an appealing political figure, Bryan was new to the business of presidential campaigning, and in casting his party adrift from its Eastern financial moorings, he was driven to improvise. The professionals, frightened by the prospect of free silver, withheld their support, and Bryan rejected the offers of those few regulars who remained loyal. Sensing the need for new rules and definitions, Bryan cast himself in the role of the crusading prophet who could purify both his party and his country—eliminating corruption in Democratic ranks, paring the campaign budget, purging the party of hacks, and emphasizing principles rather than men. As the new leader he appeared an avenging angel of the outraged American yeomanry, the people's savior stepping

THE TWO PRESIDENTIAL
CONTENDERS IN THE ELECTION OF
1896

McKinley waged his campaign
from his front porch in Canton,
Ohio, while Bryan took to the
hustings. (*Left, Ohio Historical
Society; right, Brown Brothers.*)

off his campaign train for just one more sermon to his flock. To his listeners he
invariably apologized by confessing that "a large portion of my voice has been
left along the line of travel, where it is still calling sinners in repentance." His
speeches drew on a fund of stock pietist images as he mixed indictments of the
money power, the tariff, and the gold standard with allusions to the Old Testament. His message was everywhere the same: the people must arise in their
majesty and smite the money-lenders and destroy their temple. Audiences came
to know the arguments by heart and gathered to hear confirmation of their beliefs in the Protestant virtues of hard work and a just reward. When their leader
assured them that "every great economic question is in reality a great moral
question," they understood instinctively and they cheered. As Bryan preached
the saving word of free silver his audiences saw the stone suddenly rolled away
and "the door . . . opened for a progress which would carry civilization up to
higher ground."

Republicans, following the orders of new party managers like Mark Hanna of
Ohio, willingly exchanged places with their rivals. Tossing aside their pietistic
heritage as a burden, party leaders embarked on a pragmatic course directed at
a coalition of business and labor in the urban centers of the country where most

of the votes lay. Recent Republican recognition of the need for organizational efficiency and a full party chest also dictated the choice of McKinley, bland, amiable, a solid public figure with no strikingly original ideas but plenty of presumed common sense. To McKinley's front porch in Canton came some three-quarters of a million people carried there on nine thousand railroad cars paid for by the party, to stand behind a white picket-fence and listen to homilies on the honest dollar and the full dinner pail.

McKinley's image was the invention of younger Republican managers who had come to acknowledge the liabilities of pietism in an age of industrial organization and also the need for full-time professionals, a permanent headquarters, forceful propaganda, and a full campaign chest. During the campaign, the party released an unprecedented volume of campaign literature that reached every corner of the country. Speeches, pamphlets, and newspaper editorials were carefully orchestrated to the themes of cultural and ethnic pluralism, arranged to make interest-group appeals to farmers and workers, small businessmen and big bankers, shippers, consumers, Catholics as well as Protestants, and a variety of ethnic groups to whom the gold standard was offered as the last best hope of democracy.

As election day approached, Republican leaders realized that the battle for the gold standard consisted of a number of skirmishes fought for the allegiance of a wide variety of interest groups whose loyalty could be gained and held by arguments specifically tailored to their needs. Such a strategy entailed a platform of cultural and social tolerance, ethnic and religious variety, and political flexibility, an approach that contrasted dramatically with the Democratic countercrusade for unity. It also meant a forced retreat from the military style of campaigning that had characterized the politics of equilibrium. McKinley himself summed up the new Republican mood of toleration for his followers: "We have always practiced the Golden Rule. The best policy is to 'live and let live.'" With their candidate's blessing, the Republicans turned their backs on their pietistic heritage and assumed the task of engineering a consensus sufficient to guarantee winning the election.

The returns verified the reversal of political roles. With 7 million popular and 271 electoral votes, McKinley swept the entire East and Middle West, carried California and Oregon, and held onto Minnesota, North Dakota, and Iowa. Bryan, with 6.5 million popular votes and 176 electoral votes, won the Solid South together with the plains and the mountain states.

Beneath the regional features of the election lay the deeper meaning of the political realignment. As one student of the election has noted: "The realignment of the 1890s meant that the major parties faced the new century as much different social entities than the ones that had done battle in the 1850s. The Republican

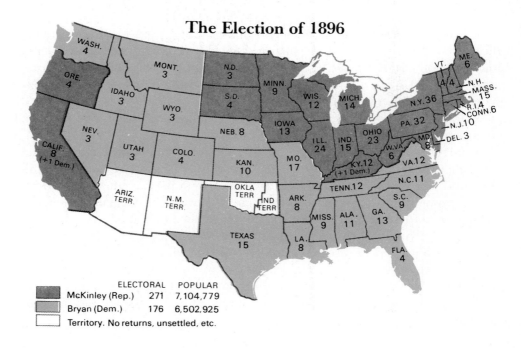

The Election of 1896

	ELECTORAL	POPULAR
McKinley (Rep.)	271	7,104,779
Bryan (Dem.)	176	6,502,925
Territory. No returns, unsettled, etc.		

party was no longer a narrowly based social vehicle in the hands of evangelical crusaders. It was a functioning integrative mechanism with a much broadened social base of support. The Democracy of Bryan was not the party of 'personal liberty,' but the instrument in the hands of 'reformers' who aimed at the creation of a moral social order." With their votes a majority of Americans declared their preference for pluralism and pragmatic accommodation and left the Democratic party to repair the damages while pondering the meaning of its defeat.

The meaning was sufficiently clear: the American electorate had repudiated the pietist countercrusade. Reforms there would undoubtedly be as the twentieth century opened, but they would not be the handiwork of a millennialist dream of purity and perfection. Political parties would have to consider and cater to the wishes of a multitude of social interests, welcoming newcomers under a broad canvas covering a wide diversity of social and cultural groups, meeting their demands, registering their complaints, and serving their needs.

Second, the election of 1896 made it clear to Americans that the organizational revolution that was transforming business and finance had also invaded politics. Just as both houses of Congress were beginning to modernize their procedures for doing the nation's business, so the two principal parties themselves had learned the value of efficient organization, continuing communications, flexible and sophisticated leaders, and above all, money with which to run their political machinery.

Finally, and most significant for the immediate future, the election of 1896 broke the grip of party regularity that had long been considered a permanent feature of the politics of equilibrium. It freed the American party system for a long-term realignment of voting patterns that would reveal the average voter as considerably more independent than the professionals had once assumed him to be. Absolute party loyalty and sustained political interest could no longer simply be assumed; voting behavior suddenly seemed more volatile and capricious than anyone had imagined. In the future, parties would have to reckon with the habits of their members, inclinations that often made them doubt the value of party rule and even mistrust the whole political process.

In defeat Bryan had uncovered a latent American suspicion of politics, a set of misgivings that had apparently been buried under the rubble of the Civil War. In his unsuccessful campaign, Bryan located this skepticism in the agrarian mind, attempted to exploit it, and failed. But by 1896 in the cities of the nation, new urban forces were already responding to a similar distrust of entrenched power and beginning to experiment with alternative ways of playing politics.

The political program of the new urban reformers, while it too promised to end machine politics and return power to the people, envisaged, not the triumph of righteousness but the rule of professionals. Experts would replace boss politics with scientifically designed administration, provide efficient and economical urban services, and stabilize the American city with man-made rather than God-given controls. The vision of social reformers organizing in American cities after 1890 centered on creating the "organic city" and liberating citizens' energies. With the stirring of these reform activities came a second and more powerful challenge to the old politics, the challenge of progressivism.

Cities in Revolt—The Rise of Urban Progressivism

The challenge of the city, announced the reformer Frederic C. Howe in 1906 after a decade of studying urban life, "has become one of decent human existence." Everywhere urban social reformers looked in the closing years of the century, they saw compartmentalization and fragmentation. Wealthy neighborhoods with million-dollar mansions were screened by parks and boulevards from teeming ghettos with dilapidated tenements and filthy streets—all too visible proof of the immense distances, social and psychological as well as economic and geographical, separating rich from poor.

It was to close the distance between urban affluence and poverty that in 1889 Jane Addams, the pioneer settlement-house worker, had moved into Hull House, a battered mansion on the corner of Polk and South Halstead streets in the heart of Chicago's Nineteenth Ward. "The streets are inexpressibly dirty," she reported, "the number of schools inadequate, factory legislation unenforced, the street-lighting bad, the paving miserable and altogether lacking in the alleys and smaller streets, and the stables defy all laws of sanitation."

Hundreds of houses are unconnected with the street sewer. . . . Back tenements flourish; many houses have no water supply save the faucet in the back yard; there are no fire escapes; the garbage and ashes are placed in wooden boxes which are fastened to the street pavements. . . . Our ward contains two hundred and fifty-five saloons; our own precinct boasts of eight. . . . There are seven churches and two missions in the ward.

In listing the needs of the Nineteenth Ward, Jane Addams summarized the main points in the urban progressive indictment of boss politics. Progressivism began as a spontaneous revolt of city dwellers convinced that they were being denied their share in the American social fund. The drive to reform the nation's cities opened with a pragmatic assessment of urban needs and quickly spawned broad coalitions of voters demanding immediate solutions to a wide range of problems: tax reforms, health regulations, streetcar fares, utility services, and city governments dominated by corrupt bosses and predatory "interests."

TENEMENTS, WASHINGTON, D.C.

Lewis W. Hine's famous photograph of the capital's black slums documents the urban progressive challenge. (*George Eastman House Collection.*)

By 1895 urban progressivism had drawn together the separate strands of a reform impulse that had originated, in the years following the Civil War, in piecemeal demands for civil service reform, railroad rate regulation, the eight-hour day, and factory legislation. The depression of the 1890s, by placing new burdens on urban consumers, bred a sudden sense of urgency and focused public attention on the shortcomings of machine rule. The key to the urban reform program, and itself the most powerful weapon in the progressive arsenal, was "invisible government," the sinister alliance between municipal authorities and business interests. The connection between "corrupt government" and "corporate arrogance" was a simple one of mutual need. In attempting to modernize their cities, machine politicians had discovered in secret agreements with transit and utility interests a handy device for supplying minimal service while lining their own pockets. At the same time, a new and unstable industry undergoing rapid reorganization saw in monopoly franchises, wholesale bribery, and kick-backs a measure of certainty in an otherwise unpredictable world. By 1890 the bargain had been sealed in most of the major cities of the country. The only real loser in this arrangement was the public.

Thus progressivism first appeared as a "people's movement" aimed at eliminating corruption and providing better services in urban transportation and other public facilities. Cutting across class and occupational lines and fastening on specific issues like dangerous railway crossings, improved sanitation facilities, or lower streetcar fares, the progressive movement in this early campaign developed a rhetoric and a style that was democratic and moralistic. The twin villains in the reformers' morality play were the businessman and the boss. His experiences as reform mayor of Detroit, Hazen Pingree concluded, had convinced him that monopolistic corporations were responsible "for nearly all the thieving and boodling with which cities were made to suffer from their servants." The muckraker Lincoln Steffens pronounced the American businessman "a self-righteous fraud." "I found him buying boodlers in Saint Louis, defending grafters in Minneapolis, originating corruption in Pittsburgh, sharing with bosses in Philadelphia, deploring reform in Chicago, and beating good government with corruption funds in New York." From the beginning progressives developed an antibusiness style that continued to obscure the real contributions of businessmen to urban reform.

The bosses offered even more enticing targets. According to Frederick Howe, Cincinnati's Boss George Cox ruled the city "as a medieval baron did his serfs."

He rose to this eminence by binding together and to himself the rich and powerful members of the community, for whom he secured and protects the franchises of street-railway, gas and electric lighting companies. They, in turn, became his friends and protectors, and through him, and for him, controlled the press and organized public opinion.

According to urban reformers, the only remedy for boss rule lay in fostering citizen coalitions to unite a fragmented community. "The very nature of city life," one progressive commentator insisted, "compels manifold cooperation. The individual cannot 'go it alone'; he cannot do as he pleases; he must conform his acts in an ever increasing degree to the will and welfare of the community in which he lives." This concept of the organic city fitted neatly the interests and ambitions of a new group of reform mayors in the 1890s who launched individual campaigns to overhaul their cities.

The first of the new reform mayors who succeeded in assembling dissatisfied urban consumers behind his reform program was Hazen Pingree, mayor of Detroit from 1889 to 1896 when he was elected governor. Pingree, who was a wealthy shoe manufacturer with a yen for politics, quickly mastered the role of "reform boss," campaigning vigorously in all the wards of the city and studiously avoiding issues of moral reform like prohibition and parochial schools, concentrating instead on the hard economic issues calculated to win him the greatest support. In the course of his several administrations, Pingree exposed bribery in a local electric light company's dealings with his predecessors and embarked on an extensive program of school and park construction. After a prolonged battle with the transit and utility interests, he succeeded in reducing streetcar and gas rates while building the city's municipal lighting plant. During the depression he initiated work relief for Detroit's unemployed and extended a variety of social service programs. Attacking Detroit's "invisible government" and replacing it with an efficient and responsive administration, Pingree set a pattern for his successors by collecting loose coalitions of voters behind a series of significant if unspectacular urban reforms.

It remained for Tom Johnson, the mercurial mayor of Cleveland from 1901 to 1909, to exploit most fully a whole new range of possibilities for leadership. Johnson had made his fortune reorganizing transit systems, and had been converted to reform on reading Henry George's *Social Problems.* After two successful terms in Congress as a reform Democrat, he returned to Cleveland to assemble the coalition with which to fight Mark Hanna and the traction interests. Energetic, tough-minded, and a consummate politician right down to the unlit cigar he waved from the nearest handy soapbox, Johnson borrowed all the techniques of the machine and improved on them. Like Pingree, he instinctively shied away from moral issues and inaugurated his reform program by arranging for a regulated system of prostitution free from police graft. Like Pingree too, he confronted the transit interests with the prospects of regulation. His most widely acclaimed achievement was the "three-cent fare," but he continued to agitate for municipal ownership of utilities, and provided the city with free public bathhouses, recreational facilities, and effective sanitary inspection.

Reform mayors who launched their careers from a platform of pragmatic opposition to the "interests" were frequently forced to confront broader questions of social welfare. Some of them, like Pingree and Johnson, and later Brand Whitlock in Toledo and Mark Fagan in Jersey City, were driven to adjust to shifting interests within their reform coalitions and to support welfare measures that extended far beyond the political and structural reforms they originally had called for. The "social justice" mayors, as they have been called, also came to question the value of strict party identification; increasingly they came to rely on the advice and services of new professionals and experts in municipal management, whose scientific concerns centered on finding more efficient and economical ways of running the city. "The fact of the matter is," "Golden Rule" Jones, reform mayor of Toledo, admitted late in his career, "that there is little hope for improvement, for progress, in the direction of scientific government in our municipalities until we shall first get the people freed from the baneful superstition of partisan politics." One route to nonpartisanship lay through increased dependence on experts; another through alliances with humanitarian reformers with their base in urban slums.

Streetcar politics was only the most visible sign of the urban revival in the 1890s. City churches, suddenly conscious of their declining membership among the working class, responded to the perceived crisis with the "institutional church" in lower-class neighborhoods. They hoped thus to spread the "social gospel" of Christianity through devices like lodging houses, reading rooms, recreational halls, and day nurseries. Then too, by 1890, groups of earnest young college graduates, many of them women, were moving to the slums to live in settlement houses modeled on London's famed Toynbee Hall. In New York in 1886, the young seminary graduate Stanton Coit founded the Neighborhood Guild on the Lower East Side, a center that soon became known as University Settlement as it began to attract young recruits from Columbia University uptown. Three years later, Jane Addams and Ellen Gates Starr moved into Hull House, where with the financial help of Chicago matrons they gathered a staff of idealistic young college graduates and set to work building a kindergarten and a day nursery for working mothers, and organizing a variety of youth clubs and an employment bureau.

By 1895 there were over fifty such settlements in major cities around the country. Settlement-house workers were invariably young (the great majority under thirty), religious (predominantly Congregationalist and Presbyterian), college-educated, single, and overwhelmingly from genteel middle-class homes. For such young intellectuals and would-be professionals, many of them with advanced training in the new social sciences taught in German universities, the city settlement offered an escape from gentility and from feelings of superfluousness and provided the chance to practice their new skills. Settlements freed their members from what Jane Addams called "the snare of preparation" for unknown careers. More important, they became the focus for a new sense of the complex social and cultural relations that defined the organic city. Teachers, housing reformers, charity organizers, health inspectors, and visiting nurses all found a congenial home in the settlements, which suddenly seemed to them miniature models of the good society. By 1900, the settlement house had established itself as an indispensable laboratory of social reform, its success measured in the years that followed by the alacrity with which city administrations institutionalized their improvements.

In experimenting with urban reform, these social pioneers discovered new techniques for coping with the bewildering variety of urban problems. In the first place, they came to rely heavily on new methods of research and fact gathering as essential to the task of re-ordering urban society. One of Jane Addams's first assignments was to collect and collate the raw data on the surrounding neighborhood; and in 1895, *Hull House Maps and Papers* appeared as the first detailed account of an immigrant community published in the United States. In 1903, Lawrence Veiller and Robert W. DeForest published their two-volume *Tenement-House Problem*, an attempt to relate urban housing to the larger city setting through the use of statistics and first-hand observation. Perhaps the most ambitious project for examining the city in its entirety was the six-volume *Pittsburgh Survey* (1909–1914) which treated politics, crime, prostitution, the family, housing, and working conditions as aspects of a functioning organism.

Social surveys underscored the need for trained personnel and scientific management. The autonomous commission staffed by trained professionals and given power to revamp tax structures, regulate transit and utility rates, and provide efficient city services quickly became the principal agency of effective urban reform. With the commission came another type of progressive reformer, the expert who saw his job as imposing order on the city in much the same way corporate businessmen were regularizing their procedures.

Still another sign of the growth of bureaucratic values was the spectacular increase in professional organizations. Economists, sociologists, political scientists, tax reformers, charity organizers, settlement-house workers, and dozens of other specialized professions had formed national societies by 1900, each with its own publications and communications network. These national organizations, besides strengthening a sense of professional community, cemented an alliance with the new universities providing the training and the facilities for scientific investigation of urban problems. In Chicago, the residents of Hull House quickly established close connections with William Rainey Harper's new University of Chicago through reform-minded academics like John Dewey, Albion Small, William I. Thomas, and Charles Merriam. In New York, economists and sociologists from Columbia University joined freelance writers and publicists at the University Settlement in analyzing city problems and working out solutions.

The settlement connection proved vital for young academicians by providing laboratories for testing new concepts of behavior and by drawing them into the exciting world of reform politics beyond university walls. Charles Merriam, the ambitious young political scientist who had trained under John W. Burgess and William A. Dunning at Columbia before joining Harper's faculty at Chicago, explained the urban challenge and the urgent need for formulating a new political science to cope with it. "The new techniques of the new time must be adapted to the new background, social and intellectual, of the new world we live in," Merriam told fellow reformers. "Politics as the art of the traditional advances to politics as the science of constructive, intelligent social control."

Businessmen and academicians often parted company, however, on the question of applying Merriam's new critical spirit. By 1900 the university had come to house historians, economists, political scientists and social theorists equipped with sharp analytical tools for dismantling old conservative myths. Charles A. Beard was only the best known of the young academicians who were beginning to question the hide-bound interpretations of American law and the Constitution as well as the penchant for ancestor-worship they encouraged. Beard's own Columbia University typified the new iconoclastic spirit. There the economist Edwin Seligman, the earnest advocate of the "New History," James Harvey Robinson, and pioneer students of administrative law like Frank Goodnow were busy probing the economic roots of political behavior. In another setting and from a different direction the political scientist Arthur F. Bentley in *The Process of Government* (1908) approached political decision-making as a pluralistic process subject to the shifting strengths of interest groups. At the University of Washington the radical historian J. Allen Smith in a book entitled *The Spirit of American Government* (1907) dismissed the Constitution as a "reactionary document" de-

MYTHS AND REALITIES

The Gilded Age abounded in racial and
social stereotypes, always crude and often
vicious. On the cover of the song sheet at
left the Irishman wears a dog's face while
the advertisement for rat poison promises
to rid the country of rats along with the
Chinese who presumably eat them. The
corrective facts appear in the photographs
above: Boss "Tim" Sullivan gives his
annual dinner for the poor; American
flags fly in New York City's Chinatown.
(*Top left, Brown Brothers; top right, Library
of Congress.*)

signed to check the forces of democracy. After 1900 the partnership between highly critical academicians and their corporate financial supporters grew increasingly strained as the professors began to question the very business civilization on which their universities now depended.

With the appearance of concepts like "social control" and "scientific efficiency," however, progressive reformers made contact with another nineteenth-century reform tradition, one that was alien to the open tolerance of reform politicians and to the democratic and humanitarian hopes of social workers. This distinctive component of urban progressivism was the belief in the transcendent importance of remodeling American city governments on the principles of efficiency and economy.

Municipal reform as a scientific movement matured in 1893 with the Conference for Good City Government, out of which came the National Municipal League. Soon a range of specialized organizations demanding the overhaul of municipal government sprang up; they combined the interests of academics and new political professionals with those of progressive businessmen intent on applying their own methods to the management of cities. The organizational zeal for scientific reform with its emphasis on economy, efficiency, and stability was part of the bureaucratic revolution that had overtaken all American society, but it was not altogether new in intent or spirit. The political goals of the scientific reformers were as old as the nation itself, and they had been renewed in various forms, generation after generation. In this latest phase, however, patrician reformers joined new businessmen in broadening their vision to include politicians who promised to return strict accountability to government at all levels. By the nineties, reform-minded Republicans, new academic specialists in tax reform and municipal affairs, and business spokesmen were busy brewing an elixir of scientific efficiency and business economy with which to restore the health of the American cities.

Constant in all phases of the movement for good government was the belief that simply by tightening the system of expenditures, consolidating power in the hands of experts, and revising the political system without particular regard for human needs and demands, reformers could manage the city. Good government, the scientific reformers reasoned, would be rigorously honest, determinedly efficient, resolutely frugal, and strictly accountable. In its initial formulation, scientific reform was neo-Federalist, designed as a check on democratic participation and aspirations; it was a modernized version of virtual representation for limiting the influence of uninformed voters whose numbers it sought to reduce through literacy tests and voter registration laws.

By the end of the century, the ancient patrician model of good government had been adapted to the modern demands of professional politicians and sophisticated businessmen. Rule by the talented few had become management by trained administrators and experts. Efficiency and economy had come to be equated with business practices of budget paring, cost cutting, tax trimming, and service chopping according to a "ledger-book ethics" of corporation accountants. To be allowed to practice as well as to preach their revivified civic morality, scientific reformers needed to win office, and this recognition led to experiments with a variety of political and structural reforms ranging from the Australian ballot, at-large elections, and voter registration laws to new commission forms, investigative bureaus, and the extension of civil service. By 1900, the original reform design had acquired the outlines of a utopia promising the extinction of parties and politics as a way of life, rule by disinterested experts supervising a trimmed-down government and using the latest scientific procedures. "Scientific" government promised a self-perpetuating bureaucratic system whose frictionless operation would ensure the efficient dispensing of goods and services.

Good government reformers considered the city a challenge that was not very different from the need for business integration and corporate merger confronting new industrialists and financiers. "Municipal government is business, not politics" read the slogan of the scientific reformers. The shaping power of the modern corporation in determining the outlook of the structural progressive reformers was reflected in their vocabulary, built on a set of useful analogies.

THE PROGRESSIVE SOCIAL WORKER'S CLIENTS

While social workers recognized that reforms ultimately depended upon the votes of men, they concentrated their efforts for immediate improvement on women and children. (*George Eastman House Collection.*)

The mayor served as *chairman of the board* of an urban *corporation* comprising big and little *stockholders,* who were expected to vote their *proxies* at annual meetings and accept their *dividends* without constantly interfering with the *managers* of the *enterprise.* It was hardly a coincidence that the waning years of the century, which saw the triumph of the corporation and the advent of scientific municipal reform, also witnessed the opening assault on the concept of a rational "public opinion," once considered the cornerstone of democratic politics. In dismissing that opinion as frivolous or perverse, scientific reformers betrayed what Frederick Howe called a "distrust of democracy," for in declining to take their instructions from the "people" they echoed the sentiments of their Federalist predecessors a century earlier in calling for the reduction of popular influence in the governing of the community. The first order of reform business, insisted Frank Goodnow, a spokesman for the scientific reformers, was recruiting cadres of loyal and politically unambitious civil servants whose combined efficiencies would permit "the business and professional class of the community to assume care of public business without making too great personal sacrifice."

For business-dominated mayors who tried to clean up city politics after 1900, urban reform meant an opportunity for Americans of the middle and upper classes, armed with new bureaucratic techniques and procedures, to repossess the field of urban politics that their predecessors had abandoned to the bosses fifty years earlier. Some of the participants in the revolt against machine politics professed not to see the contradictions between scientific efficiency and the superior claims of social democracy. Robert Merriam, a leading spokesman for a scientific politics and an active office seeker, called for "the organization of public authority" in a system linking administrative freedom with long-term democratic directives. Merriam continued to define the problem of the city as repair of the "institutional forms of democracy," and saw the progressive task as one combining the conflicting principles of autonomy and accountability in the experimental process itself.

The case for democracy was most forcefully put by Brand Whitlock, novelist, social welfare reformer, and mayor of Toledo from 1905 to 1913. Whitlock defined the "city sense" as democracy and "the spirit of goodwill in humanity" and predicted the coming of cities that should "express the ideals of the people and work wonderful ameliorations in the human soul."

This will not be accomplished by the triumph of one class over another, or by any *bouleversement* in which the processes of despotism will be reversed. . . . It will not descend upon the cities from any feudal lord or industrial baron of our time, whether in the hall of legislature or in the counting-house, however gracious and benevolent he may be. It must come up from the people themselves through patient study and careful experiment . . . and be the expression of their own best longings and aspirations.

But the great majority of reformers recognized the progressive problem for what it was, a value choice involving two widely divergent estimates of democracy and human nature. Some reformers, like the sociologist Edward A. Ross, frankly rejected the idea of democratic participation in favor of elitism. Politically, Ross argued, democracy meant not the sovereignty of the average citizen, "who is a rather narrow, shortsighted, muddleheaded creature," but the "mature public opinion" of an educated elite.

'One man, one vote,' does not make Sambo equal to Socrates in the state, for the balloting but registers a public opinion. In the forming of this opinion the sage has a million times the weight of the field hand. With modern facilities for influencing mind, democracy, at its best, substitutes the direction of the recognized moral and intellectual elite for the rule of the strong, the rich, or the privileged. . . . Let the people harken a little less to commercial magnates and a little more to geologists, economists, physicians, teachers and social workers.

The legacy of urban progressives to the twentieth century was thus a divided one. Even with the development of overlapping groups and ideas among scientific and humanitarian reformers a dual tradition emerged, polarized around conflicting values of social efficiency and democratic liberation. These contesting principles, which had combined briefly in the 1890s to unsettle the politics of equilibrium, would continue to diverge in the twentieth century, creating tensions within progressivism that would make it a varied, confused, and contradictory movement.

Suggested Readings

There are several useful guides to the politics of the Gilded Age. Leonard D. White, *The Republican Era, 1869–1901* (1958) examines the workings of the federal government. H. Wayne Morgan, *From Hayes to McKinley: National Party Politics, 1877–1896* (1969), concentrates on political organization. Daniel J. Elazar, *The American Partnership* (1962), treats federal-state relations in detail, and David J. Rothman, *Politics and Power: The United States Senate, 1869–1901* (1966), presents a fascinating account of the organizational changes in the upper house. Robert D. Marcus, *Grand Old Party: Political Structure in the Gilded Age, 1880–1896* (1971), analyzes the workings of the Republican party, and Horace Samuel Merrill, *Bourbon Democracy of the Middle West, 1865–1896*, gives a regional account of the Democrats for the same period. Vincent P. DeSantis, *Republicans Face the Southern Question* (1959) and Stanley P. Hirshson, *Farewell to the Bloody Shirt: Northern Republicans and the Southern Negro, 1877–1893* (1962), consider the race issue as it affected Republican strategy. Southern politics is perceptively treated in four important works: C. Vann Woodward, *The Origins of the New South, 1877–1913* (1951); Dewey W. Grantham, Jr., *The Democratic South* (1963); Albert D. Kirwan, *Revolt of the Rednecks: Mississippi Politics: 1876–1925* (1951); and Morgan Kousser, *The Shaping of Southern Politics: Suffrage Restriction and the Establishment of the One-Party South, 1880–1910* (1974). Mary R. Dearing, *Veterans in Politics* (1952), recounts the activities of Civil War veterans, and Marc Karson, *American Labor Unions and Politics, 1900–1918* (1958), discusses unions and politics in the opening years of the twentieth century.

A number of studies examine electoral behavior in crucial elections. Among the best are Paul W. Glad, *McKinley, Bryan, and the People* (1964); Stanley Jones, *The Presidential Election of 1896* (1964); J. Rogers Hollingsworth, *The Whirligig of Politics: The Democracy of Cleveland and Bryan* (1963). Two challenging studies, Paul Kleppner, *The Cross of Culture: A Social Analysis of Midwestern Politics, 1850–1900* (1970), and Richard J. Jensen, *The Winning of the Midwest* (1971), examine cultural factors operating in Midwestern politics during the Gilded Age and perhaps elsewhere as well.

Political biography abounds. Two of the best studies of Bryan are Paolo E. Coletta, *William Jennings Bryan: Political Evangelist, 1860–1908* (1964), and Paul Glad, *The Trumpet Soundeth: William Jennings Bryan and His Democracy, 1896–1912* (1964). For McKinley, see H. Wayne Morgan, *William McKinley and His America* (1963). On Cleveland, Horace Samuel Merrill, *Bourbon Leader: Grover Cleveland and the Democratic Party* (1957), supersedes Allan Nevins, *Grover Cleveland* (1932). Biographies of other important figures include numerous older works: Ray Ginger, *The Bending Cross: A Biography of Eugene V. Debs* (1948); Herbert Croly, *Marcus Alonzo Hanna* (1912); Nathaniel W. Stephenson, *Nelson W. Aldrich* (1930); Francis Butler Simkins, *Pitchfork Ben Tillman* (1944); Leland L. Sage, *William Boyd Allison* (1956); and Harry Barnard, *"Eagle Forgotten": The Life of John Peter Altgeld* (1938).

On the troubled 1890s, a good overview is Harold U. Faulkner, *Politics, Reform and Expansion, 1890–1900* (1959). The intellectual and cultural climate of the decade is analyzed in the idiosyncratic and amusing Thomas Beer, *The Mauve Decade* (1925), and Lazar Ziff, *The American 1890s: Life and Times of a Lost Generation* (1966). For contemporary accounts that treat the social and cultural issues in nostalgic fashion, see Harry Thurston Peck, *Twenty Years of the Republic, 1885–1905* (1907), and the first volume of Mark Sullivan, *Our Times* (6 vols., 1926–35).

Local politics continues to attract the attention of historians, and the recent literature on bosses and machines is impressive. Alexander B. Callow, Jr., *The Tweed Ring* (1966) and Seymour J. Mandelbaum, *Boss Tweed's New York* (1965) offer penetrating analyses of machine politics in New York, and so does Theodore J. Lowi, *At the Pleasure of the Mayor: Patronage and Power in New York City, 1898–1958* (1964) for a later period. For Chicago, Harold F. Gosnell, *Machine Politics: Chicago Model* (1935), is still useful but should be supplemented with Lloyd Wendt and Herman Kogan, *Bosses in Lusty Chicago: The Story of Bathhouse John and Hinky Dink* (1943), and Joel A. Tarr, *A Study of Boss Politics: William Lorimer of Chicago* (1971). Other big American cities are analyzed in Zane L. Miller, *Boss Cox's Cincinnati* (1968); Lyle Dorsett, *The Pendergast Machine* (1968); and Walton E. Bean, *Boss Ruef's San Francisco* (1952). The effect of progressive reforms is described in Melvin Holli, *Reform in Detroit: Hazen Pingree and Urban Politics* (1969); James B. Crooks, *Politics and Progress: The Rise of Urban Progressivism in Baltimore, 1895–1911* (1968); and William D. Miller, *Memphis During the Progressive Era, 1900–1917* (1957). A good study of Tammany in this period is Nancy Weiss, *Charles Francis Murphy, 1858–1924: Respectability and Responsibility in Tammany Politics* (1968). Jack Tager, *The Intellectual as Urban Reformer: Brand Whitlock and the Progressive Movement* (1968), is a sharply etched portrait of a recognizable progressive type.

26

The Progressive Impulse

In 1915, as progressive reform neared its zenith, a young professor of government at New York University, Benjamin Parke DeWitt, published a book entitled *The Progressive Movement*, in which he catalogued the political and social reforms in the United States since 1900 and pointed to their underlying unity. DeWitt, a fervent admirer of Theodore Roosevelt and an active reformer, looked behind recent campaigns and elections and discovered three interlocking progressive tendencies:

The first of these tendencies is found in the insistence by the best men in all political parties that special, minority, and corrupt influence in government—national, state, and city—be removed; the second tendency is found in the demand that the structure or machinery of government, which has hitherto been admirably adapted to control by the few, be so changed and modified that it will be more difficult for the few, and easier for the many, to control; and, finally, the third tendency is found in the rapidly growing conviction that the functions of government are too restricted and that they must be increased and extended to relieve social and economic distress.

In identifying the most urgent reform task as the redesign of American government and the recruitment of new personnel to run it DeWitt summarized the progressive belief in the primacy of politics. The progressives' reasoning made a tidy syllogism: Government at all levels was both inefficient and corrupt; because it was corrupt it neglected the needs and demands of the people, who accordingly must seize the initiative in repairing the entire system. According to this logic, the first reform task was removing unworthy and inept politicians and replacing them with trained public servants drawn from the popular ranks and equipped with the needed expertise. These new bureaucrats would see to it that government—city, state and national—performed an expanding range of functions efficiently and responsibly. Progressive reformers, in short, discovered in the uses of scientific government the materials for building a common national movement.

The progressives' keen sense of their renovative mission helped them to ignore the bewildering variety of factors that determined their goals. In the first place, there was no single "progressive type," among the leaders or the rank and file whose age, status, background, religion, and education were remarkably similar to those of their opponents. Progressives simply composed the vital center of the native-born, middle-class establishment that dominated American politics in the first two decades of the twentieth century. Educated, articulate, and eager to apply their ideas for reforming society and politics, they held no monopoly on political gentility and could be found in equal numbers in the reform wings of both major political parties.

Progressives, moreover, offered an impressive array of reform proposals: initiative, referendum, and recall; corporate regulation and social legislation of all kinds; tariff reform and banking laws; city manager plans and new budgetary procedures; immigration restriction and even prohibition. Progressive priorities differed widely according to region and interest. Farmers fought strenuously for regulation of railroad rates but ignored the plight of the industrial worker. Southern progressives rallied behind tariff and banking reform as they proceeded to disfranchise the black. Settlement-house workers grappled with the bosses for control of their cities but neglected the problems of the small-town businessman. For every progressive reformer with a comprehensive platform there were ten would-be saviors of American society with a single nostrum.

With this shifting fault line running through the first two decades of the twentieth century, it has sometimes seemed more useful to write the "obituary" of progressivism as a collectivity, approaching it, instead, as simply another form of "aggregative politics," a patchwork of divergent interest groups willing occasionally to agree on specific measures but generally unable to combine in a coherent movement.

Most progressives, however, thought otherwise. They recognized that the United States had entered a new century of consolidation, one demanding new techniques for managing what they agreed was a flourishing national enterprise. Although they admitted that there was still much wrong with America, they saw little that could not be mended by applying public authority and scientific efficiency. In the spirit of the Founding Fathers, whose buoyant nationalism they so admired, progressive reformers considered themselves the architects of a stable social order based on many of the same principles that had guided the work of their Federalist ancestors, who in their time had sought to impose system and control on a prodigal democratic people.

With their use of new political techniques and behavioral concepts, progressives were innovators, but at a deeper level of social perception they were restorationists, picking up the promise of American life where their eighteenth-century fore-bears had dropped it — with the creation of a strong national government capable of directing the energies of its citizens. If part of the progressive message calling on the "people" to seize power from their corrupt rulers seemed to invoke the spirit of Jefferson, the heart of the progressive program was the Hamiltonian demand for a new national leadership capable of composing discord and provid-ing direction. The ghosts of Hamilton and Jefferson fought over the progressive terrain with much the same intensity the two statesmen had contested each other's principles a century earlier. To the delight of his numerous progressive followers Hamilton won the victory denied him during his lifetime. If not in intent, at least in effect, progressivism marked the rebirth of original Federalist hopes for a managed republic in which men of talent and training guided the affairs of a prosperous people. After a century-long aberration chargeable to the pernicious enthusiasms of Jefferson, progressivism promised a return to order.

The Man with the Muckrake

The Muckrakers supplied progressivism with an agenda. The name was a label affixed to a new brand of reform journalists by President Theodore Roose-velt who complained that their relentless exposure of corruption in high places hindered rather than helped him in his work of improving American society. Comparing the group of headstrong publicists to Bunyan's gloomy figure who refused a celestial crown for a muckrake, the President denounced their "crude and sweeping generalizations" and their penchant for pointing the finger of civic shame. For their part the Muckrakers — Lincoln Steffens, Ida Tarbell, Ray Stan-nard Baker, David Graham Phillips, and half a hundred colleagues — accepted the label and wore it proudly as proof of their devotion to the Jeffersonian principle of a free and vigilant press.

Muckraking was the commercial product of two forces that had combined by the end of the nineteenth century: significant advances in the technology of print-ing that made it possible for the first time to produce an inexpensive, illustrated popular magazine; and the simultaneous arrival on the metropolitan scene of the reform reporter sensitive to the new social concerns of his middle-class readers and eager to exploit them. By 1900, rotary presses, linotype machines, and photoengraving had caught the attention of a group of aggressive editors whose magazine bore their personal stamp and often their names. Frank Munsey and S. S. McClure were only two of the pioneer explorers of this lucrative field, and they were quickly joined by dozens of competitors drawn to social criticism by their keen sense of the market and the prospect of sizeable profits. From the outset

Muckraking proved that reform could be a paying proposition. Gathering a staff of trained, well-paid newspapermen whom they set loose on the national community, the Muckrake editors launched an attack on the underside of American life with articles on sweatshops, tainted meat, the white slave traffic, insurance company scandals, labor racketeering, city bosses, and high finance. Effectively, they were compiling a list of all the social wrongs that enlightened readers would presumably set right.

McClure's quickly became the leader of the Muckrake pack. In the January 1903 issue of the magazine there appeared three articles exposing American social sins: Lincoln Steffens's "The Shame of Minneapolis"; an installment of Ida Tarbell's accusatory history of Standard Oil; and Ray Stannard Baker's account of the nonunion victims of the closed shop, "The Right to Work." Steffens singled out business as the cause of the nation's woes: "That's what's the matter with it. That's what's the matter with everything—art, literature, religion, journalism, law, medicine,—they're all business...." More soberly Tarbell weighed the

McCLURE'S MAGAZINE

NOVEMBER, 1903

The Labor Boss
The Trust's New Tool
By
RAY STANNARD BAKER

New York
By
LINCOLN STEFFENS

The Truth About Radium
By Cleveland Moffett

SIX SHORT STORIES

S. S. McCLURE CO. NEW YORK AND LONDON

ethical costs of monopoly and the sanctifying of business success, while Baker drew sharply etched portraits of scabs and racketeers. In an accompanying editorial McClure himself sounded the central theme in the Muckraking appeal: "There is no one left; none but all of us. . . . We all are doing our worst and making the public pay. The public is the people. We forget that we all are the people. . . ."

Beyond such moral exhortation it was difficult for the Muckrakers to go in examining the causes of the American malaise. Upton Sinclair and Charles Edward Russell urged a mild form of socialism as a corrective for predatory business behavior, and George Kibbe Turner preached salvation through business responsibility. The exuberant David Graham Phillips, whose discovery of treason in the Senate first called down the presidential wrath, warned of a power-hungry plutocracy invading the halls of state, while Steffens concentrated on municipal graft and misbehavior of statehouse rings. The thematic thread connecting their various indictments was a carefully cultivated hard-boiled tone. "If our political leaders are to be always a lot of political merchants," Steffens declared, "they will supply any demand we may create. All we have to do is to establish a steady demand for good government."

Muckraking, as Theodore Roosevelt denounced it and millions of readers reveled in it, offered both a new kind of factual reporting and an old form of moral publicity. Always extravagant and frequently sensational, the Muckrakers perfected the uses of contrast and contradiction in pointing to the disparity between venerable American fictions and startling social facts. In an article for *Cosmopolitan* on child labor in Southern cotton mills, for example, the poet Edwin Markham depicted "The Hoe Man in the Making" in the faces of "ill-fed, unkempt, unwashed, half-dressed" children penned in the narrow lanes of the mills, little victims whose dreary lives mocked the "bright courtesy of the cultured classes." The social gospelist Ernest Crosby contrasted the "appearance" of a majestic United States Senate with the reality of a "House of Dollars," a political monopoly modeled on an industrial trust. Samuel Hopkins Adams explained the national failure to regulate the food and drug industries as the result of "private interests in public murder" when "everybody's health is nobody's business."

Muckraking thus presented a technique rather than a philosophy, a popular style rather than a coherent analysis. As social critics, the journalists were curiously Janus-faced, on the one side seemingly tough-minded and factual, and on the other, romantic, moralistic, and more than occasionally sentimental. Like their millions of readers, they were the beneficiaries of a fundamental change in the idea of publicity, which they conceived of as an open-ended process of fact gathering that reflected the shifting nature of social reality. Read in this subdued light, their articles could be considered wholesome remedies and useful correctives for particular problems. Their work, the Muckrakers insisted, was never done, since an unfolding social process required constantly accommodating accepted theory to recently acquired facts, old values to new conditions.

Yet Muckraking tapped traditional moral reserves and exploited the conventional reform roles of the disinterested observer and the clear-eyed, hard-nosed investigator with his fierce desire to get "all the facts" and expose them to the sanitizing rays of moral publicity. Muckrakers liked to think of themselves as brave detectives, dashing from one hidden clue to another looking for the fragments of information that once collected and arranged would tell them what to do. Their appeal to the awakened conscience of the "people" was pure myth, serviceable enough as propaganda but scarcely an adequate description of political reality. There was also a strong bias against party government in the Muckrakers' reading of American politics as well as a weakness for conspiratorial interpretations. Their tendency to assign vast restorative powers to the masses of American voters served to justify their own roles as indispensable fact finders. Tell the people the truth, they seemed to say, and they will correct injustice forthwith! Conscience, duty, character, virtue—these were the watchwords of the Muckrakers and also a measure of their limited understanding of the problems confronting progressive America. Muckrakers identified the symptoms of disorder, but they could not isolate its causes or prescribe effective remedies. For these a clearer understanding of the workings of industrialized society was needed.

Progressives vs Politicians

The most powerful force for reforming American society came from another direction—from the ranks of businessmen, academicians, and professionals who had lately received an education in new organizational methods and now sought to apply them to the conduct of politics. These key groups in early twentieth-century America were already developing more systematic ways of doing their work along with new attitudes towards it and more sophisticated standards for measuring its performance. By 1900, professionals and businessmen were busy as never before organizing themselves according to discipline, specialty, or interest. The advantages of combination had now become obvious to groups as different as the American Sociological Association and the National Association of Manufacturers. The rise of organization was largely the work of new specialists—municipal tax experts, city planners, corporation lawyers, public health officials, market analysts, efficiency experts, and public relations men—all bent on modernizing their professions and enjoying newly acquired prestige.

Progressive businessmen and professionals shared a set of values and goals that redirected their careers and reshaped their priorities into concepts of

BOSS POLITICS: PROGRESSIVE TARGET

Progressive reformers found it difficult to compete with the city boss whose services to his clients, like those of Tammany Hall, included free barbecues. (*Brown Brothers.*)

system, control, stability, and predictability. Charity organizers realized the pressing need for accurate data and scientific procedure in drafting workable solutions to social disorganization. A giant lumber company like Weyerhaeuser came to appreciate the importance of planning and cooperation with the new experts in the Forestry Service. College professors and high school teachers now recognized the need for professional solidarity to protect their rights. Public-service lawyers, like young Louis Brandeis, suddenly realizing the complexities of new legal relations, began to experiment with the role of "counsel to the situation" and with new techniques of arbitration.

The social perceptions of this middle-class vanguard of the bureaucratic revolution stemmed from their sense of American society as a collectivity— whether a complete organism or an intergrated piece of machinery. To implement their bureaucratic values they fashioned new "scientific" operating procedures: centralizing authority in a hierarchical order rather than a democratic one; concentrating decision-making power in an energetic executive; establishing impersonal relations marked by bureaucratic function; and above all, planning for maximum efficiency. Although the bureaucratic ideal was seldom achieved either by businessmen or professionals, after 1900 it commanded increasing attention with its promise of replacing ceremonial loyalties to party and private interest with a new spirit of professional purpose and civic responsibility.

These values and procedures assumed concrete form for large numbers of progressives in the image of the modern corporation. The picture of the efficient, impersonal corporation was not drawn by big businessmen alone; it was a widely accepted model of organization that appealed to intellectuals and professionals as well as to industrialists and financiers who recognized its uses in rebuilding American politics. Progressive criticism of the trust was largely directed towards its misuse by unscrupulous promoters, not towards its seemingly rational structure. "The trust is the educator of us all," Jane Addams announced in explaining the need for new kinds of collective action. Seen in this light, the corporation appeared as a corrective of the waste and the inefficiencies of an earlier age, an actual model of organizational reform extendable, like the utopian communities before the Civil War, to a larger American society. Advocates of technology and economic innovation maintained that the new procedures had outstripped political developments, which now must catch up. Reformers had first to demolish the crumbling foundations of party politics and begin their rebuilding program by vesting power in an informed electorate willing to grant a new managerial class the power to lead.

The conservative bias of many progressive reformers could be most clearly seen in their attacks on the boss and the machine while their real intentions were frequently obscured, even to themselves, by their seemingly democratic enthusiasm. "The people are finding a way," exclaimed the progressive publicist William Allen White, who pointed in astonishment to the rapid growth of "fundamental democracy" in the American soul. A whole roster of progressive proposals for open government were billed as democratic devices for ensuring popular control at the grass roots. The direct primary and direct election of senators would release the stranglehold of the bosses on the electoral process. Referendum would send important questions of policy straight to the people over the heads of unresponsive legislators. Recall would return the power to remove officeholders to the voters, with whom it belonged. Many progressives, contemplating improvements like these, were inclined to agree with William Allen White that the machine was in "a fair way to be reduced to mere political scrap iron by the rise of the people."

Urban progressives were not hypocrites in advertising their reforms as democratic, but they did not always make it clear that by "the people" they meant not the huddled masses in center cities but solid citizens with sensible views and sober habits who had previously abdicated in favor of the bosses and their benighted clients. Below the blaring trumpets of democracy could be heard, subdued but distinct, the progressive call for the politically vanquished to return to the fray armed with new weapons.

The nerve center of urban progressivism after 1900 consisted of municipal leagues, civic federations, citizens' lobbies, commercial clubs, and bureaus of municipal research. These civic groups provided forums for the lively exchange of ideas between academicians operating out of the urban university and businessmen eager to try out their own ideas of efficiency and economy in managing their cities. From organizations like the National Municipal League and the National Civic Federation poured a flood of proposals and plans for repairing urban administrations: home rule and charter revision, ballot reform and literacy tests, citywide election schemes and city-manager plans, all of them aimed at the power base of the boss. Urban progressives, as one municipal leaguer explained, sought to make the city "an efficient business enterprise . . . a simple, direct, businesslike way of administering the business of the city." Social scientists sharpened the progressive indictment of machine politics by emphasizing waste

PROGRESS AMERICAN-STYLE

"If God had meant man to fly. . . ." But woman?
(*Library of Congress.*)

as well as corruption, denouncing the politicians' "extravagant measures" that mulcted the taxpayers. According to these new scientific experts, machine politics represented the vestiges of a nineteenth-century "sectionalism" with its futile "treaty-making by factionalism."

At first the reformers concentrated on procedural improvements. They proposed segregated budgets for economy. They introduced time clocks, work sheets, job descriptions, and standardized salaries. They developed systematic ways of letting contracts in place of the old patronage methods. But the heart of their reform program was the commission and city-manager plans, modeled on the corporation. The original idea for the city commission was the work of John H. Patterson, president of the National Cash Register Company in Dayton, Ohio, who described the ideal city as "a great business enterprise whose stockholders are the people" but one that ought to be run by "men who are skilled in business and the social sciences." Combining executive and legislative functions in a single board, at once more economical and more efficient, the commission plan spread rapidly until by 1913 over 300 cities in the United States had adopted it. The city-manager plan, a refinement of the original commission idea, further consolidated decision making in the municipal government, and by the 1920s it too had been widely adopted.

Urban progressives never succeeded in putting the political boss out of business. The profitable "business of politics" was never forced into bankruptcy, and reformers never managed to establish a permanent receivership. Nevertheless, progressivism successfully challenged boss politics by confronting it with another way of doing the business of the city. The machine's power lay in the center city, with its immigrants and working classes. Middle-class reformers generally operated from power bases in the suburban periphery. Boss politics, for all its various sins, was marked by a high degree of accountability and popular participation in the wards and precincts. Progressives tried to reduce direct popular involvement at both the voting and the officeholding level. Bosses were prodigal but democratic; reformers were economical and bureaucratic. In the tradition of the Federalists, urban progressives attempted to bring democratic society under control by arrogating the directive power in an industrial society to themselves.

Progressive success was limited. All too often procedures changed but official policy did not. Still, if the boss and his underlings proved remarkably adept at parrying the electoral thrusts of reform candidates, they could no longer ignore the increasingly strident cries for more effective government. By 1920 neither side could claim victory. The progressives' dream of a shiny, streamlined, nonpartisan administration rationally measuring and meeting citizen demands never materialized. Yet the modernizing of American cities proceeded with or without the politician's blessing. In their partial overhaul of the nation's cities the progressives scored important gains for the new bureaucratic order.

Progressivism Invades the States

The progressives who set out to reform state politics after 1900 built on urban achievements. Beginning in 1900 with the first administration of Wisconsin governor Robert M. LaFollette, reform swept across the country in the next decade transforming the conduct of state politics and bringing a change of outlook that was long overdue.

Although progressivism varied widely in the three major sections of the country, there were enough similarities to give political reform the appearance of a national movement. In the South, progressives, inheriting a number of Populist grievances, often wore the one-gallus trappings of a redneck revolt against business-minded Bourbons. By the opening years of the century one governorship after another was falling to economy-minded agrarians from upcountry or downstate—Jeff Davis's punitive rule in Arkansas, Hoke Smith's rural ascendency in Georgia, Ben Tillman's pitchfork politics in South Carolina. The Southern rebellion against the alliance of big business and Democratic regulars drew on popular sympathies and brought railroad and corporate regulation, antimonopoly laws and insurance company controls, improved public education and child labor reforms, all at the price of total disfranchisement of the Negro.

Progressivism in the Midwest and on the Pacific Coast also grew out of insurgency, usually within a Republican party perceived as too generous to railroads and corporations. Midwestern progressives drew more heavily from the arsenal of democratic political reforms like the initiative and the referendum than their counterparts in the East, who tended to rely more on administrative reforms. But everywhere the political control of state legislatures by big business made an inviting target. In New Jersey, corporate dominance by 1900 was all but complete. "We've got everything in the state worth having," a spokesman for the state's corporate interests boasted. A compliant legislature regularly dispatched two senators to Washington to represent the utility interests and the insurance companies. The chief justice of the state supreme court, the commissioner of banking and insurance, the state comptroller, the attorney general, and a majority of the state board of taxation were all former employees of the Pennsylvania Railroad.

The governors who organized the revolts against these statehouse rings headed the cast of new progressive folk heroes as tough-minded reformers who combined a proper democratic outrage with a shrewd sense of the possible. Not all progressive governors were charismatic figures; New York's Charles Evans Hughes, for example, made his reputation as a low-keyed, genteel reformer specializing in repairing the state's administrative structure. But all the progressive governors capitalized on their independence from the "interests" and organized labor and featured themselves as representatives of all the people.

The most popular of the reform governors cast themselves as Western heroes, riding into office with a mandate to clean up the state, setting about their work with grim determination, and moving on to bigger things when their job was done. Denied office by the state party machine, the reformer collected his small band of insurgents and attempted, at first without success, to take over the party. To help him in his fight he enlisted other mavericks in his posse and began to explore electoral reforms, like the primary and the direct election of senators, fixing his sights on the "interests" and eventually unhorsing the party regulars.

Once elected, the progressive governor moved quickly to neutralize his opposition by absorbing some of their numbers into his own reform coalition. He quickly learned to wield patronage with a surprising ruthlessness, and with secure majorities in the legislature proceeded to enact his reform program. His list of reforms generally included strict regulation of railroads and public service corporations, a revamped tax structure, and major pieces of social legislation to improve working conditions in the state. After a hectic term or two in which he managed to complete at least part of his rebuilding program the

"BATTLING BOB" LAFOLLETTE CAMPAIGNING

LaFollette was famous for his style of political barnstorming. (*State Historical Society of Wisconsin.*)

progressive governor moved on to the Senate where he was joined by other like-minded rebels from similar backgrounds who had the same hopes of imposing their reform designs on national politics. The career of one such progressive hero, Robert M. LaFollette, illustrates the main features of this legend of progressive reform.

LaFollette, an intense, unsmiling, self-made man in the Horatio Alger mold, was a small-town lawyer who struggled to the top of the political heap in Wisconsin and in his three terms as governor after 1900 enacted a reform program that became the envy of progressives across the country. Born in Primrose, Wisconsin in meager circumstances, the young LaFollette was a walking example of the Protestant ethic. He put himself through the new state university by teaching school, and dutifully prepared himself for a career in politics by studying for the bar. At the University of Wisconsin he came under the reform influence of President John Bascom who was just beginning to build a public service institution, a task that LaFollette himself would complete a quarter of a century later.

Short, wiry, with a shock of bristling iron-gray hair, LaFollette combined a rock-hard moralism with a combativeness difficult to match in progressive circles. He won his first office as district attorney, without the endorsement of the Republican machine, by barnstorming the countryside and haranguing rural audiences on the need for integrity and independence. In 1884, he was elected, again without the support of party regulars, to the first of three terms in Congress as the youngest member of the House. After six years as a useful but undistinguished member of the Republican contingent in Washington, LaFollette was defeated in the Democratic landslide of 1890 and came home to a lucrative law practice.

The Republican party in Wisconsin, as in a number of other states, was the effective instrument of conservative Stalwarts representing the railroad and the lumber companies. Faced with a recovery suit against their state treasurers, who had regularly dipped into the public till for twenty years, the party bosses sent an emissary to LaFollette with a bribe to secure his influence with the judge, who happened to be his brother-in-law. LaFollette promptly cried havoc and later reckoned the attempted bribe the turning point of his career. "Nothing else ever came into my life that exerted such a powerful influence upon me as that affair." In exposing the machine's crime to the voters he effectively isolated himself from the party leaders and spent nearly a decade trying to collect enough votes from Scandinavian farmers and industrial workers in Milwaukee to overthrow the machine. By 1900 he had succeeded.

LaFollette's victory won him instant national acclaim. After destroying the power of the old machine by detaching some of its leaders to his own cause, he set out to modernize Wisconsin. The "Wisconsin idea," as it came to be known, depended on a firm progressive majority in the state legislature, and this the new governor secured by campaigning personally for his supporters and then holding them strictly accountable. Soon his opponents were complaining that he had made himself the "boss" of a ruthlessly efficient machine of his own. The substance of the Wisconsin idea consisted of a set of related reforms: a direct primary law, an improved civil service, a railroad rate commission, an equitable tax program, state banking controls, conservation measures, a water power franchise act, and labor legislation. At the center of LaFollette's reform complex stood the independent regulatory commission, staffed by the new experts supplied by the state university and given wide administrative latitude. Another of LaFollette's proudest achievements was a legislative reference bureau to help amateur lawmakers draft their bills in proper form. The bureau maintained its reputation for nonpartisan service to the very end, even drafting the bill for its enemies that put it out of business.

To his many admirers across the country, LaFollette appeared a political anomaly, at once a popular leader with his feet firmly planted in the grass roots and an enthusiastic convert to scientific government. Exacting, fiercely partisan, and a consummate hater, he often seemed to view the world as a gigantic conspiracy to do in "Battling Bob." He kept ready for display at a moment's notice the image of the sea-green incorruptible who preached the virtues of direct democracy and constantly urged his followers to "go back to the people." "Selfish interests," he declared, "may resist every inch of ground, may threaten, malign and corrupt, they cannot escape the final issues. That which is so plain, so simple, and so just will surely triumph."

The other half of LaFollette's reform equation, however, was filled with facts and figures his investigatory commissions collected. His own interminable speeches came heavily freighted with statistics and percentages provided by a corps of tax experts, labor consultants, industrial commissioners, and social workers. These facts he hammered at the voters of Wisconsin in the belief that the people, once apprised of their unmistakable meaning, would hardly fail him. The conflicting principles of divine-right democracy and government by an expert elite—principles that sat uneasily on the progressive conscience—caused LaFollette little distress, convinced as he was that once they were properly informed the people would accept his proposals. The commission form, central to the implementation of the Wisconsin idea, also answered another vexing question, what to do about increased social fragmentation and incipient class conflict. Positioned above the battle of parties and interests, the commission seemingly embodied the very disinterest and altruism it was designed to foster in the people. LaFollette's growing national reputation, in fact, rested on the confidence he inspired in the belief that democracy and scientific government were not simply compatible but complementary.

An integral part of progressive reform programs in the states was a package of new laws drawn up by civic groups, women's organizations, and consumer interests that finally humanized working conditions. As late as 1900 over half of the states had no laws establishing a minimum age for workers. By 1914 every

"SHUCKING" OYSTERS, OYSTER HOUSE, BALTIMORE, MARYLAND

After 1900 progressive legislation in the states was aimed at protecting working women like these. (*Culver Pictures, Inc.*)

state but one had set an age limit on the employment of children. In most states a social justice crusade for the protection of women in industry paralleled the drive to abolish child labor. Illinois led the way in 1892, by limiting hours for women. New York and Massachusetts followed suit, and thereafter the movement spread rapidly westward. When the Supreme Court upheld the principle of state regulation of hours for women in the celebrated case of *Muller* v. *Oregon* in 1908, barriers collapsed, and by the time America entered the First World War thirty-nine states had written new laws protecting women or significantly strengthening old ones while eight of them had gone even further by enacting minimum wage laws for women. A third feature of the progressive social reform program

was the campaign for employers' liability laws and industrial accident insurance, which did away with the worst of the inequities of the old common-law doctrines of the "fellow-servant" and contributory negligence. By 1916 nearly two-thirds of the states, responding to the mounting pressure of progressive reformers, had established insurance programs.

Progressivism, taking different forms in different states, everywhere signified a shift of power within the American political system from cumbersome, interest-dominated legislatures to a new public authority vested in the executive and its supporting administrative agencies charged with the enforcement of a revitalized general will. To justify their roles as custodians of this general will, progressives unearthed a national-interest theory of politics as old as the Founding Fathers. "I would not be a dredger Congressman, or a farm Congressman, or a fresh egg Congressman," a typical progressive told his constituents in summoning up the spirit of Edmund Burke and virtual representation. "I would like to be an American Congressman, recognizing the union and the nation." If warring economic interests were chiefly responsible for the lack of direction and the low tone of American politics, progressives reasoned, then it was wise to ignore them and appeal instead to a latent public virtue. "Progressivism believes in nationalism, in individual citizenship," another reformer added. "It opposes class government by either business, the laboring, or any other class. . . ." The tendency to reject interest-group government (government as a bargaining process between blocs of big business, big labor, and big agriculture) drove progressives to embrace the concept of leadership from above—from those "good men" in whom altruism presumably ran deeper than selfishness. "While the inspiration has always come from below in the advance of human rights . . ." the California progressive William Kent insisted, the real accomplishments in the improvement of American society must always be "the disinterested work of men who, having abundant means, have ranged themselves on the side of those most needing help." In the progressive interpretation of American politics underdogs announced their needs but topdogs filled them.

Draped with the mantle of disinterested benevolence, progressivism looked like nothing so much as a renovated model of Federalism, suitably altered to fit a modern bureaucratic society. Progressives, like their Federalist ancestors, came to fear the idea of party government and class division, and sought to take the politics out of American life in the name of scientific management. For an eighteenth-century rule by republican notables they substituted leadership by experts whose skills would command the allegiance of all enlightened citizens. Most of the progressive political reforms, an analyst of American politics has noted, were "devices of political stabilization and control, with strongly conservative latent consequences if not overt justifications, and with an overwhelming non-partisan bias." In similar fashion the progressive social justice programs initiated by the states were designed to strengthen corporate capitalism by empowering

Art as Urban Experience

The great Chicago architect, Louis Sullivan, summed up the meaning of the twentieth-century city for a progressive generation of Americans when he defined it as a scene of "strife"—at once an "arena" for contending social energies and the center of a new democratic culture. For Sullivan a "culture of democracy" meant a "culture of action." His tall office buildings, as he called them, embodied the "mobile equilibrium" that symbolized for him the fusion of individual genius and the massed energies of a whole people. The architect, he explained, "causes the building by acting on the body social" following a design "struck out at a single blow." As for the building, "the force and power of altitude must be in it, the glory and pride of exaltation must be in it. It must be

every inch a proud and soaring thing, rising in sheer exaltation that from bottom to top it is a unit without a single dissenting line." Sullivan's own buildings with their sharp verticality, contrasting piers and planes, hard-edged mouldings and exuberant ornamentation represented the encased energy and power of "becoming" which their creator identified with the democratic spirit and the city.

American artists in the opening years of the century shared Sullivan's vision of the city as the focus of national life and the center of a new culture. For Robert Henri and his "black gang" of realists who gloried in their name as the Ashcan School, New York City served as a backdrop for an exciting procession of urban scenes and types which they recorded in the documentary style they had perfected

Detail from "Stag at Starkey's," George W. Bellows, *The Cleveland Museum of Art, Hinman B. Hurlbut Collection.*

"The Speilers," George B. Luks, Addison Gallery of American Art, Phillips Academy, Andover, Mass.

as newspaper illustrators—swirling crowds on gusty street corners, slum kids swimming in the East River, working girls drying their hair on a sunny tenement roof, ragamuffins gaily dancing the two-step on a crowded pavement —all the "drab, happy, sad and human" moments in the life of the metropolis. Henri's student, John Sloan, took West Fourteenth Street for his reporter's beat and painted the energy he discovered in ordinary people and familiar neighborhood scenes. George Bellows extended the idea of energy from subject to slashing technique in his famous *Stag at Sharkey's* with its two faceless fighters straining against each other. "Who cares what a prize fighter looks like," Bellows exclaimed. "It's his muscles that count."

The New York Eight were boisterously

"Cliff Dwellers," George W. Bellows, *Los Angeles County Museum of Art.*

"Steaming Streets," George W. Bellows, *Santa Barbara Museum of Art*.

"Hammerstein's Roof Garden," William J. Glackens,
Whitney Museum of American Art.

democratic and proletarian in sympathy. "A child of the slums will make a better painting than a drawingroom lady gone over by a beauty shop," insisted George Luks, the most colorful and obstreperous of the Eight. In the city's "incredible panorama" of clattering els and gigantic excavations, towering skyscrapers and shabby tenements, vaudeville houses and open-air markets, the Eight discovered an infinitely renewable America. "What a mistake we have made in life seeking for the finished product," Henri scoffed. "A thing that is finished is dead." To the Ashcan School, as to Louis Sullivan, the city promised a democratic immortality.

Another group of younger and more adventurous American artists fresh from encounters with European post-Impressionism, who exhibited at Alfred Stieglitz's Photo-Secession Gallery at 291 Fifth Avenue, also responded to the clashing energies of the city which they caught and fixed in abstract patterns and bold colors. Like the Ashcan School, the new abstract painters sought vitality in

"Hester Street," George Luks,

their work in the conviction, as Stieglitz put it, that "it is the spirit of the thing that is important. If the spirit is alive, that is enough for me." But John Marin, Georgia O'Keeffe, Marsden Hartley, Max Weber, Arthur Dove and the other modernists gathered at 291 to celebrate, not the Eight's triumph of life over art, but the liberating forces of the esthetic experience itself. The modernists, unlike the Ashcan School, were defiantly *avant garde*,

and the freedom they sought was freedom from the conventions of pictorial art and the chance to experiment with new forms with which to record a kaleidoscopic urban world. "I see great forces at work, great movements," John Marin declared, "the large buildings and the small buildings, the warring of the great and the small. . . . While these powers are at work . . . I can hear the sound of their strife, and there is a great music being played."

"Rush Hour, New York," Max Weber, National Gallery of Art, Washington, D. C., Gift of the Avalon Foundation.

The modernists, in the spirit of the progressives who often failed to understand them, approached their art as a process of experimentation and research, one demanding innovative technique and bold improvisation. "There was life in all these new things," Marsden Hartley explained in recalling the years before the First World War. "There was excitement, there was healthy revolt, investigation, discovery, and an utterly new world out of it all." Art, as the modernists conceived it, was what the instrumentalist John Dewey called "a process of doing or making," a confrontation with partially disorganized nature with its "breaks and reunions" that plunged the viewer into "the ongoing world around him." The young abstract painters were struck with the action, clash, and tension of city life which they captured in new dynamic patterns quite unlike the static forms of European cubists such as Georges Braque and

Juan Gris. The Futurist Joseph Stella found the most powerful image of conflicting urban forms in the Brooklyn Bridge, with its "massive dark towers dominating the surrounding tumult of surging skyscrapers . . . the eloquent meeting point of all the forces arising in a superb assertion of their powers, an Apotheosis." His *Coney Island,* an arrangement of splinters of light, Stella entitled "Battle of Light." Georgia O'Keeffe confessed to a fascination with New York's skyscrapers and determined to make her flowers "big like the huge buildings going up. People will be startled and look . . . ."

With the arrival of the twentieth century, the city came to dominate the imagination of artists and architects who continued to seek in it the source of a vital American art.

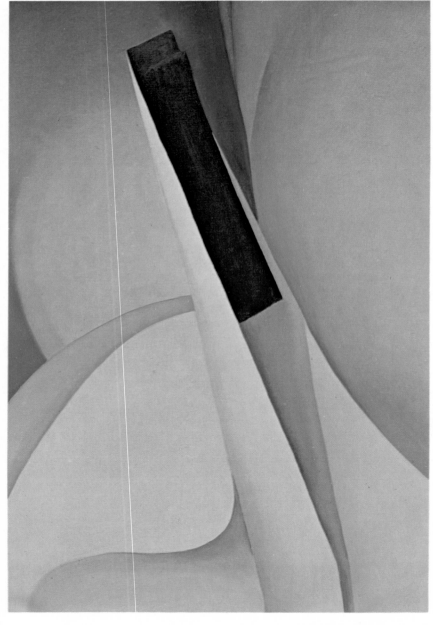

"Black Spot No. 2," Georgia O'Keeffe, *Collection of Irving Levick.*

government to help reassign responsibilities and temper the harshness of the American industrial environment. To carry out their containment policy at the national level, the progressives looked to the figure of the new statesman, and in Theodore Roosevelt they found their earthly paragon.

Theodore Roosevelt: The Progressive as Hero

In September 1901, President William McKinley died in Buffalo of an assassin's bullet, and Theodore Roosevelt, "this crazy man," as Republican managers thought him, was catapulted from his "utterly anomalous office," the vice-presidency, into the post of national leader. Blueblood, historian, student of the classics, amateur naturalist, cowpuncher and Rough Rider, Roosevelt at forty-two appeared to his millions of admirers as the last of the universal men, and to uneasy Republican managers like Mark Hanna as "that damned cowboy." With an audible sigh of relief Old Guard Republicans heard the new President announce his intentions "to continue, absolutely unbroken, the policy of President McKinley." McKinley had meant high tariffs, the gold standard, and a not-too-vigorous prosecution of the trusts. The prospect of a continuing custodial presidency reassured those congressional standpatters who feared above all a rambunctious executive. Yet within the year Roosevelt had begun to challenge congressional ascendency, and by the time he retired from his second term in March 1909, he had succeeded in creating a national progressive movement, reinvigorating American foreign policy, and laying the foundations of the twentieth-century welfare state. Well might the professionals have wondered what manner of man had fallen heir to the presidency.

Roosevelt was the product of patrician New York society, the son of a banker-philanthropist who had dabbled in genteel reforms and organized the city's upper-class contribution to the cause of the Union during the Civil War. A graduate of Harvard, where he amused his classmates with his odd earnestness and vibrancy, he immediately settled on a life in politics among the "kittle-kattle" of Spoilsmen and Mugwumps. For the moral chaos of Gilded Age politics he held the comfortable classes chiefly responsible, and with a highly developed sense of noblesse oblige he entered the New York State Assembly as a representative from one of the city's Republican silk-stocking districts. In the Assembly, where he served a single term from 1882 to 1884, he displayed the singular mixture of social conservatism, pugnacity, and political acumen that was to become his distinguishing mark. In 1886 he accepted the Republican nomination in the three-cornered mayoralty race in New York City and ran a respectable third behind winner Abram S. Hewitt and Single-Taxer Henry George. The 1880s also saw the growth of a sizable body of historical work—*The Winning of the West*, a biography of Gouverneur Morris, and another of Thomas Hart Benton—in which Roosevelt proclaimed his unqualified approval of the nationalist designs of the

Federalists, denounced Jefferson as a hypocrite, and hymned the glories of westward expansion and the fulfillment of a continental destiny.

When his first wife died in 1884, Roosevelt retired to the frontier he had described so eloquently, finding solace in Dakota ranch life filled with cowboys, frontier justice, and manly virtues. As a steadfast if unpredictable young Republican he was appointed to the United States Civil Service Commission by President Benjamin Harrison in 1889 and served in Washington until 1895, when he returned to New York to head the Board of Police Commissioners and make a name for himself with late-night prowls on the lower East Side with his journalist friend Jacob Riis in futile attempts to enforce the city's blue laws. McKinley rewarded such misplaced energy by appointing him assistant secretary of the navy despite rather than because of Roosevelt's outspoken views on behalf of American military power.

The Spanish-American War in 1898 drew Roosevelt out of the shadows of appointive office and into the limelight of electoral politics to play the nation's hero. As self-appointed leader of the Rough Riders, the First Regiment of the United States Cavalry Volunteers, he caught the fancy of a patriotic public that

followed with keen interest his dramatic if somewhat superfluous exploits in
charging up San Juan Hill, pausing now and then to exult over all "those damned
Spanish dead" as he rallied his disorderly troops. Disembarking to the tune of
"There'll Be a Hot Time in the Old Town Tonight," he was promptly elected
governor of New York and as quickly discomfited party bosses by taking a firm
progressive stand on a state factory inspection act and on another law regulating
the hours of state employees. "If there is going to be any solution of the big social
problems of the day," he warned his supporters, "it will come, not through a
sentimental parlor socialism, but through actually taking hold of what is to be
done working right in the mire." Republican leaders in New York, however,
were content to lift their governor out of the slough of reform politics and into
the clean and safe office of the vice-presidency, a piece of political miscalculation
made clear to them by an assassin's bullet.

In seeking to learn what kind of President they had acquired Americans did
not lack for answers, for Roosevelt had strong opinions on every conceivable
subject and delighted in publishing them in pungent and readable phrases. The
objects of presidential scrutiny ranged from the novels of Emile Zola (which he

THE TWO SIDES OF THEODORE
ROOSEVELT
Surrounded by the paraphernalia
of patriotism, Roosevelt campaigns
in New Castle, Wyoming, in 1903.
The more reflective man appears
in the doorway of his Dakota
ranch-house. (*Left, Library of
Congress; right, Theodore Roosevelt
Collection, Harvard College Library.*)

generally disliked) to the "full baby carriage" (which he heartily endorsed); and his advice ranged from conduct becoming both football players and would-be reformers ("Don't flinch, don't foul, hit the line hard!") to what one observer called an "unflagging approval of the Ten Commandments." A vigorous intellectual himself, with interests in birds and political bosses, trusts and big game, divorce and "practical idealism," Roosevelt collected hundreds of willing contributors to a mind already well stocked with ideas that he regularly assembled in print—not writing with a pen, as one reader put it, so much as charging with it.

Roosevelt's forceful and sometimes contradictory opinions revealed two distinct personalities. The first one was once described by a New York boss as "the most indiscreet guy I ever met," the keeper of the national conscience always ready to speak his mind. This public Roosevelt served as the confident spokesman of an aggressive American nationalism—prophet of a coming Anglo-Saxon supremacy, celebrant of military valor, unblushing advocate of power politics, and true believer in the American mission to order the affairs of the rest of the world. The national hero—"Teddy," a name he disliked—looked the part. With pince-nez adorning a bulbous nose, toothy grin stretched tight in a near grimace, a full square face with its several chins resting on heavyset shoulders, and reedy voice and pump-handle gestures, he was a cartoonist's dream!

In the role of the mad American of his generation, as he has been called, Roosevelt could and frequently did talk great nonsense. He lashed out at "radical fanatics" and the "lunatic fringe" of soft-headed reformers with equal contempt. "Sentimental humanitarians" he denounced as "a most pernicious body, with an influence for bad hardly surpassed by that of the professional criminal classes." He stressed the importance of "good blood" flowing in the veins of well-bred, self-denying gentlemen. He predicted race suicide for any of the world's people who preferred "effeminacy of character" to the "rougher and manlier virtues." For handling mobs he recommended "taking ten or a dozen of their leaders out, standing . . . them against a wall, and shooting them dead." For anarchists and socialist agitators a similar prescription—troops supplied with real bullets and "the most wholesome desire to do them harm." Americans, whether delighted or appalled by such balderdash, recognized in Roosevelt the authentic American hero, the compulsive man of action who shot from the hip and whose motto read: "Get action; do things; be sane."

The other Roosevelt, unlike the trigger-happy dispenser of justice, was a thoughtful if highly partisan student of American history with a keen appreciation of the original work of the Founding Fathers. Young progressives entering the political arena after 1900 with credentials from the new university brought with them training in new disciplines like economics and sociology. But for the slightly older progressive leaders, the study of history was still the primary tool for examining American society. Despite the rapid growth of "scientific history" in the nation's graduate schools and the appearance of the specialized monograph, much of the popular history written after 1880 continued to be the work of gentleman amateurs like Roosevelt himself, or his friends Henry Adams and the retired industrialist James Ford Rhodes, who measured the achievements and noted the shortcomings of nineteenth-century American democracy. The thrust of much of this popular history was towards political nationalism and social conservatism, whether in John Fiske's account of the Founding Fathers' rescue operation during the "critical period" or Henry Adams's search for the principles of "scientific government" in his magnificent nine-volume history of the administrations of Jefferson and Madison, or in Roosevelt's hymns to national valor in *The Naval War of 1812* and *The Winning of the West*.

This reflective, historically minded Roosevelt was the first President after Lincoln and the last of the moderns with an understanding of the eighteenth century. Beneath his dramatic account of America's rise to greatness lay a clear grasp of the original Federalist design and the men who fashioned it. National greatness, then as in his own time, seemed to Roosevelt to rest on the "power to attain a high degree of social efficiency," by which he meant "love of order" and the "capacity to subordinate the interests of the individual to the interests of the community." The Federalists, led by farseeing nationalists like Hamilton and Gouverneur Morris, had tried to teach the first Americans the same lessons that his own generation had just learned, that "the sphere of the State's action may be vastly increased without in any way diminishing the happiness of either the many or the few."

The American people, Roosevelt was convinced, had been given the wrong

"TEDDY" CORRECTS THE
HISTORICAL RECORD

George Washington is now "*Second* in war, *second* in peace, and *second* in the hearts of his countrymen." (*Library of Congress*.)

directions by a demagogic Jefferson and had drifted steadily towards the smashup
of the Civil War even as they expanded and enriched their domain. From Jefferson and his Jacksonian heirs they had acquired the illusions of little government
and the self-regulating moral order. Despite their magnificent material accomplishments in filling out a continent and building an industrial empire they had
failed to devise the political means of managing it. Only briefly during Lincoln's
war administrations had Americans caught a glimpse of true national unity and
the statesmanship required to create it. With the onset of the Great Barbecue
the original statesman's question "Will it work?" had given way to the commercial
demand "Does it pay?" and the national energy had been squandered in money
grubbing. One fact was clear at last—that Americans had to "abandon definitely
the *laissez-faire* theory of political economy, and fearlessly champion a system of
increased Governmental control." The opening years of the twentieth century,
Roosevelt was sure, represented "an era of federation and combination" that had
been foreshadowed by the age of the Founding Fathers. The President, like his
Federalist mentors, deplored class politics and called for the rule of enlightened
men of integrity whom, for the moment, he identified with the better half of the
Republican party. But wherever found, the disinterested patriot held the key to
the future. "A simple and poor society can exist as a democracy on the basis of
sheer individualism. But a rich and complex society cannot so exist. . . ." By the
time Roosevelt took over the presidency, he had acquired a clear definition of his
role as general manager of the United States even though the details of his plan
for its "orderly development" emerged only gradually from the recesses of his
conservative mind.

"Wise Radicalism and Wise Conservatism"— The Square Deal

The Roosevelt presidency saw the establishment of the regulatory principle
and the arrival of twentieth-century administrative government. What Roosevelt
and the country came to call the Square Deal, as he campaigned for reelection
in 1904, began as a loose collection of proposals for regulating national economic
development. The President inherited from Gilded Age Republicanism an old
guard of party conservatives who had built their stronghold in the Senate, where
they kept firm control over the legislative process and saw to it that any President
followed their dictates. Roosevelt was immediately forced to bargain with their
leader, Senator Nelson W. Aldrich of Rhode Island, and to agree to keep his
hands off the tariff question in exchange for a limited freedom to pursue his
interventionist concerns elsewhere. These concerns, like the interests of several
of his progressive followers, centered on the trusts.

Roosevelt shared the progressives' ambivalent views of big business. "Nothing
of importance is gained," he admitted in reviewing his policy of regulation, "by
breaking up a huge inter-State and international organization which has not

offended otherwise than by its size. . . . Those who would seek to restore the days of unlimited and uncontrolled competition . . . are attempting not only the impossible, but what, if possible, would be undesirable." Roosevelt followed most progressive thinking in considering behavior rather than mere size of the new conglomerates the test of their social utility, and in declaring it the job of the federal government to require them to operate "in the interest of the general public," whatever that might mean. To ensure their proper conduct and prevent them from fixing prices and manipulating the market, he proposed a watchdog agency modeled on the Interstate Commerce Commission, an appointive body staffed by "trained administrators, well known to hold the scales exactly even in all matters. . . ." After a sharp skirmish with big business and its spokesmen in Congress, he succeeded in 1903 in establishing the Bureau of Corporations within the new Department of Labor and Commerce to police business practices and report its findings to the public.

Publicity formed the keystone of Roosevelt's regulatory arch, and he himself perfected the art of disclosure in launching a series of actions under the Sherman Act, advising the Beef Trust of his intentions to "Destroy the Evils in Trusts, But Not the Prosperity" and insisting publicly on settling in the Northern Securities Case "the absolutely vital question" of federal power to regulate the trusts. The Northern Securities Company, together with its partners in monopoly, the United States Steel Company and the American Tobacco Company, Roosevelt considered potential forces for evil. While it was clearly impossible to "restore business to the competitive conditions" of the middle of the previous century, he considered it essential for the federal government to maintain "strict supervision" of the trust to see that it did not go wrong.

In applying his interventionist strategy, Roosevelt gave the signal to the Department of Justice in 1902 to move against J. P. Morgan's railroad combine. Morgan, he recalled with relish, "could not help regarding me as a big rival operator who intended to ruin all his interests or else could be induced to come to an agreement and ruin none." But it was power that concerned the President, who viewed the clash as one between rival sovereignties. The Supreme Court, in upholding the government's case against the railroad merger, gave Roosevelt his precedent. In the E. C. Knight case, he announced with obvious satisfaction, the Court had erroneously decided that the federal government lacked the power to break up dangerous combinations. "This decision I caused to be annulled." He failed to add what soon became obvious—that he had not thereby annulled the force of the merger movement.

Roosevelt more nearly approximated the progressive ideal of government by administration and arbitration in his handling of labor problems which he also approached with a divided mind. The test of his opinion on unions, strikes, and injunctions came early in his first administration, when the United Mine Workers struck against the anthracite coal operators, a confrontation that alarmed the whole country and provided Roosevelt with welcome public support. The miners, led by the canny union leader John Mitchell, demanded a pay increase and an eight-hour day along with acknowledgement of their right to organize the coal industry. George Baer, president of the Reading Railroad, bungled the case for the operators from the outset. He proclaimed it his "religious duty" to defeat the strikers, insisting that "the rights and interests of the laboring men will be protected and cared for—not by labor agitators, but by Christian men to whom God in his infinite wisdom has given control of the property interests of the country." Roosevelt, his interventionist hand strengthened by the obstinacy of the operators, moved quickly by calling for an investigation by his labor commissioner and using his findings to force the coal companies to compromise. When they refused, Roosevelt ordered both parties to a conference in Washington, where the operators, under the presidential threat to send in troops, finally agreed to an arbitrational panel. The Anthracite Coal Strike Commission awarded a 10 percent pay increase and a reduction in hours to the miners while refusing their demand for a closed shop. Once again, as in regulating the trusts, it was principle and procedure—the orderly disposition of grievances by disinterested men—that concerned the President.

Roosevelt's views on organized labor mirrored his convictions on big business: the ultimate test for both sides was a willingness to furnish order and stability of their own volition. If trusts tended to threaten the balance of economic power with their irresponsible aggrandizements, Roosevelt reasoned, labor also could prove disruptive and greedy. If there were "good" and "bad" trusts, there were also dependable labor leaders like Samuel Gompers and dangerous visionaries like Eugene Debs. In either case, he concluded, it was the President who had to distinguish legitimate demands from crackpot notions, and the only standard he could finally invoke was conduct. "Where in either one or the other, there develops corruption or mere brutal indifference to the rights of others, and short-sighted refusal to look beyond the moment's gain, then the offender, whether union or corporation, must be fought." Since it was the government that would have to do the fighting, the President as its principal officer must avail himself of every opportunity to consolidate his power. Roosevelt missed few such oppor-

PORK-PACKING IN CINCINNATI

The Meat Packing Act was aimed at established practices and methods like those shown in this engraving. (*The Cincinnati Historical Society.*)

tunities. "I don't think that any harm comes from the concentration of power in one man's hands," he protested to his critics, "provided the holder does not keep it for more than a certain definite time, and then returns to the people from whom he sprang." Yet winning presidential power, he would learn, was easier than relinquishing it.

Roosevelt's theory of expanded executive power proceeded logically from his belief that only "a great exertion of federal authority" could meet the needs of all the people. The most vulnerable members of a still largely unregulated commercial society were American consumers, who needed all the help they could get. In the field of consumer legislation as in his negotiations with big business and labor Roosevelt assumed the leadership of forces that had already begun to organize by 1900. The Pure Food and Drug Law, for example, passed in 1906, was the result of a carefully orchestrated public outcry and shrewd presidential timing. The law, limited though it was in providing coverage and effective procedures, capped a strenuous campaign for effective legislation by Harvey Wiley, chief chemist of the Department of Agriculture, who twice had seen his recommendations accepted in the House only to languish in the Senate, where the food and drug interests held court. Aided by a series of lurid exposés furnished by the Muckrakers, Roosevelt finally collected the votes needed to prohibit the manufacture and sale of misbranded or adulterated foods and drugs, a power wielded cautiously ever since.

Support for the Meat Packing Act (1906) also came from consumers, many of whom learned of the appalling conditions in the industry from Upton Sinclair's sensational novel *The Jungle*. In indicting the packers Sinclair traced the shipment from prairie to slaughterhouse of cows "that developed lumpy jaw, or fell sick, or dried up of old age," carcasses "covered with boils that were full of matter."

It was a nasty job killing these, for when you plunged your knife into them they would burst and splash foul-smelling stuff into your face. . . . It was enough to make anybody sick, to think that people had to eat such meat as this; but they must be eating it—for the canners were going on preparing it, year after year.

Though annoyed by Sinclair's fictionalized account, Roosevelt promised him: "The specific evils you point out shall, if their existence be proved, and if I have the power, be eradicated." An investigation by the commissioner of labor verified most of Sinclair's charges in a fact-studded report, which the President, indulging in a calculated bit of blackmail, threatened to release unless the packers accepted minimum regulation. The final bill, like most of Roosevelt's Square Deal legislation, represented a series of trade-offs—increased appropriations for inspection against removing inconvenient requirements for enforcement—and left the matter of appeal to the courts in what the President called "purposeful ambiguity." Once the industry had accepted the legitimacy of any form of federal regulation, the big packers welcomed those requirements that could be expected to drive out their small competitors. For his part Roosevelt was perfectly willing to compromise on details in order to gain the principle of federal control.

In an eagerness to sacrifice specifics for precedent, Roosevelt frequently disappointed his more determined progressive supporters who complained that he gave in too easily on points that might have been won with more determination. In the tug of war over the Hepburn Act regulating railroad rates they appear to have won their case. The Elkins Act (1903), a piece of symbolic legislation supposedly prohibiting discriminatory rebates, had been drafted by the railroad senators who refused to grant the government effective control over rate making, and Roosevelt now meant to acquire this authority. Since transportation lay at "the root of all industrial success," he explained, the need for an "orderly system" was obvious. "It is far better that it should be managed by private individuals than by the government," he admitted. "But it can only be so managed on condition that justice be done the public."

Effective regulation basically meant strengthening the Interstate Commerce Commission by investing it with the power to fix rates and make them stick, and this an administration measure passed by the House in 1905 was designed to do. In the Senate, however, Roosevelt's plans for securing what he called "additional power of an effective kind" met the stubborn opposition of Aldrich and his group of railroad senators, who decided to teach the President a lesson in the limits of executive power. Aldrich and his conservatives quickly bottled up the bill in committee, where they conducted lengthy hearings for the benefit of its enemies. Roosevelt tried a second time the next year with another bill, this one sponsored by Representative William P. Hepburn of Ohio, empowering the ICC to set reasonable rates after hearing complaints from shippers. Again Aldrich stepped in, allowed the bill to go to the floor without Republican endorsement, and looked on with detachment as one amendment after another stripped the bill of its original intent. Roosevelt countered with a hastily assembled coalition of faithful Republicans and disgruntled Democrats, only to see it collapse; he then reversed his field and managed to win over enough moderate Republicans to force Aldrich to a compromise. The final version of the Hepburn bill increased the powers of the ICC but left intact the injunction against enforcing new rates in cases under court appeal. At best the President had won a limited victory.

Roosevelt's critics accused him of violating his own standards of political morality in accepting considerably less than half a loaf. In fact the terms agreed to by the railroads and their representatives entirely satisfied him. "I want to get something through," he told Senator LaFollette, who correctly pointed out that without actual physical evaluation of railroad properties the ICC could hardly be expected to supervise the setting of rates. To those doubters who insisted that the Hepburn Act did not go far enough the President expounded his own philosophy of reform: "I believe in the men who take the next step; not those who theorize about the two-hundredth step." With the Hepburn Act the President and his progressive contingent administered a mild corrective but gained a principle.

In the case of conservation, the last main item on the Square Deal agenda, compromise again weakened principle. Though Roosevelt himself was a nature lover and preservationist by inclination, he abandoned the tradition of Thoreau and John Muir for a developmentalist strategy designed for the multiple use of the nation's natural resources. "We are prone to speak of the resources of this country as inexhaustible; this is not so," he informed a reluctant Congress in his annual message of 1907. Calling on citizens to look ahead to "the days of our children," he warned against the waste and destruction that would "result in undermining . . . the very prosperity" that ought to go down to them "amplified and developed." Yet his formula for conservation remained the same as for other national needs: expert advice from scientists committed to development rather than preservation, and a permissive governmental oversight of private interests.

These long-term limitations were obscured for the moment in the flurry of executive actions during his second term as he added 43 million acres to the national forests, withdrew from entry over 2500 water power sites and 65 million acres of coal lands, and established 16 national monuments and 53 wildlife refuges. Conservation as an issue assumed crucial significance in Roosevelt's mind as he found himself blocked by a dilatory Congress from pursuing other social justice goals. He turned, accordingly, to the management of natural resources as "the fundamental problem which underlies almost every other problem in National life," the acid test of executive power. He flouted the congressional will with a "midnight proclamation" setting aside 23 new forest reserves and then threw down his challenge: "If Congress differs from me . . . it will have full opportunity in the future to take such positions as it may desire anent the discontinuance of the reserves." While Congress fumed, he moved rapidly ahead with plans for his conservation empire. His instruments consisted of bureaus and commissions operating under executive supervision and filled with geologists, hydrologists, foresters, and engineers taking their orders from Gifford Pinchot, his volatile but capable chief forester. In 1908, sensing widespread public interest, Roosevelt called the National Conservation Congress, which was attended by 44 governors and over 500 conservation experts and out of which came the National

JOHN MUIR AND HIS LUMBERMAN
ENEMIES

The naturalist and preservationist
John Muir fought, with limited
success, to save the wilderness
from the depredations of the
lumber companies. (*Above, Culver
Pictures, Inc.; right, Courtesy of the
Sierra Club.*)

Country Life Commission and the Inland Waterways Commission, deprived of congressional support but enjoying a hearty presidential blessing.

In spite of its appearance as a popular crusade Roosevelt's conservation program was less a grass-roots movement to save the environment than an executive scheme for national resource management imposed from above. The President envisioned a grand design "systematically and continuously carried forward in accordance with some well-conceived plan" in which irrigation, flood control, forestry, and reclamation would be treated as "interdependent parts of the same problem' of American regional development. He was forced to settle for much less. Government experts and lumber company executives, for example, could agree on the need for less wasteful methods of harvesting the national abundance, but they also shared a strong distaste for the purist notions of the preservationists. Moreover, the new federal agencies, understaffed and underfinanced, quickly found themselves dependent on the services and the good will of the very private interests they were charged with policing, and soon there arose a developmental accord between them that made effective regulation difficult. Small operators, whose reputation for gouging the landscape was well earned, were sometimes driven out, but the large concerns continued to swap their expertise for the privilege of exploiting national resources under a government seal of approval. From the perspective of three-quarters of a century Roosevelt's national conservation program, like the original Federalist partnership between wealth and government, appears to have assumed rather than protected the public interest which it identified with the welfare of private groups.

The Limits of Neofederalism

Roosevelt embarked for Africa in the spring of 1909, leaving in the White House his hand-picked successor, the ponderous William Howard Taft, to "carry on the work substantially as I have carried it on," by which he meant steering both party and country between the reactionary policies of Nelson W. Aldrich and the "fool radicalism" of insurgents like Robert LaFollette. In many ways the conservation issue, soon to give Taft the first of his numerous political headaches, symbolized both the success and the limitations of Roosevelt's attempt to forge a new national purpose. Central to his plan was infusing the American electorate with the meaning of national unity and strong government, an educational task Roosevelt had performed admirably for seven years. The conservation campaign, which gradually moved to the center of the progressive consciousness, had meant a fight against sectionalism, states' rights, business particularism, and a Congress that gave them voice. To check these divisive forces and hold the allegiance of his reform followers Roosevelt revitalized the presidential office and buttressed it with new concepts of civic duty and loyalty. "I believe in a strong executive; I believe in power. . . ," he announced and then proceeded to use his power in ways that no President since Lincoln had contemplated. "Under this interpretation of executive power," he boasted in summing up his accomplishments, "I did or caused to be done many things not previously done. . . . I did not usurp power, but I did greatly broaden the use of executive power." To aid him in his work of executive renovation, he drew heavily from the ranks of progressive experts and professionals whose cause of scientific government he championed with enthusiasm. His reform program, for all its timid approach to the regulatory principle and its deference to vested interests, marked at least a step toward the orderly republic he envisioned.

If Roosevelt's utopia still lay well over the horizon in 1909, it was because he intentionally set conservative limits to the application of governmental power, and in the last analysis firmly believed in the democratic process, guided though it might be. Although he chafed under the restraints placed on him by his party and a laggard Congress, he managed both of them with consummate skill, alternately bullying and cajoling both but breaking with neither. In negotiating his limited reforms he was willing more often than not to take the shell and leave the kernel, concerned as he was with winning a principle. Yet his presidency was no mere exercise in educational politics. Roosevelt wanted results that the country would accept, and to get them he willingly used traditional political methods. When he left office, these results remained clearly etched in the minds of his progressive followers. He had raised his office to its twentieth-century position of dominance. He had laid the foundation for a governmental bureaucracy and collected the presumably disinterested professionals to manage it. And finally, he had preached with unflagging zeal the traditional virtues of altruism, integrity, and independence as indispensable to the new citizenship.

Further than this neither Roosevelt nor the nationalist-minded progressives could well go. For it was the continuing engagement in the political process—the on-going encounter with power to which he called his supporters—that all along defined his concept of the strenuous life and formed the core of his appeal for reform. Roosevelt spoke for progressives everywhere in demanding the return to service of "the man of business and the man of science, the doctor of divinity and the doctor of law, the architect, the engineer and the writer," all of whom owed a "positive duty to the community, the neglect of which they cannot excuse on any plea of their private affairs." The ordinary citizen, "to whom participation in politics is a disagreeable duty," had long since been defeated by the "organized army" of political hacks. Now, Roosevelt and the progressives believed, it was time to try the *extra*ordinary citizen wherever he could be found. Neither he nor they would have been surprised to learn that the average citizen in the common walks of life was already taking less rather than more interest in politics if the act of voting were any test. Voter turnout, which in the Gilded Age had averaged nearly 80 percent in presidential years and over 60 percent in off years, fell a full 15 percent after 1900. Whether disenchanted with the prospects of a managed republic that progressive reformers held before them or simply because they were discovering their most pressing concerns outside the political arena, the fact was that fewer Americans were troubling themselves with the duty of taking what Roosevelt called "their full part in our life."

Here indeed lay the outermost reaches of Roosevelt's progressive domain. If Jefferson's political formula had long since proved hopelessly inadequate for managing an industrial society, his original estimate of the diverse sources of American energy had not. Jefferson, never inclined to overestimate the fragility of American society, had counted the advantages as well as the dangers of sectional division, religious variety, ethnic diversity, and even class disagreement. With Roosevelt's retirement these forces of social and cultural pluralism began to take revenge on his promise of national unity as if to fulfill the original Jeffersonian pledge, first shaking the party structure and then disrupting the national social consensus which Rooseveltian progressivism had attempted to construct. In a revived Democratic party the American people would find a different variety of progressive reform, and in Woodrow Wilson a very different kind of leader.

CONEY ISLAND, 1905

The original wonderland. (*Culver Pictures, Inc.*)

Suggested Readings

An assessment of progressivism properly begins with Benjamin Parke DeWitt, *The Progressive Movement* (1915), a contemporary account that emphasizes structural reforms. John Chamberlain, *Farewell to Reform: The Rise, Life and Decay of the Progressive Mind in America* (1932), records the New Deal disillusionment with early twentieth-century reform nostrums, and Otis L. Graham, Jr., *An Encore for Reform: The Old Progressives and the New Deal* (1967), explains the opposition of many of the progressives to later and (to them) more drastic reforms. Harold U. Faulkner, *The Quest for Special Justice, 1898–1914* (1931), defines the movement as a liberal response to social problems incident to rapid industrialization and urbanization. Read together, George E. Mowry, *The Era of Theodore Roosevelt, 1900–1912* (1958), and Arthur S. Link, *Woodrow Wilson and the Progressive Era, 1900–1917* (1954), provide an excellent survey of the politics of the Progressive period. Robert H. Wiebe, *Businessmen and Reform* (1962), and Gabriel Kolko, *The Triumph of Conservatism* (1963), make parallel observations concerning the role of businessmen in the progressive enterprise but draw different conclusions. Recent interpretive essays include William L. O'Neill, *The Progressive Years: America Comes of Age* (1975); Lewis L. Gould, ed., *The Progressive Era (1973)*; and David M. Kennedy, ed., *Progressivism: The Critical Issues* (1971).

Still the best discussions of muckraking are two older works: Louis Filler, *Crusaders for American Liberalism* (1938), and C. C. Regier, *The Era of the Muckrakers* (1932), which should be supplemented by David M. Chalmers, *The Social and Political Ideas of the Muckrakers* (1964). Peter Lyon, *The Life and Times of S.S. McClure* (1963), and Harold S. Wilson, *McClure's Magazine and the Muckrakers* (1970), provide readable accounts of the career of the pioneer muckraking editor. Arthur Weinberg and Lila Weinberg, eds., *The Muckrakers* (1961), and Harvey Swados, ed., *Years of Conscience: The Muckrakers* (1962), cover a wide range of muckraking reporting. For the autobiographical accounts of two of the leading journalists, see Lincoln Steffens, *The Autobiography of Lincoln Steffens* (1931), and Ida M. Tarbell, *All in the Day's Work* (1939).

There are several good state studies of progressivism—among them George E. Mowry, *The California Progressives* (1951); Robert S. Maxwell, *LaFollette and the Rise of Progressivism in Wisconsin* (1956); Herbert Margulies, *The Decline of the Progressive Movement in Wisconsin, 1890–1920* (1968); Ransom E. Noble, *New Jersey Progressivism before Wilson* (1946); Richard M. Abrams, *Conservatism in a Progressive Era: Massachusetts Politics, 1900–1912* (1964); Hoyt L. Warner, *Progressivism in Ohio* (1964); Irwin Yellowitz, *Labor and the Progressive Movement in New York State, 1897–1916* (1965); Robert F. Wesser, *Charles Evans Hughes: Politics and Reform in New York State, 1905–1910* (1967). David Thelen, *Robert LaFollette and the Insurgent Spirit* (1976), is a brief biography of an influential Progressive leader.

Biographies of other major political figures in the Progressive era are numerous. For Roosevelt, see the lively but biased Henry Pringle, *Theodore Roosevelt: A Biography* (rev. ed., 1956); also consult the more judicious William H. Harbaugh, *The Life and Times of Theodore Roosevelt* (1961), the brief but perceptive essay by John Morton Blum, *The Republican Roosevelt* (1954), and George E. Mowry, *Theodore Roosevelt and the Progressive Movement* (1946). G. Wallace Chessman, *Theodore Roosevelt and the Politics of Power* (1969) is a short, balanced account. On Taft, Henry Pringle, *The Life and Times of William Howard Taft* (2 vols., 1939) completes his account of the two Republican Presidents; a more useful study is Donald E. Anderson, *William Howard Taft* (1973). Norman Wilensky, *Conservatives in the Progressive Era: The Taft Republicans of 1912* (1965), is a good study of the Republican regulars, and James Holt, *Congressional Insurgents and the Party System, 1909–1916* (1969), covers the careers of leading Insurgents. Biographies of other important figures include Alpheus T. Mason, *Brandeis: A Free Man's Life* (1946); Paolo E. Coletta,

William Jennings Bryan (3 vols., 1964–69); Lawrence W. Levine, *Defender of the Faith: William Jennings Bryan The Last Decade* (1965); Dexter Perkins, *Charles Evans Hughes and American Democratic Statesmanship* (1956); Richard Lowitt, *George W. Norris: The Making of a Progressive* (1963); John A. Garraty, *Right-Hand Man: The Life of George W. Perkins* (1960); Richard Leopold, *Elihu Root and the Conservative Tradition* (1954); M. Nelson McGeary, *Gifford Pinchot: Forester-Politician* (1960).

Progressive issues have been exhaustively treated in numerous recent works. James H. Timberlake, *Prohibition and the Progressive Crusade, 1900–1920* (1963), explores connections between progressive politics and moral reform. Jack Holl, *Juvenile Reform in the Progressive Era* (1971), examines a hitherto neglected aspect of progressivism. The progressive concern with eugenics and birth control is described in Donald K. Pickens, *Eugenics and the Progressive Era* (1971); Mark H. Haller, *Eugenics: Hereditarian Attitudes in American Thought* (1963); and David Kennedy, *Birth Control in America: The Career of Margaret Sanger* (1970). C. Roland Marchand, *The American Peace Movement and Social Reform, 1898–1918* (1973), traces the varied fortunes of the progressive advocates of peace. Changing patterns of morality emerge clearly from William L. O'Neill, *Divorce in the Progressive Era* (1967), and crucial developments in progressive education from Lawrence Cremin, *The Transformation of the School: Progressivism in American Education, 1876–1956* (1961). Samuel P. Hays, *Conservation and the Gospel of Efficiency* (1959), provides a revisionist account of the conservation movement, and James Penick, Jr., *Progressive Politics and Conservation: The Ballinger-Pinchot Affair* (1968), effectively recounts an imbroglio. Albro Martin, *Enterprise Denied: Origins of the Decline of American Railroads, 1897–1917* (1971), reverses a number of long-held assumptions about the regulation and management of railroads in the Progressive era. Mary O. Furner, *Advocacy and Objectivity: A Crisis in the Professionalization of American Social Science, 1865–1905* (1975), treats perceptual contradictions inherited by Progressives.

The intellectual climate of Progressivism has been described in several excellent studies. David Noble, *The Paradox of Progressive Thought* (1958), is a stylistically dense but highly rewarding examination of representative progressive intellectuals and professionals. Charles Forcey, *The Crossroads of Liberalism: Croly, Weyl, Lippmann and the Progressive Era, 1900–1925* (1961), offers a lively account of three leading Progressive publicists. Edward Moore, *American Pragmatism* (1950), is useful for understanding the reform outlook of the Progressives. Robert W. Schneider, *Five Novelists of the Progressive Era* (1965), examines the connection between reform and new American fiction. Frederic C. Jaher, *Doubters and Dissenters: Cataclysmic Thought in America, 1885–1918* (1964), traces a persistent theme of apocalypticism in a handful of nay-sayers in the Progressive years. Thomas F. Gossett, *Race: The History of an Idea in America* (1963), and I. A. Newby, *Jim Crow's Defense* (1965), follow the history of another tenacious and socially destructive myth. The best introduction to the writing of Progressive history is Richard Hofstadter, *The Progressive Historians* (1968). R. Jack Wilson, *In Quest of Community: Social Philosophy in the United States, 1860–1920* (1968), and Jean B. Quandt, *From the Small Town to the Great Community* (1970). give accounts of still another central Progressive concept. Samuel J. Konefsky, *The Legacy of Holmes and Brandeis* (1956), examines the instrumentalist heritage. Samuel Haber, *Efficiency and Uplift: Scientific Management in the Progressive Era, 1890–1920* (1964), explains the many uses of Taylorism in reshaping Progressive values. For perceptive discussions of three key intellectuals, see David Riesman, *Thorstein Veblen: A Critical Introduction* (1963); Ralph Barton Perry, *The Thought and Character of William James* (2 vols., 1935); and Sidney Hook, *John Dewey: An Intellectual Portrait* (1939).

Reflections—sometimes illuminating, always entertaining—on the meaning of Progressivism by two active Progressives are collected in William Allen White, *The Autobiography of William Allen White* (1946), and Frederic C. Howe, *The Confessions of a Reformer* (1925).

27

Progressives and the Challenge of Pluralism

In 1910 Theodore Roosevelt, after a year's trek through Africa and the capitals of Europe, returned home to a rebellion in his own party. Once apprised of the Republican split between President William Howard Taft's regulars and his own progressive followers, the "Colonel" moved quickly to return the party to his original vision of a unified national purpose. In a speech in 1910 dedicating a state park in Osawatomie, Kansas, where John Brown had clashed with Missouri ruffians a half-century earlier, he gave his program a name—the "New Nationalism." In part, Roosevelt's speech owed its clarity to his recent reading of Herbert Croly's *The Promise of American Life* (1909), a powerful indictment of American political drift with which the former President fully agreed. But in a broader sense both Croly's lengthy analysis and the clarion call at Osawatomie summarized the arguments for an organized national society that Roosevelt had formulated years before.

It was not "overcentralization," Roosevelt announced, but "a spirit of broad and far-reaching nationalism" that must guide the American people "as a whole." The New Nationalism, putting national needs before sectional interest or personal advantage, promised to bring order out of "the utter confusion that results from local legislatures attempting to treat national issues as local issues."

After enumerating the many unfinished tasks awaiting federal action Roosevelt drove home his point with a comparison still familiar to the few aging veterans of the Grand Army in his audience. "You could not have won simply as a disorderly mob," the Rough Rider reminded them. "You needed generals; you needed careful administration of the most advanced type. . . . You had to have the administration in Washington good, just as you had to have the administration in the field. . . . So it is in our civil life."

Unfortunately for Roosevelt in 1910, administration of the most advanced type was not yet a fact, as the man who was to be his chief rival in the election of 1912 correctly sensed. Woodrow Wilson, as a Southerner and a Democrat, drew on both these traditions in sounding the principal countertheme of progressivism. Wilson, a former professor of political science and president of Princeton, currently the reform governor of New Jersey, was fully Roosevelt's match as an historian and an intellectual, and in appraising the American system in 1910 he came closer to understanding the complexity of social forces at work in the nation than either of his Republican rivals.

Whereas Roosevelt's New Nationalism called for an immediate ordering of American forces and the acquiring of new duties and habits, the New Freedom, as Wilson came to call it, offered a variant reading of progressivism as a liberation movement. Wilson envisioned an open society filled with immigrants and women as well as native-born white males, Catholics and Jews along with Protestants, reformers together with politicians, and visionaries of all sorts to balance the offerings of self-proclaimed realists. In the election year 1912 the broader strokes of Wilson's New Freedom seemed to present a truer picture of American life than the more stylized renderings of the New Nationalists. But it remained to be seen whether the Democratic party, emerging from sixteen years of enforced retirement, could succeed in turning its estimate of the "generous energies" of the American people into a political program.

Changing the Progressive Guard

By 1910 it seemed that reform had slowed, as the forces of pluralism—both social and political—applied the brakes to the progressive engine. Republicanism stood in disarray, the President besieged by liberal critics within and without the party. The Democratic party showed few signs of wanting to become a national contender again. Congress, continuing to house a bipartisan faction of conservatives, appeared in no mood to complete the tasks of building a national banking system and assembling a program of business regulation. To one side stood a watchful Supreme Court, always ready to disapprove any further advances toward the social service state.

Of all the branches of the federal government, the Supreme Court was the least responsive to the problems confronting industrial society. Although it agreed to the Roosevelt administration's attempt to break up the Northern

Securities combine and the oil and tobacco monopolies, the Court was considerably less enthusiastic about the new progressive forms of administrative government. The struggle for administrative autonomy after 1890 often seemed to be waged between a handful of justices clinging tenaciously to the right of review and a clique of frustrated congressional reformers seeking to strengthen the administrative arm of government. To disgruntled reformers the judiciary's stubborn defense of its prerogatives seemed an act of usurpation, taking away from federal agencies like the Interstate Commerce Commission the power to do their job. In late progressive memory, moreover, the Court had also declared a federal income tax unconstitutional and set severe limits on the powers of the states to enact social legislation.

Progressivism invaded the Supreme Court with the appointment of Oliver Wendell Holmes, Jr. Chosen by Roosevelt in the belief he would reeducate his colleagues in judicial restraint and bring a more enlightened view of regulatory power to the Court, Holmes was already acknowledged as the most articulate of the new legal instrumentalists. Holmes, as he had repeatedly made clear, considered the Constitution not a yardstick for measuring the shortcomings of imperfect laws but a flexible instrument for meeting the "felt necessities" of the age. For Holmes, the life of the law inhered not in absolute truth—cold, formal-

TWO VIEWS OF NEW YORK AT THE OPENING OF THE CENTURY

The New York Stock Exchange on Wall Street contrasts with
Mulberry Street on the Lower East Side. (*Library of Congress.*)

istic, and abstract — but in attributes of utility — relative, approximate, and experimental. Those justices who still professed belief in natural law Holmes
dismissed as willing captives of "that naive state of mind that accepts what has
been familiar and accepted by them and their neighbors as something that must
be accepted everywhere." As for himself, the outspoken newcomer readily admitted, "I . . . define truth as the system of my limitations and leave absolute
truth for those who are better equipped."

Holmes attempted to explain his belief in the necessity of social experimentation in the famous *Lochner* case in 1905, a decision involving a New York law
that reduced the workweek for bakers to 60 hours. In a five-to-four decision the
majority declared that the law, as another of the recent "meddlesome interfer-
ences with the rights of individuals," was unconstitutional. In his dissent Holmes
lectured his colleagues on the inadvisability of intruding their laissez-faire views
into the legal process. The Constitution, he declared, had not been intended
"to embody a particular economic theory, whether of paternalism and the organic
relation of the citizen to the state or of laissez-faire." Instead it was made for
"people of fundamentally differing views, and the accident of our finding certain
opinions natural and familiar, or novel and even shocking, ought not to conclude
our judgment upon the question whether statutes embodying them conflict with

the Constitution of the United States." In a series of similar dissents over the next two decades Holmes—together with Louis Brandeis, who joined the liberal side of the court in 1916 after an epochal confirmation battle—argued the tradition of judicial restraint against an activist conservatism of a majority intent on checking the progressive drift toward a managerial society.

Congress, frequently at loggerheads with itself after 1909, made little headway against such certainty of conservative purpose. Both the Senate and the House, in fact, saw a series of encounters between aggressive Insurgents and stubborn conservatives over tariff and reciprocity matters, conservation policy, and governmental reorganization. Without the support of the President, who chose to back the Republican regulars in their holding action against the Insurgents, the immediate prospects for further reforms grew dim.

Meanwhile Taft's personal bulk and political lethargy made an inviting target for the barbs of the Insurgents. Though he came recommended as a reformer, Taft lacked Roosevelt's concern with strengthening the federal government as well as the former President's skill in managing his party. Ponderous, stubborn, unschooled in the arts of political persuasion and with none of the Colonel's popular appeal, Taft quickly made it clear that he was no crusader.

Taft's administration, accordingly, was marked by a series of political explosions. The first one was touched off by the Pinchot-Ballinger imbroglio over conservation policy. Gifford Pinchot, "Sir Galahad of the Woods," as Harold Ickes called him, accused Taft's secretary of the interior, Richard Ballinger, of neglecting his duties, and further, of unsavory conduct in validating the Bering River coal claims that had mysteriously come into the possession of the Morgan-Guggenheim syndicate. Although a congressional investigation exonerated Ballinger of any suggestion of fraud, and though the feisty Pinchot overplayed his accusatory hand by appealing to the American public, Taft's administration lost face along with the loyalty of a sizable contingent of Roosevelt progressives.

Taft compounded his political troubles with his handling of the tariff. After promising meaningful downward revision, he backed away from the ensuing congressional donnybrook and sat by while the high-tariff forces of Aldrich and the Old Guard loaded the bill with higher schedules. To the consternation of the Insurgents the President hastened to their midwestern camp, where he pronounced the Payne-Aldrich Act the "best tariff ever passed by the Republican party."

Roosevelt watched Taft's maladroit handling of his party with growing disdain that soon hardened into conviction; "a lawyer's administration" was proving itself "totally unfit" to lead the country. For like-minded progressives, who had recently formed the Progressive Republican League, there were two choices, the first to appeal to Roosevelt to intervene in party councils in their behalf and help them replace Taft with a candidate of their own, the second and more desperate measure, to bolt the Republican party and set up shop for themselves as a reform party. By 1912, Republican progressives remained sharply divided on this question.

As the election year approached, Roosevelt himself was of two minds about the best course. For two years after his retirement he remained dubious about the prospects of any "back from Elba movement" in his behalf. On the one hand, he was convinced that under the "Taft-Aldrich-Cannon regime," as he now called it, there had been little understanding of the "needs of the country." On the other, he confessed to little enthusiasm for "staggering under a load on my shoulders through no fault of my own."

Whether Roosevelt knew it or not, he had practically declared himself available with his "New Nationalism" speech at Osawatomie in 1910 as he began to assemble the pieces of the original Square Deal into an even bolder nationalist design. Composed of plans for improved regulation of corporations, physical evaluation of railroads, a graduated income tax, a refurbished banking system, labor legislation, the direct primary plus a corrupt practices act, the former President's new program, so reassuring to his nationalist followers, seemed nothing less than revolutionary to the Old Guard. Far from closing the breach

WOMEN SWIMMING IN THE SURF, CONEY ISLAND, 1910

(*Brown Brothers.*)

between the two factions of the party, the New Nationalism speech in effect threw down the gauntlet to Taft and his conservatives.

Taft's refusal "to step out of the way of Mr. Roosevelt" along with LaFollette's rival bid for progressive support finally determined Roosevelt, and he entered the contest. Six months before convention time the Colonel announced that he would accept the offer if there were signs of "a real popular movement" in behalf of his nomination and if it were tendered to him. It never was. Taft regulars, with a secure hold on the Southern "rotten boroughs," put them to good use against their old adversary. Roosevelt's hopes at the convention rested on some 252 contested seats, at least 100 of which he needed to secure his candidacy. With the credentials committee and the whole party apparatus in the hands of the regulars he succeeded in winning exactly 14 of them. Consulting hurriedly with his financial backers, George W. Perkins and Frank Munsey, who promised to see him through his long night of opposition, Roosevelt agreed to call his own convention of the vanquished to protest Taft's grand larceny by launching an independent Progressive party.

The loyal ten thousand who gathered in the Chicago Auditorium in August 1912 to hear their leader pronounce himself as fit as a "Bull Moose" and to sing with him the "Battle Hymn of the Republic" comprised a motley collection of mavericks and reformers, nationalists and big businessmen, social workers and intellectuals, all determined to stand at Armageddon. Conspicuously absent were most of the original Insurgents, who declined to make an investment in third party politics. Although the spirit of the old progressivism enveloped the Bull Moosers at Chicago and lifted their nationalist hopes, winning the necessary votes, as the Colonel and his advisers realized, would prove another matter. As Roosevelt intoned the Eighth Commandment and called down divine judgment on his betrayers, he must have known secretly that a Democratic victory that fall was all but inevitable.

If fortune was about to shine its face on the Democratic party in the election of 1912 it gave no sign. Democrats carried their own pluralist liabilities into the convention, and chief among them was their titular head and perennial candidate, William Jennings Bryan, who had labored sixteen years to undo the damages of his ill-fated experiment in political pietism. In the center ring at the 1912 Democratic Convention stood "Champ" Clark, speaker of the House and veteran Southern politician backed by the party's agrarians; William Randolph Hearst, the demagogic publisher and would-be reformer; and Woodrow Wilson, the shining knight of New Jersey progressivism. Fresh from a series of legislative encounters that had seen the passage of a direct primary law, railroad regulation, workmen's compensation, and a corrupt practices act, Wilson represented the hopes of urban progressives. Clark upheld the time-honored particularism of the Democracy.

The Democratic Convention in Baltimore in 1912 was every bit as uproarious as the Republican Convention. Clark, armed with preconvention pledges, jumped out to an early lead, which he maintained until the Wilson contingent finally broke his hold. On the forty-sixth ballot, following some timely arrangements with Alabama Senator Oscar Underwood and a deal with Chicago boss Roger Sullivan, the deadlock was ended and Wilson won the nomination. Before the Democrats adjourned, they patched up their differences in a platform that roundly condemned Republican centralization—as all Democratic platforms had unfailingly done since Reconstruction—and advertised its own brand of progressivism guaranteed to lower tariffs, break up trusts, give the banks back to the people, and destroy all special privilege.

The Election of 1912

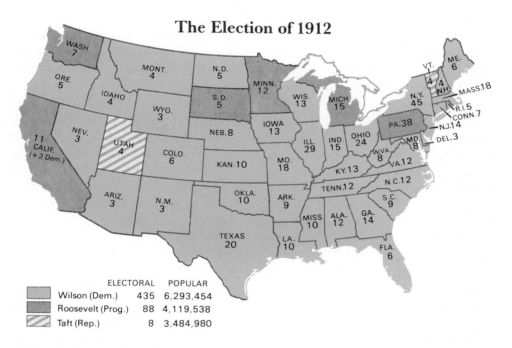

	ELECTORAL	POPULAR
Wilson (Dem.)	435	6,293,454
Roosevelt (Prog.)	88	4,119,538
Taft (Rep.)	8	3,484,980

But the heart of the Democratic promise in 1912 lay in its candidate's call for liberation from the rule of big business and big government. Wilson pictured Democratic deliverance as "coming out of a stifling cellar into the open" where the people could "breathe again and see the free spaces of the heavens." Taft's official Republicanism, according to Wilson, spelled business domination, and Roosevelt's plan for monitoring trusts simply added the power of the national government to the power of the monopolists. "We design that the limitations on private enterprise shall be removed, so that the next generation of youngsters, as they come along, will not have to become the protégé of benevolent trusts, but will be free to go about making their own lives what they will. . . ."

Whether or not American voters considered an escape from economic and political consolidation likely, enough of them—6,286,214, or 42 percent—elected Wilson President. Even with the split among Republicans, who gave Taft some 3.5 million votes, and Roosevelt's Progressive party, which garnered just over 4 million, the changing of the political guard was easily effected. It remained to be seen to what purpose.

If the intellectual roots of Roosevelt's New Nationalism reached back into the eighteenth century world of the Founding Fathers, the roots of Woodrow Wilson's New Freedom were firmly planted in Victorian verities. Wilson, who was born in Staunton, Virginia, in 1856, grew up in the heart of the Confederacy, briefly attended Davidson College, and graduated from Princeton in 1879. After a year spent studying law, for which he had no particular liking, he turned to his real interest, political science and history, studying with the great institutionalist historian Herbert Baxter Adams at Johns Hopkins and earning a doctorate there in 1886. Then came several years of climbing the academic ladder, with appointments at Bryn Mawr, Wesleyan, and Princeton where he taught for twelve years before becoming president in 1902. Wilson's books, polished though not sparkling pieces of political science and history, made a varied collection: *Congressional Government* (1885); an extended essay, *The State* (1889); a history of the Civil War years, *Division and Reunion* (1893); the five-volume *History of the American People* (1902); and *Constitutional Government in the United States* (1908).

By temperament as well as training Wilson was an academician, an educator-scholar whose calling it was to instruct a progressive generation in the science of good government. As schoolmaster to the nation, he looked the part—with a lean, angular face, a long aquiline nose adorned by a pince-nez, full pursed lips, and eyes that seemed to look through his visitors rather than at them. Distant, formal, somewhat austere in his relations with the public, he often appeared correct but cold. He recognized this reserve in himself and considered it a weakness. "I have a sense of power in dealing with men collectively," he once confessed, "which I do not feel always in dealing with them singly." There was little familiarity in the man and no feelings of camaraderie. As president of Princeton, governor of New Jersey, and chief executive, Wilson was a man one worked *for* but not *with*. Both as pedagogue and as administrator, he had a problem not so much in disciplining his followers, at which he excelled with a politeness occasionally frosty, as in gaining control over a high-voltage temper and a tendency to bridle when challenged. When opposition to his plans mounted, as it did at Princeton over the issue of the graduate school, Wilson would dig in his heels, personalize the conflict, and impute malice to his opponents while avowing the purity of his own motives.

At his best, however, Wilson could be a superb leader, directing the work of his subordinates with cool precision, holding their loyalty with ideals, and winning the American public over with his convictions of rectitude. In the few moments when his self-confidence flagged in the face of enemy attack he could be petty, vindictive, and ultimately self-destructive. But at all times he lived the role of the statesman as educator, standing before and slightly above the people to whom he sought to teach the meaning of effective government.

WOODROW WILSON CAMPAIGNING, 1912

Although his style differed markedly from Theodore
Roosevelt's, Wilson was an effective and persuasive speaker.
(*Brown Brothers.*)

   Some of the lessons Wilson taught were curiously old-fashioned—moral precepts rather than operational concepts. For him words like *liberty, justice* and
progress still possessed their mid-nineteenth-century clarity, connected as they
were in his mind with the Christian principles of "obligation," "service," and
"righteousness" that his father preached from his Presbyterian pulpit. These
were the skeletal truths around which Wilson packed such flesh-and-blood meaning as his Southern Democratic heritage afforded. His intellctual origins pre-
disposed him to an individualist and pluralist view of American politics, one in
which John Stuart Mill's definition of liberty as the absence of external restraint
ideally held sway. A Southern upbringing also left him with a generally unen-
lightened outlook on race and a quiet respect for the reasoning that had once
upheld the Lost Cause.

   Wilson sensed clearly that American life in the opening years of the twentieth

century was too amorphous, its forms too protean, to be encased in any nationalistic formula. "The life of the nation has grown infinitely varied," he reminded
his fellow Democrats in pointing to a flourishing cultural diversity. "It does not
centre now upon questions of governmental structure or of distribution of governmental powers. It centres upon the questions of the very structures and operations of society itself. . . ." In Wilson's view the most urgent American reform
task was releasing the creative impulses of a free people. Nations, he argued
with Jeffersonian logic, are renewed from the bottom up, from "the great struggling unknown masses of men" at the base of society.

> If America discourages the locality, the community, the self-contained town, she will kill
> the nation. A nation is as rich as her free communities; she is not as rich as her capital
> city or her metropolis. . . . The welfare, the very existence of the nation, rests at last
> upon the great mass of the people; its prosperity depends upon the spirit in which they
> go about their work in the several communities throughout the broad land.

What the nation most needed, Wilson announced, was the revival of the common
counsel of the working men and women in their many communities.

Americans — New and Old

Many of the men and women who did the daily work of the nation were recent
arrivals from Europe. The decade after 1900 saw the climax of a century-long
European exodus in the cresting of a wave of new immigrants from new sources.
Until roughly 1890 the great majority of immigrants had come from northern and
western Europe. Although these newcomers in their time had posed acute problems of cultural identity for native-born Amer-
icans, these paled in comparison with those
accompanying the so-called "new immigration."
In the first place the very numbers of these
newcomers appeared overwhelming to the
nativists: statistics confirmed their worst fears.
In the quarter-century before the First World
War 18 million newcomers poured down the
gangplanks, 80 percent of them from southern
and eastern Europe. In the first decade of the
century alone some 5.8 million people arrived
from Austria-Hungary, Spain, Italy, and Russia.

Another set of figures reinforced the fears of
native-born Americans. In the peak nineteenth-
century year, 1882, when more than three-
quarters of a million immigrants had disem-
barked at Atlantic ports, a third of their numbers
had come from Germany while Italy sent only
32,000 people and Russia not quite 17,000. The

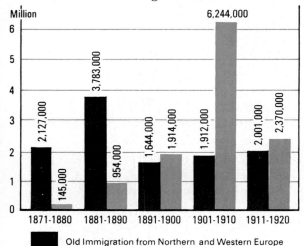

Old and New Immigration, 1871-1920

Million

6,244,000

2,127,000 · 145,000 · 3,783,000 · 954,000 · 1,644,000 · 1,914,000 · 1,912,000 · 2,001,000 · 2,370,000

1871-1880 1881-1890 1891-1900 1901-1910 1911-1920

■ Old Immigration from Northern and Western Europe
■ New Immigration from Southern and Eastern Europe

peak year in the progressive era, 1907, reversed this balance: Germany sent only 37,000 while Italy dispatched 285,000 of its citizens, the Austro-Hungarian empire another 338,000, and Russia together with the Baltic states still another 250,000 people. For the entire period 1881–1910 Italy headed the list of European exporters with 3 million immigrants. Next came the Jews, most of them from Russia, numbering about 2 million, followed by 1 million Poles by 1914. These three main groups, then, together with Magyars, Greeks, Armenians, Syrians, and Turks, attested to the results of leaving the gates ajar.

Four out of five of the new arrivals settled in the industrial cities of the Northeast and the Midwest, concentrating in areas where the jobs were. Their collective impact on these cities became clear when native-born Americans suddenly realized that 75 percent of the populations of New York, Chicago, Cleveland, and Boston were immigrants or children of immigrants. Like it or not, progressives faced a bewildering ethnic variety in the sudden presence of so many new arrivals eager to get ahead in their new land.

Economic opportunity magnetized the new immigrants as it had the old, drawing them off worn-out lands and out of the ghettos of European port cities

PASSENGERS WHO MISSED THE MAYFLOWER

Immigrants arrive in steerage. (*Culver Picture, Inc.*)

into an American setting of deprivation that at first seemed all too familiar. Once arrived, they started at the bottom of the occupational ladder doing the nation's dirty work—construction, mining, smelting, factory work, and domestic service. They usually arranged themselves in tight ethnic communities around their work, finding security in an enforced segregation. This pattern of inner-city concentration fed old-stock American fears even as it removed the "foreigners" from the suburban field of vision. Frequently, too, the newcomers elbowed their predecessors out of their neighborhoods, sending them further out along the city's extremities.

Old-stock Americans tended to assign the new arrivals a national identity that most of them did not yet possess. The vast majority of the "new immigrants" came from cultures that had long been narrowed to the locale, the region, or the village. However compact and homogeneous the immigrant enclaves in American cities seemed to outsiders, they were in fact fractured into blocks of ethnic and religious experience, each neighborhood boasting its own churches and patron saints, feast days and civic associations. In trying to impose an institutional order on their new surroundings, the new Americans mirrored the progressive search for order, but under adverse conditions and with improvised methods. By 1910, urban America had become a patchwork quilt of tightly knit and sharply contrasted peoples and cultures.

Packed into slums, exploited by native-born employers and their own contractors alike, harassed by nativist groups and earlier arrivals, fighting among themselves for a foot on the economic ladder, millions of the new immigrants at first lived marginal lives close to the edges of defeat. The going rate for piecework for young Jewish girls in New York's garment industry was 8¢ an hour. Slovak steel workers in Pittsburgh sweated a 60-hour week for $12.50. A German husband and wife team on Tenth Street on the lower East Side in 1900 could expect $3.75 for every 1000 cigars they wrapped. By working 15 hours a day the two of them could turn out 3000 cigars. Leisure for cultural and educational pursuits was a scarce commodity in America's Little Italys and Little Warsaws.

Slowly these immigrant communities acquired a measure of stability. They developed lively subcultures of their own through churches, foreign language newspapers, service organizations like the Sons of Italy and the Pan-Hellenic Union, and a growing variety of social agencies and immigrant aid societies. Edward Corsi, who became Hoover's commissioner of immigration and naturalization, recalled the clotted tenement-house life of New York's East Harlem with "five thousand human beings in one city street, as many as fifteen to a four-room flat; two, three, and even four hundred to a tenement intended for fifty." Twenty-seven nationalities all told, with Chinese laundrymen, Syrian shopkeepers, and gypsy phrenologists tossed in for good measure. On the East River the Italians; along Pleasant Avenue, the Poles, Austrians, and Hungarians; over on the West Side, Jewish shopkeepers besieged by Turks and Spaniards. And descending from the north like a new Mongol horde driving all before them, the blacks, turn-

The Lower East Side

The Jewish Immigrant District of New York City

1910

Madison Square

Union Square

GREENWICH

VILLAGE

Wholesale Garment District

Galicians

Rumanians

Levantines

Hungarians

Russians

City Hall

East River

Houston St. Ferry

Williamsburg Bridge, 1903

Grand St. Ferry

Manhattan Bridge 1909

Brooklyn Bridge 1882

East R.

- - - - Hungarian Jews
- · - · - Galician Jews (From Northwest Spain)
- - - - - Rumanian Jews
- ·· - ·· - Levantine Jews (From E. Mediterranean Seacoast)
———— Russian Jews

ing the retreat of the Irish and Germans into a rout. Scattered here and there were lonely islands of old-stock Americans "like refugees in exile."

Corsi's East Harlem supported a lusty popular culture, not the imposing façades of "opera houses, theaters, and hotels," but the reenactment of Old World pageants in cafes, rathskellers, spaghetti houses, cabarets, and dance halls. "We have Yiddish theaters and Italian marionette shows, not to mention movie and vaudeville houses. Our secondhand book shops are as good as those of Paris. So are our music stores."

Mystified by the teeming variety of immigrant life, most progressive Americans fell back on increasingly irrelevant schemes for "Americanizing" the new arrivals. At dockside civic aid societies handed out pamphlets printed in English admonishing the newcomers to be "honest and honorable, clean in your person, and decent in your talk," but these scattered in the swirl of numbers like so many pious hopes. Restrictionists followed Theodore Roosevelt in deploring the "tangle of squabbling nationalities" as "the one certain way of bringing the nation to ruin," yet the fact remained that hyphenated Americanism was the only clear avenue to full citizenship. Even the hopeful immigrant Israel Zangwill, looking forward to the day of total assimilation, described a dream rather than reality. The composer-hero of Zangwill's popular play *The Melting Pot* hears the melodies for his "American symphony" in the "seething crucible—God's crucible," where a new amalgam, "the coming superman," is being forged over divine fires. Yet Zangwill told progressive audiences what they wanted to hear, not what they saw around them.

A clearer assessment of the forces of cultural pluralism came from the more reflective of the immigrants themselves, who exposed the progressive persuasion as the myth that it was. "There is no such thing as an American," a Polish priest informed the genteel social worker Emily Greene Balch. Poland, he explained, was a nation, but the United States was simply a country—in the beginning an empty land open to all comers in turn. Immigrants, according to the newly arrived Mary Antin, were just people who had missed the *Mayflower* and taken the next available boat.

A growing number of younger progressive intellectuals responded enthusiastically to the promise of cultural pluralism. In the variety and excitement of cultural clash they found an escape from the stifling middle-class gentility of Gilded Age homes. One of them, a young radical student of John Dewey's at Columbia University, Randolph Bourne, found a title for this cultural diversity— "Trans-National America"—and hailed the United States as the "intellectual battleground of the world . . . a cosmopolitan federation of national colonies, of foreign cultures, from whom the sting of devastating competition has been removed."

Bourne's concept of America as a world federation in miniature ran headlong into the barriers of exclusivist fears. The myth of the "new immigrants" assumed a variety of ugly shapes: they were dangerously illiterate and culturally deprived; they brought with them either a benighted Catholicism or private visions of the overthrow of capitalist society; they were doomed to a permanently inferior place in the Darwinian scale of races and could never master the skills democracy demanded. Amateur and professional sociologists, Cassandras all, consulted the numbers and predicted "race suicide." The sociologist Franklin Giddings announced hopefully but somewhat ambiguously that the "softening" of the traits of "preeminently an energetic, practical people, above all an industrial people" would continue as Mediterranean instincts insinuated themselves into the American character until the original Baltic and Alpine stock had become transformed into "a more versatile, a more plastic people," at once gentler and more poetic. Giddings's prophecies raised the inevitable question that a progressive reformer put in *Charities:* "Are we not, most of us, fairly well satisfied with the characteristics, mental and physical, of the old American stock? Do we not love American traits as they are?"

The Dillingham Commission placed the imprimatur of the federal government on these progressive anxieties by making an official distinction between the already assimilated "old immigration" and the patently unassimilable "new immigration." The commission, a joint House-Senate inquiry that Roosevelt appointed in 1907, took four years to complete its 42-volume report. Although it amassed much useful information on the work patterns and living conditions of immigrants, the Dillingham Commission took for its controlling assumption the need to check the flood of new arrivals, if not with a literacy test, then through a quota system. When Congress promptly obliged by passing a literacy bill in 1913, Taft vetoed it in deference to Republican employers who still found merit in a supply of cheap labor. But the quota scheme survived the prewar debate and reemerged in postwar legislation establishing strict limits. The Dillingham Report marked a reversal in American attitudes toward cultural minorities: by 1910 restrictionist hopes flared as the more cosmopolitan aims of the pluralists flickered and died.

In the case of black Americans, white fears produced an even harsher doctrine of reaction. The progressive generation had inherited most of the ingredients for a racist myth from the nineteenth century but improved the formula with new "scientific" evidence of the biological inferiority of the Negro race. Not surprisingly, the opening years of the twentieth century saw the nearly total disfranchisement of black voters in the South. Exclusionist techniques varied from state to state: poll taxes, grandfather clauses, literacy tests, white primaries— all served effectively throughout the South to bar the great majority of Negroes from the polls. Southern liberals and progressives justified the purge with a variant of the argument Northern reformers used to exclude the immigrant, that good government required the political elimination of the inferior and the unfit. The Southern progressive Edgar Gardner Murphy pronounced sentence on the civic performance of Southern blacks when he dismissed them as a "backward and essentially unassimilable people."

Most Northern liberals continued to regard the Negro as a peculiarly Southern problem, despite mounting evidence to the contrary. "The popular mind in the old free states," lamented the progressive publicist Walter Weyl, ". . . has retreated from its uncomfortable dictatorial attitude and thrown the whole matter over to the States of the South." But it was South Carolina's racist demagogue Ben Tillman who probed the softest spot in the progressive plan for regeneration,

The pioneer documentary photographer Lewis W. Hine
(1874–1940) had acquired a degree in sociology from
Columbia when in 1908 he joined the staff of the National
Child Labor Committee as investigator-photographer. For
the committee he compiled the first American photographic
documentary, "Neglected Neighborhoods of Our National
Capital," and also served as staff photographer for *Charities*
as well as for the Russell Sage Foundation whose six-volume
Pittsburgh Survey contained a number of his photographs.
Hine's primary subjects throughout the progressive years
remained children and immigrants whose drab lives and
harsh routines he caught with unforgettable clarity. (*George
Eastman House, Inc.*)

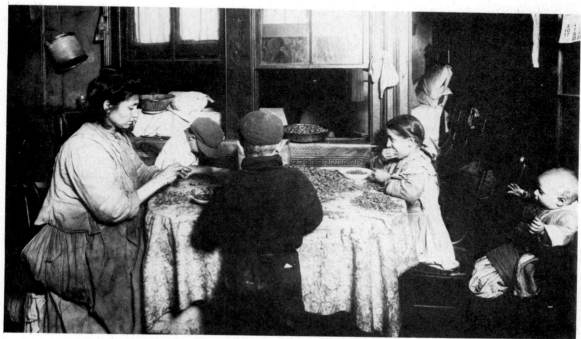

its lack of moral certainty. "Your slogans of the past—brotherhood of man and fatherhood of God—have gone glimmering down the ages," Tillman chortled. A progressive age, stripped of the moral absolutes that once sustained the abolitionist crusade, the more easily accepted the racist conclusions seemingly established by its up-to-date social science.

For the moment, however, statistics obscured the long-term meaning of the effect of industry on Southern blacks, most of whom as late as 1900 were tied to the land by tenancy and sharecropping. In that year there were less than 1 million Negroes north of the Mason-Dixon Line, and thirty years later a full 80 percent of all blacks in the United States still lived below it. Still, the intervening years saw a net gain to Northern cities of 1.4 million as even before the First World War the often illusory lure of economic opportunity and personal freedom drew blacks northward. Herded into big-city ghettos—New York's black community numbered 70,000 by the turn of the century—they were met with proscription and wholesale discrimination. As lynchings in the South slowly declined, they were replaced by their Northern counterpart, the race riot—in the small Indiana town of Greensburg in 1906; in Springfield, Illinois, two years later; and in explosive racial tensions in New York, Chicago, and Philadelphia. Blacks paid a high price for their escape from sharecropping.

Black Americans attempted to counter political proscription and economic exploitation with two limited strategies, neither very successful in overcoming white progressive prejudices. The official black spokesman, the "office broker for the race" as admiring white liberals called him, was Booker T. Washington. The son of a slave, Washington learned the gospel of self-help at Hampton Institute and put it into practice at Tuskegee, where he trained thousands of young men and women in the industrial and domestic arts. Washington presented the philosophy underlying his educational program in his famous address at the Atlanta Exposition in 1895. He urged black listeners to strike their roots in Southern soil by "making friends in every manly way of the people of all races by whom we are surrounded." To whites he offered the same suggestion, urging them to cast down their buckets among a race "whose habits you know, whose fidelity and love you have tested."

Most white liberals took Booker T. Washington to their hearts as a "credit to his race," although not all of them approved of President Roosevelt's inviting him to lunch at the White House. Washington became the symbol of the "good Negro," who knew his place and aspired only to keep it—the man of sorrows who accepted the fact of race prejudice while rejecting all its assumptions and working patiently to lift his people the few notches a dominant white society allowed them. The question Washington's program did not answer, however, was the one the Muckraker Ray Stannard Baker asked in his pessimistic analysis of American race relations, *Following the Color Line* (1908): "Does democracy really include Negroes as well as white men?"

The photographer Francis Benjamin Johnson posed this picture of a carpentry class at Hampton Institute to illustrate the kind of "useful" vocational training for blacks offered at the school. The black women going to work at the Libby, McNeill and Libby plant in Chicago during the Stockyards Strike in 1904 were probably hired as strikebreakers. (*Top, Library of Congress; bottom, Chicago Historical Society.*)

By 1900 the black progressive William E. B. DuBois, together with several Northern liberals of both races, had concluded that until Negroes gained full political rights democracy would never be theirs. Northern black leadership in the big cities appealed to a different constituency from Booker T. Washington's and offered another approach to black advancement. DuBois, a New Englander and a graduate of Harvard, followed the typical progressive route to profession-alism by studying in Berlin before returning to an academic career at Atlanta University in 1897. Like his white counterparts, he recognized the pressing need for scientific data on the actual conditions of Negro life in America. "We must not forget," he reminded his students, "that most Americans answer queries regarding the Negro a priori, and that the least that common courtesy can do is to listen to the evidence." To provide this evidence DuBois pioneered with a socio-logical study of the Philadelphia Negro, in which he presented a clear picture of life in the ghetto. In *Souls of the Black Folk* (1903) he appealed to a latent black solidarity and cultural consciousness in criticizing Washington's "gospel of work and Money." He suggested, instead, cultivating the "higher aims of life" with his plea for the "Talented Tenth," calling for programs to train and equip a black intellectual vanguard. In this early phase of his career DuBois developed an undisguised progressive program aimed at substituting "man training" for moneymaking and at cultivating "intelligence, broad sympathy, knowledge of the world" in a new elite. Increasingly after 1900 DuBois turned to the small group of progressives in the North who agreed with him in defining black issues as the need for leadership, organization, and political activism.

Although DuBois's elitist strategy and Washington's accommodationist tactics complemented each other in theory, a bitter rivalry developed between the Tuskegee Machine and the Niagara Movement of Northern radicals seeking full political and social equality. By the time the National Association for the Advancement of Colored People was founded in 1910 through the joint efforts of white neo-abolitionists like Mary Ovington and Oswald Garrison Villard and the black liberal followers of DuBois, neither moderate nor militant efforts had succeeded in denting the prejudices of most white Americans. For them the "race problem" was best solved by a system of strict segregation and the fiction of "separate but equal."

The Jeffersonian tradition of decentralization and localism worked to the distinct disadvantage of black Americans throughout the progressive years. It perpetuated sectional patterns of discrimination and fostered a national disregard for what had clearly become a fundamental challenge to democracy. Down to the New Deal of the 1930s the progressive compromise with the forces of bigotry and prejudice blocked any real hopes for a federal program to equip Negroes with political rights or to open the door for them to full economic opportunity. In the last analysis progressivism rested on racist assumptions and a supportive doctrine of localism, which had changed little since the Civil War.

The Rise of Social Feminism

The arrival of large numbers of American women on the social and industrial scene after 1900 also disrupted nationalist-progressive plans for completing the ordered society. The percentage of working women rose most spectacularly in the first decade of the century; gainfully employed women between the ages of 16 and 44 composed 21 percent of the work force in 1910. Their rapid recruitment into industry effectively dismissed the question of their suitability for factory and office work, and raised other issues in its stead. Were there certain "natural" occupations for them? Did they have the right to organize? to strike? For a raw industrial society that had not yet fashioned a general labor policy, these questions became increasingly urgent as a small group of women workers began to raise them in militant fashion after 1910.

Even more perplexing to American men in the progressive age was the question of the proper role and acceptable functions of the "New Woman," the young, educated, unmarried woman in revolt against a smothering gentility and the prospects of perpetual domesticity. In the beginning, feminist protests against an American society that seemingly offered no useful work for talented women did not threaten to disarrange the ideological formulations of progressivism. Some of the most articulate new social feminists echoed progressive demands for greater efficiency in managing American society. The radical feminist Charlotte Perkins Gilman, for example, indicted the American home for its shocking waste of human energies. The home, she scoffed, was a case of arrested development. "Among the splendid activities of our age it lingers on, inert and blind, like a clam at a horse race." By reducing the wife to a "social idiot" and subjecting the child to the constant care of an ignorant "primeval mother," the home acted as the chief deterrent to progress.

Equally subversive of the progressive program for social order was the feminist theme of liberation that Jane Addams and the legions of settlement-house women sounded in announcing the need for new social outlets for feminine energies. Addams cited not simply the inefficiencies of family arrangements but the waste of individual lives in enforced domesticity. In her widely read account of social settlements, *Twenty Years at Hull House,* she duly acknowledged the objective conditions in urban slums demanding remedial action, but also stressed the "subjective necessity" for useful work to fill the empty lives of educated women languishing in the family circle. While admitting the need to expand social democracy, she was also worried lest the feminine personality, denied a full range of experience, atrophy. Where efficiency-minded reformers like Gilman called for better organization of public resources, Jane Addams and her colleagues emphasized the release of vital creative forces.

Yet viewed as either an efficiency or a liberation movement, social feminism collected little in the way of an ideology. Even in its attempts to improve the lot of working women it mounted no concerted assault on corporate capitalism or the profit motive. Its power to unsettle an American male order stemmed from a different source. Nineteenth-century feminism had concentrated for the most part on removing legal barriers to full citizenship for women—on winning the vote and acquiring the right to hold and bequeath property. The new social feminism, fed by the ideas of European artists and intellectuals like Ibsen, Nietzsche, and Bergson, postulated a new kind of individualism and self-realization. The Western revolt against positivism and the discovery of the irrational that swept across the Atlantic in the last years of the nineteenth century provided women as well as men with new standards of social and sexual behavior not fully legitimized by the moral politcs of progressivism. It was precisely here that the challenge of feminism seemed so disquieting.

The revolt began inauspiciously as an uprising of young educated women against the concept of self-denial. When Theodore Roosevelt, as was his wont, spoke of duty as involving "pain, hardship, self-mastery, self-denial," he presumably prescribed for both sexes. It was against this male-imposed definition of duty as circumscribed by hearth and home that young middle-class women suddenly began to rebel. One of the leaders of this feminist revolt, appropriately named Lydia Commander, pointed to the decline of the Victorian ideals of humility, obedience, and self-sacrifice once "assiduously cultivated as the highest womanly virtues." Now, she declared, these qualities had fallen from grace, and the "principle of self-development" reigned supreme in the soul of the new woman. Gone too, feminists agreed, was the obsolescent notion of female innocence. "What good does it do her?" snapped Charlotte Gilman.

Subjectivity proved a two-edged sword for would-be liberated women. With the one hand it could be used to carve out blocks of experience for women that were manifestly different from men's, and with the other to cut away piled-up deprivations. The sense of victimization could lead to the demand for special protection from the oppressive force of industry—for compensatory laws against long hours, dangerous conditions, and exhausting routines. In this sense social feminism aimed not so much at equality of treatment as at special consideration. But for a more privileged class of leisured women the feminist impulse was more purely egalitarian—the demand for equal access to all the opportunities of modern life. By 1910, the "New Woman," after countless repeat performances in popular fiction and middle-class magazines, had become a stereotype. "This young person," one mother complained, "with surprisingly bad manners—has gone to college, and when she graduates is going to earn her own living . . . she won't go to church; she has views upon marriage and the birthrate, and she utters them calmly, while her mother blushes with embarrassment; she occupies herself, passionately, with everything except the things that used to occupy the minds of girls." To the late Victorian mother it seemed that her home was passing out of vogue.

One of the outlets for the growing social concerns of women before the

First World War was the women's club movement, which provided a useful if limited perspective on the problems of industrial society. The General Federation of Women's Clubs grew rapidly from an initial membership of 20,000 in 1890 to nearly a million twenty years later. The clubs were thoroughly genteel organizations, devoted, at least in the beginning, chiefly to self-culture. At no time did the federation encourage a high level of political consciousness. Nevertheless, individual branches took up issues like factory inspection and child labor, lobbied for criminal justice reforms, and even experimented with tenement-house improvements. In a variety of "study groups" middle-class women discovered an expanding range of problems: the poor quality of municipal services; urban political graft; the need for pure food and drug laws; conservation; and belatedly, the importance of the vote for women.

Women's clubs popularized rather than initiated reforms. Ultimately their most important contribution lay in their support, however tardy, for women's suffrage. Neither innovative nor consistently liberal, the General Federation of Women's Clubs did, however, succeed in shifting the interests of well-to-do women outside the home and settling them in the center of the national social spectrum.

EAST SIDE SETTLEMENT CLASS, CIRCA 1910

A settlement teacher and her pupils. (*Brown Brothers.*)

A second, more sharply focused women's organization, which gave a practical point to the humanitarian concerns of the women's clubs, was the National Consumer's League. Modeled on English precedents, the NCL grew out of the early work of the patrician charity organizer Josephine Shaw Lowell, who took up the cause of New York City's working girls late in her career. Out of her efforts in the 1890s came a small group of upper-class women who decided to use their buying power to enforce an enlightened labor policy on the city's employers. As the consumer movement spread to other cities, a national league was formed in 1899, with the remarkable administrator Florence Kelley to head it. The daughter of an abolitionist congressman, a graduate of Cornell University with advanced training in Zurich, a socialist and Illinois's first factory inspector, Florence Kelley brought impressive credentials and the skills of a superb lobbyist to her job. Under her firm guidance the National Consumers' League grew rapidly until it numbered 60 local branches in 20 states, all applying the league's White Label to approved products.

The league specialized in protective legislation for women and children, lobbying successfully for the Ten-Hour Law in Oregon and retaining Louis Brandeis to argue its constitutionality before the Court. The league also joined the campaign for establishing the Children's Bureau within the Department of Labor, and it helped its sister organization, the National Child Labor Committee, to press Congress for a child labor law. Working together in a new spirit of professionalism, the social feminists built staffs of dedicated administrators like Frances Perkins and the Goldmarks, Pauline and Josephine, who would carry their crusade against child labor and social abuse into the 1920s. These women reformers, in separating their bureaucratic methods from the profit motive, were experimenting, however provisionally, with an alternative to what the feminist Rheta Childe Dorr called the "commercial ideal" of American business.

This same spirit of education and a distaste for the commercial life also distinguished the settlement house. In contrast to England, where young men from Oxford and Cambridge took the lead in founding settlements in London's East End, women dominated the American wing of the movement from the outset. The settlements themselves, shabby remnants of a genteel society that had long ago moved out, stood in the middle of sprawling slums and quickly became the focal points for the public activities of their inhabitants. To the busy complex at Hull House, for example, or to New York's Henry Street Settlement or Boston's South End House came children of the neighborhood to nurseries and playgrounds, their mothers for classes in hygiene and domestic economy, and in the evenings, the men for lessons in English and discussions of politics.

The impulse behind settlements was religious though not sectarian, and the atmosphere in all of them—Graham Taylor's Chicago Commons, New York's University Settlement, Kingsley House in Pittsburgh—was redolent with Christian ethics. Inevitably the earnestness of young college women bent on lifting the tone of immigrant neighborhoods with lectures on Ruskin and displays of pre-Raphaelite reproductions gave rise to sneers. Thorstein Veblen dismissed the settlements as "consistently directed to the incubation, by precept and example, of certain punctilios of upper-class propriety in manners and customs." But it was not long before the settlement-house workers learned to estimate the needs of their neighbors more accurately, and cultural uplift gave way to hard practicality.

The restless energies of the residents combined with their vagueness about political means and an absence of ideology to give the settlement houses all the features of an alternative form of community. Turnover remained high, and a constant lateral mobility into the furthest reaches of the city often made them mere collecting points for members whose jobs as teachers, social workers, visiting nurses, architects, and planners kept them out in city streets. For both men and women, settlements provided a halfway house between the closed intellectual communities of college or university life and the fragmentations of a professional career, fluid arrangements of work and leisure held together by a sense of social sharing.

Education formed the core of the settlement-house experience. The educational process was initially conceived of as a one-way street down which the immigrants would march toward citizenship. Under the pressures of adversity, however, it was quickly redefined as a mutual learning experiment, one that involved genuine exchange and not simply bestowal. As Jane Addams explained to an increasingly receptive progressive public, "A settlement is a protest against a restricted view of education."

Frequently settlement-house workers borrowed and applied the progressive scientific methods of fact gathering and data analysis. And as professionals they looked out on an indeterminate world of the city, one that required continual adaptation and manipulation of means. There the similarity to progressive political reform stopped; instead of accepting specialization and compartmentalized functions they tried to transcend them or at the very least to humanize them. Their instrument was the new educational theory of John Dewey, which in defining learning as a social experience cemented together the various pieces of city life into the concept of the settlement school extending into and in turn penetrated by the larger community. The settlement-house women sought to perform their new roles as social teachers with every device at their disposal— nurseries, evening classes, lectures and lunch programs, health care and slum clearance.

When the women first founded their settlements, they carefully avoided clashes with the city bosses on the theory that urban politics was hopelessly corrupt and that their own redemptive task lay elsewhere. Soon however, they came to agree with Jane Addams that "to keep aloof from it [politics] must be to lose one opportunity of sharing the life of the community." Still, they found it difficult and often impossible to work with the unsympathetic ward boss, who distrusted them as do-gooders and rivals for the affections of his clients. Cooperation turned to confrontation over matters of garbage removal, street lighting, police protection, or the location of a neighborhood park. The most adventurous residents were driven to oppose the boss, but the contest was unequal, as Jane Addams learned to her chagrin in trying to unseat Alderman Johnny Powers in Chicago's Nineteenth Ward. She attacked Powers with every argument she could muster, capping her indictment with the charge that although he dispensed free turkeys at Christmastime he gave notoriously poor service. Yet turkeys continued to turn the political trick, and the likes of Johnny Powers generally held on to their fiefdoms.

Struggling to fend off the counterthrusts of the politicians, the settlement-house women deliberately fashioned their institutions into public forums where social opinions of every stripe could be heard. Chicago Commons, for example, featured a weekly "Free Floor Discussion" billed as "self-conscious democracy,"

SACRED MOTHERHOOD POSTER OF
THE WOMEN'S TRADE UNION
LEAGUE OF CHICAGO, 1908

(*State Historical Society of Wisconsin.*)

in which a labor leader, a college professor, an anarchist, and a businessman disposed of the future of the capitalist system. From these discussions the women themselves learned valuable political lessons as the logic connecting reform to the vote suddenly became too obvious to ignore. As Maude Nathan, an active member of the Consumers' League and a supporter of settlements, pointed out, women needed the vote to make good on their promise to improve American life. Without the franchise they were left with little more than moral suasion, while manufacturers and merchants used their voting power "to hold in terror" over the politicians. By 1910, mounting frustrations had led many of the settlement-house women to join the drive for woman's suffrage. With their discovery of the political dimension of their reform work, social feminists struck an alliance with political feminists.

The two main agencies of the suffrage movement after 1912 were the staid and cautious National American Woman Suffrage Association, headed by Carrie Chapman Catt, and its more militant offshoot, the National Women's Party, which had been organized by the formidable Quaker agitator Alice Paul. Suffragists presented two fundamentally different and even contradictory arguments. The first was well suited to the progressive temper, a conservative appeal to the instincts for order and control. Mary Putnam Jacobi, a veteran suffragist and leading woman doctor, summarized the case for women as willing instruments of political correction:

No matter how well born, how intelligent, how highly educated, how virtuous, how refined, the women of today constitute a political class below that of every man, no matter how base born, how stupid, how ignorant, how vicious, how poverty-stricken, how brutal.

The second suffragist argument singled out the interests and capabilities of women that were in need of recognition. According to this reasoning, women were uniquely endowed with humane qualities that could soften the rigors of industrial society and nurse the American polity back to health. Such was Jane Addams's explanation for women's political role: "If women have in any sense been responsible for the gentler side of life which softens and blurs some of its harsher conditions, may not they have a duty to perform in our American cities?" In arguing for the vote middle-class women could take their choice between a demand for a simple justice and the promises of a regenerative creed.

At the other end of the social spectrum stood Margaret Dreier Robins and her National Women's Trade Union League. Robins argued that the vote was essential for the working women of the nation since, she said, "The power of the police and of the courts is against them in many instances, and whenever they try to meet that expression of political power, they are handicapped because there is no force in their hands to help change it." Whatever the case for the vote for women, idealistic or purely practical, it was strengthened by the more glaring absurdities of its opponents, one of whom, a worried military officer, warned

Woman Suffrage Before the 19th Amendment

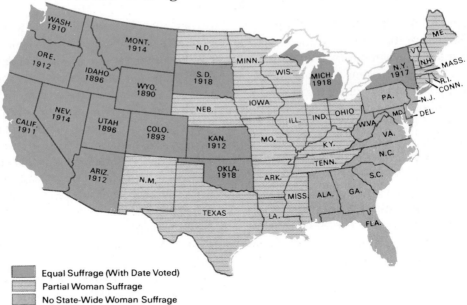

- � Equal Suffrage (With Date Voted)
- Partial Woman Suffrage
- No State-Wide Woman Suffrage

against "the dilution with the qualities of the cow, of the qualities of the bull upon which the herd's safety must depend."

The suffrage movement gathered its momentum for the assault on the federal government in the states. In 1910, Washington state gave the vote to women, and the next year California, succumbing to a high-pressure campaign, also awarded women the vote. In 1912, Arizona, Kansas, and Oregon capitulated as Theodore Roosevelt's Bull Moose party, despite the initial reservations of its leader, adopted a plank calling for national suffrage. With the presidential election of 1912 a more militant feminist strategy emerged, which concentrated on Congress and the President, neither of which was particularly sympathetic to the suffrage cause.

The leader of a small band of radicals who began to demonstrate their refusal to accept federal proscription was Alice Paul, a grimly determined feminist who had earned a doctorate at the University of Pennsylvania and spent five years in England studying Emmeline Pankhurst's disruptive tactics before returning home to try them out for herself. Intense, untiring, a stickler for principle and an able tactician, Alice Paul promptly singled out Woodrow Wilson and the occasion of his inauguration for a giant protest parade involving 5000 women, which ended in a near riot. Then, in applying the ideas of the English suffragettes, she organized an aggressive lobby, which three years later became the National Woman's party, dedicated to direct action. The National American Women's Suffrage Association, challenged by the successes of its aggressive rival, revived under Mrs. Catt's able leadership, and a reorganized board of directors redoubled its efforts to reach women at the state and local levels.

By 1917, as the country prepared for war, Wilson's administration faced two organizations of political feminists with distinctly different views of the world conflict: a small group of militants who vehemently protested American participation and demonstrated against "Kaiser Wilson" with marches and hunger strikes; and a much larger group of moderates who supported the war in the belief that peace would bring victory to women as well as to the cause of democracy. In June 1919, Congress rewarded the patience of the moderates by passing the Nineteenth Amendment, thereby giving the vote to all adult Americans regardless of sex. Yet the cause of democracy and reform, American women would soon learn, was not to be determined one way or the other by their sudden invasion of the polls. A genuine pluralist alternative to rule by male politicians never really materialized. Women, their arguments to the contrary notwithstanding, did not compose an interest group with special needs and talents, nor did their egalitarian arguments alter the course of progressivism. Proposals for a great recasting of industrial society and the reordering of American priorities properly belonged only to the socialists.

SUFFRAGETTE AT WORK

(*Brown Brothers.*)

Paradise Lost: Socialism in America

American socialism in the years before the First World War presented the odd spectacle of a lively critique of the capitalist system developed by an inventive but faction-ridden party drifting steadily away from its nineteenth-century European revolutionary moorings. Despite a collectivist ideology, socialism in action embodied a Jeffersonian pluralism that defied the bidding of progressive nationalists. In its salad days between 1900 and 1914, the socialist movement followed a pattern of checkered regionalism as old as the nation itself. Party members included industrial workers in the cities of the Northeast, old ethnics in the urban enclaves of the upper Midwest, agrarians with memories of Populism in the Plains States, hard-bitten miners and lumber stiffs from the Rocky Mountains and the Pacific Northwest, and a cadre of college-trained intellectuals preaching everything from Fabianism and Christian Socialism to revolution-for-the-hell-of-it. If socialists never quite lived up to their reputation as the chief American menace to order and decency, they nevertheless presented a case against corporate capitalism that progressives found deeply disturbing.

Socialism as a significant political force dated from the turn of the century. In 1901 disgruntled members of the Socialist Labor party, fed up with the dictatorial ways of its hard-lining Marxist leaders, bolted, and collecting other splinter groups like Eugene Debs's Social Democratic party, formed the Socialist party of America. The 94,000 votes Debs won in the presidential election of 1900 marked the beginning of a revisionist drift among a majority of American socialists towards the center and of a theory of nonviolent parliamentary socialism, a move not always clear to the embattled participants themselves.

American socialism showed two faces. To progressive outsiders it continued to threaten the replacement of their capitalist system. According to socialists, capitalism was traveling a historically determined route to oblivion, destroying small-scale enterprise, saturating international markets, and establishing spheres of influence along the way. Although the socialist account of the rise and fall of industrial capitalism touched a few raw nerves, most progressives comforted themselves with the conviction that neither class war nor the degradation of the working class in the United States appeared very likely. Yet to most Americans before the First World War the very vehemence of the socialist prophecy constituted a menace that appeared to stem from an organized conspiracy of malcontents and madmen. Accordingly, progressive society prepared to deal with its enemy and to dispose of it in the best way it knew how, by intimidation and suppression.

Socialists themselves, on the other hand, seemingly confronted the riddle of the Sphinx propounded by American developments. Their list of unanswered questions lengthened as capitalism continued to display surprising powers of recuperation. Did the immediate gains of shorter hours and improved working conditions strengthen class solidarity or simply adjust workers to a wage system over which they could exercise no real control? Could socialists accomplish more through political action—running candidates of their own—or was such politicking tantamount to betraying the interests of the working class? Was the overthrow of the capitalist order imminent, or would the takeover proceed only gradually, following the education of the workers? The socialist failure to reach agreement on such matters was taken by most progressives as proof of the absurdity of their ideas but also as a warning to a society willing to tolerate their foolishness.

Gradually, however, the center of the Socialist party began to be occupied by solid and sensible moderates—men like Milwaukee's shrewd tactician Victor Berger; New York's scarred veteran of innumerable ideological campaigns Morris Hillquit; and the "Pennsylvania Dutchman" James Hudson Maurer, who looked to an alliance with the AFL. This moderate center hoped to educate the country out of its capitalistic habits with the lessons of evolutionary socialism. They were bitterly opposed, from without by diehard members of the militant Socialist Labor Party, and also from within by their own left wing, which had converted to industrial unionism and direct action. In the years after 1900 the Socialist Party, far from solving its theoretical and organizational problems, continued to divide into camps of pragmatists and doctrinaires, "impossibilists" and "opportunists." The party, Algie Simons complained to fellow moderate William English Walling, was a precariously balanced seesaw with "a bunch of intellectuals" at one end, and on the other "a bunch of never-works, demagogues and would-be intellectuals, a veritable 'Lumpen Proletariat.'"

Of all the dissident left-wing groups careering out of the socialist orbit, the most alarming to progressives was the Industrial Workers of the World, a faction of industrial unionists led by "Big Bill" Haywood. The "Wobblies," as they were called by a derisive but apprehensive American public, rejected all forms of political action and recommended strikes and sabotage as the only way to build "the one big union." The IWW roused fear and resentment far out of proportion to its membership, which was mostly made up of unskilled and migratory workers, lumber stiffs, ore-boat hands, and all the other rejects of organizational society. The Wobblies saw their historic mission as the total destruction of capitalism and the forming of the new society "within the shell of the old." Progressives shuddered at the prospect.

During a brief and stormy existence, the Wobblies waged a bitter struggle for survival. Although they scored short-lived victories in strikes in the Pennsylvania steel town of McKees Rocks in 1907 and again in the Lawrence, Massachusetts mills in 1912, they lacked the funds and the organization for sustained unionizing drives. Their myth of the "general strike" and the vision of "One Big Union" served chiefly to rally the spirits of marginal men who dreamed of participatory democracy among the uprooted. At no time did the Wobblies threaten the American capitalist order.

Seen in proper historical perspective, the Wobblies represented the last futile attempt of a nineteenth-century frontier mentality to recover an imaginary world

without politics, where abundance automatically rewarded the natural cooperation of free men. "Big Bill" Haywood could have been addressing an audience
of progressives when he confessed his hopes for a future America:

I have had a dream that I have in the morning and at night and during the day, that there
will be a new society sometime in which there will be no battle between capitalist and wage-
earner . . . there will be no political government . . . but . . . experts will come together for
the purpose of discussing the means by which machinery can be made the slave of the
people instead of part of the people being made the slave of machinery.

Ironically, it was a progressive majority bent on finding another way of trans-
cending politics with the rule of the experts that clubbed the Wobblies' dream to
death.

Socialists themselves were burdened with many of the same liabilities as their
more radical competitors—a tradition of local autonomy, fierce rivalries for leadership, and a host of competing views on the verdict of history. The choice of
Eugene Debs, with his enduring popularity, as the spokesman for a splintered
party was proof of Socialist divisions. Tall, angular, with a shambling gait and an
easy-going manner, Debs served the party faithfully as a national walking-delegate,
captivating hundreds of thousands with homely speeches punctuated by allusions
to America's past. When Debs walked out of Woodstock jail after serving a term
for violating a federal injunction during the Pullman strike, he left a confirmed
but confused socialist. His were the home-grown talents of the moral agitator,
his heroes the abolitionists Wendell Phillips and William Lloyd Garrison. When
it came to formulating a workable collectivist strategy, Debs vacillated between

EUGENE V. DEBS CAMPAIGNING

The Socialist party candidate
makes one of his innumerable
speeches in behalf of a lost cause.
(*Brown Brothers.*)

supporting left-wing industrial unionism and endorsing the moderate parliamentarians. A spellbinder with no large fund of useful ideas, he was nevertheless an able conciliator and a durable campaigner. In 1904 he won some 400,000
votes for his party, and four years later duplicated the feat with a whirlwind tour
by rail across the country in his "Red Special," giving up to twenty speeches a
day. The big leap in Socialist party totals, however, came in 1912 when voters
gave Debs nearly a million votes in his fourth try for the presidency.

Debs personified both the ethical force of the socialist critique of capitalism
and also its besetting organizational weakness. He cared little for the hard work
of running the party and warmed to the myths of participatory democracy. "I
never had much faith in leaders," he once admitted. "I am willing to be charged
with almost anything, rather than to be charged with being a leader. . . . Give me
the rank and file every day." Even though both wings of the party criticized his
leadership, Debs remained the choice of his rank and file from the halcyon prewar days through the lean years of socialist martyrdom during and after the war.

The chief socialist contribution to the American pluralist tradition was the
example it set of the open society it sought to create. The party posed as a model
of pluralism in action—a loosely organized, tactically divided intellectual community in rough agreement in its ethical condemnation of capitalism but unable
to unite on its application. These disagreements crystallized in the lives of the
young academics, artists, and intellectuals who were drawn to socialism as much
by its promise of cultural revolution as by its economic platform. Socialist intellectuals soon made it clear that they opposed both the moral pieties of progressivism and the bureaucratic collectivism of party centrists. They made their
spiritual home in the Intercollegiate Socialist Society, the brainchild of Upton
Sinclair, which was primarily composed of students and their teachers, artists,
and intellectuals.

The membership rolls of the ISS listed some of the most impressive and varied
intellectual talent in the country and proffered a range of critical analysis extending from the Fabianism of John Spargo to the protocommunism of Louis Budenz,
the civil liberties concerns of Roger Baldwin and Alexander Meiklejohn to the
protest fiction of Ernest Poole and Zona Gale, the latent progressivism of defectors
like Walter Lippmann to the pacifism of A. J. Muste and Jessie Wallace Hughan.
Connecting these diverse personalities was a strong distaste for the commercial
spirit generated by capitalism and an abiding fear of privilege. While the solid
burghers at the center of the party fed on the ordinary fare of meat-and-potato
socialism, the intellectuals preferred the lighter diet served up by Max Eastman's
The Masses, in which variety abounded and readers were admonished to "enjoy
the revolution." More serious moderates struggling for control of the movement
objected that such lightheartedness smacked of frivolity, not to say heresy. They
railed constantly at the inhabitants of "that nebulous middle world which lies
somewhere between the Socialist movement and the world of bourgeois compla-
cency," a never-never land where undisciplined enthusiasts mixed "Socialism,

Anarchism, Communism, Sinn Feinism, Cubism, sexism, direct action and sabotage into a more or less harmonious mess."

Such complaints of workaday socialists were not altogether misguided although they betrayed a bias toward bureaucracy uncomfortably close to that of the progressives. In their most inspired moments Socialist intellectuals argued not merely the case against economic injustice but an ethical and an aesthetic set of perceptions as well. They found a Marxist world view less helpful than the pragmatic guidelines of William James and John Dewey. To them, socialism signified the preconditions for an age of altruistic experimentation, a conviction they had reached less through the study of Marx than an appreciative reading of Anglo-American revisionists like George Bernard Shaw, H. G. Wells, Graham Wallas, and Thorstein Veblen. Their expectations for socialism were as much psychological as sociological, and they combined their insights into the social creation of personality with an open-ended experimental outlook. Socialism, as redefined by the intellectuals, came to mean a rational, peaceful method of securing economic justice and social harmony.

The striking variety of American socialism, its shifting assessment of ends and means, and its inventiveness in tapping the rich reserves of American dissent made it a lively if not ultimately a powerful opponent of progressivism. Despite its brief successes on the local level the Socialist party was never a genuine political contender even before the First World War, and its greatest days were spent in vocal but isolated opposition to that war and the mindlessness of superpatriots. Its real role, like the role of the Populist party before it, was largely educational. And what it taught, more by example than by design, was the uses of secular, permissive open society. In so doing it supplied useful correctives for a compulsive progressive order from which Americans might have profited. Its disruption and decline with the coming war dealt a major setback to the Jeffersonian tradition.

The New Freedom

Woodrow Wilson's New Freedom followed the design outlined by his academic career and rested on his hopes for a strong presidency. The second half of Wilson's intellectual heritage, his scholarly background, led him to a prolonged examination of American institutions and leadership. His training at Johns Hopkins had come at a time when political scientists were beginning to set aside their preoccupation with constitutional questions and matters of sovereignty but had not yet acquired the economic and sociological techniques for examining how institutions really functioned. Wilson shared the progressive fascination with institutional politics, but his treatment of it remained curiously abstract. "My purpose," he announced in one of his books, "is to show . . . our constitutional system as it looks in operation." Yet the workaday reality of American politics was precisely what his analysis always lacked, the linking of larger social forces with political action. Despite frequent promises to "look below the surface" of American institutions Wilson was at his best in expounding a philosophy of politics that Theodore Roosevelt would have endorsed: "All the country needs is a new and sincere body of thought in politics, coherently, distinctly and boldly uttered by men who are sure of their ground." Like Roosevelt too, Wilson held that the key to effective democratic government rested in the hands of a powerful executive who offered "the best chance of leadership and mastery."

For Wilson, then, leadership, whether as head of a university, governor of a state, or President, involved a preference for governing attached to a contrary urge to dismantle concentrated federal power. These seeming contradictions—strong presidential leadership and diminution of regulatory power—were yoked together in his mind by the figure of the plebiscitarian leader like the great English prime minister, William Gladstone, who could sense the aspirations of the common people and give voice to them as commands to the parliamentarians. Yet there was a vacuum at the center of Wilson's liberalism in 1912, one that could not be filled with nineteenth-century pieties. More would be required than restoring old liberties and appealing to the "generous energies" of citizens. The federal government, in particular the power of the President, had its uses, as he clearly sensed. But the real question was whether it could be used to eliminate business coercion, break up communities of privilege, restore competition, and rescue the little man from the clutches of impersonal economic forces.

The chief architect of the New Freedom citadel was Louis Brandeis, the nation's leading progressive lawyer, who had made a career of tilting with big business. In the course of this prolonged combat Brandeis had worked out a full-blown alternative to Roosevelt s New Nationalism. His program rested on the conviction, reached by watching corporate capitalists play with other people's money, that the country was drifting steadily toward oligarchy. Financial oligarchy, he predicted, would soon become political despotism through the same processes that once had made Caesar Augustus master of Rome. In alluding to the fate of Rome, Brandeis touched a sensitive Democratic nerve in Wilson, who also feared monopoly but had not yet devised an effective plan for controlling it. Brandeis supplied the guiding concepts for Wilson's first administration. The core of Brandeis's program was a dismantling operation that would ensure the survival of regulated competition by shoring up the small businessman, breaking up the new conglomerates, returning the marketplace to free enterprise, dispersing wealth more widely, and reaching down a helping hand to the working classes.

Out of the collaborative thinking of Wilson and Brandeis came the New Freedom's arraignment of monopoly and a not altogether convincing distinction between acceptable and antisocial business behavior, which recalled Roosevelt's similar attempts. Big business, Wilson agreed, was natural and thus inevitable, but trusts, on the other hand, were artificial and wholly undesirable. "A trust is an arrangement to get rid of competition, and a big business is a business that has survived competition by conquering in the field of intelligence and economy," the President announced, in explaining how it was that he could support big business and yet oppose monopoly. Wilson was further convinced of the impracticality of Roosevelt's plans for a regulatory commission to oversee the operations of big business. "As to the monopolies, which Mr. Roosevelt proposes to legalize and welcome, I know that they are so many cars of juggernaut, and I do not look forward with pleasure to the time when juggernauts are licensed and driven by commissioners of the United States." But could the New Freedom offer a better solution? Was destroying monopoly by antitrust suits really feasible?

Before Wilson tackled the monopolies he decided, with the aid of a sizable Democratic majority in the House and a solid contigent of party stalwarts in the Senate, to make good on the perennial promise to lower the tariff. Calling Congress into special session and breaking precedent by appearing in person, he called for immediate downward revision. The Underwood Tariff slid through the House on rails greased by a willing Democratic majority but in the Senate ran into a barrier erected by Republicans and party members representing sugar and wool interests. Using patronage adroitly, Wilson turned aside the attacks of the protectionists. The Underwood Tariff lowered duties a general 10 percent, placed the manufactured goods of the trusts on the free list, and added a small income tax as compensation. Wilson had redeemed an old party pledge but had also encountered the force of an interest-group pluralism different from the single grassroots impulse he had formerly envisioned.

Tariff reform tested Wilson's talents as an honest broker, but banking reform strained them to the limit. Most Americans were mainly interested in getting more flexible credit than the Eastern banking establishment was currently providing. But there were also vestiges of Andrew Jackson's Bank War in the revived contest between big bankers in the East with their hopes for a central banking system under their direct control and smaller regional bankers in the hinterland, who sought freedom from Wall Street in a thoroughly decentralized system. Ranged between these contenders was a third group of progressives in both parties who wanted a genuinely national system under government management that would ensure stability.

The Federal Reserve Act was thus the product of conflicting interest groups with diametrically opposed notions of what the country needed. Establishing twelve districts, each with a member-owned and member-directed Federal Reserve Bank, argued, in theory at least, a certain degree of decentralization and autonomy. But the creation of a new currency—Federal Reserve notes—and a supervisory seven-member board in Washington gave the federal government an effective instrument of monetary control.

Big bankers, however, need not have fretted. Much depended on the willingness of the Federal Reserve Board to interpret its powers generously, but the urge to direct the financial working of the nation proved not very vigorous in the next two decades. The immediate effect of the Federal Reserve Act was to strengthen rather than weaken the control of New York banks by consolidating their partnership with the government. Somewhere Wilson's concept of the "people" became lost. As a stabilizing device for corporate capitalism involving a minimum amount of government interference and direction, the Federal Reserve System worked with reasonable efficiency. As a "democratic" reform intended to parcel out financial power to the people, it was an illusion. "Like most other progressive regulatory measures," a recent student of progressivism has concluded, "the banking reform of 1913 replaced uncoordinated strivings with an orderly, more centralized apparatus very friendly to the industry it was mandated to guide. The gain for efficiency was immediate, but the gain for other social goals took years and a different climate to materialize."

Wilson's approach to the trusts also represented a capitulation to the logic of the New Nationalism. The confusions of a quarter-century's attempted enforcement of the Sherman Act had made clarification essential. The question was how to proceed? What degree of monopolistic control was permissible, and what constituted undue restraint? These questions the Clayton Act, as originally drafted in 1914, tried to answer with an interminable list of "thou shalt nots." The bill listed unfair trade practices in tedious and confusing detail. Congressional debate, however, along with the anguished cries from big business made it increasingly obvious that a complete list of forbidden practices was an impossibility and that any attempt to compile such a catalogue amounted to legislative insanity. Yet if it was impossible to specify each and every example of wrong conduct—to name the particular sin—then the only alternative lay in vesting a regulatory commission with the discretionary power to make concrete applications of a very general rule. Here was the course Roosevelt and his New Nationalists had advised all along, regulation rather than proscription and dismantlement.

In reluctantly agreeing to the commission proposal, Wilson jettisoned the moral compass of the New Freedom and steered for the shores of administrative government. His intentions in securing passage of the Federal Trade Commission Act in 1914 closely paralleled Roosevelt's, a scheme he had once so airily dismissed: the creation of an objective body of dispassionate experts whose ad hoc judgments rested on scientific evidence.

As a regulatory agency empowered to mediate conflicts between public efficiency and private economic opportunity, the Federal Trade Commission disappointed its progressive champions. During the First World War its functions in checking business concentration were greatly curtailed, and after the war even its fact-finding powers invited the wrath of both big business and Congress itself. Congressional conservatives demanded an investigation of its methods.

The courts, in a series of adverse decisions, stripped the FTC of its power to define unfair practices. Business simply defied it by denying it access to company records and ignoring its rulings. Only when a much chastened commission, staffed with compliant members agreed to serve as the handmaiden of big business instead of the policeman did the attacks cease. Government by commission in the 1920s provided no cure for a raging speculative fever.

In other areas of national life as well, Wilson's pluralistic dreams of liberating the energies of "the great struggling unknown masses of men" ended in perplexity and defeat. Not the "people" of his earlier progressive imaginings but highly organized interest groups, exacting and clamorous, descended on Washington seeking protection and advancement of their affairs. In some cases Wilson's administration prove openhanded. For newly organized farmers, rural credit facilities. For labor, a workman's compensation act for federal employees. For consumer groups, a National Child Labor Act. There were limits to Wilson's receptivity to interest-group politics, however; notably, he disapproved of women's suffrage, and he refused to lift the burden of antitrust suits from the backs of labor organizations. He also tacitly supported the secretary of the interior and the postmaster general in instituting segregation in their departments and only reluctantly reversed himself when liberals objected. Not all interests, it was clear, could command the attention of a broker president.

By 1916, as Americans watched the war in Europe settle into a protracted and bloody stalemate, the Wilson administration had largely completed its progressive program. The President's initial promise of reversal and restoration had met an early death. In each of his major attempts at reform—lowering the tariff, building the Federal Reserve System, controlling the trusts—the President, although he preferred dispersion, had been driven in precisely the opposite direction. A Tariff Commission to systematize the nation's trade policies. A Federal Reserve Board to manage the monetary affairs of the country. A Federal Trade Commission to police big business. The meaning of these reforms was unmistakable. More not less government. An increase rather than a decrease in governmental agencies. A greater instead of a lesser reliance on experts and bureaucratic procedure. A supportive relation rather than a supervisory one between government and the large, organized interest groups, whose activities it presumably sought to regulate in the name of the people. And presiding over this new system of interest-group competition a President fully as powerful as the most ambitious New Nationalist could have wished.

Pluralism of a different sort from that with which Wilson entered the presidency strengthened the federal government under the New Freedom and completed Roosevelt's bureaucratic revolution. By the time America entered the World War in 1917, progressivism had erected the foundations of a democratic state capitalism designed to house a people of abundance. No one could yet foresee how the forces of the administrative state would erode nineteenth-century values. It would take the war itself to drive that lesson home.

Suggested Readings

Two good general introductions to the study of immigration and assimilation are Maldwyn A. Jones, *American Immigration* (1960), and Leonard Dinnerstein and David Reimers, *Ethnic Americans: A History of Immigration and Assimilation* (1975). The hostile reactions of native Americans is chronicled in John Higham, *Strangers in the Land: Patterns of American Nativism* (1955), and Barbara Solomon, *Ancestors and Immigrants* (1965). Their conclusions are documented in Stanley Feldstein and Lawrence Costello, eds., *The Ordeal of Assimilation* (1974), and Leonard Dinnerstein and Frederic C. Jaher, eds., *The Aliens: A History of Ethnic Minorities in America* (1970). Oscar Handlin, *The Uprooted* (2d ed., 1973), though challenged on many points by more recent studies, is nevertheless a classic; also see Philip Taylor, *The Distant Magnet* (1971), particularly for the European setting. Milton Gordon, *Assimilation in American Life: The Role of Race, Religion and National Origins* (1964), and Nathan Glazer and Daniel Moynihan, *Beyond the Melting Pot: Negroes, Jews, Italians and Irish of New York City* (1963), correct old American myths of easy assimilation.

The literature on specific minorities is extensive. Among the best collective portraits are Moses Rischin, *The Promised City: New York's Jews, 1870–1914* (1970); Arthur S. Goren, *New York Jews and the Quest for Community: The Kehillah Experiment, 1908–1922* (1970); Irving Howe, *World of Our Fathers: The Journey of the East European Jews to America and the Life They Found and Made* (1976); Humbert Nelli, *The Italians of Chicago, 1880–1920* (1970); Richard Gambino, *Blood of My Blood* (1974); Roger Daniels, *The Politics of Prejudice* (1968); Stanford M. Lyman, *Chinese Americans* (1974); Stephan Thernstrom, *The Other Bostonians: Poverty and Progress in the American Metropolis, 1880–1970* (1973).

August Meier, *Negro Thought in America, 1880–1915* (1963), is the best general assessment of black aspirations and programs during these years. George Fredrickson, *The Black Image in the White Mind, 1817–1914* (1972), contains several enlightening chapters on responses of the whites to the "race problem," and Jack Temple Kirby, *Darkness at the Dawning: Race and Reform in the Progressive South* (1972), gives an accurate estimate of the social price of progressive reform. The story of Harlem is well told in Gilbert Osofsky, *Harlem, The Making of a Ghetto, 1890–1930* (1966). For the Chicago equivalent, see Allan H. Spear, *Black Chicago* (1967). Louis R. Harlan, *Booker T. Washington: The Making of a Black Leader, 1856–1901* (1972), is a definitive account of the early years of that leader, and Elliot M. Rudwick, *W. E. B. DuBois: Propagandist of the Negro Protest* (1969), analyzes the early contributions of a mercurial black Progressive. Organizational problems and institutional developments are thoroughly covered in Charles F. Kellogg, *NAACP: A History of the National Association for the Advancement of Colored People, 1909–1920* (1970); Nancy Weiss, *The National Urban League, 1910–1940* (1974); and Joyce Ross, *J. E. Spingarn and the Rise of the NAACP* (1972).

Two readable surveys of women's rights and social feminism are Eleanor Flexner, *Century of Struggle: The Woman's Rights Movement in the United States* (1959) and Lois Banner, *Women in Modern America* (1974). Aileen Kraditor, *The Ideas of the Women's Suffrage Movement, 1890–1920* (1965), is indispensable for understanding the ideology but should be supplemented by Alan P. Grimes, *The Puritan Ethic and Woman Suffrage* (1967). William O'Neill presents an impressive range of individual portraits in *Everyone Was Brave: The Rise and Fall of Feminism in America* (1969). David Morgan, *Suffragists and Democrats: The Politics of Woman Suffrage in America* (1972), thoroughly analyzes political developments. For a useful study of the problem of work, see Robert Smuts, *Women and Work in America* (1959).

American socialism has been fully treated in a number of solid monographs: Ira A. Kipnis, *The American Socialist Movement, 1897–1912* (1952); Howard Quint, *The Forging of*

American Socialism (1953); David Shannon, *The Socialist Party of America: A History* (1955); James Weinstein, *The Decline of Socialism in America* (1967); and Daniel Bell, *Marxian Socialism in the United States* (1967). Donald D. Egbert and Stow Persons, eds., *Socialism and American Life* (2 vols., 1952), contains much useful documentary material. John H. M. Laslett, *Labor and the Left: A Study of Socialist and Radical Influences in the American Labor Movement, 1881–1924* (1970), explains a limited socialist impact on American workers. David Hereshoff, *American Disciples of Marx: From the Age of Jackson to the Progressive Era* (1967), covers a range of contributors to American socialism.

A brief but excellent survey of the rest of the radical spectrum is contained in John P. Diggins, *The American Left in the Twentieth Century* (1973). Melvyn Dubofsky, *We Shall Be All: A History of the Industrial Workers of the World* (1969), is a brilliant history of the movement; Paul F. Brissenden, *The IWW: A Study of American Syndicalism* (1919), provides useful documentation in addition, and Patrick Renshaw, *Wobblies: The Story of Syndicalism in the United States* (1967), is also valuable. Joseph R. Conlin, *Big Bill Haywood and the Radical Union Movement* (1969), improves on "Big Bill's" *Autobiography* (1929). Christopher Lasch, *The New Radicalism in America, 1889–1963* (1965), presents a persuasive indictment of cultural radicalism in the Progressive era.

On the intellectual and cultural transformation of American society after 1912 Henry F. May, *The End of American Innocence* (1959), is now standard. Lawrence Veysey, *The Emergence of the American University* (1970), analyzes the institutional growth of American higher education, and Richard Hofstadter and Walter Metzger, *The Development of Academic Freedom in the United States* (1955), recounts the struggle for academic autonomy. Joseph Blau, *Men and Movements in American Philosophy* (1952), covers the contributions of the pragmatists, and Nathan G. Hale, Jr., *Freud and the Americans: The Beginnings of Psychoanalysis in America, 1876–1917* (1971), is a detailed discussion of the development of Freudianism in the United States. Literary histories of the Age of Realism are numerous. Still the best discussions of important writers are Alfred Kazin, *On Native Grounds* (1942), and two volumes by Maxwell Geismar, *Rebels and Ancestors: The American Novel, 1890–1915* (1953), and *The Last of the Provincials: The American Novel, 1915–1925*. Jay Martin, *Harvest of Change: American Literature, 1865–1914* (1967), is a generally informative survey with good discussions of Henry James and Henry Adams. Michael Millgate, *American Social Fiction* (1964), traces the rise of a genre. Kenneth S. Lynn, *William Dean Howells: An American Life* (1970), is a sympathetic if critical assessment of a fractured artistic sensibility.

For illuminating discussions of significant contributors to the Progressive reform outlook, see two particularly valuable studies: Daniel M. Fox, *The Discovery of Abundance: Simon Patten and the Transformation of Social Theory* (1967), and Barry D. Karl, *Charles E. Merriam and the Study of Politics* (1974). James Gilbert, *Designing the Industrial State: The Intellectual Pursuit of Collectivism in America, 1880–1940* (1972), is an informative study.

Indispensable for an understanding of Wilson and the New Freedom is the magisterial Arthur S. Link, *Wilson* (5 vols., 1947–65), although the hostile John Blum, *Woodrow Wilson and the Politics of Morality* (1956), and John A. Garraty, *Woodrow Wilson* (1956), offer critical insights unavailable to the sympathetic Link; so does the psychoanalytical portrait, Alexander and Juliette George, *Woodrow Wilson and Colonel House: A Personality Study* (1956). William Diamond, *The Economic Thought of Woodrow Wilson* (1943), examines the shaky theoretical underpinnings of the New Freedom, and Melvin Urofsky, *Big Steel and the Wilson Administration* (1969), canvasses aspects of the Wilsonian labor policy.

Biographies of other important figures during the New Freedom years include Dorothy Rose Blumberg, *Florence Kelley: The Making of a Social Pioneer* (1966); Charles Larsen, *The Good Fight: The Life and Times of Ben Lindsey* (1972); Julius Weinberg, *Edward Alsworth Ross and the Sociology of Progressivism* (1972); Robert C. Bannister, *Ray Stannard Baker: The Mind and Thought of a Progressive* (1966); and H. C. Bailey, *Edgar Gardner Murphy* (1968).

28

The Path to Power
American Foreign Policy
1890-1917

For most of the nineteenth century Americans managed their affairs without a foreign policy. The defeat of Napoleon and the success of the American peace commissioners following a nearly disastrous war with England closed an era of diplomatic defeat for the new nation perched precariously on the rim of the Atlantic world and subject to the buffetings of the two major European powers. After 1815, geographical and ideological separation gave the American people an open continental field to explore and exploit. By midcentury George Washington's original prediction of a peculiar American destiny had seemingly become a providential fact. Secure in its continental fastness, its hemispheric dominance guaranteed by English sea power, the United States turned inward to expand its borders and develop its resources.

This favorable international climate together with unlimited opportunity at home fostered extravagant versions of an American 'Manifest Destiny, which at one time or another pointed to the annexation of Canada, the acquisition of Cuba, and the taking of "all Mexico." Geopolitical prophets dreamed of the Caribbean as an American lake or of the Mississippi valley as the center of a vast heartland empire that extended eastward across the Atlantic and westward to

979

China shores. But these flickering dreams of empire, like the immoderate reckonings of the farmers and the conjectures of manufacturers and shippers, were predictions rather than policy directives for a people busy planting the Garden of the World and producing an increasing variety of manufactured goods. In spite of sporadic American interest in the fate of republican movements in Europe, Manifest Destiny remained mostly an article for home consumption—exuberant and aggressive but not really for export

The slavery question also checked the American expansionist appetite after the Mexican War as the debate over its future in the territories monopolized the national attention. With mounting ferocity planters and free soilers charged each other with clandestine schemes for spreading or checking slavery in the territories. Americans, who were confronted with an insoluble moral problem, prepared for war and forgot about foreign affairs.

By the last quarter of the nineteenth century, however, the belief in a separate American destiny was being overturned by a series of developments that began to draw the United States into the vortex of international power politics. The most ominous of these signs was the sudden imperialist activity of the major European powers—first England, then France, Germany, and Russia—who proceeded to carve generous colonial portions for themselves out of the hinterland of Asia and Africa. American diplomats and their political masters in Washington watched with growing apprehension as the European powers, following the dictates of capital investment, scrambled for possessions and spheres of influence in the undeveloped regions of the world.

Still, in the course of his inaugural address in 1885 President Grover Cleveland could pause to say only a brief word about his foreign policy. His words were reassuring to those Americans who still considered foreign affairs a distraction. The genius of American institutions and the real needs of the people, Cleveland explained, dictated a "scrupulous avoidance of any departure from that foreign policy commended by the history, the traditions, and the prosperity of our Republic." In case his audience might have forgotten their primary responsibilities in contemplating European imperialism the President restated the traditional policy of the United States towards the rest of the world. "It is the policy of independence, favored by our position. . . . It is the policy of peace suitable to our interests. It is the policy of neutrality, rejecting any share in foreign broils and ambitions upon other continents and repelling their intrusion here,"

Cleveland's attitudes were embodied in the dilapidated foreign-policy establishment over which he presided. A casual and still largely amateur operation, it had no very effective fact-gathering apparatus, and although it boasted a handful of able diplomats, was saddled with a great many more political friends and nonentities. Most of the useful information trickling back to Washington from European capitals came from cosmopolitan private citizens concerned with the shifting scenes of international politics as the vast majority of their countrymen obviously were not. Until 1890, Europe seemed willing to take the American profession of international disinterest at face value as a declaration of intent to remain a second-class power. The diplomatic corps resident in Washington was not on the whole a distinguished one, and on more than one occasion a European state simply neglected to fill a vacant post that had come to appear superfluous.

Yet at the very moment when Cleveland spoke the platitudes that had passed for a foreign policy throughout the nineteenth century, new intellectual forces were beginning to collect around a different set of propositions drawn directly from a scrutiny of European imperialist scrambles. Lord Bryce, whose perceptive analysis of American government and society, *The American Commonwealth*, appeared in 1888, noted the difference between the foreign-policy influentials in England and their counterparts in the United States. In America, Bryce explained, "there are individual men corresponding to individuals in that English set, and probably quite as numerous." There were a sizable number of journalists of real ability, a handful of literary men, and not a few politicians who understood the mechanisms of power politics. Yet this American intellectual class remained isolated and disorganized, constantly subject to popular pressures and mass opinion as the "first set" in England clearly was not. "In England the profession of opinion-making and leading is the work of specialists; in America . . . of amateurs. By the time Bryce published his observation, however, a small group of congenial amateurs were already at work in Washington building the foundations of a foreign-policy establishment and beginning to call for a more active pursuit of world power.

The Origins of American Expansionism

By 1890 it began to dawn on an American foreign-policy public only recently recruited to the standards of national interest that the United States was in danger of being left behind in the race for territory and markets. A decade later the unblushing expansionist Senator Albert J. Beveridge summed up the lessons of the intervening years with the reminder that, like it or not, the American people had become the trustees "under God" of world civilization. "He has made us the master organizers of the world to establish system where chaos reigns." Not all Beveridge's countrymen agreed that destiny had mapped an imperial course for their country, but it was clear to them that they could no longer view the international scene with indifference.

A second force propelling the United States into the imperialist scramble, concern with world markets, was less easy to measure precisely. After 1875, American businessmen, bankers, industrialists, and shippers began to call for ready access to the markets of the world; their demands were given dramatic point by periodic depressions and doubts concerning the capacity of domestic markets to absorb what was generally considered a glut of manufactured goods and staples.

Still, the size of the American foreign market in the undeveloped areas of the

SENATOR BEVERIDGE'S "TRUSTEES" PACIFYING THE PHILIPPINES

(*Oregon Historical Society.*)

world remained relatively small as late as 1900, and the recurrent demand for enlarging it often spoke to promise rather than current realities. The discussion of markets provided an idiom for popular debate—a political grammar with which expansionists and antiexpansionists, interventionists and isolationists, realists and idealists, argued the proper role of the United States in world affairs. No one denied the importance of foreign markets as visible symbols of American prosperity and the chief instrument for spreading the blessings of democracy. But did the search for markets mean intervening in the domestic affairs of undeveloped and unstable countries? Did it require outright annexation? Were markets for investment capital different from markets for manufactured goods? And most troublesome of all, how could the spokesmen for expanded foreign markets catch and hold the attention of an unresponsive federal government?

A third force propelling the United States into the world arena could more properly be called a condition. The 1890s in many ways made up an American social crisis comprising severe economic dislocation, class conflict, political instability and intellectual discord. The cumulative effect of these tensions was a vague but intense popular conviction that the United States had passed the point of no return on its march to modernity. Whether or not they pondered Frederick Jackson Turner's warnings of the social consequences of the closing of the frontier, many Americans were acutely aware of the passing of an era of development in which free land and geographical mobility had been determinative. Viewed as fact or metaphor, the frontier had dominated the American imagination for two centuries, and the announcement of its closing, no matter how premature, reinforced a sense of irreversible change. In the twentieth century the concept of the frontier would enter the popular vocabulary in mythological form as the "urban frontier" and the various "frontiers" of science, technology, and education. But for the generation of the 1890s the simple extension of the concept out into space towards the equator and across the Pacific quickened a sense of mission and released pent-up feelings of humanitarianism as though the answer to their loss of certainty at home was a vigorous pursuit of democratic purpose abroad.

Across the rising ground of ideological debate leading to war with Spain in 1898 and the winning of empire, two traditional sets of partisans struggled to control an emergent American foreign policy. The actual contestants appeared in a number of guises in the quarter-century before American entrance into the First World War: upholders of international law and advocates of national power; preachers of pacifism and sponsors of preparedness; champions of arbitration and defenders of American honor. However distinct in style and manner, the participants in the great debate over the proper role for the United States ranged themselves behind two conflicting formulations of power and responsibility.

The first view of the nature of power and the future of the national state was admirably summarized for his generation by Captain Alfred Thayer Mahan, naval strategist and geopolitical theorist, in his *The Interest of America in Sea Power, Present and Future* (1897). Since governments, Mahan argued, could not be expected to act on any ground except national interest, it followed that patriotism and the will to fight were the indispensable attributes of a great people.

Not in universal harmony, nor in any fond dream of unbroken peace, rest now the best hopes of the world. . . . Rather in the competition of interests, in that reviving sense of nationality . . . in the jealous determination of each people to provide first for its own . . . are to be heard the assurance that decay has not touched yet the majestic fabric erected by so many centuries of courageous battling.

For a convincing explanation of the second and opposing view of the American mission, William Jennings Bryan reached down to the rich metaphorical soil of the Midwest. Nations, Bryan insisted, redeem only by force of example. "Example may be likened to the sun, whose genial rays constantly coax the buried seed into life, and clothe the earth, first with verdure, and afterward with ripened grain; while violence is the occasional tempest, which can ruin, but cannot give life."

Mahan's invitation to national greatness took precedence, at least for the moment, over Bryan's warnings as to its costs. Mahan had spent most of his career wandering about the world observing the kaleidoscopic patterns of European imperial politics, and now his warning to Americans was unequivocal. The United States, he announced, must quickly formulate and apply an aggressive expansionist policy based on naval supremacy and undisputed control of the world's sea lanes, a vigorous development of foreign markets, and an energetic cultivation of the domestic spiritual resources needed to sustain the new national mission.

To most Americans accustomed to the comforts of isolationism, Mahan's message came as a shock. In a Darwinian world of clashing national states, he argued, the United States must organize itself into a spiritual and military garrison ready to defend its interests with power. Mahan did not deny the existence of a universal law of conscience, but he anchored it in the concept of the national state fully apprised of its duty and prepared to perform it. In his view the "evils of war" paled before the dangers of "moral compliance with wrong." In the last analysis all depended on the disposition of the American people to take up their appointed tasks as the democratic saviors of the world and the guarantors of a Pax Americana. "The sentiment of a people is the most energetic element in national action," he insisted. The meaning of Mahan's argument was unmistakable: "Whether they will or no, Americans must now begin to look outward."

Mahan's arguments won him enthusiastic support in England and Germany, and were also warmly received by a small circle of American influentials whose own estimates of the international situation had led them to conclude that the

THE GREAT WHITE FLEET AND DIRTY BLACK SMOKE

In 1907 President Roosevelt dispatched the new American navy on a world cruise as a display of American strength. (*Brown Brothers.*)

United States must take its place among the imperialist powers. "You are head and shoulders above us all," wrote Roosevelt in promising Mahan to do all he could "toward pressing your ideas into effect." Roosevelt was joined by other important converts to the captain's doctrines: John Hay, soon to become McKinley's acerbic secretary of state; the freewheeling radical-reactionaries Brooks and Henry Adams and their protégé, Massachusetts Senator Henry Cabot Lodge; young, aggressive cosmopolitans like Richard Olney and staid conservatives like Joseph Choate; the academic popularizer John Fiske with his own version of the new Manifest Destiny; and the social-gospelist-turned-jingo, Josiah Strong, whose best-selling *Our Country* (1885) developed the evangelical case for renewal through expansion.

Until 1895 and the eruption of the Cuban crisis, however, the influence of these ambitious formulators of a "large policy" for the United States remained limited chiefly to those members of Congress with an interest in shipbuilding and naval rearmament and to a few career diplomats like William Rockhill, an old China hand with grandiose visions of his own. But gradually from this ideological core there developed a loose network of informed opinion concerning the need for expanding American opportunity, views increasingly expressed in metropolitan dailies and liberal journals and calling for a more realistic appraisal of America's needs. Still, not until 1896 and the election of McKinley would this rudimentary foreign-policy establishment gain a hearing for its proposals, and by that time it too was caught up in a mass popular uprising, partly humanitarian, partly chauvinist, demanding the rescue of the Cuban insurgents.

In the meantime the temperature of American diplomacy continued to rise alarmingly as though events in Latin America and the Pacific were responding to American demands by providing a hothouse climate for nourishing hardier

strains of diplomacy. A series of minor crises early in the 1890s served notice of America's intentions to take a firmer hand in managing international relations by asserting national interests and defending national honor whenever opportunity arose. In Samoa it was the threat of a German protectorate that brought United States naval forces steaming into the harbor at Apia in time to be destroyed by a typhoon. In Chile a barroom brawl involving American sailors ended in an American ultimatum to Valparaiso. And in Venezuela in 1895 a boundary dispute between England and an unstable and improvident Latin American state called forth a declaration of American omnipotence in the Western Hemisphere. "Today," Richard Olney, Cleveland's secretary of state, boasted to the startled British, "the United States is practically sovereign on this continent, and its fiat is law upon the subjects to which it confines its interposition . . . its infinite resources combined with its isolated position renders it master of the situation and practically invulnerable against any or all other powers." By 1896 events like these, evoking a disproportionate American belligerence, had paved the way for a popular crusade in behalf of Cuban independence.

The limits of popular pressure for expanding United States commitments, however, became clear in the abortive attempt to annex Hawaii following an American-engineered coup in the islands in 1893. Commercial interests pressed hard for annexation; Protestant missionaries welcomed the chance to finish the job of converting the heathen; global strategists stressed the key location of Hawaii athwart the trade lanes to the Asian mainland; and only a tiny group of anti-annexationists led by the venerable Carl Schurz objected on grounds of principle to taking the islands. The *Independent* summed up the traditional arguments for annexation in a timeworn metaphor: "The ripe apple falls into our hands, and we should be very foolish to throw it away."

President Cleveland, however, was fully prepared to resist the public outcry and called for an investigation of the circumstances of the recent revolution against the native queen. Convinced that the coup had been the work of a small group of powerful white planters and businessmen and that the great majority of the native population remained loyal to the monarchy, he preemptorily withdrew the treaty of annexation from the Senate. Without the overwhelming support of an aroused public and confronted by an executive firmly opposed to their designs, the annexationists were forced to bide their time. Hawaii in 1893 afforded neither the right time nor the right place for flexing American muscles. In Cuba five years later it would be different.

President McKinley's "Wonderful Experience"

In 1895, the Cuban revolution, which had been smoldering for nearly a quarter of a century, flared once again, and Spain dispatched fifty thousand soldiers to extinguish it. American sympathies, a mixture of humanitarian outrage and "jingo" bluster, instinctively went to the underdogs, who were widely credited with a wholesome intent to establish a Yankee-style republic. The insurrectionists responded to this encouragement pouring in from the North by dispatching a high-powered lobby to New York City with instructions to raise money and supplies while keeping William Randolph Hearst's and Joseph Pulitzer's reporters amply provided with atrocity stories. It was not long before the Cuban junta in New York received support from unexpected quarters—from Latin American trading interests, promoters of an isthmian canal, a variety of patriotic groups, and even trade unions. Carefully planned "spontaneous" rallies across the country whipped up sentiment for American intervention as Democrats and Populists joined their Republican rivals in denouncing Spain and calling for a declaration of support for the Cubans.

This mounting popular clamor was echoed in Congress, where two resolutions were reported out of the Senate Foreign Relations Committee: a majority report recommending immediate recognition of Cuban belligerency, and a minority report calling for active intervention. It soon became obvious to the incoming McKinley administration that the President would have to move quickly to avoid capture by a bellicose public mood that could give force but not direction to his policy.

In 1896 the exact meaning of this public concern for the fate of the Cuban revolution was not altogether clear. To the small group of advocates of the "large

THE SPANISH BRUTE
ADDS MUTILATION TO MURDER.

"THE SPANISH BRUTE ADDS MUTILATION TO MURDER"

The jingoistic tone of the American press during the Spanish-American War is revealed in this cartoon. (*Culver Pictures, Inc.*)

policy," intervention appeared a foregone conclusion. Roosevelt, who admitted to being "a quietly rampant 'Cuba Libre' man," informed Mahan that intervention was inevitable if the country was to retain its self-respect as a nation. Many expansionists agreed: the Cuban business would afford a heaven-sent opportunity for annexing Hawaii. But as for Cuba itself, no one could predict. Roosevelt himself, while angrily discounting "the craven fear and brutal selfishness of the mere money-getters" who opposed American intervention, doubted the wisdom of annexing Cuba "unless the Cubans wished it." "I don't want it to seem that we are engaged merely in a land-grabbing war," he admitted. Until war was declared there was little support for the idea of continuing United States involvement in the island even among the most vocal enthusiasts for intervention.

In the fiercely contested presidential election of 1896 the issue of Cuba had given way to domestic problems of free silver and the tariff. It took the renewed campaigns of the insurrectionists in December 1896, and the murder of their leader, Maceo, to raise the ire of an American public once again. This time the pattern of response was different; instead of planned demonstrations and organized rallies there were outbursts of protest across the country, genuinely spontaneous meetings in which businessmen joined patriots and humanitarians in demanding an end to Spanish rule. From now on McKinley's administration would have to contend with a powerful popular indignation.

At this point Spain added fuel to the interventionist fire as her troops in the island began to enforce a brutal program of reconcentration, herding suspected Cubans into makeshift camps, where they died by the thousands. Meanwhile an irresolute government in Madrid continued to agonize over the dwindling number of options left to it. A decaying monarchy, torn between rival factions of liberals and conservatives, unable to pacify the island but unwilling to give it up, Spain temporized hopelessly. Confusion was nearly as great within the McKinley administration, as the President found himself already caught in a verbal crossfire between Republican jingoes crying for justice at the point of an American sword and his conservative business backers fearful of the effects of a war on economic recovery. As popular pressure for intervention mounted, McKinley was also driven to temporize, publicly demanding promises of instant reform from Madrid while quietly reining in the jingoes in his party with promises of his own.

By 1897 the horrors of the reconcentration program had forced the President to press for firmer Spanish concessions when a series of incidents further strained relations between the two countries. First came the release of an indiscreet letter from the Spanish minister in Washington to his government in which he ungenerously but not inaccurately characterized McKinley as "weak" and "a bidder for the admiration of the crowd, besides being a would-be politician who tries to leave a door open behind him while keeping on good terms with the jingoes of his party." Then came the explosion in Havana harbor that destroyed the battleship *Maine* and multiplied rumors of Spanish complicity in what Senator Lodge called a "gigantic murder, the last spasm of a corrupt and dying society." Now at last the jingoes formed the vanguard of an aroused American public demanding retaliation in the name of justice and democracy.

McKinley's dilemma became more painful as conflicting reports of Spanish intentions came flooding in, accounts of the ministry's complete intransigence on the one hand, and assurances of its willingness to comply with demands for "full self-government" on the other. Given the choice between waiting and taking immediate action, McKinley finally capitulated. Two days after Spain had agreed to his demands for an immediate armistice and an end to reconcentration —while still declining to grant Cuban independence—the President sent a message to Congress requesting authority to intervene and restore peace in the island. By the time word of Spain's partial compliance reached Washington it was already too late: McKinley could now admit formally what had been obvious for some time, that the issue rested with Congress. Intervention, he realized, was tantamount to war, and Congress made the decision official on April 19, 1898, by recognizing that a state of war existed. Lacking a clearly defined set of goals and the diplomatic means of implementing them, caught in a domestic political crossfire, McKinley was forced to accept the prospect of what John Hay called a "splendid little war" for no very compelling reasons of national interest.

In the brief contest that followed, the United States made short work of Spain's decrepit navy and demoralized army. Commodore George Dewey's Asiatic squadron promptly demolished the monarchy's Pacific fleet in the Battle of Manila Bay, and the Atlantic squadron as easily penned up Cervera's ships in Santiago and systematically destroyed them. Spanish troops scarcely improved on this

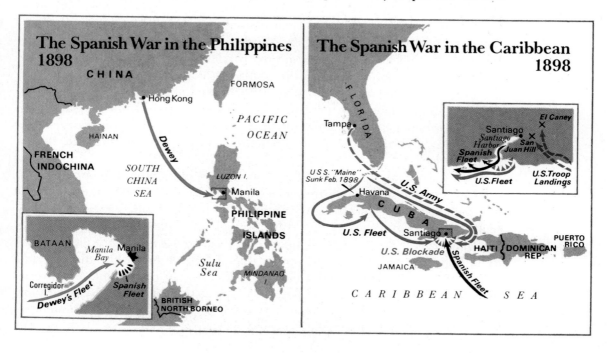

The Spanish War in the Philippines 1898

The Spanish War in the Caribbean 1898

performance against poorly trained, badly equipped, disorganized American forces. After endless confusion General William R. Shafter finally succeeded in assembling some eighteen thousand troops for an invasion of Cuba and managed to land his army, complete with press corps, foreign dignitaries, and well-wishers, near Santiago, where Roosevelt and his Rough Riders seized the lion's share of the glory in what the Colonel called a "bully fight." The Battle of Santiago capped the successes of the navy, and American soldiers settled in on the jungle heights above San Juan, where more of them died from disease than in actual combat. A small expeditionary force dispatched to nearby Puerto Rico encountered no real resistance. By August 1898, its meager military resources entirely spent and its morale shattered, Spain gave up and signed the peace protocol.

The problem of disposing of the remnants of the Spanish empire caught McKinley's administration by surprise. In the case of Cuba, Congress in an unaccountable burst of altruism had rushed through the Teller Amendment, declaring the island free and independent and disavowing any American intentions of annexation. Not for conquest nor for empire had American soldiers fought so bravely, but, as one Republican senator put it, "for humanity's sake . . . to aid a people who have suffered every form of tyranny and who have made a desperate struggle to be free." Within a year these professions of disinterest would be strained to the breaking point.

The new problem of the Philippines together with the old question of Hawaii compounded McKinley's difficulties. "If old Dewey had just sailed away when he smashed the Spanish fleet, what a lot of trouble he would have saved us," the President grumbled, confessing that he "could not have told where those darned islands were within 2000 miles"—a not entirely candid remark, since he had ordered an invasion force to Manila even before Dewey announced his victory. But with the quick collapse of Spain the barriers to empire began to fall, both within the administration and in the country at large, as groups once hostile to the idea of acquiring new territory suddenly began to weigh its advantages. Business opinion, banking and mercantile interests, church organizations, and even social reformers joined in calling for the retention of the Philippines, if not as a permanent possession, at least as a temporary way station on the route to vast Asian markets.

When the Senate came to debate the merits of annexation, the opponents of the new imperialism argued strenuously that "political dominion" was not "commercially necessary" and that the United States ought to satisfy itself with a few coaling stations and naval yards. But the logic of expansion ran against these anti-imperialists. If commercial opportunity dictated the need for political stability in both Hawaii and the Philippines, then why not go the full distance and secure it while lifting untutored peoples to the level of democratic self-government? McKinley now spoke the popular mood as previously he had failed to in presenting a narrow range of choices. It would be "cowardly and pusillanimous," he insisted, for the United States "to turn the islands back to Spain, giving them

The battleship *Maine* on the morning after the explosion, and Theodore Roosevelt surrounded by his Rough Riders. (*Above, The National Archives; left, Theodore Roosevelt Collection, Harvard College Library.*)

power again to misrule the natives." Equally "despicable" was the thought of
handing them over to England or allowing Japan to take them by default.

There is only one logical course to pursue. Spain has shown herself unfit to rule her colonies, and those [that] have come into our possession as a result of war, must be held, if we
are to fulfill our destinies as a nation . . . giving them the benefits of a christian civilization
which has reached its highest developement [*sic*] under our republican institutions.

For the moment the benefits—spiritual and material—appeared to outweigh the
costs of empire.

With the debate over the peace terms there emerged a small but vocal group
of "anti-imperialists," hastily assembled and representing a wide variety of arguments against seizing new territory. The nucleus of this anti-imperialist opposition consisted of a group of venerable mid-nineteenth-century liberals whose
advanced age and recent Mugwump obsessions with political corruption constituted their distinguishing mark and their chief liability. The veteran antislavery
campaigner Carl Schurz was 71; the free trader Edward Atkinson, 73; the Republican maverick George F. Hoar, 74; the steelmaker Andrew Carnegie, 65. Most
of the anti-imperialists hovered on the outskirts of government and party holding
long and honorable records in the cause of dissent against the Gilded Age. As an
imperial ambition caught up the majority of their countrymen they found themselves severely handicapped in preaching a doctrine of self-denial. Unskilled
in the new arts of mass propaganda, saddled with a negative program, often
distrustful of the democratic forces ranged behind the President, they were soon
outmanned and outmaneuvered by the expansionists even though they scored
some telling ideological hits on their victorious opponents.

The anti-imperialist manifesto expressed racist doubts about the wisdom of
incorporating dark-skinned, unschooled peoples. But the core of their case
against empire was the charge of betrayal of that cherished principle of national
self-determination embodied in the Declaration of Independence. It was Charles
Eliot Norton, high priest of American gentility, strangely enough, who made
this charge most indignantly:

We believe that America had something better to offer to mankind than those aims she is
now pursuing, and we mourn her desertion of her ideals which were not selfish nor
limited in their application, but which are of universal worth and validity. She has lost
her unique position as a potential leader in the program of civilization, and has taken up
her place simply as one of the grasping and selfish nations of the present day.

Some of the anti-imperialists looked back to a less complex world of a half-
century earlier, when the United States, as one defender of tradition put it, was
"provincial, dominated by the New England idea." These New England worthies,
however, were joined by younger, pragmatic critics of imperialism, like William
James who deftly probed the false "realism" of the expansionists and dissected
their specious reasoning. As the bloody and inconclusive pacification campaign in

the Philippines dragged on and the native freedom fighter Emilio Aguinaldo gave American troops a lesson in guerrilla warfare, James centered his own attack on the American penchant for substituting "bald and hollow abstractions" for the "intensely living and concrete situation." An unchecked appetite for power, he scoffed, had caused the country to "puke up its ancient soul . . . in five minutes without a wink of squeamishness."

Could there be a more damning indictment of that whole bloated idol termed "modern civilization" than this amounts to? Civilization is, then, the big, hollow, resounding, corrupting, sophisticating, confusing torrent of mere brutal momentum and irrationality that brings forth fruits like this?

Until the Philippine insurrection gave the lie to American professions of altruism, the opponents of expansion made very little headway against the winds of imperial destiny. McKinley, after wrestling with his conscience, announced that "without any desire or design on our part" the war had brought new duties for the United States to "meet and discharge" as became "a great nation." Accordingly he instructed his peace commissioners to stand firm against Spanish protests. By the terms of the peace treaty signed late in 1898 Spain agreed to dismemberment, relinquishing Cuba, the Philippines, Puerto Rico, and Guam.

In the Senate the treaty was taken in hand by the Republican faithfuls — Lodge, Spooner, Nelson, and Beveridge — who were aided in their work by Bryan's odd notion that the course of empire could only be determined in the elections of 1900. The inclination of the majority of senators for striking a balance between immediate material gains and long-term spiritual rewards was best summarized by the jingo Albert J. Beveridge: "It is God's great purpose made manifest in the instincts of the race whose present phase is our personal profit, but whose far-off end is the redemption of the world and the Christianization of mankind." Despite the warnings of the anti-imperialists that their country was descending from the "ancient path" of republican rectitude into the "cesspool" of imperialism, the Senate voted 57 to 27 to accept the treaty. Hawaii became an incorporated territory under the Organic Act of 1900. Guam was acquired as a naval station administered by the Navy Department. And Puerto Rico under the Foraker Act was attached as unincorporated territory with an elective legislature and a governor appointed by the President.

With the gathering of the colonial fruits of war with Spain and the arrival of Theodore Roosevelt in the White House, the initiative in formulating foreign policy fell to the activists who supported the President in his belief that national interest afforded the only sound base for a democratic foreign policy. "If we stand idly by," Roosevelt warned as the century opened, "if we seek merely swollen, slothful ease and ignoble peace, if we shrink from the hard contests where men must win at hazard of their lives and the the risk of all they hold dear, then the bolder and stronger people will pass us by. . . . Let us therefore boldly face the life of strife." Strife marked and not infrequently marred Roosevelt's

U.S. Marines stationed in Nicaragua. (*U.S. Marine Corps.*)

conduct of foreign policy from first to last—in Cuba and Panama and throughout
Latin America, and in American dealings with China and Japan. National interest in the Roosevelt years came to mean national egoism.

In Cuba the occupation by American forces continued as the United States
launched a program of administrative and public health reforms that culminated
in a successful campaign against yellow fever. With the Platt Amendment in 1901
the "ties of singular intimacy" connecting the United States and Cuba were drawn
even tighter by provisions for American intervention in case an unstable new
government failed to protect life, liberty, and property. Following the application of heavy pressure on the Cuban leadership this provision was written into
the constitution of the new republic in 1901 and incorporated into the treaty
between Cuba and the United States two years later. By 1903 the United States,
despite earlier disavowals, had established a virtual protectorate in the island
and reserved for itself the right of intervention in the internal affairs of its new
neighbor, a privilege it would invoke with regularity in the next half-century.

In the Philippines imposing American control awaited the outcome of the
insurrection, which dragged on until March 1901, when Aguinaldo was captured

and his scattered forces surrendered. Under the terms of the Philippine Organic Act of 1902 the United States provided a bicameral legislature and an appointed governor with broad executive powers. Although there would be numerous modifications of American rule in the islands during the next three decades, Philippine independence would not be achieved until 1946. Within a decade the dreams of a handful of "large policy" advocates had become a reality. The United States, without actually willing it, had acquired an imperial base for commercial and ideological expansion throughout the world.

Open and Closed Doors: Progressive Foreign Policy under Roosevelt and Taft

If a "splendid little war" had suddenly thrust the United States into the ranks of the world's big powers, its aftermath taught corrective lessons in the limits of American influence. The United States proved a slow and often recalcitrant pupil in the school of international power politics, and as late as the outbreak of war in Europe in 1914 still had much to learn about world affairs and the proper role of a democracy in managing them.

American education in the limits of power began in China at the turn of the century. The dream of a China market, rich and limitless, was older than the nation itself, a prime motive for original colonizing ventures and the search for a Northwest Passage. After the Revolution the dream became reality as the new nation opened markets in the Far East to compensate for the loss of old ones; and the subsequent age of clipper ships continued to feed American hopes for untold riches in the fabled Orient. Still, by century's end less than 2 percent of the foreign trade of the United States involved China, and it was with expectations of expanding this slim total that commercial and banking interests, concession hunters and investment seekers apprehensively watched European power rise rapidly in the Far East. If the United States meant to establish its own foothold on the Chinese mainland, it would have to move quickly.

The fatal weakness of the Manchu dynasty had recently become apparent in China's disastrous war with Japan in 1894–95. In the wake of China's defeat, the chief European powers joined Japan in descending on the moribund empire with demands for extended spheres of influence, trade concessions, and leases. Once again, as in the case of the Monroe Doctrine seventy-five years earlier, American and British interests coincided on the point of equal market opportunity. Again the British Foreign Office proposed a joint statement, only to be met by the preference of McKinley's administration for a unilateral American pronouncement. The result was a series of notes dispatched to the European capitals and Tokyo by Secretary of State John Hay that took the form of a self-denying ordinance binding the major powers not to interfere with vested rights within their spheres of influence or to infringe the tariff rights of the Chinese

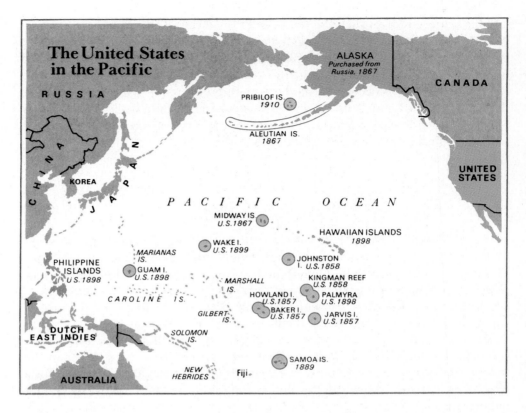

The United States in the Pacific

government. On receiving what were at best equivocal responses, Hay boldly proclaimed a general acceptance of his principles of the Open Door that he welcomed as "final and definitive."

Hay's optimistic reading of the intentions of the major powers with respect to China was soon tested by the Boxer Rebellion, a series of militant antiforeign riots that isolated the international community in Peking and invited a retaliatory rescue expedition (including 2500 American soldiers fresh from the Philippines) to lift the siege and punish the Chinese nationalists. Again the road lay open to further Chinese concessions leading to the dismantlement of the empire. Now Hay was forced to improvise a second circular note, this one announcing that the United States intended to maintain the territorial integrity of the Chinese empire. Here was a radical departure in American diplomacy — not simply a commitment to preserve equal economic opportunity on the mainland but a pledge to uphold the sovereignty of China. The American education in the limits of unilateral assertion was about to begin.

The Open Door policy, it was clear from the outset, would be just as controlling of imperialistic ambitions as the determination of England and the United States could make it. Events quickly dispelled American hopes for equal investment opportunity. The Chinese empire lay in shambles, its days numbered before revolution toppled the dynasty in 1911. England, accepting the inevitable, hastened to make overtures to Japan acknowledging that country's predominant interests on the mainland. Meanwhile rivalry between Russia and Japan over railroad and mining concessions in Manchuria led to the outbreak of war. Japan in a series of smashing victories played to perfection the role of "underdog," so attractive to Americans, and forced Russia to accept the mediational offices of Roosevelt, who suddenly appeared in the unfamiliar guise of peacemaker.

Although the Portsmouth Treaty, which Roosevelt forced on an unhappy Russia, established Japan as the dominant power in the Far East, the principles of the Open Door were scarcely advanced. In a secret agreement in 1907 Russia and Japan agreed to divide Manchuria, Mongolia, and Korea into dual spheres of influence with "special interests." Roosevelt, in recognizing Japan's special interests in Manchuria in the Root-Takahira Agreement (1908), presided over the ceremonial closing of the Open Door. Conceding that the Open Door was "an excellent thing" so far as it could be upheld by general diplomatic agreement, Roosevelt admitted that the policy simply disappeared once a nation like Japan chose to disregard it. The Open Door had ended in failure. It would take the Taft administration's abortive attempt to send American capital by diplomatic pressure "into a region of the world it would not go of its own accord" to revive interest in prying open the door to Manchuria, and here too hopes for American economic penetration would outstrip performance.

In the Moroccan crisis of 1905–06 Roosevelt managed to salvage at least some of the splinters of the Open Door as he improved his performance as peacemaker. The crisis grew out of conflicting French and German interests in North Africa, a clash in which American concern, according to Roosevelt's secretary of state, Elihu Root, was not strong enough "to justify us in taking a leading part." Nevertheless, Roosevelt broke a century-long tradition of nonintervention by actively directing the Algeciras Conference (1906). The terms of settlement, following Roosevelt's intentions, checked German penetration of North Africa for the moment, united France and England in solid opposition to the kaiser, and reaffirmed for the United States the principles of the Open Door. Roosevelt, who already distrusted German military power, professed himself entirely satisfied with the outcome at Algeciras and boasted of having stood the kaiser on his head "with great decision." Yet imperial Germany soon righted itself, and it was clear that a temporary departure from a policy of nonentanglement in European affairs was not to be repeated in the second Moroccan crisis of 1911, which Taft studiouly avoided. Despite Roosevelt's assertion of an American interest in the European balance of power, he was unable to overturn a century-long tradition of isolation or to provide compelling reasons for abandoning it. An American foreign policy of realism reached its outer limits at Algeciras.

No such doubts concerning the United States role as policeman inhibited progressive foreign policy in the Caribbean, where economic interests and preponderant American power combined in a shortsighted policy of constant intervention. In Latin America interference in the internal affairs of unstable republics quickly became a habit. Behind this pattern of continual interference lay rapidly expanding American economic interests, not simply in trade but in banking, investments, and the development of natural resources, all of which seemingly required a favorable political climate and the willingness to grant generous economic concessions to the Colossus of the North.

Troubles for Progressive policymakers began in that "infernal little Cuban republic," as Roosevelt called it in confessing to a recurrent urge to "wipe its people off the face of the earth." Four years after the removal of American forces in 1902 the troops were back again in another attempt to restore order. A policeman's lot, the President agreed, was not a happy one. "All that we wanted from them was that they would behave themselves and be prosperous and happy so that we would not have to interfere." Instead, the Cubans persisted in playing at revolution and "may get things into such a snarl that we have no alternative save to intervene—which will at once convince the suspicious idiots in South America that we do wish to interfere after all, and perhaps have some land hunger." The President neglected to add what was beginning to be obvious to interested European observers—that it was not land hunger but the hope of establishing economic hegemony in Latin America that dictated an interventionist strategy.

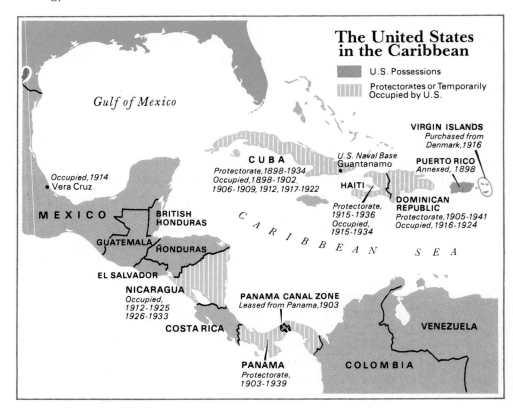

A policy of constantly interfering in the domestic affairs of neighbors required an explanation from the United States; and Roosevelt provided this in the famous "corollary" to the Monroe Doctrine in his annual message to Congress in 1905. The occasion once again as in Cleveland's administration ten years earlier was a fiscal crisis in Venezuela, where a chronically unstable and corrupt dictatorship refused to honor its debts. In 1903 Germany took it upon herself to nudge the Venezuelan government toward a more conciliatory stance by bombarding Fort San Carlos and was dissuaded from further reprisals only by prompt American condemnation of the "outrage." To forestall similar European moves to protect investors, Roosevelt offered his corollary. "Chronic wrong-doing," he admitted, would inevitably invite the wrath of "civilized" nations determined to safeguard their investments in Latin America. Since the Monroe Doctrine effectively prevented them from intervening directly, the United States, "however reluctantly," might be forced to step in "in flagrant cases of such wrongdoing or impotence." In short, denying to the major powers spheres of influence in China under the Open Door was to have no equivalent in Latin America, which rightfully belonged to the United States even if it had to undertake the work of an "international police power" itself.

The meaning of the Roosevelt "corollary" immediately became clear in the Dominican Republic in 1905, when after considerable urging from the United States the government agreed to request American assistance in straightening out its finances, advice which Roosevelt, despite congressional reservations, was more than willing to provide. With the control of the Dominican customshouse safely in American hands the United States had succeeded in forestalling German intervention once more but at the cost of a policy that would continue to breed hemispheric ill will throughout the twentieth century.

The problem of Panama and American acquisition of the rights to an isthmian canal offered the clearest example of a Progressive foreign policy based on narrow and shortsighted national interest. The decision to abandon the Nicaraguan route, which had intrigued America for over a century, was made at the behest of high-powered lobbyists of the New Panama Canal Company, successor to the defunct French company that had tried and failed to complete the Panama enterprise. The ingenious combination of French adventurers and American entrepreneurs succeeded in convincing Roosevelt, Mark Hanna, and other Republican leaders of the distinct advantages of the Panama route, and managed, with the help of a few carefully placed investments in the future of the Republican party, to win congressional support for their lucrative deal. By 1902 all that remained was to convince the inept government of Colombia of the benefits about to be conferred on it by civilization.

For a while negotiations proceeded smoothly The Hay-Herran Treaty of 1903 tendered to the United States the rights to a canal zone six miles wide for the bargain-basement price of $10 million plus an annual rental of $250,000. Then

DIGGING THE PANAMA CANAL

(*Panama Canal Company.*)

suddenly Colombian patriots, preparing to overthrow a corrupt dictatorship and awakening to the fact that they were being swindled, forced the Colombian Senate to withdraw the treaty. Colombia, it became clear to Roosevelt, was about to up the ante even if it meant incurring the famed presidential wrath.

Roosevelt denounced his new opponents as "inefficient bandits" and "contemptible little creatures" who were willfully blocking the march of progress. His initial scheme frustrated, the President accepted an alternative plan for a pocket revolution engineered by the promoters of the canal and a handful of native dissidents, who proceeded to establish Panamanian independence with the blessings of the United States and the help of the American navy. The new state of Panama, following hasty recognition by the United States, willingly obliged her benefactor by granting the terms for the canal that Colombia had refused. Roosevelt had his canal project, the Panamanian patriots their revolution, and the canal promoters their prospects of profits. Roosevelt never ceased defending his part in the affair. "If I had followed traditional conservative methods I would have submitted a dignified State paper of probably 200 pages to Congress and the debates on it would have been going on yet; but I took the Canal Zone and let Congress debate; and while the debate goes on the Canal does also."

With this bald assertion of executive power and national egoism Roosevelt drew together the strands of his progressive diplomacy. His diplomatic style, in the first place, was a highly personal one, proceeding from the assumption that most of the issues in foreign affairs were best handled, as he said, "by one man alone." Although he used his secretaries of state John Hay and Elihu Root effectively on occasion, just as frequently he bypassed them and seldom gave them credit for decisions that rightly or wrongly he considered his own. Determined to play a lone hand, he also fumed at the constant interference of the Senate and its tampering with what he considered an executive prerogative. Deliberative bodies, he insisted, were virtually useless when there was "any efficient work" to be done. It was for the President alone to take charge of foreign policy in the same way that he formulated domestic priorities of reform and reorganization. After he had retired from office, Roosevelt compiled for his admirers a list of the Latin American countries in which he had been forced to intervene, and prefaced his remarks with the boast that given the opportunity, he would have intervened in a number of others. Such actions, he boasted, would have been "simply in the interest of civilization, if I could have waked up our people so that they would back a reasonable and intelligent foreign policy which would have put a stop to the crying disorders at our very doors."

"Crying disorders"—here was the key to the passageway leading from domestic to foreign policy. Order in Asia, Roosevelt was to learn, lay beyond the reach of American power. In Europe, where his leverage was greater, Roosevelt could combine plans for a balance of power with predictions of a perpetual Anglo-American ascendency throughout the world. But it was at home in the Western Hemisphere that the benefits of order and stability seemed to him greatest even though the long-term costs in good will eventually proved prohibitive.

Although it fell to Roosevelt to preside over the transformation of territorial imperialism into a policy of economic penetration, his language betrayed an ignorance of his historical function. He spoke constantly of "honor, territorial integrity and vital interests" as the only basis for an American foreign policy, but his concepts lacked substance. His speeches rang with the clichés of "righteousness" and "duty," as he mixed moralism and nationalism in a blend of power politics that glossed over the economic motives he never clearly acknowledged. The central theme running through his pronouncements on foreign policy concerned the dangers of American preoccupation with domestic prosperity that threatened to turn righteous citizens into a mere "assemblage of well-to-do hucksters" who cared nothing for what happened beyond their borders. But to argue the case for an aggressive foreign policy purely in terms of altruism was to ignore the very economic forces that increasingly determined American activities, particularly in Latin America, namely, investment opportunity, concessions, corporate resource development, and other forms of economic penetration—all requiring political and economic stability essential to the continued exploitation of colonial economies. Roosevelt's rhetoric tended to conceal the fact that as President he became if not the captive at least the confederate of the very economic forces he presumably distrusted. In substituting dollars for bullets the Taft administration displayed no such squeamishness in confronting the reality of economic imperialism.

The marriage of economic policy and power politics that Roosevelt had failed to legitimize received its awaited sanction from the Taft administration. Taft's choice of a secretary of state, the corporation lawyer Philander C. Knox, was itself proof of the growing intimacy between the investment community in Wall Street and the State Department. Knox, who was given a freer hand in formulating policy than Roosevelt had accorded his predecessors, was the chief architect of a democratic state capitalism that came to be known as "dollar diplomacy." Dollar diplomacy involved using American export capital together with preponderant political power to appeal, as Taft explained, "alike to idealistic humanitarian sentiments, to the dictates of sound policy and strategy, and to legitimate commercial aims."

Dollar diplomacy also represented the extension of the principles of domestic progressivism into foreign policy. Investment capitalists were instructed to pursue a policy of development and economic penetration in undeveloped areas under conditions of stability and profitability to be ensured by the government. Knox himself explained how the system worked to the advantage of all parties: "If the American dollar can aid suffering humanity and lift the burden of financial difficulty from States with which we live on terms of intimate intercourse and earnest friendship, and replace insecurity and devastation by stability and peaceful self-development, all I can say is that it would be hard to find better employment." Yet Knox was not always successful at convincing American capitalists that his course was wise.

Even though the Taft administration proved more willing than its predecessor to declare openly an economic motive, it did not alter the pattern of success and failure—conspicuous success in attracting investment in Latin America, where the bankers were more than willing to go, and nearly total failure in the Far East, where they were not. In attempting to open China once more to American capital Taft met the determined resistance of British, French, and German bankers against including their American counterparts into a consortium to finance and build the Hukuang Railway in China, an ill-considered project that was never completed. By dint of considerable diplomatic pressure applied to the Chinese emperor Knox succeeded in gaining admission to the consortium but needlessly made trouble for himself by a carelessly conceived experiment in state capitalism in Manchuria. The scheme backfired when both Russia and Japan objected and American bankers lost interest. Like Hay's original scheme, the Taft administration's attempt to open the door to American capital in Asia ended in complete failure.

No such difficulties were encountered in Latin America, where American capital was already streaming in. Here a combination of supersalesmanship and regular government intervention to protect American investments—in Nicaragua, Guatemala, the Honduras, and Haiti—continued to open the sluice gates to American capital.

The legal framework within which dollar diplomacy sought to realize its economic objectives was provided by the progressive faith in arbitration with which Taft hoped to defuse international crises in much the same way mediational panels in domestic affairs theoretically depoliticized economic conflict. Twenty-five arbitration treaties had been signed in the last days of the outgoing Roosevelt administration, and Taft sought to extend the application of the principle to all "justiciable" issues. The Senate, however, promptly eliminated the procedures for discussion in every case in which the United States might be presumed to have a "vital interest." Nevertheless, an arbitration scheme designed to complement dollar diplomacy lived on as a progressive panacea, drawing the immediate attention of Woodrow Wilson and his secretary of state—the "Prince of Peace," William Jennings Bryan. There would be continuities as well as new departures in the missionary diplomacy of Woodrow Wilson.

"The Organized Force of Mankind": Wilsonian Diplomacy and World War

The progressive years saw internationalists, peace groups, and idealists regroup into a broad coalition behind the principles of missionary diplomacy, moral publicity and open covenants. In repudiating both Roosevelt's role of big brother to the benighted and Taft's "dollar diplomacy," Woodrow Wilson entered office with an appeal to national altruism that warmed the hearts of moralists everywhere. "My dream is that as the years go on and the world knows more and more of America," Wilson told a Fourth of July audience in 1914, "it . . . will turn to America for those moral inspirations which lie at the basis of all freedoms . . . and that America will come into the full light of day when all shall know that she puts human rights above all other rights and that her flag is the flag not only of America but of humanity." Yet three months earlier Wilson had ordered the occupation of Vera Cruz to vindicate American honor.

It was not the least of early twentieth-century American paradoxes that both these widely divergent formulations of foreign policy led unerringly to a continuing involvement of the United States throughout the world and direct, forcible intervention in the affairs of neighboring states almost constantly. Both the demands of national interest and the less precise requirements of moral mission ended in the application of raw power. By 1917, America's arrival as a world power had long been established, but it remained to be seen what uses would be made of the material resources of the United States in reordering a world at war. Americans joined the fighting still seeking an answer to this question.

Like most Americans before 1914, Woodrow Wilson had given little serious thought to the specifics of an American foreign policy. Diplomatic problems had not figured prominently in the campaign of 1912, and to their solution Wilson brought only a widely shared set of assumptions which constituted the conventional wisdom of an active peace movement in the United States. In the years that followed, the President served as the mouthpiece of this movement, taking many of its principles for his own and fashioning them into a theoretical alternative to balance-of-power politics.

By 1910 a belief in a coming age of international harmony had become a staple item in the ideological stock of numerous progressive intellectuals and professionals for whom worldwide communications, an international technology, and the uses of arbitration seemed to point to a new world order. The American peace movement consisted of a variety of groups and interests: traditional church-affiliated peace societies and new secular foundations like Andrew Carnegie's Endowment for International Peace; students of international law intent on building new legal frameworks; preachers of disarmament; and prophets of a vast people-to-people crusade. Common to many of these peace advocates was a peculiarly American set of assumptions that made their movement an adjunct to domestic progressive reform. There was the belief, for example, that the path to world order had been first discovered by the United States as it progressed from a loose confederation of sovereign states to a genuine union of loyal citizens. From similar beginnings, the promoters of peace reasoned, might well come an age of international harmony and democratic striving.

Attached to this golden vision of an Americanized world order was a faith in arbitration itself as a transnational mechanism for resolving tensions and conflicts, whether in a Hague Court, a body of international law, or bilateral "cooling off" treaties. Much of the appeal of the peace movement lay in its remoteness from the realities of clashing national ambitions that descended on an unsuspecting American public in 1914.

These progressive preferences led Wilson to examine the hopes of the peace advocates at just the time when many of them were beginning to retreat to a more comfortable faith in enlightened national self-interest. Wilson's language, like the vocabulary of his chief rival, Theodore Roosevelt, was unrelievedly abstract. But whereas Roosevelt, a self-declared "realist," argued the unexamined propositions of national "honor" and "integrity," Wilson translated these terms into the language of altruism. National interest narrowly construed he equated with "selfishness" and the rule of unbridled materialism. "Balance of power," in his mind, meant unstable coalitions of aggressive interests. The outlook of "average" people the world over, on the contrary, was becoming "more and more unclouded" as national purposes fell more and more into the background and the "common purpose of enlightened mankind" took their place. The time was not far distant when these "counsels of plain men" would come to replace the "counsels of sophisticated men of affairs" as the best means of securing peace. Then the statesmen of the world would be forced to heed the "common clarified thought" or be broken.

Here in embryonic form lay Wilson's plan for an alternative system of world politics, which had begun to take shape in his mind even before war broke out in Europe. Wilson's language proved fully equal to his vision as he assumed what critics called his "papal role" in preaching a humanitarian theology. "I do not know that there will ever be a declaration of independence or grievances for mankind," he told a Fourth of July audience at Independence Hall in Philadelphia in 1914, scarcely a week before the outbreak of war, "but I believe that if any such document is ever drawn it will be drawn in the spirit of the American Declaration of Independence, and that America has lifted high the light which will shine unto all generations and guide the feet of mankind to the goal of justice and liberty and peace." The President, noted the editors of the *New Republic* wryly, uttered nothing that might sound trivial at the Last Judgment.

The first fruits of this Wilsonian "missionary" spirit were bitter ones for the promoters of Dollar Diplomacy. Wilson quickly dashed the hopes of the outgoing Taft administration for continued economic penetration in China as he denounced the scheme for railroad financing as a violation of Chinese sovereignty. In the delicate negotiations over the Panama Canal tolls he argued that American exemption betrayed a "dishonorable attitude" on the part of the United States, and at the risk of dividing his own party he secured a repeal. Then in October 1913, in his famous Mobile address, he completed the reversal of Dollar Diplomacy by promising to emancipate Latin America from its "subordination" to "foreign enterprise."

Yet in Latin America, where the interests of business were real and compelling, Wilson found it impossible to reverse his predecessors' policy of intervention, and his formal disavowal of American interference ended in bitter irony. The chief contradiction of missionary diplomacy lay in the fact that under Wilson the United States intervened in the affairs of its neighbors more often than ever before. Military occupation of Haiti in 1915. Financial supervision in the Dominican Republic in 1916. Renewed controls in Cuba in 1917. And minor meddling in behalf of American investors throughout the Caribbean. Moralistic though he was, Wilson was not blind to the operation of economic motives nor deaf to the appeals of investors. His difficulties in Latin America largely resulted from his tendency to identify the beneficent workings of American capital with the welfare of "the submerged eighty-five per cent" of native populations to whom he wanted to bring the blessings of parliamentary democracy. This was the real meaning of his announced intention "to teach the South American republics to elect good men."

Mexico served as the testing ground for these theories of moral diplomacy and proved them wanting in political realism. In 1911, following a quarter-century's oppressive rule, moderate constitutionalists led by Francisco Madero overthrew the Mexican dictator, Porfirio Diaz. The new government received the prompt recognition of the Taft administration. Then, less than two years later, Madero himself fell victim to a counterrevolutionary coup directed by one of his lieutenants, Victoriano Huerta, who murdered his former chief and seized the presidential office. This was the situation confronting Wilson as he took office.

Wilson, outraged by Huerta's brutality, lost no time in denouncing him as a thug and a butcher, and refused to recognize his government. His refusal rested partly on a genuine moral revulsion and partly on the knowledge that England had accorded Huerta recognition in the hope of gaining further economic concessions. Although economic and strategic concerns usually appeared on the periphery of Wilson's moral vision, they were never quite out of sight. He continued to insist that the United States must never abandon morality for expediency and "never condone iniquity because it is convenient to do so." But in Mexico profits for American investors and parliamentary democracy for the Mexican people seemed to him wholly compatible.

Wilson's heroic remedy for Mexico mixed strong disapproval of a "government of butchers" with plans for replacing Huerta with the liberal rule of Venustiano Carranza, another constitutionalist who had succeeded in rallying opposition to the dictator. The President seized the occasion for toppling Huerta when a boatload of American sailors were arrested and unlawfully detained in Tampico. Wilson demanded an immediate apology, and his administration found itself in the strange diplomatic posture of demanding a twenty-one-gun salute from a government it would not recognize. When Huerta predictably refused, Wilson ordered the occupation of Vera Cruz, an exercise that cost the lives of nineteen Americans and a great many more Mexicans. Under relentless pressure from the United States and besieged by the forces of the constitutionalists, Huerta resigned and fled to Spain in 1914. Yet Carranza's liberal regime proved no more willing to tolerate American intervention than the deposed dictator had. Only the timely offer of the ABC Powers (Argentina, Brazil, Chile) to mediate the dispute allowed Wilson to withdraw the American forces and save diplomatic face temporarily.

The second act of the diplomatic crisis in Mexico opened with the attempt of Pancho Villa, bandit leader and unsavory associate of Carranza, to overthrow his chief and take power by provoking a war with the United States, a piece of strategy that very nearly worked. On January 10, 1916, Villa and his band stopped a train at Santa Ysabel in the northern provinces, took 17 Americans off, and shot 16 of them. Then in March, Villa raided the tiny New Mexico town of Columbus, burned it flat, and killed 19 more American citizens. Wilson responded, as Villa had hoped he would, by dispatching General John J. Pershing

MEXICAN-AMERICAN RELATIONS, 1916–1917

Pancho Villa's raid on a New Mexico town and his murder of American citizens called for a U.S. punitive expedition led by General John J. Pershing. (*Left, Brown Brothers; below, Culver Pictures, Inc.*)

on a punitive expedition, which chased the bandit chief some three hundred miles back into Mexico without managing to catch him.

Once again Carranza's diplomatic temper flared, and his government demanded the immediate withdrawal of American troops. Faced now with the nearly certain prospect of war with Germany, Wilson could only comply. "We shall yet prove to the Mexican people that we know how to serve them without first thinking of ourselves," he had promised. But in 1917 Villa roamed the Mexican countryside, an unstable Carranza government lurched toward yet another constitutional crisis, and Wilson had little to show for his five-year labor in the Mexican vineyard. Now, however, his attention was fixed on Europe.

The outbreak of the First World War caught the Wilson administration and the entire country by surprise. At first the news that Austria had invaded tiny Serbia occasioned little American concern beyond traditional sympathy for the underdog. Since neither European nor American diplomats yet realized the scale of the coming catastrophe, it was not difficult for Wilson to declare American neutrality and call on all citizens to remain "impartial in thought as well as in action." Behind the proclamation of neutrality lay the President's belief that the war would be short and end in a settlement that the United States, from its Olympian station above the battle, could help arrange. And behind that sanguine expectation lay still another conviction that the terms imposed by America would usher in a new moral order.

As the war dragged into its second year, all of Wilson's hopes for remodeling the world of power politics came to hinge on a doctrine of neutrality that itself depended on two misconceptions. First, developments quickly showed that the United States was not and could not be unconcerned with the outcome of the war. The fact was, as shrewd observers had pointed out before war broke out, that England, in upholding the European balance of power from the early 1800s, had directly contributed to American growth and well-being. An Anglo-German conflict was thus bound to affect the United States in crucial ways.

The first year of the war drove home the force of this observation. England monopolized access to the information defining the meaning of the war and skillfully manipulated its advantage until the President and his advisers came to realize, as one of them put it, that "Germany must not be permitted to win this war." By 1915 the administration began, half consciously, to act on this assumption. The American economy was placed at the disposal of the Allies, who despite the embarrassing presence of imperial Russia, were presumed to be fighting autocracy and militarism in the name of democracy. Trade with the Allies was proclaimed "legal and welcome." When Allied credit soon evaporated, American bankers rushed to the rescue with credits and loans that totaled $2.5 billion by the time America entered the war in 1917. Wilson continued to press both England and Germany for a settlement, but when neither side agreed, he tended to excuse the former and blame the latter for the disastrous military stalemate.

The second misconception underlying Wilson's doctrine of neutrality grew out of his failure to credit the logic of total war or to acknowledge the effect of modern technology. The submarine had made the traditional rights of neutrals obsolete. Both combatants as they grappled for an economic stranglehold on the other were forced to resort to novel practices that were clear violations of established precedent. England extended the right of search and visit to new lengths and established a paper blockade that virtually extinguished the rights of neutrals. Yet diplomatic exchange with England settled into a predictable pattern of violation, protest, discussion, and eventual resumption of the objectionable practice.

With Germany, on the other hand, diplomatic exchange soon grew brittle and strained as Wilson's language became increasingly terse. The use of submarines, which struck without warning or provision for the safety of passengers and crew, touched a raw nerve in the American people as yet unacquainted with the techniques of total war. When in May 1915, a German U-boat without warning torpedoed the British liner *Lusitania* with the loss of 128 American lives, Wilson initiated an angry dialogue that became more and more strident in the next year and a half. Germany quite correctly pointed out that the ship carried contraband of war, but that fact hardly weakened Wilson's determination to apply the old rules. For the President the sinking of the *Lusitania* demonstrated "the practical impossibility of employing submarines in the destruction of commerce without disregarding those rules of fairness, reason, justice and humanity, which all modern opinion regards as imperative." In resolving to hold Germany "strictly accountable" Wilson put the United States on a collision course: if the German government decided that unrestricted submarine warfare was worth the risk of bringing the United States into the war against it, the President would have little freedom to maneuver. By 1917 he had lost that initiative.

In the meantime, following the *Lusitania* incident, Germany agreed to comply with Wilson's terms. Then in 1916, with the attack on the unarmed French passenger ship *Sussex* in the English Channel, which resulted in injury to American citizens, the meaning of "strict accountability" suddenly became clear to the President. Submarine warfare, he informed Germany, "of necessity, because of the very character of the vessels employed," was "incompatible" with the "sacred immunities of noncombatants." Unless the imperial government agreed to abandon its methods forthwith, the United States would have no choice but to sever relations preparatory to declaring war. Germany agreed to discontinue the practice but only with the proviso that the United States call on England to lift the blockade. The German government reserved the right to rescind its pledge until Britain agreed. The President's options were dwindling fast.

Wilson's growing indignation reflected another, more personal anxiety. For three years he had continued to pile on the conventional concept of neutral rights a load of moral principles that the original construction had not been designed to carry. Now he was forced to admit that the United States might not be able to impose its will on warring Europe without joining the Allies. A nation that had been "too proud to fight" and had reelected him on the slogan "He kept us out of war" now faced the prospect of securing a "peace without victory" only as a participant. The meaning of this new commitment was not lost on Wilson, who now sought to define his mission to his countrymen as nothing less than the building of a system of collective security to replace a bankrupt system of balance of power. If compelled to fight, the United States would fight for utopia.

In January 1917, a week before Germany announced its decision to resume unrestricted submarine warfare, Wilson described his vision of a new world order to the Senate. The United States, prepared by "the very principles and purposes" of its humanitarian policy, must rebuild the machinery of diplomacy. Its terms for peace would "win the approval of mankind" and not merely "serve the several interests and immediate aims of the nations engaged." Wilson proposed a perpetual league of peaceful nations as an integral part of the settlement, a collective instrument, which he described as "so much greater than the force of any nation now engaged or any alliance hitherto projected" that governments and their leaders would bend to its dictates. The future of the world would thus come to depend, not on a balance of power, but on a community of opinion, not on "organized rivalries," but on an "organized peace." He proposed, in short, a concert of moral force made up of peoples who with their open covenants openly arrived at could enforce their collective will for national self-determination, democratic government, and lasting peace. To skeptical senators, particularly those in the Republican ranks, Wilson explained that his were at once "American principles" and "the principles of all mankind."

A week later the German imperial government renewed its submarine attacks in a desperate gamble to win the war before the United States could rescue England and France. In March, German submarines without warning sank four unarmed American merchantmen, and on April 2, 1917, Wilson appeared before a joint session of Congress to request that it accept the war that had been "thrust" upon the United States. By a vote of 82 to 6 in the Senate and 373 to 50 in the House, Congress agreed to the presidential request.

The United States, its citizens would learn from a year and a half of war and another year of peacemaking, had arrived at a position of world power that only a few of their number would have predicted thirty years earlier. The nation had gone to war with Spain on the flimsiest of pretexts and built an empire on its victory. But in the intervening years, most Americans, far from accepting imperial responsibilities, had agreed to neglect the chores of maintaining an empire, and except at home in their own hemisphere, had conveniently forgotten their regenerative mission. Now as their President called on them to fight another and infinitely greater war, the precise nature of their moral contribution still eluded them. For a sense of the right direction they still relied on Wilson.

WAR BOND RALLY

The American people prepare for war. (*Brown Brothers.*)

The President, for his part, having determined on war as the only option left open to him, indulged in a prophecy and a private confession in contemplating his course. "We are at the beginning of an age," he told the country, "in which it will be insisted that the same standards of conduct and of responsibility for wrong done shall be observed among nations and their governments that are observed among individual citizens of civilized states." But privately in the solitude of the White House on the eve of his appearance before Congress, he made another prediction. To Frank Cobb, the editor of the New York *World*, he admitted to fears about the unintended effects of going to war. "Once lead this people into war," he told Cobb, "and they'll forget there ever was such a thing as tolerance. To fight you must be brutal and ruthless, and the spirit of ruthless brutality will enter into the very fibre of our national life, infecting Congress, the courts, the policeman on the beat, the man in the streets." The meaning of his prophecy of a new international order awaited the outcome of the war, but the prediction of the domestic dangers in fighting it proved all too accurate.

Suggested Readings

The boundaries of scholarly criticism of American foreign policy after 1890 are established in two different surveys. George F. Kennan, *American Diplomacy, 1900–1950* (1951), points to consistently unprofessional and uninformed leaders as the chief difficulty, while William Appleman Williams, *The Tragedy of American Diplomacy* (1959), cites economic expansion as the source of a peculiar kind of American imperialism. Robert E. Osgood, *Ideals and Self-Interest in America's Foreign Relations* (1953), evaluates the assumptions of both parties to the great debate over means and ends. Richard W. Leopold, *The Growth of American Foreign Policy* (1962), is an excellent survey, which should be combined with John A. S. Grenville and George B. Young, *Politics, Strategy, and American Diplomacy, . . . 1873–1917* (1966). Two other readable accounts of the emergence of an American foreign policy are Foster R. Dulles, *America's Rise to World Power, 1898–1954* (1955), and for backgrounds Richard W. Van Alstyne, *The Rising American Empire* (1960). Rubin F. Weston, *Racism in U.S. Imperialism: The Influence of Racial Assumptions on American Foreign Policy, 1893–1946* (1972), examines race prejudice as a component of U.S. foreign policy. William Appleman Williams, *The Shaping of American Diplomacy* (1956), is a highly useful source.

The origins of the American expansionism in the 1890s are carefully examined in Walter LaFeber, *The New Empire: An Interpretation of American Expansion, 1860–1898* (1963), and Milton Plesur, *America's Outward Thrust, 1865–1890* (1971). David Pletcher, *The Awkward Years: America's Foreign Relations under Garfield and Arthur* (1962), offers a meticulous analysis of early fumblings in the 1880s.

There are several excellent studies of the rising diplomatic crisis in the 1890s—among them Ernest R. May, *Imperial Democracy: The Emergence of America as a Great Power* (1961), and the same author's exploratory essay, *American Imperialism: A Speculative Essay* (1968); H. Wayne Morgan, *America's Road to Empire: The War with Spain and Overseas Expansion* (1965); David Healy, *United States Expansionism: The Imperialist Urge in the 1890's* (1970). The influence of the navy and the role of Mahan are explored in Peter Karsten, *The Naval Aristocracy* (1972), and William Livezey, *Mahan on Sea Power* (1947). Charles H. Brown, *The Correspondents' War: Journalists in the Spanish-American War* (1967), covers the reporters' beat. Robert L. Beisner, *The Anti-Imperialists, 1898–1900* (1968), and E. Berkeley Tompkins, *Anti-Imperialism in the United States: The Great Debate, 1890–1920* (1970), assess the arguments and futile activities of the opponents of expansionism. Leon Wolff, *Little Brown Brother* (1961), gives an outraged account of the Philippine insurrection and the American pacification program.

Areas of growing American interest and control have been well covered in a number of careful monographs: Merze Tate, *The United States and the Hawaiian Kingdom* (1965); Howard F. Cline, *The United States and Mexico* (1953); A. Whitney Griswold, *The Far Eastern Policy of the United States* (1938); Charles Vevier, *The United States and China, 1906–1913* (1955); Charles E. Neu, *The Troubled Encounter: The United States and Japan* (1975); and Samuel F. Bemis, *The Latin American Policy of the United States* (1967). John Hay's intentions in announcing the Open Door policy are thoroughly canvassed in Tyler Dennett, *John Hay* (1933), and the unforeseen results in Marilyn B. Young, *The Rhetoric of Empire: American China Policy, 1893–1901* (1968); Warren Cohen, *America's Response to China* (1971); Thomas McCormick, *China Market: America's Quest for Informal Empire, 1893–1901* (1967); Jerry Israel, *Progressivism and the Open Door: America and China, 1905–1921* (1971); and Paul A. Varg, *The Making of a Myth: The United States and China, 1899–1912* (1968). Other detailed studies of aspects of progressive foreign policy include Charles E. Neu, *An Uncertain Friendship: Theodore Roosevelt and Japan* (1967); Akira Iriye, *Across the*

Pacific: An Inner History of American–East Asian Relations (1967); and Edward Berbusse, *The United States in Puerto Rico* (1965).

On Roosevelt's foreign policy formulations, Howard K. Beale, *Theodore Roosevelt and the Rise of America to World Power* (1956), is still standard; see also Raymond A. Esthus, *Theodore Roosevelt and the International Rivalries* (1970). Robert A. Hart, *The Great White Fleet: Its Voyage Around the World* (1965), is a highly readable account of Roosevelt's colorful gesture. Dwight C. Miner, *Fight for the Panama Route* (1966), tells a complicated story well, and Akira Iriye, *Pacific Estrangement: Japanese and American Expansion, 1897–1911* (1972), explains Roosevelt's many problems in that area. Walter V. Scholes and Marie V. Scholes, *The Foreign Policies of the Taft Administration* (1970), analyzes the workings of Dollar Diplomacy, and Dana G. Munroe, *Intervention and Dollar Diplomacy in the Caribbean, 1900–1921* (1964), examines its consequences. Sondra R. Herman, *Eleven Against War: Studies in American Internationalist Thought, 1898–1921* (1969), studies a variety of peace types, and Bradford Perkins, *The Great Rapprochement: England and the United States, 1895–1914* (1968), is indispensable for understanding American attitudes towards the First World War.

The most comprehensive discussions of Wilsonian diplomacy from a presidential perspective are to be found in the volumes of Link's *Wilson*. P. Edward Haley, *Revolution and Intervention: The Diplomacy of Taft and Wilson with Mexico, 1910–1917* (1970), is an even-handed examination of Mexican policy, and so is Robert Freeman Smith, *The U.S. and Revolutionary Nationalism in Mexico, 1916–1932* (1972), for the later period. Robert E. Quirk, *An Affair of Honor: Woodrow Wilson and the Occupation of Veracruz* (1962), criticizes the President for his misguided actions in that unfortunate affair, and Clarence C. Clendenen, *The United States and Pancho Villa* (1961) is adequate. Hans R. Schmidt, *The United States Occupation of Haiti, 1915–1934* (1971), surveys the problems presented by the unstable republic in the Progressive search for order in the Caribbean. Harley Notter, *The Origins of the Foreign Policy of Woodrow Wilson* (1937), tests the theoretical underpinnings of Wilsonian diplomacy.

Neutrality and American intervention in the First World War fascinated a Depression generation preparing for war and produced a number of notable accounts, from the acerbic Walter Millis, *The Road to War* (1935), to the scholarly Charles Seymour, *American Neutrality, 1914–1917* (1935), and Edwin Borchard and W. P. Lage, *Neutrality for the United States* (1940). More recent literature on Wilsonian neutrality and its premises is extensive. Among the best accounts are Ernest R. May, *The World War and American Isolation, 1914–1917* (1959); John M. Cooper, Jr., *The Vanity of Power: American Isolation and the First World War, 1914–1917* (1969); Ross Gregory, *The Origins of American Intervention in the First World War* (1971); Daniel M. Smith, *The Great Departure: The United States in World War I, 1914–1920* (1965); and Carl P. Parrini, *Heir to Empire: U.S. Economic Diplomacy, 1916–1923* (1969). Link's *Wilson* contains a meticulous account of the gradual shift in the President's assessment of the war, and Edward Buehrig, *Woodrow Wilson and the Balance of Power* (1955), examines his various strategies.

29

Progressivism and the Great War

By the time the United States entered the war in April 1917, all the European powers were rapidly approaching exhaustion. After three years of stalemate Germany was suffering from starvation and the imminent collapse of civilian morale. Austria-Hungary managed to continue the war only by imposing martial law. Russia, crippled by astronomical losses that had led to the overthrow of the czarist regime a month earlier, stood on the brink of a second Bolshevik revolution. France, its national will shattered, faced widespread mutiny in her armies. England, having sacrificed an entire generation of young men to German machine guns since 1914, was beset with severe manpower shortages both at home and in the field.

The original predictions and plans of both sides—Germany's for a six-week war and the Allies' for rolling back the enemy on two vast fronts—had long since been buried under mounds of casualties. Both sides, driven by contrasting but strangely complementary illusions, had succeeded in proving that in total war it is the war that wins. Shared strategic obsessions with artillery barrages and massed infantry assaults on entrenched positions had created a mirror image war of appalling senselessness and butchery. Two million casualties on the Western Front in 1916 had failed to move the line of advance for either side, and the war had descended once again into the trenches that stretched in an unbroken line from the sea to the mountains. A week after Wilson addressed Congress in April 1917, the British launched still another frontal attack in the Ypres sector of the front, and in five days gained 7000 yards at the cost of 160,000 dead and wounded.

Although the United States entered the war late and suffered proportionately fewer losses, the meaning of the slaughter lingered in the American imagination for a generation. In a scene in F. Scott Fitzgerald's *Tender Is the Night,* one of the characters leads a party of sightseers across the Somme valley after the war. "See that little stream," he says, "We could walk to it in two minutes. It took the British a whole month to walk to it—a whole empire walking very slowly, dying in front and pushing forward behind. And another empire walked very slowly backward a few inches a day, leaving the dead like a million bloody rugs." American soldiers in the last year of the war followed the footsteps of their British and French predecessors. In joining the Allies, the United States committed its forces to a war in which a grisly paradox awarded ultimate defeat to the side that won the most battles. Woodrow Wilson's hopes for a just peace, it is clear in retrospect, died along with more than 100,000 American soldiers on the Western Front.

It took eight months for American troops to join in the fighting on the Western Front in effective numbers and nearly a year before they were decisively engaged in helping to turn back the final German offensive. In the meantime the Allied cause hung in the balance. In November 1917, Lenin and the Bolsheviks overthrew the provisional government, established a party dictatorship and took Russia out of the war, releasing badly needed German divisions for a last offensive on the Western Front. In the spring drive along the Somme beginning in March 1918, the Germans routed the British and penned up the French but without making a decisive breakthrough. In May and June the American Second Division was dispatched to the Marne, where it bolstered sagging French defenses. In the first big American engagements of the war, United States forces halted a German advance at Château-Thierry and slowly drove the enemy out of the Belleau Wood. These American actions were only preliminaries to the great Allied counteroffensive, which in the late summer began to push the German army back toward its frontier. By September the American commander, General John J. Pershing, who had stubbornly held out for an independent command, had over a half a million men at his disposal, a number that would double by the end of the war. In October, Pershing, in concert with British and French offensives elsewhere along the line, opened a massive American drive out of the Argonne Forest aimed at the railhead at Sedan—the last sustained American action of the war. On November 3, Austria-Hungary collapsed, and on the same day the German navy mutinied at Kiel, thus raising the specter of another communist revolution. Six days later a general strike in Germany led by the

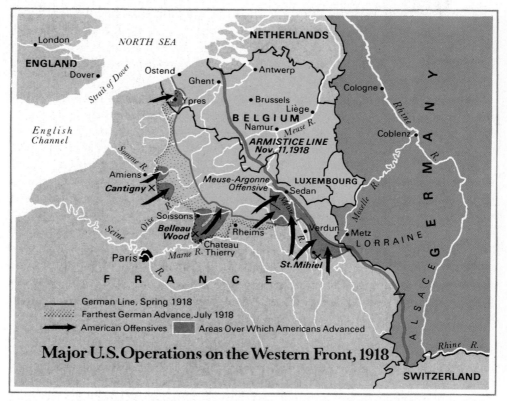

Major U.S. Operations on the Western Front, 1918

— German Line, Spring 1918
⋯⋯ Farthest German Advance, July 1918
→ American Offensives ▮ Areas Over Which Americans Advanced

Independent Socialists forced the Kaiser to abdicate, and a coalition of socialists and liberals proclaimed the republic that forty-eight hours later accepted Wilson's Fourteen Points as the basis for an armistice. The Great War was over.

The American entry, it was immediately clear, had brought badly needed troops and supplies to the Allies at a critical moment. American soldiers had supplied the preponderance of power needed to win the war. Equally important was the contribution of the United States in replenishing reduced stockpiles of food and materiel with its "bridge of ships," replacing the merchantmen sunk by German submarines, and experimenting successfully with the convoy system, which in the last analysis saved the Allies. The American contribution was essential, and it came at a crucial time. Yet despite the provisional German acceptance of the Fourteen Points as the agenda for peacemaking, the American war effort had not wiped out the national fears and hatreds embodied in wartime secret agreements and arrangements among the partners nor had it established the moral climate either at home or in Europe that, as Wilson knew, was essential to lasting peace.

With the American entrance a conflict which had already grown fiercely ideological became a crusade for democracy. All the powers had secured control over the actions and opinions of their civilian populations as they accepted the logic of total war. But the United States action completed an ideological shift for the Allies by defining the struggle in religious terms as one between the forces of peace and democracy against the dark powers of militarism. In submitting his Fourteen Points, and by explaining American war aims as nothing less than "the right of those who submit to authority to have a voice in their own government" and "a universal dominion of right by . . . a concert of free peoples," Wilson hardened the resolve of his allies to seek an unconditional surrender and a punitive peace. Perhaps the greatest irony of the First World War lay in the President's determination to inject into it a democratic ideology, which would make his own role as the even-handed peacemaker an impossible one.

Total war also imposed an organizational logic on the participants, all of whom were forced to adjust to the national need for centralization and control. Early in the war Germany recruited civilian administrators for its War Raw Materials Department, which established efficient mechanisms for allocating manpower and materiel. England organized its dwindling resources under the Defense of the Realm Act, which provided for full mobilization of all available manpower. France, its Northern industrial provinces lost for the duration, used the powers of government to relocate factories and regulate the production of food. Once in the war, the United States followed the same pattern in building a war machine, enlisting civilians in the war effort, and improvising the bureaucratic controls demanded by the emergency. By the time the war ended in November 1918, Wilson's administration had completed an organizational revolution that brought the power of government into nearly every phase of American life.

War and the Health of the State

For some progressives the coming of the war seemed a heaven-sent opportunity to consummate the American promise. The war, they confidently predicted, would bring genuine national unity and an end to class and ethnic division. It would discredit dangerous radicalism by infusing the citizens of the nation with a new spirit of patriotism. The demands of the war, moreover, would destroy all selfish materialism and preoccupation with profits and replace them with the higher goals of service and sacrifice. National preparedness and mobilization, central features of the New Nationalism, would foster moral virtue and civic purity in soldiers and civilians alike. Those progressives who continued to define their basic purpose as creating a new American morality saw in the impending war effort the outlines of what one of them called a "true national collectivism" to be built out of efficiency, social control, altruism, and revived moral purpose.

On a less ethereal plane many more progressives responded with enthusiasm to the organizational and reform opportunities furnished by the war. Those

AMERICAN BOYS AT WAR

Above, Fifteenth regiment on Fifth Avenue. (*Library of Congress.*) Top left, American field hospital in church ruins at Neuilly in the Argonne Forest. (*Library of Congress.*) Top right, American forces move up on the road to Grand Pré. (*Library of Congress.*) Bottom, A machine-gun platoon advances on a German entrenched position. (UPI *photo.*)

reformers who approached their work as a form of moral cleansing—of vice, alcohol, and prostitution—viewed the war as a chance to purify democracy at home while saving it abroad. "Long live social control," one of them exclaimed, "social control, not only to enable us to meet the rigorous demands of the war, but also as a foundation for the peace and brotherhood that is to come."

In fact, the war advanced the more restrictive progressive hopes in measurable ways. The preparedness campaign furthered the ideal of universal military service as a school of citizenship. The various Americanization programs aimed at controlling the immigrant took on new life. Prohibitionist hopes soared, and women's suffrage suddenly seemed a near thing. Even city planners, social justice workers, child labor reformers, and other progressive humanitarians warmed to the prospects of a domestic reformation in the midst of foreign war.

The war seemed to hold the greatest promise for progressives in administration and public policy, in closing the distance between the original New Nationalist emphasis on efficiency, administrative centralization, and executive power and the New Freedom faith in fact-finding, voluntary cooperation, and democratic participation. "We must speak, act, and serve together," Wilson reminded the nation. Efficiency quickly became the watchword for a new managerial elite that came to Washington with proposals for a planned war effort. Wesley C. Mitchell, a professor-turned-bureaucrat who joined the Division of Planning and Statistics of the War Industries Board, explained the appeal of government service to the professionals and businessmen who signed up for the duration. "Indeed I am in a mood to demand excitement and make it up when it doesn't offer of itself. I am ready to concoct a new plan for running the universe at any minute. . . ." Efficiency as the dominant progressive ideal attached itself to the image of the war machine turning out men and materiel automatically without the interference of politcs or partisanship. Slogans defined the renewed progressive purpose—"Elimination of Waste," "Standardization of Production," "Conservation of Resources," "Centralized Control," and above them the Wilsonian device "Democratic Autocracy."

The American performance fell far short of the progressive ideal. The most urgent task for the war state was mobilizing industry. Even before war was declared, Congress established the Council of National Defense, an advisory body composed of cabinet members and industrial and labor leaders charged with taking an inventory of the national resources. Out of the council's preliminary survey came the War Industries Board, which attempted. at first without success, to control production, arrange purchases, allocate scarce resources, and regulate labor relations. The War Industries Board failed to function effectively until Congress overhauled it, conferring near dictatorial powers on the President. Wilson brought the Wall Street banker Bernard Baruch to Washington to head the agency early in 1918 and gave him sweeping powers to establish priorities and increase production. Baruch's agency, however, was hampered in its work throughout the war by inadequate information. The continuing lack of needed data, Baruch complained, was "the greatest deterrent to effective action." By the end of the war the WIB was just beginning to unsnarl the problems of production.

In addition to regulating industrial production Wilson moved quickly to bring food and transportation under control. To head the Food Administration he appointed Herbert Hoover, who used his powers under the Lever Act to extend government control over the production and distribution of staples. Hoover's problems were complicated by poor harvests, and he was forced to experiment with price-fixing devices and a massive consumer education campaign to limit consumption. The strategy succeeded, first in doubling and then in trebling the amount of food that could be exported to starving Europe. Hoover's management of food production represented the primary accomplishment of wartime progressivism.

Managing the nation's railroads proved even more difficult, as Wilson first experimented unsuccessfully with a voluntary system under the Railroads War Board. Attempts to increase rolling stock and equalize traffic broke down completely in December 1917. Congress demanded an investigation, out of which came a revised United States Railroad Administration given effective power. Gradually the Railroad Administration extricated itself from confusion, and by

THE WAR ON THE HOME FRONT

Victory gardens were one way Americans at home could contribute. (*Brown Brothers.*)

the end of the war it too, like the War Industries Board, was beginning to function efficiently.

The Fuel Administration, headed by the progressive Harry A. Garfield, followed Hoover's lead in the Food Administration by seeking to stimulate coal production with price supports designed to guarantee profits, and less successfully, with schemes for rationalizing production and distribution. Shipping and the construction of a carrying fleet presented the Wilson administration with its most difficult problems. Here the challenge was deceptively simple: to build or commandeer ships faster than German U-boats could sink them. The progressive solution—the Emergency Fleet Corporation, originally an adjunct of the United States Shipping Board—proved inadequate. Divided leadership played havoc with planning, and the heads of the competing administrative agencies spent half the war quarreling over priorities and conflicting programs. Wilson finally removed them and put the competing interests under a single head. By September 1918 the Emergency Fleet Corporation had built only 500,000 tons of new shipping, less than German submarines had sunk in an average month in early 1917.

The labor policy of the Wilson administration was aimed at including the American workingman into the wartime partnership of business and government, as a junior partner but one entitled to his fair share of war prosperity. Yet here too a workable labor policy was slow in developing. Not until April 1918 did Wilson move to establish the National War Labor Board, with the power to adjudicate disputes between labor and management. Under the direction of ex-President William Howard Taft and the progressive labor lawyer Frank P. Walsh, the National War Labor Board heard over a thousand cases during the war involving three-quarters of a million workers. In general, Wilson's labor policy was a generous one designed to tolerate if not encourage unionism, establish an eight-hour day, avert strikes through arbitration, and provide limited increases in wages. The WLB also attempted to extend its influence into policymaking, with the creation of the War Labor Policies Board under the direction of Felix Frankfurter who sought to regularize and direct the flow of labor into crucial war industries. Frankfurter, however, like Baruch in the WIB, lacked the data needed to devise an effective plan, and once again progressive hopes outdistanced bureaucratic performance.

The progressive experiment in wartime planning was hardly an unqualified success. Lacking more than the rudiments of a national bureaucracy at the outset, Wilson's administration necessarily fumbled and temporized, dispersing rather than centralizing power through a host of overlapping and competing agencies. Not surprisingly, confusion and inefficiency resulted, as progressive bureaucrats groped their way toward centralization, learning slowly from their many mistakes. When the Armistice came the American war machine was just beginning to produce at a level approaching full capacity.

The most important consequence of the national war effort was the completion of the alliance between big business and the government. To an extent the pact was inevitable since it was only within those consolidated national industries that needed managerial talent could be recruited. To Washington accordingly, came the leaders of business and industry primed with patriotism but also determined to advance the interests of their sector, which they quickly identified with the national good. Wilson's appointment of Bernard Baruch was only the most visible symbol of this new alliance. From the ranks of railroad management, from big steel, heavy industry, finance, and banking came the self-appointed leaders of national mobilization, all bringing a measure of expertise but with it demands for stability and predictability in their industries that could only be furnished them by government.

Big business profited from the war directly and indirectly—directly in the form of arrangements like the cost-plus contract guaranteeing high levels of profit, indirectly in an education in the uses of government power to provide incentive and reward. Labor fared less well. Wartime inflation, climbing from a cost-of-living base of 100 in 1913 to 203.7 in 1920, cut deeply into wage increases. Farmers benefited from a substantial rise in real income during the war, a gain that would quickly disappear with the return of peace. But corporate profits skyrocketed in the years between 1914 and 1919, increasing threefold by the time America entered the war and leveling off in the following years at an annual 30 percent. Gains in the steel industry ranged from 30 percent to 300 percent. In the lumber industry they averaged 17 percent. In oil, 21 percent. In copper, 24 percent. Even with the moderate excess-profits tax and steeper levies on higher incomes the war made an estimated 42,000 new millionaires. If the progressive programs of Theodore Roosevelt and Woodrow Wilson had sought, at least in part, a more equitable distribution of American wealth, the war tended to reverse their hopes by piling up profits in the upper reaches of the economy.

A second limitation of the wartime experiment with state capitalism stemmed from the limited progressive experience with bureaucratic management before the war. American bureaucracy in 1917 was still in its infancy, and the relative handful of federal agencies at the policymaking level—the Federal Reserve Board, the Federal Trade Commission, and other fledgling agencies—had yet to assert their powers fully. Inevitably, the wartime administrative apparatus creaked and strained under the pressures of mobilization. Ambitious reorganizational schemes were never carried out. Programs broke down. Authority almost always overlapped, and agencies collided over matters of precedence and priority. By a method marked by more trial and error than most progressives expected, the United States moved hesitantly from administrative chaos to some bureaucratic order at war's end. The wartime administrative apparatus could the more readily be dismantled once the war ended because it had never really functioned efficiently in the first place. Businessmen, convinced of the advantages accruing to the wartime partnership with government, were nevertheless willing

AMERICAN WOMEN WAGE WAR

New York chorus girls prepare to defend the city. (*Brown Brothers.*)

to dissolve the formal ties, leaving in their place a gentlemen's agreement that promised the benefits of government support without the threat of regulation.

If the gains for the federal bureaucracy brought by the war proved partial and temporary, the same was not true of the wartime campaign for loyalty and uniformity. Here the original progressive dream of an aroused and patriotic citizenry turned into a chauvinist nightmare, and the country experienced a crisis of civil liberties.

The American people responded to the war with a spontaneous burst of nationalist fervor, which triggered a chain reaction of repression and hysteria. In the first months of the war hundreds of thousands of self-styled patriots banded together in vigilante-like groups bearing impressive titles—the American Defense Society, the National Security League, the American Anti-Anarchy Association, even the Boy Spies of America—and dedicated to hunting out heresy wherever they found it. The leaders of these grassroots purges were usually the "leading men" in the local community, businessmen, professionals and merchants, who combined more useful work for the Red Cross and Y.M.C.A. with the witch-hunting escapades common to superpatriots in any age. Wilson's administration, unable or unwilling to check such popular excesses, joined in purging dissent. The result was a fevered public uprising against nonconformity of all kinds and the ruthless suppression of American liberties.

The war hysteria fed a progressive appetite for national unity that had gone unchecked by a tradition of civil liberties. The absence of a libertarian concern with protecting basic freedoms, the central weakness in the progressive program, made a domestic war on liberalism all but inevitable. Patriots and vigilantes, equipped with ropes, whips, tar and feathers, and all the other instruments of intimidation, enjoyed a ritualistic field day complete with flag-kissing ceremonies and forced declarations of loyalty. The victims of this reign of righteous terror were mainly marginal people, uneducated or disaffected, isolated and without power. In Bisbee, Arizona, the "best" people rounded up some 1200 striking miners led by the IWW, piled them into freight cars, and sent them across the state line into the desert, where they were left stranded. In Montana a mob dragged the Wobbly organizer Frank Little out of his boardinghouse and hanged him from a railroad trestle. Soon the federal government itself joined in the campaign to crush radical dissent: in September 1917, Justice Department agents rounded up 113 officers and organizers of the IWW and impounded five tons of material with which to arraign and convict them.

Out of these spontaneous acts of suppression came loose national organizations and federations, perversions of the original progressive consumer and reform leagues, dedicated to rooting out subversion and punishing disloyalty. With support from local and state law-enforcement agencies the National Security League and the Council of Defense fixed on new targets—the Non-Partisan League in North Dakota, intent on nothing more seditious than interest-group politics; and the People's Council of America for Peace and Democracy, a band of pacifists widely condemned as "traitors and fools." Within six months of Wilson's declaration of war a rigid censorship combined with political repression had reached into the American press, schools and universities, the churches, and even the new movie industry.

This mass popular reaction formed the base of a pyramid of repression supporting a middle range of official and semiofficial bodies from citizens councils to state administrative agencies, like the Minnesota Commission of Public Safety, which became a model for the rest of the country. Other states passed criminal syndicalism laws aimed primarily at left-wing dissenters but designed as dragnets for a variety of nonconformists as well. Soon the traditional American distinction between public and private had dissolved in a welter of competing patriotic agencies.

The apex of the national system of extralegalism was completed by the federal government itself with an increasing range of agencies and activities, chief among them the omnibus Committee on Public Information headed by the progressive journalist George Creel and charged with mobilizing public opinion behind the war. Perfecting the progressive technique of moral publicity, Creel encouraged a voluntary censorship program and turned to the new public relations industry for a national cadre of opinion shapers who launched a propaganda campaign of frightening proportions. Creel's committee also coordinated the work of local patriots, advising them and publicizing their activities as contributions to the war effort.

The second weapon in the government's domestic arsenal was an administrative technique inherited from prewar progressivism, deportation of undesirable aliens and radicals. The efficiency of the deportation device lay in an administrative process not subject to judicial oversight, a form of executive justice that provided maximum freedom for administrators and minimum safeguards for the rights of the accused. The original mechanisms for the swift removal of undesirables had been created by the Immigration Act of 1903, and the war simply gave widened scope to these summary actions.

The main contributions of the federal government to the national hysteria were the Espionage Act of 1917 and the Sedition Act of 1918, twin declarations of bankruptcy, like the Federalist Alien and Sedition acts, by a society that had reached its conceptual limits. The Espionage Act provided fines up to $10,000 and twenty years in prison for anyone convicted of causing insubordination, mutiny, or disloyalty in the armed forces by "false reports or false statements." The law also empowered the postmaster general to withhold mailing privileges to newspapers and periodicals deemed subversive, a power that Wilson's appointee, Albert S. Burleson, turned into a formidable weapon against dissent. With Wilson's knowledge if not always with his approval, Burleson wielded discretionary power with a vengeance in banning Socialist periodicals like *The Masses* and Victor Berger's *Milwaukee Leader* and even a Single-Tax journal for suggesting that more revenue be raised through taxation. If Eugene Debs was convicted and sentenced to ten years in prison under the Sedition Act for telling a Socialist audience that the master class causes wars while the subject class fights them, most of the victims of such heresy hunting were faceless people guilty of nothing more scurrilous than the opinion that John D. Rockefeller was a son of a bitch who helped start a capitalist war.

The Sedition Act of the following year was designed to close the few loopholes in the Espionage Act through which thousands of "spies" and "traitors" were presumed to have escaped. The new law provided punishment for anyone who should "utter, print, write or publish any disloyal, profane, scurrilous, or abusive language about the form of government in the United States, or the uniform of the Army or Navy" or any sentiments intended to bring the government or the military "into contempt, scorn, contumely, or disrepute." More than 1500 Americans were tried and more than 1000 convicted under these laws. As Senator Hiram Johnson pointed out, this meant simply, "You shall not criticize anything or anybody in the Government any longer or you shall go to jail."

In some measure the war hysteria constituted an aberration, a sudden departure from good sense and a betrayal of progressive ideals. But at a deeper level most of the excesses were traceable to original progressive sins, either of omission or commission. Discretionary power vested in administrative agencies, which was a progressive innovation, supplied the flexibility and promptness considered essential, but only at the expense of regular processes amenable to judicial oversight. Used to facilitate policymaking and to free administrators from constant interference by the legislature, the progressive device had its merits. But applied indiscriminately to the ideas and opinions of citizens, the new administrative process forcibly illustrated all the dangers inherent in a policy cut adrift from accountability and control.

The war crisis lowered the principle of administrative autonomy to the level of license. In the case of Postmaster General Burleson, for example, even the President was unable to check misguided enthusiasm and the personal conviction that no American should be allowed to "say that this Government got into the war wrong." "It is a false statement," Burleson insisted, "a lie, and it will not be permitted." Such arbitrary power lodged either in the federal bureaucracy or in the lower echelons of state and local administrations inevitably fostered an alarming national irresponsibility by subjecting opinion and expression to the whims and caprices of petty officials freed, as one of them boasted, from "exaggerated sentimentalism [or] a misapplied reverence for legal axioms."

It would have been difficult in any case for Wilson's administration to have curbed the patriotic passions of a generation preoccupied with rescuing a sense of national unity from the repeated onslaughts of a vigorous cultural pluralism. But the wartime policy of the federal government was tantamount to issuing wholesale hunting licenses to superpatriots in tracking down and destroying dissent—in Christian pacifists, liberal reformers, socialists, anarchists, but also in a host of cultural as well as political radicals opposed to the war. The origins of this cultural rebellion against genteel restraints and nineteenth-century pieties lay deep in the prewar experience. The war simply brought to the surface cultural conflicts that since the turn of the century had pitted a moralistic progressive elite against a vanguard of intellectual and artistic radicals. By 1917 a major shift in the intellectual life of the country had already been documented in a series of confrontations, some symbolic and others real, between an inherited system of unified truth and the powerful forces of cultural revolt.

The Little Rebellion: Progressivism and the Challenge of Culture

On February 17, 1913, the International Exhibition of Modern Painting opened in the cavernous Sixty-ninth Regimental Armory on Twenty-sixth street in New York City. To the music of a military band, beneath rafters festooned with huge banners and pine boughs visitors strolled through a maze of sixteen hundred paintings, drawings, prints, and pieces of sculpture. The Armory Show, two years in the planning, took for its motto "The New Spirit," which was emblazoned on a mammoth replica of the Massachusetts Pine Tree Flag, a message that many American viewers translated as "the harbinger of universal anarchy." A non-juried show organized by practicing artists to display works "usually neglected," the exhibition had been originally conceived of as a strictly American affair, and it was actually dominated numerically by American work, which made up three-quarters of the show. The initial plans had been scrapped, however, for the more ambitious idea of a vast international retrospective tracing the rise of modernism from its nineteenth-century sources in Goya, Ingres, and Delacroix through the French realist Courbet to impressionism and the bewildering canvases of post-impressionists, expressionists, and cubists. It was not the dark looming shapes of Albert Pinkham Ryder that outraged progressive patrons, or the realistic cityscapes of the "New York Eight" with their conventional images and brushwork, but what one critic called "the imported ideology" of the new European artists—Picasso, Matisse, Brancusi, Picabia, Leger, Rouault, Kandinsky, Duchamp, and Lehmbruk. Their collective impact on the progressive eye carried the force of revolution. The staid art critic Kenyon Cox, a reliable guide for many a confused progressive, admitted to spending "an appalling morning"

at the show, where he had witnessed the "total destruction of the art of painting." "To have looked at it is to have passed through a pathological museum where the layman has no right to go. One feels that one has seen not an exhibition, but an exposure."

The Armory Show collected into a single public symbol the disparate meaning of European modernism. In the bold, thin colors of Matisse's *The Red Studio* or the splashes of one of Kandinsky's *Improvisations* or the frozen motion of Duchamp's *Nude Descending a Staircase,* Americans registered the results of a perceptual revolution that had transformed the European intellectual and artistic world and now threatened to overrun the United States. Here made visible were the effects of the revolt against nineteenth-century positivism and formalism—in Nietzsche, Bergson, Sorel, Freud, Ibsen, Strindberg—the all too apparent fruits of recent explorations into the unseen and unknown, the irrational and the relative, yielding new definitions of time, energy, force, and will. For those progressives who chose to examine the work of the modernists, the Armory Show took on the dimensions of a crisis.

The progressive crisis rose directly out of the challenge to a comfortable realism and moralism in the outlook of the average American, who firmly be-

MAY BAR YOUNGSTERS FROM CUBISTS' SHOW

"Crazy-Quilt" Art Is Not for School Children's Eyes, Says Teacher.

USES MANY HARSH WORDS

Chicago Record-Herald

Instructor Declares Exhibit Is Nasty, Lewd, Immoral and Indecent.

3/27/13

Public school children of Chicago, always urged by their teachers to view the beauties of the Art Institute, may be asked by the same teachers to stay away from the building—and all because of cubist art.

Nasty, obscene, indecent, immoral, lewd and demoralizing were a few of the adjectives used yesterday by W. C. Strauss, art instructor of Waller High School, Orchard and Center streets, after a careful inspection of the international exhibition of modern art.

THE ARMORY SHOW MAKES NEWS

Autographed menu for the dinner given by Armory artists for members of the press; below left, *Chicago Record-Herald* news story; below right, "Seeing New York with a Cubist: The Rude Descending a Staircase—Rush Hour on the Subway." (*Menu from Walt Kuhn Papers, Archives of American Art, Smithsonian Institution.*)

SEEING NEW YORK WITH A CUBIST

The Rude Descending a Staircase
(Rush Hour at the Subway)

lieved in the solid reality of the objective social world and in the power of "good art" to represent it. Socially useful art, most progressives believed, was the art of representation, if not always laden with a moral at least carrying an educative function. There was a lingering idealism in the progressive world view that rested uneasily with the new pragmatic techniques of social analysis. These two halves of the progressive outlook were held together by the firm conviction that science and the scientific method, complicated and baffling as they might seem to the layman, would ultimately prove the unity of truth and reinforce an inherited doctrine of progress. The Armory Show upset this unexamined progressive assumption.

Progressivism had reluctantly come to terms with the "Ashcan School," the group of New York realists whose paintings of street scenes and city types drew from the same sources as those of the urban progressive reformers. Like Whitman with his cosmic self, the New York Eight sought to encompass the whole urban scene with their illustrator's techniques and documentary style. The social realism of the Eight most progressives had learned to understand and accept—a direct involvement with the pictorial aspects of twentieth century urban life; the casting out of the twin devils of Puritanism and Philistinism; and the celebration of the role of the artist as the protean Whitmanesque figure spending "delightful days drifting among people" and recording his "independent personal evidence" of the wonders of democracy. "The tramp sits on the edge of the curb," the Eight's spokesman, Robert Henri, explained. "He is huddled up. His body is thick. His underlip hangs. His eyes look fierce. . . . He is not beautiful, but he could well be the motive for a great and beautiful work of art." Progressives engaged in similar explorations of city life agreed, for they shared Henri's insistence on "fundamental law" and those universal axioms "controlling all existence." By 1910 realism had broken the Genteel Tradition's grip on the American imagination without, however, dissolving its view of objective reality.

It was just this sense of the manageability of their world that gave progressives the confidence to reform and improve it. Experimenting with the new tools of social and psychological analysis and new definitions of change helped sharpen the progressive method, but they also strengthened the belief that the world was plastic after all and could be molded into a controlled environment. The recent knowledge explosion in American universities had shaken but not destroyed the progressive faith in what Theodore Roosevelt called "realizable ideals" and the belief that "the great facts of life are simple." The conviction that at bottom art and politics amounted to the same thing made the Armory Show a troubling spectacle for most American viewers because it threatened not simply aesthetic preference but belief in the possibilities of planning and social control. The "detestable things" wrought by Picasso, Matisse and Duchamp—"degraded, indecent, and insane"—seemingly disclosed the lurking presence of the unpredictable and the unmanageable, of flux and formlessness. A Matisse painting reminded Gelett Burgess of the havoc a "sanguinary" girl of eight, "half-crazed with gin," might wreak on a blank wall with a box of crayons. In choosing a revolutionary theme for their exhibition the organizers of the Armory Show were only following the path their European counterparts had taken for over a century, but American viewers took their political challenge literally and responded in kind. As one hostile critic announced: "The exploitation of a theory of discords, puzzles, ugliness and clinical details is to art what anarchy is to society, and the practitioners need not so much a critic as an alienist." Artistic madness would surely lead to barbarism.

There was a natural flow of antimodernism from aesthetic into political channels. "The United States is invaded by aliens," warned the archconservative Royal Cortissoz, "thousands of whom constitute so many acute perils to the health of the body politic. Modernism is of precisely the same heterogeneous alien origin and is imperiling the republic of art in the same way." Like the millions of new immigrants, modernism had swept away "normal conventions" and eternal verities with anarchistic doctrines "prompted by types not yet fitted for their first papers in aesthetic naturalization—the makers of true Ellis Island art." The Armory Show showed clearly the dangers of leaving the aesthetic gates ajar.

Modernism in the Armory Show presented progressive viewers with a symbolic dilemma: how to ensure the improvement of American society without underwriting revolution. Once again as in all other matters American, it was Theodore Roosevelt who had the last word on the Armory Show. "It is vitally necessary," the retired President reminded his followers, "to move forward to shake off the dead hand of the reactionaries; and yet we have to face the fact that there is apt to be a lunatic fringe among votaries of any forward movement." Still, the problem remained—how to give support to the sane and deny it to the dangerous.

On a June evening less than four months after the Armory Show this problem acquired renewed urgency. At the Battery in New York City one thousand silk workers from Paterson, New Jersey, stepped off the ferry and marched in a solid phalanx up Broadway and into Madison Square Garden. There, before a crowd of 15,000, they proceeded to reenact the events of their prolonged strike against the mill owners. Spectators watched a new form of proletarian art, social drama as participatory ritual. The Paterson Pageant was the brainchild of the young radical journalist John Reed and a handful of socialist intellectuals and artists, who dreamed of fashioning a new mass art out of working class grievances and the formal protest of the intellectuals.

The Paterson strike had been triggered by the decision of the mill owners to increase the work load for unskilled silk weavers and dyers already living on the edge of destitution. Most of the workers in the Paterson dye houses and mills, some 25,000 in all, were new immigrants from Italy, Russia, and eastern Europe, a large number of them young girls earning an average wage of $6 or $7 a week. The IWW entered the town in the winter of 1913 to help organize this unpromising material around the immediate issues of shorter hours and higher wages. "Big Bill" Haywood, fresh from his triumph in the Lawrence textile workers' strike, joined the young Wobbly agitator Elizabeth Gurley Flynn and the romantic syndicalist Carlo Tresca in teaching the Paterson workers that it was "far better to starve fighting than to starve working." By February they had succeeded in uniting the unskilled workers and shutting down the town.

The AFL, in trying to break the strike with their skilled workers, fed the progressive tendency to identify the immigrant with radicalism. Yet throughout the spring the ranks of the strikers held firm. Forming committees, appointing pickets, and arranging rallies, the Wobblies held their forces together against mounting retaliation. The mill owners fought back, stirring up hatred of "outside agitators," enlisting the services of the clergy and the merchants of the town, and dispatching police to break up picket lines and disperse meetings. "The IWW preaches sabotage; the AFL practices it," one observer noted acidly. By spring the police had arrested nearly 2000 strikers, put an end to the Sunday marches, and were indulging themselves liberally in clubbings and beatings. "There's a war in Paterson," John Reed reported to his fellow intellectuals. "But it's a curious kind of war. All the violence is the work of one side—the Mill Owners."

Reed had reason to know. Like many of the Greenwich Village socialists and radicals, he had made the Sunday excursion to Paterson to see for himself the clash between the workers and the bosses. Reed, whom Walter Lippmann once accused of the inordinate desire to get himself arrested, did just that and spent a few days in the Paterson lockup before returning to New York to write his indictment of the owners for Max Eastman's *The Masses*. A volatile cultural radical without any clear sense of ideological direction as yet, Reed dreamed of rallying the artists and intellectuals to the side of the strikers as the beginning of a permanent alliance of forces for the radical reconstruction of American life. This was the idea he brought back to the socialite Mabel Dodge's salon, the gathering place of New York's radical literati: An "oppressed" minority of cultural radicals must unite with other outsiders in progressive America under the banner of cultural revolution and proceed to make the world over.

Out of the plannning sessions at Mabel Dodge's evenings and out of recesses of her pocketbook came the plans for a gigantic pageant to raise money for the strike fund and educate liberal fellow travelers in the lessons of solidarity. Reed threw himself headlong into the project, spending eighteen hours a day on the script, drilling a thousand performers into a theatrical company, designing the massive sets with John Sloan and Robert Edmond Jones. By June he was ready, Sloan's huge factory scenes and red curtains in place, and his cast primed for performance.

The pageant caught the spirit of solidarity that Reed had sensed on his visit to Paterson. As it opened, throngs of workers moved down the center aisle to linger in front of the huge gray mills before entering to the sound of whirring machines. Suddenly the chant began—"Strike! Strike!"—growing louder and more insistent until the workers came pouring out of the factory doors and life moved outside the empty, dark mills. In front of the dead industrial husks the workers reenacted the scenes of the strike—mass picketings, police harassment, the clash between strikers and scabs where a worker was killed, the climactic funeral procession.

The audience, many of them workers admitted at 25¢ a seat, joined in booing the police, chanting strike slogans and lustily singing the *Internationale.* "This kind of thing," exclaimed the liberal journalist Hutchins Hapgood, "makes us hope for a real democracy, where self-expression in industry and art among the masses may become a rich reality, spreading a human glow over the whole of humanity." For a brief moment it seemed to Reed and his radical cultural critics that they had succeeded where progressives had signally failed in forging new weapons for social justice out of the materials of mass art.

But life did not imitate art, and the pageant brought a cresting of radical hopes for cultural reconstruction that quickly receded. The spectacle, originally intended to replenish the strike fund, actually yielded a check for $150. The 24,000 strikers who had not participated began to question the dubious benefits bestowed on them by the intellectuals. "Bread was the need of the hour," Elizabeth Gurley Flynn complained, "and bread was not forthcoming." The gulf between art and politics could not be bridged by ceremonial: in the summer the skilled workers broke ranks and returned to the mills. Then the mill owners in a series of shop-by-shop settlements that conceded nothing to the unskilled workers shattered their morale and routed the IWW leadership. By summer's end the Paterson workers were back at work on their employers' terms. Reed's script for the oppressed workers of America acting out "the wretchedness of their lives and the glory of their revolt" had failed to close the distance between the intellectual vanguard and the working class.

Artists and Scientists: Critics of Progressivism

Other critics of progressivism before the First World War perceived different divisions in American society and suggested other ways of closing them. In 1914 Walter Lippmann published his *Drift and Mastery,* and a year later Van Wyck Brooks his caustic essay *America's Coming-of Age,* two demands for an immediate reassessment of progressive aims and aspirations. Lippmann and Brooks, with their manifestos of modernism, represented a new intellectual type, the publicist directing his criticism towards a diversified group of fellow intellectuals, political leaders, and opinion shapers who composed the progressive elite. Neither journalists in a traditional sense nor philosophers, they saw themselves as cultural commentators whose task it was to direct the flow of American life through channels of publicity and informed criticism towards new national goals. They represented a new fraternity of cultural critics who sought to elevate their roles to the realms of public power through their analysis of American society.

Van Wyck Brooks, who had recently graduated from Harvard, where he studied under William James and George Santayana, was first and foremost a spokesman for the "Little Renaissance" in American art and culture that swept across the country after 1912. By the time Brooks issued his challenge to progressivism the signs of cultural rebellion against the Genteel Tradition were everywhere. Harriet Monroe had begun publishing her *Poetry: A Magazine of Verse* and introducing the work of new poets like Hart Crane, T. S. Eliot, Ezra Pound, Robert Frost, Carl Sandburg, and Amy Lowell. In Margaret Anderson's *Little Review* readers could sample themes ranging from anarchism to sexual freedom. In the same year that Brooks issued his summons to progressivism, the Provincetown Players were experimenting with the one-act plays of Eugene O'Neill. Theodore Dreiser had already completed his naturalistic explorations of American business in *The Financier* (1912) and *The Titan* (1914). Edgar Lee Masters's *Spoon River Anthology* appeared in 1915; Edwin Arlington Robinson's *Man Against the Sky* and Sherwood Anderson's first novel, a year later. Brooks joined the growing circle of artists and intellectuals in Greenwich Village following a brief teaching career at Stanford and at the Worker's Educational Association in Cambridge, England. In the Village he met Lippmann, who urged him to add his share to the literary renaissance by scrutinizing the "noble dream" of an American democratic culture in the light of the "actual limitations of experience" in the early twentieth century. Brooks promptly obliged with what he called an address to his own "homeless generation" of artists and intellectuals.

Brooks defined the basic American duality as the cultural split between "Highbrow" and "Lowbrow" a fatal division that had paralyzed the creative will of the nation. The American dilemma, he was convinced, stemmed from the conflict between a "quite unclouded, quite unhypocritical assumption of transcendent theory" and the "catchpenny realities" of a business civilization. Between these poles lay a cultural wasteland in which no true community could thrive. Brooks traced the roots of this American schizophrenia to the original sin of Puritanism, "the all-influential fact in the history of the American mind." To Puritanism in its many forms could be attributed both the "fastidious refinement" of current tastes and the predatory "opportunism" of American moneymakers.

Like the progressive historian Vernon L. Parrington, who was compiling the materials for the first volume of *Main Currents of American Thought*, at the same time, Brooks presented sets of paired opposites to prove his case: Jonathan Edwards and Benjamin Franklin, Henry Wadsworth Longfellow and Mark Twain, James Russell Lowell and Walt Whitman. These were the products of a binary culture, figures standing on opposite sides of an "unbridgeable chasm between literate and illiterate America." Throughout the nineteenth century the

WORLD WAR I POSTER

(*The New-York Historical Society.*)

divorce of the real and the ideal had resulted in an "orgy of lofty examples, moralized poems, national anthems and baccalaureate sermons" until the average progressive citizen was now "charged with all manner of ideal purities, ideal honorabilities, ideal femininities, flag-wavings and skyscrapings of every sort." In the meantime the American progressive landscape had become "a stamping ground" for every greedy commercial impulse of every individual businessman who held that "society is fair prey for what he can get out of it."

Brooks peered below the political surface of American society and pointed to the shortcomings of the progressive approach to reform. Progressivism with its moral certainties and good-government shibboleths had failed to solve the fundamental problem of modern industrial society, the "invisible government" of business. So far, the efforts of well-meaning reformers to alter American priorities had amounted to "the attainment of zero." Progressivism had simply consolidated the rule of "commercialized men." Of what use was it to tinker with political mechanisms, indulge a social conscience, or "do any of the other easy popular contemporary things" unless the quality of American life could also be improved? "To cleanse politics is of the least importance if the real forces of the people cannot be engaged in politics; and they cannot be so engaged while the issues behind politics remain inarticulate."

Here Brooks reached the core of the cultural radical critique of progressivism: Meaningful improvement of American society would require more than rationalizing a business system, more than the cheerful cooperation of business and government whether in the name of the New Nationalism or the New Freedom. "Business," Brooks declared, "has traditionally absorbed the best elements of the American character, it has been cowed by no sense of subjection, it has thriven in a free air, it has received all the leaven, it has occupied the centre of the field." Nothing would answer now but the massive shift of American energies "from the plane of politics to the plane of psychology and morals"; otherwise progressivism would have failed in its regenerative mission. When the First World War broke out, Brooks still had hopes for the cultural rebellion of which he was a spokesman. Three years later, America's entrance into the war broke these hopes on the rocks of the war state.

Walter Lippmann also discerned a split in twentieth-century American life that progressivism had failed to repair, but his definition concerned the conflict between the "sterile tyranny of taboo" bequeathed by the nineteenth century and his own generation's desire "to be awake during their own lifetime." For Lippmann the problem reduced itself to acquiring an education in the "discipline of democracy." "Drift" resulted from the capricious rule of old "bogeys"; "mastery" meant applying the scientific method to politics. Like Brooks, though for different reasons, Lippmann faulted progressive reformers for their lack of rigorous thought. The New Nationalism, although it had examined some of the worst abuses of industrialism, still spoke the language of an outmoded moralism, and the New Freedom continued to make false promises of a return to an era of competition. "You would think that competitive commercialism was really a generous, chivalrous, high-minded stage of human culture," Lippmann scoffed, instead of "an antiquated, feeble, mean, and unimaginative way of dealing with the possibilities of modern industry." Unlike Brooks and the cultural radicals, Lippmann championed the cause of business consolidation and the rule of industrial statesmen who in their own way sought to transcend politics by lifting decision making out of the marketplace to the level of scientific management. "They represent the revolution in business incentives at its very heart. For they conduct gigantic enterprises and they stand outside the higgling of the market, outside the shrewdness and strategy of competition. The motive of profit is not their personal motive. That is an astounding change."

Lippmann agreed with Brooks on the need for relocating American energies outside politics, but he differed dramatically on the means. Whereas the cultural radicals sought to challenge and hopefully destroy the rule of big business, Lippmann hoped to rationalize and reform it. First, "You have to go about deliberately to create a large class of professional businessmen." Next, "You have to encourage the long process of self-education in democracy through which unions can develop representative government and adequate leadership." And finally, "You have to devise a great many consumers' controls." Equipped with these three devices for depoliticizing industrial society, Americans could proceed to reconstruct the entire social and cultural order. Out of this recasting of priorities, he predicted, would come a true cooperative society, neither strictly capitalistic nor wholly collectivist, but a new commonwealth made up of managers, workers and consumers, each applying the instruments of measurement and control provided by science.

If American entrance into the First World War threatened the foundations of Van Wyck Brooks's radical reconstruction of American culture, it brought a welcome test for Lippmann's pragmatic liberalism and his plans for a businessmen's government. Brooks deplored the war as a betrayal of his dreams; Lippmann embraced it as an instrumentalist challenge. By 1917 these two critical views of progressivism had been institutionalized in two very different magazines—*The Seven Arts,* which Brooks and his cultural radical friends Randolph Bourne and James Oppenheim founded in 1916 and nursed through a year of precarious existence; and *The New Republic,* which Lippmann together with the liberal nationalists Herbert Croly and Walter Weyl had launched in 1914. The war records of these two periodicals testified to the divergent fortunes of cultural radicalism and liberal nationalism under the conditions of war. *The Seven Arts* announced its intention of speaking to "that *latent* America, that *potential* America" lying beneath the "commercial-industrial national organization," and it lasted just a year before succumbing to the fervor of the patriots.

Brooks's mantle fell on the diminutive figure of Randolph Bourne, who more clearly than any of the other opponents of the war saw the coming defeat of "that America of youth and aspiration" standing below the battle. In "War and the Intellectuals," the most scathing of his attacks on Lippmann and the prowar liberals, Bourne ridiculed the "war technique" of liberal reform that had led the intellectuals to the illusion that they had willed the war "through sheer force of ideas." In accepting the war, Bourne charged, *The New Republic* editors had necessarily aligned themselves with the least democratic forces in American society, those neanderthal interests still clinging to mystical notions of the national state and economic privilege. The war, Bourne concluded, provided an escape hatch for progressives, who had become prisoners of their own conceptions of the good society. The collapse of *The Seven Arts* after a year of minority opposition and Bourne's untimely death marked the end of the cultural radical attempt to reconstruct progressivism by supplying it with higher priorities.

Lippmann and the other editors of *The New Republic* continued to cling to the belief that they could direct a democratic war and help write a liberal peace. The American entrance, Lippmann explained soon after Wilson's declaration of war, would prove "decisive in the history of the world," since the United States could now proceed to "crystallize and make real the whole league of peace propaganda." Nor did he fear the effects of war psychology on the prospects of liberalism: in October 1917 he offered his services to the administration and was appointed secretary of the Inquiry, Wilson's hand-picked body of experts charged with preparing the American position at the peace table. Croly, who remained in his editorial post at *The New Republic,* quickly became disillusioned as he realized the nature of the liberal impasse both at home and abroad. From inside the administration, Lippmann's hopes for the prospects for a liberal peace remained high. Congratulating Colonel House on the administration's "victory" in securing Allied support for Wilson's Fourteen Points, Lippmann hailed the achievement as "brilliant" and "prophetic." "The President and you have more then justified the faith of those who insisted that your leadership was a turning point in modern history." Eighteen months later, discouraged by the President's failure at Versailles, Lippmann joined the ranks of the "tired radicals" seeking to defeat the treaty.

The Ordeal of Woodrow Wilson

In his address to Congress on January 8, 1918—the low point in the American war effort—Woodrow Wilson outlined the steps the United States and its allies would have to take in order to ensure a postwar world "made fit to live in." Wilson's Fourteen Points presented a blueprint for peacemaking drawn to his progressive specifications. Central to his plan was the principle of "open covenants openly arrived at," the extension to the international scene of the New Freedom ideal of moral publicity. Balancing this first point in a moral equation was the fourteenth, calling for "a general association of nations . . . formed under specific covenants for the purpose of affording mutual guarantees of political

PRESIDENT WILSON EMBARKS FOR PARIS, DECEMBER
1918

(*Brown Brothers.*)

independence and territorial integrity to great and small states alike." The
main substantive points in Wilson's utopian calendar included a general disarmament, complete freedom of the seas, an equitable adjustment of colonial
claims in the interests of the populations involved, and a series of specific provisions based on the principle of linguistic nationalism for territorial settlements
throughout Europe. These were the lofty terms that Wilson, in the face of the
mounting opposition of his war partners, attempted to impose at the peace table.

In trying to achieve his aims, Wilson was driven by his own intensely moral
nature as well as by circumstance to make several costly miscalculations. Part
of his predicament inhered in the Fourteen Points themselves. What, for example, did his principle of national self-determination mean and by what general
formula could it be applied? What adjustments might be required when linguistic nationalism failed to coincide with economic viability or strategic aims?
Then, how could a new Soviet regime with an exportable totalitarian ideology
be accorded "an unhampered and unembarrassed opportunity" for political
development? How, in short, could he as the self-declared representative of the
only disinterested power at the peace table establish in each and every instance
his claim on the enlightened conscience of mankind?

A related set of problems and misconceptions stemming from the same fervor concerned his political position at home. Who but Wilson himself could convert the Allies to his program and ensure the triumph of his cherished principle of collective security? Determined to play the dominant role at the Paris conference, he insisted on making his peace program a partisan issue in the fall elections of 1918 by warning that a Republican victory would constitute a repudiation of his leadership and his vision. Republicans, who already had grown restive under an unofficially nonpartisan war policy, now retaliated by accusing the President himself of partisan dealings. In 1918 they regained control of both houses of Congress. If the Republican victory did not quite constitute a vote of no confidence, it did serve notice on Wilson that the spirit of party politics had been revived and would be decisive in settling the fate of his program.

Even more serious was Wilson's refusal to include Republican leaders among his advisers. Former President Taft, Charles Evans Hughes, and a number of other party notables had expressed cautious interest in the idea of a league of nations, and their calculated exclusion isolated the President from the moderate internationalism he would so desperately need. On the eve of his departure for Europe in December 1918, there were already ominous signs of a growing presidential detachment from the realities of domestic politics, as Wilson began the retreat into the recesses of his moralistic nature. "Tell me what is right," he urged his advisers as he prepared for the conference, "and I'll fight for it."

THE COUNCIL OF FOUR

From left to right: Vittorio Orlando of Italy, David Lloyd George of England, Georges Clemenceau of France, Woodrow Wilson. (*National Archives.*)

Wilson fought tenaciously, even heroically, for his Fourteen Points against overwhelming odds. But in forgetting the first rules of politics and ignoring the domestic disarray he had left behind, he fatally compromised his position.

In Lloyd George of Great Britain, Clemenceau of France, and Orlando of Italy, the President confronted national leaders, who as he came to understand, spoke for their countrymen as he could not. The Allies had suffered grievously during the war, and their spokesmen could count on popular support at home for a punitive peace, one that would assign war guilt to Germany, strip it of all possessions, exact enormous reparations, and provide all the necessary safeguards against future aggression. To counter these narrow nationalistic aims, Wilson brought with him to Paris only the Fourteen Points and his vision of a new concert of power. Despite his initial popularity with the peoples of Europe his lone voice became increasingly lost in the clamor of competing chauvinisms. The American story of the peace deliberations was one of a moralist's mounting frustration and forced retreat from idealism.

The first of the Fourteen Points to be jettisoned was the utopian concept of "open covenants." Soon after the opening of the conference the plenary sessions gave way first to a Council of Ten dominated by the heads of state and their foreign ministers, and then to a Council of Four composed of Wilson, Lloyd George, Clemenceau, and Orlando, meeting behind closed doors. The press, barred from working sessions, became almost wholly dependent on news releases handed out after each plenary session. Wilson compounded his communications problems by withdrawing coldly from his colleagues on the council and ignoring most of his advisers, who also complained of his aloofness. Cut adrift from presidential oversight, the American staff floundered in confusion and frustration. Wilson, announcing that he had no desire "to have lawyers drafting the treaty of peace," played a lone hand at Paris and quickly spent all his reserves of moral capital.

On some of the specific issues of the peace settlement the President was partially successful in moderating the original demands of his partners. After an epochal battle of wills with the cynical Clemenceau, who likened his adversary to Jesus Christ bearing the Ten Commandments, Wilson forced France to agree to a multinational defense pact but at the cost of the immediate return to France of Alsace-Lorraine, the French occupation of the Rhineland, and huge reparations to be paid by Germany. On the question of the former German colonies he abandoned the principle of "impartial adjustment" but salvaged his plan for a mandate system under League auspices. For Poland he secured a corridor to the sea at the expense of linguistic nationalism, and in the Austrian Tyrol and Trentino he presided over the transfer of some 200,000 Germans to Italy. When he refused to agree to a similar transfer of a strip of the Dalmatian coast, he precipitated a crisis by appealing to the Italian people for national self-restraint over the heads of their representatives, a tactic that only hardened nationalist resolves and further discredited him with his colleagues. Self-determination of peoples, a legacy of nineteenth-century romantic nationalism, was honored in the breach at Paris as often as it was successfully applied.

But it was on reparations that Wilson suffered his most telling defeat. France originally proposed the preposterous figure of $200 billion, and England seemed unwilling to settle for much less. Clemenceau and Lloyd George, under heavy pressure from their respective publics, overrode Wilson's objections to such crippling demands and forced him to accept the inclusion of civilian damages and military pensions in the final assessment of Germany. The President, pushed beyond the limits of endurance, ill and confused, agreed to the principle of massive repayments and allowed the fixing of the specific amount to be postponed. A Reparations Commission in 1921 set the indemnity at $56 billion without regard to Germany's ability to pay or to the political consequences to a struggling Weimar Republic.

Throughout the agony of daily defeat Wilson was sustained by his hopes for the League of Nations and the work of drafting the covenant. The League, he told himself, would correct the mistakes and make good the deficiencies of the peace settlement to which it must be firmly tied. "Settlements may be temporary, but the action of nations in the interest of peace and justice must be permanent," he explained in presenting his handiwork to the plenary session in February 1919:

This document . . . is not a straitjacket, but a vehicle of life. A living thing is born . . . it is at one and the same time a practical document and a humane document. . . .

Wilson considered the League the vital center of the treaty: whatever the failings of the peacemakers — and Wilson now realized they were legion — the League would correct them. Moreover, by tying the League so closely to the treaty, the President hoped to forestall his congressional opponents by presenting them with a complete legal package that they would have to accept or reject as a whole. That they might succeed in rejecting his great work he never seriously considered.

It was Article X, the "heart of the covenant" in Wilson's view, that became the great symbolic issue that eventually destroyed his dream. Article X provided that

the members of the League undertake to respect and preserve as against external aggression the territorial integrity and existing political independence of all the Members of the League. In case of any such aggression or in case of any threat or danger of such aggression the Council shall advise upon the means by which this obligation shall be fulfilled.

For Wilson, Article X represented the triumph of moral force. The details of applying sanctions against future offenders concerned him less than the simple recognition by the nations of the world of his principle of collective security. This principle, at least, he had managed to rescue from the ruins of the treaty, and he meant to defend it at all costs.

In part the League, on which Wilson pinned all his hopes, represented the application of the progressive idea of commission government to the field of international affairs. Like a federal commission designed to free policymaking from the whims of politicians, the League with its various branches and agencies would provide the means for defusing international crises and resolving conflicts through arbitration. But in another and more profound sense Wilson's League of Nations was simply the culmination of inherited nineteenth-century liberal principles and a doctrine of progress. In the President's mind the League symbolized the old American truths and moral assumptions that neither the sophisticated instrumentalism of a Walter Lippmann nor the scoffings of cultural radicals like Van Wyck Brooks had been able to unsettle. As American institutions and legal instruments reformed the rest of the world, so the myth declared, and as the beneficent workings of trade and commerce gathered peoples together in harmony and abundance, the old selfish national interests would gradually die out until some day a worldwide legal community would rise in place of the old system of balance of power. Wilson, having witnessed four years of international slaughter and stood by while the nationalists at the peace conference imposed a punitive peace on Germany, was convinced that the time had come for building such an international moral order. While he was willing to concede much—and in fact had conspicuously failed to control the peace conference—he was not prepared to compromise on the League of Nations nor on the question of the role his country would have to play in its creation.

Wilson's utopian commitment led him to overlook two fundamental problems. The first resulted from attaching the League to the treaty: in joining an international agency to a Carthaginian peace, the Allies had merely fashioned an instrument of enforcement and put it in the hands of the victors. Connected to this contradiction of means was a second question of intent. Was the League intended to facilitate change or to prevent it? Was it designed simply to enforce a victor's peace, or would it adjust shifting balances of national power, incorporate new members, and provide for ordered change? No amount of Wilsonian rhetoric about "the general moral judgment of mankind" could obscure the basic confusion of purpose in his attempt to replace international power relations with a utopian community of moral force.

Wilson returned in the summer of 1919 to a nation already in the throes of reaction. The shadow of the Russian Revolution, which had fallen over the peace table, now lengthened across the Atlantic. The threat of revolution strengthened the forces of the right everywhere in Europe as conservatives rushed to defend their states from the Bolshevik menace. To Americans the Soviet challenge appeared particularly ominous because it threatened to destroy their own revolutionary tradition. Here was no mere political rearrangement sensibly completed and solicitous of property rights and personal liberties, but a vast social upheaval with a collectivist ideology that was the antithesis of Western capitalist democracy. The immediate American response to the new Soviet regime was twofold: an abortive attempt to strengthen the counterrevolutionary forces in Russia by land-ing troops (soon withdrawn) at Murmansk and Vladivostok, and the tendency at home to see Reds everywhere. By the summer of 1919 the "Red Scare" had taken full possession of the public imagination as a wartime fear of subversion was suddenly transformed into dread of imminent revolution.

Wilson also felt the full force of a congressional reaction that had been building since the Armistice. War mobilization had concentrated unprecedented power in the executive branch of the government, thus completing the political cycle that had begun with Theodore Roosevelt's presidency. But now, with reconversion and demobilization, the pendulum began to swing the other way, as Congress moved firmly to reassert its control over foreign affairs as well as domestic policy.

The legislative resurgence had already acquired a highly partisan cast with the revival of the Republican party, which with forty-nine seats in the Senate now enjoyed a two-vote margin over its rivals. Presented with the opportunity to check Wilson's power by modifying the terms of American participation in the new League of Nations, they scarcely could be expected to resist. Republicans also were preparing themselves for rolling back wartime controls and curb-ing the regulatory power of federal agencies, whose activities they now tended to equate with socialism. They reasoned that if the wartime prosperity could be maintained and the gains to business ensured at the same time the supervisory powers of the federal government were curtailed, then an incoming Republican administration, on which they counted, might well build a new dynasty based on voluntary cooperation. The League was only the most obvious issue with which Republicans aimed to reestablish themselves in contention once again.

Yet on the question of acceptance of Wilson's treaty and American participa-tion in the League of Nations, the Republican members of the Senate remained divided. On the right of the party stood some dozen or fifteen "Irreconcilable" stalwarts, isolationists opposed to nearly any continued international involvement. At the other end of the spectrum were the "Mild Reservationists," supporters of the League in principle but concerned with the extent of Wilson's commitment to collective security and anxious to reduce it. Ranged between these two ideological poles were the "Strong Reservationists," making up the majority faction and tak-ing their orders from Henry Cabot Lodge. Lodge combined a cordial hatred of the President with a narrow nationalism that had not changed since the Spanish-American War. The "Strong Reservationists," willing to consider United States participation only on their own terms, were fully prepared to force on the Presi-dent significant reservations limiting the extent of American commitments and making the Congress rather than the chief executive the final judge of their appli-cability. Within his own party, Wilson could count on solid internationalist sup-port, but it was clear at the outset of the struggle that he would have to detach a sizable number of Republican moderates from Lodge's control if he were going to win acceptance for his project. By July 1919, Wilson faced a formidable but not an impossible task, one that would require great patience and even greater flexibility.

For his part, Lodge followed a clever strategy contrived to exploit every advantage over his adversary. He packed the Senate Foreign Relations Committee with his followers; conducted interminable hearings that gave a voice to every conceivable opponent of the League; courted right-wing businessmen like Henry Clay Frick and Andrew Mellon, who had swung over to his side; and loaded the Treaty down with amendments. By fall his original forty-five amendments had been reduced to fourteen reservations, one for each of Wilson's initial Fourteen Points. The first reserved to the United States the sole right to decide whether it had fulfilled its obligations under the covenant and gave the power of withdrawal from the League to Congress. The second, directed at the controversial Article X, was also aimed unerringly at Wilson's greatest weakness. It provided the primary check to the President's hopes for full American participation by stipulating that the United States would accept no obligation to enforce the collective security provisions of the covenant without the consent of Congress in each and every case. Other reservations rejected any mandates assignable to the United States; reserved the right to determine which questions involving American interests might be submitted to the League; and withdrew the Monroe Doctrine from the international arena altogether. Taken together, Lodge's reservations were significant though hardly crippling modifications, as the subsequent history of the League would show.

Yet, as Lodge hoped, Wilson believed otherwise; he consistently refused to make a realistic assessment of the damage done to his vehicle. He was unwilling to consider the specific circumstances under which the United States might be called on to apply sanctions, either economic or military, because basically he was convinced that full discussion and debate in the forum of the League would make any such drastic appeal unnecessary. For him the real question was simple: Was the United States prepared to make the significant moral gesture towards peace and international security? Would the American people see to it that the Senate carried out its obligation? Although the actual struggle with the Senate grew complicated with proposals and counterproposals, amendments, reservations, and interpretations, Wilson's position remained essentially the one he had taken in presenting the treaty to the Senate: "The stage is set, the destiny disclosed. . . . We cannot turn back. We can only go forward, with lifted eyes and freshened spirit, to follow the vision."

His own vision led him away from Washington on an 8000-mile tour of the nation, during which he gave forty speeches explaining to the American people the importance of the League to their future security and welfare. In taking his case to the country Wilson was violating one of his own precepts. "The Senate," he once wrote, "is not . . . immediately sensitive to [public] opinion and is apt to grow, if anything, more stiff if pressure of that kind is brought to bear upon it." Now President Wilson ignored Professor Wilson's stricture. His tour carried him further and further away from political reality and the central problem of securing the consent of the Senate. Although he referred frequently to specific issues and explained the limited nature of the American commitment, it was to the theme of principle that he returned obsessively as he reduced the question to one of conscience:

You have no choice, my fellow citizens. . . . You cannot give a false gift. . . . Men are not going to stand it. . . . There is nothing for any nation to lose whose purposes are right and whose cause is just. . . . The whole freedom of the world not only, but the whole peace of mind of the world, depends upon the choice of America. . . . I can testify to that. . . . The world will be absolutely in despair if America deserts it. . . .

Worn out and distraught, collapsing under the weight of his moral mission, Wilson suffered a stroke in Pueblo, Colorado, on September 25 and was rushed back to Washington where a week later a second stroke left him paralyzed. Isolated by his illness from his followers and advisers, locked in a private moral world, Wilson in effect had spoken his last word on the treaty. Loyal Democrats received their presidential orders: vote to reject the treaty with the Lodge reservations. On November 19, 1919, the treaty with the reservations failed of adoption by a vote of 39 for and 55 against, with loyal Democrats joining the Irreconcilables to defeat it. Wilson still hoped to make the presidential election of 1920 the occasion of a giant referendum on the League, but his advisers along with more objective observers knew the fight was over. The President's dream had died.

Domestic discord in 1919 mirrored the collapse of Wilson's moral world. A calendar of violence marked the decline of original progressive hopes.

In January shipyard workers in Seattle struck for higher wages, organized a general strike, and paralyzed the city. At the request of the mayor the federal government dispatched the Marines.

In May four hundred soldiers and sailors sacked the offices of the Socialist New York *Call* and beat up the staff.

In the summer of 1919, race riots erupted in 25 cities across the country, the most serious outbreak in Chicago where 38 were killed and over 500 injured.

In September the Boston police force struck for the right to unionize, and the city experienced a wave of looting and theft until leading businessmen and Harvard students restored order.

In September 350,000 steelworkers struck for the right to unionize and an eight-hour day.

In November a mob in Centralia, Washington dragged the IWW agitator Wesley Everest from jail and castrated him before hanging him.

In December agents of the Labor Department rounded up 249 Russian Communists and deported them to Finland.

THE WALL STREET BOMBING, 1920

(*Brown Brothers.*)

There were Americans in 1919 who recalled Wilson's definition of the progressive task six years earlier as "the high enterprise of the new day." "Our duty is to cleanse, to reconsider, to correct the evil without impairing the good, to purify and humanize every process of our common life without weakening or sentimentalizing it." For those who remembered there could be little doubt that the new day had ended.

Suggested Readings

Three good surveys of the military conduct of the war are Edward M. Coffman, *The War to End Wars: The American Military Experience in World War I* (1968); Hanson W. Baldwin, *World War I* (1962); and Russell F. Weigley, *The American Way of War* (1973). Fredric L. Paxon, *American Democracy and the World War* (3 vols., 1936–48) provides massive treatment of the war years at home and in the field. John G. Clifford, *The Citizen Soldiers: The Plattsburg Training Camp Movement, 1913–1920* (1972), describes the preparedness movement.

Immediately following the war the participants on the home front took the measure of their difficulties and accomplishments in numerous monographs useful for their impressions: Benjamin Hibbard, *Effects of the Great War Upon Agriculture in the United*

States and Great Britain (1919); Grosvenor Clarkson, *Industrial America in the World War* (1923); Gordon Watkins, *Labor Problems and Labor Administration in the United States during the World War* (1920); George Creel, *How We Advertised America* (1920). More recent studies are at once more accurate, better balanced, and generally critical. Robert Cuff, *The War Industries Board* (1973), discusses in detail the overwhelming problems confronting the board, and Charles Gilbert, *American Financing of World War I* (1970), carefully analyzes a difficult subject. Frank L. Grubbs Jr., *The Struggle for Labor Loyalty: Gompers, the A. F. of L., and the Pacifists, 1917–1920* (1968), describes the war efforts of labor leaders. Theodore Saloutos and John D. Hicks, *Agricultural Discontent in the Middle West, 1900–1939* (1951), contains an account of the growing plight of the farmers, as the opening section of George Soule, *Prosperity Decade* (1947), does for the American economy as a whole. Daniel R. Beaver, *Newton D. Baker and the American War Effort, 1917–1919* (1966), surveys the contributions of a great organizer. George T. Blakely, *Historians on the Homefront: American Propagandists for the Great War* (1970), is an unsettling account of misplaced patriotism. Seward W. Livermore, *Politics Is Adjourned: Woodrow Wilson and the War Congress, 1916–1919* (1966), recounts the fate of wartime bipartisanship.

The years since World War II have seen a growing number of incisive studies of American civil liberties during and after the First World War. Beginning with Zechariah Chafee, *Free Speech in the United States* (1941), the list includes Harry N. Scheiber, *The Wilson Administration and Civil Liberties, 1917–1921* (1960); Donald M. Johnson, *The Challenge to American Freedoms* (1963); H. C. Peterson and Gilbert Fite, *Opponents of the War, 1917–1918* (1957); William Preston, Jr., *Aliens and Dissenters: Federal Suppression of Radicals, 1903–1933* (1963); Robert K. Murray, *Red Scare: A Study of National Hysteria, 1919–1920* (1955); and Paul L. Murphy, *The Meaning of Freedom of Speech . . . Wilson to FDR* (1972). Stanley Cohen, *A. Mitchell Palmer* (1963), paints a portrait of a national villain.

For the effects on the social and cultural life of Americans during the war, see the selections in David F. Trask, ed., *World War I at Home: Readings on American Life, 1914–1920* (1969), and Arthur S. Link, ed., *The Impact of World War* (1969). Paul A. Carter, *The Decline and Revival of the Social Gospel* (1954), traces the history of a key religious concept through the war, and Ray Abrams, *Preachers Present Arms* (1933), describes the recruitment of segments of the ministry to the war state. A. Hunter Dupree, *Science and the Federal Government* (1957), considers how war cements ties between government and the scientific community, Arthur Waskow, *From Race Riot to Sit-In, 1919 and the 1960's* (1966), and William Tuttle, Jr., *Race Riot: Chicago and the Red Summer of 1919* (1970), analyze the most serious of the racial disturbances during and after the war. Robert L. Friedheim, *The Seattle General Strike* (1964) dissects an important event. Wesley M. Bagby, *The Road to Normalcy: The Presidential Campaign and Election of 1920* (1962) opens the political door on the Twenties.

The immediate shock of war as experienced by artists and intellectuals is described in Stanley Cooperman, *World War I and the American Novel* (1967), and its lingering effects in Malcolm Cowley, *Exiles Return: A Literary Odyssesy of the 1920's* (1951), and Frederick J. Hoffman, *The 20's* (1955). There are two good discussions of American art in the early twentieth century: Sam Hunter, *American Painting and Sculpture* (1959), and Barbara Rose, *American Art Since 1900: A Critical History* (1967), which should be read together with her *Readings in American Art Since 1900: A Documentary Survey* (1968). John I. H. Bauer, *Revolution and Tradition in Modern American Art* (1967) provides useful commentary on the Ashcan School. For the Armory Show, see Milton Brown, *The Story of the Armory Show* (1963), and also the best brief discussion of its revolutionary meaning for American art, Meyer Schapiro, "Rebellion in Art," in Daniel Aaron, ed., *America in Crisis* (1952). The confused response of one practitioner of the strenuous life can be found in Theodore Roosevelt, "A Layman's Views of an Art Exposition," *Outlook 29*, March 9, 1913.

The best approach to the intellectual history of the Progressive years is through the writers themselves. Significant works of social and political analysis, now considered classics, include Jane Addams, *Twenty Years at Hull House* (1910); Randolph Bourne, *Youth and Life* (1913) and a collection of Bourne's war pieces, *War and the Intellectuals* (1964), edited by Carl Resek; Louis Brandeis, *Other People's Money* (1914); Van Wyck Brooks, *America's Coming of Age* (1915); Charles H. Cooley, *Human Nature and the Social Order* (1922); Herbert Croly, *The Promise of American Life* (1909); John Dewey, *School and Society* (1899); W. E. B. DuBois, *Souls of the Black Folk* (1903); Charlotte Perkins Gilman, *Women and Economics* (1898); Walter Lippmann, *Drift and Mastery* (1914); John Reed, *Insurgent Mexico* (1914) and *Ten Days That Shook the World* (1919); Walter Weyl, *The New Democracy* (1912).

On the diplomacy of war and peacemaking, Arno J. Mayer, *Political Origins of the New Diplomacy, 1917–1918* (1959) and *Politics and Diplomacy of Peacemaking: Containment and Counterrevolution at Versailles, 1918–1919* (1967), are both ponderous and provocative. N. Gordon Levin, *Woodrow Wilson and World Politics: America's Response to War and Revolution* (1968), focuses on the presidential strategies as does Warren Kuehl, *Seeking World Order: The United States and World Organization to 1920* (1969). Two works by Thomas A. Bailey, *Woodrow Wilson and the Lost Peace* (1944) and *Woodrow Wilson and the Great Betrayal* (1945), detail Wilson's tragic postwar course. On the opposition to the League, Ralph A. Stone, *The Irreconcilables: The Fight Against the League of Nations* (1970), is admirable, and John Garraty, *Henry Cabot Lodge* (1953), offers a sympathetic but not uncritical appraisal of Wilson's archenemy. On Soviet-American relations, see George F. Kennan, *Russia Leaves the War* (1956), and *The Decision to Intervene: Prelude to Allied Intervention in the Bolshevik Revolution* (1958). Peter G. Filene, *Americans and the Soviet Experiment* (1967), and Christopher Lasch, *The American Liberals and the Russian Revolution* (1962), consider the varied American reactions to the Revolution. Betty M. Unterberger, *America's Siberian Expedition* (1956), explains the failure of that misguided action. Lawrence E. Gelfand, *The Inquiry: American Preparations for Peace, 1917–1919* (1963), is an account of the role of President's advisers at Versailles. Paul Birdsall, *Versailles: Twenty Years After* (1973), assesses the peacemaking from the perspective of a later crisis.

1890 In *Louisville, New Orleans, and Texas Railroad v. Mississippi,* Supreme Court upholds segregation in railroad cars.
Sherman Anti-Trust Act passed in attempt to regulate monopolies in restraint of trade.
Sherman Silver Purchase Act passed, resulting in depleted gold reserves.
Yosemite National Park created.
General Federation of Women's Clubs formed.
William James's, *Principles of Psychology;* William Dean Howells's, *A Hazard of New Fortunes.*
Force Bill.
McKinley Tariff raises duties to average 49.5 percent.

1892 Populists organize in Saint Louis and nominate General James B. Weaver for President.
Grover Cleveland elected President.
John Muir forms Sierra Club.
Homestead strike in Carnegie steel mills.

1893 Financial panic sends United States economy into four years of depression.
Repeal of Sherman Silver Purchase Act.
Conference for Good City Government inaugurates urban progressive reform movement.
Pullman strike; Eugene V. Debs jailed.
Attempt to annex Hawaii following American-engineered coup thwarted by Cleveland.
Frederick Jackson Turner, in "The Significance of the Frontier in American History," announces closing of the frontier.
Formation of Anti-Saloon League.

1894 "Coxey's Army" of unemployed marches on Washington, where it is quickly dispersed.
Pullman strike, one of 1,394 strikes in this year, broken by General Managers Association and federal troops; Debs jailed.
Chicago World's Fair opens.
Henry Demarest Lloyd, *Wealth against Commonwealth,* exposé of Standard Oil Company.
Wilson-Gorman Tariff lowers some tariffs, makes average rate 39.9 percent.

1895 In *U.S. v. E. C. Knight Co.,* government

1902 Roosevelt launches antitrust action against Northern Securities Company.
Newlands Act establishes Bureau of Reclamation for financing irrigation projects.
Roosevelt settles anthracite coal strike through arbitration.
Oliver Wendell Holmes appointed to Supreme Court.
United States returns civil government to Republic of Cuba.

1903 Bureau of Corporations established within new Department of Commerce and Labor.
W. E. B. DuBois's *The Souls of the Black Folk.*
Hay-Herran Treaty with Republic of Colombia giving United States 99-year lease on Canal Zone is rejected by Colombia.
Roosevelt aids revolt in Panama.
Hay-Bunau-Varilla Treaty gives United States full sovereignty in Canal Zone.
United States-Cuba reciprocity treaty forms close economic ties between both countries.
Citizens Industrial Association formed to secure open shop in American industry.
Wright brothers make their first flight.

1904 Roosevelt corollary to Monroe Doctrine.
Lincoln Steffens's *The Shame of the Cities.*
Roosevelt reelected, defeating Democrat Alton B. Parker and Socialist Eugene V. Debs.
Anna Howard Shaw becomes head of National American Woman Suffrage Association.
Northern Securities case.

1905 *Lochner v. New York;* Supreme Court declares unconstitutional New York law regulating hours for bakers.
Niagara Movement formed to agitate for integration and civil rights for blacks.
Industrial Workers of the World formed.
Roosevelt mediates in Russo-Japanese War.

1906 Hepburn Act passed, strengthening powers of Interstate Commerce Commission.
Pure Food and Drug Act.
Upton Sinclair's *The Jungle.*
Meat Inspection Act.
John Spargo's, *The Bitter Cry of Children,*

1912 Woodrow Wilson elected President, defeating Republican regular William Howard Taft, Progressive "Bull Moose" Theodore Roosevelt, and Socialist Eugene Debs.
Lawrence (Massachusetts) Strike against American Woolen Company, led by IWW.

1913 Sixteenth and Seventeenth Amendments ratified, authorizing federal income tax and providing for direct election of senators.
Underwood Tariff lowering rates.
Federal Reserve System created.
Armory Show in New York City.
Dayton, Ohio, adopts first major city manager plan.
Patterson Strike.

1914 First World War begins; Wilson declares American neutrality.
Wilson orders occupation of Vera Cruz.
Clayton Anti-Trust Act.
Panama Canal opened.
Smith-Lever Act.
Federal Trade Commission created to regulate business practices.
"Ludlow Massacre"; National Guard attacks tent colony of strikers in Ludlow, Colorado, killing 11 women and 2 children.

1915 United States troops occupy Haiti.
United States recognizes Carranza government in Mexico.
Germans declare unrestricted submarine warfare and sink *Lusitania* with loss of American lives.
Preparedness movement.
D. W. Griffith's movie *The Birth of a Nation.*

1916 Wilson reelected, narrowly defeating Charles Evans Hughes.
House-Grey Memorandum on United States efforts for negotiated peace.
American troops occupy Dominican Republic.
Louis Brandeis appointed to Supreme Court.
Tariff Commission created.
Adamson Act establishing eight-hour day on interstate railroads.
Keating-Owen Act regulating child labor (later declared unconstitutional).

address.
United States intervenes in boundary dispute between Britain and Venezuela as Secretary of State Richard Olney declares nation "practically sovereign on this continent."
Spain sends troops to quell Cuban revolution.
Stephen Crane's *The Red Badge of Courage.*

1896
Cuban rebel leader Maceo murdered, resulting in American popular support for Cuba.
Plessy v. Ferguson establishes "separate but equal doctrine."
McKinley elected President, defeating Bryan and "Free Silver."

1897
Delôme Letter calling McKinley "weak" and "a would-be politician" intercepted, worsening American and Spanish relations.
Dingley Tariff raises duties to new high of 57 percent.

1898
Spanish-American War: United States acquires Philippines, Puerto Rico, and Guam, and annexes Hawaii.

1899
Hay's "Open Door" notes to world powers calling for "equal and impartial trade" in China and preservation of "Chinese territorial and administrative" integrity.
Senate ratifies peace treaty with Spain.
John Dewey's *School and Society,* pioneer progressive education tract.
United States, Germany and Great Britain partition Samoa.

1900
Foraker Act establishes civil government in Puerto Rico.
McKinley reelected President, defeating Bryan once again.
Robert La Follette elected to his first term as progressive governor of Wisconsin.
Theodore Dreiser's *Sister Carrie,* naturalistic novel causes literary stir.
National Civic Federation founded by labor leaders and important industrialists.

1901
Hay-Pauncefote Treaty.
Theodore Roosevelt becomes President after McKinley assassinated.
Platt Amendment.
Formation of United States Steel Corporation.
Insular cases.

settles French-German conflict in Morocco.
Black troops accused of involvement in Brownsville, Texas, riot.

1907
Financial panic; Roosevelt turns to J. P. Morgan and the bankers for help.
William James's *Pragmatism.*
Roosevelt appoints Dillingham Commission to investigate immigration problem.

1908
William Howard Taft elected President, defeating Bryan and Debs.
Louis Brandeis argues sociological brief in *Muller v. Oregon* as Court upholds state law regulating hours for women.
Root-Takahira Agreement; United States recognizes Japan's interests in Manchuria.

1909
Payne-Aldrich Tariff raising rates to protect Eastern manufacturers provoke opposition of South and Midwest.
Taft inaugurates Dollar Diplomacy in China and Latin America.
United States intervenes in Haitian and Nicaraguan finances.
National Association for the Advancement of Colored People founded.
Herbert Croly's *The Promise of American Life.*

1910
Taft fires Gifford Pinchot, chief forester.
Woodrow Wilson elected New Jersey governor.
Roosevelt's "New Nationalism" speech at Osawatomie, Kansas.
Women enfranchised in state of Washington.
Mann-Elkins Act.

1911
Triangle Shirtwaist Factory fire in New York City's East Side kills 146 women, leading to investigation and revision of state factory code.
Frederick Winslow Taylor's *Principles of Scientific Management,* pioneer work on industrial efficiency.
Marines sent to Nicaragua.
"Dissolution" of Standard Oil and American Tobacco trusts.

establishing provisional government; "October Revolution" engineered by Bolsheviks.
Draft Act.
Espionage Act.
Purchase of Danish Virgin Islands.
Creation of War Industries Board.
Lansing-Ishii Agreement.
First Pulitzer prizes awarded.

1918
Wilson's Fourteen Points outlining administration's peace aims.
United States troops at Belleau Wood.
Saint Mihiel salient, first United States offensive.
Meuse-Argonne offensive.
Sedition Act providing severe penalties for expressing "disloyal" opinions.
Armistice; Germany defeated.

1919
Schenck v. U.S., upholding Espionage Act and government curtailment of free speech during wartime.
Abrams v. U.S., upholding Sedition Act.
Eighteenth Amendment prohibits sale or manufacture of alcoholic beverages.
Steel strike.
Race riots in Chicago, East Saint Louis, and Washington.

1920
Great Red Scare.
Defeat of Versailles Treaty by Senate.
Nineteenth Amendment gives vote to women.
Warren G. Harding elected President, defeating James M. Cox and Eugene Debs.

During the late 1950s and the 1960s, Pop
artists such as Johns adopted images from
advertising, comic strips, and all forms of
popular culture as subjects for their work.
During the sixties the symbol of the
American flag was used in many guises to
rally both opponents and supporters of
government policy. (*Collection of Mr. and
Mrs. Burton Tremaine, Meridan, Connecticut.*)

PART SIX

Modernizing the Republic

1920 to the Present

ROBERT H. WIEBE

The First World War shattered some hopes beyond repair. Never again would a cultural vanguard expect a sweeping, almost spontaneous revolution in values with such happy zest as the Greenwich Village radicals did on the eve of the war. Never again would Americans bring such a shining optimism to international affairs as they did when Woodrow Wilson called them to battle for universal democracy and justice. A certain faith in the world's moral wholeness and its natural improvement had been irreparably lost. Yet these casualties of the war were themselves an important preparation for the nation's future. As the high ideals of the progressive years deflated, Americans entered the 1920s with a sharper focus on material goals. The greater willingness of Americans to find salvation through the economy set them on the path into the modern era.

The core of modern American society was a national economy that acquired its basic form in the 1920s. Beginning with the industrial consolidations of the late nineteenth century, the main subdivisions of the economy—the business of production and distribution, the centers of finance, skilled labor, and commercial agriculture—had become increasingly organized, increasingly committed to nationwide cooperation, and increasingly alert to the usefulness of the government in Washington. The First World War accelerated these trends. By the middle of the 1920s, the components of America's modern economy had co-alesced into a national system, and during the next half-century the system's essential character did not fundamentally alter.

Along with this national economic system came four primary problems that shaped modern American history. The dramatic occurrences of the modern era—the Great Depression, the Second World War, the onset of the Cold War, and the upheaval of the 1960s—certainly influenced the ways in which Americans tried to solve these problems. So in a much smaller way did the changes of Presidents and political parties in Washington. But as the nation swung from prosperity to depression, from peace to war, and from confidence to doubt, it was always this set of four problems that gave continuity to America's development.

First, how should Americans maintain a strong economy? In the 1920s, the new economic system seemed quite capable of running itself. Without direction, however, it ended in the ditch of depression, and a majority of Americans turned for help to the national government. Yet for a quarter of a century after the Great Crash of 1929, the nation's leaders failed to settle on a generally acceptable means of using the government's powers. Not until the early 1950s did Republicans and Democrats alike come to rely on Washington's fiscal authority, particularly the huge national budget, to guarantee a steady, healthy economy.

A fiscal solution gained bipartisan approval partly because it promised maximum government support for the whole economy with minimum interference in private economic affairs. A similar combination of support and restraint answered a second primary problem in modern America. How should authority be divided between national and local politics? What made this problem so sensitive was a growing separation between the two levels. National politics concentrated more and more exclusively on national economic issues. Local politics, on the other hand, continued to be steeped in a variety of traditional ethnic and cultural concerns. Different leaders, different standards, and different needs at the two levels of politics threatened to disrupt government. During the 1930s, the Democratic party under Franklin Roosevelt struck a tacit bargain that gave national leaders a free hand in devising general economic policy and local leaders a wide discretion in setting cultural and ethnic rules for their domains. In 1953, as the Republican Dwight Eisenhower entered the White House, this compromise seemed even sturdier than it had been under the Democrats.

A third primary problem involved personal rather than political guidance. What values should govern the individual in modern society? Some Americans adapted their values to fit the specialized occupations in a modern economy. Others, finding little prestige in their routine jobs, looked elsewhere for meaning in their lives. Though almost all Americans participated in the expanding consumer economy, some did so wholeheartedly and some warily. A great many wondered if they could even survive as individuals in an impersonally organized society. Such a wide range of responses demanded an equally varied array of alternative answers, and by midcentury American society seemed to offer the individual an appropriate mixture of personal values.

America's economy made it the world's most powerful nation, yet America's tradition held it aloof from international commitments. What role should the United States play in world affairs? In resolving this fourth primary problem, Americans tried to find a middle ground between immersion and withdrawal. Even the Second World War did not destroy America's urge to balance the need for involvement with the tradition of detachment. After the war, however, America's leaders interpreted the challenge of Soviet communism as too critical to allow a peacetime detachment, and through the global policy of containment, they cast the nation's future with a worldwide involvement in international affairs.

By the early 1950s, an initial round of asking and answering was completed. In the process, Americans had greatly increased the burdens on their national government. What happened in Washington intimately affected this web of solutions, and any number of actions there might unravel the entire pattern, forcing a new search for answers. During the late 1950s and 1960s, the policies of the national government did precisely that. A drive for uniform racial and cultural standards, highlighted by the movement for black rights, disrupted the balance between national and local power. An attempt to determine the destiny of Indochina, producing the Viet Nam War, eroded popular support for containment. These conflicts, in combination with deepening doubts about the future of the individual, triggered an open revolt against modern American values, first among well-to-do youths and then among millions of wage earners and townspeople throughout the nation.

In the 1970s, just as the national government was experimenting with a new compromise between national and local power in domestic affairs and a new balance between detachment and involvement in world affairs, the economy lost its equilibrium. International forces caused the greatest disturbance, and no purely American policy could tame them. In approximately a ten-year span from the middle of the 1960s to the middle of the 1970s, therefore, all four primary problems in modern American history had reemerged to demand a fresh set of answers. These problems, so thoroughly embedded in American society, defied any final, absolute solution. Their history was the history of modern America, and as each generation provided new answers, it wrote another chapter in the continuing American story.

The Emergence of Modern Politics

As their first order of business in the 1920s, Americans wanted to settle the issues that had carried over from the war years. But while they were placing those issues to rest, they also began the long process of developing a new system of politics. The most striking quality of the new politics was its division of interests between national and local affairs. In national affairs, modern politics concentrated on economic matters, seeking a nationwide policy that would best serve the economy as a whole. In local affairs, on the other hand, politics continued to mix people's economic ambitions with their ethnic, cultural and moral concerns. These differences were masked for a time, first by a general enthusiasm for America's prosperity and then by a common preoccupation with America's depression. Yet throughout the late twenties and early thirties, the gap between national and local politics was widening. During Franklin Roosevelt's first term as President, the emerging system of modern politics faced its initial crisis. After years of depression, were America's leaders capable of finding a national policy that actually benefited the whole economy? And how could such a policy bridge the gap between national economic needs and the cultural sensitivities of local politics? By the midthirties, a crucial set of answers to these questions was beginning to materialize.

The Reactionary Impulse, 1920–1924

Rarely had the voters faced such a lackluster pair of presidential candidates as they did in 1920. Each of the two major parties, turning away from the late examples of a strong chief executive, nominated a political mediocrity from Ohio. For the Democrats, Governor James M. Cox offered the best alternative to the stricken but still ambitious President Wilson. The Republicans selected the weak, affable Senator Warren G. Harding in order to break a convention deadlock. During the campaign, Cox talked as if he had lost his way in national affairs, and Harding relied almost exclusively on empty platitudes. But the handsome senator at least showed Americans a warm smile and a friendly manner. In November 1920, that genial personality, along with a nationwide accumulation of grievances against the Democrats, gave Harding an overwhelming 61 percent of the popular vote. Cox carried no states outside the South.

An era, it seemed, had ended. America now had a passive, conservative President with no taste for reform and no ambition for either national or international ventures. Promising the nation a return to "normalcy," Harding entered the White House with no apparent goals of any sort. Some observers concluded that he was trying to recapture the spirit of the McKinley years, when the chief executive had watched benignly while other people ran the country. They might better have cited the spirit of the Grant administration, for Harding allowed a swarm of greedy men to infest the government, corrupt many of its offices, and ruin his own reputation.

PRESIDENT HARDING AND FRIEND

President Warren G. Harding said "yes" to his friends too often, and his administration ended in scandal. *(Brown Brothers.)*

In an inconspicuous house on K Street, members of an "Ohio gang" with connections in the justice department sold immunity from federal prosecution. Charles Forbes, a chance acquaintance whom Harding appointed director of the Veterans' Bureau, fled the country in 1923 to avoid punishment for misusing millions of public funds. Most sensational of all, a long congressional inquiry in 1923 and 1924 exposed the bribes and backroom deals behind the private leasing of government oil lands on Teapot Dome in Wyoming and Elk Hill in California. For his part in the "Teapot Dome Scandal," Secretary of the Interior Albert Fall, whose lean frame, broad-brimmed hat, and drooping handlebar moustache made him look for all the world like a Hollywood sheriff, became the first cabinet officer in history to serve a jail sentence. Harding's close associate Attorney General Harry Daugherty barely escaped being the second. By a measure of morality or energy or ideology, the contrast between Harding's crowd and the administrations of Theodore Roosevelt and Woodrow Wilson could not have been more striking.

Harding's promise of normalcy echoed the desire of millions to purge their country of troubles and reclaim a mythical, harmonious past. Adapting the nation's oppressive wartime tactics to peacetime needs, a host of private citizens and public officials set out to eliminate organized radicalism in the name of 100 percent Americanism. They completed the destruction of the Industrial Workers of the World (IWW). Legally elected members from the Socialist Party were not even allowed their seats in the House of Representatives and the New York Assembly. During the Great Red Scare of 1919–20, Attorney General A. Mitchell Palmer twice ordered extensive raids on America's fledgling Communist party and came very close to annihilating it. "America," the evangelist Billy Sunday proudly declared, "is not a country for a dissenter to live in."

Although some prominent citizens sharply condemned the excesses of the Red Scare, antiradicalism remained a powerful force early in the 1920s. One of its victims was the Non-Partisan League, an alliance of respectable farmers, lawyers, and merchants that was active in an arc of states around North Dakota. Seeking freedom from distant businessmen and bankers, the Non-Partisan League wanted to use the credit of the state government so that local farmers could store their crops and market them at the best prices. Yet after winning control of the North Dakota government, the Non-Partisan League discovered that private bankers would not buy and sell North Dakota's state bonds. During the recession of 1921–22, the bankers' boycott succeeded in undermining the League's "socialist" program.

Antiradicalism also contributed to the drives against organized labor. Immediately after the war, businessmen and their allies created "open shop" committees throughout the nation to smash the unions in the American Federation of Labor. The leaders of the AFL were themselves vigorous antiradicals, but they still could not protect their own unions from sweeping charges that all labor organizations were somehow socialist and un-American. The steel companies crushed an ambitious organizing drive in their industry in 1919, and two years later the biggest meat packers cleared the unions from their plants. Under heavy attack, union membership fell from a peak of over 5 million in 1920 to about 3.6 million in 1923. Union morale suffered even more than statistics could reveal.

Because radicalism was invariably called an alien influence, immigrants generally suffered in the climate of the early twenties. Sometimes radicals and aliens were merged in a single stereotype of the bewhiskered, bomb-throwing foreigner. But the rising hostility to immigration came mostly from another kind of concern about a lost racial and cultural purity. Before the First World War, many "native Americans"—white, Anglo-Saxon, and Protestant—became convinced that they needed special protection against the deluge of Catholics and Jews from southern and eastern Europe. Some accused the immigrants of flooding the labor market and lowering the American standard of living. Others, citing the newcomers' support of corrupt political bosses, declared them unfit to vote. Advocates of prohibition condemned their saloons, and urban reformers condemned their living habits By 1920, innumerable Americans were justifying these prejudices with racial theories that categorized the "dirty little dark people" of southern and eastern Europe as a genetically inferior breed who were mongrelizing the American population.

Despite a minority who defended both the immigrants and the American tradition of open gates, public debate in the early twenties largely focused on the best techniques for restriction. The government's first attempt, the Literacy Test of 1917, had failed because, contrary to common belief, most immigrants could read and write. The opponents of immigration soon adopted a much more effective device, annual immigration quotas by nationality. Between 1921 and 1924, Congress considered various formulas for these quotas. In 1921, it used 3 percent of the number of foreign-born in the 1910 census as the basis for each European country's quota. In the comprehensive National Origins Act of 1924, Congress substituted 2 percent of the foreign-born in the 1890 census as an interim measure until experts could prepare the long-range solution, an annual limit of 150,000 immigrants divided according to the percentage of each European nation's historical contribution to the white population in the United States.*

The justification for these laws was explicitly defensive and nostalgic. Restrictionists idealized the racial qualities of an earlier America. At each stage in the legislative sequence, Congress discriminated more harshly against southern and eastern Europe, where by far the largest number of potential immigrants lived. Not only did the act of 1924 place a ceiling on immigration that was less than

---

*The complicated calculations on national origins were not completed until 1929. Some version of this quota system remained in effect until 1965, when Congress in a new law used the nation's need for skills as the basis for deciding who should be admitted.

one-fifth of the normal prewar flow; it assigned the English, Germans, and Scandinavians higher quotas than they were able to fill and closed the door on the Italians, Polish, and Russians. In a direct slap at the Japanese, the law totally excluded Asiatics. Seldom had Congress managed to embitter so many people here and abroad with a single law.

Of all the reactionary movements in the early 1920s, none equaled the Ku Klux Klan. In 1920 two talented promoters, Edward Clarke and Elizabeth Tyler, took charge of a small Southern organization with a name famous from the days of Reconstruction. By capitalizing on the attractions of its fraternal secrecy, white-hooded rituals, and elaborate titles, they built the Ku Klux Klan into a nationwide organization of about 4 million members by 1924. Its primary enemies were alienism and immorality, and in fighting them, the Klan often resorted to intimidation and violence. The fiery cross and the midnight whipping became its symbols of justice.

Basically the Klan was a collection of local organizations that adapted their purposes to fight the particular enemies of each community. In the Oklahoma oil fields, a local Klavern boasted of transforming "'no counts' of men and females . . . almost [into] a 'Sunday-School class.'" Its counterpart in Calypso, North Carolina, announced, "All the Catholic gold in the universe can't buy our manhood and our liberty." In Denver, the Klan opposed labor unions and welfare programs. But the Klan also stretched its influence into state and national politics.

A KU KLUX KLAN INITIATION NEAR BRUNSWICK, MARYLAND, JUNE 28, 1922

Ghostly rituals gave the fraternity of the fiery cross an aura of special power, but the KKK was rarely a well-mobilized force. (*Brown Brothers.*)

Early in the 1920s, its leaders claimed political control of states as varied as Oklahoma, Oregon, and Indiana. The Klan's national spokesmen supported every campaign against radicals and immigrants, and Klansmen regularly flooded their congressmen with letters. The most important issue at the Democratic National Convention of 1924 was the place of the Klan in that party's affairs.

Though the Klan quickly aroused a vigorous national opposition, it remained a formidable presence in American politics because it represented only an exaggerated, somewhat disreputable version of a common impulse. Its themes were a lost unity and a lost virtue. It pined openly for a mythical America of hard-working, churchgoing, small-town citizens, all of whom were white, Anglo-Saxon, and Protestant. Like other Americans in all walks of life, Klansmen expected public policy to reflect their cultural, moral dreams. And in a variety of areas, including such economically significant ones as immigration and labor organization, just this kind of concern was still shaping public policy in the early twenties.

The Modern Economy, 1920–1929

Running parallel to these reactionary trends were fundamental changes that prepared the way for America's future. Though no single change made dramatic headlines, they combined to complete an economic revolution that had been under way for more than a quarter of a century. An important cluster of these changes involved the organization of the economy. Since the turn of the century, a varied array of groups in business, labor, agriculture, finance, and the professions had been forming throughout the nation. Each group was organized according to the special economic function it performed—lumber companies, retail druggists, railroad workers, investment bankers, civil engineers, and the like. Each of them wanted to stabilize its own economic sphere with its own rules. Each expected long-range planning to increase its efficiency and its income. Each recognized the importance of linking its activities with the activities of other economic groups around it. Taken together, they created a nationwide system of interest groups that were integrated by a common national outlook, a common concern for the health of the whole economy, and a common belief in the value of cooperation and coordination.

The most successful means of business stabilization was oligopoly, the domination of an industry by a few large firms. By 1920, oligopolies controlled almost every basic industry needing a heavy investment of capital. In railroading, for example, a handful of corporations, approximately equal in strength, divided the nation's territory among themselves. In the automobile industry, Ford and General Motors set the standard for a much more competitive but highly profitable market. In steel, one huge firm, United States Steel, rose above the other corporations—which were called Little Steel—to become the industry's informal leader. No matter what the variations, however, oligopoly always simplified the problems of industrial coordination by limiting the number of companies that had to agree on a common business policy. To facilitate long-range planning, these large corporations were themselves organized into several specialized departments, such as purchasing, finance, and production. The giants of industry had come a long way since the railroad pioneer James J. Hill had declared, "No one man can run more than ten thousand miles of railroad." In the 1920s no one thought to try. Management teams, working through elaborate corporate structures, coordinated the nation's big business.

In industries such as clothing manufacture, building construction, and most branches of retailing, where many small firms competed, trade associations were an alternative way of minimizing competition. About two thousand trade associations already existed in 1920, and they continued to multiply. Ranging from secret price-fixing pacts to occasional lunch meetings, the trade associations shared a commitment to pooling information so that common knowledge might stabilize their industries and increase their profits. Although they seldom coordinated business affairs as effectively as the oligopolies did, the trade associations still represented a significant step in the same general direction of cooperation and planning.

Most businessmen expected their wage earners to participate in these movements toward coordination and cooperation. Unlike the captains of industry of the late nineteenth century, who had usually treated wage earners much as they did hunks of ore or gears in the machinery, the modern business managers considered laborers as human beings whose efficiency would increase as their morale and incentive improved. Specialists in personnel policy organized company recreational programs for the employees, prepared chatty company bulletins, and invited workers to suggest improvements in the firm's procedures. To encourage a cooperative group spirit, some corporations sponsored their own company unions and shop committees. More and more of the unions in the AFL and the Railroad Brotherhoods accepted such company policies in an effort to salvage a place for themselves in the economy of the twenties. Under an accommodating new president, William Green, the AFL in 1925 listed the improvement of industrial productivity as one of its primary objectives. "[The] new, suave, discreet unionism," as one commentator noted late in the 1920s, "talks the language of the efficiency engineer and busies itself about ways and means of increasing output."

For good reason, successful commercial farmers regarded themselves as businessmen. As chemical fertilizers and the gasoline engine were revolutionizing agriculture, only the wealthy investor, applying these resources on a large scale and purchasing the latest improvements, could expect substantial profit from modern farming. These "agribusinessmen," like their industrial counterparts, sought to coordinate their affairs, and they too organized. Local farm bureaus distributed information about scientific farming techniques and through the

In the 1920s, America's "agribusiness" became integrated into a national economic system. *(Library of Congress.)*

national organization, the American Farm Bureau Federation, lobbied for favorable government policies. In addition, cooperative marketing associations in such agricultural specialties as wheat and dairying tried to maintain a steady level of profits throughout the year for their members. The cooperatives acted so much like any other business organization that the same men who had staffed Bernard Baruch's War Industries Board in 1918 could become the most prominent advisers of the farm cooperatives during the 1920s.

Bankers acted as auxiliaries to these various business groups. The wizards of Wall Street no longer dominated American business as they had twenty years earlier. The regional structure of the new Federal Reserve System encouraged the development of other financial centers in such cities as Chicago, Minneapolis, and San Francisco. Bursts of prosperity after 1915, and again after 1923, not only hastened this financial decentralization but also increased the number of important corporations that could be their own bankers. During the 1920s, companies as diverse as Eastman Kodak, Aluminum Corporation of America, Ford, and Sears, Roebuck were routinely financing business expansion from their own vast profits. As a service agency, banking organized itself into specialized subdivisions that matched the needs of its business clients.

The professions formed a second band of auxiliaries to business. Lawyers had been specializing in contracts, taxation, and labor policy right along with the growth of modern business, and this close interaction between business needs and legal services continued during the 1920s. Engineering organizations, which had shown some interest in broad social reforms before the war, now concentrated their attention on business efficiency. A variety of economists, statisticians, psychologists, sociologists, and educators also adopted the stance of a willing helper to the nation's business. And where an important profession, such as chemistry, was not adequately developed, powerful industries encouraged its growth.

Changes in government came in tandem with the organization of these economic interests. Because the new network of groups was national in both scope and outlook, only the national government could meet its needs. But the government was expected to be a helper, not a director of the economy. Its tasks were to encourage the development of economic groups and smooth the cooperation among them.

The heaviest burdens of economic service fell on the executive branch. Even the election of an incompetent President did not seriously weaken the national executive. To the most critical executive posts, Harding appointed able men who were enthusiastic about the latest economic trends. Under Herbert Hoover, the Department of Commerce convinced manufacturers that they should standardize the production of items ranging from wood screws to fan belts, distributed business statistics to help the trade associations, enabled the major broadcasting companies to stabilize the new radio industry, and at every opportunity publicized the virtues of business cooperation. Secretary of Agriculture Henry C. Wallace was equally dedicated to the modern economy. He expanded his department's scientific research, its collection of agricultural data, and its promotion of orderly national and international marketing. The new Federal Power Commission, originally a collection of cabinet officials, did whatever it could to further the private development of America's hydroelectric resources, and such established departments as the Forestry and Fisheries Services and the Bureau of Mines also placed their skills at the disposal of their business constituents.

The independent commissions, which had expanded so impressively during the Progressive era, also adapted to assist business cooperation. Through the Transportation Act of 1920, the Interstate Commerce Commission received extensive authority over almost all areas of the railroad industry. But instead of using these broad powers to issue commands, the ICC certified the agreements that the major railroads and their organized business customers negotiated in the commission's offices. The Federal Trade Commission, which had exposed the monopolistic practices of large corporations during the war years, was transformed into a service agency for the trade associations, where businessmen met in private, agreed on a suitable method of cooperation, and departed with the government's blessing. Only the Federal Reserve Board, which Harding filled with cronies and deserving Republicans, failed to meet the new standards of government service. However, the New York Regional Board, under a reputable banker Benjamin Strong, substituted as headquarters for national banking policy.

The Supreme Court gave the modern economy the protection of the law. In *U. S.* v. *United States Steel* (1920), the Court allowed the nation's largest corporation to dominate its industry just as long as some competitors survived; and throughout the decade, the justices looked favorably on the oligopolies. Because the trade associations were a relatively new form of business cooperation, they posed a more complex problem for the Court. In 1921 and 1923, it condemned the associations' information pools as restraints of trade. Then in the *Maple Flooring Manufacturers' Association* case of 1925, the Court changed its mind: trade associations, like oligopolies, were legal if they did not eliminate all signs of competition in their areas of business. Meanwhile, the Court was placing narrow limits around the labor unions. Led by its new chief justice, William Howard Taft, whom Harding appointed in 1921, the Court sharply restricted organized labor's right to picket and boycott, and it watched approvingly as the lower courts expanded the use of injunctions against striking workers. In addition, the Supreme Court overturned a national child labor law in *Bailey* v. *Drexel Furniture Co.* (1922) and a state minimum wage law in *Adkins* v. *Children's Hospital* (1923).

Perhaps the government would have been a less willing helper if the modern economy had not performed miracles during the 1920s. As the interest groups and government services were forming a national network, the economy recovered from the sharp recession of 1921–22 and flourished grandly until late 1929. Manufacturing output as a whole rose 64 percent during the twenties, and after the postwar recession, the Gross National Product (GNP), one measure of the economy's overall strength, climbed a substantial 5 percent a year. The leaders of the boom were the automobile and construction industries. Both the number of automobile sales and the value of construction more than tripled between 1915 and 1925, then continued to rise. Moreover, these two leaders spread their benefits widely to such related industries as steel, petroleum, rubber, and cement.

How the economy worked impressed people even more than how much it produced. A broad range of manufacturing plants, following the lead of Henry Ford, introduced the moving assembly line, a revolution in factory procedure. Time and motion studies further refined the efficient use of labor. Through electricity in industry and the gasoline engine in agriculture, the amount of horsepower per worker rose well over 50 percent during the twenties. As a consequence of these changes, output per working hour increased an astonishing 35 percent, almost double the gains of the previous decade. America, it seemed, had answered all the riddles of economic growth. Throughout the decade, a stream of delegations came from abroad in hopes of discovering the secret of American productivity.

Contemporaries declared the arrival of a "New Era." Praise for the nationwide spirit of cooperation filled the air. As the number of strikes declined dramatically, spokesmen for the new industrial harmony boasted that America had resolved forever the conflict between labor and capital. Former critics of American society now became its ardent champions. Socialism was "reactionary," said John Spargo, once a leader of the Socialist party, and American capitalism offered "the greatest hope for mankind." "I can find no historic parallel, outside of the great religious revivals, with which [the New Era] has much in common," marveled a veteran of the social gospel. "Standards of ethics have probably changed more extensively than in any corresponding period in history." From the vantage point of the Great Depression, it would be easy to ridicule the most grandiose claims of the decade: poverty on the verge of abolition, a chicken in every pot and two cars in every garage, anyone with self-discipline and common sense a millionaire. But during the late 1920s, almost no one rose to challenge these visions.

The Politics of the New Era, 1924–1929

The first political test of confidence in the New Era began in August 1923 when President Harding, while touring the western states, died of a heart attack. Harding's Vice-President, Calvin Coolidge, an obscure Massachusetts politician of no apparent talents, suddenly inherited the White House. During his early months in office, the corruption that had spread through Harding's administration oozed to the surface and soon became public knowledge. Compounding the Republican party's troubles, a collection of dissident farm spokesmen, union officials, Socialists, and reformers nominated their own presidential candidate for 1924, the tough old progressive, Robert LaFollette, whose strongest appeal would be to normally Republican voters.

But as the journalist Bruce Blivin noted, most Americans reacted to the corruption among Harding's associates as nothing more than "a scandal of personality."

"Silent Cal" Coolidge, the model of small-town New England values, was able to overcome the crisis simply by demonstrating the old-fashioned Yankee virtues of tight-lipped integrity and tight-fisted frugality. At the Republican Convention of 1924, on a rising curve of prosperity and optimism, Coolidge's party nominated him for a full term. With scarcely any effort, Coolidge swamped his ineffectual Democratic opponent, the Wall Street lawyer John W. Davis, by 382 electoral votes to 136. Although LaFollette received an impressive personal tribute of almost 5 million popular votes, he carried only Wisconsin.

Coolidge's triumph coincided with a new calm in national affairs. The angry, volatile issues of the early twenties were rapidly subsiding. When Coolidge appointed the moderate Harlan Stone attorney general in 1924, the national government abandoned the cause of antiradicalism. The Communist party, practically outlawed early in the decade, appeared on the ballots of thirty-four states in 1928. As steady a voice of 100 percent Americanism as the *Saturday Evening Post* recalled the Red Scare almost apologetically as "nothing but the last symptom of war fever." At the annual meeting of the American Legion in 1925, one committee complained: "Americans have become apathetic to the monotonous appeal of the patriotic exhorter. The utmost ingenuity is frequently necessary to obtain publicity in the campaigns which the national convention has directed us to undertake." Vigilante activities also declined dramatically. Between 1922 and 1926, the American Civil Liberties Union reported, the number of disrupted public meetings dropped from 225 to 21.

The last public furor over the events of the Red Scare illustrated how much had changed since the early twenties. In 1921, two immigrant anarchists, Nicola

CALVIN COOLIDGE AND HERBERT HOOVER

No love was lost between Coolidge (left) and Hoover (right). Together, however, they symbolized solid values and sound leadership during the prosperous New Era. *(Culver Pictures, Inc.)*

Sacco and Bartolomeo Vanzetti, were tried for the murder of a paymaster in South Braintree, Massachusetts. In a courtroom echoing with antiradical rhetoric, the two anarchists were convicted and sentenced to death. For years, legal appeals delayed their execution. The bias of the trial, and the dignity and eloquence of the prisoners during their long ordeal, attracted a wide range of liberal and radical sympathizers, who fought fervently for their pardon. But the cause failed. As large crowds here and abroad mourned in public, Sacco and Vanzetti died in the electric chair in August 1927. Even more striking than the campaign of protest was the opposition to it. Now the conservatives were on the defensive. Prominent citizens who once would have screamed "Bolshevik!" remained remarkably quiet while an embarrassing legacy from the past ran its course. They considered the issues of immigrants and radicals already settled. It was time to enjoy the prosperous New Era.

Few Presidents have encountered as meek a Congress as Coolidge faced after 1924. Almost no one in Washington wanted to rock the cart. Although the costs of government in the New Era were about two and a half times higher than they had been in 1915, the President seldom had to justify his expenditures. The President's Bureau of the Budget, relying heavily on the advice of the United States Chamber of Commerce, decided on the level of government spending. After 1924, congressional appropriations were an almost perfect carbon for the bureau's recommendations. In 1926, even the controversial tax program of Secretary of the Treasury Andrew Mellon was enacted. To release more money for private investment, Congress lowered the rate of income tax for the very wealthy from 46 percent to 26 percent and cut inheritance taxes in half.

The only significant signs of a congressional rebellion came over farm policy. Commodity prices, which fell precipitously in 1921, revived sluggishly during the 1920s. In 1929, net farm income was still $3 billion lower than it had been in 1919. The farm lobby, demanding immediate assistance, proposed that the government sell part of the farmers' output in a protected, high-priced domestic market and dispose of whatever Americans did not buy in the lower-priced world market. In 1927 and again in 1928, Congress passed a McNary-Haugen bill to implement this program. Twice Coolidge vetoed it. Yet the actual difference between the farm lobby and the Coolidge administration was not very great. The administration's solution also sought to regulate the marketing of agricultural products. When prices fell, the commodity cooperatives would receive temporary government payments while they stored their products. As prices improved, the cooperatives would gradually sell their surplus and repay the government. The farm lobby, in fact, included this scheme in its second McNary-Haugen bill. Therefore, everyone appeared optimistic in 1929 when Congress created the Federal Farm Board, with an unprecedented $500 million in government credit to help the cooperatives market their products at the best prices.

But beneath the smooth surface of national economic politics, a very different spirit was bubbling away in local affairs. In the best years of the New Era, about two-thirds of the nation's families fell below an annual income of $2,500, which experts considered adequate in the twenties. These families had only an indirect stake in the economic system that was forming on the national level. Most wage earners were not union members, and most farmers never joined the agricultural organizations. Very small businesses everywhere—the neighborhood grocer, the secondhand shop, the little variety store—belonged to no economic league or trade association. Even a number of those Americans who were somewhat better off remained outside the New Era's organizational structure. The United States Chamber of Commerce discouraged membership in towns under 5000, and businessmen there kept largely to themselves. The Chicago Bar Association, the strongest of its kind in the nation, enrolled only half of the city's licensed lawyers in the late 1920s.

For most of these Americans, a neighborhood or a community bounded their lives. They cared very much about jobs and income, but they tried to manage such problems locally. Their networks were personal ones, woven through families, friendships, and contacts. They reinforced these strands with a high degree of cultural consciousness. Outside the cities, that usually meant pride in being white, Anglo-Saxon, and Protestant. These same qualities were also important in the cities, but there a great variety of groups were trying to preserve their

MAIN STREET, BINGHAM, UTAH, 1927

(Courtesy Utah State Historical Society.)

ethnic differences. Black, brown, yellow, or white skin, Italian, Polish, German, or Irish ancestors, Catholic, Protestant, or Jewish religion, all drew critical social lines.

Such tight local attachments made any kind of broad organization extremely difficult. The Ku Klux Klan had been an exception early in the twenties. Then in 1924 and 1925, widely publicized exposés of corruption in the Klan and the conviction of Indiana's leading Klansman, David Stephenson, for the sex murder of his secretary, demoralized that organization. By 1928 its membership fell to about 200,000. The Anti-Saloon League, once a formidable power in national politics, also collapsed in the late twenties. Equally important, few people in national affairs seemed to care any more about the cultural and moral standards that still mattered a great deal to millions of Americans. Although former members of the Klan did not discard their old beliefs about foreigners, Catholics, and radicals, no strong voice spoke for them in Coolidge's Washington. They became what the Klan had always claimed to be, an "Invisible Empire."

Local politics remained the one natural center for this mixture of economic, cultural, and moral concerns. In the towns and the countryside, they dominated innumerable county organizations in which friendship and family ties, not efficiency and expertise, determined who would receive most of the jobs and favors of local politics. In the wards of the large cities, similar private bargains tied individuals, families, and cultural groups into little political alliances. Another set of private bargains entwined government officials with a web of criminal activities in prostitution, gambling, and bootlegging. The boxer, Billy Conn, growing up on the streets of Pittsburgh, was twenty years old before he realized that the police were also paid by the city government. On a large scale, these many personal arrangements became political machines, which thrived during the 1920s. Though they were known by the names of the bosses—Tom Pendergast in Kansas City, Big Bill Thompson in Chicago, Ed Crump in Memphis, Frank Hague in Jersey City, and James Michael Curley in Boston—their roots were decentralized and popular.

During the New Era, it required an exceptionally powerful force to draw these insular, local alliances into national affairs. The strongest magnet was the Eighteenth, or "Prohibition," Amendment, which banned the production and sale of liquor. Put into effect in January 1920 and enforced by the strict Volstead Act, the Eighteenth Amendment began its career in an atmosphere of high optimism. Drinking, declared William Jennings Bryan, was as dead an issue as slavery. But countless Americans decided otherwise. An insatiable demand for liquor in the big cities and a considerable market elsewhere in the nation created a massive business out of illicit production and distribution. As one investigating commission ruefully noted, "Few things are more easily made than alcohol." A little machinery and a bathtub transformed any thirsty citizen into a distiller. Moreover, the long boundary of the United States was a sieve for illegal imports. To police these many violations, the Treasury Department employed about 2000 officials. Herbert Hoover later estimated that effective enforcement would have required at least 250,000.

Millions of locally oriented Americans considered Prohibition an insufferable violation of their rights. Not only did the "wets" make a travesty of the law in their neighborhoods and communities; they increasingly demanded action from state and national governments. In 1923, New York repealed its state law to enforce Prohibition. By 1930, six other states had followed New York's lead. With equal fervor, millions of locally oriented "drys" regarded Prohibition as the keystone of American morality. Not only did they give teeth to Prohibition in their localities; they sponsored stern state laws to uphold the "noble experiment." In Michigan, a fourth offense under the Prohibition law meant life imprisonment. Basically, the story of Prohibition was this stream of local passions pouring through the nation and battling in the name of irreconcilable truths.

From these same wells came the emotions that made Alfred E. Smith the most controversial politician of the 1920s. A capable governor of New York, who very much wanted to be President, Al Smith touched the nerve centers of local politics. He was a Catholic, a wet, and a self-taught immigrant's son who wore Tammany Hall's traditional brown derby askew and spoke in the accents of Manhattan's lesser known avenues. The thought of Al Smith in the White House roused feelings of wonder and horror across the nation. Self-conscious ethnic groups in the Northern cities gave him their fanatic devotion. White Protestant Democrats in the rural South looked on Smith as the Antichrist. At the Democratic National Convention of 1924, Smith's friends and enemies fought over his nomination for an incredible ninety-five ballots before turning in exhaustion on the one hundred and third to John W. Davis. Despite the absence of a serious competitor in 1928, Southern delegates allowed Smith's nomination for President with the most profound misgivings.

The election of 1928 provided a unique meeting ground for the conflicting spirits of national and local politics. To oppose Smith, the Republicans chose Herbert Hoover, by all odds the most important political spokesman for the New Era. After an impressive early success in business, Hoover won renown during the First

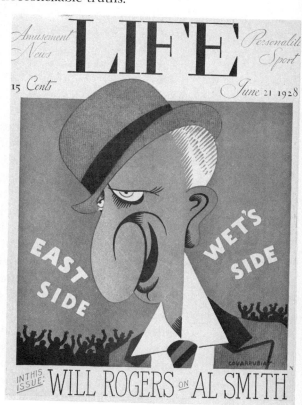

AL SMITH ON THE COVER OF "LIFE" MAGAZINE, 1928

Loyal to Tammany and hostile to Prohibition, Al Smith could never escape the image of the New York ward boss who had made good. (*Culver Pictures, Inc.*)

The Election of 1928

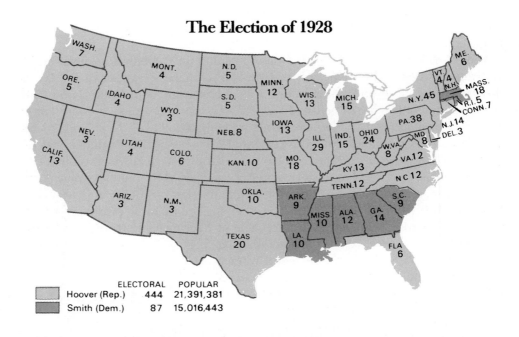

ELECTORAL POPULAR
Hoover (Rep.)   444   21,391,381
Smith (Dem.)   87   15,016,443

World War as an administrator, first of international relief, then of agriculture. There was already talk of Hoover as President in 1920. Instead, he served in the cabinets of Harding and Coolidge, and made himself the unofficial center of the executive branch: "Secretary of Commerce and assistant secretary of everything else." He was serious and shy, extremely proud and highly ambitious. Too formidable for Coolidge, who heartily disliked him, and too independent for many professional politicians, who preferred a weaker man, Hoover still went after the nomination with absolute confidence in his ability to be President. Successful Americans overwhelmingly supported him. Of those listed in *Who's Who,* for example, 87 percent endorsed his candidacy.

Al Smith wanted to pitch his campaign at the level of national policy. An essentially conservative man who later opposed the New Deal, the Democratic candidate thought of himself as an eminently qualified leader for the existing economic system, not as a product of New York City's Lower East Side. To oversee his campaign, Smith selected a prominent executive in General Motors, John J. Raskob, rather than a professional politician. The partisans of local politics, however, would not let Smith transcend his origins. In November 1928, Smith's name on the ballot drew large, jubilant majorities in the industrial cities, but it also sent millions of Protestant townspeople to the polls with literally a religious commitment to Hoover and put seven formerly Democratic Southern states in the Republican column. Hoover, the shining symbol of the New Era prosperity, swept to victory with 444 electoral votes against Smith's 87.

The Crisis of Depression, 1929–1935

Hoover had served at the creation of the New Era. Now, as President, he would preside at its triumph. At the inauguration of the "Great Engineer" in March 1929, who could have predicted that disaster was just six months ahead? By 1929, countless Americans were convinced that the nation was riding an escalator of unlimited progress, and increasing numbers of them were expressing this happy faith with investments in the stock market. If tomorrow would inevitably be more prosperous than today, why not buy some of tomorrow at today's prices? This reasoning had already pushed up prices on the New York Stock Exchange by 40 percent in 1927, then another 35 percent in 1928, to heights that bore no relation to the actual growth of the nation's corporations. Yet the Great Bull Market charged heedlessly onward. With scarcely a pause, stock prices continued to climb week after week until by September 1929 they stood a dizzying 400 percent above their level of only five years earlier.

Spasms of doubt shook the stock market in September and early October. Then on October 23, 1929, confidence died. For almost a week the stock exchange was a mad scene of frantic sellers, elusive buyers, and exhausted clerks struggling to record the wreckage. By October 29, all the paper profits of 1929 had been lost. Early in November the gains of 1928 disappeared, and during the summer of 1930 the hopes of 1927 also dissolved. Finally, on June 8, 1932, the stock market hit bottom, 50 percent below its modest level at the time of Coolidge's inauguration.

The collapse of the Great Bull Market had severe effects throughout the economy. Because the frantic speculation attracted a large portion of the nation's short-term credit, the heavy losses of late 1929 dried up the normal flow of loans to both individuals and companies. Banks, some of them deeply implicated in the speculation, sharply retrenched their activities and deepened the crisis. Retrenchment accentuated every weakness in the New Era economy. Because of a markedly unequal distribution of income, most Americans could buy only the bare necessities without credit. As purchases de-

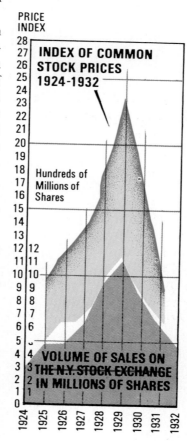

PRICE INDEX

INDEX OF COMMON STOCK PRICES 1924-1932

Hundreds of Millions of Shares

VOLUME OF SALES ON THE N.Y. STOCK EXCHANGE IN MILLIONS OF SHARES

clined, thousands of small businesses, just making it in good times, now folded. Many farmers, also just making it before the crash, could no longer meet their mortgage payments. Business failures and farm foreclosures further sapped the resources of the banks that had been financing them. Soon the downward spiral was pulling the strong as well as the weak into a national depression.

During the next three years the economy, like a tin can in a vise, was relentlessly squeezed to half its size. Some indicators, such as labor income, salaries, and national income, fell somewhat less than 50 percent; others, such as industrial production, manufacturing wages, dividends, and farm income, somewhat more. The human costs were incalculably higher. Millions already living on the edge of poverty could afford no decline in farm income, no shorter hours of work. And the unemployed, about 30 percent of the labor force by early 1933, soon had nothing. The chicken once promised for every pot had gone into charity's soup kettle, and each year longer and longer lines of hungry, bewildered people formed in front of it with their empty bowls.

Hoover's response to depression was clear and firm. If the principles behind the New Era were correct, as everyone seemed to believe, Americans should follow them strictly and prosperity would surely be just around the corner. "Progress is born of Cooperation . . . ," the President reminded the nation. "The Government should assist and encourage these movements of collective self help by itself cooperating with them. . . ." For the large corporations, Hoover sponsored meetings at the White House to establish common industrial policies.

Depression struck Americans with a numbing force. Their savings irretrievably lost, customers mulled helplessly around the closed, empty banks. Where there were no jobs month after month, there was eventually no hope. Impoverished families took what shelter they could find, forming dismal shanty slums called "Hoovervilles." (*Brown Brothers, Library of Congress, Chicago Historical Society, Library of Congress.*)

For the trade associations, the Federal Trade Commission held a Trade Practices Conference to strengthen their stabilizing agreements. For labor, Hoover won a promise from business leaders to spread the work in their firms rather than simply fire some percentage of their employees. For agriculture, the new Federal Farm Board issued large amounts of credit so that the commodity cooperatives could keep their products off the market and halt the decline in farm prices. And for suffering Americans everywhere, Hoover used the President's office as clearinghouse and coordinator for private relief. Between 1929 and 1932, donations for relief increased about eightfold, a remarkable accomplishment by any previous standard.

Of all the President's problems, finance was the most difficult. Financiers had been expected to act as facilitators of business enterprise. Instead, they had fed the Great Bull Market. Hoover, who never trusted Wall Street bankers, took a certain grim satisfaction in the stock market crash, as his first terse announcement in October 1929 implied: "The fundamental business of the country—that is, the production and distribution of goods and services—is on a sound and prosperous basis." As the depression deepened, he insisted that the nation's big bankers fulfill their obligations to the economy by collecting a huge reservoir of credit for America's flagging industry. Financial leaders stalled, then refused. In 1932, the President reluctantly accepted the necessity of a new government credit agency, the Reconstruction Finance Corporation. That year, the RFC invested an astonishing $1.5 billion in private enterprise, mostly in a few large corporations that were considered the key to economic recovery. Hoover, who also watched Europe's banking disasters in 1931 intensify America's depression, left office with his original convictions unshaken. "We have been fighting for four years to preserve the system of production and distribution from . . . [the] failure of the financial and credit system."

From 1929 to 1932 the President acted positively, often vigorously, according to the principles of the New Era. If recovery had followed, he would have been a hero, tough enough in crisis to protect the American way. But in 1932 the national economy teetered on the edge of total collapse. Employers discarded their programs for spreading the work, and during the winter of 1932–33, another 3 million joined the over 12 million already without jobs. Relief inundated state and local governments without the funds to meet them. As commodity prices continued to fall, the Federal Farm Board simply ran out of credit and ceased to function. Farmers burned their corn and left their cotton unpicked because it no longer paid them to market the crop. In some Midwestern county seats, silent men with hunting rifles closed the courts so that their mortgages could not be foreclosed. More than five thousand banks had failed since 1930, and early in 1933 the entire financial structure of the nation began to crumble.

These signs of calamity brought out Hoover's poorest qualities. When thousands of war veterans marched to Washington in an appeal for bonuses, the President thought he heard revolution in their cries for a little cash, and in July

1932 he allowed the army to drive them away. Hoover's deep, personal antagonism to socialism kept him from supporting federal appropriations for state and local relief. Such narrow principles gave no comfort in a hungry land. "I have a remarkable job for you," the wry humorist Will Rogers had Hoover saying to his administrator of relief; "you are to feed the several million unemployed." "With what?" asked the official. "That's what makes the job remarkable." Even before the 1932 election, a majority of Americans had turned away from their President. The old prosperity slogans came back to haunt him. Now it was "a chicken in every garage." Clusters of makeshift hovels for the unemployed became "Hoovervilles."

Hoover's failure expressed the new, demanding standard by which Americans judged their President. During the New Era, when the economy appeared to operate by itself, relatively little was expected of the President as an individual. But the economy was now thoroughly national, and when it broke down, only the national government had the scope and authority capable of repairing it. Because the executive branch dominated the national government, people naturally looked there for help. Atop the executive branch stood the President, and the longer the depression lasted, the more he alone seemed the one person who could lead them out of the wilderness. By 1932 millions who had no other place to turn were blaming Hoover in a harsh, personal way for the nation's troubles.

Hoover, renominated at the gloomy Republican Convention of 1932, still refused to believe that the nation would reject him. But almost everyone else recognized 1932 as a Democratic year. The leading Democratic contender bore a magic name in American politics. Franklin D. Roosevelt, a distant cousin of

The Election of 1932

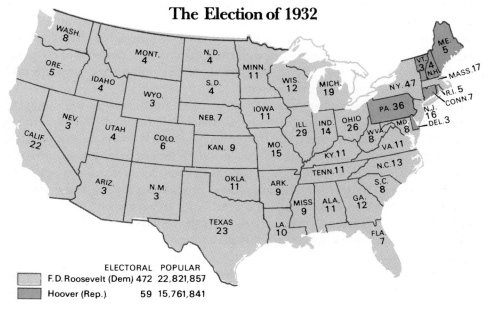

ELECTORAL POPULAR

F.D. Roosevelt (Dem) 472 22,821,857

Hoover (Rep.)   59 15,761,841

Theodore, had been assistant secretary of the navy in the Wilson administration and had then run as the vice-presidential candidate in the futile Cox campaign of 1920. Despite an attack of poliomyelitis in 1921 that paralyzed him from the waist down, Roosevelt had returned to public office in 1929 as governor of New York. Slow, careful preparation gave him a large bloc of delegates before the 1932 convention. A bargain with John Nance Garner of Texas, which made "Cactus Jack" the vice-presidential candidate, sealed his nomination. That November, riding to victory on the waves of popular sentiment that repudiated Hoover, Roosevelt received 472 electoral votes to the hapless Hoover's 59.

Once in office, Roosevelt revealed a unique capacity for leadership. Beneath an easy public style and a gracious private manner lay a keen, calculating mind that always sought to control people and events. Unlike Hoover, Roosevelt welcomed the challenge of selling his programs to a demoralized nation. A master of popular phrasing and simple analogies, he sent his strong, warm voice into millions of homes through radio "fireside chats" that were bits of genius in the use of a mass medium. Roosevelt made a great variety of people feel that he intuitively understood and sympathized with them. Always he radiated confidence. The tilt of Roosevelt's chin and the cocky angle of his cigarette holder invariably gave the sense of a man looking upward. The din of demands around his powerful office never ruffled him. To preserve his personal control, he waited just as long as possible before committing himself to a policy, serene in the faith that he could charm the impatient, make the decision, and soothe the disappointed.

Some critics later claimed that Roosevelt was a politician without any clear purpose in domestic affairs. They were wrong. Roosevelt entered the White House with as firm an attachment as Hoover's to the New Era, and until 1935 he remained extremely loyal to its principles. He wanted business to organize, industry by industry, and agriculture, commodity by commodity. With help from an efficient labor force and a supporting network of finance, he believed, these private groups could generate prosperity through their own natural patterns of cooperation. The government had only to assist them in regaining their strength and finding their proper places in the system.

What set Roosevelt so sharply apart from his predecessor was his willingness to experiment with a great variety of schemes to achieve this goal. Such openness in the nation's President attracted a wide range of newcomers to Washington and surrounded him with a curious but strikingly effective group of advisers. As secretary of the treasury, Roosevelt brought in his close friend and neighbor from Hyde Park, Henry Morgenthau, whose predictable loyalty and conscientiousness made him indispensable to the President. In agriculture Roosevelt appointed the son of Harding's secretary of agriculture, Henry A. Wallace, whose broad liberal vision compensated for his inattention to details. Another liberal Republican, Harold Ickes, became secretary of the interior and watched over his domain with a fierce jealousy and a scrupulous honesty. Along with Harry Hopkins, the tough, dedicated administrator of relief, these proved to be the President's most valuable assistants. But the new regime also drew kinds of people who had never before influenced government policy: an obscure Montana professor named M. L. Wilson with a proposal for limiting agricultural production; Raymond Moley, Rexford Tugwell, and Adolph Berle of Columbia University, the "Brains Trust" of Roosevelt's 1932 campaign, with ambitions to improve the economy's organization; and social workers with plans to aid the unemployed, the disabled, and the aged. These and many more recruits joined the veterans from the business and agricultural associations to help Roosevelt provide a "New Deal" for America's ailing economy.

An experimental President, an eager pack of advisers, and a receptive Congress combined to produce an explosion of government actions in 1933. (See chart page 1082.) They ranged from manipulations in the gold value of the dollar to emergency credit for farm mortgages, to a Civilian Conservation Corps (CCC), which gave jobs in rural conservation to unemployed urban youths. Two measures from this array formed the heart of the early New Deal. One was the National Industrial Recovery Act of June 1933. The less significant half of the law created the Public Works Administration (PWA), with a $3.3 billion appropriation that was supposed to generate jobs and invigorate the economy. But Secretary Ickes, its director, moved with such extreme caution that PWA had no appreciable effect on the depression. The far more important half of the National

PRESIDENT FRANKLIN ROOSEVELT VISITS A CIVILIAN CONSERVATION CORPS (CCC) CAMP

Hope at last! FDR's grand smile, infecting everyone around him, seemed to promise America a brighter future just ahead. Seated third from the left is Secretary Harold Ickes. On Roosevelt's left are Secretary of Agriculture Henry A. Wallace and Roosevelt's adviser, Rexford Tugwell. (*Associated Press.*)

Industrial Recovery Act authorized each specialized segment of business to prepare a code of self-governance and established the National Recovery Administration (NRA) to supervise the process.

As chief of NRA, the President chose General Hugh S. Johnson, a brash,
noisy veteran in government affairs, who immediately launched a circus of a
campaign to rally all Americans behind his program. Through parades, speeches,
and assorted hoopla, Johnson made the Blue Eagle, NRA's emblem of cooperation, almost synonymous with the New Deal itself, and he counted on public
opinion to make it almost synonymous with Americanism. "When every American Housewife understands that the Blue Eagle on everything that she permits
to come into her home is a symbol of its restoration to security," the general
roared in characteristic bombast, "may God have mercy on the man or group
of men who attempt to trifle with this bird."

In NRA's first four months, business groups wrote over seven hundred constitutions to govern their affairs. Where one or more large firms dominated an
industry, NRA relied on them to prepare the codes; where no firm dominated,
NRA turned to a trade association. Although the codes varied from industry
to industry, they usually included some agreement on prices, wages, and the
acceptable limits of competition. The only integration among them was a common commitment to stabilization, a common freedom from antitrust prosecution, and a common dependence on the industrial groups themselves to regulate
their own members. Johnson exalted the spirit of cooperation and swore at the
"slackers," but never coerced the businessmen.

Section 7a of the National Industrial Recovery Act authorized workers to
organize and bargain in their own behalf, and some labor leaders, notably John
L. Lewis of the United Mine Workers, acted as though the government was now
their sponsor:"THE PRESIDENT WANTS YOU TO JOIN THE UNION!"

THE NRA

The dream behind the National Recovery
Administration (NRA) was progress
through unity. In this cartoon, worker and
manager look like loving brothers, and
both like dutiful nephews of their Uncle
Sam. (*Library of Congress.*)

Neither "union" nor "bargaining," however, had yet acquired a clear legal meaning. Company unions, many little organizations representing fractions of an industry's employees, and countless techniques for consultation between managers and workers fitted these elastic terms. The Roosevelt administration did not encourage an independent labor movement. When Ickes established the Labor Policy Board in the oil industry, for instance, he selected a company unionist, an independent unionist, and an economist. In fact, labor representatives rarely served on the governing boards that policed the industrial codes. Under NRA, labor remained dependent on management.

The second basic law of the early New Deal was the Agricultural Adjustment Act, which arrived in May 1933. By including almost every kind of farm program that had been proposed during the twenties and early thirties, the law constituted a grab bag of alternatives. There were provisions for marketing agreements, commodity loans, export subsidies, government purchases, and the latest favorite, a restricted allotment of acreage among farmers who raised a given crop. During its first months, the Agricultural Adjustment Administration (AAA) gave highest priority to cash relief and paid farmers to plow under their crops and slaughter their livestock in midseason, a bitter expedient with so much hunger in the nation. The long-term goal of the law, however, was to increase farm income to a level of "parity" with its income just before the First World War.

To achieve parity, AAA relied on the organized farmers in each subdivision of agriculture to select the program appropriate to their product. George Peek and Chester Davis, who headed AAA, were old friends of the farm associations and worked easily with them, especially the American Farm Bureau Federation. What looked like a concentration of power in Washington, therefore, was actually a scattering of powers among commercial farmers. Aside from temporary government coercion to limit the production of cotton and tobacco, the New Deal's farm policy preserved the essentials of the New Era. The national government delegated most of its authority to farm groups so that they could make their own decisions and largely administer them.

Elsewhere in the New Deal the same bustle, the same openness, and the same principles prevailed. Like Hoover, Roosevelt and many of his advisers considered finance particularly guilty of causing the depression. "The money changers have fled from their high seats in the temple of our civilization," the President bitingly said of the bankers in his inaugural address. While congressional investigations were revealing how bankers had speculated with their own institution's deposits, new laws sought to hold finance within proper bounds. Through the Glass-Steagall Act of 1933, Congress required banks to separate their investment in securities from normal commercial banking. The next year it placed the stock exchange under the regulation of the Securities and Exchange Commission (SEC). In 1935, Congress outlawed holding companies that had been formed in the 1920s for no other purpose than the sale of stock, and it gave the SEC authority to dissolve other questionable holding companies. Aside from these punishments for past sins, however, finance received an impressive array of government assistance. Roosevelt, immediately after his inauguration in March 1933, declared a brief "Bank Holiday" in order to check a nationwide financial panic. The Reconstruction Finance Corporation then pumped loans into the banks that were still solvent. In addition, Congress created the Federal Deposit Insurance Corporation in 1933 so that ordinary citizens would no longer lose their savings when a bank failed. New executive agencies, especially the Home Owners Loan Corporation, underwrote farm and housing mortgages. In 1935, when Congress consolidated the regulatory powers of the Federal Reserve System in a centralized board of governors, the government had completed a national framework of supports around American finance. The effect of these laws was to place both the prestige and the credit of the government behind the everyday decisions of private bankers. Within a short time, even the SEC was depending on the more enlightened brokers and financiers themselves to stabilize the stock exchanges. As Chairman William O. Douglas stated in 1938, "Government regulation at its best should be residual."

The New Deal responded to the pressing problem of public relief with an equally restrained use of government power. Though Roosevelt did not hesitate about requesting funds in 1933, he shared a common belief that only desperate circumstances could justify national money for relief. The New Deal's first relief agency was appropriately named the Federal Emergency Relief Administration (FERA). During 1933 and 1934, Congress voted relief funds as if each new contribution would surely be the last. When an initial appropriation of $500 million for FERA proved inadequate, Roosevelt drew an additional $400 million from Ickes's PWA for a hastily devised program of work relief. In February 1934, Congress finally authorized more funds for FERA. Harry Hopkins, Roosevelt's administrator of relief, employing a small staff, relied on private groups and local governments to distribute most of the money. "Nothing in the new Federal Act was meant to change that local responsibility, nor did the Federal Administration have any intention of doing so," an expert on public relief con-

Trying to Revive the System
Principal New Deal Measures, 1933–1935

"Bank Holiday"	March 1933
Federal Emergency Relief Act, creating	
Federal Emergency Relief Administration (FERA)	May 1933
Agricultural Adjustment Act, creating	
Agricultural Adjustment Administration (AAA)	May 1933
Tennessee Valley Authority (TVA)	May 1933
Home Owners' Loan Corporation	June 1933
National Industrial Relations Act, creating	
National Recovery Administration (NRA)	June 1933
Federal Deposit Insurance Corporation	June 1933
Civil Works Administration (CWA)	November 1933
Securities and Exchange Commission (SEC)	June 1934
Public Utility Holding Company Act	August 1935

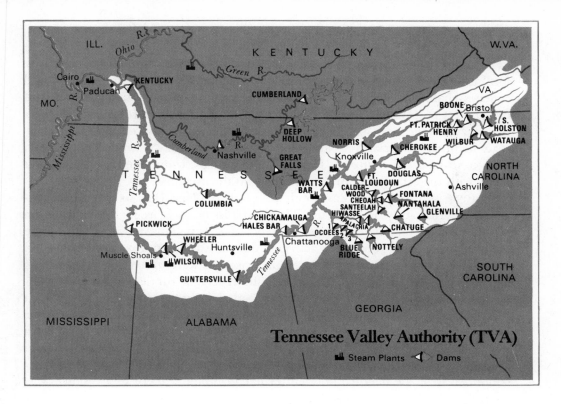

Tennessee Valley Authority (TVA)

Steam Plants ◄► Dams

cluded. To the starving, all that mattered was a little help had finally come.

The most daring government venture of the early New Deal was the Tennessee Valley Authority (TVA). Its origins lay in a long, inconclusive debate during the 1920s over the disposition of a dam at Muscle Shoals, Alabama, that the government had started to build in wartime but never completed. When Henry Ford, widely regarded in the 1920s as a great public benefactor, offered to lease and develop it, Senator George Norris of Nebraska, a tenacious old progressive, skillfully blocked the proposal and in time convinced a majority of his colleagues that the government itself should develop the dam. During the 1920s, however, no one anticipated the vast undertaking ahead. Beginning in 1933, Muscle Shoals became merely the point of departure for a new concept in regional rehabilitation, which soon gained international fame. The Tennessee Valley Authority, with sweeping administrative powers over a domain that wound through seven southern states, embarked on two decades of activity that created a network of dams and canals, rejuvenated the soil and protected it against floods, and harnessed electric resources to service millions of homes and thousands of new businesses.

From the outset, TVA challenged the customary rights of private enterprise by selling the electric power it generated. Because of this, conservatives probably hated it the most of all the New Deal programs. Nevertheless, TVA's directors had not completely abandoned the principles of the New Era. At every step, they worked through the existing, organized groups in their region. Chambers of commerce, leagues of bankers, commercial farming associations, and their local associates from the Department of Agriculture and the state agricultural colleges channeled the TVA's information, chose its demonstration farms, and distributed many of its political benefits. The same local groups were TVA's primary allies in the long legal battle with the private utility companies over the issue of public electricity, a battle that TVA did not fully win until 1939. Even such a striking departure as TVA, in other words, cooperated as closely as it could with the established private interests in the area.

In 1934, shortly before Raymond Moley left the New Deal to become its conservative critic, he commented, "This administration is as far from socialism or communism as any group ever assembled in a national government." The sheer quantity of government activities during 1933 and 1934 misled a good many people into believing that profound changes were under way. Despite the broadened range of government services, however, the fundamentals of the New Era remained intact. Subsequent speculation about a critical moment in March 1933 when American society might have taken a radical turn made little sense because the nation's leaders in March 1933 had no radical intentions. With fresh faces and tactics, through experiments and expedients, the New Deal fought to preserve a particular economic system that had formed during the 1920s and that continued to shape national policy after five grinding years of depression.

The New Deal at the Crossroads, 1935–1936

But the New Deal was not working. By late 1934, NRA was a shambles, the victim of the businessmen's self-serving codes, widespread violations of these same rules, and bitter criticism from almost every section of American society. The depression refused to lift. Though unemployment had declined since the darkest months of early 1933, it was about as bad as it had been the day Roosevelt was elected. Net farm income was a dismal 50 percent of its level in 1929, and the food shortages caused by a cruel drought on the Great Plains accounted for most of the price increases since 1933. Only corporate profits were making strong gains in 1934.

As confidence in the New Deal dwindled, millions of angry, suffering people appeared to be finding new leaders and new causes. From Louisiana came the shrewd, flamboyant Huey Long, who promised to make "every man a king." By appealing to the poor forgotten whites of his state, Long had become not only governor in 1929 but actually the ruler of Louisiana through an extensive, ruthless political machine. Elected to the Senate in 1930, the Louisiana Kingfish was soon using it as a forum to spread the gospel of Share Our Wealth, a simple, sweeping program that would expropriate the wealth of the very rich in order to provide all families with a $5,000 homestead and an annual income of about $2,500. From a suburb of Detroit came the rich radio voice of a Catholic priest, Charles Coughlin, who castigated Wall Street, called for the nationalization of the banks, and demanded an immediate, massive monetary inflation. From Long Beach, California, came Dr. Francis E. Townsend, who envisaged prosperity spreading to everybody through monthly government payments of $200 for each unemployed person over 60. All three campaigns were rapidly accelerating in late 1934 and early 1935.

Long, Coughlin, and Townsend spoke in the language of local politics, where the appeal of a popular, common sense economics had always remained strong. As years of depression eroded the hopes and evaporated the resources in countless neighborhoods and communities, the people whose lives were rooted there desperately sought ways of bringing opportunity back to their localities. To many of them, the neat, mechanical answers of Share Our Wealth, inflation, and old age pensions sounded just right. In the tradition of free silver in the 1890s and radical antimonopoly in the progessive years, these proposals promised at a stroke to give ordinary Americans a decent life without elaborate laws or government regimentation.

No one ever knew how many Americans accepted these formulas for prosperity. Though Long, Coughlin, and Townsend each claimed millions of adherents, none formed an effective organization. The imposing façades of Long's Share Our Wealth clubs, Coughlin's National Union for Social Justice, and Townsend's Old Age Revolving Pensions clubs covered a thoroughly scattered, locally oriented following that defied a head count. Partly because no one could estimate their strength, these movements caused considerable anxiety in Washington. The New Dealers in Congress and the White House had such nebulous, rumbling threats very much in mind as they considered their next moves against an obstinate depression.

In January 1935, Roosevelt set the New Deal into fresh winds by calling for a huge work relief program and a comprehensive social security measure. Three months later, Congress laid the foundation for the Works Progress Administration (WPA). The very size of the appropriation indicated how central the New Deal suddenly considered relief. With almost $5 billion, or ten times the amount originally given to FERA, the WPA absorbed about half the government's total expenditures. Like its predecessors, the act contained in its title the word *emergency*. By 1935, however, very few people thought that local or private contributions could ever again carry the burdens of relief in a depression. Hopkins, who administered the WPA, now emerged as Roosevelt's most powerful lieutenant. Through his large staff, the WPA supervised an extraordinary variety of projects, ranging from theatrical productions to road maintenance, that on the average employed over 2 million of American's jobless. Although WPA wages could not match Huey Long's $2,500, they were a blessed step above nothing.

The Social Security Act of August 1935 was more cautious in approach but more lasting in influence. It established a national system of old-age insurance that was funded by a tax on workers' wages and an equivalent tax on their

employers. The act also taxed employers to finance a varied set of state programs for unemployment compensation, and it offered the states matching
grants to aid dependent mothers and children and the disabled. In all, the
Social Security Act was a conservative version of schemes for social insurance
that had been discussed since the early 1900s. The poorest Americans, who had
no wages to tax or whose jobs fell outside the scope of the law, received no
protection at all. Payments did not even start until 1942. Nevertheless, if the
act did not equal the generosity of the Townsend Plan, it coped with the same
ills. Moreover, social security was an expandable formula, and later Congresses
gradually extended its range, until by the mid-1970s it covered almost all employees and many more of life's hazards.

Liberal congressmen produced a third basic law, which the President after
months of hesitation finally endorsed. The National Labor Relations Act, or
the Wagner Act, of July 1935 marked a startling shift in New Deal policy. Before
1935, the government had considered labor primarily as a dependent part of
industry. With the Wagner Act, however, the New Deal committed itself un-
equivocally to supporting unions that were independent of management. Not

SENATOR HUEY LONG OF LOUISIANA

Long, Roosevelt's most powerful
critic, expressed the anger and
frustration of poor people who
had not benefited from the early
New Deal. (Culver Pictures, Inc.)

only did the law bar company unions, but it also outlawed any form of company discrimination against members of an independent union. The National Labor Relations Board (NLRB), which was created to supervise the act, could conduct an election among a company's employees to ensure their free choice of a bargaining agent, and it could compel employers to comply with the new rules.

The first important consequence of these three ground-breaking acts was a powerful release of emotions. During 1935 and 1936, the New Deal, and above all Roosevelt himself, generated nationwide passions of hope and hate that would run like a high-voltage charge through the next two decades of American politics. If the New Deal neither cured the depression nor saved the nation from suffering, it communicated a humane concern when no one else seemed to care. The legislation of 1935, offering millions of hard-pressed Americans a bit of help, simultaneously held out the promise of much more to come. The Works Progress Administration kept innumerable families from a bottomless pit of despair. Social Security raised miraculous visions of a decent life in old age. The Wagner Act told countless wage earners that the government now stood with them instead of with their bosses.

What gave hope at the bottom of society spread horror at the top. Among many people with a strong stake in the existing system—bankers, lawyers, corporation executives, and doctors—these same laws created images of a chaotic society where demagogues were inciting the masses against everyone else's privileges. Year after year, an inability to explain what had gone wrong with the economy or predict what the government would do next had been deepening their frustration. Conservative doubts about the New Deal in 1933 turned into charges of incompetence in 1934, then outright hatred in 1935. No more irrational but much more powerful than the millions who loved Roosevelt, the wealthy foes of the New Deal had the means of making their feelings heard. They spoke from chambers of commerce and bar and medical and banking associations. They formed new organizations such as the American Liberty League, which spent millions to discredit the New Deal. Through newspapers, radio, and venomous little rumors ("Polio? Syphilis!"), they mounted a furious assault on the man even more than his administration.

Such an intense involvement with Roosevelt tended to obscure a second basic issue that accompanied the New Deal's economic policy. In destitute localities everywhere, the prospect of any assistance, of course, was a godsend. But how would it be distributed? By the efficiency standards of a distant bureaucracy or the personal judgments of local politicians? As the battles over Al Smith demonstrated, the Democratic party had been collecting a particularly combustible mixture of ethnic groups during the twenties. The elections of 1932 and 1934 added even more urban cultural blocs to the party's new majority. If the government's programs interfered with the sensitive, local standards of these groups, the New Deal coalition might disintegrate.

The Long and Coughlin movements, in the tradition of local politics, appealed directly to the Democratic majority's racial and religious feelings.* But the Roosevelt administration, national and economic in orientation, hoped to avoid all issues that might disturb these local cultures. After 1929, when hard times gave impetus to the drive against Prohibition, the national Democratic party had led the campaign for the Twenty-first Amendment, which in December 1933 repealed the Eighteenth and left the rules governing alcohol to local choice. Overjoyed to have Prohibition behind them, the New Dealers expected to concentrate exclusively on the problems of depression. It never dawned on them, for example, to revive the old Progressive wars against immigrant radicals or prostitution. Though Roosevelt selected the first woman to hold a cabinet post, Secretary of Labor Frances Perkins, neither Perkins nor Roosevelt's active wife, Eleanor, nor anyone else in the New Deal wanted to revive the movement for women's rights. By 1935, the old crusades were over, and no one in the Roosevelt administration was recommending a new one.

In many ways, the New Dealers were impressively liberal on matters of race and religion. Secretary of Interior Harold Ickes was a veteran member of the National Association for the Advancement of Colored People. Eleanor Roosevelt spoke eloquently for racial and religious equality. In the 1940s, Henry Wallace became one of the most prominent white champions of black rights. The President himself appointed a Jew as secretary of the treasury, an ironic reply to the anti-Semitic hallucination about a Jewish plot to control world finance. By inclination, however, all the New Dealers, including Ickes and Wallace, ignored ethnic problems as much as they could. They wanted to frame public policy in economic, not ethnic, terms and that predisposition prepared them to compromise with the values of their local constituents.

The pattern of decentralized administration that already characterized NRA and AAA supplied the broad formula for satisfying these local values. In return for the right to formulate general economic policy, national Democratic leaders would allow local politicians to distribute public funds in their own areas by their own standards. New Deal money in the South underwrote white Protestant cultures. In the large cities, its funds passed through urban political machines to the families and cultural groups who voted for them. Congress, by rejecting an amendment to the Wagner Act that would have required racial equality on the job, left the issue of bias in the unions to the labor leaders themselves. The immediate responses to these policies were politically heartening. Enthusiasm for the New Deal ran high in the South. In such cities as Pittsburgh and Kansas City, the New Deal's relief laws shored up the existing political machines, and in Chicago, WPA funds actually saved the budding Democratic

---

*Long himself was assassinated at the Louisiana State House in September 1935. Others, notably the Reverend Gerald L. K. Smith, tried to reach his national audience through religious and racial prejudice.

organization of Mayor Edward Kelley. These beneficiaries ranked among the
Roosevelt administration's most dedicated supporters. Meanwhile organized
labor declared Roosevelt its champion.

The primary political test of the New Deal's latest departures came in the
elections of 1936. Roosevelt's Republican opponent was the honest, uninspired
governor of Kansas, Alfred Landon. Coughlin, Townsend, and the remnants
of Long's legions gathered to form the Union party and nominate Representative
William Lemke of North Dakota for President. Although Coughlin personally
promised 9 million votes for Lemke and the *Literary Digest* predicted Landon's
election from a poll of those still able to afford telephones, most people expected Roosevelt to win. The margin of victory, however, would serve as the
critical index to the New Deal's success. Experts laughed at the estimate of
James Farley, Roosevelt's political aide and postmaster general, that the President
would carry every state except Maine and Vermont. Yet in November exactly

ROOSEVELT SUPPORTER

By 1936, Roosevelt's devoted partisans saw him as
their personal, towering champion in the White
House. (*Library of Congress.*)

that happened. Along with huge Democratic majorities in Congress, the election gave Roosevelt a breathtaking 523 electoral votes to a mere 8 for Landon. The woebegone Union party did not even collect a million popular votes, and Coughlin announced his retirement from politics.

The Democratic triumph of 1936 ratified the New Deal's policies in the two most crucial areas of modern politics. First, it placed responsibility for the national economy squarely in the lap of the government. After 1936, most Americans looked to the leaders in Washington to guarantee their economic welfare, and the popular economics of people like Long, Coughlin, and Townsend never again won a mass following. The wealthy haters of Roosevelt had to bide their time and fight another day. Second, the landslide of 1936 justified the New Deal's balance between national and local power. Broad economic policy from Washington and local control over cultural matters proved a brilliantly success-ful formula. How federal funds were spent ranked on a par with how much was spent. Nevertheless, these two answers only set a general direction for political policy. No one had yet resolved precisely how the national govern-ment should exercise its authority over the economy. Nor could anyone foresee how future pressures might affect the New Deal's ad hoc, unwritten agreement on local autonomy in cultural and ethnic affairs. The election of 1936 was a point of departure to a destination still unknown.

Suggested Readings

The best general guide to national politics during the 1920s and 1930s is a combi-nation of John D. Hicks, *Republican Ascendency, 1921–1933* (1960), and William E. Leuchten-burg, *Franklin D. Roosevelt and the New Deal, 1932–1940* (1963), an outstanding survey. Though less authoritative, George H. Soule, *Prosperity Decade* (1947), and Broadus Mitchell, *Depression Decade* (1947), provide an abundance of information on the national economy for these same years. Thomas C. Cochran, *American Business in the Twentieth Century* (1972), gives a clear overview of its subject, and Paul L. Murphy, *The Constitution in Crisis Times, 1918–1969* (1972), presents a full account of the Supreme Court's decisions. George B. Tindall, *The Emergence of the New South, 1913–1945* (1967), sets that region in a national context. A provocative interpretation of "The Age of Corporate Capitalism" appears in William Appleman Williams, *The Contours of American History* (1961).

Numerous books examine portions of the emerging modern economy. *Strategy and Structure: Chapters in the History of Industrial Enterprise* (1962), a pathbreaking volume by Alfred D. Chandler, Jr., analyzes the organization inside giant corporations, while Louis Galambos, *Competition and Cooperation: The Emergence of a National Trade Association* (1966), traces the pattern of organization among the scattered firms in cotton textiles. Allan Nevins and Frank Ernest Hill, *Ford: Expansion and Challenge, 1915–1933* (1957), covers the peak years of the flivver king's career. On labor the best study is Irving L. Bernstein's well-written *A History of the American Worker, 1920–1933: The Lean Years* (1960). Grant McConnell's *The Decline of Agrarian Democracy* (1953) centers on the American Farm Bureau Federation.

Robert K. Murray, *The Harding Era* (1969), and Donald R. McCoy, *Calvin Coolidge*

(1967), generously assess these Presidents and their policies. The major political scandal of the 1920s is explained in Burt L. Noggle, *Teapot Dome* (1962). David Burner's perceptive study, *The Politics of Provincialism* (1967), recounts the pulling and hauling in the Democratic party during the New Era, and William H. Harbaugh, *Lawyer's Lawyer: The Life of John W. Davis* (1973), evaluates the party's losing candidate in 1924. An interesting picture of the politics of natural resources emerges from Donald C. Swain, *Federal Conservation Policy, 1921–1933* (1963), and Norris Hundley, Jr., *Water and the West* (1975). The politics of commercial agriculture is the subject of Gilbert C. Fite's *George W. Peek and the Fight for Farm Parity* (1954). Theodore Saloutos and John D. Hicks, *Agricultural Discontent in the Middle West, 1900–1939* (1951), provides greater detail on farm groups and their programs. For the limitations of liberal reform, see LeRoy Ashby, *The Spearless Leader: Senator Borah and the Progressive Movement in the 1920's* (1972), Richard Lowitt, *George W. Norris: The Persistence of a Progressive, 1913–1933* (1971), and Arthur Mann, *LaGuardia: A Fighter against His Times, 1882–1933* (1959). In *Seedtime of Reform: American Social Service and Social Action, 1918–1933* (1963), on the other hand, Clarke A. Chambers discovers a maturing process during the twenties.

The best introduction to the ethnic and cultural issues of the twenties is John Higham's excellent *Strangers in the Land* (1955), which analyzes American nativism to 1925. David M. Chalmers, *Hooded Americanism* (1965), is a lively history of the Ku Klux Klan, and Kenneth T. Jackson, *The Ku Klux Klan in the City, 1915–1930* (1967), is an important supplement to the story. G. Louis Joughin and Edmund M. Morgan, *The Legacy of Sacco and Vanzetti* (1948), remains the richest account of events surrounding the trial of these men. The rise and fall of the "noble experiment" is traced in Andrew Sinclair, *Prohibition: The Era of Excess* (1962). Joseph R. Gusfield, *Symbolic Crusade* (1963), explores the emotional force behind Prohibition, and Norman F. Furniss, *The Fundamentalist Controversy, 1918–1931* (1954), reviews the antimodernist legislative campaigns. How cultural issues have been translated into politics is described generally in Oscar Handlin, *Al Smith and His America* (1958), and more specifically in J. Joseph Huthmacher, *Massachusetts People and Politics, 1919–1933* (1959).

John Kenneth Galbraith's clear essay, *The Great Crash, 1929* (3rd ed., 1972), marks the end of the New Era. Arthur M. Schlesinger, Jr., *The Crisis of the Old Order* (1957), the first volume of his *The Age of Roosevelt*, evokes the desperate confusion of economic depression, and so does the early portion of William Manchester's *The Glory and the Dream* (1974). In *The Lords of Creation* (1935), Frederick Lewis Allen captures the drama of the Wall Street debacle. More on the human meaning of the Great Depression can be found in Federal Writers' Project, *These Are Our Lives* (1939), and Studs Terkel, *Hard Times: An Oral History of the Great Depression* (1970). Joan Hoff Wilson's *Herbert Hoover: Forgotten Progressive* (1975) is the best general evaluation of that controversial President. Fuller accounts of government policy during Hoover's administration appear in Albert U. Romasco, *The Poverty of Abundance* (1965), Jordan A. Schwarz, *The Interregnum of Despair* (1970), and Harris G. Warren, *Herbert Hoover and the Great Depression* (1959).

Volumes 2 and 3 of Arthur Schlesinger's *The Age of Roosevelt—The Coming of the New Deal* (1958) and *The Politics of Upheaval* (1960)—provide a thorough and readable account of Franklin Roosevelt's first administration. The essays in John Braeman et al., eds., *The New Deal, I: The National Level* (1975), expand portions of the story; essays in the second volume, *The State and Local Levels* (1975), survey the experiences of government outside Washington. James T. Patterson, *The New Deal and the States* (1969), analyzes the tensions between national and state power. The most valuable work on the National Recovery Administration and other policies pertaining to business is Ellis W. Hawley, *The New Deal and the Problem of Monopoly* (1966). Organized labor's course is followed in

Irving Bernstein's *A History of the American Worker, 1933–1941: Turbulent Years* (1970). Val N. Perkins, *Crisis in Agriculture* (1969), details the beginning of the Agricultural Adjustment Administration. On the most innovative New Deal policy, C. Herman Pritchett, *The Tennessee Valley Authority* (1943), supplies basic information; Philip Selznick, *TVA and the Grass Roots* (1949), analyzes the Authority's social orientation; and Thomas K. McCraw, *TVA and the Power Fight, 1933–1939* (1971), traces the principal challenge to the Authority's program. Grace Abbott, *From Relief to Social Security* (1966), covers the record of public assistance, and Roy Lubove, *The Struggle for Social Security, 1900–1935* (1968), explains the origins of the Social Security Act. Michael E. Parrish, *Securities Regulation and the New Deal* (1970), is an illuminating monograph on that area of public policy. Two interesting studies—Paul K. Conkin, *Tomorrow a New World: The New Deal Community Program* (1959), and Jane DeHart Mathews, *The Federal Theater, 1935–1939* (1967)—suggest the breadth of interests affected by the New Deal. A sample of the sharp historical debates over the New Deal is collected in Alonzo L. Hamby, ed., *The New Deal* (1969).

On Roosevelt himself, the best study for the New Deal years is James MacGregor Burns, *Roosevelt: The Lion and the Fox* (1956). Frank Freidel's massive biography, *Franklin D. Roosevelt* (4 vols. to date, 1952–73), has carried FDR through his first critical months in the White House. Additional insights into the Roosevelt household appear in Alfred B. Rollins, Jr., *Roosevelt and Howe* (1962), and Joseph P. Lash, *Eleanor and Franklin* (1971). Among the many published journals and memoirs by participants in the New Deal, Raymond Moley's critical *After Seven Years* (1939) and Rexford G. Tugwell's appreciative *The Democratic Roosevelt* (1957) are especially useful. J. Joseph Huthmacher, *Senator Robert F. Wagner and the Rise of Urban Liberalism* (1968), and Paul A. Kurzman, *Harry Hopkins and the New Deal* (1974), are complimentary accounts of these important men. Otis L. Graham, Jr., *An Encore for Reform* (1967), explores the generally unfavorable responses of the old progressives to the New Deal, and George Wolfskill, *The Revolt of the Conservatives* (1962), describes the outrage of the American Liberty League.

The world of local politics appears largely in glimpses. In combination, John M. Allswang's *A House for All People: Ethnic Politics in Chicago, 1890–1936* (1971), Edward R. Kantowitz's *Polish-American Politics in Chicago, 1888–1940* (1975), and Humbert Nelli's *Italians in Chicago, 1880–1930* (1970) sketch an interesting picture for one big city. Arthur Mann, *LaGuardia Comes to Power: 1933* (1965), uses an important election in New York City to analyze its political roots. The relation between the New Deal and the local bosses is considered in Bruce M. Stave, *The New Deal and the Last Hurrah: Pittsburgh Machine Politics* (1970), and Lyle W. Dorsett, *The Pendergast Machine* (1968). Charles J. Tull, *Father Coughlin and the New Deal* (1965), and T. Harry Williams, *Huey Long* (1969), examine the New Deal's leading competitors in local politics, and David H. Bennett, *Demagogues in the Depression* (1969), chronicles their decline. The cultural values of the New Dealers themselves are summarized in E. Digby Baltzell, *The Protestant Establishment* (1964).

31

The Development of Modern Politics

When the New Deal changed course in 1935, it abandoned the vision of the economy that had dominated public policy since the First World War. During the 1920s and early 1930s, policymakers sought harmony among the nation's big economic units: business, labor, agriculture, and finance. With encouragement from Washington, it was assumed, business would lead the other units in a coordinated march to prosperity. After 1935, these big economic blocs broke into smaller and smaller subdivisions, each demanding its own policy to serve its own interests. As the economy fragmented, government officials groped for a new understanding of how the economy worked and how prosperity could be achieved. The Second World War gave them a crucial clue. With a vast increase in government spending during the war, the economy revived dramatically. Nevertheless, it took many more years of angry debate to settle on a fiscal policy that would sustain an economy of countless special interests. Meanwhile, a growing number of Americans were insisting that the government also tackle the nation's racial and cultural problems. As a new economic policy developed in the 1950s, attention was already shifting to racial and cultural issues that would mark the next phase of modern politics.

The New Deal Loses Its Way, 1936–1941

At the peak of his popularity in 1936, a confident Franklin Roosevelt prepared for a triumphant second term. His political base was secure. Federal assistance to wage earners, farmers, and the unemployed, in combination with a restrained use of national power in local affairs, had created a massive Democratic majority in Congress and attracted a passionate loyalty to the President himself. Now the challenge was to devise a policy expressing the government's broad responsibility for the American economy. Could the New Deal expand on the impressive but still tentative departures of 1935?

Roosevelt's first objective had already been dictated by the Supreme Court. In the tense climate of 1935 and 1936, as the New Deal was expanding its scope, the Court grew increasingly rigid. Drawing on precedents that in some instances had been conservative in the 1890s, a bare majority of five justices attacked the national government's primary source of power over the economy, regulation of interstate commerce. Mining and farming, in the Court's view, were local, not interstate, activities. By implication, these interpretations jeopardized a full range of the New Deal's policies in industry and agriculture. Moreover, a narrow construction of interstate commerce automatically cast doubts on the government's authority to regulate labor-management relations through the Wagner Act, and to tax employers and employees through the Social Security Act.

The most publicized of the Court's many decisions during 1935 and 1936 were the *Schechter* case (1935), striking down the National Recovery Administration (NRA), and *U. S.* v. *Butler* (1936), invalidating the tax on food processing in the Agricultural Adjustment Act. Neither decision crippled the New Deal. The NRA, a loosely worded delegation of powers to the executive that all nine justices condemned, was already dead by 1935. The Court's judgment merely gave it a decent burial. Following the *Butler* decision Congress continued the New Deal's basic farm program under the guise of soil conservation. But the Court's willingness to assault two such important laws, along with so many other threatening precedents in 1935 and 1936, forced a confrontation between the Roosevelt administration and the Supreme Court. As the President stated, the New Deal could not function with a "horse and buggy" conception of interstate commerce.

Reading his victory in 1936 as a mandate to storm this conservative outpost, Roosevelt submitted a judiciary reorganization bill to Congress in February 1937. The President requested the right to enlarge the Court from nine to a maximum of fifteen members if those justices over seventy years old did not voluntarily resign. Although Roosevelt's purpose was to create his own Court majority, he pretended that the issue was judicial efficiency. The existing Court, the President claimed, could not manage its heavy load of work, a charge that the magisterial Chief Justice Charles Evans Hughes easily refuted. To this deviousness, Roosevelt added an unusual ineptness. When Congress resisted his plan, Roosevelt refused either to negotiate or to compromise, and his heavy-handed pressure on the legislators strengthened the opposition. Instead of pitting the New Deal against the Court, Roosevelt's course set Congress against the President. By the summer of 1937, Roosevelt's bill was lost.

In the end, the conservatives did lose their judicial stronghold. During the congressional fight, the Court in *NLRB* v. *Jones and Laughlin Steel* (1937) upheld the Wagner Act by a margin of one vote. "A switch in time saved nine," the wags declared. A rapid sequence of retirements from the Court soon enabled the President to appoint a majority who were thoroughly committed to the New Deal. Beginning in 1937, the Court executed a dramatic reversal. By the time of *U. S.* v. *Darby* (1941), it had authorized a sweeping regulatory power over interstate commerce and validated all the principal legislation of the New Deal. But the price of victory was high. Roosevelt's clumsy attack on the Court severely tarnished his reputation as a leader. In the future, even Democratic congress-men would feel much freer to vote against the President.

The labor movement also strained the New Deal coalition. As the Wagner Act passed, the labor movement split into warring camps. John L. Lewis, president of the powerful United Mine Workers, led a group of dissident unions out of the craft-oriented AFL in order to organize the semiskilled and unskilled workers in the major mass production industries. The rebels eventually formed the Congress of Industrial Organizations (CIO), while the skilled trades remained in the AFL. Looking at the leaders of the two organizations, there seemed to

NINE OLD MEN, FROM "NEW MASSES," MARCH, 1937

The "Nine Old Men" of the Supreme Court as partisans of the New Deal saw them in 1937. Yet Roosevelt's attack on the court alienated many more Americans than it rallied to his cause. *(Brown Brothers.)*

be no contest. Lewis's dramatic flair and imaginative leadership made him a national attraction in the mid-1930s second only to Roosevelt, and the shaggy giant of the CIO appeared capable of demolishing the AFL's mild little William Green with words alone. "Explore the mind of Bill Green," the advocates of labor compromise had suggested to Lewis. "I have done a lot of exploring in Bill's mind," Lewis declared, "and I give you my word there is nothing there." But the AFL proved to be a resourceful enemy that mobilized local opposition to the CIO, collaborated with employers who were fighting the new unions, and helped antiunion congressmen brand the CIO a communist organization.

In addition, the CIO faced a formidable challenge from the unorganized industries themselves. Employers from the docks of San Francisco to the textile mills in North Carolina used murder, gas, beatings, and intimidation to demoralize their workers and block the CIO's unionizing efforts. The first crisis in this rough, uncertain struggle began in December 1936, when workers at a number of General Motors affiliates sat inside the company plants to gain recognition for their new organization, the United Auto Workers (UAW). Ignoring court orders to evacuate the buildings, receiving supplies from their friends outside, and turning back the police in "The Battle of the Running Bulls," the auto workers, with the help of cooperative state and national politicians, achieved the CIO's first great victory. In February 1937, General Motors and the UAW signed a peace pact. Illegal sit-down strikes quickly spread nationwide.

STEEL STRIKE RIOT, CHICAGO

Passions and dangers surrounded the organizing drives of the CIO. A movie camera captured this moment of terror when Chicago policemen assaulted steel strikers and their families in May 1937. (*Associated Press.*)

Meanwhile, a CIO drive in the steel industry won a second stunning success. In March 1937, U. S. Steel, the very symbol of the open shop in America's mass production industries, ended a bitter strike by recognizing the steelworkers' union. Almost all the corporations in "Little Steel," however, adamantly refused to follow suit, and bloody reprisals stalled the organizing campaign there. In the "Memorial Day Massacre" outside Republic Steel's plant in Chicago, for example, police shot into a fleeing crowd, killing or wounding dozens of strike sympathizers. In fact, there was an epidemic of industrial violence in 1937.

The turmoil of sit-down strikes and local warfare broke an uneasy truce over labor policy within the Democratic party. While an exasperated Roosevelt condemned management and labor alike by declaring "a plague on both your houses," Democratic factions in Congress angrily debated the sins of employers and unions. Fortunately for the CIO, a partisan National Labor Relations Board (NLRB) continued to fight vigorously in behalf of the new unions. By 1941, with almost 10 million members divided between the AFL and the CIO, the union movement had safely passed the first round of crisis. In the process, however, it had made a host of enemies, Democrats as well as Republicans.

A growing hostility to the labor movement decreased the likelihood that the government would assist other Americans to organize in their own behalf. Tenant farmers, for example, were particularly in need of the government's help. Always the poor relations in an era of commercial agriculture, they had suffered cruelly from depression and drought in the 1930s. The AAA, which distributed benefits only to landowners, offered the destitute tenants almost no relief. In 1935, when some of them formed the Southern Tenant Farmers' Union, landlords and sheriffs crushed their organization. When reformers in the Department of Agriculture argued the tenants' cause, they were fired.

Trying New Departures
Principal New Deal Measures, 1935–1938

Works Progress Administration (WPA)	May 1935
Wagner Act, creating National Labor Relations Board (NLRB)	July 1935
Social Security Act	August 1935
Bankhead-Jones Farm Tenancy Act, creating Farm Security Administration (FSA)	July 1937
Fair Labor Standards Act	June 1938

The first serious attempt to reverse this tide was the Bankhead-Jones Farm Tenancy Act of 1937. Through a new agency, the Farm Security Administration (FSA), the law provided credit with which tenants could purchase the farms they were working. In addition, the FSA explored ways to develop a diversified, cooperative community life for small farmers and to protect the interests of the forgotten farm laborers. The FSA was one logical extension of the New Deal's innovations in 1935, a rural counterpart of the program for organized labor. But in 1937, the opposition of the established agricultural organizations and the flagging reform spirit in Congress kept its budget small and its future precarious.

The only solid expansion of the New Deal came in the Fair Labor Standards Act of 1938. After much wrangling, Congress established a minimum wage level and an official rate of time and a half for overtime work, and it abolished child labor. With wholesale exemptions in agriculture, special dispensations for Southern employers, and minimum wage scales that were meager even by a depression standard, this law, like the Social Security Act, was neither general in its coverage nor generous in its provisions. Yet in combination with Social

Security and the Works Progress Administration (WPA), the Fair Labor Standards Act reinforced a fundamental new assumption. The national government should protect the economic welfare of its poorer citizens.

By 1938, the New Deal was obviously drifting. Its thin list of accomplishments in two years reflected above all the absence of a clear purpose. Once Roosevelt and his advisers had lost faith in the ability of organized business to bring back prosperity, they simply could not decide where to lay the foundations for a sound economy. None of the available alternatives seemed very promising. Roosevelt did sign two laws strengthening the rights of small businessmen. The Robinson-Patman Act of 1936 sought to protect independent retailers against such huge chains as A & P and Woolworth, and the Miller-Tydings Act of 1937 legalized "fair trade" agreements, or fixed retail pricing, in behalf of similar small firms. The President also authorized the justice department to bring more antitrust suits against big business. Yet Roosevelt never longed for the old days of small-unit competition, and the administration's new antitrust policy did not try to destroy giant corporations. Some advisers suggested a closer alliance between the New Deal and the unions, but Roosevelt neither understood organized labor's raw battles nor trusted John L. Lewis, its outstanding leader. The President also refused to believe that government spending could cure the depression. He even helped to cause a new economic crisis in 1937 by sharply reducing the government budget. Although Roosevelt

The burdens of the thirties crushed America's tenant farmers. In the dust bowl of the Great Plains, drought was as devastating as depression. (*Library of Congress, United States Department of Agriculture, Library of Congress.*)

was profoundly disturbed by the vision of "one-third of a Nation ill-nourished, ill-clad, ill-housed," he did not know how, in the long run, to solve the problem.

On Capitol Hill, an informal coalition of Republicans and conservative, largely Southern Democrats moved into the vacuum of leadership. With no clearer purpose than the liberals, they concentrated primarily on opposing "socialist" measures that would enlarge the national government's responsibilities, or "giveaway" programs that would expand its services. In the spirit of the 1920s, many of them still equated prosperity with a self-regulating economy. All of the conservatives used "New Dealer" as a dirty word. Roosevelt returned their feelings, but he could not check their rising power in Congress. When he tried to "purge" a few prominent opponents in his own party during the offyear elections of 1938, he not only failed but actually publicized his declining authority over the legislature.

In this confusion of uncertain purposes, vague rhetoric, and mutual suspicions, the one sharp focus fell on Roosevelt himself. Reformers, as their fortunes waned, considered him more important than ever. To conservatives, "that man in the White House" embodied the evils of their time. Roosevelt accentuated this tendency to personalize national politics. By 1939, the nation's parlor game was guessing whom the President might designate his successor. Characteristically, Roosevelt kept a serene silence, held the spotlight on himself, and at the last minute allowed the Democratic convention of 1940 to nominate him for an unprecedented third term. The prospect of a third term stirred all the latent emotions about Roosevelt, the aspiring dictator, and Roosevelt, the indispensable man. As the President knew very well, FDR would be the issue of the 1940 campaign.

This time, the Republicans selected a candidate able to challenge Roosevelt. Wendell Willkie, a former utilities executive who had once led the fight against TVA, was an inspired amateur in national politics. Liberal enough to attract independent voters yet conservative enough to satisfy most opponents of the New Deal, Willkie eagerly took on "the Champ" in a vigorous presidential campaign. With arms akimbo and eyes sparkling, he became the first Republican candidate in twenty years to

"Come along. We're going to the Trans-Lux to hiss Roosevelt." *(Library of Congress.)*

elicit a warm popular response as he toured the nation. "Well, muss my hair and call me Willkie!" a common saying in 1940, expressed an easy affection that almost no American had bestowed on solemn Herbert Hoover or bland Alfred Landon. But charm was also Roosevelt's special strength. Moreover, the New Deal's combination of national aid and local autonomy continued to be an extremely successful political formula. Though a few former allies, such as John L. Lewis and Vice-President Garner, deserted the President, most of the voters did not. In November 1940, Roosevelt and his new running-mate, Henry Wallace, won by a substantial margin, 449 electoral votes to 82 for Willkie.

Even before 1940, Roosevelt's attention had increasingly turned outward to the world, where wars in Asia and then in Europe were threatening to engulf the United States. Both Roosevelt and Willkie devoted as much time in their campaigns to foreign affairs as to domestic issues. Following the election, the President immersed himself in the problems that on December 7, 1941, would culminate in war. As Roosevelt later phrased it, he was already discarding the mantle of "Dr. New Deal" and preparing to don a new one, "Dr. Win-the-War." The passing of the New Deal left the government's economic role in limbo. Through humanitarian statements and innovative programs, the Roosevelt administration aroused nationwide expectations that the government would help the needy and support the economy. Yet the sum of the New Deal's efforts neither cured the depression nor established an economic policy. Other leaders would have to bridge the gap between popular hopes and government actions.

Wartime Prosperity and Postwar Confusion, 1941–1947

The Second World War solved the depression. Before the war was over, net farm income almost doubled and corporate profits after taxes climbed 70 percent. From a total of over 8 million unemployed in 1940, the curve dropped below a million by 1944. Moreover, an abundance of jobs and an industrial wage scale that rose 24 percent drew into the labor market an additional 7 million workers, half of whom were women. There had been no economic boom like it in American history.

Economic organization for a worldwide conflict required an extraordinary expansion of government power. The War Production Board, the Office of Price Administration, the War Manpower Commission, the Office of Defense Transportation, and the War Food Administration each had broad authority to manage its subdivision of the economy. Beginning in October 1942, the skillful South Carolina politician James F. Byrnes ruled above these agencies through the Office of Economic Stabilization, and subsequently the Office of War Mobilization.

The problems most bedeviling to the wartime agencies were allocating scarce resources and controlling inflation. Because the United States was blessed

BOEING AIRPLANE FACTORY

The Second World War sent America back to work.
(Library of Congress.)

with an abundance of natural resources, its own raw materials were sufficient
for most wartime programs. When a shortage of rubber created a crisis, the rapid
development of synthetic rubber soon resolved it. The shortage of skilled labor,
however, defied solution. Not only did the armed services absorb over 15 million
men and women, but civilians could not resist hopping from job to job in search
of better wages. "Stabilization," or job-freeze, orders from Washington had
little effect on labor turnover, and Roosevelt's proposal in 1944 to draft workers
into an industrial army collapsed in the face of united opposition from employers and unions alike.

Prices soared during the early months of the war. The Office of Price Administration (OPA), under the able but politically obtuse economist Leon Hender-
son, lacked the power to control inflation because Congress refused to check
the rise of agricultural prices. Only late in 1942, when James Byrnes took charge
of the entire mobilization program, did a semblance of order begin to emerge.
By mid-1943, a broad ceiling over prices, wages, and rents finally stopped the

upward spiral. Although the cost of living increased about 33 percent during the war, relatively little of that occurred after the summer of 1943.

Finance posed a third basic wartime problem. Though more than half the costs of war accumulated as a national debt, massive new funds still had to be raised. The answer came in the revolutionary Revenue Act of 1942, which established America's modern structure of taxation. The heart of the measure was a steeply graduated income tax that for the first time covered most middle-income and lower-income groups. As a result, the number of families paying income tax quadrupled, and by 1945, revenues from the tax stood twenty times above their level in 1940. To ease the pain yet increase the flow, the government took most of these taxes directly from the paychecks rather than demand them in a lump once a year.

Inside the intricate framework of wartime rules, however, extreme decentralization prevailed. The tax laws contained numerous loopholes for the wealthy. Thousands of local draft boards decided who should fill the quotas for military service. To get the planes and tanks and beef and wheat it needed, the government simply offered to pay a lot of money. With industries, it signed lucrative contracts guaranteeing costs, profits, and large tax writeoffs. Companies negotiated these contracts through the various bureaus of the wartime government, then fought with one another for the labor and raw materials all of them needed. After the government allowed farm prices to skyrocket for a year, it continued to subsidize many farmers at a level above the market price for their products. Even the unpopular OPA, which rationed such scarce commodities as gasoline, meat, shoes, and sugar among a nation of grumbling consumers, exercised little control over the widespread violation of its rules. The government's chief administrators intervened only when the many small decisions below them had created a hopeless mess.

In the wartime scramble for advantage, reforms were pushed aside. The conservative coalition in Congress, growing a bit with each election, proceeded to trim the New Deal. As the unemployed came back to work, Congress in 1942 terminated the WPA. Calling the Farm Security Administration a "communist" center, its opponents abolished the FSA's social programs for the rural poor. The one child of the

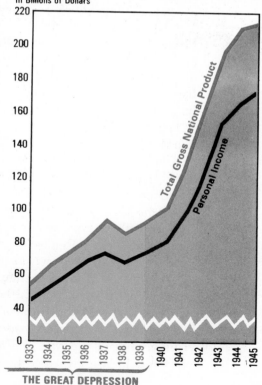

Recovery of the National Economy

In Billions of Dollars

Total Gross National Product

Personal Income

THE GREAT DEPRESSION

thirties to thrive during the war was the revitalized union movement. In 1941, two more citadels of the open shop—Ford and the corporations in Little Steel—surrendered. During the war itself union membership rose 40 percent. Even more important, many employers, in an effort to hold their workers and maintain production, actually bargained with the unions for the first time. Yet here also the conservatives had their say. Although the number of strikes remained quite low between 1941 and 1945, important ones in the coal and railroad industries during 1943 triggered an angry public reaction, and Congress responded with the Smith-Connally Act, which authorized the President to postpone a strike for thirty days and seize a plant that had been struck. Strikers could be fined and imprisoned.

Above all, the conservatives fought every executive agency that tried to make economic plans for the postwar years. Not one of them survived the congressional budget cuts. As the war drew to a close, the only significant preparation for peace was the Servicemen's Readjustment Act of 1944, popularly known as the GI Bill, which provided unemployment compensation, medical care, mortgage funds, and educational subsidies for the returning veterans. Roosevelt, growing old and ill, did nothing to arrest the confusion. Investing all his energies in world problems, the President left the home front to his subordinates. When the Democrats nominated him for a fourth term in 1944, he campaigned listlessly against Thomas E. Dewey, the smooth, capable Republican governor of New York. Roosevelt still won handily, 439 to 99 electoral votes. Perhaps the nasty Democratic comment that no one wanted "little Tom Dewey sitting on two Washington telephone books" at a peace conference captured the essence of Roosevelt's strength. At a momentous juncture in world affairs, the President had an appropriately grand international prestige. But domestically, America had no leader at all entering 1945.

The man who actually presided over the nation's transition to peace was Harry S Truman. An able Missouri judge during the late 1920s and early 1930s, Truman came to the Senate in 1935 and built a reputation for hard work, party loyalty, and stubborn determination. At the 1944 convention, Democratic leaders selected the reliable, unobtrusive Truman to replace Vice-President Wallace, whose desire to expand the New Deal and usher in the "century of the common man" had alienated the conservatives in his party. Yet no one seemed to have considered Truman seriously as a possible President. Roosevelt, it appeared, would live forever. Then on April 12, 1945, only a few weeks after his fourth inauguration, the President died and an era ended. Millions mourned in public; thousands celebrated in their clubs; and Truman, no more prepared than the nation, suddenly found himself the chief executive.

The most experienced leader would have had difficulty guiding America's economy out of the war. Truman simply floundered. Even before Japan surrendered in August 1945, he could not withstand the popular pressures for a rapid demobilization of the armed forces and a rapid dismantling of most wartime regulations. Industries now made their own decisions in their own behalf, and during the first postwar year corporate profits shot up 20 percent. Strikes spread across the nation. By January 1946, 3 percent of the labor force, including auto, steel, electrical, and packinghouse workers, were simultaneously on strike. When a new round of strikes occurred that spring, a furious President went before Congress to threaten the railroad workers with an army draft even though the Railroad Brotherhoods had already cancelled the strike. The only broad national controls governed prices, and a feud between the President and Congress needlessly allowed these to end all at once in June 1946, producing the highest rate of inflation in the nation's history. Farm prices rose almost 14 percent in a month and nearly 30 percent before the end of the year. As the saying went, "To err is Truman." "Had Enough?" asked the Republicans.

Apparently many Americans had, for the offyear elections of 1946 cost the Democrats 11 seats in the Senate and 54 in the House. When the Eightieth Congress convened in 1947, the Republicans were the majority party for the first time since Hoover's administration. With the cooperation of conservative Democrats, they could even override the President's veto. Yet the Eightieth Congress had little to offer as an alternative to Truman's erratic policies. Its primary contribution was the Taft-Hartley Act of 1947, a culmination of the congressional antagonism toward unions that had been growing for a decade. A complicated law, Taft-Hartley required financial reports from the unions, restricted their political activities, and prohibited a list of "unfair" labor practices. It also empowered the President to postpone a major strike for an eighty-day "cooling off" period and allowed state governments to pass antiunion "right to work" laws. But despite these new rules and the howls they brought from the unions, labor-management relations proceeded much the same after Taft-Hartley as before.

The paralysis in public policy that was afflicting the government had far deeper causes than political quarrels in Washington. Fundamental changes were occurring in the economy, and no one yet knew how to deal with them. By 1936, it was no longer practical to picture the economy in terms of big interdependent units: business, labor, agriculture, and finance. Government officials, instead of trying to design one policy for each of these large blocs, increasingly responded to the special claims of much smaller economic units. After 1936, there were no more NRAs for all of American business, just a "little NRA" for coal, another program for oil, particular legislation for retailers, a special antitrust policy for oligopolies, and on and on. Civil war in the labor movement publicized the very different grievances separating carpenters from steelworkers, from longshoremen from hatmakers—a decentralization of interests far greater than just a division between the AFL and the CIO. By the late 1930s, wheat growers and dairy farmers and cotton producers and cattle grazers were all demanding programs specifically designed for their commodities. It became more and more difficult to pretend that there was any unified, national agricultural interest.

The Second World War hastened this fragmentation. Beneath a shell of administrative centralization, innumerable special interests fought for the government's favors. The stakes were high, the rules loose, and the results chaotic. Each economic interest grew accustomed to caring for itself in the Washington jungle. By the end of the war, the big economic blocs of an earlier era were in thorough disarray. Such broad organizations as the U. S. Chamber of Commerce, the National Association of Manufacturers, and the American Bankers Association, once the voices of basic economic groups, now spoke for no one in particular. The American Farm Bureau Federation was rapidly losing strength, and the Department of Agriculture came to rely less and less on it to administer the government's farm programs. As the AFL and the CIO began making peace and preparing for their merger in 1955, both organizations were experiencing a similar decentralization. Strong industrial unions in the CIO exercised the same kind of independence that the affiliates of the AFL had long enjoyed, and neither central headquarters had much success trying to discipline such stubborn organizations of the Longshoremen and the Teamsters. Even the oligopolies were less integrated than they had once been. The latest wave of corporate consolidations, which eventually produced such conglomerates as Litton Industries, Textron, and Kaiser Industries, favored purely financial combinations of distinct and often very different kinds of business firms.

Paralleling this fragmentation of interests, a permanent, professional bureaucracy formed in Washington to deal with each specialized subdivision of the

The Growth of Union Membership

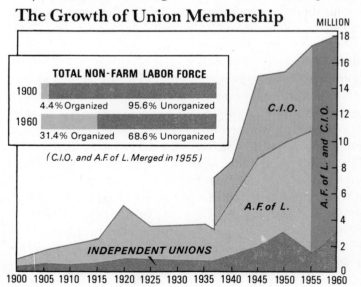

economy. Before 1935, when the national government acted largely as a service center, administrators tended to behave as if they were temporary and would soon leave the government to follow private careers. By 1936, however, the government had become the economy's vital center, and its new responsibilities appeared likely to remain for a long time. Officials in the Works Progress Administration (WPA), the enlarged bureaus of agriculture, the growing Tennessee Valley Authority (TVA), and many other agencies settled in for the duration. Then during the war, the government bureaucracy swelled to four times its size in 1939. In a hubbub of crash programs and quick decisions, no one closely supervised its myriad economic activities. Even after demobilization, the number of civilian employees more than doubled the government's prewar level. Administrators had grown accustomed to running their own little domains and protecting them from higher authorities. Almost every office along the miles of Washington corridors was linked to some private group and a few friendly congressmen. In sum, these many alliances between public officials and private interests made a broad public policy extremely difficult to create.

As this pattern of decentralization developed, the economic importance of the national government loomed larger than ever. No one could miss the intimate connection between government policy and the nation's phenomenal economic growth during the war. America's Gross National Product (GNP) rose a breathtaking 67 percent. Government expenditures accounted for an equally astonishing 40 percent of the total GNP. *Government*—singular and capitalized—arrived as an everyday term to designate this huge center of money and power. With the shadow of the Great Depression still across people's thoughts, the national government's vast authority became inseparably connected with long-term, peacetime prosperity. In the Full Employment Act of 1946, Congress accepted the government's responsibility for maintaining a healthy economy. But Congress carefully avoided specifying how. This sprawling, government-oriented economy had been changing too rapidly, and neither the Democrats nor the Republicans had found a satisfactory technique for managing it.

Local Politics Comes to Washington, 1936–1947

While leaders in Washington were grappling with the problems of the economy, the racial and cultural concerns of local politics gradually rose again to influence national affairs. For a time, it appeared that the informal bargain between the New Deal and local Democrats might keep the two levels separate. By granting local politicians wide authority over the distribution of federal funds, the Roosevelt administration did insulate itself from most local pressures during its second term. James Farley, Roosevelt's master of patronage, managed government appointments with a keen eye to the needs of both the administration and local politics, and the Democratic city bosses continued to give Roosevelt their loyal support. A diffuse anti-Semitism spread through the Great Plains and the northern industrial cities, but it never surfaced in national politics. Although some Southern whites considered the Farm Security Administration and the new industrial unions a threat to local rights, the FSA's programs for black tenant farmers never really materialized, and the CIO received little help trying to organize workers in the towns and small cities of the South. Nor did the New Deal's principal reforms in Indian affairs disturb local politics. After decades of government neglect and hostility to Indian culture, the Roosevelt administration sponsored the Indian Reorganization Act of 1934, an attempt to allow Indians tribal self-government and at least some economic autonomy. Nevertheless, the law required no change in local white policies toward Indians.

The Second World War broke this deceptive calm in national affairs. As the power of the national government rapidly expanded, it inevitably became entangled with local politics. The most shocking example occurred on the West Coast immediately after the Japanese attack at Pearl Harbor. A large majority of whites along the West Coast continued to nurse a traditional hostility toward Asiatics. Following a surprise attack on American territory, they readily believed rumors of a Japanese "fifth column" in the United States that was planning extensive sabotage and communicating with enemy submarines off America's shore. The government, they cried, must destroy the danger from within. These popular, bipartisan emotions found a willing servant in Lieutenant General John DeWitt, who headed the Army's Western Defense Command. Responding to DeWitt's request, Washington gave the general broad powers in February 1942 to solve the Japanese problem as he chose.

At the outset, DeWitt planned to use stronger measures against the 40,000 alien Japanese (immigrants who by law were denied the right to become American citizens) than against the 70,000 who were American citizens by birth. But that distinction quickly disappeared. Early in 1942, DeWitt ordered all Japanese Americans along the coast of Washington, Oregon, and California and from southern Arizona to abandon their homes. From temporary stockades, they were transported to ten island centers where the Army Relocation Authority guarded them for the duration. In *Korematsu* v. *U. S.* (1944), the Supreme Court upheld these policies on grounds of national security. Along with their liberty, Japanese Americans lost about $350 million in property and income.

Concentration camps for 110,000 Japanese Americans were an embarrassment to the Roosevelt administration, which was simultaneously fighting to empty the Nazi concentration camps in Europe. Officially, the Japanese Americans were in "relocation centers." After the initial wave of panic passed, government officials discussed ways of reversing their policy and releasing the prisoners. Once again, local hostilities prevailed. The Roosevelt administration was told that no communities would accept the Japanese Americans. As the common argument went, Japanese Americans would be mobbed if the government did not protect them inside the camps. Instead, the Army compromised during 1943 and 1944 by issuing extended leaves to 35,000 Japanese Americans. Finally, in January 1945, the gates were opened to everyone.

A second challenge came from black Americans who were losers in local politics. Between the two world wars, racial problems that had once been considered peculiarly Southern became clearly national. Close to a million blacks left the South during the 1920s, almost double the number who had emigrated in the previous decade. Even in depression, when the unemployed crowded the large cities, 400,000 more came North. Then during the early 1940s alone, another million responded to the wartime jobs that beckoned from Los Angeles to Boston. By 1950, approximately one-third of America's black population lived outside the South.

In two important respects, the Northern urban experience altered black attitudes. First, it encouraged their assertiveness. During the same years that whites argued over the racial merits of immigration, urban blacks were also manifesting a stronger racial consciousness. Claude McKay, Langston Hughes,

"RELOCATION"

A relatively prosperous Japanese-American family awaits its fate early in 1942. Imprisonment during the war cost them everything. *(Library of Congress.)*

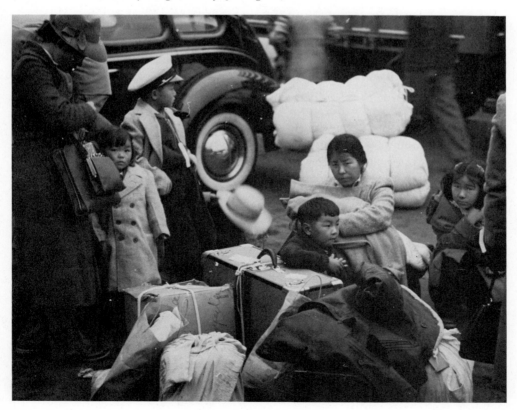

Black Population, 1920-1930

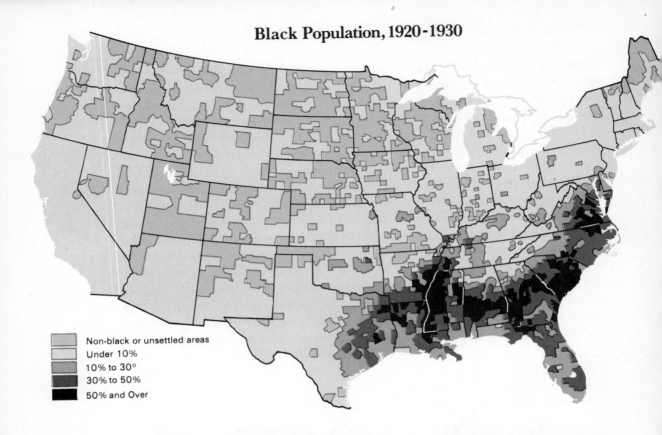

Non-black or unsettled areas
Under 10%
10% to 30°
30% to 50%
50% and Over

Countee Cullen, and other contributors to the "Harlem Renaissance" of the 1920s wrote eloquently about the black spirit. Early in the twenties, millions of blacks found inspiration in the African nationalism of Marcus Garvey, an immigrant from Jamaica whose Universal Negro Improvement Association promised racial glory in the Empire of Africa.* Moreover, in some cities, blacks secured a place for themselves in the urban political machines. Under Tom Pendergast in Kansas City and Big Bill Thompson in Chicago, for example, black bosses represented their wards and negotiated with organized crime much as the white bosses were doing.

Second, the Northern urban experience stimulated a national movement for black rights. Each large city contained a core of black leaders who were aware of the modern nationalizing trends around them and eager to use them in behalf of their own people. Their primary organization was the National Association for the Advancement of Colored People (NAACP), and their primary spokesman was Walter White, the talented writer and persistent lobbyist who in 1931 began his long tenure as national secretary for the NAACP. When the Great Depression made it clear that only the national government could signifi-

---

*Garvey's conviction in 1923 for mail fraud disorganized his movement, and nothing comparable arose to take its place.

cantly improve the position of blacks in America, the NAACP pressed two kinds of arguments on the government's leaders. One, appealing to their conscience, demanded racial equality. The other, appealing to their political interests, offered to trade black votes for black rights. Unlike the Southern cotton fields, the Northern cities lay in competitive, two-party states with large electoral votes, and the NAACP tried to convince the Democratic party in particular that urban blacks could tip the balance in these states.

The New Deal's response was extremely disappointing. In matters of personal discrimination, Roosevelt's circle responded with sensitivity and imagination. In 1939, when the world-famous contralto Marian Anderson was denied the use of Constitution Hall in Washington because she was black, Harold Ickes arranged for a dramatic concert at the steps of the Lincoln Memorial. Eleanor Roosevelt's warmth and kindness to people of all races made her a national institution. But in basic matters of civil and economic rights, the Roosevelt administration changed very little. It refused to take a strong stand against lynching. Without special protection for black wage earners, the New Deal's labor policies sometimes resulted in even fewer jobs for blacks. Its agricultural programs in the South were administered through white channels and did nothing to loosen the bonds of black peonage. In the Department of Agriculture, black county agents who complained about white favoritism were fired. Although blacks did benefit from national relief, they often stood last in line. The New Deal left blacks to fight for their share through local politics, where their rewards were meager.

With these frustrations in the background, A. Philip Randolph, the shrewd president of the Brotherhood of Sleeping Car Porters, introduced a new tactic in the fight for blacks rights. Early in 1941, as the economy was mobilizing in anticipation of war, Randolph rallied blacks throughout the nation for a mass march on Washington that would publicize America's racial discrimination around the world and possibly disrupt the early stages of war production. Randolph's price for canceling the march was President Roosevelt's intervention in behalf of black workers. Despite his irritation at Randolph's threat, Roosevelt on June 25, 1941, issued a precedent-setting executive order that banned discriminatory hiring "because of race, creed, color, or national origin," both within the national government and throughout its expanding scheme of war-related contracts. The executive order also established the Fair Employment Practices Committee (FEPC) to oversee these rules.

But it was the need for labor, not the weak FEPC, that expanded economic opportunities for blacks during the war. Both in the war industries and in the armed services, Jim Crow rules gradually weakened under the pressure of an increasingly severe manpower shortage. Meanwhile, racial tensions were mounting, especially over access to housing and public facilities in the swollen industrial areas of the large cities. During the summer of 1943, these emotions exploded from coast to coast in a series of violent racial encounters. The worst of the riots occurred in Detroit, a primary center of war production, where 500,000 newcomers, including 60,000 blacks, had been squeezed in since 1940. On a hot Sunday in June 1943, a fight between teenage whites and blacks ignited two days of guerrilla warfare and widespread looting. Twenty-five blacks and nine whites were killed, hundreds wounded, and millions of dollars in property lost. By then, some Democrats were openly worrying about "the Negro vote." Yet every national election between 1936 and 1944 seemed to verify the political wisdom of Democratic policies. If blacks were really discontented, why did they vote as heavily Democratic as any other urban group? Wait until after the depression, the Roosevelt administration had told its black critics. Wait until after the war, it told them in the early 1940s.

After the war, impatient black leaders insisted that the time had finally come. They had two reasons to feel some optimism. First, they were joined by a growing number of Northern whites who had committed themselves to a movement for equal black rights. This alliance had produced a string of FEPC laws in such states as New York, New Jersey, Massachusetts, and Connecticut, and now it

The migration of the blacks started from the fields and towns of the South and took them to the slums of the northern cities. Although still on the bottom rung, they at least found opportunities in the North to protest, as this call for a demonstration in the mid-forties illustrates. A civil rights movement was forming. *(Library of Congress, Chicago Historical Society.)*

was mobilizing for a national campaign against racial discrimination. Second, the elections of 1946, returning Republican majorities in several Northern states that had previously been Democratic, gave new force to the old argument of the NAACP. Black votes might indeed make the critical difference in a closely balanced national election. The shifting tides of party politics had invested a racial group with the same kind of importance that the economic groups in labor, agriculture, and business traditionally held. In the future, national campaigns would have to adapt to this distinctive political bloc.

Solving the Riddle of Economic Policy, 1948–1954

Although most Democratic leaders prayed that Truman would not run for President in 1948, he did. With little choice, less enthusiasm, and no hope, the national convention dutifully nominated him. The odds against Truman's success were prohibitive. Liberal Democrats judged him too conservative, and conservative Democrats judged him too liberal. Both considered him weak. Immediately after Truman was nominated, two additional parties appeared to attract the votes of dissident Democrats. The Progressive party, in the tradition of American parties with that name, depended on the reputation of one man, Henry Wallace. As former secretary of agriculture, Vice-President, and secretary of commerce under Roosevelt, he brought to the Progressives the prestige of the New Deal. And because Wallace's liberalism had flowered during the 1940s, he contributed his own fervent calls for world peace and domestic reform. In Birmingham, a new States' Rights Democratic party formed out of a general dislike for the New Deal legacy and a specific hostility to the regular party's appeal to the blacks. The "Dixiecrats" nominated Governor J. Strom Thurmond of South Carolina and dreamed of carrying the entire South. Above all, Truman faced a formidable Republican opponent in Governor Dewey of New York, who had done better against the indomitable Roosevelt in 1944 than any of the three Republican candidates preceding him. The only argument among the experts was the margin of Dewey's victory.

Truman made fools of the experts in 1948 because he responded so shrewdly

The Election of 1948

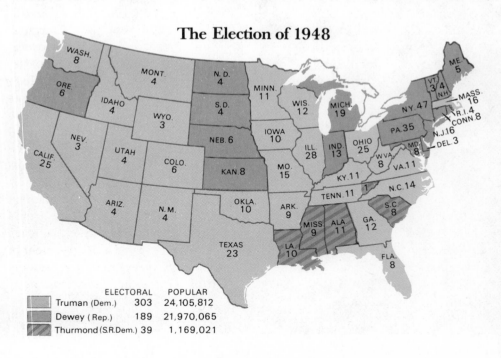

	ELECTORAL	POPULAR
Truman (Dem.)	303	24,105,812
Dewey (Rep.)	189	21,970,065
Thurmond (S.R.Dem.)	39	1,169,021

to the prevailing disorganization in political and economic affairs. In a nation of innumerable, scattered interest groups, no one knew how to provide effective leadership. Using a carefully devised strategy, the President shifted the blame for weak leadership to the Republican majority in the Eightieth Congress, which he scorned as the "Do-Nothing Congress." After the nominating conventions, he called Congress into special session and challenged the Republicans to enact their program. Of course little happened. The general paralysis in public policy appeared to be specifically a Republican malady.

Without a systematic program of his own, Truman compiled a long list of favors and promises. He reminded the unions that he had vetoed the Taft-Hartley Act of 1947 and that Republican votes had overridden him. He reminded business groups of tax benefits and government contracts. He promised parity to everything a farmer could produce. He recommended enlarging the TVA, increasing public housing, and broadening Social Security. He favored government aid to education. At the national convention in 1948, Mayor Hubert Humphrey of Minneapolis had led the successful drive for a firm platform on black rights, including a permanent FEPC and federal laws against lynching and poll taxes. Truman not only endorsed this platform; he took the cause to Harlem, where no presidential candidate had ever campaigned. Even more striking, the President embarked in 1948 on the long, difficult course of desegregating the armed forces.

Dewey took the high road, blandly promising a sound, sane administration. But the bantam rooster from Missouri, fighting his way through an arduous cross-country campaign, ran for President like a county politician. His remark to one audience told the meaning of the entire campaign: "Vote your own interests." In 1948, Truman's provincialism was sophisticated national politics. By November, Wallace, who increasingly seemed the candidate of the Communist party, had lost almost all support. Thurmond kept only the four Southern states which he had controlled in July. And Truman, with 303 electoral votes to Dewey's 189, scored the most stunning upset in modern politics.

Truman's victory demonstrated how many groups now looked to the national government for assistance. His second term revealed the constraints on the government in responding to them. Truman gave his many promises a name, the "Fair Deal," but few of them survived the next four years. Congress rejected federal aid to education, national health insurance, and a permanent FEPC. Although the President held to his purpose of desegregating the armed forces, he did not lead a general campaign for blacks' rights. In 1950, when the Supreme Court ruled against segregation in interstate commerce, neither Truman nor the Interstate Commerce Commission seriously tried to implement it. Most of Thurmond's Dixiecrats returned to the regular Democratic party without severe strain.

The laws that did pass minimized the national government's influence in guiding social change. The Housing Act of 1949, which renewed a program that had started during the New Deal, made Washington a financier, but not a planner, of public housing. Local governments and private groups decided who would get the benefits from public housing in their areas. Legislation subsidizing hospitals and medical research followed this same pattern. Appropriately, these bills carried the names of such conservative or moderate senators as Robert Taft of Ohio and Lister Hill of Alabama, for each law followed the safe tradition of a detached and indirect government support.

By the end of the 1940s, therefore, two basic conditions for a successful economic policy had been clarified. Such a policy had to meet the needs of innumerable small interest groups, and it had to remove the national government as far as possible from the affairs of these groups. The ideal means did lie immediately at hand. The government's fiscal powers expanded remarkably during the 1940s. Although national expenditures dropped with the end of the war, they still remained six or seven times greater than in the 1930s, and double the New Deal's percentage of the GNP. The wartime tax laws and their successors bound almost all Americans into the government's financial network. By 1946, the national debt had also risen sevenfold above the level of 1939, and funding this giant debt automatically made the government a dominant force in the nation's credit system. Moreover, the Federal Reserve's Board of Governors in Washington exercised an important general control over the nation's monetary affairs.

Adjusting the national budget, funding the national debt, regulating national monetary policy—here were precisely the mechanisms that the postwar economy could tolerate. The fiscal machinery operated just as effectively with any number of small interests. It did not require direct government interference with private groups or individuals. At the same time, it formed a broad national authority over the whole economy. If the economy faltered, the government could ease credit, lower taxes, and increase its deficit. If an economic boom threatened inflation, the government could tighten credit, raise taxes, and shrink the deficit.

Truman, however, was not the person to shape the government's fiscal powers into an acceptable public policy. First, neither the President nor his closest advisers felt free to manipulate government finance. Truman, much like Roosevelt before him, disliked budget deficits on principle and periodically led stern attacks on government spending. His narrow secretary of the Treasury, John Snyder, refused to consider the national debt as anything besides an unfortunate government expense. Second, Truman's prestige as a leader collapsed. The Korean War, beginning in June 1950, brought a sharp inflation and growing frustration over international affairs. In 1951 and 1952, evidence of corruption among Truman's associates and in the Justice Department sullied the administration's reputation. The President's own combative, unpredictable behavior added to the discontent. According to opinion polls in 1952, less than one in four Americans approved of his presidency.

Broad bipartisan approval for a policy of fiscal controls required a new President with a fresh start. The Republicans, looking toward the 1952 elections, vowed that this time they would be the ones to name the new President. The two important candidates for the Republican nomination were the brusque, efficient Robert Taft, son of a President and leader of his party in the Senate, and Dwight D. Eisenhower, hero of the Second World War and favorite of the party's moderates. Taft had established a long record of opposition to Washington bureaucracies and government interference with business. At the same time, as a practicing politician, he accepted the primary results of the New Deal and acknowledged a government responsibility to protect the economy. Eisenhower, on the other hand, had established his record in the army, where the general demonstrated an impressive talent for diplomacy as well as command.

DWIGHT D. EISENHOWER

In Ike, the Republicans finally found a winner. A war hero with such a smile was unbeatable in the fifties. (*Magnum.*)

Though Eisenhower said he favored a "balanced budget," the code words of conservative Republicanism, his attitude on domestic affairs was largely a mystery.

In a bitter contest, Eisenhower defeated Taft for the Republican nomination in 1952. Despite Taft's impressive strength among party regulars, the Republicans could not resist an immensely popular war hero. The Democrats had even more difficulty finding a candidate. A folksy campaign by the liberal Tennessee senator, Estes Kefauver, replete with handshakes, barbecues, and coonskin caps, gave him an early lead in a crowded field, but Truman refused his blessing. Instead, the Democrats finally drafted the circumspect governor of Illinois, Adlai E. Stevenson. That fall, against an eloquent but outclassed Stevenson, the general transformed his radiant smile, unaffected manner, and shining reputation into an overwhelming 442 electoral votes to Stevenson's 89.

By November, it was becoming clear that Eisenhower, even more than the conservative Taft, retained a nostalgic attachment to an earlier age. An army career had spared Eisenhower the kinds of policy adjustments that Taft had been making in the 1930s and 1940s, and the general had never abandoned the principles of the New Era. He prized individualism and visualized its operation through private groups—"political, industrial, church, school, labor," as he put it. "It has been a group effort, freely undertaken, that has produced the things of which we are so proud," Eisenhower announced, and he expected his administration to serve this "American way of life." "Free enterprise," "private initiative," and the dangers of "regimentation" peppered his conversations. He regarded TVA as "creeping Socialism." On election night, 1952, when Eisenhower finally broke loose from the happy mob, he placed his first telephone call to Herbert Hoover.

Eisenhower gathered so many wealthy opponents of the New Deal into his cabinet that it was popularly described as "nine millionaires and a plumber"— and the "plumber," Secretary of Labor Martin Durkin, soon resigned. The President and most of his cabinet shared a common purpose. They agreed that rich deposits of oil just off America's shore should be relinquished to the states, and in 1953, Congress passed such a law. They also proposed distributing federal revenues to the states. In cooperation with Secretary of the Treasury George Humphrey, the President set out to slash the national budget and minimize the government's influence in the economy. Eisenhower had no disagreement with the statement of Secretary of Defense Charles E. Wilson, former president of General Motors, that "what was good for our country was good for General Motors, and vice versa." Nor did he object when Secretary of Commerce Sinclair Weeks tried to fire the chief of the Bureau of Standards for reporting that a useless commercial battery additive, AD-2X, was useless. Secretary Weeks thought it should be allowed a "test of the marketplace."

Nevertheless, Eisenhower's attempt to revive the past quickly failed. Private groups welcomed favors, but almost none of them wanted responsibilities.

Bipartisan leagues of businessmen, union leaders, and professionals demanded more money and more assistance, not less, from Washington. The farm associations were horrified when Eisenhower recommended phasing out their subsidies. State and local governments recoiled at the thought of managing their own little economies.

Public confidence broke during a recession in 1953 and 1954. When Eisenhower responded with a firm assurance of no more New Deals and a willingness to wait for prosperity's return, he met a nationwide hue and cry. Reluctantly but realistically, the President reconsidered. By March 1954, the Eisenhower administration had committed itself to protecting the economy with fiscal countermeasures, and when the recession had passed, the President gave due credit to "the automatic workings of the fiscal system."

A stamp of approval from these impeccably conservative Republicans largely ended debate over the government's new approach to economic maintenance. By 1954, substantial majorities in Congress stood ready to support the economy by adjusting taxes and federal spending. The Federal Reserve Board and the Treasury Department both agreed that they should fund the national debt and regulate interest rates so that credit would expand in a weak economy and contract during inflation. In fact, the secretary of the Treasury now ranked with the secretaries of state and defense as government leaders. So many people accepted these fiscal techniques so fast because they seemed so neutral. They did not inhibit the stream of favor-seeking and favor-dispensing that flowed through Washington's busy offices. Liberals could still plan to expand government services and conservatives could still hope to preserve the government's detachment. For the Invisible Hand that had guided Hoover's cooperative commonwealth in the 1920s, the national government of the 1950s substituted the Barely Visible Hand of fiscal manipulation, and in the process it temporarily solved one of the knottiest problems in modern politics.

Local and National Politics Collide
1948–1954

As the government was unraveling the economic puzzle, the second fundamental problem in modern politics, national-local relations, grew more and more tangled. The prominence of black rights in the campaign of 1948 made race relations the most likely source of tension between national and local politics. But during his second term, Truman defused the issue by proceeding very cautiously on civil rights. Adlai Stevenson, the Democratic candidate in 1952, was more moderate on the subject than Truman. In addition, the NAACP was concentrating its primary energies on the Supreme Court, which attracted far less attention than the President or Congress. In *Smith* v. *Allwright* (1944), the Court had outlawed all-white primary elections in the South. Then in *Sweatt*

v. *Painter* (1950), it broadened an earlier ruling against segregated professional schools. The NAACP, behind its chief counsel, Thurgood Marshall, quietly prepared a legal assault on all segregated facilities.

Instead of black rights, it was anticommunism that disrupted the balance between national and local politics. A new wave of antiradicalism began to build after 1935, when enemies of the New Deal accused it of adopting communist ideas, and patriotic groups attacked the public schools for teaching radical doctrines. The House Committee on Un-American Activities, established in 1938, gave lurid publicity to the charge that communists dominated the new industrial unions. Congress captured the spirit of this vague antiradicalism in the Smith Act of 1940, which set criminal penalties for teaching or advocating violent revolution, or for belonging to an organization that did either. Despite the wartime alliance with the Soviet Union, anticommunist rhetoric remained fairly common during the early 1940s, and immediately after the war, both the House Un-American Activities Committee and numerous state antisubversive committees moved into action against an ever widening range of ideological dangers.

In 1947, the Truman administration declared international communism the enemy of the United States. Prominent Americans of both parties echoed the alarm. Between 1947 and 1949, communist governments spread across Eastern Europe and China, and in 1949 the Soviet Union exploded its first atomic bomb. Throughout the nation—in government, in the labor unions, in the communications industries, in public and private education—a variety of oaths and reviews screened those who were suspected of communist sympathies. The Justice Department, using both the Smith Act and the new Internal Security Act of 1950, prosecuted some members of the Communist party and forced the rest to disband. After a dramatic series of public hearings, Alger Hiss, once a respected official in the State Department, was convicted of perjury in January 1950 for denying that he had passed government information to a Soviet agent. In June came the shock of the Korean War, followed by arrests that eventually led to the execution of Julius and Ethel Rosenberg as Soviet spies. America seemed to be a monolith of anticommunism.

But inside this apparent consensus lay two profoundly different anticommunisms. One expressed the natural preoccupations of national politics. Appearing in strength around 1947, this anticommunism sought to defend the United States against an international challenge: the Soviet Union, the league of communist countries it headed, and the espionage system it directed. Abroad, this anticommunism tried to contain the power of the Soviet Union. At home, it concentrated above all on communists in government, because the enemy's agent at a crucial spot in the government could seriously damage the nation's defense. Hence, the revelations about Alger Hiss greatly aggravated these worries.

The other anticommunism expressed the fears and frustrations of locally oriented Americans. Their communism was a pervasive web of dangers that might appear in the guise of atheism, sexual freedoms, strange accents, civil rights, or whatever most threatened a particular group's sense of security. Although this anticommunism also spoke of national defense and international conflict, it equated these issues with threats to a locality's cultural and moral standards. The actual sources of danger might well be some of the leaders in national politics. Splintered, diffuse, and eruptive, this was the truly popular anticommunism.

These two anticommunisms, the one emphasizing power and the other emphasizing sin, were irreconcilable. From a national vantage point, the many state and local committees that in the name of anticommunism attacked textbooks and library catalogues and civil libertarians were part of an aimless witchhunt. What possible relevance could these matters have to an international contest with Soviet Communism? As one lawyer summarized the work of the Broyles Commission in Illinois, it "almost completely skirted . . . the operations of the Communist party in Illinois," and it failed totally "to uncover evidence of actual subversion within the state." But such committees in Illinois, California, New York, Maryland, and elsewhere were not looking for that kind of communism. As the Broyles Commission stated, "Liberalism" was its enemy, and the educational system, the commission's primary target, was an excellent place to begin the battle. Sophisticated "Eastern internationalists" in the State Department were an equally logical target. The State Department's opposition to the Soviet Union did not affect such judgments, for they relied on a local definition of communism.

In February 1950, a month after the conviction of Alger Hiss, an undistinguished first-term Republican senator from Wisconsin, Joseph McCarthy, elbowed forward to make anticommunism his personal crusade. For more than four years, this canny politician frightened government officials with charges of communist infiltration in their departments, staged melodramatic investigations of suspected enemy agents, exercised a powerful influence over government appointments, and won a large following. According to a national poll early in 1954, three out of five Americans with an opinion about McCarthy favored his activities.

McCarthy opened his campaign by claiming he had a list of authentic communists who were still employed by the State Department. Some thought he said 205. The senator later settled on 57. During Truman's administration, he continued a scattergun attack on the State Department and helped to make "communism" a noisy issue in the elections of 1952. After Eisenhower's inauguration, McCarthy broadened his anticommunist fire until he hit the army itself early in 1954. Few politicans cared to risk an encounter with the Wisconsin slugger, because McCarthy quickly acquired a reputation for defeating his political enemies at the polls. Eisenhower also refused to engage him, saying privately, "I will not get into the gutter with that guy."

SENATOR JOSEPH MCCARTHY UNDER A HALO OF
LIGHTS AND HIS AIDE ROY COHN AT THE ARMY-
MCCARTHY HEARINGS IN 1954

To millions of Americans in the early fifties, these
were fearless patriots who defended the nation
against an insidious network of communists. *(Wide
World.)*

The key to McCarthy's success was his ability to use the national issue of
communists in government as a source of strength in the Senate, and the local
issue of domestic subversion as a source of strength among millions of citizens.
McCarthy repeatedly claimed that the sole purpose of his investigations was
the exposure of communists in government, and after the Hiss conviction,
no one in Washington could lightly dismiss that possibility. As cool a head
as Senator Taft endorsed McCarthy's freewheeling search for spies. When
McCarthy failed to find any Soviet agents, however, he shifted his attack to the
books that his suspects had written, the reforms that they had supported, and
the people who had associated with them. McCarthy invariably identified communism as "Godless" and usually discovered its American disciples among the
wellborn, well educated, and well placed.

Despite the special attention that McCarthy attracted, others used even more
extreme language. In 1952, Senator William Jenner of Indiana declared, "I
charge that this country today is in the hands of a secret inner coterie which

is directed by agents of the Soviet Union." Democrats, including Truman, made important contributions to the harsh anticommunist climate. What set "McCarthyism" apart was its capacity to bring a rough-hewn version of local politics inside the national government. Violating the customary procedures of the Senate, McCarthy impugned the personal integrity of his critics and called them "gutless." The State Department, instead of selecting officials for their knowledge and skills, had to listen when it was told to "get rid of the alien-minded radicals and moral perverts."

Years of such confusion in the standards of government eventually became intolerable. When McCarthy attacked the upper echelons of the army in 1954, his growing opposition in Washington began to organize. The senator and his aides did not fare well in a televised series of "Army-McCarthy" hearings. In August 1954, the Senate created a select committee to review charges of senatorial misconduct against McCarthy, and that December, by a vote of 67 to 22, his colleagues condemned him. Without authority in the Senate, McCarthy faded into obscurity.

McCarthyism was simultaneously unique and representative. The special style of the Wisconsin senator and the special circumstances encouraging its success were passing matters. But the collision that McCarthyism caused between national and local politics would occur again and again in later years. By 1954, the centrality of the national government in American life was an indisputable fact. The scope and significance of its powers made it a magnet for almost every ambitious group in American society. Washington irresistibly attracted those issues that had once been hidden in the nation's neighborhoods and communities. If the national government could solve America's economic problems, why could it not also solve America's racial and cultural problems? As the national government fulfilled the New Deal's promise in economic management, therefore, it critically altered the New Deal's balance between national and local authority, and ushered in a new phase of modern politics.

Suggested Readings

William E. Leuchtenburg's *Franklin D. Roosevelt and the New Deal, 1932–1940* (1963) stands alone as a guide to the late years of the New Deal. However, Paul K. Conkin's essay, *The New Deal* (rev. ed., 1975), offers a shrewd assessment of its limitations. Joseph Alsop and Turner Catledge, *The 168 Days* (1938), reports the battle over the Supreme Court, and Paul L. Murphy, *The Constitution in Crisis Times, 1918–1969* (1972), reviews the relevant Court decisions. On the struggles of organized labor, the best survey is Irving L. Bernstein, *Turbulent Years* (1970). More information on the institutional warfare among the unions appears in Walter Galenson's detailed *The CIO Challenge to the AFL* (1960) and Philip Taft's sympathetic *The A. F. of L. from the Death of Gompers to the Merger* (1959). Sidney Fine, *Sit-Down* (1969), captures the drama of a crucial strike in the automobile industry, and Jerold S. Auerbach, *Labor and Liberty: The LaFollette Committee and the New Deal* (1966), examines one form of government assistance to the new unions. The bottom of the rural economy is explored in David E. Conrad, *The Forgotten Farmers: The Story of Sharecroppers in the New Deal* (1965), in Pete Daniel, *The Shadow of Slavery: Peonage in the South, 1901–1969* (1972), and most feelingly in James Agee and Walker Evans, *Let Us Now Praise Famous Men* (1941). Sidney Baldwin's *FSA* (1968) is an appealing history of the New Deal's major effort to help the rural poor. Barry Dean Karl, *Executive Reorganization and Reform in the New Deal* (1963), and Richard Polenberg, *Reorganizing Roosevelt's Government: The Controversy over Executive Reorganization, 1936–1939* (1966), discuss an important political struggle in the late thirties. These studies along with two other fine books— Richard S. Kirkendall's *Social Scientists and Farm Politics in the Age of Roosevelt* (1966) and James T. Patterson's *Congressional Conservatism and the New Deal* (1967)— help to explain the decline of reform.

The domestic side of the Second World War has received little attention from historians. Richard Polenberg, *War and Society: The United States, 1941–1945* (1972), provides a useful overview. Something of the relations between government and business is revealed in Bruce Catton, *The War Lords of Washington* (1948), and Donald M. Nelson, *Arsenal of Democracy: The Story of American War Production* (1946). Joel Seidman, *American Labor from Defense to Reconversion* (1953), deals primarily with government policy. On the other hand, William Henry Chafe, *The American Woman: Her Changing Social, Economic, and Political Roles, 1920–1970* (1972), includes a valuable discussion of women in the wartime economy. Roland A. Young, *Congressional Politics in the Second World War* (1956), reviews the legislative record. On specific laws, Davis R. B. Ross, *Preparing for Ulysses* (1969), explains the GI Bill, and Stephen K. Bailey, *Congress Makes a Law* (1957), analyzes the Full Employment Act.

A growing literature examines the place of racial minorities in modern America. Two surveys— John Hope Franklin, *From Slavery to Freedom* (3rd ed., 1969), and August Meier and Elliott M. Rudwick, *From Plantation to Ghetto* (rev. ed., 1970)— ably cover the years after 1920. Nathan Irvin Huggins, *Harlem Renaissance* (1971), minimizes the cultural significance of its subject. On the very different aspirations of Marcus Garvey and his followers, the best assessments are E. David Cronon, *Black Moses* (1955), and Thomas G. Vincent, *Black Power and the Garvey Movement* (1971). St. Clair Drake and Horace R. Cayton, *Black Metropolis* (2 vols., rev. ed., 1962), remains a valuable study of the Chicago ghetto. Raymond Wolters, *Negroes and the Great Depression* (1970), tells a grim story of the thirties, and Dan T. Carter's smoothly written *Scottsboro* (1969) recounts the most notorious abuse of justice in the South during that decade. The most important organizations serving blacks are discussed in Langston Hughes, *Fight for Freedom: The Story of the NAACP* (1962), and Nancy J. Weiss, *The National Urban League, 1910–1940* (1974). Also see Walter White's autobiography, *A Man Called White* (1948). Richard M. Dalfiume's *Desegregation of the United States Armed Forces* (1969), traces the most striking public gain for blacks during the Truman years. In *Black Bourgeoisie* (1957), E. Franklin Frazier offers a sharp analysis of relatively well-to-do blacks. Roger Daniels, *Concentration Camps, USA* (1971), is a brief study of the persecution of Japanese Americans during the Second World War; Jacobus ten Broek et al., *Prejudice, War and the Constitution* (1954), provides many of the details. Wilcomb E. Washburn, *The Indian in America* (1975), is a solid survey with an extensive bibliography.

Although there is no authoritative account of Harry Truman's administration, Cabell Phillips, *The Truman Presidency* (1966), is a reasonable introduction. Merle Miller, *Plain Speaking: An Oral Biography of Harry S. Truman* (1974), helps in understanding the President's quality of mind. A considerably more sophisticated study, Alonzo L. Hamby's *Beyond the New Deal: Harry S. Truman and American Liberalism* (1973), analyzes the place of the Truman administration in a modern democratic tradition. A good place to begin exploring the election of 1948 is Samuel Lubell, *The Future of American Politics* (1952). Susan M. Hartmann, *Truman and the 80th Congress* (1971), covers important background in Washington. The meaning of Henry A. Wallace's third-party candidacy is evaluated in Norman D. Markowitz, *The Rise and Fall of the People's Century* (1973), and detailed in Allen Yarnell, *Democrats and Progressives* (1974). V. O. Key, Jr., *Southern Politics in State and Nation* (1949), is a mine of information on its subject. On particular areas of public policy, William C. Berman, *The Politics of Civil Rights in the Truman Administration* (1970), and Richard O. Davies, *Housing Reform during the Truman Administration* (1966), are both careful studies. Allen J. Matusow's *Farm Policies and Politics in the Truman Years* (1967) makes a thorough assessment in its field. More critical appraisals of the President appear in Barton J. Bernstein, ed., *Politics and Policies of the Truman Administration* (1970), especially the essays by Bernstein himself. J. Joseph Huthmacher, ed., *The Truman Years* (1972), contains an excellent bibliography.

The best source on the growing Republican challenge to the Democrats is James T. Patterson's appreciative biography of Robert A. Taft, *Mr. Republican* (1972). Herbert S. Parmet, *Eisenhower and the American Crusades* (1972), is a good general account of the Eisenhower presidency, and Gary W. Reichard, *The Reaffirmation of Republicanism* (1975), contains a fuller examination of Eisenhower's early years in office. *The Ordeal of Power* (1963), a thoughtful appraisal of Eisenhower's presidency by Emmet John Hughes, is also most valuable on the early years. Additional material appears in Robert J. Donovan's chatty *Eisenhower: The Inside Story* (1956) and Sherman Adams's *Firsthand Report* (1961), the memoir of Eisenhower's chief domestic aide. The momentous changes in the government's fiscal powers and policies are discussed in Herbert Stein, *The Fiscal Revolution in America* (1969). For a dissent from the new fiscal orthodoxy, see Milton Friedman and Anna J. Schwartz, *A Monetary History of the United States, 1867–1960* (1963).

No domestic subject since the New Deal has attracted such scholarly attention as the anticommunist issue after the Second World War. Robert Griffith and Athan Theoharis, eds., *The Specter: Original Essays on the Cold War and the Origins of McCarthyism* (1974), Earl Latham, *The Communist Controversy in Washington* (1966), and Walter Gellhorn, ed., *The States and Subversion* (1952), suggest the wide range of topics and interests that were involved. Athan Theoharis, *Seeds of Repression* (1971), and Richard M. Freeland, *The Truman Doctrine and the Origins of McCarthyism* (1972), place a heavy responsibility for the rise of popular anticommunism on the Truman administration, and Alan D. Harper, *The Politics of Loyalty: The White House and the Communist Issue, 1946–1952* (1969), significantly tempers that judgment. Robert Griffith, *The Politics of Fear* (1970), analyzes McCarthy's sources of power in the Senate. In *The Intellectuals and McCarthy* (1967), Michael Paul Rogin blames conservative academicians for inflating the record of McCarthy's popular appeal. On the most sensational espionage cases, see Walter and Miriam Schneir, *Invitation to an Inquest* (1965), which explores the Rosenberg case, and Allen Weinstein, *Perjury! The Hiss-Chambers Conflict* (1977).

32

Modern Culture

As the economy was modernizing, so were the everyday lives and hopes and worries of countless Americans. A national consumer market, a revolution in transportation, and new means of mass communication guaranteed that almost everyone would feel the effects of this modernizing process. But the response to it varied widely. From the most positive of these responses came a set of values that gave Americans a new understanding of their lives and a new morality for guiding behavior. The old-fashioned ways, however, refused to capitulate. Adjusting to survive in the twentieth century, America's traditional values continued to fight for a place in the modern era. The most consistent common denominator between these competing sets of values was concern for the individual. Where in an organized, mechanized modern society did the individual fit? This disturbing question proved so difficult to manage that a series of clear answers did not develop until midcentury.

The Consumer Paradise

During the 1920s, a cornucopia of consumer delights spread before the nation. Abandoning the time-honored rules to buy cautiously, fear debt, and save each small surplus, Americans made consumer credit a national necessity, and it soon became available through a great variety of convenient, local outlets.

To one visitor from abroad, the entire nation was a "rapturous whirl of making and spending."

The most prized of the consumer treasures was the automobile. By 1920, new techniques of automobile production and heavy investments in plant equipment had prepared the way for mass marketing, and by the end of the decade, the number of registered cars almost equaled the number of families. For innumerable Americans, it was a case of love at first sight. Talk about the car, care of the car, accessories for the car occupied them as much as using the car. It emancipated people from a set of channels fixed by their homes, neighborhood shops, and jobs. Once the front porch had been the family gathering place on a pleasant evening. Now families piled into the car, and the new houses no longer had front porches. When a country housewife was asked why her family had a car but not a bathtub, she replied, "Bathtub? You can't go to town in a bathtub!" Indeed, a whole range of new freedoms came with the car. One horrified old-timer called it a "House of Prostitution on wheels."

A second group of consumer goods relied on the spread of electricity into family dwellings. The Midwestern utilities magnate Samuel Insull pioneered the revolutionary process of selling a metered electrical service to households, and other companies soon recognized the genius of his scheme. Though Insull's unwieldy empire of utility companies collapsed after the Crash of 1929, his influence lived on in millions of American homes. By the end of the twenties, two out of three households had electricity, in contrast to one out of five before the war. By 1940, with help from the New Deal's Rural Electrification Administration (REA), the proportion had risen to four out of five households.

Into the new electrical outlets, Americans plugged lamps, refrigerators, washing machines, and toasters, each a special object of joy and discussion during the twenties. Above all, electricity brought the radio. In November 1920, the crackling sounds of America's first radio station, KDKA at East Pittsburgh, opened a modern era of personal mass communication. By 1923, over 500 stations with much improved equipment were broadcasting to the nation. Most homes with electricity had radio sets. Other Americans gathered to listen at their local bars or clubhouses. While the car was dispersing Americans in search of their individual pleasures, the radio was bringing them back home on schedule to catch their favorite shows.

Consumer services as well as consumer goods poured from the cornucopia of the 1920s. Personal expenditures for recreation more than doubled between 1919 and 1929. Across an entire range of public entertainment—theatres, sports, amusement houses—the twenties were bonanza years, in part because the family car rapidly broadened the scope of potential customers. The lord of the entertainment world was a relative newcomer, motion pictures, which during the twenties grew from a scattering of nickelodeon shows and occasional full-length features to a systematized $2 billion industry with a steady flow of films and a dazzling array of stars. Not only did "movie houses" appear in

ROADSIDE BILLBOARDS, 1929

Sexual and racial stereotypes
abounded in standardized ads for
the national consumer market.
*(State Historical Society of
Wisconsin)*

almost every town and neighborhood in the nation; their ornate grandeur
marked them as centers of community life. By 1929, the average weekly attendance at these palaces of culture exceeded 80 million.

The pattern of modern consumerism, once set, did not appreciably change
during the next twenty years. A shortage of money in the thirties, and a shortage of material in the early forties, slowed the consumers' purchases without
significantly altering their preferences. Attendance at the movies and other
kinds of public entertainment dropped slightly in the 1930s but quickly returned to its earlier level in the following decade. At the beginning of the depression, most Americans clung tenaciously to their old cars. Only in the late
thirties did they again begin to purchase new ones in quantity. Then after the
war temporarily halted automobile production, Americans rushed to buy an
unprecedented number of new cars during the late forties. The sale of most
household appliances followed a similar curve. The number of radio sets, however, multiplied throughout the depression, and during the thirties and early
forties, the stars of radio enjoyed their golden age of popularity.

In its broad effects, modern consumerism nationalized America's sounds
and sights and experiences. Millions heard the same broadcasts, watched the
same movies, and bought the same kinds of cars. Moreover, the few corporations that dominated the major consumer industries increasingly homogenized
the output. In radio, the formation of the National Broadcasting Company in
1926 and the Columbia Broadcasting System in 1927 superimposed network
programming over a previously decentralized industry. The number of local

radio stations actually declined after 1927. From a handful of gigantic studios such as Warner Brothers and Metro-Goldwyn-Mayer came the standardized films that were characteristically "Hollywood" productions. Ford, General Motors, and Chrysler, which made 83 percent of America's automobiles by 1930, were soon synchronizing industrywide shifts in car styling. Along with a rapid expansion of chain stores and a continuing consolidation of newspaper owner-ship, these strong oligopolistic trends were systematizing everything in the con-sumer market from nuts to news. A flourishing industry of advertising made its friendly radio voices a part of American family life, and they transformed such nationally distributed products as Campbell soups and Pepsodent toothpaste into household words.

Modern Values

Among the images coming out of these national centers of communication was a new model for the good life. As the modern economy developed, it relied more and more heavily on the efficient fulfillment of specialized tasks. Some specialties, including those in such business-related occupations as management, banking, merchandising, and advertising and such professions as law, medicine, engineering, and economics, became so important to the economy that success in any of these careers was itself the source of a person's prestige in modern America. In the 1920s, perhaps 3 million Americans had the skills, or the success, to claim membership in these exalted ranks. In addition, as the nation's population grew from 106,466,000 to 123,077,000, or about 15 percent, during the twenties, the number of white collar workers rose 40 percent to over 14 million. Many of these white collar workers also thought of themselves as part of a specialized economic system.

The greater the emphasis on occupational success, the less people felt bound by traditional rules of behavior. What happened away from work increasingly belonged to a separate realm of individual discretion. From this crucial division of occupational life from private life came a new, often exhilarating freedom to enter the consumer market and simply enjoy oneself. During leisure hours, clothes became a matter of personal taste rather than an expression of solid character. The styles of the 1920s, appropriate to their modern meaning, emphasized freedom: the arrival of new colors and patterns for men, the departure of corsets and hobbling long skirts for women. Both men and women now smoked casually in public, and cigarette sales climbed 250 percent during the decade. The symbol of the exciting new freedom was the "Flapper." With hair bobbed, face painted, and cigarette in hand, she airily waved goodbye to yesterday's rules. Her flattened breasts, loose-fitting clothes, and short skirt gave her the appearance of a modern Peter Pan, seizing the pleasure of the moment in the spirit of eternal youth.

Nothing more clearly announced a new attitude toward private freedom than the changing responses of successful Americans to Prohibition. In 1920, most national spokesmen dutifully endorsed the Eighteenth Amendment. By 1924, however, such prominent citizens as the industrialist Pierre du Pont, the dean of the settlement workers Graham Taylor, and the philanthropist John D. Rockefeller, Jr., were leading a widespread defection from the cause. In 1926, an insignificant group, the Association against the Prohibition Amendment, was reorganized with a board of directors that read like a roster of the national elite. Soon a great many city and state organizations were arguing the case for repeal before chambers of commerce, bar associations, and other professional groups. By 1932, about three-fourths of the readers of *Literary Digest*, a rough index to the opinion of successful Americans, favored repeal of Prohibition.

The reasoning of these prominent citizens was simple. By making illegal an act that millions refused to consider wrong, Prohibition artificially created a new class of criminals, spread disrespect for the law, and then increased taxes to pay for the enforcement. Repeal of the Eighteenth Amendment would return the authority over liquor to state and local governments, where it be-

A FLAPPER AND A SPORT, SOME BOOZE, A FLIVVER, AND A SMOKE

For successfu Americans, the sins of the nineteenth century became the pleasures of the twentieth. *(Culver Pictures, Inc)*

NEW YEAR'S NUMBER!

JANUARY 3, 1925

PRICE 15 CENTS

JUDGE

"THEY'RE OFF!"

longed. On the surface, it was a weak argument. Many other unpopular laws increased the crime rate and were far more expensive to police. Because the enforcement of Prohibition was always haphazard, its costs had little effect on taxes. In other areas, the opponents of Prohibition welcomed the expansion of national authority over state and local powers. Actually, their entire case depended on a single assumption. It simply did not matter very much if people drank. Prohibition, in Pierre du Pont's phrase, was "a nuisance and menace"— or, more accurately, a menace *because* it was merely a nuisance. In a proper state of affairs, using alcohol would be an individual choice.

As the areas of private discretion expanded, leisure in general came to have a new meaning. Free time acquired a therapeutic purpose. Leisure activities no longer had to be justified as morally beneficial but simply as a salutary way for individuals to release their tensions and return refreshed to their jobs. The best expression of the new meaning for leisure was the annual vacation, a segregated bloc of time specifically for recuperation. Once the prerogative of a very small, prosperous minority, the annual vacation became widely accepted during the twenties. Early in the 1920s, according to a study by the sociologists Robert and Helen Lynd, most white-collar employees in Muncie, Indiana, assumed for the first time in their lives that they had a right to an annual vacation, and many received one with pay. As a rule, the movement to conserve natural resources fared poorly during the 1920s, but the notable exception was an enlargement in the National Park Service. Parks were now a valuable public facility, where the nation's city dwellers could turn once a year for revitalization.

A higher premium on personal freedom meant a lower premium on sin. Although church membership increased a striking 31 percent between 1916 and 1926, so did the emphasis in white-collar congregations on a soothing, largely undemanding religion that stressed good human relations rather than sin and salvation. Not every liberal Protestant welcomed Bruce Barton's best-selling *The Man Nobody Knows* (1925), which transformed Jesus into a vigorous executive who had taken "twelve men from the bottom ranks of business and forged them into an organization that conquered the world." Nevertheless, few liberal Protestants during the twenties expressed much concern of any kind for theological details or even denominational distinctions. To many of them, Catholicism now seemed less an evil religion than an odd but purely private choice. The anti-Catholic furor surrounding Al Smith's presidential campaign in 1928 simply makes no sense from a modern Protestant perspective.

Nor did the long-standing association between sex and sin. During the twenties, a variety of psychologists, including the American disciples of Sigmund Freud, told Americans to consider sex a human need to fulfill: the more complete the satisfaction, the healthier the individual. Repression and guilt only warped the personality. Public displays of affection no longer implied loose morals. Even premarital sex was a legitimate subject for discussion. Margaret

Sanger, America's pioneer advocate of birth control who had once been a pariah in respectable circles, now won the approval and even the financial support of many well-to-do Americans. Though too much "petting" remained a parental worry and any hint of "free love" was sharply condemned, sex emerged in the twenties as a subject for rational examination instead of moral taboo.

The new values covering recreation, religion, and sex found their strongest support in metropolitan areas. During the 1920s, cities of 100,000 or over grew more than twice as fast as the population as a whole. White-collar workers, who were increasing in numbers at about the same rate, congregated in and around these cities and reinforced one another's values. An urban way of life became their standard of America's progress, and they used it to judge the rest of the nation. Instead of praising the little red schoolhouses in the countryside, urban educators recommended their consolidation to lower costs and modernize instruction. Efficiency experts wrote despairingly about the incompetence of county governments. The farther that life was removed from the styles of the big city, the less attractive it appeared. The descriptions of the small town as a prison in Sherwood Anderson's *Winesburg, Ohio* (1919) and Sinclair Lewis's *Main Street* (1920) met a warm reception from urban readers.

The new urban standard was particularly hard in its judgment of the South. In 1925, Henry L. Mencken, the critic, essayist, and high priest of the new urban culture, visited Dayton, Tennessee to report on the trial of a high school biology instructor, John Scopes, who had broken a state law by teaching Darwin's theory of evolution. Because the trial pitted the famous criminal lawyer Clarence Darrow against William Jennings Bryan, the aging champion of evangelical Protestanism, it became a national spectacle. An urban audience, unable to comprehend why anyone would legislate against science, treated the Scopes trial like a carnival of freaks. As Mencken described the "anthropoid rabble" of Tennessee protecting themselves "from whatever knowledge violated their superstitions" and climaxing an outdoor religious revival with a sex orgy, the modern caricature of the South was taking shape. Sharecropping, soil leaching, and unmechanized farming retarded Southern agriculture. A crude racism appeared to dominate its society, and a narrow Protestant theology seemed to tyrannize its spirit. Both support for Prohibition and opposition to Al Smith thrived there. When Erskine Caldwell's *Tobacco Road* appeared in 1932, many successful Americans were already prepared to accept this picture of a stunted life on Georgia's barren soil as the true South.

Modern Families and Careers

Modern values also reshaped the role of the family in American life. In the white-collar world around the cities, men no longer relied heavily on the family to maintain their reputations. Occupations were their primary sources of prestige, and they brought their reputations home from their offices. Extramarital sex, especially in the large cities, became increasingly acceptable. Even in Sinclair Lewis's small city of "Zenith," the hero of *Babbitt* (1922) could have a brief affair without damaging his career. Wives, on their part, were expected to counter their husbands' drift away from the family. Advertisements promised miraculous results from a better dinner, a cleaner house, or any number of enticing domestic surprise. Advice columns revealed how to soothe a tense, weary man at the end of the workday. Accompanying the new explicitness about sex, a thriving cosmetics industry encouraged wives to enhance their charms as a means of holding husbands within the home.

Unlike the nineteenth-century wife, who had been solemnly charged with preserving society's morals, her modern counterpart had no such high responsibilities. And in a system of values that honored expertise, her talents as a homemaker could never compete with the claims of business and the professions. As women's traditional sphere shrank, however, other opportunities beckoned. The residential areas that men from their downtown offices called "bedroom towns" became uniquely female domains, where women moved and talked and acted much as they chose during the daytime hours. With radically less

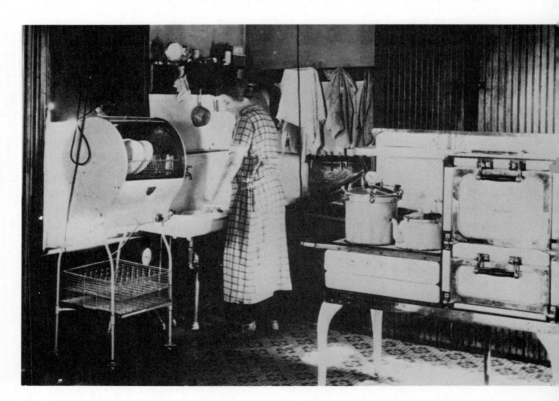

The life of the modern woman mixed tradition with change. She remained chief cook and bottle washer, but new appliances dramatically altered her kitchen. She was still responsible for rearing the children, but she had greater control over the number of children. Mass media fed her with fantasies about love and beauty, but mass transportation expanded her freedom of movement and activities. *(State Historical Society of Wisconsin, Culver Pictures, Inc.)*

Margaret Sanger dares to tell the truth about Birth Control

For centuries the world has played a game of "hush" about the one most important fact of marriage. Even to-day tens of thousands of women are doomed to a life of hopeless, helpless drudgery—and their children are doomed to privation and neglect because the mother simply cannot give so many of them the proper care or support.

Words alone cannot tell the terrible sacrifice in wasted bodies and blasted lives that has been exacted from women every year. Words alone cannot express the untold suffering tens of thousands

"Why is it," Mrs. Sanger asks, "that the women of Australia, New Zealand, Holland, France, and many other nations are permitted to know the truths that can save them from this terrible suffering while the women of America must still endure the agonies to which they are [. . .] Margaret Sanger [. . .] he intelligence [. . .] to deny to [. . .] h has brought [. . .] s, and life it- [. . .] other nations. [. . .] the storms of

birth control. It is a startling revelation of a new

this daring and heroic author points out that women who cannot afford to have more than one or two children, should not do so. It is a crime to herself, a crime to her children, a crime to society.

A Priceless Possession

Now Margaret Sanger's message to all women, contained in "Woman and the New Race," is made available to the public. A special edition of this vital book has been published in response to the overwhelming demand. Order your copy of this wonderful book at once, at the special edition price of only $2. Then if after reading it you do not treasure it as a priceless possession return it to us and your money will be refunded.

It is not even necessary to send a penny now. Just the coupon will bring your copy of "Woman and the New Race." It is bound in handsome, durable gray cloth, printed in clear readable type on good quality book paper and contains 286 pages, sent to you in a plain wrapper.

When the book is delivered at your home, pay the postman the special low price of $2 plus the few cents postage But mail the coupon at once. Tear it off before you turn this page.

Partial List of Contents

*Woman's Error and Her Debt
Cries of Despair
*When Should a Woman Avoid Having Children
Two Classes of Women
Birth Control—a Parent's Problem or Woman's
*Continence — Is it Practical or Desirable
Women and the New Morality
*Are Preventive Means Certain
Legislating Women's Morals
*Contraceptives or Abortion

[. . .] die. Ignorance on this all-important subject has put me where I am."

Truth Publishing Company

Is the Husband or Wife to Blame?

surveillance than their grandmothers had experienced, they purchased the bulk of the family's consumer goods, and consequently their preferences had a powerful influence on the local consumer market.

Modern mothers and fathers reared their children to enter the same kind of occupationally oriented world in which they lived. The home, it was assumed, could provide very little of the knowledge that children would later need to make their way in twentieth-century society. Modern Americans looked outside the home for expert advice on almost every subject, from maintaining the family car to balancing the family budget. With the founding of *Reader's Digest* in 1922 and *Time* in 1923, they even had convenient, expert summaries of the latest news and views about their contemporary world. Hence, as parents, they were expected to be intermediaries between their children and an array of specialists who did know about their children's psyches, health and education.

Because parents had a relatively small part in equipping their children for successful adult careers, they had to prepare their sons and daughters to accept directions from outside the home. The preparations began early. Parents in the twenties and thirties were warned against the dangers of an excessive emotional attachment to their children or a domineering authority over them. Mothers heard about the perils of the Oedipus complex. Manuals on child care gave specific instructions on cuddling and comforting. Playwrights such as Sidney Howard and Tennessee Williams made the clutching, overbearing mother a central character in the American theater. In the movies of the 1930s and 1940s, such actors as Lewis Stone and Spencer Tracy modeled the modern role of the father: a superficially gruff, basically agreeable man who footed the bills, fussed with his pride, and eventually allowed the children to have their way.

The critical phase in the children's preparation for adulthood occurred during adolescence. Beginning in the 1920s, a well-developed and widely publicized youth culture provided adolescents with an acceptable means of rebelling against their parents and declaring themselves ready for the occupational world. Although the details varied decade by decade, the essentials remained the same. Along some sensitive frontier of values — sex during the 1920s, for example, or social reform during the 1930s — adolescents stepped just across the adult boundary and derided their lagging parents. When parents objected, their children accused them of hypocrisy or irrelevance. To divide the ages further, adolescents adopted their own special jargon, and they made very effective uses of dance and dress. Unlike the square dances and waltzes of the nineteenth century that had combined the generations, the Charleston in the 1920s and jitterbugging in the 1930s and 1940s required such limber joints that older people risked catastrophe if they tried it. Young men chose sufficiently outlandish clothes to make father look foolish in them. Young women chose sufficiently revealing ones to contrast their firm flesh with mother's signs of age. Modern parents not only subsidized the youth culture; they were told to worry if their children did not fully participate.

At each stage in child rearing, schools exercised a greater and greater influence. During the twenties and thirties, the public school system underwent a considerable expansion and adaptation. The elementary grades, which changed the least, increasingly served as feeders into the high schools, now important institutions in their own right. Enrollment in secondary schools doubled during the 1920s, and then rose another 50 percent during the 1930s. In 1920, one-sixth of America's adult population had high school diplomas; in 1940, one-half held them. Indeed, secondary education became so significant to white-collar families that some of them chose a place to live on the basis of the local high school's reputation. The Winnetka System under Carleton Washburne, for example, made that Illinois community nationally famous.

What modern families sought in a school system was a combination of instruction in the basic skills and socialization for modern America. The current trends in "progressive" education favored precisely this combination. The modern high school tried to prepare young minds that, as one committee of educational experts stated in 1929, "will be suited to the changing situations" of modern society. Even ethics "differed in different occupations," the journalist Lincoln Steffens noted in 1931. "And an ethical practitioner formed and fitted into one occupation . . . is apt to be disqualified thereby for another occupation, morally as well as technically." Therefore, the more progressive high schools taught

THE JUKEBOX CULTURE AROUND 1940

Modern adolescents used music and dance to create their own world apart from prying adults. (*Library of Congress.*)

general methods of thinking and a general open-mindedness rather than a specific body of truths and moral absolutes.

If young people could make a successful adjustment in high school, it was assumed, they would be prepared for a happy, rewarding life in modern America. Aptitude tests and counseling centers, both suddenly prominent in the high schools of the 1920s, guided them into the proper occupational areas, or for an increasing number, to college for further specialization. Those who then entered the best white-collar occupations had the satisfaction of discovering that they had acquired a superior mental power. According to a variety of publicists during the twenties, individuals who mastered a specialty in business or the professions developed a general capacity for rational thought that placed them in a select minority. By implication, the majority of Americans, in Mencken's blunt but revealing term, were "boobs," a highly suggestive public that could be manipulated by a foresighted few.

Along with this belief came a popular psychology called behaviorism, which contained a simple, persuasive formula for mass manipulation. As the psychologist John B. Watson explained the human personality, a clear stimulus produced in the individual a predictable response, and the regular repetition of such stimuli established a habit that with occasional reinforcement made the response self-generating. With the right message and the right means of communication, therefore, a rational minority who understood this process could influence an almost limitless number of people.

During the 1920s, behaviorism became an article of faith among successful Americans and gave many of them extraordinary confidence in their powers of social control. A number of otherwise routine white-collar jobs, particularly selling, now seemed fraught with significance. The insights into mass manipulation even offered a fresh view of history. "Galileo failed because he was an investigator and not a salesman," one psychologist revealed in 1925. "Consequently, he could not get his goods marketed . . . . His competitors, Aristotle, Moses, and the church fathers, had monopolized the market, and their stockholders would not let him do business." Advertising developed into an especially honored field. A new group of experts in personnel management also used the same basic formula of mass manipulation to guarantee employers a loyal and productive work force.

Successful Americans of many different persuasions accepted this assumption of a two-tiered society: a minority of manipulators and a mass to be manipulated. Neither liberal nor conservative, it simply came with America's modern values. What Republican businessmen in the 1920s applied to the sale of their goods, New Dealers in the 1930s applied to the sale of their reforms. In return for a sincere interest in the public welfare, the Roosevelt administration expected popular support, not popular demands. By the Second World War, these habits of modern leadership were so ingrained that businessmen and reformers alike automatically went about the tasks of "selling" the war, "conditioning" the public for bad news from the battlefront, and experimenting with better ways to improve American "morale."

Response of the Traditionalists

From the lower of these two tiers, modern America looked quite different. Most people's jobs did not belong in the specialized upper ranks of the economy and therefore brought very little national prestige. Moreover, mass communication made it impossible to ignore the disparity between their own lives and the lives of successful Americans. Millions of Americans with unskilled or routine jobs did hope that they, or their children, would eventually rise on the occupational ladder. Yet almost all of them found the modern values unacceptable to some degree. They chose instead to follow a long American tradition and live by local values. In a rural community or a city neighborhood, they judged one another by family reputations, church preferences, work habits, and a variety of other personal characteristics that established a standard of prestige and a scale of morality specifically designed for their own locality.

The pattern of resistance to the modern ways varied a great deal from place to place and even from individual to individual. During the twenties and thirties, some local pockets of opposition, particularly in the countryside, confronted the new values directly and repudiated them wholesale. Condemning the new liberalism in dressing, drinking, dancing, smoking, and sex, they refused to consider such behavior a matter of private choice and set firm rules against the modern hedonism. The most common agency of moral discipline was the church. As membership in the Protestant churches expanded, a large majority continued to belong to the evangelical denominations. Many Baptist and Methodist congregations, with a history of serious concern about their members' public behavior, banned the new ways as sins. Smaller bodies of Lutherans and Seventh-Day Adventists were even stricter about such practices as dancing and smoking. From evangelical Protestantism came the political pressure behind Tennessee's antievolutionary law of 1925, which precipitated the famous Scopes trial. In other Southern states as well, including Texas and Mississippi, state officials cooperated in keeping Darwin's theories out of the classroom. In the northern cities, the Catholic church often set its considerable weight against modern values, especially those on sex. Like the public schools in areas where evangelical Protestantism predominated, the Catholic parochial system carefully instructed its pupils in religious morality. According to nationwide studies in the late 1920s and 1930s, a majority of American schoolchildren were still receiving this kind of traditional, moral education.

"CHURCH SUPPER," *painting by James B. Turnball*

In reaction to modern values, millions of Americans
idealized an older, simpler society that was rooted in the
family, the church, and the community. *(Courtesy of
Mr. & Mrs. Carroll Martin.)*

Nevertheless, only a minority of Americans in a few localities totally rejected the new ways. A compromise between modern and traditional values was much more common. Almost all Americans wanted some share in the new culture, but a great many of them hoped to participate without feeling that it would corrupt them. At the beginning of the twenties, for example, motion pictures were exploiting sex so avidly that a majority of state legislatures threatened to censor them. In 1922, the movie industry responded with the Hays Office, Hollywood's center for self-censorship, which designated what parts of the female anatomy had to be covered, what language was taboo, and how justice must triumph in the end. These moral formulas created just the right aura of respectability. Without basically altering the movies, they appeased the critics and assured a mass audience.

Other mass media also enhanced their popularity by catering to traditional values. Magazines and newspapers told countless stories of how the time-honored virtues of honesty, thrift, and perseverance had enabled ordinary people to weather their troubles and win in the end. To vast daytime audiences, such radio soap operas as *Ma Perkins' Family* and *Just Plain Bill* recounted the trials and tribulations of familiar, local individuals who preserved their simple goodness under the most extraordinary hardships. Norman Rockwell's famous covers for the *Saturday Evening Post,* depicting the comforts of life in the family and the small town, ennobled many of the same traditional values.

In a traditional local setting, trusting other people required a feeling of intimacy with them. Sunday supplements responded to this need with articles on the private lives and endearing habits of prominent Americans, and radio stations featured informal, personal interviews with a variety of otherwise anonymous leaders. The popularity of both Franklin and Eleanor Roosevelt benefited immeasurably from the warm, friendly personalities they communicated to a traditionalist public. The President's battle with polio, his hobbies, and his anecdotes, all gave indispensably human qualities to the nation's leader. Far more than any other President's wife, Eleanor Roosevelt traveled throughout America to express her own personal concern for the needs of its citizens. Her syndicated newspaper column, *My Day,* an unpretentious account of her thoughts and affairs, significantly lessened the distance between the nation's First Lady and a large, attentive body of readers.

Perhaps the most important need of those Americans whose jobs neither carried much prestige nor paid very well was some evidence that they could still succeed without abandoning their values. During the 1920s, an abundance of publicity assured them that the avenue upward was not only broad but especially well-traveled by individuals of solid character and good habits. Salesmanship offered a particularly enticing route because it held out the prospect of success without a highly specialized training. Throughout the twenties, a popular passion for the salesman's skills was fed by numerous manuals, lectures, and correspondence courses that promised to reveal the secrets of the art to any ambitious American. The example of certain businessmen encouraged hopes of an even more dramatic rise to riches. If immigrants such as the utilities magnate Samuel Insull, the banking king A. P. Giannini, and the movie mogul Samuel Goldwyn could make it to the top, American society must still be rewarding the traditional virtues of hard work and high ambition.

No one's reputation benefited more grandly from such reasoning than Henry Ford's. Here was a country boy who had turned a mechanical genius and dogged persistence into a fabulous fortune and international fame. He had mastered the modern economy so thoroughly that everyone came to him to learn the best techniques of mass production and distribution. Yet he had never capitulated to the slick ways around him. He attacked the evils of Wall Street, belittled the significance of higher education, and demanded strict moral standards from his workers. He could even give new values the sound of old truths: "One day some one brought to us a slogan which read: 'Buy a Ford and Save the Difference.' I crossed out the 'save' and inserted 'spend'—'Buy a Ford and Spend the Difference.' It is the wiser thing to do. Society lives by circulation, and not by congestion."

The depression seriously damaged this American dream. After 1929, Ford's popularity declined drastically, and no businessman ever replaced him. Not even the prosperous 1940s revived the vision of a simple rise from humble origins to the pinnacle of the corporate system. A great many Americans still retained their commitment to the old-fashioned virtues. During the 1930s, for example, the child actress Shirley Temple became the movie industry's most valuable property for projecting an image of triumphant innocence amidst widespread corruption—both the imaginary corruption of the screen play and the publicized corruption of life in Hollywood. But the avenues to fame and fortune were increasingly obscure. Dale Carnegie's phenomenally popular *How to Win Friends and Influence People* (1936), the counterpart for the 1930s of the salesmen's manuals of the 1920s, promised wonders for its readers if they would only master an elementary set of rules. Yet unlike the literature of salesmanship, Carnegie's book was quite vague about where the ambitious but poor individual should look for his success. A critical element of hope was dwindling in the lives of millions of Americans.

Dangers to the Individual

The dimming prospects for individual success were only one part of a large, complicated problem that disturbed the followers of modern and traditional ways alike. How could individuals in any walk of life preserve their integrity in a nationalized, systematized society? Here, in a general sense, was a problem for all modern America. Signs of a new concern for the individual were already appearing before 1920. The American Civil Liberties Union, which had originated as an emergency committee to defend dissenters during the First World

War, remained after the war as a permanent center to protect the individual's freedom of speech, religion, assembly, and press under the First Amendment. Even before the war, America's most creative poets, Ezra Pound and T. S. Eliot, had started a trek to Europe of young writers and artists who felt stifled by American culture. A Lost Generation, the writer Gertrude Stein called these intellectual exiles. In 1920, America's greatest playwright, Eugene O'Neill, won the first of four Pulitzer Prizes for *Beyond the Horizon*, launching his long, agonizing exploration into the power of irrational forces over the individual's fate. From such scattered beginnings developed a broader and broader survey of the dangers for the individual in modern society.

The first danger to receive serious attention was the dehumanizing quality of modern society's organization. During the 1920s, the best of the so-called antiwar novels—John Dos Passos's *The Three Soldiers* (1921), e. e. cummings's *The Enormous Room* (1922), and Ernest Hemingway's *A Farewell to Arms* (1929)— said relatively little about war itself. Instead, they used the war as a means of portraying the individual's jeopardy inside an impersonally mobilized society. In 1923, critics gave a warm reception to the American version of Karel Capek's play *R. U. R.*, introducing the robot as modern society's citizen, and to *The Adding Machine*, Elmer Rice's biting comedy on the effects of dull, routine work.

Of all the routine tasks in modern America, intellectuals considered work on the assembly line the most threatening to the individual. In fact, it was less wearing than a fruit harvest, less demanding than a sweatshop, and less dangerous than a coal mine. But factory labor combined monotony and mechanization in a way that communicated a special danger to people who were already worried about modern society's depersonalization. After Sherwood Anderson had exposed the evils of the small town in *Winesburg, Ohio*, he turned to the assembly line, where he found the conveyer belt a relentless master over its wage slaves. Henry Ford's plant produced cars at the price of humanity, the young pastor Reinhold Niebuhr noted in his journal. One of the most acclaimed scenes in an American movie was Charlie Chaplin's rebellion in *Modern Times* against the intolerable discipline of the assembly line and his glorious escape through a maze of giant gears and monstrous machinery. America's great challenge, the cultural critic Lewis Mumford wrote in 1934, was to make "the machine . . . our servant, not our tyrant." By the 1930s, it became commonplace for intellectuals to condemn everything about the factory as ugly and alien.

Critics were also disturbed about an all-consuming passion for goods and money. The New Era, Suzanne La Follette acidly concluded, was testing the proposition "that human beings can live a generally satisfactory life . . . so long as they are kept powerfully under the spell of a great number of mechanical devices. . . ." During the 1920s, old progressives as dissimilar as the moralistic Westerner George Norris and the patrician Easterner Gifford Pinchot warned of the corrosive influence that the pursuit of money was having on American values. John Dos Passos made this corrupting passion a central theme in his

CHARLIE CHAPLIN IN "MODERN TIMES"

Charlie Chaplin, a Pied Piper for the working stiffs, romps
through the dehumanizing machinery of a modern factory.
(Culver Pictures, Inc.)

powerful, rambling trilogy *USA* (1930–36). In the 1930s, the nineteenth-century
pioneers of corporate enterprise received the indelible label "robber barons."
No part of the nation's heritage suffered more severely at the hands of American
writers than the success ethic, which such important novels as F. Scott Fitzgerald's
The Great Gatsby (1925) and Theodore Dreiser's *An American Tragedy* (1925)
attacked for its destructive effects on the individual. In *I'll Take My Stand* (1930),
twelve Southern intellectuals combined the worship of money with "the tempo
of industrial life" and the cult of machinery to prove that their region's agrarian
tradition offered the sole "defense of the individual" in modern America. To
the surprise of both authors and publisher, the book won an enthusiastic national
following.

   As urgent as many of these critics sounded, they were rarely either desperate or radical. They located danger spots in America's industrial order. Rather

Varieties of Reality

The meaning of art in modern America expanded and blurred. A profusion of photographs, illustrations, movies, buildings, landscapes, fashions, and handicrafts hopelessly muddied the traditional questions about the appropriate subjects of art, the necessary training for artists, and the proper cultivation of the viewers. Could advertising qualify as art? Were the creators of comic strips artists? Did mass production destroy artistic taste or generate new forms of democratic art? Yet the endless quarreling over these unanswerable questions could not hide the timeless qualities of the debate. Now as before, each aspiring artist tried to determine *what* people saw and *how* they saw it. Each of these many images promised its viewers a special insight into what was real, rather than merely superficial or transient. And these competing visions of reality, in turn, reflected the main lines of tension in modern American culture.

Images, like other modern goods, were mass distributed, and however unwittingly, Americans consumed them along with the myriad products of their society. As Americans took sides in a cultural conflict, therefore, they received images that helped them to understand their choices. During the 1920s and 1930s, for example, an aversion to city life was visualized in small groups of country people: a warm family gathering, an easy intimacy among friends, a mutual support between generations. The images of urban-industrial progress, on the other hand, were oriented toward things rather than people. Long, dramatic views of a factory, skyscraper, or center city communicated the expansive grandeur of American technology. Americans came to know these images so well that in the 1960s environmentalists needed only a slight shift in focus to make ironic statements about modern progress. A tip of the camera accentuated the smoke belching from the factory. A longer view of the city juxtaposed its skyline with urban blight. By the sixties, the country town was slipping from memory, and the visual alternative to the city leaped past civilization to the wilderness. The image of pure nature, however, was a study in contemporary American frustration, for it also offered no human comfort. As soon as people entered the virgin wilderness, they defiled it.

THE SATURDAY EVENING POST

MARCH 9, '29

5c. The Copy 10c. in Canada

Samuel M. Vauclain—William Hazlett Upson—James Warner Bellah
Wesley Stout—Eleanor Mercein—Samuel Crowther—Booth Tarkington

Erich Hartmann/Magnum.

For Americans without personal knowledge of small-town life, Norman Rockwell's famous drawings defined it as simple, friendly, and unaffected. In this fashion, Rockwell's imaginary town became part of modern America's reality. In contrast to Rockwell's cozy, vibrant town, the untouched wilderness had no place for people. Beneath this beautiful vision ran an undercurrent of hopelessness about modern American society.

Another group of artists sought reality in a complex relation between the emotions of the viewers and the essential components of what they saw. They probed the same subjects of nature and urban-industrial society, but they rephrased these issues in abstract images. The flowering of American abstraction came in the years after the Second World War when Willem de Kooning was expressing the dynamism of modern life in rugged blocks and explosive colors, and the controversial Jackson Pollack was extending visual horizons with his flowing lines and subtle uses of depth. Then in the 1960s, as many Americans rebelled against the clutter and complexity around them, painters of the "minimalist" and "op art" schools responded to these new yearnings with simple geometric abstractions.

Abstract artists, like other modern experts, developed techniques of expression that required special training simply to understand, let alone to use. Significantly, their strongest defenders were professional and business people whose own success depended on expertise. Every subdivision of knowledge, they assumed, had special rules for understanding. But modern abstractionists, unlike the pioneers of the Armory Show in 1913, reached a nationwide audience. For millions of skeptical Americans abstract art was an incomprehensible jumble of shapes and colors. In art as in other areas of knowledge, they demanded a common sense reality that anyone could grasp.

"Ashville," Willem de Kooning,
The Phillips Collection, Washington.

"Cathedral," Jackson Pollock,
Dallas Museum of Fine Arts.

Willem de Kooning, a major contributer to America's renaissance in painting after the Second World War, gave new vitality to the European cubist tradition. More innovative than de Kooning, Jackson Pollock was particularly ingenious in adapting modern technology to his art, as the aluminum paint on this canvas demonstrates. In the 1960s the trends moved away from Pollock's complexity toward a simple, almost photographic reality. The reputation of Edward Hopper, whose best paintings had been completed three decades earlier, rose impressively. Almost no signs of life intruded on Hopper's brilliant, haunting scenes, and the loneliness of his stark art touched widespread anxieties about the individual's survival during the sixties.

"House by the Railroad," Edward Hopper,
The Museum of Modern Art.

The popular arts satisfied these demands. Through constant repetition the popular arts drilled a few simple images of truth and beauty into the American consciousness. The most familiar of all was the smooth, sexy, welcoming woman. From the Hollywood vamp of the twenties to the Petty girl of the forties to the *Playboy* centerfold of the sixties, a composite model of female beauty shaped ⸻ tions about women and women ⸻ about themselves. The popular ⸻ brated the virtues of certain oc⸻ der the auspices of the New Dea⸻ public murals and bas-relief sc⸻ fied manual labor with scenes of ⸻ lar men and women in the fields ⸻

Photo by Milton H. Greene.

Sex and violence—sometimes singly, sometimes in combination—dominated the popular arts after the Second World War. Mass-marketed stereotypes of sex and beauty reached their peak with the era of Marilyn Monroe, who exercised an extraordinary influence over American dreams and behavior. The vision of history's most horrible weapon as an awesome fantasy of color and clouds greatly strengthened the modern connection between violence and beauty.

During the Second World War these handsome titans became soldiers and sailors. In fact, the Second World War introduced an elaborate esthetic of violence that made instruments of destruction into objects of beauty: the gleaming fleets of battleships and bombers, then the eerie majesty of the atomic bomb's mushroom cloud. The beauty of violence remained after the war as an important theme of the popular arts. A particularly striking example appeared in the climactic scene of the movie *Bonnie and Clyde,* which transformed the mutilation of the heroine's body into an arresting, slow-motion dance of death.

U.S. Energy Research and Development Administration.

In reaction against these mass-produced images, some Americans swung to the other extreme and praised the beauty of almost anything unique. The market for handicrafts and homemade art objects thrived during the 1960s and 1970s. What popular primitivism lacked in refinement it contributed in personal expression, and its proponents contrasted the reality of a rough-hewn people's art with the artificiality of a slick commercial art. The urge for self-expression also spread into "street art," a new public outlet for the emotions of assertive, often angry city dwellers. None of the older art forms had to give way for the newcomers. A contemporary people's art simply added to the artistic variety of modern America.

Subway Graffitti. Was it art or vandalism? The answer lay in the cultural standards of the beholder.

Naar/Alskog/Photo Researchers, Inc.

than demand an end to modern society, they usually cautioned the individual to keep a safe distance from its most threatening centers. The individual's protection, in other words, was an intelligent detachment. The clearest summary of this view appeared in Hemingway's *A Farewell to Arms*, where Lieutenant Frederic Henry, an American who had volunteered for the Italian ambulance corps early in the First World War, watched the impersonal forces of the war devour more and more people around him until they verged on swallowing him, too. He deserted—a sane and courageous act as Hemingway described it. Escaping to Switzerland, he found fulfillment briefly in a love affair with Catherine Barkley. Yet even when her death left Frederic Henry absolutely alone, his core of inner strength enabled him to survive in an insensitive universe.

The individual's lonely detachment failed to satisfy a growing number of Americans who in some fashion felt overwhelmed by the forces surrounding them. The response to these feelings of powerlessness was an elaborate set of images and myths, a special culture of compensations that spun a dream-like web of strength around the individual. Some of them envisaged a perfect defense for the otherwise vulnerable individual. During the depression, for example, a flood of advertisements promised males a physical strength so great that no one would dare to challenge it. The most famous of these appeals, a mail-order course in "Dynamic Tension," guaranteed that any man could relive the fairy tale of its sponsor's life. Charles Atlas, a huge man whose mound of muscles rippled from every ad, had himself been "a 97-pound weakling" before he discovered the secret he would now divulge.

The new mass media created a striking array of fantasies about the perfect defense. Some were comic: Charlie Chaplin's carefree little tramp weaving his way among bullies and cops and puffing, pompous officials; a dutiful, intent Buster Keaton wheeling and spinning past impossible dangers to complete the appointed task; the infinitely resilient pseudoblacks in *Amos 'n Andy*, the most popular radio program of the 1930s, who were always scheming, always losing, but always ready to try again. Or the fantasies might be brutal. The cult of the movie antihero surrounding James Cagney in *Public Enemy* and Edward G. Robinson in *Little Caesar* idolized a swaggering ruthlessness that cleared every obstacle with a Tommy gun. The most popular fantasy of toughness continued to be the classic Western hero, brave and handsome, who killed faceless bad men in the good man's cause and faceless Indians in the white man's cause. During the Second World War, in the midst of bombs, tanks, and machine gun blasts, Hollywood's Westerner-as-GI even overcame the awesome threats of modern warfare.

No clear line divided Charles Atlas from the Western hero, or the Western hero from Superman, yet somewhere along the way the meaning of the fantasy shifted from the perfect defense of the individual to the individual's vaulting leap into a wonder world of success. America's new culture of compensation was also filled with images of an all-conquering power. As public restraints on the subject of sex relaxed, both the movies and the popular magazines spread a modern version of the traditional rags-to-riches tale. In its nineteenth-century form, the hero had won the rich man's daughter through his sterling character and her father's approval. In the modern variation, however, physical charm alone catapulted the hero to the top. The rich man's daughter, finding the poor but virile man irrisistible, convinced an angry father that she could not live without him. The mirror image of this tale, a sexually charged Cinderella story, sent the poor but beautiful woman into the arms of a rich, adoring husband.

The "star" system that came to dominate the entertainment industry during the 1920s reflected this popular involvement with an all-conquering power. The stars themselves seemed to have such powers; the irresistible lover Rudolph Valentino thrilling millions of moviegoers; the "Galloping Ghost" Red Grange scoring five touchdowns in one game; the courageous young Gertrude Ederle swimming the English Channel; even the publicized flagpole sitters staying awake and alive days on end. Accentuating the personal qualities of success, American audiences showed a strong preference for the idiosyncratic star who ignored many of the usual rules of the game. Fans loved the erratic slugger Jack Dempsey more than the boxing machine Gene Tunney, and the high-living, casual "Sultan of Swat," Babe Ruth, more than the intense, consistent batting champion, Ty Cobb.

Against this background Charles Lindbergh, the star of stars, rose to fame. In May 1927, while liberally financed and elaborately organized competitors were stalled on the ground, this unknown pilot became the first person to complete a solo airplane flight from New York to Paris. Americans instantly made the quiet, handsome Midwesterner a national idol. Lindbergh's triumph, as millions interpreted it, was the accomplishment of an indomitable individual. Both literally and figuratively, the "Lone Eagle" had soared beyond the ordinary individual's constraints to his purely personal success. Moreover, Lindbergh's sudden fame did not appear to affect his traditional virtues of modesty, simplicity, and self-reliance. Of all the decade's stars, Lindbergh had the greatest and most lasting popularity.*

The star system also encouraged Americans to picture themselves, or their children, leaping to fame and fortune. The entertainment world not only made its stars fabulously rich; it also seemed to reward them instantaneously. Stars, according to popular mythology, were "discovered." As the prospects of an immediate success in business or the professions dimmed, the vision of boys as athletes and girls as actresses shaped more and more American dreams. The fewer the alternatives, the more passionate the involvements. In the late 1930s, the heavyweight champion Joe Louis was almost worshipped in the black

---

*The tragic kidnaping and death of Lindbergh's son produced a new surge of public interest in 1932. Then in 1941, Lindbergh's advocacy of a negotiated settlement with Hitler's Germany sharply diminished his popularity.

CHARLES LINDBERGH AND THE "SPIRIT OF ST. LOUIS"

An adoring public believed that Lindbergh, through strength of character, had achieved a personal triumph over his society's impersonal forces. *(Culver Pictures, Inc.)*

ghettos. In some urban neighborhoods, the kings of organized crime, who emerged in the 1920s with Prohibition, were equally compelling models of power and success.

One threat to the individual, the emptiness of old age, required a separate cluster of compensations. For two reasons, the problems of the aged were growing more severe in modern times. First, as the average life expectancy for an American rose from 47 years in 1900 to 68 years in 1950, the proportion of old people increased dramatically. Second, as the numbers expanded, the sources of self-respect for the aged were shrinking. Wherever America's modern values prevailed, old people could scarcely avoid feeling useless. Knowledge in a specialized society was supposed to be advancing too rapidly for an older generation to master. Only the young could keep pace with America's highly technical and increasingly complex progress. As children reached adulthood, therefore, parents had good reason to feel that their best years were gone and that the future, which belonged to the young, opened a huge void before them.

Beginning in the 1920s, many older Americans earnestly set about the task of tricking the fates and staying young. The market for bright clothes and beauty aids, cosmetic surgery and dentistry, wigs and elixirs, all thrived. After 1922, F. Scott Fitzgerald recalled, the revelry of the Jazz Age "was a children's party taken over by elders." At the same time, a veil fell over the process of dying. Pictures of old people invariably showed them smiling, alert, and vigorous. A special literature, including Walter Pitkin's very popular *Life Begins at Forty* (1932), told Americans to think positively about their later years, and a multiplying number of settlements for old people, particularly in Florida and California, promised a happy, relaxed retirement for those who could afford to buy it. Despite these compensations, however, Americans occasionally heard a cry of resentment from their abandoned elders. During the 1930s, the Townsend movement for old-age pensions, which drew its greatest strength from the retirement communities of California, was both an expression of economic need and a demand for attention. Although Social Security responded to the economic problem, nothing was done about the human importance of these forgotten Americans.

Answers for the Individual

During the twenties and thirties, the individual received a good deal of general advice and a variety of palliatives. But what failed to appear was a clear statement of the individual's situation and future prospects in modern society. A new round in search of an answer to this problem began rather vaguely in the depression, when a number of public leaders and intellectuals tried to conceive of the individual as part of a broad social enterprise. New Deal enthusiasts attacked the evils of "rugged individualism" and foresaw a new age of social responsibility. The reputation of the philosopher John Dewey, America's leading advocate of a social ethic, rose impressively during the 1930s. Moreover, as depression crippled America, one group of intellectuals looked abroad to the Soviet Union as a model of the healthy society. A few of them also took the next logical step and applied Karl Marx's theories of class conflict to American society. Only through class consciousness, they argued, could the individual find security. But in most cases, the affair between American intellectuals and the Soviet Union was a brief infatuation. Never willing to relinquish the individual in favor of the class, they were revolted by the bloody Soviet "purge" of the late thirties, and increasingly they became convinced that Americans would have to develop their own kind of social consciousness.

At best, the search of the thirties offered a hope for tomorrow, but not a solution for today. John Steinbeck, who had once been attracted by Marxism and who continued to have a strong social conscience, captured this tentative quality at the end of his finest novel, *The Grapes of Wrath* (1939). Steinbeck told the grim story of an impoverished Oklahoma farm family, the Joads, tracing them from their uprooting early in the depression through their futile quest for a fresh start in California. Then on the last page of his poignant novel, Steinbeck sketched in a few sentences a vision of a new fellow feeling just beginning to surface in America.

For a great many Americans, that spirit of a collective endeavor finally arrived with the Second World War. In 1940, Hemingway's hero from the 1920s reappeared in *For Whom the Bell Tolls* as Robert Jordan, who was no longer alone because he had found a social commitment. This time Hemingway's hero was fighting in the Spanish Civil War. Instead of deserting, as Frederic Henry had done in *A Farewell to Arms*, Robert Jordan chose to die for human values in the battle against fascism. A year later, the former pacifist Robert E. Sherwood, winner of four Pulitzer Prizes, announced his conversion to the same crusade in his play *There Shall Be No Night.*

After the attack on Pearl Harbor in December 1941, the sense of a shared enterprise spread throughout America. In ways that no government propaganda could have achieved, all kinds of people linked all kinds of activities to a common cause: welding for the war effort, waking an hour early for the car pool, keeping tin cans for the scrap metal drive, saving war stamps for a war bond. Nothing eliminated the conflicts in a complex society, yet to a remarkable degree, whatever an American did had a larger social meaning attached to it. For a brief period, the individual seemed to require no special reinforcements. Even in the midst of military combat, Bill Mauldin's extremely popular cartoons of the grunts Willie and Joe pictured them slogging through the muck of war with their sense of reality and their instinct for survival firmly intact.

"Just gimme a coupla aspirin. I already got a Purple Heart."

(Drawings copyrighted 1944, renewed 1972, Bill Mauldin; reproduced by courtesy of Bill Mauldin.)

Then as soon as the war ended, the spirit of a common cause dissolved. The news told only of selfish strikers, business profiteers, and greedy farmers. The government seemed no more than an arena for squabbling interests. Where were the truly national goals? According to *The Best Years of Our Lives*, Hollywood's outstanding movie of the 1940s, the soldiers, who had sacrificed the most, had to fight still another battle at home to preserve their dignity in an ungrateful society. In fact, what had the war meant? In its aftermath, total war raised questions about the threat of a technological barbarism that could no longer be confined simply to the evils of fascism.

In these sobering postwar years, four answers emerged to define the place of the individual in modern American society. Though each of the four communicated a very different message, all of them dealt in some way with the clash between modern and traditional values, and all of them responded in some fashion to the issues and images of the vulnerable individual. Taken together, these four answers were a creative summary of the central problems in modern American culture.

One answer told the individual to learn the rules of the modern occupational system, abide by them, and succeed. The wartime economy intensified the demand for greater numbers of specialists with higher levels of skill, and immediately after the war, Americans turned to the schools to fill this demand. Bands of citizens campaigned to improve instruction in the basic skills. Funds flowed freely into the entire educational system. Between 1945 and 1950, expenditures in the public schools more than doubled; even more impressive, enrollment in higher education doubled. Just as the importance of the high school had dominated the 1920s and 1930s, so the importance of higher education dominated the years after the Second World War. Now only colleges and graduate schools could satisfy a complex economy's need for specialized training. The greatest single impetus to college enrollment came from the GI Bill of 1944, which eventually subsidized the education of about 8 million former servicepeople. Along with the sheer numbers it funded, the GI Bill helped to democratize opportunities in higher education and hence in the upper ranks of business and the professions as well.

In *Death of a Salesman* (1949), the young playwright Arthur Miller created a brilliant morality tale of why and how to use these broadening opportunities. Miller's drama was immediately acclaimed one of America's greatest plays. Through the story of Willy Loman, it provided an excruciating lesson on how to fail in modern America. Willy lived by a weakened, vulgarized version of the traditional American dream of success. In the 1920s, when salesmanship had seemed the right avenue for a self-made man, Willy chose that career with visions of a swift rise to wealth and importance. Instead, he became trapped in the endless, weary rounds of meager sales, humiliating failures, and interminable debts. Willy desperately hoped that his sons, who idolized him, could still realize his dream of quick riches, and he taught them the only values he knew: a personal style, a winning appearance, and an eye for the main chance would achieve the miracle of success. Under their father's guidance, Biff and Hap approached manhood athletic, shallow, and morally stunted. Biff, discovering the fraud of Willy's life, turned in impotent rage on his father. Hap became a petty cheat. Willy, broken and psychotic, completed his dream by committing suicide, under the pathetic delusion that his life insurance payment would somehow catapult Biff to greatness.

During the hopeful years, while Willy and the boys were polishing the car and talking of Biff's future as an athlete, Bernard, the scrawny kid next door, mooned after the popular Loman boys. But Bernard was also winning the highest grades in his high school class. As the Loman nightmare unfolded, Bernard left to learn a specialty and returned a self-possessed, well-balanced adult, who was sufficiently eminent as a young lawyer to argue a case before the Supreme Court. His father Charley, cool and clear-eyed, had simply relinquished his son to

America's system of specialized occupations. "And you never told him what to do, did you?" a bewildered Willy asked his neighbor. "You never took any interest in him." Instead of an embittered Biff to plague him, Charley enjoyed an easy, warm relation with the adult Bernard, who dropped by whenever his busy schedule allowed. Bernard's success explained Willy's failure. Modern America's avenue upward had been there all the while, but Willy's dream had hidden the only legitimate path to success.

The second of the postwar answers began by acknowledging that the individual did indeed face serious problems in the modern world. Like the earlier critics of America's machine culture, a variety of intellectuals, educators, and publicists now warned that science and technology by themselves were amoral. Like the defenders of America's traditional values, they declared that the individual would have to find an anchor of values outside of science. Such a task, they said, required finding the fundamental principles in civilized life, and only the humanists — the philosophers and poets and theologians — could lead that search.

The quest for basic values was a nationwide preoccupation in the late forties. Some scholars explored the American past to discover its essentially American qualities, giving special attention to such brooding spirits as Thoreau, Melville, and the Puritans. Others examined the far richer resources of the Western tradition. Adults were guided along the peaks of that tradition in well-received classes on the "Great Books" of Western civilization. In colleges throughout the country, new and often required courses tried to distill wisdom not only from a long span of time but also from a breadth of subjects, such as an interdisciplinary examination of American culture or a humanistic understanding of science. The most intriguing innovation in college education was Chancellor Robert Hutchins's program at the University of Chicago that integrated the entire subject matter of the undergraduate curriculum in a unified course of study.

The fascination with fundamentals produced a strong reaction against the pragmatist's faith in an experimental, evolving truth. John Dewey, who more than any other intellectual leader was identified with a scientific method in ethics, became a particular target of attack in the late 1940s. Dewey's old friends, such as the philosopher Sidney Hook, joined his old enemies, such as the journalist Walter Lippmann, in condemning the effects of scientific relativism. Others blamed Dewey for the intellectual deficiencies they found in American public education. Dewey's critics wanted certainties in place of his open-ended pursuit of truth. In foreign policy, for example, they sought to define a single, unwavering "national interest" to guide America's international affairs. In civil liberties, they assigned to the freedoms of the First Amendment an absolute, timeless meaning that no judiciary, they asserted, should ever alter.

The critics of scientific relativism accused it of arrogance as well as fuzziness. The human mind, they claimed, was incapable of solving all of the world's problems through a scientific method. This line of opposition, which acquired the name realism, found its most effective spokesman in Reinhold Niebuhr, a theologian who in his own career had moved from an optimistic Christian socialism to the humbling doctrines of Martin Luther. Niebuhr began by placing ultimate truth beyond the human reach in God's inscrutable wisdom. Therefore, all actions reflected an inevitable human fallibility, and all choices involved moral risks. Nevertheless, people could not throw up their hands and quit. Individuals had a moral responsibility to choose among alternatives and to act on their choices. The necessity of choosing from an inherently imperfect knowledge defined the human predicament. Americans, Niebuhr declared, must learn to accept these human limits and abandon their simple faith in a man-made progress. Instead, they should meet each situation as it arose, and without arrogance, commit themselves to a course that held the best promise of fulfilling their moral obligations. Niebuhr's complex commandments were praised more than they were studied. But in the simplified image of the sober individual strengthened through self-knowledge and humility, his message had a remarkably wide appeal during these anxious years.

The third of the postwar answers was a defiant statement in behalf of the sovereign individual. Setting the individual at odds with modern society, it told him to overcome the dangers around him through his own powers. In a few instances, this answer was addressed to the specialist. Ayn Rand's best-selling novel *The Fountainhead* (1943), for example, glorified the right of the creative professional to discard society's ordinary rules in order to realize his genius, and in the postwar years, Rand cults mushroomed on college campuses. Usually, however, the hero had no special training and no resources except his core of inner strength. During the forties, a mass audience learned about this hero through the movies, particularly those starring Humphrey Bogart, and through a flood of inexpensive paperbacks that suddenly covered the drug stores and newsstands.

Soon after the publication of his first book in 1947, Mickey Spillane became the undisputed king of this new paperback market. In less than a decade, 30 million copies of his novels had been sold, a record far surpassing any competitor's. His initial title revealed his central theme: *I, the Jury*—and judge and executioner. Spillane's hero was a tough, resourceful private detective named Mike Hammer, who radiated an irresistible power. Good people willingly helped him; weak ones crumbled before him. Beautiful, sensuous women, looking past his lumpy face to the inner man, desired him. Though often battered, he always survived through a "gimmick" or a bit of Hammer luck. Enemies understood that nothing would deter him. When Hammer set upon organized crime, for example, the entire Mafia quaked, for they knew that he would bring them a personal, bloody justice.

Although Spillane drew on a full tradition of fantasies about the all-conquering individual, he more than any of his predecessors gave them a contemporary urban setting. The metropolis, Mike Hammer declared, was a formless "monster," teeming with ominous forces. City culture was dehumanized and city government corrupt. In the urban jungle, Spillane's hero had no alternative but to devise his own code of values. It required an exceptional courage, an extraordinary effort of will, to break free from this threatening human mass. Those who succeeded, however, became true individuals and survived. Obviously, Spillane's message had touched a popular nerve. Not only the sale of his books but also the number of his imitators indicated that his, of all the postwar answers, found the widest audience.

The fourth of the postwar answers was the most pessimistic. It expressed such despair that it seemed to forecast the individual's destruction. In the late forties, Americans were listening for the first time to those Europeans who had already peered inside a soulless society and found no individuals there. Franz Kafka's nightmares of man as vermin, of a nameless subject wandering through a fathomless system to a death he came to welcome, were suddenly relevant. A much larger public responded so attentively to the accounts of a devouring social organization in Aldous Huxley's *Brave New World* (1932), Arthur Koestler's *Darkness At Noon* (1941), and George Orwell's *1984* (1949) that their contents became clichés. Because Orwell and Koestler were describing a communist system, Americans had a choice of reading their books as justifications for a free Western society. Instead, many Americans used them as a frame of reference for discussing the dangers in their own lives.

The Second World War, as it was viewed in retrospect, contributed significantly to this new spirit of despair. The best of the American war novels—Norman Mailer's *The Naked and the Dead* (1948), Irwin Shaw's *The Young Lions* (1948), and James Jones's *From Here to Eternity* (1951)—did not simply surround their characters with danger, as the war novels of the 1920s had done. Now individuals were sucked into the very center of destruction, and all characters were equally exposed to the stray bullet. No personal choice or inner strength affected these human specks that were being tossed by the fates.

Above all, "The Holocaust" and "The Bomb" posed the most profoundly disturbing problems of the postwar years. After Germany's surrender in 1945, the numbing facts about the Nazi's Jewish policy began to filter back to the United States. Rationally and efficiently, the German government had applied the best techniques of modern organization to systematically destroy 5 million human beings. Had the Germans, in the process, revealed an essential truth about the impersonal mobilization of power in modern society? Again in 1945, American atomic bombs demolished the Japanese cities Hiroshima and Nagasaki. The bomb juxtaposed scientific genius and human annihilation so sharply, challenged the concept of civilization so directly, and symbolized the terrors of death so vividly that it left even the most resolute Americans unable to express its import.

The uniquely American way of expressing despair about the individual's lot appeared in a new image, "the Southern." In 1949, the Southerner William

HIROSHIMA, 1945

Was modern society on the brink of suicide?
The awful power of the atomic bomb raised
fundamental questions about the meaning of
science, progress, and civilization. *(U.S. Air Force.)*

Faulkner, with his finest writing already behind him, received the Nobel Prize
for literature. He had recently risen to public prominence, and a favorite intellectual game of the late forties was unraveling the family histories in Faulkner's
Yoknapatawpha County, the fictional Mississippi setting for his greatest works.
A year earlier, the young Tennessee Williams had been awarded a Pulitzer Prize
for *A Streetcar Named Desire*, the second of two stunning dramatic successes in the
1940s that established him as a leading playwright. These two, along with other
gifted Southern writers such as Carson McCullers and Flannery O'Connor,
created a composite image unlike anything Americans had ever encountered.

Understanding the Southern depended on an appreciation of the Western,
for intentionally or not the Southern was a systematic attack on America's oldest

myth of individual strength. In the Western, one man entered an open plain that was as stripped of constraining institutions as he himself was of a constraining past. There he confronted a direct challenge, and by a clear moral choice he overcame it. He was the pure individual: a man alone, a man of simple, sovereign convictions, a man of action whose problem, once met, dissolved in a cleansing rite of violence. Not only had the movies, the radio, comics, and pulp fiction expanded the audience for this myth since the 1920s; such thoughtful writers as Hemingway had borrowed from it. The Western hero continued to stand tall in postwar America.

Like the Western, the Southern also used a regional stereotype to communicate a national message. Just as countless Americans associated the West with a new, formless land, many regarded the South as a decaying, backward region. This popular caricature helped Southern writers reach a national audience. In contrast to the Western's openness, the world of the Southern was a suffocating prison —a town or household or room in which the inmates were held by invisible shackles they could never break. Dreams and memories bound them to the dead as well as the living. Unlike the direct challenge in the Western, the hovering, atmospheric problems in the Southern were impalpable. The Southern world was filled with human vulnerability. Children were caught in a whirl of adult terror and adults locked in a desperate battle for sanity; amorality was in power and sadism at large; bodies were deformed and brains addled. In these struggles, contrary to the gun fights of the Western, women managed more effectively than men. Maleness and impotence were common companions in the Southern.

Where the Western hero acted, the characters in the Southern talked. They stabbed one another with words, searched in vain for the meaning of their lives with words, and covered their own anguish with words. Occasionally someone's hopelessness or passion would explode in violence, but violence only complicated the problems that no one would ever resolve. In *A Streetcar Named Desire*, Tennessee Williams let loose a caricature of the Western hero, the physical-sexual-nonverbal Stanley Kowalski, and he wrecked the fragile human defenses around him. Perhaps no more than a small minority listened carefully to the agonizing message of the Southern. Nevertheless, an exceptionally talented cluster of modern writers had finally questioned whether or not the individual could survive.

At midcentury, Americans reached a pause in the process of creating a modern culture. Their commitment to mass consumerism was firmly established. So was a widespread concern for the fate of the individual. Beyond these general areas of agreement, however, American culture remained a loose cover over a great variety of attitudes and aspirations. Both modern and traditional values still had their adherents. Some Americans were trying to combine elements of the two, as the postwar search for fundamental values illustrated. But a new clarity in the debate over the individual's place in modern America actually sharpened the differences among competing camps. It was questionable if Arthur Miller's

Bernard, Reinhold Niebuhr's Moral Man, Mickey Spillane's Mike Hammer, and Tennessee Williams's Stanley Kowalski all belonged to the same human race. To coexist, these conflicting beliefs required a good deal of mutual tolerance—or mutual indifference. Whether or not an increasingly nationalized American society would contain such leeway became one of the crucial problems for the next quarter-century to resolve.

Suggested Readings

America's modern culture is explored in detail in Daniel J. Boorstin, *The Americans: The Democratic Experience* (1973). Another broad study, Rowland Berthoff's *An Unsettled People* (1971), emphasizes the deficiencies in American individualism. William E. Leuchtenburg, *The Perils of Prosperity, 1914–32* (1958), has particularly revealing chapters on the consumer culture of the twenties and the changes in values accompanying it, subjects that are also covered in Frederick Lewis Allen's *Only Yesterday* (1931). There is a perceptive analysis of the new sexual morality in Christopher Lasch's *The New Radicalism in America [1889–1963]* (1965). Isabel Leighton, ed., *The Aspirin Age* (1949), contains a lively set of essays on the culture of the twenties, and Freda Kirchway, ed., *Our Changing Morality* (1924), offers a sample of present-day ponderings on the new values. A broad picture of the city's dominance in twentieth-century society appears in Zane L. Miller, *The Urbanization of Modern America* (1973); some of the effects of urbanization on suburban values are discussed in Peter J. Schmitt, *Back to Nature* (1969). Carl Bode, *Mencken* (1969), assesses the leading spokesman for the new urban culture. An intriguing section in Gilman M. Ostrander, *American Civilization in the First Machine Age: 1890–1940* (1970), defines the place of youth in modern society, and John R. Seeley et al., *Crestwood Heights* (1956), examines the importance of the schools in modern suburban life. Three books evaluate women's part in the new culture. William L. O'Neill, *Everyone Was Brave: The Rise and Fall of Feminism in America* (1969), and William Henry Chafe, *The American Woman* (1972), trace the decline of earlier trends toward emancipation, while J. Stanley Lemons, *The Woman Citizen: Social Feminism in the 1920s* (1973), concentrates on women's continuing action after the First World War. In *Birth Control in America* (1970), David M. Kennedy adds a critical analysis of Margaret Sanger's career.

Several books illuminate the values of important institutions and occupations. James W. Prothro, *Dollar Decade* (1954), summarizes the attitudes of businessmen during the twenties; Morrell Heald, *The Social Responsibilities of Business, Company, and Community, 1900–1960* (1970), views them from a longer perspective. Otis Pease, *The Responsibilities of American Advertising* (1958), covers developments in a thriving business. The engineer's dedication to business values is the subject of Edwin T. Layton, Jr., *The Revolt of the Engineers* (1971), and the social scientists' dedication to the same values is the subject of Loren Baritz, *The Servants of Power* (1960). Roy Lubove, *Professional Altruists* (1965), describes the businesslike efficiency of social workers. The section on the United States in Reinhard Bendix's *Work and Authority in Industry* (1956) investigates the strategy of the new specialists in personnel management. Also see Milton Derber, *The American Idea of Industrial Democracy, 1865–1965* (1970). The effects of the new culture on education are analyzed in Patricia Albjerg Graham, *Progressive Education from Arcady to Academe: A History of the Progressive Education Association, 1919–1955* (1967), August Hollingshead, *Elmtown's Youth* (1949), and Solon Kimball and James E. McClellan, Jr., *Education and the New America* (1962). Edward A. Krug, *The Shaping of the American High School, 1920–1941* (1972),

Wieruille, Jim

Quizes	Exam #1	Total Pts	Mid-Term
7	79	~~250~~	117
7	83	280	227
8		300	243
8			
8			
9			
9			
9			
9			
10			
10			

$$\begin{array}{r} 11.3\\ 150\overline{)1706}\\ \underline{1059}\\ 1200\\ 1200\\ \end{array}$$

$$\begin{array}{r} 113\\ \underline{18}\\ 135 \end{array}$$

provides basic information on the modern high school, and Christopher Jencks and David Riesman, *The Academic Revolution* (1968), explores the modern university.

Traditional values in modern America have attracted much less scholarly attention. Two interesting books analyze these values under challenge: Ray Ginger's *Six Days or Forever? Tennessee v. John Thomas Scopes* (1958), and Don S. Kirschner's *City and Country: Rural Responses to Urbanization in the 1920s* (1970). *Middletown* (1929) and *Middletown in Transition* (1937), classic studies of Muncie, Indiana, by Robert S. Lynd and Helen Merrell Lynd, reveal a mixture of traditional and modern values. Lawrence Chenoweth, *The American Dream of Success* (1974), describes the modern version of a traditional quest, and Donald B. Meyer, *The Positive Thinkers* (1965), examines modern variations of the equally traditional doctrine of self-help. Other books cast light on traditional values through the study of popular heroes. In *The Hero* (1959), Kenneth S. Davis discusses the fame of Charles Lindbergh. Reynold M. Wik, *Henry Ford and Grass-Roots America* (1972), explains the automobile magnate's powerful appeal, and Keith T. Sward, *The Legend of Henry Ford* (1948), contrasts the public image with the actual record.

The best account of modern relativism is Morton G. White, *Social Thought in America: The Revolt against Formalism* (rev. ed., 1957). Three excellent books discuss early discontents with relativism and various quests for certainty: Donald B. Meyer, *The Protestant Search for Political Realism, 1919–1941* (1960), Edward A. Purcell, Jr., *The Crisis of Democratic Theory: Scientific Naturalism & the Problem of Values* (1973), and David A. Hollinger, *Morris R. Cohen and the Scientific Ideal* (1975). The appeal of another kind of authority is examined in John P. Diggins, *Mussolini and Fascism: The View from America* (1972). Several fine books explore the intellectual consequences of the Depression: Charles C. Alexander, *Nationalism in American Thought, 1930–1945* (1969), Arthur A. Ekirch, *Ideologies and Utopias: The Impact of the New Deal on American Thought* (1969), R. Alan Lawson, *The Failure of Independent Liberalism, 1930–1941* (1971), Richard H. Pells, *Radical Visions and American Dreams: Culture and Social Thought in the Depression Years* (1973), and William Stott, *Documentary Expression and Thirties America* (1973). Other studies trace ideas in creative writing. Alfred Kazin, *On Native Grounds: An Interpretation of Modern American Prose Literature* (1942), is a stimulating essay. Frederick J. Hoffman, *The Twenties* (rev. ed., 1966), discusses American fiction in an artistically critical decade. The strains of both modern society and depression are revealed in Maxwell Geismar's *Writers in Crisis: The American Novel, 1925–1940* (1942), and Daniel Aaron's *Writers on the Left* (1961). Thomas R. West, *Flesh of Steel* (1967), deals with the effects of the machine on the literary imagination. Of course, the creative writers themselves remain our indispensable sources. The best survey of the fine arts is Oliver W. Larkin, *Art and Life in America* (rev. ed., 1960). On architecture, see John Burchard and Albert Bush-Brown, *The Architecture of America* (1961).

The ferment in values after the Second World War has yet to find a historian. Something of the concern for the individual is communicated in two important sociological studies, David Riesman et al., *The Lonely Crowd: A Study of the Changing American Character* (1950), and C. Wright Mills, *White Collar: The American Middle Class* (1951). Alexander Meiklejohn, *Free Speech and Its Relation to Self-Government* (1948), and Hans J. Morgenthau, *In Defense of the National Interest* (1951), illustrate the demand for fixed values. Also see Carl L. Becker, *Freedom and Responsibility in the American Way of Life* (1945). Robert M. Hutchins, *The Conflict in Education in a Democratic Society* (1953), and Arthur E. Bestor, Jr., *Educational Wastelands: The Retreat from Learning in Our Public Schools* (1953), discuss the place of fundamentals in education. The new tough-minded approach to social values is revealed in Arthur M. Schlesinger, Jr., *The Vital Center* (1949), Max Ascoli, *The Power of Freedom* (1949), and Reinhold Niebuhr, *The Irony of American History* (1952).

CHAPTER

33

International

Power

The last, great thrust of modernization occurred in America's international relations. It came last because nothing between 1920 and 1940 forced the United States to make a fundamental change in its approach to world affairs. Without doubt, the United States was already the world's greatest power in 1920. In agriculture, industry, and finance, it towered above its competitors. Invulnerable itself to serious attack, the United States had the military potential to punish almost any nation it selected. The officials who conducted America's foreign relations during the twenties and thirties recognized, moreover, an inevitable connection between the security and prosperity of their own nation and the actions of other nations throughout the world. Yet an overwhelming majority of Americans, including the nation's leaders, had not abandoned the traditional belief that the United States should stand apart in the family of nations, carefully preserving the right to make its own decisions and to cooperate with other nations only as it chose.

The challenge that the nation's leaders faced, therefore, was to find a policy compatible with both their awareness of an interconnected world and their urge to retain America's freedom of action. Although opponents within the government accused one another of being "internationalists" or "isolationists," almost all shared a common desire to strike some reasonable balance between America's involvement and its detachment. It was the Second World War that disrupted this consensus. During the war and its troubling aftermath, the United States became far more enmeshed than it had ever been in world affairs, and Americans groped for a way to reconcile their vast international authority with their tradition of detachment. But the old balance was lost. By the early 1950s, the United States had committed itself to a systematic, world-wide containment of communism. With that commitment, America turned away from the tradition of detachment and entered a new era in foreign affairs.

A New International Order, 1920–1929

Immediately after the First World War, the strongest influences on America's foreign policy were pulling it out of international affairs. The war itself, disillusioned Americans were saying, had exposed the extensive moral rot in European civilization. This same sickness was now destroying the chances for a just peace. Some Americans feared that bolshevism would spread from Russia throughout the continent because European society was too weak to resist it. The widespread desire to insulate America from these European diseases drastically diminished support for President Wilson's League of Nations. After March 1920, when the Senate finally rejected the League, few Americans seemed to mourn its passing. As the perceptive Protestant minister John Haynes Holmes noted in 1920, "We still regard international affairs as existing in a realm altogether removed from our ordinary . . . standards."

Once the issue of the League had been settled, however, the American government demonstrated that it certainly was not withdrawing altogether from international affairs. As the Harding administration took office in 1921, the most threatening area of the world was the Far East, where friction between the United States and Japan had been mounting for several years. Not only were American leaders worried about Japan's imperial ambitions on the mainland of Asia, and possibly in the Philippine Islands, but they also fretted over Japan's longstanding defensive alliance with Great Britain, which linked a European friend to their Asian rival. With the Far East in mind, Charles Evans Hughes, Harding's austere and able secretary of state, used the growing concern over a worldwide naval armament race as justification for calling an international conference.

During the winter of 1921–22, representatives from industrial nations with interests in East Asia, except for the Soviet Union, met in Washington. To everyone's surprise, Hughes insisted that the delegates act as well as talk. Consequently, the Washington Conference produced three important agreements. All of them sought in some way to freeze the existing balance of power and privileges in East Asia. One, the critical Four-Power Treaty of nonaggression among the United States, Japan, Great Britain, and France, superseded the troublesome Anglo-Japanese Alliance. A second agreement, the Five-Power

Even in a group Harding's
Secretary of State Charles Evans
Hughes seemed to stand alone.
But at the Washington Conference
of 1921–1922, that tough
independence got results. *(Wide
World.)*

Treaty, added Italy to the big four and established tonnage limitations on major
warships according to a ratio approximating the current strength of these
nations. Finally, the Nine-Power Treaty committed all imperial nations to the
principle of equal opportunity inside an independent China—the American
doctrine of the "Open Door."

Through this new framework, the United States hoped to stabilize relations
in the Far East in such a way that America could act as a world power without
elaborate diplomatic involvements or military investments. By signing these
treaties, the United States acknowledged a crucial interconnection among the
policies of the world's industrial nations. But these agreements also minimized
the need for close international cooperation. Although the treaties included
provisions for mutual consultation, they were basically a structure of rules rather
than a system for collective action. Americans assumed that once these rules were
established, they would allow the United States to pursue its own objectives in
its own way.

To a very different set of problems in Europe, the United States applied a similar formula of stabilization and limited participation. The Harding administra-

tion signed treaties with each of the defeated Central Powers that copied the settlements of the Paris Peace Conference—with one primary exception. These treaties excluded any commitment to international enforcement. At the same time, the United States was demanding that its former European allies repay the large loans it had granted them during the war. European nations deeply resented this interpretation of the war debts as a business transaction. They tried to convince the United States that at the very least, they should repay American loans only to the extent that Germany was paying them the war reparations promised in the Versailles Treaty. Officially, the United States refused to acknowledge any connection between the debts and reparations. Unofficially, however, the American government did take the lead in organizing financial assistance for Germany's weakened economy through the Dawes Plan (1924) and the Young Plan (1929). As Germany recovered sufficiently to pay reparations, the former Allied Powers then made some payments on their war debts, and the United States did not press them very hard for more. In other words, the United States was willing to help manage a complex problem in international finance just so long as it did not involve a formal government commitment.*

That same aversion to new commitments surfaced repeatedly during the twenties. America's relations with the League of Nations remained very cautious and strictly unofficial. After a prolonged debate over whether or not the United States should enter the World Court, the League's unintimidating judicial arm, the Senate finally voted to join in 1926. But the Senate attached so many special conditions to America's participation that the other members of the World Court refused the terms. A year later, the French government publicly invited the United States to negotiate a bilateral renunciation of war. The Coolidge administration, however, considered the prospect of such a treaty too close to an alliance with France. Coolidge's secretary of state, Frank B. Kellogg, instead insisted on an extremely broad statement outlawing war and an invitation for all nations to sign it. More than sixty governments eventually ratified the Paris Peace Pact of 1928.** "An international kiss," snorted Missouri's sour Senator James Reed. Nevertheless, the Paris Peace Pact, with no mention of enforcement, was extremely popular in the United States.

A similar mixture of involvement and detachment characterized Washington's role in America's economic expansion. During the 1920s, assistance in developing foreign markets ranked high among the new areas of government service. As the budget for the Department of Commerce grew sixfold between 1921 and 1932, the department invested heavily in surveys of foreign markets, advisory personnel for business groups abroad, and publicity on the opportunities

---

*The depression of the 1930s, by stopping this flow of investments, reparations, and debt payments, once again made the war debts a bitter issue.
**The Paris Peace Pact of 1928 was sometimes called the Kellogg-Briand Peace Pact.

for economic expansion. It even competed with the Department of Agriculture in trying to enlarge the international market for farm products. Beginning in 1922, the State Department also introduced a new service for international investors. Bankers could submit their proposed loans to foreign governments for the State Department's review. The department would then evaluate them and issue judgments of "objection" or "no objection." The State Department rarely opposed these loans, and its statements of "no objection" appeared to be a government stamp of approval in marketing the foreign bonds.

At the same time, government officials almost always acted as though America's private business activities, once under way, would take care of themselves. In Latin America, the economic interests of the United States spread extensively during the 1920s, and the government, like the internationally minded businessmen, hoped that the United States would have a near monopoly on foreign investments there. But the government's leaders grew increasingly unwilling to support these interests with force. Washington was gradually repudiating the "Roosevelt Corollary" to the Monroe Doctrine, which had made the United States a policeman over Latin America's unstable, defaulting governments. American policymakers much preferred using persuasion to using the marines. Some government officials, particularly Herbert Hoover, even tried to discourage the most risky private loans to Latin America for fear that United States military forces might later be asked to collect such loans.

The desire to stabilize world affairs took precedence over America's private economic expansion. Where Washington committed itself to a policy, businessmen had to fit their interests within that policy. For example, the United States operated from a somewhat misty conviction that the future of China would determine the future of East Asia. Though American trade and investment overwhelmingly favored Japan, not China, the government continued to view Japan as the greatest threat to its Asian policy. After all, foreign trade remained about 5 percent of the national income during the 1920s, and foreign investments never reached 3 percent of the nation's total assets. It was difficult to argue that the health of the American economy required drastic diplomatic measures abroad. Only where the United States had no other clear goals did business interests predominate. In the Middle East, for instance, the government allowed American oil companies to conduct their own diplomacy during the twenties. When they negotiated a place for themselves in the world petroleum cartel, Washington ratified the results.

Overall, the United States used its great power quite cautiously during the twenties. The tentative quality of its international involvement was best revealed in the attitudes of the most influential official in Washington, Herbert Hoover. Despite his impressive efforts as secretary of commerce to assist business abroad, Hoover firmly believed that America had to rely on the strength of its domestic economy. Against the advice of many economists and big businessmen, he favored the high Fordney-McCumber Tariff of 1922 and the higher

Hawley-Smoot Tariff of 1930, both formidable barriers to international commerce. The solution to America's farm problems lay at home, he said, for the United States would soon be consuming its entire agricultural output. An admirer of Woodrow Wilson, Hoover blamed Europe for the failure to make a constructive peace in 1919, and he never altered his poor opinion of America's wartime allies. Hoover doubted that the United States and Japan could reach a lasting accommodation in the Far East. Yet he abhorred war and would have sacrificed almost anything to avoid it. It required no leap of the imagination for Hoover, at the outbreak of the Second World War, to advocate a detached and defensive "Fortress America."

International Disintegration, 1930–1941

The Great Depression of the thirties was worldwide. By 1931, the German economy was virtually bankrupt, the British credit system was tottering, and the foundation beneath every other industrial nation was badly shaken. By 1933, whatever faint chances had once existed for a cooperative international response to the depression disappeared, and each major power looked to its own resources for a solution. Economic nationalism thrived, as government after government moved first to protect its weakened domestic interests from outside competition. Simultaneously, some powers also tried to renew their strength through military imperialism.

The first of the military imperialists to strike was Japan. When depression pinched its lifelines of commerce, Japan looked more avidly than ever to its most natural area for economic expansion, the Asian mainland. But Japan could expect little profit in China as long as it was plagued by civil wars and carved into many spheres of foreign influence. Beginning in September 1931, Japan's Kwantung Army, which was stationed in Manchuria, took the initiative by seizing all of this rich northern province. Twelve months later, Manchuria became the Japanese puppet state of Manchukuo. Tokyo then sought to extend its sway southward by making a vassal of China's most successful warlord, Chiang Kai-shek. Chiang, whose first priority was defeating the Chinese Communists under Mao Tse-tung, eluded the Japanese until the summer of 1937, when the Japanese government released its impatient army to conquer all of China. By October 1938, Japan had occupied China's most important cities. Both Chiang's Nationalists and Mao's Communists, however, kept resistance alive in the countryside.

An even more formidable imperialism emerged in Germany. Against a background of economic chaos, the National Socialist party worked its way into the German government early in 1933, established its leader Adolf Hitler as dictator, and proceeded to eliminate its opponents. For a time, outsiders refused to take the militaristic pomp, the crude racism, and the ranting leaders of the Nazis seriously. But the new government proved ingenious in attracting German

ADOLF HITLER REVIEWING TROOPS

Goose-stepping soldiers and Nazi salutes symbolized a
new German power that shook the foundations of
Europe in the late 1930s. *(Brown Brothers.)*

loyalties and mobilizing its economic resources. As the Nazis consolidated their
power at home, they also asserted it abroad. Hitler, repudiating the Versailles
Treaty as a "stab in the back," pulled Germany out of the League of Nations
in 1933 and two years later announced that Germany would rearm. In 1936,
German troops occupied the Rhineland provinces, which the Versailles Treaty
had demilitarized. In March 1938, demanding the political unification of all
German people, Hitler sent his soldiers into Austria, and Germany annexed it.
That September, the Sudeten territory of Czechoslovakia fell to Germany. In
March 1939, Hitler seized the rest of Czechoslovakia and took aim at the former
German lands along the Baltic Sea. By early summer of 1939, the German
military was poised at the border of Poland.

As a minor accompaniment, Italy also joined the new imperialists. The Fascist Benito Mussolini, who had arisen as Italy's dictator in 1922, longed to make his nation the great power of the Mediterranean. But the opportunistic Duce had to settle for lesser glory. In October 1935, hoping to distract Italians from their economic woes at home, Mussolini ordered his army into Ethiopia, and the following May, Italy annexed it as a colony. Two months later, civil war in Spain offered Mussolini another chance to extend Italy's influence in the Mediterranean. Between 1936 and 1938, Italian military intervention in behalf of General Francisco Franco's army, more than matching the assistance that France and the Soviet Union gave to the Spanish Republicans, made a critical difference in this war. By 1939, Franco's reactionary Falange ruled Spain. The canny Franco, however, remained independent of both Mussolini and Hitler, who had also aided his cause. The alliance that did emerge during the Spanish Civil War was the Rome-Berlin Axis, which firmly bound those two dictatorships by 1939.

None of the mechanisms for international stabilization so optimistically developed during the 1920s could halt these waves of violence. The Washington Conference's limitations on naval armament, which had been restated at the London Naval Conference of 1930, were now discarded in the rush for more power. Japan's expansion into China erased the Open Door doctrine of the Nine-Power Treaty. In 1933, Japan and then Germany simply walked out of the League of Nations. The League's attempt to impose economic sanctions against Italy for its invasion of Ethiopia failed abysmally, and in 1937, Italy also withdrew from the League. Even the normal channels of diplomacy were clogged with accusations, suspicions, and deceptions.

Consequently, each nation that felt threatened by the new imperialism adopted its own course. No European power had the energy to confront Japan. Britain and France, though fretful about their own imperial interests in Asia, neither condoned nor seriously challenged Japan's conquests. The Soviet Union and France were particularly vehement in condemning Hitler's advances. Yet neither trusted the other sufficiently to take an effective joint stand. Moreover, both Hitler and Mussolini, by keeping the hopes for compromise alive with hints of moderation, discouraged a collective retaliation. It was British Prime Minister Neville Chamberlain who most earnestly explored these prospects of a peaceful settlement. Unlike France and the Soviet Union, England reacted very mildly to Italy's intervention in Spain. When Hitler's demand for the Sudetenland precipitated a European crisis, Chamberlain carried the primary burdens of diplomacy that culminated in the Munich Conference of September 1938. At Munich, England and France agreed that Germany and other Central European states could divide about one-third of Czechoslovakia among themselves. In the wake of the Munich Conference, Chamberlain returned to London with promises of "peace in our time."

When Hitler devoured the rest of Czechoslovakia in March 1939, Chamberlain's illusion of peace dissolved. Britain and France committed themselves to a defense of Poland and frantically prepared for war. Then in August 1939, Germany and the Soviet Union, Europe's most implacable foes, shocked the world by signing a nonaggression pact. With the Nazi Wehrmacht prepared to strike at Poland, all eyes fixed on Berlin.

America's mixture of involvement and detachment had no way of reckoning with military imperialism. Either the United States would have to expand its commitments and cooperate with other nations, or it would have to separate itself even farther from the new centers of danger. Hoover's secretary of state, Henry L. Stimson, tried the first alternative and failed. When Japan occupied Manchuria in 1931 and 1932, an outraged Stimson explored ways by which the United States could join in a collective international response. As an outsider, however, the United States could not collaborate effectively with the League of Nations. And the Nine-Power Treaty on the Open Door in China, a vague document at best, contained no sanctions against a violator. Hoping at least to keep the path open for a stronger American policy in the future, Stimson this time was blocked by the President. Hoover publicly declared that the United States would participate in neither military nor economic sanctions against Japan. What emerged was a purely American and purely moral condemnation of Japan. The "Hoover-Stimson Doctrine" of 1932, relying on the Paris Peace Pact's repudiation of war, stated that the United States would refuse diplomatic recognition to a military aggressor's territorial gains.

A second way to expand international cooperation was to bypass the imperialists themselves and concentrate instead on lifting the depression. President Hoover tried to follow this route. By declaring a moratorium on war debts in 1931, he eased the impact of an international crisis in finance. Then as Hoover was leaving the White House in 1933, he contended that the United States must take the lead at a forthcoming London Economic Conference in order to stabilize the world's chaotic finances. Hoover's successor disagreed. Roosevelt, by refusing America's cooperation in the middle of the negotiations, destroyed the London Conference and aligned himself with the popular sentiment at home that the United States could solve its depression alone. Democrats preferred a far less demanding form of international cooperation, lower tariffs. They argued that by increasing the flow of trade, international tensions would ease and the prospects of world peace improve. With Secretary of State Cordell Hull in command, Congress passed the Reciprocal Trade Agreement Act of 1934, so that the State Department could negotiate these lower tariffs with other nations. Although the United States signed many such agreements, they had no effect on either the worldwide depression or the rise of militarism.

In the mid-thirties American sentiment appeared overwhelmingly to favor a greater detachment from a troubled world. Congress expressed this opinion on several occasions. The Tydings-McDuffie Act of 1934, which set a schedule of independence for America's Philippine colony, promised to remove a particularly dangerous outpost of American responsibility. The Johnson Debt-Default Act of 1934, establishing the narrowest possible definition of America's friends and enemies abroad, denied American credit to any foreign government that had not honored its war debt. Then between 1935 and 1937, Congress enacted a series of neutrality laws to close off the routes that had led into the previous war. It embargoed arms and munitions to belligerents, banned using American vessels to ship them, prohibited arming American merchant ships, and proscribed extending credit to belligerents. Later, the neutrality laws would be ridiculed as a scheme to "Keep America Out of the First World War." Americans, not yet knowing any other war, praised these laws as their protection against the madness of a world in arms.

As the pace of the new imperialism accelerated between 1937 and 1939, American attitudes began to change in two important respects. First, a growing majority of Americans concentrated their feelings of horror and hatred on Japan and Germany. The full-scale invasion of China in 1937 gave Americans their first appalling revelations of what a modern air force could do to an urban population. On the eve of the Second World War, the bombing of China's cities produced the same kind of humanitarian outcry in America that bayoneted babies had roused during the First World War. Although most Americans would not realize until the mid-1940s how literally the Nazis sought to exterminate the Jews, news about mass arrests and concentration camps increasingly identified Hitler's anti-Semitism as a threat to all civilized values. Japan and Germany, a majority of Americans concluded, were the centers of an insane barbarism.

A second change in attitudes involved the potential danger from Germany and Japan. Americans who understood their own society as a system of interest groups thought of the world also in terms of interrelated national interests and international spheres of influence. Many of them believed that the United States and Latin America formed a sphere of reciprocal interests, with the United States investing in the Latin American economies, processing their raw materials, and selling finished products in their markets. Early in the thirties, some Americans were willing to accept Japan and Manchuria as a comparable sphere. The more vigorously the new imperial systems grew, however, the more they seemed bent on absorbing the whole world. If Japan controlled all China, would its sphere not expand throughout the western Pacific and Southeast Asia? If Germany dominated Europe, how could it possibly be excluded from the Western Hemisphere? By lumping all of the expansive powers together as "fascist," Americans increasingly found themselves pondering the ultimate danger. Could America itself survive in a world of fascist spheres?

One natural reaction to these worries was to consolidate America's power in the Western Hemisphere. Under Roosevelt's "Good Neighbor Policy," the United States formally abandoned any claim to intervene in a Latin American state. The State Department actively pursued reciprocal trade in Latin America,

THE NAZI THREAT

(Library of Congress.)

and this region was exempted from the new prohibitions governing American neutrality. As Germany and Japan became ever more menacing, the United States sponsored agreements in 1936 and 1938 that made an external threat to one nation in the hemisphere the common concern of them all. At least the United States would protect the "American sphere."

In September 1939, Germany invaded Poland. As Hitler prepared to divide that unhappy land with the Soviet Union, Britain and France declared war on Germany. That winter the world waited. Then in April 1940, Germany began a lightning sweep through Western Europe, taking Norway, Denmark, the Netherlands, and Belgium. By June, France itself had fallen. Only Britain remained. Though German bombers devastated its cities and German submarines squeezed its lifeline of supplies, an invasion of England never came. Instead, the Nazis turned eastward late in 1940 and, with feeble assistance from their Italian ally, conquered the Balkans. In June 1941, Hitler launched the fateful thrust of the war, an attack into Russia. The Nazi-Soviet pact of 1939 had been a calculated expedient between enemies, enabling Hitler to conquer the heart of Europe and the Russians to seize a portion of Poland, the Baltic states of Latvia, Lithuania, and Estonia, and a slice of Finland. Now the Nazis were ready to smash their last great opponent on the continent, and the German war machine roared across a broad eastern front against Russia's primary cities.

While Germany was swallowing Europe, Japan extended its authority southward into French Indochina—ostensibly to tighten the blockade of China but actually to control a new area rich in natural resources. Just ahead lay the precious oil and rubber of Southeast Asia. In September 1940, Japan joined the Axis powers in a defensive Tripartite Pact. It was a tentative connection. Many Japanese leaders never trusted Hitler or wanted their nation's destiny tied to a European power. Yet from the outside, Tokyo's link with Berlin and Rome gave the impression of a unified fascist force rolling toward global domination.

Before September 1939, President Roosevelt seemed to be a firm believer in America's detachment from the world's turmoil. In 1932, to increase his chances for the presidential nomination, he abandoned the cause of America's entry into the League of Nations. Soon after taking office, he undermined the London Economic Conference. In fact, Roosevelt showed little interest in any foreign affairs outside the Western Hemisphere. The President did not seriously contest the neutrality laws of the mid-thirties, and he seldom hazarded an opinion of any kind about the state of the world. Although his private concerns obviously rose toward the end of the decade, his public statements remained very broad. In October 1937, Roosevelt did use the suggestive word *quarantine* in a speech on the evils of war and aggression. But when commentators took it to imply coercion or collective action against the fascist powers, the President angrily denied any such thought. After the Munich Conference in 1938, Roosevelt congratulated the leaders in England and France for their efforts to keep the peace.

Because the President's influence over foreign policy was always very strong in a time of crisis, even the subtle shades in Roosevelt's thinking became critically important after September 1939. Early in his career, Roosevelt came to believe that a great power such as the United States should play an important role in world affairs. His background and training equated Anglo-American culture with civilization, and his instincts told him that Germany was the nation's enemy. Unlike many of his contemporaries, Roosevelt never questioned either the wisdom or the justice of America's entry into the First World War. As foreign affairs occupied more and more of the President's attention, these attitudes increasingly shaped American policy. Characteristically, Roosevelt avoided hard commitments as long as he could, and in the process kept personal control over the government's decisions. The selfless Harry Hopkins, moving into the White House as Roosevelt's intimate adviser and mirroring his ideas on world affairs, was FDR's favorite envoy.

Between the outbreak of war in 1939 and Germany's "Blitzkrieg" in 1940, America hugged its shore. In 1939, the United States induced the nations of Latin America to join it in declaring a huge neutrality zone between Europe and the Western Hemisphere. Although England and France purchased war materials in the United States, the terms were "cash and carry." By law, Americans could provide neither credit nor shipping for a belligerent. Almost everyone hoped a major war would never develop. When Germany's conquest of Western Europe destroyed that hope, a new pattern of American opinion began to form. During 1940 and 1941, a rising majority of Americans wanted the United States to stand behind Britain's resistance to Hitler. At the same time, a declining but substantial majority wanted the United States to remain at peace. The rough guideline became "all aid short of war."

For a time, Roosevelt followed these potentially conflicting sentiments. During the presidential campaign of 1940, the "Battle of Britain" raged furiously as German bombers and submarines swarmed around the isolated isles. Roosevelt, despite a hard contest with the Republican Wendell Willkie, risked a dramatic violation of traditional neutrality in an effort to relieve the British. In September 1940, the President announced an exchange of fifty old American destroyers for the lease of British bases in the Western Hemisphere. The Destroyer Deal formally declared America's commitment to the British cause. Nevertheless, the Roosevelt administration resisted close diplomatic or military cooperation with Britain and generally refused to prepare for a wartime alliance.

But the pressure of events was forcing a hard choice between involvement and detachment. By the winter of 1940–41, Britain's situation appeared desperate and a German invasion imminent. Britain's dwindling assets in the United States could not begin to pay for the war materials it needed. Roosevelt, with growing popular support behind him, chose involvement. Describing the United States as the "arsenal of democracy," Roosevelt proposed an almost unlimited British access to American production and credit. An "America First" movement, which attracted such prominent men as Robert E. Wood of Sears, Roebuck, the labor leader John L. Lewis, and the hero of the twenties Charles Lindbergh, fought frantically against the legislation. Nevertheless, in March 1941, Congress passed the open-ended Lend-Lease Act, wiping out the last traces of American neutrality. Lend-lease, its opponents cried, was a Grim Reaper's AAA that would "plow under every fourth American boy." Publicly, Roosevelt tried to calm these fears of war. In private, however, he knew that the United States and Britain were now partners, pooling resources and coordinating plans against a common foe.

To ensure the delivery of these essential supplies, American convoys carried them closer and closer to the British Isles. In April 1941, the United States extended its patrols to the mid-Atlantic. Then in July, following Germany's invasion of Russia, American convoys moved a big step closer to the English ports by escorting the supplies as far as Iceland. A month later, the American navy expanded its protection to cover British merchant ships as well as American. Meanwhile, along the Atlantic sealanes, the Americans and British collaborated in locating and attacking German submarines. In September, one German submarine, as it fled from the U.S.S. *Greer*, fired at the American destroyer. Roosevelt, pretending that the submarine had been the aggressor and likening German power to a "rattlesnake" that was coiled to strike at the Western Hemisphere, ordered American ships to "shoot on sight." By October, Congress authorized convoys to land in Britain. "All aid" to Britain could not stop "short of war." Though most Americans did not yet know it, their second world war had already begun.

During these crucial months of 1940 and 1941, Asian affairs appeared to be less volatile and less important. Most Americans agreed that Japanese imperialism posed some kind of threat, but few could define it. Roosevelt himself did not have precise objectives in Asia, and he left the negotiations with Japan largely to his crusty secretary of state, Cordell Hull. Hull insisted that Japan honor the Nine-Power Treaty of 1922 on the Open Door. In effect, that meant a Japanese withdrawal from the mainland of Asia. As leverage, the United States imposed an increasingly tight embargo on trade with Japan, a policy that did indeed have a sharp effect on the Japanese economy. During most of 1941, conciliatory forces in the Japanese government under Prince Fuminaro Konoye, the prime minister, sought some way of mollifying the United States short of a complete Japanese capitulation. Although Konoye would not reopen the question of Manchuria, he proposed a Japanese military withdrawal elsewhere on the Asian mainland in exchange for a friendly Chinese government and American economic cooperation. But Hull was unrelenting. Before serious negotiations could begin, he insisted, Japan must first declare its acceptance of the Open Door throughout the area of Japanese expansion.

By the summer of 1941, the two nations were drifting towards war. In July, Japan completed its occupation of Indochina, and Roosevelt retaliated by freezing Japanese assets in the United States. Appraising their limited resources, Japan's leaders realized that if they had to fight the United States for their empire, the time had come. Though Prince Konoye continued to explore various formulas of compromise, his power at home was waning. Washington remained unresponsive. In October 1941, the more militant Hideki Tojo replaced Konoye as prime minister, and Japan prepared for war. As Japan mobilized, one last effort at negotiations failed. Meanwhile, because American intelligence had broken Japan's secret code, Washington knew that a Japanese attack of some kind was pending. Roosevelt's inner circle guessed that it would strike in Southeast Asia. But no one anticipated what was to come, and no one was ready. At dawn on December 7, Japanese planes roared across the naval base at Pearl Harbor, Hawaii and crippled America's Pacific force. By waiting instead of negotiating, Roosevelt had been given an event that dissolved the nation's doubts and propelled it into total war.*

---

*Within a few days after the attack on Pearl Harbor, an exchange of war declarations — Britain with Japan, Germany and Italy with the United States — completed the alignment of powers until August 1945, when the Soviet Union entered the war against Japan.

PEARL HARBOR, DECEMBER 7, 1941

Out of the wreckage of Pearl Harbor came a powerful
American commitment to win the war. *(Official Navy
Photograph.)*

World War, 1941–1945

Between December 1941 and May 1945, the United States, unlike its allies,
was continuously engaged in two very different wars. In the Pacific theater,
where victory hinged on control of the seas, the United States fought almost
alone. In the European theater, where victory could be won only on the continent, the United States contributed to a complex, collective effort.

During the early months of the war, both theaters offered a dismal picture
of retreat and jeopardy. Japanese units swept away the remnants of resistance
in Southeast Asia, occupying the Netherland East Indies (Indonesia), capturing
the British base at Singapore, and penetrating to the frontier of India. Japan's
naval victory in the Java Sea assured its control of the western Pacific. In May
1942, the last of America's small, isolated force in the Philippines surrendered
to the Japanese. Germany's successes were even more ominous. Its fleet of
submarines, which had been held in check before December 1941, unleashed
a devastating attack on the Atlantic supply lines. The Nazi's mechanized divisions under General Erwin Rommel drove across North Africa into Egypt,
threatening the Suez Canal. Above all, a renewed offensive in Russia spread

German troops from the outskirts of Leningrad in the north to the gates of Stalingrad in the south. Into the late fall of 1942, the greatest disaster, a Soviet collapse, loomed as a strong possibility.

How could the United States best use its massive resources to alter the balance of the war? In broad strategic matters, the answers came quickly and clearly. The European theater had priority over the Pacific. Food and war materials, which under lend-lease had been moving to Russia before Pearl Harbor, were the immediate contributions that the United States could make to Soviet survival. Despite the menace of the German submarines, the quantity of these supplies swelled each month. Finally, to relieve the pressure on the Soviet army, American and British forces had to launch a "second front" as soon as possible somewhere in the west.

The men who ultimately made these decisions were President Roosevelt and Prime Minister Winston Churchill, Britain's brilliant, calculating war leader. Their personal collaboration had begun at the Atlantic Conference of August 1941, which declared to the world that the United States and Great Britain stood together against the Axis. From December 1941 to January 1943, through a series of private meetings, the two men grew closer. Although Russia's fate also hung on the decisions that Roosevelt and Churchill made, the Soviet Union remained a distant ally, declaring its needs and awaiting a response from the Western powers.

The initial American impulse was to open at least a token second front in Western Europe during 1942. Sobered by the logistical difficulties of a quick attack on France, however, Roosevelt and his advisers reluctantly accepted Churchill's alternative of a North African campaign. In November 1942, an

SIEGE OF LENINGRAD

Their city surrounded by German troops, citizens of Leningrad dip water from a broken main. More than 600,000 died of starvation during the two-year seige. *(Associated Press.)*

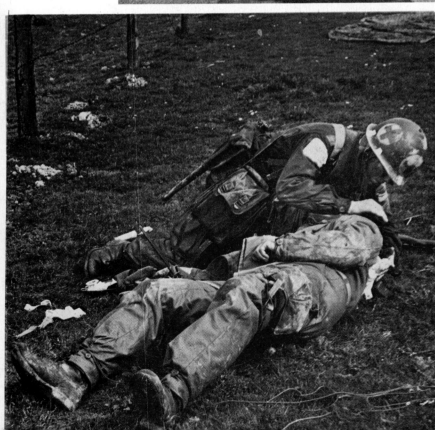

Anglo-American force under General Dwight D. Eisenhower invaded French Morocco and Algiers and by the following May eliminated Axis power throughout North Africa. Meanwhile the Soviet Union had won the pivotal engagement of the European war. In an effort to crack Russia's resistance before another winter froze his army in place, Hitler gambled recklessly on an assault against Stalingrad. During the winter's war of 1942–43, a relentless Soviet counterattack not only saved Stalingrad but actually cost Germany half a million troops. The following summer, the Soviet army took the initiative and began its drive westward toward Berlin.

In 1943, Churchill again convinced Roosevelt to postpone an attack on France. That July, in the most dubious strategic decision of the war, an allied force landed in Sicily, then in September crossed into Italy. Although Italy immediately surrendered, German troops filled the vacuum from the north and stalled the allied army. It was not the second front that the Soviet Premier, Josef Stalin, thought he had been promised. Russian soldiers continued to bear the primary burden of the ground war against Germany, and Stalin was furious.

Not until June 6, 1944, did the United States and Britain finally establish a successful second front in France. Under General Eisenhower, the allies executed a brilliant landing at Normandy. Then in August, another force invaded southern France, and that same month Paris fell. In September, British and

FRANCE, 1944

The photographer Robert Capa captures the horrors of war and joys of peace: the Normandy invasion, a wounded soldier, liberated Paris. *(All from Robert Capa,* Images of War, *Copyright © 1964.)*

American troops entered Germany itself. Even before the Normandy landing, the Russian army was pressing toward Poland, East Prussia, and the Balkans. Except for a desperate Nazi counterattack at the German-Belgian border—the "Battle of the Bulge" in December 1944—Germany's army collapsed inside the allied vise. By the end of April, Russian troops were fighting in the streets of Berlin. Following Hitler's suicide, German officers capitulated on May 7, 1945.

The critical contributions to victory in Europe had been Russian lives and American productivity. About 16 million citizens of the Soviet Union died in the conflict with Germany. By contrast, British losses were about half a million, and American losses in both theaters of war about 250,000. The United States had indeed served as the arsenal of democracy. By 1942, America's war production equaled the combined output of the Axis powers; by 1944, it doubled the enemy's total. In 1943 and 1944, when Germany could no longer slow the delivery of American goods, the Nazis fell beneath a crushing wave of war materials. America's schedule of production became Germany's timetable of defeat.

In Asia, the United States confronted a weaker but more remote foe. Because Congress had authorized a program of naval construction well before Pearl Harbor, the American fleet was able to return in strength to the Pacific less than a year after Japan's devastating surprise attack. In May 1942, even as Japan was absorbing the Philippines, a successful American attack on Japanese shipping in the Coral Sea secured Australia. A month later, a Japanese naval force was repulsed near Midway Island, west of Hawaii. Then in November 1942, the American navy won a three-day battle off the Solomon Islands near Australia, and the balance of sea power shifted back to the United States.

Still, the pace of the Pacific war remained slow during 1943. The European theater continued to have priority, and the logistics of the Pacific campaign denied any chances for a sudden, grand success. On the assumption that only an occupation of Tokyo itself could end the war, naval forces under Admiral Chester Nimitz and a combination of American, Australian, and New Zealand ground forces under General Douglas MacArthur began a grim, two-pronged assault toward the Japanese mainland. Nimitz's command had to sweep the myriad islands in the central Pacific. From the south, MacArthur's command had to struggle through the jungles of New Guinea, then converge with Nimitz's on the Philippines.

Early in 1944, as America's productive capacities expanded to serve both the European and the Pacific wars, the drive to Japan gained momentum. By summer, the United States controlled the central Pacific. Then in October, with General MacArthur dramatically leading his troops to the site of a humiliating defeat early in the war, American forces invaded the Philippines. That same month, in the Battle of Leyte Gulf, Japanese naval power was destroyed. Ferocious Japanese resistance continued to keep casualties high. As late as March 1945, a month's fight for the tiny island of Iwo Jima left 20,000 Americans dead and wounded. But Japan itself now lay open to systematic bombing.

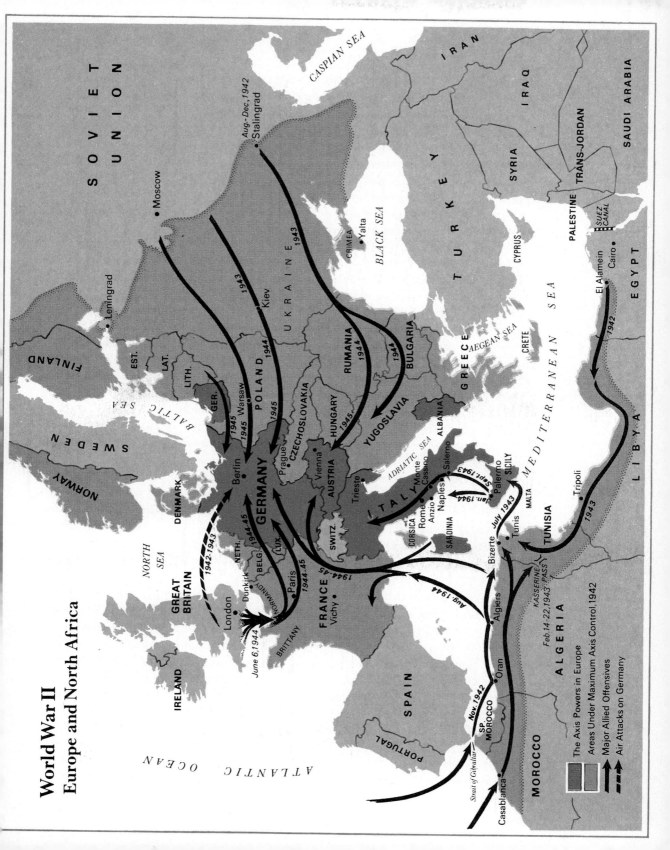

World War II
Europe and North Africa

Napalm raids burned its compact cities, one by one. In March 1945, a single attack on Tokyo killed more than 80,000. When Germany surrendered in May 1945, an utterly exposed Japan was already tottering.

Strangely enough, the climactic blow of the Asian war had been in preparation even before Pearl Harbor and had been originally aimed at Germany, not Japan. In 1939, refugee physicists from Europe, fearing the potential of Germany's military technology, began urging the American government to explore the possibility of an awesome new atomic bomb before the Nazis could develop it. Within a year the project was under way. In utmost secrecy, groups of scientists at separate laboratories struggled against time to master the secrets of the atom. They learned to control a chain reaction of atomic fission so that it would generate enormous power. Then they translated this discovery into a technically practical military device. In July 1945, the task was finally completed at a lonely center in Los Alamos, New Mexico, under the direction of the physicist J. Robert Oppenheimer. By then, however, Germany had fallen. A new, inexperienced President, Harry Truman, sat in the White House. An array of military and civilian advisers counseled the President to use the new weapon against Japan, and Truman agreed. On August 6, a single bomb demolished the city of Hiroshima, immediately killing about 80,000 and maiming and poisoning thousands more. Three days later, just as the Soviet Union declared war on Japan, a second bomb razed Nagasaki. On August 14, Japan agreed to surrender.

Although Roosevelt did not live to celebrate the final victory, his leadership set the nation's course to the eve of surrender. At two levels, that leadership was notably effective. Roosevelt was an inspired spokesman of hope, not only for Americans but also for yearning people throughout the world. Even before Pearl Harbor, Roosevelt and Churchill had sketched ideals for the postwar world in the Atlantic Charter, which drew heavily on the Wilsonian principles of political self-determination, free economic exchange, and international cooperation. Roosevelt's broad goal of the "Four Freedoms"—freedom from want and fear, freedom of speech and religion—met an enthusiastic international response.

On a very practical level, Roosevelt was also a skilled mediator among quarreling, competing wartime interests. He maneuvered among the many military demands of Americans and allies alike, giving a little, taking a little, but never losing command. Of all the challenges to these negotiating talents, the greatest was the Soviet premier, Josef Stalin. Between the Bolshevik Revolution of 1917 and the German invasion of Russia in 1941, Soviet-American relations had been an almost unrelieved story of mutual hostility. Until 1933, the United States did not even recognize the Soviet Union. Americans responded in disgust to the Nazi-Soviet pact of 1939 and the Russian war against Finland that winter. Even after the United States and the Soviet Union became wartime allies, their exchanges were often sharp, especially over the delays in a second front. Stalin's suspicious nature complicated each problem.

World War II in the Pacific

Legend:
- Areas Under Japanese Control, 1942
- Major Allied Offensives
- Major Allied Air Operations

Map labels:

ALASKA

BERING SEA

ALEUTIAN ISLANDS
Attu
Kiska 1943

KURILE IS.

SOVIET UNION

RUSSIANS 1945

OUTER MONGOLIA

MANCHURIA
Peking
Nanking

CHINA

KOREA
Tokyo
Hiroshima
Nagasaki
Shanghai

JAPAN

Iwo Jima 1945
Okinawa 1945

FORMOSA
Hong Kong

INDIA

BURMA
Ledo
Lashio
Rangoon
Stilwell Rd.
"The Hump" 1943
Burma Rd.
Kunming
Chungking

FRENCH INDO-CHINA
THAILAND

MALAYA
Singapore

SUMATRA

NETHERLANDS INDIES

BORNEO
CELEBES
JAVA
TIMOR

PHILIPPINE ISLANDS
LUZON
MINDANAO

PACIFIC OCEAN

Limit of Farthest Japanese Expansion

Wake I.

MARIANA IS.
Saipan
Guam 1945

CAROLINE IS.
Eniwetok
Kwajalein 1944

MARSHALL IS.

GILBERT IS.
Tarawa 1943

SOLOMON IS.
Guadalcanal 1942

Bismarck Sea
NEW GUINEA
Port Moresby 1942
1943

CORAL SEA 1942

1944-45

Midway I.
June 3-6, 1942

HAWAIIAN ISLANDS
Pearl Harbor Dec. 7, 1941

EQUATOR

AUSTRALIA

INDIAN OCEAN

THE SURRENDER OF JAPAN

At the microphone a magisterial Douglas
MacArthur presides as Japan surrenders. *(U.S. Army
Photograph.)*

Although no one person could have overcome this history of obstacles, Roosevelt did manage to open a dialogue with the Soviet dictator. At the depths of
Russia's wartime doubts in 1943, Stalin, Churchill, and Roosevelt arranged
their first joint meeting, which took place that November and December in
Tehran. During the conference, Roosevelt distanced himself from Churchill
and responded in a conciliatory way to Stalin's proposals. When the Big Three
met again at the much more important Yalta Conference of February 1945,
the American President adopted a similar stance toward his colleagues.

As an architect of national policy, however, Roosevelt was extremely vague.
The President was thoroughly committed to the allied policy of "unconditional
surrender," and he tried as best he could to bury the long-range problems of
the postwar world beneath the short-term needs of a military victory. But
fighting a war to win it did not establish an international program. Unlike
Churchill and Stalin, Roosevelt had almost no traditional goals that he could
actually transfer to a map of the postwar world. Moreover, the President had no
inclinations to draw one. In his wartime exchanges with Churchill and Stalin,
Roosevelt chided the British on the sins of their empire, talked of future Soviet-
American cooperation, but whenever possible, avoided specific commitments.

Only on the issue of international organization did the Roosevelt administration show itself decisive. At the Bretton Woods Conference of 1944, the

United States took the lead in developing a program for international monetary stabilization. The American dollar became the basis for most monetary transactions. To facilitate international finance, the conference planned two new agencies, the World Bank and the International Monetary Fund. The International Monetary Fund, in turn, belonged to a far more elaborate organization that was also developing during the war, a new league of nations. Once again, it was the Roosevelt administration that led the movement for another attempt at worldwide collective security.

Cordell Hull, tenaciously devoted to the concept of world organization, deserved the primary credit for negotiating a postwar United Nations (UN). Recalling Woodrow Wilson's disaster, the secretary of state wooed the Senate and included prominent Republicans in the planning of a new league. At every opportunity, Hull pressed America's wartime allies for firm commitments to an international organization. When the secretary retired in 1944, the hardest work had been done. Despite British fears for its empire and Soviet fears for its security, their representatives joined delegates from forty-six other nations in San Francisco to found a world organization. Overcoming a final Soviet resistance, the delegates signed the Charter for the United Nations in June 1945. The heart of the UN lay in the small Security Council, where the important decisions were made and each great power had a veto. The General Assembly, representing all members, served as an arena for discussion and broad pronouncements. Surrounding this legislative core, a host of agencies fulfilled specialized international functions; and presiding over the entire structure, the Secretary-General's office administered the UN's programs. In July 1945, the United States Senate overwhelmingly approved America's participation.

International organizations were only mechanisms, not policies, and the war did not create a new American foreign policy. What it did change was America's orientation toward international affairs. The primary lesson of the war, as almost every American leader interpreted it, was the importance of power. In the past, they argued, American diplomacy had relied far too exclusively on moral principles and good intentions. The ultimate guarantee of a just cause was an adequate military force and the will to use it. Blaming the Second World War on the failure of democratic nations before 1939 to confront the fascist aggressors, Americans made *Munich* and *appeasement* synonymous with diplomatic suicide.

By itself, this reasoning encouraged neither a greater international involvement nor a detachment from world affairs. It could justify both Wendell Willkie's expansive plea for "One World" and Congresswoman Clare Booth Luce's inturning rebuttal—"Globaloney!" Many Americans continued to hope that without sacrificing America's military strength, the nation could regain its traditional balance between involvement and detachment. Air power became the most popular means of achieving that goal. Even during the war, the presence of American troops abroad seemed fundamentally unnatural. Almost everyone expected the soldiers to come home and stay home after the war. For emotional as well as logistical reasons, therefore, Americans increasingly favored a powerful air force to provide a maximum of protection with a minimum of involvement. As the fighting came to an end, the Chief of Staff, General George C. Marshall, was planning the nation's postwar defense in these terms.

Roosevelt's thoughts about a new league of nations also reflected the recent emphasis on power. As a young man, Roosevelt had accepted the Wilsonian vision of an evolving general plan for world organization that would express an international consensus about peace and justice. By the Second World War, however, the President shifted his focus to some form of regional policing. He even settled on the international policemen: the United States, the Soviet Union, Great Britain, and China. In other words, the heart of Roosevelt's conception was no longer a "solemn covenant," just four strong, alert nations enforcing the peace in their natural regions of influence. Later, when the great powers could not cooperate inside the UN and the United States bypassed it in favor of military alliances, America altered Roosevelt's tactics without violating his assumptions about the connection between power and collective security.

Cold War, 1945–1950

On April 12, 1945, a change in Presidents made a critical difference in the nation's foreign affairs. Roosevelt had paid no attention to Harry Truman, the Vice-President who was pushed on him at the 1944 convention. Senator Robert Taft once said, in rejecting the office, that the Vice-President had nothing to do except "inquire about the President's health." Truman had not even done that. Stunned by Roosevelt's death, he suddenly found himself chief executive without adequate knowledge about America's international involvements or a clear postwar policy to guide him.

Within two years after Truman took office, the United States and the Soviet Union were engaged in a "Cold War" along a line approximating the location of their victorious armies in the summer of 1945. Though no experienced observer expected a placid transition from war to peace, relatively few people seemed to have anticipated or welcomed such bitter animosity. Despite an apparent desire in the United States and the Soviet Union for some accommodation, a core of problems between the two nations proved so intractable that they destroyed the capacity to compromise on any other issue. The underlying causes of this rift were extremely complex, and for decades reasonable people would differ sharply over their meaning. The immediate source of conflict, however, was obvious to everyone. What should be the postwar disposition of Germany and Eastern Europe?

At the Yalta Conference Roosevelt, Churchill, and Stalin took an initial step toward resolving this complicated package of problems. Stalin stated the Soviet position in detail. For Germany, which had invaded Russia twice in thirty years, he demanded a harsh settlement that would strip it of the potential to make war and send massive reparations in machinery and labor to the Soviet Union. In Eastern Europe, which had been Germany's avenue for invasion, Stalin wanted friendly governments from Poland in the north to the edge of Greece in the south. Where Stalin was rigid and determined, Roosevelt was vague and agreeable. The gravely ill President seemed to accept Stalin's argument that these measures were essential to Russian security. It was Churchill, not Roosevelt, who futilely resisted $20 billion as an estimate for German reparations. Again it was Churchill, more than Roosevelt, who forced the insertion of "free and unfettered elections" into the Yalta agreement on the postwar Polish government. Neither Churchill nor Roosevelt challenged a general Soviet sphere of influence covering Hungary, Rumania, Bulgaria, and Yugoslavia.

All parties regarded the agreements at Yalta as no more than the outline for a later settlement. But instead of proceeding toward a full-scale peace treaty, the Soviet Union and the United States each began reshaping the Yalta decisions to suit its own ends. Stalin made it clear that the elections in Poland would have to choose his candidates. Truman not only attacked Russia's coercion of Poland; he now challenged the entire concept of a Soviet sphere in Eastern Europe. Meanwhile, the United States abandoned plans for a harsh peace in Germany and tried to preserve its remaining economic strength. As a temporary measure, Germany had been divided into American, British, French, and Russian zones of military

ROOSEVELT AND CHURCHILL AT YALTA

Between 1941 and 1943, Roosevelt and Prime Minister Winston Churchill developed an exceptionally close wartime partnership. (*Library of Congress.*)

occupation. By treating these zones as self-contained administrative units, the United States was able to shield the western industrial portions of Germany from most Soviet demands for reparations.

By summer, Soviet-American tensions were so high that any meeting between Stalin and Truman was in doubt. In July 1945, however, the two did confer at Potsdam. Although the allied leaders issued bland statements of unity and Stalin renewed a promise to declare war on Japan, it was an unhappy conference. The crucial exchanges concerned Germany. Unable to find a common ground, the great powers accepted the separate ground that each one already held. The Soviet Union could set its own policy in the eastern zone of Germany; the United States, Great Britain, and France would determine policy in their western zones. The divisive issue of German reparations was cast vaguely into the future. After Potsdam, neither Truman nor Stalin sought another summit meeting.

There were many other sources of Soviet-American friction in 1945 and 1946. At the San Francisco conference to found the United Nations, the Russian delegates came close to disrupting the proceedings. The Soviet Union continued to view the UN as a league of potential enemies and often obstructed its work. Moreover, to contest American and British influence in the Middle East, Russia kept its troops in Iran and withdrew them early in 1946 only after strong protests. On its part, the United States abruptly ended economic aid to the Soviet Union after Germany's defeat, despite Russia's desperate need for assistance. Bluntly, Truman made any future aid dependent on a Soviet acceptance of American policies. In addition, the United States excluded Russia from the occupation government of Japan, as it already had from the occupation government of Italy.

Yet each of these problems by itself was either negotiable or tolerable. Only the issues of Germany and Eastern Europe defied any accommodation. In what Soviet officials construed as an assault on their vital interests, the Truman administration pursued a policy of reconciliation with Germany and demanded independent governments throughout Eastern Europe. The German zones rapidly became permanent eastern and western spheres; the Soviet Union tightened its authority over Poland and the Balkans. "From Stettin in the Baltic to Trieste in the Adriatic," Churchill declared in a speech at Fulton, Missouri, "an iron curtain has descended across the Continent." More and more stories of mass killings, deportations, and labor camps filtered through that curtain. Although there were moments of hope for a year after the Potsdam conference, the main trend in Soviet-American relations ran strongly toward suspicion and anger. By late 1946, even the occasional hopes disappeared.

What led the United States to confront the Soviet Union in Europe? The answer had four parts. The most elusive but perhaps the most important element was a powerful tradition of mutual distrust. There was a natural inclination in both the United States and the Soviet Union to regard the other nation as the "communist" or "capitalist" enemy. Because leaders in each nation viewed their Soviet or American counterparts as inherently expansionist, feelings of distrust easily turned into fears of aggression. Moreover, the wartime habit of dividing the world into diametrically opposing camps encouraged people to understand their postwar problems through similar concepts. By substituting *communism* for *fascism*, many Americans found a convenient answer to a perplexing, worldwide array of problems. In the process, this way of thinking made each little conflict still another sign of fundamental differences. After a clash with Russia's delegates over the charter for the UN, the influential Republican senator, Arthur Vandenberg, noted in his diary: "The basic trouble is that we are trying to unite two incompatible ideologies."

The second part of the answer concerned American expectations following a victorious war. It seemed that the United States, never before so paramount above all other nations, should be able to control the terms of a postwar settlement. Indeed, some saw no limit to America's influence. An "American Century" is commencing, declared the prominent publisher Henry Luce. It was difficult to accept the conflicts and confusions of the postwar world as normal. It was doubly irritating to meet the rigid opposition of a former ally, the Soviet Union. Because most Americans assumed that an able President could manage those international problems, a very heavy burden fell on the inexperienced Truman. Such a high level of popular expectations and low level of popular patience made a hard line in foreign affairs increasingly probable in 1945 and 1946.

The third element in America's postwar policy was Truman's personal inclination toward a hard line. By temperament, he was a fighter. Reporting his first sharp exchange with Soviet Foreign Minister Molotov, Truman wrote with obvious relish, "I gave it to him straight 'one-two to the jaw.' " The same man who thoroughly enjoyed his "Give 'em Hell, Harry" campaign for the presidency in 1948 also found it natural to "get tough" with the Russians in 1945 and 1946. In a characteristically Truman manner, the President wrote his secretary of state in January 1946, "I'm tired of babying the Soviets." Moreover, Truman took pride in his ability to reach a decision promptly, then hold to it firmly. After a meeting with J. Robert Oppenheimer over the moral implications of the atomic bomb, the President snapped: "Don't ever bring the damn fool in here again. He didn't set that bomb off. I did. This kind of snivelling makes me sick." With the unyielding Russians on one side and the pugnacious Truman on the other, the possibilities of a compromise were always slender.

Truman's advisers made the fourth contribution to America's postwar foreign policy. In his bewildering first months as President, Truman had three groups of counselors in foreign affairs. He inherited one group from the Roosevelt administration. Secretary of War Henry Stimson, Secretary of Commerce Henry Wallace, and Roosevelt's personal aide Harry Hopkins all considered themselves experts in world affairs. Whenever they looked at Truman, they saw the giant shadow of FDR behind him. Understandably, the new President found it hard to fit these advisers into a distinctively Truman administration, and one by one they dropped away. Hopkins and Wallace, who shared Roosevelt's optimism about postwar cooperation between the United States and the Soviet Union, were particularly unhappy about Truman's hard line with Stalin. By the fall of 1945, Hopkins was lamenting, "we are doing almost everything we can to break with Russia, which seems so unnecessary to me." After a long period of strain, Wallace finally cut his ties with the Truman administration in September 1946, when he declared in an important speech: " 'Getting tough' never brought anything real and lasting—whether for school yard bullies or businessmen or world powers. The tougher we get, the tougher the Russians will get."

By choice, Truman turned for advice to a group of political associates from his days in Congress. One of these, James Byrnes, became secretary of state in July 1945. Following an impressive career in Congress, on the Supreme Court, and as "Assistant President" in charge of America's wartime mobilization, Byrnes took his new office on the assumption that he would guide both the President and the nation into the postwar world. Though Byrnes was a firm anticommunist, he was also a bargainer. As a professional politician, he had emphasized mediation and adjustment, not flat commands. As secretary of state, he preferred a similar approach. In his scheme of things, Stalin was the international counterpart to a stubborn city boss. As long as Byrnes prevailed, an element of flexibility remained in America's relations with the Soviet Union.

Discreetly at hand stood a third group of advisers, whose base of operations was the State Department. As America's world affairs increasingly demanded a wider range of diplomatic services, the State Department emerged as a significant center of government power, with extensive connections in those business, military, and publishing circles that affected its work. The expanding department attracted an able and strong-minded set of leaders, including W. Averell Harriman, the son of a railroad magnate and ambassador to Great Britain and the Soviet Union, George Kennan, a career diplomat with special talents as a writer and planner, and Dean Acheson, a wellborn lawyer who had found his true calling in the State Department. Through such men as Harriman, Kennan, and Acheson, the department offered Truman something that his other advisers failed to provide, the outlines for a systematic world policy.

As the leaders in the State Department interpreted Soviet behavior, the Russians were following a long-term plan to destroy all capitalist societies. Communist ideology made them fanatics. Despite the needs of their war-ravaged nation, Soviet officials kept a large army mobilized after Germany's surrender. State Department leaders thought that if weakness in a neighboring country gave the Russians the opportunity, they would brutally use this military might. The Soviet army had already attempted such a probe in Iran. From its base in Central Europe, it could strike at any time into the devastated, chaotic nations of Western Europe. To counter this broad threat, the United States, too, needed a long-term plan. American power had to meet Soviet power on a global scale. Otherwise, as Harriman warned, the Russians would pursue their goal of world domination by continuing to build "tiers [of satellites], layer on layer," until they crushed the forces of freedom. Only a firm stand could stop them. As the history of fascism proved, appeasement merely whetted a dictator's appetite.

By the end of 1946 as the United States hovered at a momentous turn in its foreign policy, Truman was ready to follow the State Department's guidance. Unlike Secretary Byrnes, who never completely downed a feeling that Byrnes, rather than Truman, really should have been Roosevelt's successor, the leaders in the State Department invariably acted as obedient servants. Truman, who came to take great pleasure in his office, resented his secretary's independent ways and welcomed this respectful advice from the State Department. With the patrician Dean Acheson, the earthy President developed a beautifully synchronized relationship. Above all, Truman and the department's spokesmen agreed that it was high time to get even tougher with Russia.

In January 1947, Byrnes was replaced as secretary of state by General George Marshall, a man of flawless integrity but limited imagination who funneled ideas from the State Department. In February, one of Roosevelt's four policemen, Great Britain, informed Washington that it was retiring from the force. American, not British, aid would have to save the conservative government in Greece, which was racked with civil war. President Truman, addressing Congress in March on aid to both Greece and Turkey, dramatically announced the new "Truman Doctrine." "At the present moment in world history nearly every nation must choose between alternative ways of life," Truman declared. One alternative was freedom and democracy.

The second way of life is based upon the will of a minority forcibly imposed upon the majority. It relies upon terror and oppression, a controlled press and radio, fixed elections, and the suppression of personal freedoms. I believe that it must be the policy of the United States to support free peoples who are resisting attempted subjugation by armed minorities or by outside pressures.

Simultaneously, the State Department was preparing strategy for a general European defense "against totalitarian pressures." The Marshall Plan, which took shape in the summer of 1947, eventually sent more than $12 billion in American aid to its European allies, including West Germany, and enabled their shattered economies to achieve a minor miracle in recovery. Though the communist nations of Europe were officially invited to participate, the price was a breach in Russia's security system for Eastern Europe. American leaders expected the Russians to refuse. Bitterly denouncing its Western enemies, the Soviet Union obliged, and it demanded the same of its own European allies. Hungary in May, then Rumania in December, fell absolutely under Russian control.

In February 1948, turmoil inside Czechoslovakia, the very symbol of a liberated Europe, allowed the Communist party there to take power. Communications across the Iron Curtain virtually ceased. That spring, rumors raced through

THE BERLIN AIRLIFT

In 1948 the Berlin airlift expressed America's resolve to
keep any further European territory from communist
control. *(Black Star.)*

Washington that a real war was imminent. Instead, between April and June 1948,
the Soviet Union cut the transportation lines to Berlin. Buried deep in the Russian section of Germany, the former capital, like the country as a whole, was
administered through zones. Now the American, British, and French zones of
Berlin were under seige. The United States responded with an impressively
organized air lift that brought essential supplies to the citizens in these isolated
zones. In May 1949, the Russians finally abandoned the blockade. More than any
other event, the Berlin Blockade seemed to verify the Truman administration's
warnings about Soviet aggression. Domestic opposition to the Cold War collapsed
beneath the weight of the blockade, and anti-Soviet sentiments spread in Western
Europe.

Riding the momentum of these changes at home and abroad, the Truman
administration completed negotiations for the North Atlantic Treaty, a pact of
mutual assistance among twelve nations that was signed in April 1949.* Although

*The eleven other nations were Belgium, Canada, Denmark, England, France, Holland,
Iceland, Italy, Luxembourg, Norway, and Portugal. Greece, Turkey, and West Germany
soon joined.

the wording of the treaty was general, almost everyone interpreted it as the guarantee of American military support in case of a Soviet attack in Europe. In January 1949, Dean Acheson, the primary architect of Truman's European program, became secretary of state and received proper credit for this sweeping commitment of American power. Meanwhile, the Federal Republic of Germany emerged out of the western zones of occupation and was set on its way to independence. To each of these steps, the Soviet Union responded with a countermeasure: the German Democratic Republic in the east, then the Warsaw Pact with its European satellites.

With breathtaking speed, the United States had fundamentally changed its role as a peacetime world power. Between March 1947 and April 1949, an entire structure of precedents collapsed. During the rise of fascism in the 1930s, the United States had withdrawn more and more tightly into the Western Hemisphere. Now through the Truman Doctrine, the United States made an open-ended offer of assistance to nations everywhere in the world. Instead of demanding payment of its war debts, as the United States had done after the First World War, the government devised the Marshall Plan to underwrite the economies of Western Europe. In 1940, even the fall of continental Europe had not brought the United States into the Second World War. In 1948, danger to the single city of Berlin threatened to trigger a third world war. In 1927, Americans had shied away from a simple bilateral renunciation of war with France. In 1949, the North Atlantic Treaty placed eleven other nations under the shelter of American power.

In spite of these profound changes, however, the United States still did not have a clear foreign policy. What areas of the world did the Truman Doctrine cover? Under Acheson's guidance, the Truman administration concentrated on Europe and left the rest of the world in limbo. How did the United States plan to defend the nations that fell under its protection? No one expected American troops to spread throughout the world. Some people, including the influential columnist Walter Lippmann, hoped that American economic aid would enable groups of nations to organize their own regional leagues of defense. In his inaugural address of 1949, the President encouraged this kind of vision. "Point Four" of that address raised the possibility of exporting more technological skills and fewer weapons to the world's needy nations.

Two critical events of 1949 underlined the importance of these unresolved problems. One occurred in Asia, where Mao Tse-tung's Communists poured out of Manchuria, drew popular support as they moved, and swept through China, driving Chiang Kai-shek's tattered remnants to the island of Formosa (Taiwan). Even before the end of the Second World War, American officials began their futile attempts to mediate between Chiang's Nationalists and Mao's Communists. Special American missions, including a highly publicized one in 1945 and 1946 under General Marshall, warned Chiang about the corruption in his government, dangled the prospect of economic assistance before the two camps, and struggled to arrange a truce between their armies. Unwilling to force a compromise on

Chiang yet unable to intervene effectively in his behalf, the United States invested some military aid and much larger amounts of hope in his cause. By 1949, the Truman administration could only say that its tactics had not worked.

The old American assumption that China held the key to all Asia exposed the Truman administration to charges of criminal neglect. Because America was the world's preeminent power, many argued, it could have saved China. By a reasonable construction of the Truman Doctrine, the United States should have. Instead, a vast territory and huge population had fallen to the enemy. Adding China to the Soviet sphere in Eastern Europe produced an appalling total effect. Simple maps blacked out the recent losses, and simple arithmetic summarized the human costs. When Congressman Richard Nixon of California totaled the people inside and outside the communist domain, he concluded that "in 1944 . . . the odds were 9 to 1 in our favor. Today . . . the odds are 5 to 3 against us."

Before the communist victory in China, Americans had been comforted by the belief that people elsewhere, once free to choose, would select something like the American way. The struggle against evil persisted, but as that sturdy liberal senator, Robert Wagner of New York, said, "History is on our side." In the administration's most cogent justification for the Truman Doctrine, George Kennan of the State Department relied on these premises to outline what would happen if the United States applied a steady, patient pressure along the perimeter of the com-

PRESIDENT TRUMAN WITH DEAN ACHESON ON HIS RIGHT AND
GEORGE MARSHALL ON HIS LEFT

The creators of America's containment policy remained in office to grapple with the Korean War. (Wide World.)

munist sphere. In time, the communist domain would erode from its own weaknesses, and gradually more and more people would select freedom. The Chinese Revolution struck at the heart of this faith. For another quarter-century, the United States not only refused to recognize the communist government of China; many Americans also clung to the belief that the Chinese, given a choice, would still follow the tough old warlord Chiang.

The second critical event of 1949 was the detonation of an atomic bomb by the Soviet Union. In 1945 and 1946, mutual distrust between the United States and the Soviet Union destroyed the chances for an international control over atomic weapons. The bomb remained exclusively American, and its monopoly enabled the United States to expand its international commitments without spreading its military forces abroad. The Truman Doctrine seemed to say that American aid alone could protect its allies. The bomb would deter a large-scale Soviet intervention. A few months before the Soviet's atomic test, Secretary Acheson told the Senate Foreign Relations Committee that the North Atlantic Treaty Organization (NATO) would require no more than token American soldiers in Europe. Truman gave this claim the ring of truth in 1949 by insisting on a reduced military budget. No American leader seriously contemplated using the bomb. Nor did any of them want the monopoly broken. Just having the bomb was enough.

How thoroughly the United States had relied on its monopoly in atomic weapons became clear after that monopoly was broken. The United States itself was suddenly, terribly vulnerable. America's new security program for Europe no longer had teeth. In the scramble for alternatives, some government officials actually did suggest a preemptive atomic strike at the Soviet Union. Moreover, if Soviet society was inherently inferior, as Americans had been repeatedly told, how had it manufactured its own bomb so soon? Spies must have stolen American secrets. The Federal Bureau of Investigation proceeded to uncover Julius and Ethel Rosenberg, who were charged with passing information about the bomb to the Soviet Union, found guilty, and executed. Judge Irving Kaufman who sentenced the Rosenbergs to death in 1951, expressed the anger of a nation that had been stripped of its primary protection:

. . . your conduct in putting into the hands of the Russians the A-bomb . . . has already caused, in my opinion, the Communist aggression in Korea, with the resultant [American] casualties exceeding fifty thousand and who knows but that millions more of innocent people may pay the price of your treason. Indeed, by your betrayal you undoubtedly have altered the course of history. . . .

Containment, 1950–1953

The Korean War, beginning in June 1950, completed America's global policy of "containment." As the problems of 1949 demonstrated, neither the geographical extent of America's anticommunism nor the methods enforcing it had been carefully examined. Without firm solutions on both of these issues, the

United States would continue to stumble from incident to incident. Appropriately, the place of decision was East Asia, where the Chinese Revolution had just forced Americans to rethink both the scope and the tactics of their foreign policy.

In 1945, during the Soviet Union's brief war against Japan, Russian troops moved across Manchuria into the Korean peninsula before American troops could land from the sea. The two armies hastily agreed to occupy northern and southern halves of the peninsula, divided at the 38th parallel, until their governments could settle the fate of this Japanese territory. As so often happened after the war, delays, Soviet-American tensions, and then the Cold War transformed a momentary convenience into a permanent solution. Under the auspices of the UN, which assumed responsibility for a Korean settlement, the United States backed one government in South Korea. The Soviet Union sponsored a rival government in North Korea. Each Korean government claimed the whole of the peninsula, and each was itching to fight for it. Because Korea had little significance in the complex contest between the Soviet Union and the United States, neither power closely supervised its dependent government before 1950.

As if in spite, the Korean pawns moved themselves in June 1950. Under circumstances that remain obscure, the two Korean armies clashed, and the superior northern force began rolling southward. Although the Truman administration had not prepared for a crisis in Korea, it was ready to act. After sending the South Koreans light reinforcements from Japan, the United States took advantage of Russia's absence from the Security Council of the United Nations to place America's cause under the authority of the UN. On June 27, the Security Council endorsed intervention. Officially, therefore, the United States did not fight a war in Korea; it cooperated in a UN police action.

The Shifting Front in Korea

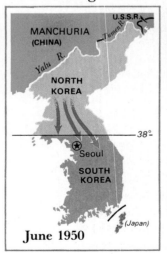

June 1950

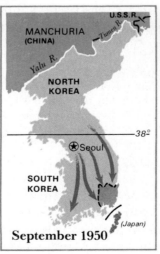

September 1950

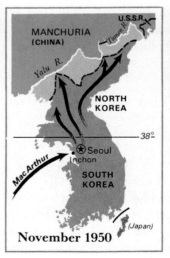

November 1950

July 1953

Within a few days American troops were struggling to stem the South Korean retreat. During the summer, America's military power under General Douglas MacArthur did reverse the battle and drove the North Korean army past the 38th parallel back through its own territory to the Chinese border. The original purpose of the war had been protection of South Korea's territory. Now the goal seemed to be unification of the entire Korean peninsula. In November, large Chinese reinforcements surprised the American forces and pushed them once again below the 38th parallel. By early 1951, the war settled into a grudging, bloody struggle along the original boundary. Shortly after Eisenhower's inauguration in 1953, an armistice between the opposing armies more or less reestablished the division at the 38th parallel. A formal peace never came.

Though this stalemate war aroused widespread resentment in the United States, the range of opposition was quite narrow. Critics filled the air with might-have-beens and should-have-beens that censured Truman and Acheson as short-sighted, fumbling leaders, but they almost never questioned the appropriateness of American military intervention. Nor did the administration's critics rally much support for a big war against either China or Russia. The center of such ambitions was the imperious General MacArthur, whose belligerent and insubordinate behavior after China's entry into the war forced Truman to recall him from Korea in April 1951. As the hero of two wars and the successful director of America's occupation government in postwar Japan, MacArthur received an adoring welcome home after his recall. As the advocate of Asian conquest, however, MacArthur won no important endorsements. Even the free-swinging Joe McCarthy knew enough to avoid that crusade. In response to a thoroughly unpopular war, the large majority of Americans repudiated their President but ratified his policy.

The elections of 1952 solidified this point. Foreign policy loomed larger than in any presidential campaign since 1916, and discontent with the Korean War dominated these concerns. According to the opinion polls, only one in four Americans thought that the United States was winning the Cold War; only one in four approved of Truman's presidency. Yet neither the Republicans nor the Democrats broke from the administration's Korean policy. Both Eisenhower and Governor Adlai Stevenson supported the concept of a limited war. Both promised to settle it as promptly as possible. After declaring that he would "go to Korea" himself in an effort to end the fighting, Eisenhower took office in a climate of expectations that he, far better than Truman, could make Truman's policy work.

With the Korean War came answers to the two most perplexing questions in America's international affairs. After several years of hesitation, the government interpreted the words in the Truman Doctrine literally. Any nation willing to cooperate with America's worldwide anticommunist policy became a member of the Free World. Some of these members, such as England and Canada, were old and trusted democratic friends. Others were recent enemies. West Germany was now preparing to enter NATO. In 1951, over the vehement protests of the Soviet

Union, the United States signed a formal peace with Japan and incorporated it, along with Australia, New Zealand, and the Philippines, in America's expanding scheme of defensive alliances. Still other members of the Free World, such as Spain and South Korea, were authoritarian states. Nevertheless, as John Foster Dulles, the Republican party's leading expert on foreign affairs, said to the government of South Korea, its nation formed one "part in the great design of human freedom." Even a desire to remain neutral in the Cold War indicated an indifference to "human freedom."

Officially, every member of the Free World had equal importance in America's global policy. Before June 1950, both General MacArthur in Japan and Secretary Acheson in Washington had suggested that South Korea fell outside America's primary line of defense. War followed, and the government vowed never to repeat that mistake. Viewing the communist camp as one interrelated whole and the Free World as another, American policymakers interpreted a weakness in either bloc as the sign of greater changes to come. Yugoslavia's refusal to accept Soviet dictation after 1948, for example, kindled hopes for the

THE PENTAGON

The Pentagon in Washington was the imposing symbol of America's new military establishment, a crucial link in the containment policy. (*Library of Congress.*)

liberation of all Eastern Europe. Korea, as the expression went, pointed like a dagger at Japan. Clusters of free nations were likened to rows of dominoes, where the tipping of one toppled the rest. From these concerns came the cardinal rule that would dominate the next two decades of American foreign policy. The Free World must not relinquish a single additional piece of territory. No more Munichs; no more Chinas.

Just as firmly, the United States resolved the problem of tactics. Containment depended primarily on military power. Years of debate about the best way of assisting friendly nations ended in a resounding victory for military aid, which Congress not only increased but also distributed throughout the Free World. In Western Europe, the United States pressed its allies, including West Germany, to rearm and integrate their military strength. At home, the United States embarked on a long-range program of military preparedness that included the development of tactical units against local aggression, elaborate surveillance systems to gather military intelligence, and the construction of a far more lethal nuclear weapon, the hydrogen bomb. In addition, it explored better means for delivering a nuclear attack by air, from the sea, and through a network of foreign bases. Lacking a monopoly of nuclear weapons, Americans sought a clear military advantage over the Soviet Union, because ultimately, the proponents of containment argued, communist totalitarianism would respond only to power. The Department of Defense, which the National Security Act of 1947 had created to coordinate the army, navy, and air force, participated closely in decisions on foreign affairs. And the Central Intelligence Agency (CIA), which had also been established by the National Security Act, came of age as an important center of secret international relations.

Containment was a popular policy. An almost continuous string of international crises since the Second World War argued the necessity of a broad, consistent approach to world affairs. Moreover, Americans had several years to grow accustomed to the idea of a new policy. Beginning with the Truman Doctrine in 1947 and culminating in the Korean War, the nation's leaders prepared the way through stages of greater and greater international responsibility. Each additional step received widespread publicity and extensive explanation. By the early 1950s, a global program of military preparedness seemed the most sensible means of protecting the Free World and actually lessening the risks of nuclear holocaust.

Various groups of Americans found other reasons for endorsing containment. Intellectuals who were horrified by the communist controls over free expression welcomed the new policy. National leaders who thought naturally in terms of long-range planning and stability admired containment as an example of sound international management. Under the containment policy, corporations with foreign interests received a more consistent government support than ever before. Almost by definition, the links between American business and a foreign nation strengthened the cohesion of the Free World. Cultural and religious groups whose compatriots abroad were persecuted under communism gave containment a particularly zealous support.

Finally, containment appealed to the powerful American tradition of personal courage. The widely acclaimed movie *High Noon,* a parable on the Cold War, illustrated this connection. The hero (sober, freedom-loving America) discovered that the citizens of a western town who had once fought for their freedom (allies from the Second World War) lacked the stamina for another confrontation with a band of terrorists (fascism once, communism now). Although the hero was opposed by his pacifist bride (America's well-meaning but misguided critics of force), he knew his duty and went to meet the gunmen. At a critical moment, his bride saw the light and shot the last of the villains. The two of them (America united) then drove away, leaving the shamed townspeople with a security they had done nothing to preserve. As statesmen of the Cold War from Arthur Vandenberg to Richard Nixon said, it took "guts" to hold the line.

Government officials, citing the alternative of total war, called containment a moderate policy. Yet no one could deny that it was an astonishing departure from the past. Instead of a cautious balance between involvement and detachment, the United States had chosen wholesale, worldwide involvement. Containment required the government to concern itself not only with the foreign policy but also with the domestic affairs of a great variety of nations. In response to almost every international issue, the United States applied the same general test. What would help the communists and what would strengthen anticommunism? Critics abroad considered that test too narrow to deal with the world's diversity. America, they complained, was the first nation in history to move directly from childhood to senility in its foreign policy. But Americans replied that the solution to all other problems hinged on the outcome of this global contest between communism and freedom. There would be ample time to test these conflicting viewpoints, for the United States had set its course in world affairs for the next twenty years.

Suggested Readings

L. Ethan Ellis, *Republican Foreign Policy, 1921–1933* (1968), is a sound introduction to the postwar years. However, the most influential work on America's international affairs is William Appleman Williams, *The Tragedy of American Diplomacy* (rev. ed., 1962), an essay on the dominance of economic expansion in the nation's foreign policy. Joan Hoff Wilson's excellent book, *American Business and Foreign Policy, 1920–1933* (1971), analyzes this process of economic expansion, and Herbert Feis, *The Diplomacy of the Dollar: First Era, 1919–1932* (1950), provides insight into the State Department. Harold G. Moulton and Leo Pasvolsky, *War Debts and World Prosperity* (1932), follows a difficult subject in considerable detail. The best discussion of the London Economic Conference appears in Frank Freidel's *Franklin D. Roosevelt: Launching the New Deal* (1973). Lloyd C. Gardner's *Economic Aspects of New Deal Diplomacy* (1964) emphasizes an insatiable urge for profits.

A clear, reliable survey of United States policy in East Asia is presented in Warren I.

Cohen, *America's Response to China* (1971). Akira Iriye's *After Imperialism: The Search for a New Order in the Far East, 1921–1933* (1965) places American policy in an international setting. The crucial postwar treaties on Asia are covered in Thomas H. Buckley, *The United States and the Washington Conference, 1921–1922* (1970). In *Herbert Hoover's Latin American Policy* (1951), Alexander DeConde finds a liberalizing trend. Peter G. Filene, *Americans and the Soviet Experience, 1917–1933* (1967), traces responses from the Bolshevik Revolution to America's recognition of the Soviet Union, and Robert Paul Browder, *The Origins of Soviet-American Diplomacy* (1953), describes the frustrated hopes for economic gain accompanying recognition.

America's reaction to the early imperialist crisis in Asia is explored in Sara R. Smith, *The Manchurian Crisis, 1931–1932* (1948), Richard N. Current, *Secretary Stimson* (1954), and Robert H. Ferrell, *American Diplomacy in the Great Depression: Hoover-Stimson Foreign Policy, 1929–1933* (1957). Dorothy Borg's *The United States and the Far Eastern Crisis of 1933–1938* (1964) continues the story into the full-scale Sino-Japanese War. The title of Arnold A. Offner's *American Appeasement: United States Foreign Policy and Germany, 1933–1938* (1969), indicates the author's approach to the years when Hitler was consolidating power. Alton Frye, *Nazi Germany and the American Hemisphere, 1933–1941* (1967), minimizes Hitler's transatlantic ambitions.

The most thorough account of diplomatic events leading to the Second World War is the two-volume study by William L. Langer and S. Everett Gleason, *The Challenge to Isolation, 1937–1940* (1952), and *The Undeclared War, 1940–1941* (1953), a detailed justification of American policy. Herbert Feis, *The Road to Pearl Harbor* (1950), is a much more limited version from the same point of view, and Robert A. Divine's two volumes, *The Illusion of Neutrality* (1962) and *The Reluctant Belligerent* (1965), are only slightly more critical. In the last hurrah of a great historian, Charles A. Beard, *President Roosevelt and the Coming of the War, 1941* (1948), indicts FDR for maneuvering the nation into war. Manfred Jonas, *Isolation in America, 1935–1941* (1966), and Wayne S. Cole, *America First: The Battle against Intervention, 1941–1941* (1953), present the basic facts about the domestic opposition to the government's policies, and Warren F. Kimball, *The Most Unsordid Act: Lend-Lease, 1939–1941* (1969), discusses the issue that aroused the fiercest resistance. Complexities that the Roosevelt administration ignored are examined in Paul W. Schroeder's *The Axis Alliance and Japanese-American Relations, 1941* (1958), and the official in Tokyo who reported these complexities is the subject of Waldo H. Heinrichs, Jr., *American Ambassador: Joseph C. Grew and the Development of the United States Diplomatic Tradition* (1966). Roberta Wohlstetter, *Pearl Harbor: Warning and Decision* (1962), analyzes the controversy surrounding the Japanese strike at Hawaii.

Gordon Wright, *The Ordeal of Total War, 1939–1945* (1968), gives an overview of the European theater during the Second World War; A. Russell Buchanan, *The United States in World War II* (2 vols., 1964), covers America's military activities in both the European and the Pacific theaters. A famous naval historian, Samuel Eliot Morison, tells of the conflict at sea in *The Two-Ocean War* (1963). Morison's *Strategy and Compromise* (1958) and Kent Roberts Greenfield's *American Strategy in World War II: A Reconsideration* (1963), evaluate broad questions of military policy. Forrest C. Pogue, *George C. Marshall* (3 vols. to date, 1963–73), has followed the career of Roosevelt's chief of staff to 1945. The best introduction to America's foreign relations during these years is Gaddis Smith, *Diplomacy during the Second World War, 1941–1945* (1965). Herbert Feis, *Churchill, Roosevelt, and Stalin* (1957), examines the critical issues besetting the grand alliance. Two useful books—Robert A. Divine, *Second Chance: The Triumph of Internationalism in America during World War II* (1967), and Diane Shaver Clemens, *Yalta* (1970)—chart paths into the postwar years. Specifically on the President's leadership, the concluding volume of James MacGregor

Burns's biography, *Roosevelt: The Soldier of Freedom* (1970), finds a good deal of drift in the White House. Robert A. Divine, *Roosevelt and World War II* (1969), is a keen and generally favorable appraisal. Valuable material on two of Roosevelt's advisers appears in Robert E. Sherwood, *Roosevelt and Hopkins* (rev. ed., 1950), and John Morton Blum, ed., *From the Morgenthau Diaries: Years of War, 1941–1945* (1967). H. Bradford Westerfield, *Foreign Policy and Party Politics: Pearl Harbor to Korea* (1958), deals with the contribution of Congress. On the development of the atomic bomb, see Walter S. Schoenberger, *Decision of Destiny* (1969). Martin J. Sherwin, *A World Destroyed: The Atomic Bomb and the Grand Alliance* (1975), and Barton J. Bernstein, *The Atom Bomb: The Critical Issues* (1976), explore its international implications.

The history of the Cold War is a caldron of controversy. Two judicious guides are John Lewis Gaddis, *The United States and the Origins of the Cold War, 1941–1947* (1972), which tends to justify American policies, and Walter LaFeber, *America, Russia, and the Cold War, 1945–1966* (1967), which tends to criticize them. For a pungent taste of the battle, however, read on the one hand Herbert Feis, *From Trust to Terror: The Onset of the Cold War, 1945–1950* (1970), the last in his series of volumes explaining modern American diplomacy; and on the other hand Gabriel Kolko, *The Politics of War: The World and United States Foreign Policy, 1943–1945* (1968), and Joyce and Gabriel Kolko, *The Limits of Power: The World and United States Foreign Policy, 1945–1954* (1972), a thorough condemnation of Washington's policy. A number of careful, recent studies have added substantially to our knowledge of the critical problems dividing the United States and the Soviet Union immediately after the war: Thomas M. Campbell, *Masquerade Peace: America's UN Policy, 1944–1945* (1973), Lynn Etheridge Davis, *The Cold War Begins: Soviet-American Conflict over Eastern Europe* (1974), George C. Herring, Jr., *Aid to Russia, 1941–1946* (1973), Bruce Kuklick, *American Policy and the Division of Germany: The Clash with Russia over Reparations* (1972), and Thomas G. Paterson, *Soviet-American Confrontation: Postwar Reconstruction and the Origins of the Cold War* (1973). On issues that hardened the pattern of the Cold War, see Joseph I. Lieberman, *The Scorpion and the Tarantula: The Struggle to Control Atomic Weapons, 1945–1949* (1970), W. Phillips Davison, *The Berlin Blockade* (1958), and Robert E. Osgood, *NATO* (1962). The origins and the course of America's postwar policy in East Asia are discussed in Kenneth E. Shewmaker, *Americans and Chinese Communists, 1927–1945* (1971), Herbert Feis, *The China Tangle* (1953), Tang Tsou, *America's Failure in China, 1941–1950* (1963), and Akira Iriye, *The Cold War in Asia* (1974).

Lloyd C. Gardner, *Architects of Illusion: Men and Ideas in American Foreign Policy, 1941–1949* (1970), is a perceptive essay on the men who won control of America's postwar foreign policy, and Thomas G. Paterson, ed., *Cold War Critics: Alternatives to American Foreign Policy in the Truman Years* (1971), is a collection of essays on the men who lost. Additional information on the shapers of American policy appears in George Curry, "James F. Byrnes," in Vol. 14 of *American Secretaries of State and Their Diplomacy* (1965), Robert H. Ferrell, *George C. Marshall* (1966), which is Vol. 15 of the same series, Gaddis Smith, *Dean Acheson* (1972), which is Vol. 16, and Arnold A. Rogow, *James Forrestal* (1964), a study of the first secretary of defense. The writings of the participants themselves include these particularly useful books: Dean Acheson, *Present at the Creation* (1969), Lucius Clay, *Decision in Germany* (1950), George F. Kennan, *Memoirs, 1925–1950* (1967), and Arthur H. Vandenberg, Jr., ed., *The Private Papers of Senator Vandenberg* (1952).

For the background to the Korean War, see Leland M. Goodrich, *Korea: A Study of U. S. Policy in the United Nations* (1956). The policy struggles accompanying the war are discussed in John W. Spanier, *The Truman-MacArthur Controversy and the Korean War* (1959), and Trumbull Higgins, *Korea and the Fall of MacArthur* (1960). The indefatigable journalist I. F. Stone raises some intriguing questions in *Hidden History of the Korean War* (1952).

34

The Consequences
of Modernization

The process of modernization that dominated American history during the second quarter of the twentieth century was also a process of nationalization. Modern politics drew more and more problems, and hence more and more public attention, into the orbit of *national* affairs. America's modern culture established *national* values in such areas as the meaning of success, the right to a private freedom, and the way to rear children, and it gave *national* voice to the plight of the individual in modern society. As international turmoil was producing America's worldwide policy of containment in the late forties and early fifties, foreign affairs became a matter of general *national* importance.

By the early 1950s, these modernizing, nationalizing forces integrated American society far more tightly than ever before. But the hope that integration meant unity, and that a united American society guaranteed a smooth, stable progress, proved to be illusory. Instead, nationalization created a critical imbalance in the lives of a growing number of Americans. New national rules in racial and cultural affairs threatened the traditional local autonomy of millions of white citizens. Other Americans rebelled against the nation's extensive international involvements, particularly its war in Viet Nam. Still others believed that nationalization was crushing them as individuals.

"National" usually meant "the national government." Just as Washington had become the center for more and more of the ambitions in modern America, so it now became the focus for more and more of the discontents with modern society. Nationalization, in other words, politicized America's hopes and hates. Even those who feared for their survival as individuals increasingly blamed their problems on the policies of the national government. During the late 1960s, a powerful surge of these many emotions poured into national politics and precipitated a crisis. The nation's political leaders had their hands full just trying to identify what had gone wrong, and at the end of the sixties, it was still not clear that they would be able to surmount this crisis.

Unity and Progress

In retrospect, Americans tended to scorn the 1950s as a time of mass conformity and bad taste. Where was the urge to reform, they asked? Did people want nothing more than a house in the suburbs and a job with a pension? What kind of standards glorified plastic, chrome, and neon? Questions like these missed too much of the decade. The 1950s, like the 1920s, were years of fulfillment. The large problems of the past seemed to be solved. As the bitter strikes and angry rhetoric of the postwar years subsided, so did most worries about a selfish, fragmented society. Despite two recessions during the decade, the

SUBURBAN DEVELOPMENT

Sometimes the sewers went in and sometimes they did not, but in the 1950s nothing could halt the stampede to the suburbs. *(State Historical Society of Wisconsin.)*

GNP rose by 50 percent. Never before had America offered its citizens such a grand array of services for their health, welfare, and pleasure. Echoing the claims of the 1920s, the publicist Peter Drucker told Americans that their society had passed *"beyond Capitalism and Socialism."* Millions believed that in solving the problems of the past, they had also learned how to solve the problems of the future. Not only had they constructed the good society; they knew how to maintain it as well.

This sense of control over America's destiny drew on three primary sources of strength. One was the resurgence of mass consumerism. After the economic frustrations of the Great Depression and the material shortages of the Second World War, the consumer extravaganza of the 1950s gave Americans their most persuasive evidence of a healthy, progressive society. In a variety of ways, its effects seemed increasingly democratic and unifying. The sheer quantity of services and goods suggested a more democratic consumer market. By the 1950s, leisure activities were absorbing 15 percent of the GNP. Between 1945 and 1957, the amount of consumer credit rose a breathtaking 800 percent, and as it swelled, it brought a full complement of revolving charge accounts, easy payment plans, and credit cards. The widespread use of such light, relatively inexpensive materials as plastics, aluminum, and transistors reinforced the belief in consumerism's democratic qualities. Not only did these new materials expand the range of inexpensive goods; they created a mass market for the duplicates of goods that

had once been luxury items, like silk stockings and fine-grained furniture. Because cheaper materials led to a much more rapid turnover of approximately the same products, critics complained of a shabby industrial policy of "planned obsolescence." All Americans felt the consequences in such mundane ways as the accumulation of consumer trash and the decline in repair services. But these were side effects that the consumer society of the 1950s appeared quite willing to tolerate.

Another sign of democratization was the nationwide rush to the suburbs. An extensive development of urban highways and a record level of automobile sales enabled many different kinds of Americans to pursue their dreams outside the city limits. The construction industry faced an almost insatiable demand for housing. During the depression and war years, the number of new dwellings had averaged about 300,000 a year. During the fifties, the average ran almost four times higher. Instead of the "bedroom towns" of the 1920s that had relied on the services of the inner city, the suburbs of the 1950s provided their residents with an increasingly self-contained life. Business firms, following the rush to the suburbs, displayed their wares along miles of commercial avenues and inside countless shopping plazas. By the late 1960s, there were even more jobs in the suburbs than in the cities. To encompass this sprawling, cloverleaf culture, Americans used a new word, *suburbia*.

In its broad effects, the consumerism of the fifties appeared to be drawing Americans closer together. A network of highways was quickly spreading across the nation. Between 1946 and 1956, state governments tripled their investment in road construction, and the Federal Highway Act of 1956 committed the national government to subsidizing over 40,000 miles of superhighways that would connect America's major cities. In the high-powered, postwar cars, Americans found their range of travel greatly expanded. The airplane shrank distances even more dramatically. Between 1947 and 1957, as passenger service grew fourfold, the airlines became a normal, accepted means of travel. Most impressive of all, television was transformed from a curious new toy into a staple of the American home. Fourteen thousand families had TV sets in 1947; ten years later 35 million families owned them. By driving, flying, or simply watching at home, Americans were discovering one another, it was assumed. Nobody, no place, needed to be strange or distant in a land of rapid transportation and instant communication.

Moreover, Americans appeared to unite just by acting as consumers. Common cars and clothes, common houses and vacations, common foods and recreations, gave the impression of a single national commitment to the same good life. In 1933, the Roosevelt administration had issued a three-cent postage stamp to symbolize unity in a society of large, economic blocs: a farmer, a businessman, a laborer, and a housewife, each in distinctive dress, marched shoulder to shoulder "in common determination." In the consumer society of the 1950s, a comparable image of unity would have shown an assortment of shoppers in the same style of clothes filling their carts with the same standardized products.

By the 1950s, consumerism had become a way of thinking. At a Moscow trade exhibit in 1959, Vice-President Richard Nixon engaged Soviet Premier Nikita Khrushchev in a famous "kitchen debate" inside a model American home. To each of Khrushchev's arguments about the superiority of communism to capitalism, the Vice-President pointed to the consumer goods immediately at hand, and back in the United States, a large majority of Americans applauded Nixon's logic. Consumerism also enabled Americans to evaluate the state of their society. An old device, "standard of living," won a wide new popularity in the 1950s because it could survey the entire population by measuring consumption. How much could a family purchase? What way of life did these purchases represent? How did one family's purchases compare with the purchases of other families? Standard of living and its cousin, "cost of living," became the most common American techniques for identifying public problems and formulating their solutions.

A second broad source of public confidence was faith in the experts. Following the awesome discoveries in atomic physics, the mass distribution of "wonder drug" antibiotics, and the conquest of poliomyelitis, scientists reached a new peak of prestige. More eagerly than ever, Americans looked to the nation's experts for personal guidance. Psychoanalysis achieved its pinnacle of popularity. Counseling specialists and home beautification advisers, tourist handbooks and sports manuals, all flourished. "Culture vultures" joined record and book clubs, studied brochures on the mysteries of painting, and subscribed to theater series so that they could experience the best of the arts. After a partial eclipse during the depression, advertising and public relations returned to full public favor. Scarcely a government program appeared without an attractive acronym like HUSKY, SHAPE, or VISTA. Farm subsidies became thrifty investments in a "soil bank," and the recession in 1953 a "rolling readjustment."

Like mass consumerism, faith in the experts had long been a standard part of modern society, and it continued to express itself in standard ways. The campaign to improve the educational system, for example, gained even greater momentum during the 1950s. Attacking the vagueness of the schools' "life adjustment" programs, reformers demanded rigorous instruction in the basic skills of the experts. Curricular "tracks" in the best suburban and private schools were linked so well with higher education that the brightest high school students, especially in science and mathematics, were able to prepare themselves for advanced college work. Between 1940 and 1960, costs per student more than quadrupled in the public schools, and expenditures in higher education rose more than sixfold. With the National Defense Education Act of 1958, the national government also invested in the education of scientists and engineers who seemed in dangerously short supply. In all, it was another impressive vote of confidence in the social value of expertise.

The distinctive new element in the 1950s was a faith in the unique powers of massed expertise. Reflecting the modern sense of an integrated society, an increasing number of Americans looked on the experts as a vast, national pool of

MAN AND MACHINE

Although very few understood the mysteries of modern technology, Americans banked their future on the computerized knowledge of the expert. (*Henri Cartier-Bresson/Magnum.*)

skills that could be used in various combinations to suit particular problems. Scientifically coordinated teams, rather than just scientifically trained individuals, held the key to the future. It required precisely such a cluster of specialists to harness the atom, to operate on the human heart, to measure public opinion, or to run a giant corporation. Moreover, these teams now had a marvelous new technological aid, the computer, which promised impartial answers to the world's most complicated questions. No lone genius could match the scientific range of computerized team research.

A gamut of images about science, management, and success was altered along with this new faith. The clearest expression of these changes came in response to America's space program. In 1957, the Soviet Union shocked Americans with the successful launching of a "Sputnik" spacecraft. After considerable public discussion about the weaknesses in American policy and technology, President John Kennedy countered the Soviet challenge in 1961 by promising to place a man on the moon before 1970. Amply financed and widely publicized, the Mercury program to orbit the earth, the Gemini program to maneuver in space, then the Apollo program to reach the moon filled the decade with televised countdowns, blastoffs, reentries, and splashdowns. Americans of all ages watched with fascination as scurrying teams of specialists readied the crafts and clicking computers monitored their flights. The climax of the Apollo flights occurred on July 20, 1969, as Neil Armstrong descended to the surface of the moon before a billion television witnesses, declaring it "one small step for man, one giant leap for mankind."

In the midst of these extremely intricate operations sat the crews of astronauts—trained, disciplined, yet relaxed. They were the group heroes of the 1960s. Even their personalities seemed to merge into a composite of the healthy, balanced American male. Various Americans saw what they wanted in the flight of the astronauts: the interplanetary Western, the verification of a science-fiction future, the triumph of ordinary American virtues, or the waste of national resources. For a good many Americans, however, the astronauts exemplified the values of massed expertise. In the 1920s, the nation had idolized Charles Lindbergh as the "Lone Eagle" who transcended his impersonally organized society. Inside the fantastic gear of the space explorer, his counterparts in the 1960s were cheered for achieving glory through an incredibly complicated team effort.

A third source of confidence during the fifties was government management. Once again, the popular faith in government management derived from a modern sense of the nation's wholeness, and this vision of wholeness made Washington the natural overseer of America's welfare. Clearly, the government's most important obligation was to maintain a healthy economy. By 1954, it stood ready to fulfill this task by adjusting the national budget, funding the national debt, and controlling national monetary policies. Beyond a general obligation to the economy, however, effective government management did not require systematic plans for the entire nation. On the contrary, the government usually responded to the demands of private groups, trying to give something to all of them without capitulating fully to any one of them.

Under President Dwight Eisenhower's light rein, the government followed these guidelines at a cautious pace. Indeed, the unspectacular qualities of government during the Eisenhower years contributed to a feeling of security among the nation's major interest groups. Many businessmen who had once been mortal enemies of a big bureaucracy enjoyed easy and profitable relations with the government during the fifties. Farm groups, after being frightened in 1953 by talk of a free market for agricultural products, soon learned that their subsidies would not disappear. During the early 1950s, as during the 1940s, the debates over farm policy mostly revolved around the exact level of government price supports for specific agricultural products. Farm groups continued to seek a guarantee of "parity," which was their estimate of a just price for their output. Then in 1956, the emphasis in farm policy shifted with the introduction of the soil bank, a government program that paid farmers to remove land from cultivation. For those scientifically advanced farmers who could grow more and more on less and less acreage, the soil bank proved a bonanza. The merger of the AFL and the CIO in 1955 under a tough, conservative president, George Meany, strengthened the political position of a third set of interests, organized labor. Although most unions were unenthusiastic about the Eisenhower administration itself, the AFL-CIO continued to have many allies in Congress. Minor restrictions on their financial affairs in the Landrum-Griffin Act of 1959, like the earlier restrictions in the Taft-Hartley Act, scarcely affected the unions' policies.

Changes in government management reflected the changes in American society. As the importance of the experts and mass consumerism rose, for example, government officials grew more sensitive to their needs. By the early 1950s, physicists, chemists, biologists, engineers, hospital administrators, and a variety of other scientific groups had become part of the Washington establishment. During the fifties, professionals ranging from pediatricians and vocational rehabilitaters to experts in race relations and urban planning found secure places for themselves in the government bureaucracy. The clearest new response to consumers came from the federal judiciary. In the *Schwegmann* decision of 1951, the Supreme Court struck down a basic part of the "fair trade" law of 1937, which had enabled merchants to maintain fixed retail prices regardless of the competition. When Congress enacted the new Federal Fair Trade Act in 1952, the courts made it so difficult to enforce that it steadily lost authority. By the 1960s, price-cutting retail chains and discount houses spread nationwide. Moreover, the Supreme Court also broadened the consumer's right to claim damages from the manufacturers of defective consumer products. A long tradition of legal issues between big business and small business was being overshadowed by a modern set of legal issues between business and the consumer.

No one coordinated Washington's vast apparatus of government. On paper, it looked as though the executive branch was the center of control. In 1950, Congress added to its extensive powers by giving the President the right to appoint his own chairmen to the independent regulatory commissions. Now each new administration could have an immediate influence on the policies of the "Big Six": the Civil Aeronautics Board, the Federal Communications Commission, the Federal Power Commission, the Federal Trade Commission, the Interstate Commerce Commission, and the Securities and Exchange Commission. Then in 1953, the new Department of Health, Education and Welfare (HEW) combined a great variety of services and programs under one executive chief. Nevertheless, the larger the executive branch grew, the more its authority was scattered among innumerable offices and subdivisions. As powerful a politician as President Eisenhower's principal domestic aide, Sherman Adams, could do no more than respond to the issues of government one at a time as they came to him. Fortunately for the President, the tests of good management required only a strong economy and a satisfied constituency of private interest groups. By these standards, the government functioned very well during the 1950s. Although Americans often grumbled about incompetent bureaucrats, they generally approved the results of bureaucratic government.

World Order

In foreign policy, as in domestic affairs, the United States presented a new face of national unity and common purpose during the fifties. After the Korean War, no significant group of Americans challenged the basic outlines of the nation's containment policy. Both Republicans and Democrats defined international communism as a worldwide conspiracy that was directed from its headquarters in

Moscow. The United States, they told the nation, must gird for a long, taxing struggle against the enemy.

The consensus on foreign policy covered strategy as well. Containment envisaged a worldwide league of so-called free nations encircling communist territory and sealing off its avenues of expansion. To complete this circle, the United States negotiated a variety of agreements with nations outside Europe. The most ambitious of these was the Southeast Asia Treaty Organization (SEATO) of 1955, which allied France, Great Britain, and the United States with Australia, New Zealand, Pakistan, the Philippines, and Thailand. In addition, the United States encouraged its allies in the Middle East to form the Central Treaty Organization (CENTO) of 1959.* As some critics promptly noted, neither organization was strong or comprehensive. Of the countries on the mainland of Southeast Asia, only Thailand entered SEATO. No Arab nation belonged to CENTO. Nevertheless, in combination with the North Atlantic Treaty Organization (NATO), these treaties formed a symbolic global ring around the communist domain. Formidable or not, they were a logical expression of containment's purposes.

America's reliance on military power to contain communism went almost unchallenged. Although Democrats and Republicans hotly debated the adequacy of each other's defense proposals, they were trying to prove themselves even more committed than their opponents to military preparedness. The Eisenhower administration, borrowing a term from women's fashions, proposed a "New Look" in America's military program. Politically, it appealed to the economy-minded, who were promised, in Secretary of Defense Charles Wilson's blunt phrase, "more bang for the buck." But militarily, the New Look represented only a slight shift away from ground and naval forces in favor of air and missile power. Some critics of the New Look, such as Professor Henry Kissinger of Harvard University, charged that the Eisenhower administration's heavy reliance on nuclear weapons removed too much flexibility from the nation's military policy and left it unable to meet a variety of small, local communist thrusts. Other critics, including Senator John Kennedy of Massachusetts, warned of a general decline in the nation's military power. Not many Americans paid attention to these complaints, and not much changed after Kennedy became President in 1961.

The popular confidence in containment relied on a broad faith in government management and massed expertise. The wonders of science figured just as prominently in international as in national affairs. The latest developments in ballistic missiles, supersonic jets, and nuclear-powered submarines became standard parts of the American vocabulary and standard images of American defense. Under President Eisenhower, the United States established a worldwide, electronic Distant Early Warning System (DEW Line) that would alert the nation's

---

*The members of CENTO were Great Britain, Iran, Pakistan, and Turkey.

military power in case of an enemy attack. Under President Kennedy, a "Hot Line" was installed in 1963 to provide instant communication between the White House and the Kremlin in case of the ultimate emergency. Abroad as at home, skillful managers plus modern technology equaled national security.

But foreign and domestic affairs were linked by much more than this abiding faith in managers and experts. Unlike any other peacetime era, military expenditures now dominated the national budget. Their size alone, fluctuating around 60 percent of the government's total costs, made military expenditures crucial to maintaining a healthy economy. In addition, the government's military contracts were concentrated in the scientifically sophisticated areas of industry. Directly or indirectly, the military program financed the research behind America's most important technological innovations. Moreover, such giant corporations as General Electric, General Motors, and Douglas Aircraft subcontracted portions of their military work, creating a much wider web of economic dependence around the government's initial investment. If the government terminated a big defense contract, therefore, it might send shock waves through a large section of the economy and undo the government's efforts to sustain prosperity.

A former general first popularized the phrase that most Americans used to describe these arrangements. President Eisenhower, always unhappy over the accumulation of power in Washington and always skeptical of budget demands from the military, devoted part of his final State of the Union address to warn the nation about this "military-industrial complex." During the sixties, more and more Americans came to picture the military-industrial complex as a diabolical force directing the nation's foreign policy. Actually, the government awarded military contracts in the same piecemeal fashion as it did the rest of its benefits, and the military-industrial complex remained much too decentralized to act in concert. But the sum of its influences was profound. In the past, mobilizing the nation for war had disrupted the economy. Now disarming the nation for peace threatened to disrupt the economy even more.

"Multinational" corporations formed a second new strand connecting the domestic economy with world affairs. Before the Second World War, almost all the subdivisions that American corporations established abroad had remained small dependent outposts of the parent companies. After the Second World War, however, corporate expansion entered a new phase. From soft drinks to automobiles to electronics, American industries gravitated to the capital-poor nations of the postwar world, where production costs were low, governments encouraging, and ready markets inviting. Even more important than the quantity of foreign subsidiaries were their special qualities. An increasing proportion of them duplicated the parent company's full corporate structure and dropped roots in the societies where they were planted. By the 1950s, these corporate offshoots were thriving on every continent, with a particularly large number in Canada and the economically advanced countries of Western Europe. Still tied to their parent companies in the United States yet assimilated into the lives of foreign nations, they gave a new transnational cast to the American economy.

Multinational corporations were only the most striking part of a massive business expansion after the Second World War. In 1946, America's private investments abroad approximated their level in 1929. During the next decade, foreign investments tripled. By the end of the 1960s, they stood almost ten times higher than in 1946. Much of this money went in search of minerals that the United States either lacked or used at a faster rate than it produced. Oil alone accounted for more than a third of these investments. The spread of American capital abroad, taken as a whole, expressed the economy's increasing dependence on resources and markets and government policies around the world.

A clear purpose in international affairs, a managerial approach to international problems, and a growing economic stake in international stability all contributed to the continuity in American foreign policy during the Eisenhower and Kennedy administrations. John Foster Dulles, who as secretary of state between 1953 and 1959 was largely responsible for the conduct of American policy, moved naturally with these currents. His experience in diplomacy began in 1907. As Eisenhower commented, only half in jest, "Foster has been studying to be secretary of state since he was five years old." During his legal career Dulles had worked sympathetically with some of America's most internationally oriented businessmen. Moreover, he was religiously anticommunist.

Foreign affairs continued to follow the primary lesson of the Truman years: lose no more people or territory to communism. Secretary Dulles subscribed so deeply to this lesson that he was willing to risk thermonuclear war in its behalf. To resolve any doubts on the subject, Dulles reminded the world in January 1954 that behind America's policy lay a "great capacity to retaliate, instantly, by means and at places of our own choosing." The first test of the secretary's "brinkmanship" began only a few months later in 1954. China opened a bombardment of several islands less than ten miles from its coast that Chiang Kai-shek, over a hundred miles away on Formosa (Taiwan), had fortified as his outposts. In the Formosa Resolution of January 1955, Congress authorized the President to protect both Formosa and these offshore islands. For brief periods in 1955 and again in 1958, there was at least a possibility of thermonuclear war over two rocky dots in the Formosa Strait named Quemoy and Matsu. But China did not press the attack, and the principle of containment was preserved.

Far closer to home, another crisis arose as Eisenhower was completing his second term. In 1959, an intensely nationalistic and charismatic Cuban, Fidel Castro, toppled the dictator Fulgencio Batista and set about breaking Cuba's economic dependence on the United States. Castro's assertiveness and Washington's hostility to his revolution produced a quick rupture. The Eisenhower administration established the main lines of a policy that its successor then continued: an economic boycott of Cuba, an attempt to isolate it politically in the Western Hemisphere, and an encouragement for Cuban counter-revolutionaries. There were also secret American plans to assassinate Castro. Castro came to rely

FIDEL CASTRO AND
NIKITA KHRUSHCHEV.

It was a happy moment for Castro
and Khrushchev but an ominous
one in Washington, where their
embrace was interpreted as a
grave threat to containment.
(*Wide World.*)

much more on Soviet assistance than he had anticipated, and soon the Cuban
government formally committed itself to communism. Not only had the cardinal
rule of containment been violated; the breach had occurred just off the Florida
coast.

Castro became an American obsession. President Kennedy, who controlled his
administration's foreign policy and shared Dulles's commitment to containment,
entered office in 1961 with a powerful urge to eliminate Castro. When the CIA
promised a successful counterrevolution in Cuba if it could only land a cadre of
Castro's opponents on the island, Kennedy allowed the CIA to continue training
a small army of Cuban émigrés in preparation for such an attack. On April 17,
1961, an ill-equipped émigré force of 1400 made a disastrous thrust at Cuba
through the Bay of Pigs, where the invaders and America's reputation promptly
sank together. As sponsor of the invasion, the United States was guilty of violating
another nation's basic rights. As manager of America's foreign policy, the President was vulnerable to charges that he had done either too much or too little in
assisting the émigré army.

The Bay of Pigs was background to a much graver crisis a year later. After the
émigré attack, both Castro and Soviet Premier Khrushchev, a tough but erratic

gambler, calculated that missile bases in Cuba would improve their bargaining positions with the United States. Secretly, a flow of Soviet materials and technicians began moving by supply ships to Cuba. American intelligence learned about the missile sites in 1962 as they were being constructed. The existing arsenals of intercontinental missiles defined the balance of military power between the Soviet Union and the United States, and Soviet missiles in Cuba did not alter that balance. As one American official phrased it, the Cuban missile sites had a "psychological and political rather than military" meaning. Kennedy, rejecting advice to bomb the sites at once, announced on October 22, 1962, that the United States would set a naval blockade around Cuba and demanded an immediate halt to the missile traffic. The world held its breath. Then a day after the blockade went into effect a dozen Soviet supply ships turned from their course and went home. Russia dismantled the bases, America promised to honor Cuba's sovereignty, and in the United States, Kennedy emerged from the ordeal a hero.

Khrushchev also designated another point of crisis. The rough-hewn Soviet premier came to full power in 1958 determined to break the stalemate of the Cold War. He especially bridled at the impasse over Berlin, the sole Western outpost in the Soviet sphere. In an effort to force a new settlement for Berlin, he not only threatened to restrict Western access to the city, he declared that the Soviet Union and East Germany might have to decide Berlin's future by themselves. Off and on between 1958 and 1962, that isolated city once again became a potential center of war. The peak of danger occurred in the summer and fall of 1961, when the communists erected a wall across Berlin to seal their section of the city. Kennedy responded with the preliminary moves toward a war mobilization. The President called for military reserves, increased civil defense, and reinforced the American garrison in Berlin. Although the Berlin Wall remained, the crisis passed. By 1962, neither side wanted to press the other on the issue of Berlin.

In each area of crisis—the offshore islands, Cuba, and Berlin—the United States basically sought to preserve the status quo. Indeed, American policy expressed a general opposition to major changes and upheavals. In 1958, that urge led Eisenhower to land fourteen thousand American troops in Lebanon, in an attempt to keep the bitter, tangled rivalries of the Middle East from toppling governments that were friendly to the United States. Between 1960 and 1964, a similar impulse lay behind the financial and diplomatic assistance that the United States gave to a United Nations police force in the Congo (Zaire), where a chaotic civil war was racking this former Belgian colony. American policy outside of Europe was accurately described as antirevolutionary. In even broader terms, it was antidisruptive. In July 1956, for example, President Gamal Nasser of Egypt vented his anger at the Western powers by seizing the Suez Canal. From a mixture of motives and a mistaken impression that the United States would support them, England, France, and Israel coordinated military forces in October to humble Nasser and retake the canal. The United States, however, broke from its

BUILDING THE BERLIN WALL

With the wall came the threat of war.
(*Magnum.*)

allies. Coldly cooperating with the Soviet Union, the Eisenhower administration worked through the United Nations to halt the war and return the canal to Egypt.

This strong desire to stabilize international affairs tempered America's foreign policy throughout the Eisenhower and Kennedy years. Despite loose Republican promises during the 1952 campaign to "roll back the iron curtain" in Europe and "unleash" Chiang Kai-shek's army on China, the Eisenhower administration carefully avoided either course. When East Germans rioted in 1953 and Hungarians revolted against their government in 1956, the United States did nothing to provoke a wider conflict. In East Asia, the United States made an explicitly defensive treaty with Formosa in 1955, and on several other occasions Secretary Dulles assured Americans that the leash on Chiang Kai-shek was very tight indeed. Eastern Europe and China, already lost to the enemy, would have to await the long-range successes of containment.

The longer America's containment policy lasted, the more it acquired the characteristics of a ceaseless international game that should be played according to a careful set of rules. The first, tentative moves to regularize the competition of the Cold War occurred soon after President Eisenhower took office. Stalin's death in 1953, coinciding with a new administration in Washington, reopened the possibility for some exchange between the Soviet and American governments, which since 1947 had been yelling at one another half way around the world. Very gingerly, diplomats from the two superpowers began to explore a number of delicate problems, including a settlement for Germany and a limitation on armaments. In 1955, they actually signed a peace treaty for Austria.

The symbol of hope for a new era of "peaceful coexistence" was the summit conference between Soviet and American heads of state, comparable to the ones Roosevelt, Churchill, and Stalin had held during the Second World War. World-wide pressures for such a conference grew too strong for either great power to resist. In July 1955, for the first time in ten years, the President of the United States and the Premier of the Soviet Union, along with their counterparts from Britain and France, sat down together at a meeting in Geneva. Less formally, Eisenhower and Khrushchev met again at Camp David, Maryland, in September 1959. Although Americans spoke optimistically about a new "spirit of Geneva" in 1955 and then a new "spirit of Camp David" in 1959, the next two summit conferences were disasters. Just before an eagerly anticipated meeting at Paris in 1960, an American U-2 spy plane had been downed far inside Russia and its pilot, Francis Gary Powers, displayed to the world as proof of America's hostile intentions. Khrushchev's angry attacks at Eisenhower wrecked the Paris meeting. Then at Vienna in 1961, the distrust between Khrushchev and Kennedy ruined the chances for an effective conference. For a time, the vogue of the summit ended.

Nevertheless, the underlying forces for stabilization continued to operate. Both the United States and the Soviet Union found the management of their inter-national spheres a complicated, frustrating, and expensive task. Both had poor success appealing to the so-called neutral countries outside the two spheres. Both were deeply committed to consumer satisfactions at home. Moreover, as the weapons of nuclear annihilation piled higher and higher in the arsenals of both nations, their leaders were to some degree sobered by the incredible power they could unleash. "We have arrived at that point," Eisenhower acknowledged in 1954, "where war does not present the possibility of victory or defeat." His counterpart in the Soviet Union, Georgi Malenkov, had already admitted as much a year earlier. Each of these parallel developments applied a slight brake of caution to the diplomacy of the Cold War. Gradually, the trends seemed to be moving from a volatile Cold War to a predictable Cold Peace.

Presidential Leadership

Each additional step in the process of modernization placed a heavier burden of management on the President. The responsibilities for maintaining a sound economy that had arrived with the Great Depression never left the White House. During the 1940s, world war and cold war also made the President the focus of America's international security. Although foreign affairs had traditionally been his special duty, never before had they carried such profound consequences. In

"I SAID — WE SURE SETTLED THAT DISPUTE, DIDN'T WE!"

(Frank Miller cartoon in the Des Moines Register *May 6, 1963. Wide World.)*

the thermonuclear age, international relations became literally a matter of life and death. By the 1950s, the President alone seemed capable of ensuring the nation's unity, stability, and progress.

Under this massive weight of responsibilities, the meaning of the presidency changed in two important respects. First, the office was separated from the normal patterns of electoral politics. Beginning with Eisenhower's triumph in 1952, the vote for President no longer followed the same curve as the nationwide vote for other Democratic and Republican candidates. Franklin Roosevelt's rising and falling majorities had roughly paralleled the majorities of the Democratic party. Even Harry Truman's surprising victory in 1948 had coincided with a similar Democratic revival. After 1952, however, the presidential vote set a course of its own. In 1954, the Democrats recaptured both houses of Congress and continued to hold them, usually by substantial majorities. By contrast to this steady, partisan line, the presidential returns swung in big loops that expressed specific, quadrennial choices between individuals.

As Americans detached their President from party politics, they were developing a new relation with him that had relatively little to do with the electoral process. Its crucial components were television and national opinion polls. The President spoke personally to all the people through television; they responded directly to him through opinion polls. The entire nation and America's indispensable leader, it seemed, were engaged in a unique, continuous dialogue. A presidential election was merely the most formal and dramatic moment in the dialogue. Between elections, a string of opinion polls charted results that were widely interpreted as substitute elections, continually measuring the success of the nation's leader. Any overwhelming endorsement of the President, such as Eisenhower's runaway victories in the 1952 and 1956 elections or Kennedy's impressive ratings in the opinion polls of 1961 and 1962, became a sign of national strength. By the same token, a sharp drop in Truman's ratings during 1951 and 1952 signaled a severe national problem. Americans, in other words, made their month-by-month judgments of the President into a bedside graph of America's health.

The second significant change in the presidency involved the requirements for effective national leadership. The complex nature of the President's tasks forced him to act simultaneously as a mobilizing leader for the whole nation and as a cautious manager of America's intricate foreign and domestic affairs. As early as the 1930s, Roosevelt had understood this need for an inspiring moderation. FDR, however, served during a bitterly partisan period when no one could hope to transcend parties and represent all the people. Moreover, his leadership was identified not with steady management but with great emergencies: depression, then war. Truman was the last of the openly partisan Presidents. The Missouri scrapper seldom allowed anyone to forget that he was a Democrat, and his quick temper, sharp tongue, and unpredictable ways clashed with the image of a smooth manager.

Eisenhower was the first to meet the modern demands on the President. The general's background allowed him to appear a man above the clamor of special interests. Each landmark in his military career—wartime commander of the Allied armies of Europe, Chief of Staff, and commander of NATO's forces— suggested the highest level of nonpartisanship. Even as President, Eisenhower liked to think of himself as a nonpartisan leader. He projected an instinctive fairness that promised to reunite the nation after the harsh years of Truman and McCarthy. Although his temper and tongue could match Truman's, Eisenhower held them in public. Eisenhower never mastered the art of a formal television speech, but he was irresistibly attractive in casual shots. His incomparable smile, strong stride, and easy yet authoritative manner made him everybody's Ike. In a special sense, Eisenhower seemed able to speak to all Americans at home and speak for them abroad.

Eisenhower strengthened his position as national leader by delegating much of the controversial work of his administration. While his secretary of state used the militant language of the Cold War, the President spoke in a moderate, conciliatory tone. The world identified Dulles with "brinkmanship." It identified Eisenhower with "Atoms for Peace," a program to share America's scientific knowledge that the President first proposed in 1953 and then elaborated in 1955. In election years, Eisenhower almost always took the high ground of broad, bland pronouncements. Vice-President Nixon was the administration's partisan voice, and every two years he flayed the Democrats with a rawhide campaign rhetoric.

The Eisenhower formula was unbeatable. In the campaign of 1956, the Democrats again set the cultivated phrasemaker Adlai Stevenson of Illinois against the President, and again Eisenhower easily defeated him, 457 electoral votes to 73. As long as Eisenhower remained in the White House, no one else seemed very important as a national leader. At the nominating conventions of 1960, the men who filled this vacuum were Richard Nixon and John Kennedy. The choice of Nixon established a logical corollary to the modern presidency. The Vice-President, borrowing a reflected glory from the nation's one, indispensable leader, became the President's natural successor. Muting his earlier partisanship, Nixon conducted his campaign like the heir apparent who would continue the

The Election of 1960

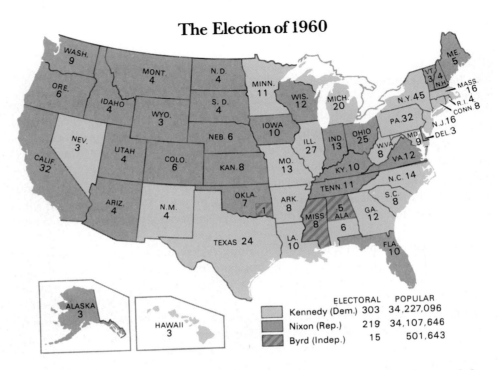

	ELECTORAL	POPULAR
Kennedy (Dem.)	303	34,227,096
Nixon (Rep.)	219	34,107,646
Byrd (Indep.)	15	501,643

policies of Eisenhower's popular rule. The Democrats, sensing the need for a new name to replace Stevenson, chose the youthful senator from Massachusetts, whose well-organized and liberally financed primary campaign gave him a considerable edge over his competitors. In the closest presidential race since the late nineteenth century, the inexperienced Kennedy received a scant 100,000 votes more than the uninspired Nixon.

When Kennedy entered the White House in 1961, the modern role of the President was already well defined. In place of his predecessor's nonpartisan background, Kennedy's large family fortune conveyed a similar detachment from the scramble of economic interests. In place of Eisenhower's reputation for fairness, Kennedy's record of personal courage in the Second World War suggested that he, too, would make a strong, even-handed leader. Like the combination of Dulles and Eisenhower, Kennedy also tried to balance militancy and moderation in his foreign policy. After the Cuban missile crisis of 1962, for example, came the Test Ban Treaty of 1963, in which the Soviet Union and the United States agreed to stop contaminating the atmosphere with their nuclear tests. Kennedy was particularly imaginative in associating the President's office with broad national goals. Under Kennedy's sponsorship, a wide assortment of studies and reports attempted to define America's primary objectives. It was Kennedy who recognized the special attraction of a journey to the moon as a truly national enterprise that would stand apart from domestic jealousies and make sense to Americans of all types and ages. Beginning in 1961, the President's Peace Corps, through which American volunteers took their skills to the world's poor nations, had a somewhat comparable appeal.

INAUGURATION OF JOHN F. KENNEDY

Presidents past and future gathered in 1961 as Chief
Justice Earl Warren administered the oath of office to John
Kennedy. Adlai Stevenson on the far left and Associate
Justice William O. Douglas on the far right, both of whom
had wanted the office, watched solemnly from the fringes.
Dwight Eisenhower, Lyndon Johnson, and Richard Nixon
stood in the front row. *(Wide World.)*

Kennedy's most impressive contributions to the new leadership involved the
intangibles of style and charm. He made a striking appearance on television, as
he had already demonstrated in his televised debates with Nixon during the 1960
campaign. As President, Kennedy continued to make excellent use of the
medium, both formally and informally. The youngest elected President in history
at forty-three, he radiated health and vigor. Appropriate to his administration's
image of youthful adventure, Kennedy's program acquired the name of the New
Frontier. At times, the handsome President's private affairs seemed to loom
larger across the nation than his public actions. Through the eager cooperation
of the news industry, the President and his stunningly attractive, photogenic
family entered everybody's lives as their familiars: Jack and his wife Jackie, their
children Caroline and John, Jr., the President's brother Bobby, and the rest of
the vibrant Kennedy clan.

Nothing better illustrated this intimate bond between Kennedy and the public
than America's response to the President's assassination in Dallas on November
22, 1963. For a long, mournful weekend, the nation immersed itself in every

detail of the tragedy and its aftermath. Through television, Americans traced the President's motorcade, saw Kennedy jarred by an explosion of shots, shared the vigil outside the hospital, witnessed the incredible murder of the prime suspect Lee Harvey Oswald, and then followed the doleful state funeral through the gray streets of Washington. No event had ever been so thoroughly national and yet so intensely personal. More than a decade later, with important questions about the assassination still unanswered, millions could re-create those "six seconds in Dallas" as if their lives, too, had hung in the balance.

After Kennedy's successor, Lyndon B. Johnson, had been in office only a few months, the Democratic party nominated him for a presidential term in his own right. Although Johnson had neither the towering prestige of Eisenhower nor the brilliant charm of Kennedy, he did have a long record of moderate congressional management and a brief but striking record of presidential leadership. To challenge Johnson in 1964, the Republicans selected the deeply conservative senator from Arizona, Barry Goldwater, along with an equally conservative candidate for Vice-President. Goldwater represented a wing of the Republican party that opposed city bosses and government bureaucrats, labor unions and farm subsidies, welfare payments and poverty programs. That fall, the Arizona senator, an honest, articulate man, spoke his mind freely. He promised thorough, drastic changes in government policy, including a considerably more aggressive foreign policy. Johnson skillfully kept his campaign within the standard presidential mold of dynamic temperateness. If anyone had doubted the popular appeal of the modern presidential model, this election must have settled the issue. In a remarkably clear contest between the images of unifying moderation and factional extremism, Johnson overwhelmed Goldwater, 43 million votes to 27 million.

The Crisis in National–Local Relations

The confidence of the fifties had created such optimism about the powers of national management that some Americans came to believe that every problem had a national, managerial solution. Most followers of this faith were successful Americans, whose careers flowed with the currents of modernization. National in orientation and outlook, they turned naturally to the government in Washington for the skills and authority necessary to solve America's problems. But a fine line separated their optimism from arrogance. As the national government enlarged the scope of its responsibilities, it generated new problems faster than it solved old ones. The first sign of these unexpected consequences appeared in an increasingly angry clash between an expansive national government and a threatened world of local white power.

One of President Eisenhower's earliest appointments was a new chief justice of the Supreme Court. He chose the affable California Republican, Earl Warren, who had been an extremely popular governor and the party's vice-presidential candidate in 1948. Although Warren was classified a "liberal Republican," he was also a skilled mediator who had no record of interest in social experimentation. He had even participated in the drive to intern Japanese Americans during the Second World War. His appointment seemed to augur a safe, middle-of-the-road Court.

As Earl Warren became chief justice in 1953, the most significant issue pending before the Supreme Court was racial segregation in the public schools. Precedents that challenged the doctrine of "separate but equal" educational facilities for blacks had been accumulating for more than a decade, but the Supreme Court had phrased them in cautious, narrow terms. Many observers expected a similar wording from the moderate new chief justice. Instead, in the unanimous decision of *Brown* v. *Board of Education* (1954), Warren boldly declared separate educational facilities inherently unequal and inhumane. The long legal march of the National Association for the Advancement of Colored People had reached its objective. At a stroke, the Court undercut the entire structure of Jim Crow laws.

SEGREGATED CAFÉ AND CIVIL RIGHTS DEMONSTRATOR

The discipline, drama, and fellowship of the civil rights movement won it nationwide support in the late fifties and early sixties. *(Left, Denny Lyman/Magnum; right, Bruce Davidson/Magnum.)*

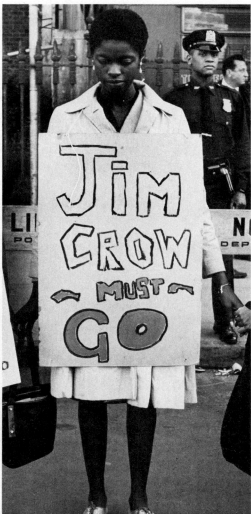

Few successful white Americans could debate Warren's conclusions. No ethnic standard had a logical place in their occupational world, and a rigid pattern of Jim Crow drinking fountains and bus seats seemed particularly irrational. In the postwar years, segregation had become an obvious affront to America's modern values. At home, it clashed with the ideal of an open society, in which citizens were free to acquire all the skills they could learn and buy all the goods they could earn. Abroad, it jeopardized America's chances of bringing people with brown or black or yellow skin into a worldwide anticommunist league. Prominent Southern liberals increasingly joined the critics of segregation. By the 1950s, nationally minded Americans regarded Jim Crow as an anachronism that a modern society could no longer tolerate.

They considered education an excellent place to begin racial desegregation. Because successful Americans were sensitive to the relation between skills and success, they immediately recognized the serious consequences of an inferior education. Moreover, they believed that completely dismantling the caste system would require slow, careful adjustments over many years. If children in integrated schools grew up free of prejudice, these new generations, coming one after another, would eventually eliminate the last traces of racial hate. Time and the power of education lay on the side of progress. In this spirit of optimistic caution the Supreme Court declared in 1955 that school desegregation should proceed "with all deliberate speed."

During the next decade, the conflicts over racial segregation reinforced these initial desires to abolish it. It was the opponents of segregation who could almost always claim to be law-abiding, orderly, and moderate. Southern whites, on the other hand, threw all manner of legal obstacles in the path of integration, ranging from the novel constitutional doctrine of "state interposition" between the national government and its citizens to the substitution of private segregated schools for the public system. With increasing firmness, the federal courts removed each one. In 1957, when Governor Orval Faubus of Arkansas defied a court order to desegregate the schools of Little Rock, it required a wall of soldiers to protect the thin line of black children from a taunting crowd of adult whites. Individual blacks faced a roughly comparable experience as they tried to enter the state universities in Alabama and Mississippi. In 1957 and 1960, Congress passed two mild civil rights laws that allowed the federal courts to intervene in behalf of disfranchised blacks. A number of Southern politicians reacted as if the right to vote were a subversive doctrine.

During the same years, blacks and whites also confronted each other directly over segregation. Blacks took the initiative, and their movement quickly became identified with the particular style of an intense, eloquent young minister from Montgomery, Alabama, Martin Luther King, Jr. Not yet twenty-seven years old, he emerged in 1955 as the nationally publicized leader of a local boycott against Montgomery's segregated buses. Through words and example, King provided blacks with a creative combination of the Christian love that their churches taught, the strategy of peaceful mass resistance that the Hindu, Mahatma Gandhi, had formulated, and the self-discipline that relatively well-to-do blacks had long used to defend their rights in America's caste system. While King was inspiring his fellow blacks, he was also attracting wide support among successful whites. Non-violent protest suited their standards of orderly behavior and peaceful change so well that many of them heralded King as one of America's statesmen.

In 1960, black students throughout the cities of the South applied King's tactics in a dramatic wave of "sit ins" that desegregated numerous restaurants, then a variety of other public accommodations. The following year the Congress on Racial Equality (CORE), an even older center of peaceful resistance, sponsored black and white "Freedom Riders" on a harrowing bus trip into the South that publicized the illegal segregation in interstate travel. This pillar of Jim Crow also toppled. As in the case of Little Rock, the violent responses to these protests strengthened the bond between successful whites and black moderates. In 1963, when King led a movement against segregation in Birmingham, Alabama, na-tional television vividly recorded the cattle prods, fire hoses, and snarling dogs that local police used to intimidate the blacks. Murders relating to the civil rights movement that year in Birmingham and the next summer in Mississippi could not be prosecuted in the Southern courts. King's Southern Christian Leadership Conference (SCLC) and its offspring, the Student Non-Violent Coordinating Committee (SNCC), seemed the embodiment of rationality by contrast to the revived Ku Klux Klan, the raucous rhetoric of local Southern politics, and the partiality of Southern white justice.

The accelerating pace of events gave the movement for black rights a new tempo and a new urgency. White sympathy for King's inspired moderation con-tinued to rise in the summer of 1963 when a quarter million Americans drama-tized the plight of the blacks by marching peacefully through Washington and gathering at the Lincoln Memorial. There they heard King's moving message of hope: "I have a dream that one day [in the Deep South] . . . little black boys and black girls will be able to join hands with little white boys and white girls and walk together as sisters and brothers."

What was missing was strong political leadership. The White House had largely held aloof from the civil rights movement. President Eisenhower, who later cursed his choice of Earl Warren as chief justice, stated privately "that the Supreme Court decision [on school desegregation] *set back* progress in the South at least fifteen years. . . . We can't demand *perfection* in these moral questions." No one was less happy than Eisenhower when the posturing Governor Faubus forced the President to intervene in Little Rock. Kennedy, though much less attached to local customs than his predecessor, was equally cautious as he began his term. Despite campaign promises to end racial discrimination in public hous-ing with "a stroke of the presidential pen," he delayed almost two years before signing the appropriate executive order. In 1963, Kennedy delivered an im-portant address in support of black rights and called for new legislation in their

behalf. However, Kennedy's pressure on Congress still lagged behind his words.

Lyndon Johnson filled the void in leadership. Always a restless soul, he had pushed his way out of the Texas hills as a youth, entered Congress in the 1930s, then moved up to the Senate in 1949. During Eisenhower's two terms, Johnson was generally regarded as the most powerful Democrat in Washington. An exceptionally skillful legislative director, he combined a relentless energy, a keen understanding of politics, and a driving ambition for greatness. A good many people were surprised in 1960 when Johnson accepted the nomination for Vice-President. But the shrewd Texan, who had watched Nixon step from that office to the Republican presidential nomination, knew just what he was doing.

By temperament, Johnson was always prepared to lead. With Kennedy's grave scarcely sealed in November 1963, the new President was already mobilizing for action, and during his first two years in office he compiled an astonishing record. Some of the measures he sponsored had originated with the Kennedy administration. Others were Johnson's own. Declaring a "War on Poverty," the President convinced Congress to invest billions of dollars in training the unemployed, supporting community development, reviving impoverished regional economies, and expanding educational services in the slums. As headquarters for the war, Congress in 1964 created the Office of Economic Opportunity (OEO). In addition, the Education Act of 1965 marked the beginning of massive federal aid to the public and parochial schools. Finally, after decades of discussion, medical insurance (Medicare) was included under Social Security.

In each of these two extraordinary years, President Johnson guided an important civil rights law through Congress. The Civil Rights Act of 1964, emphasizing coverage more than enforcement, deepened the national executive's involvement in almost every area of the expanding movement for equality: voting, public accommodations, schools, employment. The Civil Rights Act of 1965, concentrating on the franchise, made it possible for the national government to act as official registrar for black voters in the South. Under the provisions of the new law, the lists of eligible black voters rapidly expanded. Johnson, who cherished the tradition of the New Deal, assumed that his administration could facilitate the rise of black Americans much as the Roosevelt administration had assisted the poor thirty years earlier. In effect, the War on Poverty was a selective anti-depression program, and a high proportion of these impoverished Americans were blacks. The Civil Rights Acts of 1964 and 1965 completed a framework for racial reform that in many ways resembled the New Deal's labor policies of the late 1930s. They established a uniform structure of rules, centralized the admin-

BLACK AND WHITE TOGETHER

Massive yet orderly, the March on Washington in 1963 gave a powerful impetus to the biracial civil rights movement. *(Bob Adelman/Magnum.)*

"You Mean These Apply To The Riff-Raff Too?"

(From the Herblock Gallery, *Simon and Schuster,*
1968.)

istration of these rules, and relied on a sympathetic federal judiciary to enforce them.

Johnson's legislative success ended one phase of the movement for black rights. Its rationale had actually been stated in 1944 by Gunnar Myrdal's *An American Dilemma*, which dominated the understanding of race relations for the next twenty years. In this massive study that Myrdal prepared for the Carnegie Foundation, the Swedish scholar defined antiblack prejudice as the one great contradiction to the "American Creed," a nationally accepted set of beliefs in equality, opportunity, and justice for everybody. Behind the civil rights movement lay a faith that this American Creed would inevitably triumph over its antiblack contradictions. The Warren Court depended on the creed to give social authority to its legal rulings against segregation. Martin Luther King depended on the creed as a national white conscience that his strategy of civil disobedience could stir. The Johnson administration depended on the creed to rally the last holdouts behind a national program to eliminate racial inequalities from American life. Because of their common faith in the creed, a disciplined black minority and a well-to-do white minority had been able to work together in the cause of black rights. As a climax to the biracial civil rights movement, successful whites enthusiastically applauded in 1964 when King rose in Oslo to receive the Nobel Prize for Peace.

Contrary to the hopes of the civil rights movement, millions of whites understood the American Creed not as a common system of national values but as a justification for their particular set of local values. Turning inward, they continued to build their lives around family networks, cultural identities, and special local ways. In the 1960s, about half of America's white wage earners still lived in "ethnic, religious, and social enclaves relatively untouched by [the postwar years] and emphatically personal in character." Even those who had moved tried to stay within traveling distance of "home" and often retained very close ties with their families and old friends. Christianity in local America ranged from a ritualistically rich Catholicism, to the kind of evangelical Protestantism that made the revivalist Billy Graham a national hero, to such fundamentalist denominations as Jehovah's Witnesses. Beneath the glare of national TV, the gossipy, personal AM radio stations reflected these local values. Sports provided another outlet for a fierce local attachment. When the Chicago Black Hawks played in Detroit, or the New York Knicks in Boston, they were openly, honestly hated. In Brooklyn, nothing could ease the deep sense of cheat when the Dodgers—"dem Bums!"—departed in 1958 for Los Angeles.

Attempts to draw local Americans into a uniform system of national rules arrived like an enemy invasion. In most cases, local Americans could not grasp the legal and bureaucratic procedures behind such rules. As a study in 1970 revealed, a majority of Americans were "functionally illiterate" in the face of tax forms, insurance claims, credit contracts, and similar fine print. In the 1950s and 1960s, plans for urban improvement seldom took into account the local ways of life they were disrupting. The acronym for one local organization spoke the feelings of innumerable Americans from the inner city: SOUR—Stamp Out Urban Renewal. In the countryside as well as the city, it was becoming harder each year for Americans to protect their local networks.

In many localities skin color was a primary means of separating insiders from outsiders. White wage earners increasingly worked with people of other colors but still refused to accept such people in their neighborhoods, schools, parks, and taverns. During the fifties, these insular feelings exploded in anger throughout the South, where the civil rights movement first concentrated. But temperatures were also rising in the North. During the 1950s, every Northern city suffered from a housing shortage that dated from the slowing of home construction late in the 1920s. Indeed, there was a growing pressure on all kinds of city resources, partly as a result of new migrations. Rural blacks and whites who had been replaced by mechanical cotton pickers, consolidated farms, and mechanized coal mining poured into the city slums. So did Mexican Americans and Puerto Ricans, who were trying to escape their own grinding poverty. In a crowded arena of competitors, racial antagonisms turned into hate. When King took his civil rights campaign north in 1964, the ferocity of the white reaction matched anything he had encountered in the South.

By itself, the civil rights movement would have tipped modern America's delicate balance between national and local authority. Establishing national rules in such an extremely sensitive area of local white privilege guaranteed a local revolt. But civil rights did not come alone. A broader movement for national uniformity accompanied the movement for black rights and threatened an array of traditionally local powers. Because the Supreme Court figured so prominently in this nationalizing process, the Warren Court came to symbolize a wholesale assault on local America, and "Impeach Earl Warren" was its popular slogan of resistance. Between 1956 and 1965, the Court significantly narrowed the local power to censor obscenity. Beginning with the *Mallory* decision of 1957 and culminating in the *Escobedo* and *Miranda* decisions of 1964 and 1965, it set standards of police procedure to protect the rights of suspected criminals. In 1962 and 1964, the

ONE ANSWER TO NATIONAL AUTHORITY

(Danny Lyon/Magnum.)

Court outlawed prayers and Bible readings in the public schools. During these same years, notably in *Baker* v. *Carr* (1962), the Court also required the creation of state election districts that would approximate the rule of "one person, one vote."

Each of these changes challenged a basic local right. Censorship of movies, pornography, and schoolbooks was a widely used means of preserving local values. As the fear of street crime spread in the cities, many people thought they could no longer walk in their neighborhoods if the police were hobbled in pursuit of suspected criminals. The local truths of religion, a majority of Americans continued to believe, belonged in the schools just as they did in the home. Gerrymandering the cities was the customary way for small towns to ensure that the state legislature would protect their rights against outside intrusions.* In some instances, city dwellers wanted to gerrymander the suburbs for similar reasons.

The period of acute crisis in local power commenced in 1957. That year, Congress passed the first civil rights law since Reconstruction, federal troops entered Little Rock to enforce school desegregation, and the Warren Court embarked on its most active period. By 1965, the local barriers against national

---

*Gerrymandering is the drawing of grossly unequal election districts.

power appeared to be smashed. Washington officials were registering black voters in the rural South. The Warren Court had defined its broad national domain. As local governments complained of a budget squeeze, fresh funds for the war on poverty were bypassing almost all of the white neighborhoods in favor of the people economically below them. Not only did the public welfare rolls swell enormously in the mid-1960s, but some agents of OEO were even organizing welfare recipients to demand more. Until 1964, the President and Congress indicated from time to time that they had not completely forsaken the old balance. But when President Johnson called for a Great Society in January 1965, he officially committed his administration to a vigorous national management over matters that once were privileges of the locality. That year, Congress responded with large majorities for the President's program.

Nationally oriented Americans had convinced themselves that their understanding of equality, opportunity, and justice was everybody's American Creed. As they used this creed to make national policy, they assumed that no one would seriously question the new policy's impartiality. Everyone, they believed, would soon accept it as a nonpartisan, nonpolitical fact of life. But this nationalizing process had just the opposite effect. Instead of creating a nonpolitical consensus, it ignited a fresh political conflict. Actually by 1965 not a great deal had changed in the local white world. Only a small percentage of black children attended integrated classes. Many communities still found ways of keeping Christianity in and alien books out of their schools. Police procedures altered very little. Nevertheless, when locally oriented whites saw a solid phalanx in the national government arrayed against them, they prepared to fight for their traditional rights.

The Decline of Containment

A second crisis in Washington's management occurred in international affairs. Here also the nation's leaders tried to impose their understanding of events on people who lived by very different values. In this case, it was the doctrine of containment that clashed with other people's aspirations, and it was a variety of nations throughout the world that challenged America's right to thwart their own, distinctive ambitions.

From the beginning, containment was a specifically American policy. Relatively few other nations gave anticommunism the same overriding importance that the United States assigned to it. The more the Cold War stabilized and the more economically independent America's allies became, the more these allies resisted America's particular interpretation of world affairs. In Europe, France led the resistance. By refusing to join an integrated continental military force in 1954, France destroyed America's plans for a European Defense Community (EDC). Then after 1958, the Paris government under its imperial President, Charles de Gaulle, furnished a continuing center for European criticism of American policy. More subtly, Japan also maneuvered for greater independence from the United

States. No sooner had the American occupation ended in 1951 than Japan sought full control over its territory and policies. Here, as in Western Europe, the desire to trade with communist nations contributed to the tension, for the United States opposed almost all economic relations between the two international spheres.

Although the world's agrarian nations had a meager share in the prosperity of the 1950s, many of them, too, were marking their own separate paths. The electric names in Africa and Asia were fervent nationalists such as Gamal Nasser of Egypt, Kwame Nkrumah of Ghana, Jawaharlal Nehru of India, and Sukarno of Indonesia. In a variety of ways, these leaders struggled to develop their nations without sacrificing independence to either side in the Cold War. Extremely sensitive to pressures from the great powers, they retaliated in anger when the United States or the Soviet Union appeared to dangle economic aid as an incentive to enter its camp. Because the United States was allied to their former imperial masters in Europe, the recently emancipated colonies especially set themselves against a future that would be known as the "American Century."

In the face of these nationalist assertions, Secretary Dulles held tenaciously to the principles of containment. He threatened France with an "agonizing reappraisal" of America's support, and he condemned the trend toward neutralism among the agrarian nations. As best he could, he minimized the importance that such countries as India and Pakistan, or Greece and Turkey, assigned to their own feuds. After Dulles's retirement in 1959, however, the world's variety started to break through the monolithic conceptions of the Cold War. With Kennedy's inauguration, officials in Washington began exploring ways of responding to these diverse international ambitions. The new President, who expected to build his reputation in foreign affairs, encouraged fresh ideas about America's policies. He promised to accept the new nations of Africa and Asia on their own terms and to negotiate with the established nations as equals. In 1961, Kennedy announced the "Alliance for Progress" with Latin America that would use economic aid from the United States to improve the quality of life in this hemisphere. The Peace Corps also placed local human needs above international military policy.

Nevertheless, in the day-to-day conduct of foreign affairs, Kennedy, his primary adviser on foreign policy, McGeorge Bundy, and his secretary of state, Dean Rusk, gave priority to the containment of international communism. During the 1960 campaign, Kennedy had claimed that Soviet military advances left the United States at the wrong end of a "missile gap." Though no one ever found the gap, the new President still worked hard to expand America's military capabilities. Twice he demanded and received substantial increases in the military budget. Moreover, military assistance continued to dominate the budget for foreign aid. In Latin America, the guide to American policy was not the Alliance for Progress but isolating Castro's Cuba and insulating other countries against a similar revolution.

Under Kennedy's successor, even the exploration of alternatives dwindled. Johnson came to office in 1963 with a longstanding, firm commitment to containment, and he showed little patience with new ideas on world policy. Unlike Kennedy, he relied heavily on his advisers in foreign affairs. By backing the requests from the Pentagon and the State Department, Johnson hoped they would manage international problems while he concentrated on domestic affairs.

With this cast of mind, Johnson met the primary international challenge of his administration, a civil war in Viet Nam. America's involvement in Viet Nam dated from 1950, when the United States first supplied aid to the French in their attempt to recapture their Indochinese colony. France still lost the battle of the jungles to Ho Chi Minh's communist army, and in 1954 an international conference at Geneva created three independent states from the former French territory: Laos, Cambodia, and Viet Nam. Viet Nam was temporarily divided between a communist north and a noncommunist south pending national elections and unification.

After the French defeat, the United States assumed responsibility for containing communism throughout Indochina. As Dulles explained, one primary reason for sponsoring the Southeast Asia Treaty Organization in 1955 was to provide a "cover" over Indochina. With American support, the leaders in the southern portion of Viet Nam repudiated the Geneva plan for national elections and established a permanent state, South Viet Nam. As Kennedy took office, the anticommunist governments in both South Viet Nam and neighboring Laos were in jeopardy. South Vietnamese guerrillas who had been fighting the corrupt government in Saigon consolidated their forces as the National Liberation Front (NLF). Kennedy responded by expanding America's covert military assistance, including the organization of raids inside North Viet Nam, where some of the rebels were trained and supplied. The conflict in Laos stabilized, but not the one in South Viet Nam. The more American the war in Viet Nam became, the broader the guerrilla resistance to Saigon grew.

Johnson rode the momentum of America's involvement into a major war. In 1964, he inflated a small naval encounter off the Vietnamese coast as a calculated attack by North Viet Nam on an American ship, and in the "Gulf of Tonkin" Resolution the Senate granted the President wide discretion in defending America's forces in Viet Nam. Starting seriously in 1965, Johnson enlarged the American contingent in Viet Nam until by 1968 it exceeded half a million men. Under the code name Operation Rolling Thunder, massive bombing raids struck North Viet Nam, which now sent its own troops into the south. Squads of American planes followed the winding jungle trails of Indochina in an attempt to block the flow of troops and supplies from the north. Johnson abruptly dismissed each overture to compromise.

Johnson's plan in Viet Nam grew out of a central assumption in America's containment policy. As Kennedy's military adviser General Maxwell Taylor stated it, the communists had to be taught that a war for national liberation was "costly," not "cheap." Or in Dulles's words of 1954, communist guerrillas had to "suffer damage outweighing any possible gains from aggression." Johnson's strategy was to increase the level of punishment until the price of continuing the war became too high and the enemy would quit. Because the guerrilla foe was so difficult to locate, the military relied more on broad coverage than precise assaults. America's tactics included chemical defoliants, carpet bombing, and napalm. Inevitably they took a terrible civilian toll in search of the hidden enemy. Meanwhile, the Johnson administration issued optimistic statements about the progress of the war.

The Vietnamese did not respond according to plan. Under increasing attack, neither North Viet Nam nor the NLF weakened. During January and February of 1968, in a dramatic demonstration of their continuing strength, the communists launched the "Tet Offensive" into the primary cities of South Viet Nam, which had been considered well beyond the reach of the guerrilla armies. Even before the Tet Offensive, American opposition to the war had already been rising. Like Hoover's prosperity, Johnson's victory in Viet Nam stayed just around the corner too long. In the jargon of the sixties, the "credibility gap" had spread too wide. Saigon eventually reported a count of communist casualties that exceeded the total Vietnamese population. As the military draft quotas mounted each year, so did the number of evaders. In 1968, draft resistance erupted nation-

WAR IN VIETNAM

Who was the enemy in Viet Nam? Perhaps this
Vietnamese woman knew, but increasing
numbers of Americans could not say. *(Magnum.)*

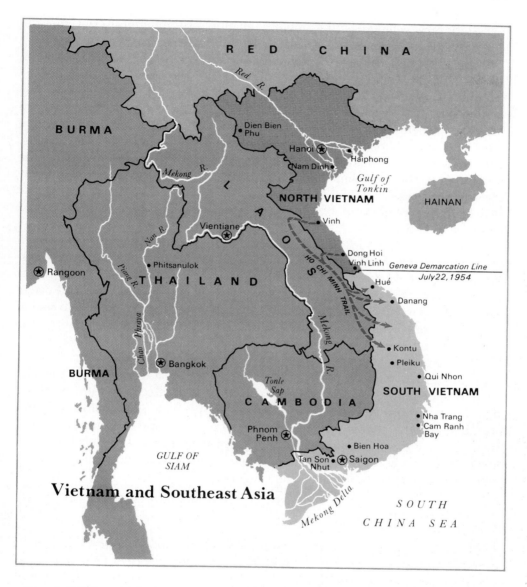

Vietnam and Southeast Asia

wide. J. William Fulbright, the chairman of the Senate Foreign Relations Committee, who had once trusted Johnson to conduct the war in his own way, became one of its sharpest critics, and a growing body of disillusioned Democrats sided with Fulbright against the President. With the Tet Offensive, television coverage and news dispatches increasingly emphasized the futility and brutality of the war. "Bombing, bombing! Why do you always write bombing?" an angry officer demanded at a military briefing for reporters in Saigon. "It's air support, not bombing!" On March 31, 1968, a frustrated Johnson turned the corner. Before a nationwide television audience, he announced an end to the escalation of the

war and a new willingness to negotiate. Then in a stunning postscript, the subdued President said that he would not seek reelection.

Once a popular faith in containment would have strengthened American
support for the war. By the late 1960s, however, the Viet Nam crisis just accelerated the general decline of America's global policy. Communism, according
to the logic of containment, was a single international system directed from
Moscow. Yet throughout the 1960s, astonished Americans had been learning
more and more about a bitter hostility between China and the Soviet Union.
The Soviet-Chinese feud not only shattered a cardinal principle behind the
Cold War; it also contributed to the growing American awareness of a highly
diverse, subdivided world. The Viet Nam War, instead of being an integral
part of America's global policy, increasingly seemed a separate issue that could
be solved by itself.

In one more way Viet Nam hastened the decline of containment. Foreign
governments that had been harboring resentment against the world's greatest
power took the war as an occasion to express these feelings and declare their
independence of Washington. Even yesterday's imperialists in Western Europe
joined in the worldwide criticism of American policy in Viet Nam. No nation
altered its basic relations with the United States. But America's isolation over
Viet Nam did hurry the international decentralization that had been under
way for more than a decade.

By 1968, the American policy of containment was disintegrating. As the Viet
Nam War demonstrated, containment could not deal effectively with the rising
nationalist passions among the world's agrarian peoples. Nor could it respond
adequately to the growing independence among the world's industrial nations.
In the early fifties, containment had appeared to be a model of global management. Now this outworn policy, which the United States seemed unable to use
or to abandon, had become a manager's nightmare.

The Lament of the Individual

Meanwhile a third crisis was brewing among the very Americans who were
supposed to be the primary beneficiaries of modern society. In the 1950s,
a well-trained and well-paid minority, holding jobs with national prestige in
business and the professions, presumably sat atop American society and epitomized its confidence. Yet the same nationalizing forces that gave them power
and prestige also shrank their importance as individuals. The more systematized their society, the less significant, or even distinguishable, any one person
was in its operations. Perhaps, as the most critical voices of the late forties had
implied, there really were no individuals in a modern, bureaucratic society.

During the 1950s, successful Americans told one another to find their personal security in the impersonal forces governing their society. They praised
the unifying effects of mass consumerism. They expected the computer to make

sense out of the complex social problems around them. Sufficient megatons of "nuclear deterrent," they said, would preserve the Free World. The publicist Peter Drucker asked Americans to picture the "Industrial Enterprise" as their social model. According to the economist John Kenneth Galbraith, huge "countervailing powers," or nationwide interest groups, maintained the healthy balance inside American capitalism.

But where were the individuals in this scheme of abstractions? The countercurrents of doubt began to swell. One source was a set of images particularly associated with the thermonuclear age. Such popular novels and movies as *On the Beach* and *Fail-Safe* touched the deep fears of a world dying in its contaminated atmosphere and a flaw in the computerized balance of terror triggering the ultimate holocaust. The audience for a dehumanizing science fiction expanded. The most intriguing new American writer of the 1950s, J. D. Salinger, and the most talented new American dramatist of the 1960s, Edward Albee, both emphasized the individual's agonizing, inescapable vulnerability in modern society. Many young writers accentuated the individual's isolation by using ordinary conversation as a way of hiding rather than communicating their

RUSH HOUR, NEW YORK CITY

Routinized jobs in impersonal institutions made even successful Americans wonder about the meaning of their lives. A thousand clowns, one popular movie of the sixties called them. *(Abigail Hayman/Magnum.)*

characters' feelings. Only when the characters talked to themselves in lonely, interior monologues did they honestly express their emotions. Novelists such as Saul Bellow and Joseph Heller relieved their own grim assessments with a wild laughter at the individual's preposterous fate in modern society. The escape through humor found its most popular common denominator in the "sick joke" of the 1960s.

The malaise that these writers expressed was also affecting attitudes toward work. During the 1950s, employers noted that white-collar employees were inquiring more often about fringe benefits like vacations, company cars, and retirement plans than about the challenges of the job itself. By the 1960s, many corporations were discovering a new problem of morale among those executives who ran the company's daily affairs. Rising rates of absenteeism and declining rates of efficiency expressed the refusal of "middle managers" to devote themselves to jobs that no longer seemed to reward them. Indeed, white-collar efficiency had become a pervasive problem. Studies revealed that, on the average, an office of white-collar employees devoted about 50 percent of their potential labor to the job. In the fifties, large audiences followed the television series *Ben Casey*, whose utterly dedicated doctor-hero never shed his white coat or left his patients. By the 1960s, Ben Casey had become a grind. Somewhere outside of the job lay an elusive something called "fulfillment," and more and more successful Americans set out to find it.

It was a wide-ranging quest. Some cultivated their avocations instead of their vocations. It became increasingly common for well-to-do Americans to find their primary satisfactions from boating or bridge or travel or tennis. With the rise of avocationalism came a redefinition of leisure as something much more basic in life than simply a means to recuperate. A cult of the wilderness, condemning the artificiality of modern society and praising experiences with raw nature, enjoyed a new vogue. The glorification of nature was in part a reaction against the biological devastation that an indiscriminate use of insecticides was causing throughout America. In a chilling best-seller, *Silent Spring* (1962), Rachel Carson eloquently publicized this modern blight. Reaction against the taste and quality of mass-produced goods helped to generate an interest in personal craftsmanship. From a modest beginning in the "do-it-yourself" kits of the 1950s, this involvement with manual skills made workmanship an increasingly important part of white-collar America's full life.

The most general expression of the individual's modern quest was a nationwide fascination with personal power. Human manipulations that had once been considered ethically questionable became matters of public pride in the fifties and sixties. Experts explained how they had "sold" political candidates to the voters. Books coached Americans on games of "one upmanship" in their everyday relations with friends and acquaintances. Commentators and historians praised the "strong" Presidents. Because the preoccupation with power was a mass phenomenon, it found a variety of popular outlets. The crunching game of football arrived as America's leading sport. Its competitors adapted as best they could through shortened fences and livelier balls in baseball, the "big game" in tennis, the "dunk" in basketball, and the "power play" in hockey. High-speed auto racing attracted more and more fans. By the 1960s, everybody's car could be a personal vehicle of power: Cougar, Wildcat, Thunderbird, Stingray, Mustang. Promises of power suffused the advertising of everything from perfumes to breakfast foods. Its values saturated the movies and television, most drippingly in the James Bond shows and their many "superspy" imitators but just as thoroughly in the children's cartoons and the movies' technicolor shots of mutilation and bloodshed. According to some experts, the most common cause of alcoholism, the nation's greatest addiction, was a compensation for the feelings of powerlessness.

Against this background of doubting and searching, bands of well-to-do white youths came into the streets as the hippies and flower children and dropouts and rebels of the 1960s. Though a minority of their age group, they were so obvious and so audible that they always seemed far more numerous than they actually were. They clustered in the parks to smoke and sing. They crowded the sidewalks around college campuses. They became the most committed white partisans of black rights and the bulwark of a marching, chanting peace movement. Beginning with the Free Speech Movement at Berkeley in 1964 and culminating in the nationwide, decentralized Students for a Democratic Society (SDS), their protest groups rallied many more young people behind specific campaigns for student rights and social justice. Suburban high school students copied both their programs and their tactics. By 1967 and 1968, student strikes were commonplace. So were the pockets of young people who collected to experiment with communal life, drugs, and poverty. In the late 1960s, the largest of these colonies occupied much of the Haight-Ashbury district of San Francisco.

In many ways, these young dissenters were carrying out just one more variation of the modern adolescent rebellion. All the standard elements of the past forty years were there. Increasingly hard, acid rock set a musical barrier between the generations. Adults were accused of hypocrisy, and adult authority was condemned. Trust no one over thirty, the rebels declared. Even their primary areas of rebellion—dress, language, drugs, and sex—were the familiar ones from the 1920s. When young people in the 1960s wore workclothes or exotic clothes or no clothes, screamed four-letter words, substituted narcotics for alcohol, and claimed the right of sexual intercourse on demand, they were extending the very domains of personal freedom that well-to-do Americans of four decades earlier had explored.

At the same time, this noisy rebellion supplied a penetrating commentary on the contemporary life of successful Americans. It focused on the most sensitive problems of the individual in modern society. In response to a dehumanizing bureaucracy, the young dissenters assaulted the nation's important institutions: the government, the political party, the corporation, and the university.

Some of them ostentatiously rejected the products of these institutions—the government's laws, the party's candidates, the corporation's goods, the university's degrees—and many more young people cheered them on. In response to the individual's feelings of loneliness, they emphasized community and loyalty and love. Rejecting professionalism, they exalted individual fulfillment. Craftsmanship, nature, and a "whole earth" were almost holy causes. A few rebels tried to build an entire life around these new values in self-sufficient rural communes. The young dissenters even reflected their society's preoccupation with power. The abuse of power, they claimed, lay at the root of America's social evils. "Power to the people" would bring a new era of justice.

As they probed the primary doubts in their parents' lives, the young rebels split an older generation. A minority defended the right of their sons and daughters to a dissenting life style. Often these adults found courage to act out their own feelings. Some marched for civil rights and peace. Others, acknowledging the need for a new intimacy in human relations, experimented with "encounter" and "sensitivity" groups and greater sexual freedom. A few joined the dropouts. But a majority of successful adults opposed the new youth movement. By pushing their private anxieties into public, the young rebels threatened the balance that older people were maintaining between adult responsibility and its discontents. The more extreme the adolescent rebellion, the more widespread the opposition became. By 1970 the young radicals had lost almost all their sympathizers.

The most lasting outgrowth of the rebellious sixties was the movement for women's rights. No rational grounds existed for excluding women from a full range of white-collar occupations. Like race or culture, gender was irrelevant to a skills standard. Yet only in the private realm away from work did women enjoy anything approximating the freedom of successful men. As dressing styles, leisure activities, and public behavior increasingly became "unisex," men continued to keep the best jobs. By the 1960s, close to half of the women in America held paying jobs, partly because close to half the marriages in America ended in divorce. A significant proportion of women received lower salaries or wages than men did for the same work, and an even larger percentage of women were blocked somewhere along the ladder of promotion in their occupations. Meanwhile, women's responsibilities at home scarcely changed. The widespread concerns about individual fulfillment, the anxieties about powerlessness, and the increasing doubts about the quality of American consumerism, all had particularly sharp application in the lives of women. In the critical climate of the 1960s, some of them began to strike out against restraints and indignities.

In 1963, Betty Friedan's *The Feminine Mystique* broke the silence. By the end of the decade, a host of books and articles was analyzing the evils of the modern doll's house. The drive for black rights contributed a vocabulary to communicate women's feelings of oppression and, in 1966, the acronym for a

WOMEN DEMAND THEIR RIGHTS

Justice on the job represented the mild side of a broad and varied women's movement. (*Magnum.*)

new pressure group, the National Organization for Women (NOW). ("What do you want?" the civil rights marchers chanted. "FREEDOM!" "When do you want it?" "NOW!") The recent emphasis on personal power helped women to identify and expose a "machismo" cult of swaggering masculinity. Moreover, it justified their own demands for more power. Young women in particular were determined to start with a new set of rules, and some of them insisted on immediate, wholesale changes in the relations between men and women. A few even tried physical assaults on the "male chauvinist pigs." But this temporary phase was far less important to the success of the women's movement than America's modern occupational values. Where a standard of skills prevailed, women's rights to an equal opportunity was an unquestionable claim. Quite promptly, both the federal courts and the national executive committed themselves to enforcing equal access to jobs, and equal pay for equal work.

Early in 1968, the forces of protest and reform seemed on the verge of capturing the national government. The summer before, a quarter million Americans had marched quietly through Washington in behalf of peace in Viet Nam. Both their number and their discipline gave the movement a new respectability. The inheritor of this strength was a thoughtful, enigmatic Democratic senator from Minnesota, Eugene McCarthy, who in November 1967 opened his campaign for President on a peace platform. In January and February 1968, as the

Tet Offensive exposed the military failure of America's policy in Viet Nam, McCarthy was touring New Hampshire in preparation for the first presidential primary. That March, the quixotic candidate no one had taken seriously received almost as many votes as President Johnson himself.

Within a few weeks after the New Hampshire primary, Johnson quit the race. A second peace candidate, Robert Kennedy, entered the lists. The boyish Bobby Kennedy, who had been attorney general in John Kennedy's administration and then senator from New York, attracted an even more zealous following than his older brother had, and a majority of Americans assumed that in time he also would be President. The favorite of the youth movement, however, was still McCarthy. His willingness to fight a lonely battle and his cool, moral style converted tens of thousands of college students, "Clean for Gene" with shaves and neckties, into campaign workers. Meanwhile, through sit ins, rallies, and strikes, more radical students were applying heavy pressure on the major universities to support a great variety of causes for social justice.

Actually, the ground beneath the reform movement was already eroding. In April 1968, a sniper caught Martin Luther King on the balcony of a Memphis hotel. At the news of his assassination, black ghettos across the country erupted in violence. In death as in life, King could not channel the emotions of the Northern ghettos toward peaceful resistance. Although King gathered many loyal partisans in the Northern cities, he also encountered a very different, angry spirit, especially among younger blacks. This, in a broad sense, was the spirit of Black Power. At one level, Black Power was a reasoned explanation of American race relations. In *Black Power* (1967), for example, Stokely Carmichael and Charles Hamilton denied the existence of the American Creed, which had underpinned the civil rights movement. On the contrary, they argued, white values were best expressed in a self-serving institutional structure that made blacks a colonial people inside American society. Only a racially proud movement that was exclusively black could hope to break these institutional shackles. At another, more popular level, however, Black Power was a volatile expression of ghetto frustrations, a release of raw feelings that sometimes struck in fury at the most immediate sources of oppression in the ghettos themselves.

Less than a week after the adoption of the Civil Rights Act of 1965, the ghetto area of Watts in Los Angeles exploded in riot and flames. More black riots scorched almost every major city during the next three years, burned miles of the Detroit ghetto in 1967, and spread nationwide at the word of King's murder in 1968. Meanwhile, new black leaders were demanding exclusive control over the movement for black rights and draining support from King's biracial civil rights campaign. In place of King's cause, the spreading spirit of Black Power strengthened such groups as the ascetic, business-minded Black Muslims and the militant, socially minded Black Panthers. Successful whites were left in confusion. Some of them still read the autobiographies of Malcolm X and Claude Brown as moving accounts of how individual blacks had survived against extraordinary odds. These were also triumphs by white values. But the slashing ghetto despair that burned people's own homes belonged to another world, and fiery assaults from the unknown just frightened them.

The people who could best appreciate this rage were locally oriented whites, who were also rising in retaliation against outside domination. As the national threats to local power intensified, these whites struck back along two lines. One was an attempt to reassert control over what they regarded as their own local institutions. In the Northern cities, they fought against the racial integration of the schools, especially when integration meant busing black and white children. Numerous white Catholics in such cities as New Orleans, Philadelphia, and Boston actively resisted their church's policies of integration. Urban politicians attacked the local agencies of OEO and lobbied in Washington to disband it. In the towns as well as the cities, bumper stickers reading "Support Your Local Police" signaled a growing opposition to judicial restraints and supervisory review boards. The Crime Control Act of 1968, which generally endorsed strong police action, was considered a significant victory in this cause. In many white communities, Mayor Richard Daley of Chicago became a hero when it was reported that he had instructed the police to maim looters and kill arsonists during a ghetto riot.

The second line of counterattack was aimed at the youth rebellion. In the tradition of community control, locally oriented whites set out to suppress a wide range of unacceptable behavior. "Sideburns . . . shall not extend lower than the bottom of the ear opening and shall be uniform width," the regulations of the Louisville Fire Department stated. "Beards, goatees or any other extraneous facial hair will not be permitted." Opinion polls showed consistently large majorities favoring severe punishment for drug users, including marijuana smokers. By 1968, the Viet Nam War was unpopular throughout the United States. But in almost every locality, waving a Viet Cong flag or burning an American one, as television reported some radicals doing, ranked as a far greater evil than the war. By local values, affluent students had no right to insult their nation or squander its educational privileges. The New York police who cracked heads while breaking a campus strike at Columbia University in 1968, the townsmen who took a crowbar to the flower children, or the construction workers who roamed lower Manhattan beating up long-haired youths were expressing the feelings of innumerable fellow citizens. In May 1970, when four students at Kent State University were killed for no apparent reason by the National Guard, a nationwide poll tallied four out of five Americans on the side of the guardsmen.

Kent State typified the ending of the decade. University administrators relied more and more on the local police to control student unrest. Law enforcement agencies killed, jailed, or scattered the leadership of the Black Panthers. After 1967, the peace marches in Washington were battling, antagonistic affairs, and the peace organizations, always a quarreling lot, fragmented. Occasionally a happy episode broke the pattern. In the summer of 1969, "the nation of Woodstock," perhaps 400,000 young people, gathered at White Lake, New York, for a rock festival and a holiday frolic. But a few months later in Altamont, California, an attempt to repeat the joys of Woodstock dissolved in bloodshed.

These rising waves of anger swept over the presidential campaign of 1968. In June, while celebrating an important victory in the California primary, Robert Kennedy was assassinated by a moody young Jordanian, Sirhan Sirhan. Eugene McCarthy, now the sole leader of the peace movement, unaccountably allowed his own drive for the presidential nomination to lose momentum. That August in Chicago, while policemen were banging their way through a parkful of young demonstrators outside convention headquarters, the Democrats nominated a very different Minnesota politician, the talkative, middle-of-the-road Vice-President, Hubert Humphrey. The most vital force in the fall campaign was Governor George Wallace of Alabama, candidate of the American Independent party. As the advocate of "poor folks" against invading bureaucrats and decent citizens against subversive youths, Wallace gave local whites their first authentic spokesman in a presidential contest since Al Smith. Even more impressive than the 10 million votes Wallace eventually received, the nationwide enthusiasm for Wallace's cause revealed the depth of America's discontent.

In general, harsh and negative feelings dominated the campaign of 1968.

Richard Nixon, who had returned to win another Republican nomination, promised to impose law and order on a permissive society. The Democrat Humphrey likened the peace marchers to the appeasers of Hitler. In striking contrast to the fifties and early sixties, no one spoke any longer for a common American purpose. America's nationalizing trends had divided people into hostile camps, and for a time, no national manager could win the confidence of a broad majority. Except for the economy, which remained strong, the old problems of modernization had simply returned in new forms. As they converged in the politics of the late sixties, some Americans wondered if their society could survive the onslaught.

STUDENTS AND POLITICS, 1968

College students entered national politics with an unprecedented passion in 1968. Their fervor gave electric vitality to Eugene McCarthy s primary campaigns. Then at the Democratic convention in August, delegate votes and police clubs silenced McCarthy's youth brigade. In the gloomy aftermath, young radicals had the last word. *(Left, Robert Azzi/Nancy Palmer Photo Agency; middle, Mallock/Magnum; right, Costa Manos/Magnum.)*

Suggested Readings

William E. Leuchtenburg, *A Troubled Feast: American Society since 1945* (1973), is a lively introduction to the postwar years and contains a good bibliography. The confidence of the 1950s glows from *U. S. A., the Permanent Revolution* (1951) by the Editors of *Fortune* and from *The Big Change: America Transforms Itself, 1900–1950* (1952) by Frederick Lewis Allen. A similar confidence, with minor reservations, appears in the writings of various intellectuals: Peter F. Drucker, *The New Society* (1950), John Kenneth Galbraith, *American Capitalism* (1952), Daniel J. Boorstin, *The Genius of American Politics* (1952), and Daniel Bell, *The End of Ideology* (1960). From a more critical perspective, four books are particularly useful in assessing the contemporary political economy. C. Wright Mills, *The Power Elite* (1956), explores what later came to be called the military-industrial complex. Grant McConnell, *Private Power and American Democracy* (1966), and Theodore J. Lowi, *The End of Liberalism* (1969), analyze the dangers to the public interest from pressure-group politics. John Kenneth Galbraith, *The New Industrial State* (1967), examines the influence of corporate managers in national economic policy.

The history of politics during the confident years focuses largely on the presidency. Herbert S. Parmet, *Eisenhower and the American Crusades* (1972), and more briefly Charles C. Alexander, *Holding the Line: The Eisenhower Era, 1952–1961* (1975), cover the general's two terms. Marquis W. Childs, *Eisenhower: Captive Hero* (1958), gives valuable background. Both James MacGregor Burns, *John Kennedy* (1960), and Theodore C. Sorensen, *Kennedy* (1965), are useful political biographies. On Kennedy's administration, Arthur M. Schlesinger, Jr., *A Thousand Days* (1965), is appreciative and revealing. Jim F. Heath, *John F. Kennedy and the Business Community* (1969), emphasizes the President's conservative inclinations. In *The Promise and the Performance: The Leadership of John F. Kennedy* (1975), Lewis J. Paper tries to strike a balanced judgment. Rowland Evans and Robert Novak, *Lyndon B. Johnson* (1966), helps to explain the powerful chief executive. For legislation during the fifties and sixties, James L. Sundquist, *Politics and Policy: The Eisenhower, Kennedy and Johnson Years* (1968), is indispensable. John Barlow Martin's *Stevenson of Illinois* (1976), the first volume of a biography, examines the hero of the liberals who twice lost to Eisenhower. Theodore H. White's *The Making of the President, 1960* (1961) includes shrewd observations on Nixon's losing campaign. Barry Goldwater speaks for himself in *The Conscience of a Conservative* (1960). In a deceptively entitled study, *Revolt of the Moderates* (1956), Samuel Lubell explains moderate voting behavior that affected presidential politics. Richard E. Neustadt, *Presidential Power* (1960), is an analysis of leadership that reputedly influenced John Kennedy. Insights into the political turmoil of the late sixties appear in Eric F. Goldman, *The Tragedy of Lyndon Johnson* (1969), Tom Wicker, *JFK and LBJ* (1968), Penn Kimball, *Bobby Kennedy and the New Politics* (1968), and Lewis Chester et al., *An American Melodrama: The Presidential Campaign of 1968* (1969).

Donald R. Matthews, *U.S. Senators and Their World* (1960), and William S. White, *Citadel: The Story of the U.S. Senate* (1957), contain interesting material on another center of political power. John D. Weaver, *Warren* (1967), and Leo Katcher, *Earl Warren* (1967), praise the controversial chief justice, and Milton R. Konvitz, *Expanding Liberties* (1966), evaluates some of the Warren Court's important decisions. How the national government has affected modern urban affairs is analyzed in Mark I. Gelfand, *A Nation of Cities* (1975). A crucial new political bloc is examined in Robert Gilpin and Christopher Wright, eds., *Scientists and National Policy-Making* (1964), and Don K. Price, *The Scientific Estate* (1965).

John W. Spanier, *American Foreign Policy since World War II* (rev. ed., 1973), is a clear, largely favorable summary. On the internationalization of American business, see Raymond Vernon, *Sovereignty at Bay: The Multinational Spread of U. S. Enterprise* (1971), and

Mira Wilkins, *The Maturing of Multinational Enterprise: American Business Abroad from 1914 to 1970* (1974). In *The Politics of Oil*, Robert Engler examines some effects of internationalization. Paul Y. Hammond, *Organizing for Defense* (1961), discusses the place of the military in twentieth-century America; Warner R. Schilling et al., *Strategy, Politics, and Defense Budgets* (1962), analyzes specific decisions in military policy. Maxwell D. Taylor, *The Uncertain Trumpet* (1960), is a prominent general's appraisal of the Eisenhower years that influenced the Kennedy administration. The sources and consequences of America's military foreign policy are explored in Richard J. Barnet, *Roots of War* (1972), and Alexander L. George and Richard Smoke, *Deterrence in American Foreign Policy* (1974).

Michael A. Guhin, *John Foster Dulles* (1972), praises one architect of American foreign policy for his flexibility, and Herman Finer, *Dulles over Suez* (1964), gives a detailed account of the international furor that the secretary of state raised in 1956 and 1957. A dangerous issue that spanned the Eisenhower and Kennedy administrations is examined in Jack M. Schick, *The Berlin Crisis, 1958–1962* (1971). Richard J. Walton's *Cold War and Counterrevolution* (1972) takes a negative view of Kennedy's foreign policy. The decline of Kennedy's Alliance for Progress is traced in Jerome Levinson and Juan de Onís, *The Alliance That Lost Its Way* (1970). On the Cuban missile crisis, Henry M. Pachter, *Collision Course* (1963), provides a basic summary, and Graham T. Allison, *Essence of Decision* (1971), offers an intriguing set of alternative explanations.

Most writers on the war in Southeast Asia condemn the United States. *The Indochina Story* (1970) by the Committee of Concerned Asian Scholars is a particularly striking example, while Donald S. Zagoria, *Vietnam Triangle: Moscow, Peking, Hanoi* (1967), is one of the relatively few defenses of American policy. Henry Brandon, *Anatomy of Error: The Inside Story of the Asian War on the Potomac, 1954–1969* (1969), and Arthur M. Schlesinger, Jr., *The Bitter Heritage: Vietnam and American Democracy, 1941–1966* (1967), seek a middle ground. David Halberstam's fascinating *The Best and the Brightest* (1972) dissects the policy-making in Washington, and Frances Fitzgerald's excellent *Fire in the Lake* (1972) analyzes the consequences of this policy in Vietnam. J. William Fulbright, *The Arrogance of Power* (1967), expresses the opposition from Congress. A notorious massacre of civilians in Vietnam and the official attempts to hide it are exposed in Seymour M. Hersh, *My Lai 4* (1970).

The hopes and concerns of the civil rights movement are revealed in Martin Luther King, Jr., *Why We Can't Wait* (1964); Howard Zinn's account of young activists, *SNCC: The New Abolitionists* (1964); and Charles E. Silberman's *Crisis in Black and White* (1964), a liberal white's summary of the issues. The sources of black militancy emerge from *The Autobiography of Malcolm X* (1965), Charles V. Hamilton and Stokely Carmichael, *Black Power* (1967), Eldridge Cleaver, *Soul on Ice* (1968), and James Forman, *The Making of Black Revolutionaries* (1972). Claude Brown, *Manchild in the Promised Land* (1965), is an eloquent statement on life and survival in the ghetto. On the travail of civil rights leaders, see Chandler Davison, *Biracial Politics: Conflict and Coalition in the Metropolitan South* (1972), David L. Lewis, *King: A Critical Biography* (1970), and August Meier and Elliott Rudwick, *CORE* (1973), the account of an organization transformed by the sweep of events. *Report of the National Advisory Commission on Civil Disorders* (1968) and Robert M. Fogelson, *Violence as Protest* (1971), reflect the sense of complexity that came to surround the issue of black rights. Two important studies of poverty in America are Michael Harrington, *The Other America* (1962), and Harry M. Caudill, *Night Comes in the Cumberlands* (1963).

The literature of the youth rebellion begins with Jack Kerouac's *On the Road* (1957) and more or less ends with Charles A. Reich's *The Greening of America* (1971). The world against which these well-to-do youths rebelled is discussed in William H. Whyte, *The Organization Man* (1956), and Scott Donaldson, *The Suburban Myth* (1969). Theodore

Roszak, *The Making of a Counter-Culture* (1969), attempts to probe the rebellion's inner meaning, and Abbie Hoffman, *Steal This Book* (1971), expresses something of its style. Philip E. Slater's *The Pursuit of Loneliness* (1970) contrasts the rebel culture with establishment culture. In *Young Radicals* (1968), Kenneth Keniston analyzes leaders in the rebellion. Kirkpatrick Sale, *SDS* (1973), is a sympathetic study of its most prominent campus organization. Tom Wolfe comments on the culture of Haight-Ashbury in *The Electric Kool-Aid Acid Test* (1968). There are perceptive essays on radicalism in Joseph Boskin and Robert A. Rosenstone, eds., *Seasons of Rebellion* (1972). The most enduring portion of the rebellion, the movement for women's rights, is examined in William Henry Chafe's *The American Women* (1972). Three outstanding books—Betty Friedan, *The Feminine Mystique* (1963), Kate Millett, *Sexual Politics* (1970), and Robin Morgan (comp.), *Sisterhood is Powerful* (1970)—suggest the range and force of the movement.

Sources on the resistance to national liberalism and young radicalism are scattered. Arthur B. Shostak's *Blue-Collar Life* (1969) summarizes an array of studies on white urban wage earners and their families. Bennett M. Berger, *Working-Class Suburb* (1960), Herbert J. Gans, *The Levittowners* (1967), and William Kornblum, *Blue-Collar Community* (1974), add substantially to this analysis. Herbert J. Gans, *The Urban Villagers* (1962), and Sam Bass Warner, Jr., *The Urban Wilderness* (1972), include perceptive accounts of how government policies have damaged inner-city life. In *Small Town in Mass Society* (1958), Arthur J. Vidich and Joseph Bensman describe the defenses of townspeople against external authority. Peter Binzen, *Whitetown, U. S. A.* (1970), discusses urban dwellers in rebellion against such authority, and Numan V. Bartley, *The Rise of Massive Resistance* (1969), and Neil R. McMillen, *The Citizens' Council* (1971), trace an earlier rebellion in the South. The new explicitness about ethnic identities is explored in Michael Novak's *The Rise of the Unmeltable Ethnics* (1972).

35

Stabilization

By election time 1968, such broad, optimistic visions as John Kennedy's New Frontier and Lyndon Johnson's Great Society seemed part of a distant past. The news was a daily bombardment of conflicts: teachers versus students, hawks versus doves, professionals versus hard hats, men versus women, whites versus blacks. Countless Americans were preparing for even more trouble. Elementary schools taught children to be wary of strangers, particularly the friendly ones. Gun sales continued to climb. So did the hiring of private police.

In this climate of suspicion, political leaders changed both their style and their objectives. Rather than speak the confident language of unity and progress, they acknowledged America's divisions and tried to fit some of its pieces into a stable coalition. The most important of these new leaders was the victor in the presidential race of 1968, Richard Nixon. Entering the White House with scarcely more than 43 percent of the popular vote, Nixon began at once to broaden his political base. Four years later, he had satisfied the popular desires for "law and order" and "peace" so ably that he ranked among the most successful Presidents of the twentieth century. It was an astonishing political triumph. Although economic and personal disasters soon toppled Nixon, his new departures in both domestic and foreign affairs continued to dominate American policy in the mid-seventies.

National and Local Power

Richard Nixon first attracted national attention in the late 1940s when as a congressman from California, he helped to link the former State Department official Alger Hiss with communist espionage. That success, in addition to his reputation as a reliable Republican, made him a senator, then the Vice-President under Dwight Eisenhower. After his fractional loss to John Kennedy in 1960 and his failure to become governor of California in 1962, Nixon suffered a temporary eclipse. But he fought tenaciously to win a second presidential nomination in 1968. This time, in another extremely close contest, he defeated the Democrat Hubert Humphrey and George Wallace, the third-party candidate.

Nixon took office under a cloud. A minority President and a stiff, uninspiring speaker, he also attracted a particularly deep hostility from his opponents. Intellectuals nursed a hatred for "Tricky Dick" Nixon unlike anything a new President had faced in this century. In a short time, however, the shrewd chief executive was surprising enemies and friends alike with his political skills. The first item on the new President's agenda was to redress the balance between national and local power. Through policies that were sometimes called a "Southern strategy" and sometimes an appeal to the "Silent Majority," Nixon immediately set about allaying fears that the national government was antagonistic to local control. He started with the Supreme Court. Four vacancies offered Nixon the best opportunity since Franklin Roosevelt's second term to recast its philosophy. And because the Democratic Senate rejected two of his early

The Election of 1968

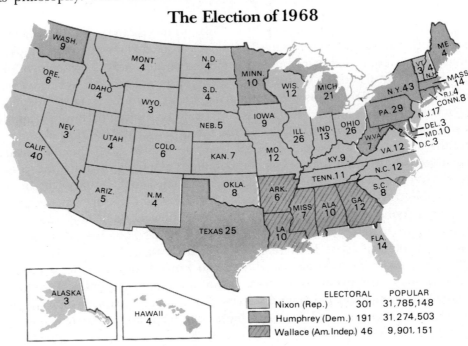

	ELECTORAL	POPULAR
Nixon (Rep.)	301	31,785,148
Humphrey (Dem.)	191	31,274,503
Wallace (Am. Indep.)	46	9,901,151

RICHARD NIXON

There was little warmth in his political style, but
Nixon proved to be an extraordinarily successful
President during his first term. *(Newsweek/Wally
McNamee.)*

nominees who had dubious, segregationist credentials, the President's intention of creating a conservative judiciary received nationwide attention.

Beginning with a new chief justice, the politically astute Minnesota Republican
Warren Burger, Nixon's appointments did reorient the Supreme Court. Gradually it turned back toward the principles of local autonomy. The police received wider latitude in dealing with suspected criminals. After a period of
doubt about the legality of the death penalty, the Burger Court in *Furman*
v. *Georgia* (1972) decided that state legislatures only needed to be more specific
about which crimes deserved the death sentence.

One of the most volatile issues of the seventies, busing schoolchildren to
achieve racial integration, required more time to manage. The Supreme Court
had established a long, consistent record of support for desegregation, including a crucial endorsement of busing in 1971. The first signs of an accommodation did not occur until 1974. That July, in *Milliken* v. *Bradley,* the Burger Court

ruled against a busing plan for metropolitan Detroit that would have incorporated the suburban schools, 98 percent white, with the city schools, 65 percent black. "No single tradition in public education is more deeply rooted than local control over the operation of schools," the chief justice declared in the spirit of the old balance. The national government would "deprive the people of local control" if it imposed its authority across the jurisdictional boundaries of the metropolitan area. Nevertheless, even after this decision, the federal courts continued to enforce busing in Boston, where crowds of angry whites fought against the legal orders, and in Louisville, where the city and its suburbs were, in fact, part of a common plan.

Meanwhile members of the Nixon adminstration were echoing the values of local America. When a presidential commission recommended minimal supervision over pornography, Nixon dismissed its findings as "morally bankrupt." The President also condemned current trends in sexual freedom and demanded stern punishment for drug offenders. Through Attorney General John Mitchell, the administration publicized its cooperation with local police forces, and in May 1970, when tens of thousands of antiwar protesters came to Washington, the Justice Department responded with mass arrests and makeshift detention corrals. Nixon, who had once been the partisan voice of the Eisenhower administration, used Vice-President Spiro Agnew in a similar way. Through Agnew, the administration heaped scorn on "an effete corps of impudent . . . intellectuals," accused the television networks of news distortion, and locked horns with such nationally prominent newspapers as the New York *Times* and the Washington *Post*. In the previous twenty-five years, only Joseph McCarthy and George Wallace had expressed the popular hostility to modern values as effectively as Agnew did.

The administration's assault on modern values was part of a general effort to redress the balance between national and local authority. The new balance of the seventies tried to assure different groups in American society that they had domains of their own. The proud declaration of a Polish or Italian or Jewish identity became increasingly acceptable. From West Virginia to North Dakota, rural communities reasserted their right to control the local schools and censor the books they used. Through the programs of revenue sharing and block grants that the Nixon administration introduced, local governments received additional federal money to manage more or less as they chose. At the same time, nothing significantly abridged the privileges of successful Americans. The leading suburban and private schools operated as they always had. National economic policy remained the province of a national elite. In fact, the personal freedoms of well-to-do Americans continued to expand, most notably as a result of the Burger Court's decision in *Roe* v. *Wade* (1973), which legalized abortions.

The balance of the seventies did, however, halt new national programs in behalf of racial minorities. Early in the 1970s, for example, groups of Indians

CÉSAR CHAVEZ AND THE NATIONAL
FARM WORKERS

Despite the iron determination of
Chavez, the cause of the Chicano
farm workers declined in the
seventies. *(Michael Dobo/Stock
Boston.)*

drew attention to their history of oppression and ostracism by temporarily
occupying a number of public places that were linked with their past. Some
of these protests were peaceful, as at Fort Sheridan, Illinois, and some were
violent, as at Wounded Knee, South Dakota. Neither tactic won concessions
from the national government. During the sixties, Mexican Americans who
labored in California's "farm factories" had formed the National Farm Workers
Association under the patient and persistent César Chavez, and the new organization received considerable support from reformers and unionists. Robert
Kennedy had been its outstanding national partisan. But after Kennedy's
death, the Chicanos found no prominent champion in Washington. Beset by
the combined opposition of commercial farmers and a rival Teamsters union,
the fortunes of the National Farm Workers Association dwindled during the
seventies.

In addition, the Nixon administration dismantled the Office of Economic
Opportunity, which had been encouraging local black organizations, and announced a period of "benign neglect" in the government's policies for racial
equality. As the percentage of black pupils in all-black schools dropped below
20 percent, a rising percentage in Congress opposed busing as a way of achieving a closer racial balance in the schools. President Nixon, by expressing his

personal dislike for busing, strengthened this opposition. The only inviting avenues to a greater black power were now local, not national, and blacks did try to follow them. Early in the seventies, blacks became mayors of several important cities, including Cleveland, Atlanta, Los Angeles, and Detroit. Yet the big cities, in turn, were suffering from a severe budget squeeze. During the fall of 1975, for example, New York City almost went bankrupt. Hence, this kind of political power was diminishing just as blacks were acquiring it.

The new balance received a broad popular approval. Opinion polls in the mid-seventies registered two out of three Americans against busing, two out of three for the death penalty, three out of four against legalized marijuana, and almost everyone for greater protection against crime. These attitudes were crucial to Nixon's overwhelming reelection in 1972. That summer, a serious, liberal senator from South Dakota, George McGovern, won the Democratic nomination for President following his success in the primaries. Everything about McGovern's candidacy suggested danger to the new balance. He wanted to renew the war on poverty and use the government's authority in behalf of black rights. His support among well-to-do college students was as enthusiastic as Eugene McCarthy's had been four years earlier. McGovern refused to endorse harsh measures against street crimes and drug violations, and he appeared indifferent to such issues as Bibles in the schools and the suppression of obscenity. In November 1972, only Massachusetts and the District of Columbia gave majorities to McGovern. With 521 of 538 electoral votes, Nixon, a marginal leader less than four years before, scored one of the most impressive political victories of modern times.

A Flexible Diplomacy

Stability at home depended on stability abroad. The bitter controversy over Viet Nam continued as Nixon took office in 1969, and he knew that, one way or another, he had to end the war. Like his predecessors, Nixon was committed to containing communism in Southeast Asia. But to this task, the President brought his own assumptions about a sound policy. Remembering Eisenhower's settlement of the Korean conflict in 1953, Nixon concluded that in an unpopular war most Americans would choose the withdrawal of their own troops over a clear-cut military victory. Second, the President believed that the United States should be willing to increase the punishment of a stubborn enemy considerably above the levels the Johnson administration had inflicted.

Nixon's strategy in Southeast Asia, therefore, combined a wider, freer use of military power with a gradual removal of American troops. Initially, the President hoped that a more daring application of ground forces could still shift the military balance in Viet Nam. Through tactical invasions of Cambodia in 1970 and Laos in 1971, the American command tried to cut the supplies and disperse the armies that the enemy was concentrating in South Viet Nam.

When a coup established a friendly government in Cambodia, the United States equipped its army. Now it was openly an Indochinese war. But an Indochinese war merely created an Indochinese guerrilla opposition without affecting the balance of power in Viet Nam. The longer Nixon managed the war, the more he came to rely on bombing raids that exceeded even the massive ones under Johnson.

Meanwhile, the President was reducing the number of American troops in Viet Nam from over half a million in 1969 to under 100,000 in 1972. The South Vietnamese army, the President said, would soon be capable of fighting the ground war alone. Because these withdrawals significantly lessened American criticism of the war, they gave Nixon more time to reach some kind of settlement with the North Vietnamese. He needed the leeway, for the failure of his Indochinese strategy strongly argued for compromise. During the final months of Johnson's presidency, the United States and North Viet Nam had opened a forum for these negotiations in Paris, and after 1969, delegates from the two nations used it alternately to storm at one another and to explore the possibilities of peace.

The crisis in the negotiations occurred just after the election of 1972, when the scale of America's air attacks implied that it might indeed try to bomb North Viet Nam "back into the Stone Age." In January 1973, both sides modified their demands just enough to sign a peace agreement. In effect, the settlement allowed the war to continue without American troops. Through a tortured use of the language, Nixon was able to call the agreement "peace with honor" because technically it satisfied the standard rule of containment. No new territory had been relinquished to the communists. But the Indochinese paid an appallingly high cost in blood and misery for that honor. In two more years, even the illusion of containing communism dissolved. After appearing to hold their own against the communist armies, America's allies in South Viet Nam and Cambodia collapsed abruptly in the early months of 1975. Suddenly, communist governments ruled everywhere on the mainland of Southeast Asia except Thailand, and American power was eliminated. Once the shock of surprise had passed, few Americans tried to keep the issue of Indochina alive. Hawks and doves alike agreed that the war had been the most disastrous in American history.

During the final years of the Indochinese War, the Nixon administration was also responding to the worldwide problem of containment's crumbling structure. Here it showed exceptional imagination. In the most important series of events during Nixon's presidency, the United States dramatically improved its relations first with China, then with the Soviet Union. The deepening hostility between China and Russia, and the desire in each of these two nations to devote more energy to internal affairs, raised the possibility that one or both of them might welcome an accommodation with the United States. Early in 1971, Nixon seriously began investigating this opportunity. Feelers indicated that China was receptive to an American overture. While leaders in

SAIGON, MAY 1975

As the communist armies rolled toward Saigon, Americans
fought off their own allies in the panic to evacuate.
(*Associated Press.*)

Washington and Peking made small public gestures of moderation, Nixon's
adviser Henry Kissinger was meeting secretly in China with Premier Chou En-lai.
In the summer of 1971, the President broke the astonishing news that he personally would visit China.

After turning its back to the People's Republic of China for more than twenty
years, the United States acknowledged its existence with the chief executive's
presence. The entire affair was international theater at its best. In a rush of
discovery, millions of Americans learned something of the revolution that had
been transforming the world's largest nation. Then they watched on television
as their President crossed containment's invisible barrier in February 1972 to
shake hands with the leaders of "Red China." Though relations between the
two governments remained cautious, the United States finally abandoned the
cause of Chiang Kai-shek, accepted China in the United Nations, and prepared
the way for a broader interchange.

Also during 1971, the administration was moving silently toward détente with Russia. The Soviet Premier, Leonid Brezhnev, who was anxious to limit the range of Russia's international involvements, willingly grasped a chance to lessen the tensions with its chief rival. Once again, private diplomatic discussions on the possible areas of agreement came first. Once again, the President surprised the world by announcing a visit to the Soviet Union in May 1972. Nixon picked up a thread that had been lost at the futile summit conferences of 1960 and 1961. Soon after his trip to China, he traveled to Moscow, where he had an extremely cordial meeting with the very officials whom Americans had recently considered the masterminds of international conspiracy.

Like the new relations with China, the Soviet-American détente yielded few specific returns. The two nations reached some agreement on regulating their nuclear weapons, welcomed each other's citizens more liberally, and negotiated a sale of American wheat to Russia that unfortunately occurred just on the eve of a sharp rise in the American price for grain. And except for Brezhnev's reciprocal visit to the United States in 1973 and another wheat deal in 1975, nothing more concrete emerged from détente during the next few years. Many of the old antagonisms proved to be very much alive. Nevertheless, beginning in 1972, longstanding fears of thermonuclear war eased. The world's super powers were prepared to confer about any serious international problem.

The fresh departures with China and the Soviet Union, in turn, were part of an even broader reorientation of American diplomacy. The world's heterogeneity that the Kennedy administration recognized and the Johnson administration tried to ignore became the starting point in foreign relations during the Nixon administration. The new diplomacy relied on principles similar to those prevailing in America's domestic politics: bargain with a group at a time, work to minimize the friction among allies, keep promises as loose as possible, and assume the need for continuing renegotiations. Just as these techniques were used to manage varied interest groups at home, so they were expected to deal with an equally diverse set of international interests. In domestic affairs, Americans tested their effectiveness by such traditional guidelines as the victory of a political party or a rise in the standard of living. In world affairs, however, Americans had no comparable way of measuring the success or failure of these bargaining tactics. By the mid-1970s, America had moved full circle around the years of containment and operated once more without a systematic policy in its foreign relations.

Nixon's collaborator in this transformation was Henry Kissinger, a German-born professor from Harvard who first served as the President's adviser and then in 1973 became secretary of state. Kissinger personified the new diplomacy of evolving bargains and ad hoc arrangements. Under both Nixon and his successor Gerald Ford, Kissinger was the man in motion, negotiating the Paris accord with North Viet Nam, preparing the way for Nixon's visits to Peking and Moscow, shuttling between Israel and the Arab nations, touring the capitals of Europe, and searching for a settlement of the Cyprus War between Greece and Turkey. The substance of the nation's foreign policy seemed to be Kissinger grappling with one problem after another. As a result, many Americans held this one man responsible for the ups and downs of world affairs. In the summer of 1974, when international problems appeared to be abating, Kissinger was acclaimed the one indispensable man in Washington. Six months later, when détente with the Soviet Union was losing its freshness, hostilities were threatening in the Middle East, and Southeast Asia was falling to the communist armies, disillusioned critics called the secretary of state an utter incompetent. In another six months, Kissinger was presiding over a historic agreement between Egypt and Israel, and once again his reputation soared.

Kissinger's incessant travels gave the impression that the United States was immersed in every one of the world's problems. Actually, the trend ran in the opposite direction. During the era of containment, the slightest change anywhere on the globe had some meaning for America's anticommunist policy. By the 1970s, however, a great many international events no longer mattered very much. In 1974, Washington remained quite calm when new leaders and governments suddenly appeared in an array of countries throughout the world, including France, Germany, Israel, Greece, and Japan. In September 1975, when the Organization of American States (OAS) in the Western Hemisphere lifted its boycott of Cuba, few Americans even knew about this break in the chain of containment.

Each event, in effect, had to prove its own importance. Nothing better illustrated the new approach than the Nixon administration's response to the collapse of the Bretton Woods agreement, which since 1944 had regulated international monetary exchanges by the American dollar. Instead of scrambling to reassert its leadership of the Free World, the United States decided to let all national currencies fluctuate in price on an open world market. Beneath the hustle of the new diplomacy, the United States was reclaiming some of its old heritage, a detachment from international affairs. Above all, a large majority of Americans wanted to avoid "another Viet Nam." During the winter of 1975–76, for example, foreign intervention in the new African nation of Angola set the Soviet Union and Cuba against the United States and South Africa on opposite sides of a civil war. Congress, with a strong public sentiment behind it, moved promptly to place tight limits around America's involvement.

Despite these changes in orientation, many of the traditional assumptions behind containment continued to shape America's foreign affairs. National security was still equated with a full arsenal of nuclear weapons. Beginning in 1969, the United States and the Soviet Union engaged in lengthy Strategic Arms Limitation Talks (SALT), but the pattern of the arms race did not significantly change. In fact, the political opposition to disarmament was rising late in 1975. The United States still preferred firmly anticommunist governments as

its allies, and particularly in Latin America, it still considered aggressive reformers an international danger. Using the familiar language of the Cold War,
President Ford justified America's sponsorship of a military coup in Chile as
"in the best interest of the people in Chile and certainly in our best interest."
The critical difference was that these actions no longer belonged to a cohesive
global policy. They had become pieces of an old policy in search of a new framework.

An Erratic Economy

One of the few remaining areas of confidence during the late 1960s had
been the state of the economy. Yet no sooner did Nixon take office than this,
too, posed serious problems of stabilization. Because Congress had lowered
taxes just as the heaviest financing of the Viet Nam War was about to begin, the
government's policy generated a great surge of purchasing power that practically
guaranteed inflation. Prices were already rising sharply as Nixon became President. At the same time, the economy grew sluggish. From 1969 to early 1971,
as the percentage of unemployed increased to about 6 percent, the GNP scarcely
changed, its worst record in more than a decade. Late in 1971, the pinch eased.
For several months, the GNP rose impressively, unemployment eventually fell
below 5 percent, and the rate of inflation, while still disturbingly steep, showed
some signs of abating. Then in 1973 a crisis struck. Inflation took off at an
annual rate of about 10 percent, unemployment mounted until it also approached
10 percent, the GNP slumped almost 5 percent a year, and the stock market
dropped precipitously. Now the economy recalled memories of the thirties.

Almost every American blamed the President for these troubles. After all,
he was the manager of the national economy. By the 1970s, however, the scope
of the President's economic power had appreciably narrowed. The government
manipulated the national budget, the national debt, and national monetary
policy on the assumption that these domestic actions would produce a predictable
set of domestic reactions. To combat inflation, the government taxed surplus
income and tightened credit. To stimulate economic growth, it increased the
national deficit and lowered interest rates. But the wave of inflation that swept
over the United States in 1973 also flooded the world, overwhelming all national economies and bringing rates of increase elsewhere that were considerably
higher than America's. Basic resources ranging from grains and sugar to oil
and aluminum soared in price. The United States could not control any of them.
When world inflation was superimposed on an American recession, the standard
techniques of economic management no longer worked. Attacking the recession risked an even wilder inflation. Attacking inflation risked an even deeper
depression. In an earlier day, America's economy had dominated the rising
and falling curves of the international cycle. Now the United States was just

one of several great powers, and it tossed in the same winds that were shaking the rest of the world.

No President, therefore, could satisfy the popular demands that were placed on him. Both Nixon and Ford relied heavily on psychological tactics, both hoped that time would operate on their side, and both, when forced to choose, emphasized the problem of inflation over the problem of recession. In 1971, Nixon dramatically opened his battle against inflation with a temporary freeze on wages and prices, which publicized the administration's concern and prepared the way for a long-term program. In what was called Phase II, the freeze was lifted from most of the economy, and the executive applied intensive persuasion to hold wages and prices to modest rates of increase. By 1973, it was assumed, the executive could largely withdraw, set broad guidelines, and let the economy function normally in Phase III. Fortunately for the President, Phase II coincided with an economic revival and a steadying rate of inflation. Unfortunately for Nixon, Phase III began just as international inflation was ready to skyrocket, and a hastily devised Phase IV was lost in the updraft.

President Ford took office in midflight. After a futile try at positive thinking, which included the distribution of WIN (Whip Inflation Now) buttons, Ford reluctantly accepted the need for tax cuts and a sizable budget deficit early in 1975. The Democratic Congress enthusiastically endorsed these antidepression measures. In the long run, however, Ford insisted that Congress pair tax cuts with spending cuts, and he used his veto again and again to reduce appropriations. That combination no longer qualified as an antidepression policy. With prices still rising about 10 percent a year, Ford concentrated his attention on inflation. Opinion polls late in 1975 indicated that about three out of four Americans agreed with his priorities.

While the nation was wrestling with recession and inflation, two other trends emerged from these economic hardships. One involved the so-called ecology movement, which had spread during the 1960s in an effort to halt an urban-industrial society's damage to the physical environment. Images of an uncontaminated earth where man and nature were once again in harmony aroused a deeply embedded set of emotions. In a crescendo of cries, more and more successful Americans of all ages demanded relief from the dangers of chemical sprays, industrial wastes, and automobile exhaust. Veteran conservationists found an eager, new audience. "Organic" foods and "recyclable" products became increasingly popular in the consumer market. Beginning with the Clean Air Act of 1963, the national government responded by establishing a series of antipollution standards to protect both the atmosphere and the waterways.

In local America, however, the ecology crusade had a very mixed, sometimes hostile reception. Higher antipollution standards usually implied higher costs and perhaps fewer jobs. In America's vacation lands, environmental pres-

WIN (WHIP INFLATION NOW)

In his first months as President, Gerald Ford hoped that a
higher public morale would lower the rate of inflation.
(*UPI photo.*)

ervation often seemed the rich person's way of stopping latecomers from making
their fortunes. As the economy faltered, the ecology movement stumbled with
it. Neither Nixon nor Ford sympathized with the movement, and they willingly
gave precedence to profits and jobs over purification. Local governments, which
carried the primary burdens of enforcement, bent to the wishes of their local
industries, which usually led the opposition to the antipollution standards.
Although a widespread awareness and a continuing set of national guidelines
guaranteed that the ecology movement would not disappear, it became sub-
ordinated to the issues of inflation and recession.

The second of these trends was a movement toward national self-sufficiency,
which had been growing while America's commitment to the Cold War diminished. As the United States had to share more and more of its world power,
it could exercise less and less control over its international economic relations.
One of the primary threats that Cuba posed in the 1960s, for example, was its
encouragement for other agrarian countries to nationalize American-owned

assets. Beginning in the early 1960s, the United States suffered periodically from an adverse balance of payments, with too much capital leaving the country and not enough coming in. Though the United States had once helped European nations solve a comparable problem, no one offered to return the favor.

These vague, nagging irritations about an unreliable world came sharply into focus with the energy crisis of 1973–74. The immediate cause of the crisis was another round in the Middle Eastern conflict between Arabs and Israelis. After decades of clear military superiority over any combination of Arab opponents, Israel suddenly found the balance of forces much closer to even in a bloody, protracted war that began late in 1973. A primary reason for the new military balance was the financial support that the oil-producing Arab nations now gave to the war against Israel. To underline their commitment, these nations imposed a producers' boycott on petroleum in behalf of the Arab cause. That winter, every important industrial nation, except the Soviet Union, suffered an oil shortage. When a pause in the war occurred early in 1974 and the boycott ended, the Arab producers more than doubled the price of oil and in one

THE GAS CRISIS, 1973

(Allan Tannenbaum photo)

bold stroke altered the flow of international finance. Years before, the columnist Joseph Alsop had warned that hands from the Middle East pressed on Europe's jugular. Industrial nations everywhere felt the pressure in 1974, and in response to this awesome Arab power, they began withdrawing diplomatic support from Israel.

During the winter of 1973–74, millions of Americans feared that they might not have enough oil to heat their homes. Morning after morning, weary commuters scoured the city for an open service station, then waited in line for a few gallons of gasoline. Though the policy of American oil companies was more responsible for these domestic shortages than the boycott, the most publicized villains were the petroleum-rich Arab nations. The United States government seemed utterly helpless. Neither bluster nor persuasion affected the Arab producers. Because only the United States held reasonably fast in support of Israel, many Americans also worried about the possibility of being drawn into a Middle Eastern war just as they were escaping a Southeast Asian war. Such a striking lesson in America's vulnerability, coupled with the tendency in hard times to draw people's attention toward domestic problems, gave a strong impetus to the movement for American self-sufficiency. Total isolation was inconceivable, but a maximum degree of economic autonomy became one of the most popular national objectives.

A Cloudy Horizon

The early seventies, like the late forties, were years for sober reassessment. In ways reminiscent of the period just after the Second World War, Americans of many different kinds were demanding a return to the basics. Professions that had been subjected to radical pressures during the late sixties renewed their exclusive commitment to the values of expertise. "Permissive" child rearing fell into disrepute, and parents pledged their allegiance to clear authority and salutary discipline in the home. Yet unlike the postwar years, the 1970s revealed no new sources of strength. By now, the miracle cures of the 1950s had become thoroughly entangled in the very problems that people were struggling to resolve. The computer, rather than answering the big social questions, seemed only to verify the complexity and intractability of the nation's primary challenges: racial inequality, the culture of poverty, drugs, violence, crime. Neither desegregation nor the war on poverty had improved the relative economic standing of America's black population, which suffered severely in the recession of the 1970s. Even consumerism was suspect. To beat inflation and conserve energy, Americans were told, they should buy less, eat less, drive less, and heat less.

Early in the 1970s, prominent Americans also discovered a new, personal danger in the manipulative techniques that were originally meant to influence the masses. Through Daniel Ellsberg, a disillusioned expert from the Department of Defense, the nation's leading newspapers received classified documents exposing the government's secret maneuvers and systematic lies about the Indochinese War. Although the Nixon administration fought to suppress them, these documents were published serially during 1971, then compiled as *The Pentagon Papers*. Ellsberg himself became the target of a bizarre government plot of character defamation that included burglarizing his psychiatrist's office. Each year, more such stories appeared. President Johnson had approved the electronic surveillance of Martin Luther King, Robert Kennedy, and Spiro Agnew. Kissinger had requested wiretaps on his own aides and President Nixon had authorized one on his own brother. Military intelligence had spied on an array of liberal politicians and the FBI had compiled dossiers on an even longer list of them. The director of the FBI, J. Edgar Hoover, had waged a personal vendetta against King. The Internal Revenue Service had audited income tax returns on the basis of a citizen's political activities. The unfolding record revealed a technique gone berserk, or perhaps just democratic. People who had once thought they belonged to a minority of manipulators now saw themselves as part of the mass to be manipulated.

One widespread effort to protect the individual against manipulation was the consumer movement of the 1960s. In 1965, a zealous young lawyer named Ralph Nader emerged as the movement's chief spokesman with the publication of *Unsafe At Any Speed*, a detailed analysis of the automobile hazards being manufactured in Detroit. A shabby attempt by General Motors to discredit him only enlarged his fame. Through the efforts of young volunteers called "Nader's Raiders," a variety of additional exposés rapidly followed. By the end of the decade, innumerable journalists, scientists, and local committees were spreading the gospel of consumer standards, and polls indicated a large majority behind the cause. Millions of Americans even thought Nader should be President. Yet in spite of new legal guidelines in such areas as automobile safety, credit contracts, product labeling, and food adulteration, the consumer movement dwindled in the 1970s. There were many protests against inflation, but they had little cohesion or consistency. Consumers were everybody in general and nobody in particular—and exceedingly hard to organize. Nothing arose to replace the movement.

The soul searching of the late 1940s had inspired a new faith in "realism." Many Americans had concluded that if they accepted the world's complexity and the human mind's limitations, they could move step by step toward sounder,

CITY SMOG

The sickly haze of the cities was a subject of talk far more than action in the seventies. *(Elliott Erwitt/Magnum.)*

wiser policies. But the reassessments of the early 1970s seemed only to produce fatalism, a feeling that vast national and international problems defied solution. The novelist Kurt Vonnegut captured the mood in an exchange between two middle-aged men who were pondering a prospective world population of 7 billion:

> "I suppose they will all want dignity," I said.
> "I suppose," said O'Hare.

That same sense of the individual trapped in a web of forces characterized such important novels as Joyce Carol Oates' *Them* (1969) and Joseph Heller's *Something Happened* (1974), as well as a number of fine movies.

Americans at least discovered that the mightiest individuals were not necessarily more secure then they. One of the most publicized series of events during the Nixon years was the fall of the great men. Each new scandal in the sequence was more shocking than the last, and each punishment set a historic precedent. First came Abe Fortas, an associate justice of the Supreme Court whom President Johnson, in his final days, tried to make Earl Warren's replacement as chief justice. When a congressional inquiry in 1969 revealed that Fortas had profited unduly from his office, the pressure forced him to resign from the Court. Fortas was followed by Judge Otto Kerner, a liberal Democrat with an unusually high reputation for integrity, who had chaired the important Presidential Advisory Commission on Civil Disorders. Found guilty of accepting bribes while he had been governor of Illinois, Kerner went directly from his place on the circuit court to jail.

Next came Vice-President Agnew, national champion of law and order and current favorite to win the Republican nomination for President in 1976. Early in 1973, the Justice Department reconstructed a long history of secret payments that engineering firms, in return for government contracts, had been making to Agnew throughout his rise in Maryland politics. Couriers even sat in the Vice-President's anteroom waiting to deliver the cash. After a frantic attempt to save his career, the Vice-President suddenly resigned in October as part of a bargain with the Justice Department. Agnew received a light sentence for evading income tax but avoided the much more serious penalties for extortion and bribery.

The loss of the Vice-President was stunning enough. Yet Agnew was only the prologue. As he fell, the President himself was toppling. In June 1972, five men were arrested for burglarizing Democratic headquarters at the Watergate Apartments in Washington, D. C. After a flurry of attention, the story slipped from sight. Despite the connection between the burglars and the Republican Committee to Reelect the President, Nixon's Democratic opponent, Senator McGovern, could rouse little interest in the incident during the fall campaign. Then in the spring of 1973, one of the burglars decided to cooperate with the

THE FALL OF VICE-PRESIDENT SPIRO AGNEW

(Oliphant © 1973 Denver Post.)

government investigators. As he was talking, John Dean, a close presidential adviser, joined him. Behind these two, a longer line of penitents began to form.

The stories they told spread in two directions. One traced a variety of activities through the executive's most powerful offices: the use of campaign contributions to win government favors, the illegal handling of those funds, devious techniques for making the President a millionaire, and assorted tactics of political sabotage to ensure Nixon's reelection. Although it was a sordid view through the keyhole of national politics, it attracted far less attention than the second trail of evidence, which carried the planning and suppressing of the Watergate burglary to Nixon's inner staff—John Dean, Attorney General John Mitchell, and a pair of hard, ascetic organization men, H. R. Haldeman and John Ehrlichman, who were the President's principal domestic aides. Would the trail lead to the President's desk?

For more than a year, Nixon fought to block it. In public, the President repeatedly declared his innocence. In private, he plotted ways of obstructing a grand jury under the tenacious Judge John Sirica and a Senate investigating committee under the skeptical old-timer, Sam Ervin of North Carolina. Forced to accept a special Watergate prosecutor within the Justice Department, Nixon in October 1973 fired the first one, Archibald Cox of the Harvard Law School, because Cox was preparing to sue for the evidence that the President would not relinquish. Cox's replacement, the conservative Houston lawyer Leon Jaworski, proved just as dogged and carried his demand for the evidence to the Supreme Court.

JOHN DEAN TESTIFYING BEFORE THE SENATE SELECT
COMMITTEE

(Magnum.)

The evidence in question lay in a vault of tapes recording almost every conversation that had been held in President Nixon's private office. These tapes, which Nixon strangely chose to clutch rather than destroy, eventually wrecked his defenses. Someone tried erasing portions of the tapes. The White House issued an edited transcript from them. Finally, the President decided to withhold them altogether. But in July 1974, the Supreme Court unanimously awarded the tapes to Judge Sirica's grand jury and, through the grand jury, to all the hounds at bay. As the House of Representatives was preparing to vote articles of impeachment against the President, Nixon acknowledged much of what the tapes would verify about his involvement in the Watergate affair almost from the day of the burglary. Admitting the facts but denying any guilt, Nixon resigned as President on August 9, 1974.

The last and mightiest fall set the most astonishing precedents. After receiving 97 percent of the electoral vote, the President—the indispensable leader—had been driven from office in midterm. Moreover, his replacement had been elected to no office higher than representative from the Fifth Congressional District of Michigan. Gerald Ford, whom Nixon selected in 1973 to replace the departed Agnew, had a mandate for national leadership only from the two houses of Congress. What might have caused an upheaval actually calmed the nation, for the prestige of the President now relied more on opinion polls than on election returns. Well before Nixon's capitulation, the most persuasive proof that he should resign lay in a steady stream of reports that only about one in four Americans was supporting his presidency.

Ford responded to the challenge of public confidence with just the right tactics. In his initial address as President, he promised to represent almost everyone except the atheists. His manner was unaffected, amiable, and open — a perfect contrast to Nixon's. Though temperamentally and ideologically conservative, he knew the ways of political compromise from his years as minority leader in the House of Representatives. Rather than adopt a bold executive brand of leadership, Ford retained his own cautious, congressional style. His programs, offering a little for this group, a little for that one, read like committee reports to the House. When opinion polls showed three out of four Americans behind the new President, Ford had weathered the crisis.

An equally important reason for the smooth transition between Presidents was a nationwide cynicism about all Washington politics. During the presidential crisis, no message appeared more clearly in the opinion polls. When a majority first expressed the belief that Nixon was lying about Watergate, four out of five also judged him no more corrupt than his predecessors. On the eve of his resignation, one out of two wanted the Senate to impeach Nixon but only one out of four thought it would. Much the same spirit prevailed during the election of 1974, when scarcely more than a third of the eligible voters cast their ballots.

As if to counteract this widespread cynicism, the news media presented Nixon's fall as a morality play. They focused on the individual, Richard Nixon, and interpreted his disgrace as a lesson to prove that even the most exalted would suffer for the sin of pride. Such an orientation also eased the transition between Presidents, because it made Nixon's resignation the solution to the nation's outstanding problem. Many people who subscribed to this interpretation sharply criticized President Ford late in 1974 for issuing a blanket pardon to Nixon and thus blocking legal action against the former chief executive. At the very least, the argument went, Nixon should confess his guilt before he earned a pardon. As one after another of Nixon's associates stood trial and received punishment, the curtain slowly fell on the morality play. Appropriately, the New York *Times* summarized the prison sentences for Mitchell, Haldeman, and Ehrlichman in February 1975 by calling them "The Price of Arrogance."

As Americans celebrated their bicentennial, they might have taken satisfaction from two centuries of constitutional government, a century of remarkable economic development, half a century of national security in a war-plagued world, and a quarter of a century of expanding minority rights. Instead, the

OPERATION SAIL, NEW YORK HARBOR, JULY 4, 1976

The most popular exhibit on the bicentennial Fourth of July
said nothing about America's revolutionary heritage, its
unique institutions, or its future promise. (*Associated Press.*)

prevailing tone was quiet. A bumper sticker neatly caught the tentative, drifting mood: "Yesterday sex was dirty and the air was clean." Economic troubles, which had dampened the centennial celebration in 1876, the Columbian Exposition in 1893, and the "Century of Progress" World's Fair in 1933, once again muted the cheers. The talk of an American Century in the forties, the voices of national confidence in the fifties, and the cries for social reform in the sixties had all subsided. Americans appeared to be waiting for someone, or something, to define a new set of objectives that would mark the path into a new era.

Suggested Readings

Accounts of Richard Nixon include a favorable one in Earl Mazo and Stephen Hess, *Nixon: A Political Portrait* (1968), and an unfavorable one in Garry Wills, *Nixon Agonistes* (1970). In *Kissinger* (1974), Marvin and Bernard Kalb raise Nixon's reputation in foreign affairs by deflating claims that Kissinger dominated the President. Harland B. Moulton, *From Superiority to Parity: The United States and the Strategic Arms Race, 1961–1971* (1973), discusses some preliminary moves toward détente. The presidential records of Lyndon Johnson and Nixon have stirred interest in the office of chief executive. Among recent books on the subject are George E. Reedy, *The Twilight of the Presidency* (1970), Arthur M. Schlesinger, Jr., *The Imperial Presidency* (1973), which is sharply critical of Nixon, and Otis L. Graham, Jr., *Toward a Planned Society: From Roosevelt to Nixon* (1976), which contrasts Nixon's approach to planning with the approach of Franklin Roosevelt. The Watergate affair has generated a special group of studies. Carl Bernstein and Bob Woodward, the reporters who helped to expose the affair, tell a fascinating tale of investigation and deception in *All the President's Men* (1974). Their sequel, *The Final Days* (1976), deals with Nixon during the year before his resignation. Jonathan Schell, *The Time of Illusion* (1976), is also illuminating on the Watergate period.

A number of fine books argue the need for reconsideration after the sixties. Christopher Lasch, *The Agony of the American Left* (1969), analyzes the limitations of contemporary radicalism, Alexander M. Bickel, *The Supreme Court and the Idea of Progress* (1970), the limitations of the judiciary, Robert L. Heilbroner, *An Inquiry into the Human Prospect* (1974), the limitations of the world economy, and Andrew Hacker, *The End of the American Era* (1970), the limitations of Washington's managerial leadership. On the other hand, Daniel Bell is reasonably confident about America's future in *The Coming of Post-Industrial Society* (1973). On two controversial issues, Martin Hoffman's *The Gay World: Male Homosexuality and the Social Creation of Evil* (1968) presents the case for homosexuals, and David F. Musto's *The American Disease* (1973) traces the history of federal policy on narcotics. A general account of a minority that has failed to find support in Washington is Matt S. Meier and Feliciano Rivera, *The Chicanos: A History of Mexican Americans* (1972).

1920 Suspected radicals arrested in Palmer raids, height of Red Scare.
Senate rejects Versailles Treaty and U.S. entry in League of Nations.
Nineteenth Amendment guarantees women's suffrage.
First commercial radio station begins operation.
Sinclair Lewis's *Main Street* published.
Warren G. Harding elected President defeating James M. Cox.

1921 First bill restricting immigration passed.
Washington Conference limits naval tonnage among major powers.
Collapse of farm prices precipitates serious recession.

1922 Nationwide coal strike accompanied by violence.
Fordney-McCumber Tariff raises protective rates.
Recovery from 1921 recession begins.
Supreme Court strikes down child labor laws.

1923 U.S. Steel agrees to abandon twelve-hour day.
Teapot Dome, other Harding administration scandals exposed.
Harding dies in San Francisco; Calvin Coolidge becomes President.
Supreme Court strikes down minimum wage for women.
Founding of *Reader's Digest* and *Time Magazine*.

1924 Bonus Bill enacted, providing benefits to First World War veterans.
National Origins Act sets restrictive immigration quotas.
Snyder Act guarantees U.S. citizenship to American Indians.
Calvin Coolidge elected President defeating John W. Davis.

1925 John T. Scopes convicted of violating Tennessee law against teaching evolution.
F. Scott Fitzgerald's *The Great Gatsby* published.

1926 U.S. "joins," then quits World Court in treaty dispute.
Revenue Act lowers taxes on corporations, wealthy individuals.
First scheduled commercial airplane flights begin.
National Broadcasting Company, first radio network, formed.

1934 Frazier-Lemke Bankruptcy Act helps farmers regain lost property.
Federal Housing Administration founded to insure home mortgages.
Father Charles Coughlin, Detroit "radio priest," starts National Union for Social Justice.
Dr. Francis Townsend wins wide support for old age pension plan.

1935 Works Progress Administration funds public works.
Public Utilities Holding Company Act attacks utilities trusts.
Supreme Court, in Schechter decision, strikes down NRA.
Wagner Act affirms collective bargaining rights, sets up NLRB.
First Social Security Act adopted.
Revenue Act of 1935 increases taxes on wealthy.
Senator Huey P. Long of Louisiana leads national "Share Our Wealth" movement until assassinated in Baton Rouge.
Congress of Industrial Organizations begins rift of industrial unions from American Federation of Labor.
Senate rejects U.S. membership on World Court again.
Italy invades Ethiopia.

1936 Supreme Court strikes down AAA and New York minimum wage law.
CIO, sit down strikes paralyze rubber, auto industries.
Playwright Eugene O'Neil receives Nobel Prize for Literature.
Spanish Civil War erupts.
Roosevelt elected President defeating Alfred Landon in landslide.

1937 Roosevelt proposes courtpacking scheme; Congress buries it.
Supreme Court, reversing earlier positions, upholds Wagner Act.
CIO, officially expelled from AF of L.
Ten killed in "Memorial Day Massacre" during Chicago steel strike.
Bankhead-Jones Farm Tenancy Act helps tenants and small farmers.
Japan invades China.

1945 First electronic digital computer completed.
Roosevelt defeats Thomas E. Dewey to win fourth term as President.
FDR, Churchill, Stalin meet at Yalta, agree to divided occupation of Germany; further agreements reached at Potsdam.
Americans recapture Philippines.
Roosevelt dies; Harry S Truman becomes President.
U.S. drops atomic bombs on Hiroshima and Nagasaki in Japan.
Germany and Japan surrender.
Fifty nations meet in San Francisco to sign United Nations charter.

1946 Military demobilization brings major reductions in army, navy.
Wage and price controls end.
Evangelist Billy Graham holds first mass revival meeting.

1947 Taft-Hartley Act restricts power of unions.
National Security Act consolidates military under Defense Department.
Truman Doctrine promises U.S. support to "free peoples," establishing "containment" policy and marking start of Cold War.
U.S. launches Marshall Plan to help rebuild Western Europe.
Jackie Robinson becomes first black to play major league baseball.

1948 Truman integrates armed forces by executive order.
U.S. airlifts supplies to West Berlin during communist blockade.
Organization of American States established.
U.S. first nation to recognize new state of Israel.
Truman elected President defeating Dewey in surprising upset.

1949 Housing Act authorizes government slum clearance, urban renewal.
William Faulkner receives Nobel Prize for Literature.
Chinese Communists defeat Nationalists, win control of nation.
Soviet Union detonates its first atomic bomb.
U.S., Western Europe form North Atlantic Treaty Organization.

1950 Senator Joseph McCarthy launches crusade

1928
- Charles Lindbergh makes first solo trans-Atlantic airplane flight.
- *The Jazz Singer*, first feature sound film, released.
- Kellogg-Briand Pact outlaws war "as instrument of national policy."
- Stock market boom begins.
- Herbert Hoover elected President defeating Al Smith.

1929
- William Faulkner's *The Sound and the Fury* and Thomas Wolfe's *Look Homeward Angel* published.
- Stock market crashes.
- Agricultural Marketing Act starts federal farm price stabilization.

1930
- Smoot-Hawley Tariff raises protective barriers.
- Sinclair Lewis becomes first American writer to receive Nobel Prize for Literature.
- Congress rejects U.S. membership on World Court.

1931
- European financial collapse worsens Depression in U.S.
- Japan invades Manchuria.

1932
- Bonus Army of unemployed veterans dispersed by federal troops during march on Washington.
- Riots among unemployed break out in Dearborn, Michigan.
- Reconstruction Finance Corporation founded to help troubled businesses.
- Stimson Doctrine establishes U.S. opposition to Japanese expansion.
- Franklin D. Roosevelt elected President defeating Hoover.

1933
- Emergency Banking Act halts major national banking crisis.
- Glass-Steagall Act establishes Federal Deposit Insurance Corporation.
- National Industrial Recovery Act authorizes wage-price codes for industries and funds public works.
- Agricultural Adjustment Act begins modern policy of farm supports.
- Civilian Conservation Corps provides public employment for youths.
- Tennessee Valley Authority, government power project, established.
- Prohibition repealed by Twenty-first Amendment.

1939
- Hitler seizes Austria; England concedes Czechoslovakia to Germany at Munich.
- Vinson Naval Expansion Act authorizes U.S. naval growth.
- Germany invades Poland, starting Second World War.
- Roosevelt declares American neutrality.
- Russia, Germany sign pact, demoralizing U.S. Communist Party.
- Neutrality Act authorizes "cash and carry" sale of munitions.
- John Steinbeck's *The Grapes of Wrath* published.
- First commercial trans-Atlantic air service begins.
- NBC begins first commercial television broadcasts.

1940
- Germany captures Belgium, Holland, France.
- German invasion of England thwarted in Battle of Britain; Winston Churchill becomes prime minister.
- Congress approves new funds for American preparedness.
- Roosevelt defeats Wendell Wilkie, wins third term.

1941
- Congress approves Lend-Lease, American supplies to Allies.
- American rearmament accelerates.
- Roosevelt bans racial discrimination in government and defense industry hiring.
- Germany invades Soviet Union.
- FDR, Churchill meet in Atlantic Conference to prepare Anglo-American alliance.
- Japan attacks Pearl Harbor; U.S. enters war.
- Penicillin used effectively in treating humans.

1942
- U.S. forms alliance with Britain, USSR, 23 other nations.
- Government wage and price controls established.
- Federal government evacuates 110,000 Japanese-Americans from California.
- American troops driven from Philippines.
- U.S. inflicts first major defeat on Japan at Battle of Midway.

1943
- Race riot in Detroit leaves 34 dead.
- FDR, Churchill plan Allied campaigns at Casablanca.
- FDR, Churchill, Stalin meet for first time at Teheran.
- Soviets defeat Germans at Stalingrad.
- Allies invade Italy.
- Americans drive Japanese from Guadalcanal.

1944
- U.S. Navy defeats Japan in Battle of Leyte Gulf. Allies invade France; recapture France, Belgium, Luxembourg.
- "G.I. Bill of Rights" guarantees education and other benefits to veterans.

...ing charges.
- Communist troops invade South Korea; United States leads UN military force in opposing them. UN troops in Korea push communists back above original border.
- Chinese enter war in Korea, push UN forces South.

1951
- Twenty-second Amendment limits Presidents to two terms.
- War in Korea bogs down; peace talks begin at Panmunjom.
- Truman removes Douglas MacArthur from command in Korea.

1952
- Supreme Court invalidates government seizure of steel mills after strike.
- U.S. completes development of hydrogen bomb.
- Peace talks in Korea break down.
- General Dwight D. Eisenhower elected President defeating Adlai Stevenson.

1953
- Armistice signed, ending Korean War.
- Earl Warren named Chief Justice of Supreme Court.
- Julius and Ethel Rosenberg executed as spies, sparking wide protests.

1954
- Supreme Court, in *Brown* v. *Board of Education of Topeka*, orders integration of all public schools.
- First White Citizens Councils formed in South to resist integration.
- Senate censures McCarthy after Army-McCarthy hearings.
- Massive retaliation doctrine increases U.S. reliance on nuclear weapons.
- U.S. joins Asian nations in anti-communist Southeast Asia Treaty Organization.

1955
- Martin Luther King, Jr., leads bus boycott in Montgomery, Alabama.
- AF of L, CIO. merge, electing George Meany president.
- Eisenhower and Soviet Premier Bulganin meet in Geneva.
- Salk polio vaccine introduced.

1956
- Highway Act begins construction of interstate highway system.
- Soviet troops crush Hungarian Revolution.
- Israelis and Arabs open hostilities; Britain, France occupy Suez.
- Eugene O'Neill's play *Long Day's Journey Into Night* produced.
- Eisenhower again defeats Stevenson for President.

1957 Federal troops enforce school desegregation in Little Rock, Arkansas.
Civil Rights Commission created to investigate racial discrimination.
Eisenhower Doctrine promises U.S. aid to Middle East against communists.
Soviet Union launches Sputnik, first man-made satellite.

1958 Agricultural Act lowers price supports for farmers.
First commercial jet airplanes begin operation.
Economic recession begins, helping Democrats to election victories.

1959 Alaska, Hawaii admitted to Union.
Fidel Castro overthrows Fulgencio Batista, controls Cuban government.

1960 Civil Rights Act expands court power over state voting laws.
Blacks stage first sit-in, at Greensboro, North Carolina lunch counter.
American U-2 spy plane shot down over USSR, destroying scheduled Eisenhower-Khrushchev summit meeting in Paris.
Cuban-American relations deteriorate; Castro develops ties to USSR.
First birth control pills marketed.
John F. Kennedy defeats Richard M. Nixon for President.

1961 U.S. breaks diplomatic relations with Cuba.
Peace Corps established.
American-backed invasion of Cuba at Bay of Pigs fails.
Freedom rides begin in South, challenging segregation.
Communists erect wall between East and West Berlin.
U.S. increases military aid to South Viet Nam.
Joseph Heller's *Catch-22* published.

1962 Supreme Court, in *Baker v. Carr*, subjects legislative apportionment to federal scrutiny.
Federal marshalls help James Meredith enroll at University of Mississippi.
Rachel Carson's *Silent Spring* warns of environmental dangers of pesticides.
John Glenn becomes first American to orbit earth.
Kennedy orders naval blockade of Cuba, forcing Soviets to remove offensive missiles from island.

1963 Nuclear Test Ban Treaty ratified.
Supreme Court in *Gideon v. Wainwright* guarantees right to defense counsel.
Betty Friedan's *The Feminine Mystique* launches new women's rights movement.

1964 King receives Nobel Prize for Peace.
Civil Rights Act bans discrimination in public accommodations.
Gulf of Tonkin Resolution authorizes President to retaliate against aggression in South Viet Nam.
Johnson announces national War on Poverty.
Twenty-fourth Amendment bans poll tax.
Johnson elected President defeating Barry Goldwater in landslide.

1965 Congress approves flurry of Great Society legislation, including Medicare, federal aid to education, urban renewal funds.
Civil rights demonstrators clash with police in Selma, Alabama.
Race riot in Watts section of Los Angeles leaves 28 dead.
Ralph Nader's *Unsafe at Any Speed* launches consumer advocacy movement.
Johnson sends American combat troops to Viet Nam; bombing of North begins.

1966 Supreme Court, in *Miranda v. Arizona*, requires police to inform suspects of rights upon arrest.
Black Panther Party formed.

1967 Thurgood Marshall becomes first black appointed to Supreme Court.
Twenty-fifth Amendment provides for appointment of new Vice-President in case of vacancy.
Race riots in Newark, Detroit leave 66 dead.

1968 National Advisory Commission on Civil Disorders warns of "two societies, one black, one white — separate and unequal."
Columbia University paralyzed by student disorders.
Johnson withdraws from presidential race.
Martin Luther King, Jr. assassinated.
Senator Robert F. Kennedy assassinated.
Poor Peoples Campaign sets up tent city in Washington.
Civil Rights Act forbids housing discrimination.
Police and demonstrators clash during Democratic Convention in Chicago.
Richard Nixon defeats Hubert Humphrey in close presidential election.

1969 Nuclear Non-proliferation Treaty, banning spread of atomic weapons, ratified.
Supreme Court orders immediate school integration.
Two Americans first to land on moon.

1970 Environmental Protection Agency established.
American Indian Movement founded.
American forces invade Cambodia; four students killed in Ohio during nationwide campus protests.

1971 Supreme Court paves way for forced busing to achieve integration in *Swann v. Charlotte-Mecklenburg Board of Education*.
New York Times, Washington Post print previously secret Pentagon Papers, study of U.S. involvement in Viet Nam.
Twenty-sixth Amendment lowers voting age to 18.
Amtrak establishes government corporation to run passenger trains.
U.S. stops convertibility of dollar into gold, ending run on dollar.
Wage-price freeze and controls imposed.

1972 Nixon visits China, Soviet Union in effort to better relations.
Congress approves Equal Rights Amendment, guaranteeing women's rights; sends it to states for ratification.
Supreme Court, in *Furman v. Georgia*, bans death penalty as presently administered.
Five men arrested burglarizing Democratic headquarters in the Watergate; *Washington Post* ties them to high White House aides.
Nixon reelected in landslide over George McGovern in presidential election.

1973 Treaty of Paris halts fighting in Viet Nam; U.S. troops and prisoners of war return to U.S.
Senate Watergate Committee begins hearings on Nixon scandals; existence of tapes of presidential conversations disclosed.
Vice-President Agnew resigns after charges of bribe-taking; Gerald Ford appointed to succeed him.
Supreme Court, in *Roe v. Wade*, strikes down anti-abortion laws.
Arab oil boycott of U.S. creates energy shortage.
Nixon fires Watergate Special Prosecutor Archibald Cox.
Members of American Indian Movement occupy Wounded Knee, South Dakota.

1974 Worst economic recession since 1930s.
Supreme Court orders Nixon to release subpoenaed tapes.
House Judiciary Committee recommends impeachment on three counts.
Nixon resigns the presidency; Ford becomes President.
Ford pardons Nixon.

1975 South Viet Nam and Cambodia fall to communist governments.

1976 United States celebrates 200th anniversary of independence.
Supreme Court, in *Gregg v. Georgia*, upholds death penalty under certain conditions.
Carter defeats Ford in presidential election.

Declaration of Independence

IN CONGRESS, JULY 4, 1776

THE UNANIMOUS DECLARATION OF THE THIRTEEN UNITED STATES OF AMERICA

When, in the course of human events, it becomes necessary for one people to dissolve the political bands which have connected them with another, and to assume, among the powers of the earth, the separate and equal station to which the laws of nature and of nature's God entitle them, a decent respect to the opinions of mankind requires that they should declare the causes which impel them to the separation.

We hold these truths to be self-evident: That all men are created equal; that they are endowed by their Creator with certain unalienable rights; that among these are life, liberty, and the pursuit of happiness; that, to secure these rights, governments are instituted among men, deriving their just powers from the consent of the governed; that whenever any form of government becomes destructive of these ends, it is the right of the people to alter or to abolish it, and to institute new government, laying its foundation on such principles, and organizing its powers in such form, as to them shall seem most likely to effect their safety and happiness. Prudence, indeed, will dictate that governments long established should not be changed for light and transient causes; and accordingly all experience hath shown that mankind are more disposed to suffer, while evils are sufferable, than to right themselves by abolishing the forms to which they are accustomed. But when a long train of abuses and usurpations, pursuing invariably the same object, evinces a design to reduce them under absolute despotism, it is their right, it is their duty, to throw off such government, and to provide new guards for their future security. Such has been the patient sufferance of these colonies; and such is now the necessity which constrains them to alter their former systems of government. The history of the present King of Great Britain is a history of repeated injuries and usurpations, all having in direct object the establishment of an absolute tyranny over these states. To prove this, let facts be submitted to a candid world.

He has refused his assent to laws, the most wholesome and necessary for the public good.

He has forbidden his governors to pass laws of immediate and pressing importance, unless suspended in their operation till his assent should be obtained; and, when so suspended, he has utterly neglected to attend to them.

He has refused to pass other laws for the accommodation of large districts of people, unless those people would relinquish the right of representation in the legislature, a right inestimable to them, and formidable to tyrants only.

He has called together legislative bodies at places unusual, uncomfortable, and distant from the depository of their public records, for the sole purpose of fatiguing them into compliance with his measures.

He has dissolved representative houses repeatedly, for opposing, with manly firmness, his invasions on the rights of the people.

He has refused for a long time, after such dissolutions, to cause others to be elected; whereby the legislative powers, incapable of annihilation, have returned to the people at large for their exercise; the state remaining, in the mean time, exposed to all the dangers of invasions from without and convulsions within.

He has endeavored to prevent the population of these states; for that purpose obstructing the laws for naturalization of foreigners; refusing to pass others to encourage their migration hither, and raising the conditions of new appropriations of lands.

He has obstructed the administration of justice, by refusing his assent to laws for establishing judiciary powers.

He has made judges dependent on his will alone, for the tenure of their offices, and the amount and payment of their salaries.

He has erected a multitude of new offices, and sent hither swarms of officers to harass our people and eat out their substance.

He has kept among us, in times of peace, standing armies, without the consent of our legislatures.

He has affected to render the military independent of, and superior to, the civil power.

He has combined with others to subject us to a jurisdiction foreign to our constitution, and unacknowledged by our laws, giving his assent to their acts of pretended legislation:

For quartering large bodies of armed troops among us;

For protecting them, by a mock trial, from punishment for any murders which they should commit on the inhabitants of these states;

For cutting off our trade with all parts of the world;

For imposing taxes on us without our consent;

For depriving us, in many cases, of the benefits of trial by jury;

For transporting us beyond seas, to be tried for pretended offenses;

For abolishing the free system of English laws in a neighboring province, establishing therein an arbitrary government, and enlarging its boundaries, so as to render it at once an example and fit instrument for introducing the same absolute rule into these colonies;

For taking away our charters, abolishing our most valuable laws, and altering fundamentally the forms of our governments;

For suspending our own legislatures, and declaring themselves invested with power to legislate for us in all cases whatsoever.

He has abdicated government here, by declaring us out of his protection and waging war against us.

He has plundered our seas, ravaged our coasts, burned our towns, and destroyed the lives of our people.

He is at this time transporting large armies of foreign mercenaries to complete the works of death, desolation, and tyranny already begun with circumstances of cruelty and perfidy scarcely paralleled in the most barbarous ages, and totally unworthy the head of a civilized nation.

He has constrained our fellow-citizens, taken captive on the high seas, to bear arms against their country, to become the executioners of their friends and brethren, or to fall themselves by their hands.

He has excited domestic insurrection among us, and has endeavored to bring on the inhabitants of our frontiers the merciless Indian savages, whose known rule of warfare is an undistinguished destruction of all ages, sexes, and conditions.

In every stage of these oppressions we have petitioned for redress in the most humble terms; our repeated petitions have been answered only by repeated injury. A prince, whose character is thus marked by every act which may define a tyrant, is unfit to be the ruler of a free people.

Nor have we been wanting in our attentions to our British brethren. We have warned them, from time to time, of attempts by their legislature to extend an unwarrantable jurisdiction over us. We have reminded them of the circumstances of our emigration and settlement here. We have appealed to their native justice and magnanimity; and we have conjured them, by the ties of our common kindred, to disavow these usurpations, which would inevitably interrupt our connections and correspondence. They, too, have been deaf to the voice of justice and of consanguinity. We must, therefore, acquiesce in the necessity which denounces our separation, and hold them, as we hold the rest of mankind, enemies in war, in peace friends.

We, therefore, the representatives of the United States of America, in General Congress assembled, appealing to the Supreme Judge of the world for the rectitude of our intentions, do, in the name and by the authority of the good people of these colonies, solemnly publish and declare, that these United Colonies are, and of right ought to be, FREE AND INDEPENDENT STATES; that they are absolved from all allegiance to the British crown, and that all political connection between them and the state of Great Britain is, and ought to be, totally dissolved; and that, as free and independent states, they have full power to levy war, conclude peace, contract alliances, establish commerce, and do all other acts and things which independent states may of right do. And for the support of this declaration, with a firm reliance on the protection of Divine Providence, we mutually pledge to each other our lives, our fortunes, and our sacred honor.

JOHN HANCOCK [President]
[and fifty-five others]

Constitution of the United States of America

PREAMBLE

We the people of the United States, in order to form a more perfect union, establish justice, insure domestic tranquillity, provide for the common defense, promote the general welfare, and secure the blessings of liberty to ourselves and our posterity, do ordain and establish this CONSTITUTION for the United States of America.

ARTICLE I

Section I

All legislative powers herein granted shall be vested in a Congress of the United States, which shall consist of a Senate and a House of Representatives.

Section II

The House of Representatives shall be composed of members chosen every second year by the people of the several States, and the electors in each State shall have the qualifications requisite for electors of the most numerous branch of the State Legislature.

No person shall be a Representative who shall not have attained to the age of twenty-five years, and been seven years a citizen of the United States, and who shall not, when elected, be an inhabitant of that State in which he shall be chosen.

Representatives and direct taxes shall be apportioned among the several States which may be included within this Union, according to their respective numbers, *which shall be determined by adding to the whole number of free persons, including those bound to service for a term of years and excluding Indians not taxed, three-fifths of all other persons.* The actual enumeration

NOTE: Passages that are no longer in effect are printed in italic type.

shall be made within three years after the first meeting of the Congress of the United States, and within every subsequent term of ten years, in such manner as they shall by law direct. The number of Representatives shall not exceed one for every thirty thousand, but each State shall have at least one Representative; *and until such enumeration shall be made, the State of New Hampshire shall be entitled to choose three, Massachusetts eight, Rhode Island and Providence Plantations one, Connecticut five, New York six, New Jersey four, Pennsylvania eight, Delaware one, Maryland six, Virginia ten, North Carolina five, South Carolina five, and Georgia three.*

When vacancies happen in the representation from any State, the Executive authority thereof shall issue writs of election to fill such vacancies.

The house of Representatives shall choose their Speaker and other officers; and shall have the sole power of impeachment.

Section III

The Senate of the United States shall be composed of two Senators from each State, *chosen by the legislature thereof,* for six years; and each Senator shall have one vote.

Immediately after they shall be assembled in consequence of the first election, they shall be divided as equally as may be into three classes. The seats of the Senators of the first class shall be vacated at the expiration of the second year, of the second class at the expiration of the fourth year, and of the third class at the expiration of the sixth year, so that one-third may be chosen every second year; *and if vacancies happen by resignation or otherwise, during the recess of the legislature of any State, the Executive thereof may make temporary appointments until the next meeting of the legislature, which shall then fill such vacancies.*

No person shall be a Senator who shall not have attained to the age of thirty years, and been nine years a citizen of the United States, and who shall not, when elected, be an inhabitant of that State for which he shall be chosen.

The Vice-President of the United States shall be President of the Senate, but shall have no vote, unless they be equally divided.

The Senate shall choose their other officers, and also a President *pro tempore*, in the absence of the Vice-President, or when he shall exercise the office of President of the United States.

The Senate shall have the sole power to try all impeachments. When sitting for that purpose, they shall be on oath or affirmation. When the President of the United States is tried, the Chief Justice shall preside: and no person shall be convicted without the concurrence of two-thirds of the members present.

Judgment in cases of impeachment shall not extend further than to removal from office, and disqualification to hold and enjoy any office of honor, trust or profit under the United States: but the party convicted shall nevertheless be liable and subject to indictment, trial, judgment and punishment, according to law.

Section IV

The times, places and manner of holding elections for Senators and Representatives shall be prescribed in each State by the legislature thereof; but the Congress may at any time by law make or alter such regulations, except as to the places of choosing Senators.

The Congress shall assemble at least once in every year, and such meeting *shall be on the first Monday in December, unless they shall by law appoint a different day.*

Section V

Each house shall be the judge of the elections, returns and qualifications of its own members, and a majority of each shall constitute a quorum to do business; but a smaller number may adjourn from day to day, and may be authorized to compel the attendance of absent members, in such manner, and under such penalties, as each house may provide.

Each house may determine the rules of its proceedings, punish its members for disorderly behavior, and with the concurrence of two-thirds, expel a member.

Each house shall keep a journal of its proceedings, and from time to time publish the same, excepting such parts as may in their judgment require secrecy; and the yeas and nays of the members of either house on any question shall, at the desire of one-fifth of those present, be entered on the journal.

Neither house, during the session of Congress, shall, without the consent of the other, adjourn for more than three days, nor to any other place than that in which the two houses shall be sitting.

Section VI

The Senators and Representatives shall receive a compensation for their services, to be ascertained by law and paid out of the treasury of the United States. They shall in all cases except treason, felony and breach of the peace, be privileged from arrest during their attendance at the session of their respective houses, and in going to and returning from the same; and for any speech or debate in either house, they shall not be questioned in any other place.

No Senator or Representative shall, during the time for which he was elected, be appointed to any civil office under the authority of the United States, which shall have been created, or the emoluments whereof shall have been increased, during such time; and no person holding any office under the United States shall be a member of either house during his continuance in office.

Section VII

All bills for raising revenue shall originate in the House of Representatives; but the Senate may propose or concur with amendments as on other bills.

Every bill which shall have passed the House of Representatives and the Senate, shall, before it become a law, be presented to the President of the United States; if he approve he shall sign it, but if not he shall return it with objections to that house in which it originated, who shall enter the objections at large on their journal, and proceed to reconsider it. If after such reconsideration two-thirds of that house shall agree to pass the bill, it shall be sent, together with the objections, to the other house, by which it shall likewise be reconsidered, and, if approved by two-thirds of that house, it shall become a law. But in all such cases the votes of both houses shall be determined by yeas and nays, and the names of the persons voting for and against the bill shall be entered on the journal of each house respectively. If any bill shall not be returned by the President within ten days (Sundays excepted) after it shall have been presented to him, the same shall be a law, in like manner as if he had signed it, unless the Congress by their adjournment prevent its return, in which case it shall not be a law.

Every order, resolution, or vote to which the concurrence of the Senate and House of Representatives may be necessary (except on a question of adjournment) shall be presented to the President of the United States; and before the same shall take effect, shall be approved by him, or being disapproved by him, shall be repassed by two-thirds of the Senate and House of Representatives, according to the rules and limitations prescribed in the case of a bill.

Section VIII
The Congress shall have power

To lay and collect taxes, duties, imposts, and excises, to pay the debts and provide for the common defense and general welfare of the United States; but all duties, imposts and excises shall be uniform throughout the United States;

To borrow money on the credit of the United States;

To regulate commerce with foreign nations, and among the several States, and with the Indian tribes;

To establish an uniform rule of naturalization, and uniform laws on the subject of bankruptcies throughout the United States;

To coin money, regulate the value thereof, and of foreign coin, and fix the standard of weights and measures;

To provide for the punishment of counterfeiting the securities and current coin of the United States;

To establish post offices and post roads;

To promote the progress of science and useful arts by securing for limited times to authors and inventors the exclusive right to their respective writings and discoveries;

To constitute tribunals inferior to the Supreme Court;

To define and punish piracies and felonies committed on the high seas and offenses against the law of nations;

To declare war, grant letters of marque and reprisal, and make rules concerning captures on land and water;

To raise and support armies, but no appropriation of money to that use shall be for a longer term than two years;

To provide and maintain a navy;

To make rules for the government and regulation of the land and naval forces;

To provide for calling forth the militia to execute the laws of the Union, suppress insurrections, and repel invasions;

To provide for organizing, arming, and disciplining the militia, and for governing such part of them as may be employed in the service of the United States, reserving to the States respectively the appointment of the officers, and the authority of training the militia according to the discipline prescribed by Congress;

To exercise exclusive legislation in all cases whatsoever, over such district (not exceeding ten miles square) as may, by cession of particular States, and the acceptance of Congress, become the seat of government of the United States, and to exercise like authority over all places purchased by the consent of the legislature of the State, in which the same shall be, for the erection of forts, magazines, arsenals, dock-yards, and other needful buildings; — and

To make all laws which shall be necessary and proper for carrying into execution the foregoing powers, and all other powers vested by this Constitution in the government of the United States, or in any department or officer thereof.

Section IX

The migration or importation of such persons as any of the States now existing shall think proper to admit shall not be prohibited by the Congress prior to the year 1808; but a tax or duty may be imposed on such importation, not exceeding $10 for each person.

The privilege of the writ of habeas corpus shall not be suspended, unless when in cases of rebellion or invasion the public safety may require it.

No bill of attainder or ex post facto law shall be passed.

No capitation, or other direct, tax shall be laid, unless in proportion to the census or enumeration herein before directed to be taken.

No tax or duty shall be laid on articles exported from any State.

No preference shall be given by any regulation of commerce or revenue to the ports of one State over those of another; nor shall vessels bound to, or from, one State, be obliged to enter, clear, or pay duties in another.

No money shall be drawn from the treasury, but in consequence of appropriations made by law; and a regular statement and account of the receipts and expenditures of all public money shall be published from time to time.

No title of nobility shall be granted by the United States: and no person holding any office of profit or trust under them, shall, without the consent of the Congress, accept of any present, emolument, office, or title, of any kind whatever, from any king, prince, or foreign state.

Section X

No State shall enter into any treaty, alliance, or confederation; grant letters of marque and reprisal; coin money; emit bills of credit; make anything but gold and silver coin a tender in payment of debts; pass any bill of attainder, ex post facto law, or law impairing the obligation of contracts, or grant any title of nobility.

No State shall, without the consent of Congress, lay any imposts or duties on imports or exports, except what may be absolutely necessary for executing its inspection laws: and the net produce of all duties and imposts, laid by any State on imports or exports, shall be for the use of the treasury of the United States; and all such laws shall be subject to the revision and control of the Congress.

No State shall, without the consent of Congress, lay any duty of tonnage, keep troops or ships of war in time of peace, enter into any agreement or compact with another State, or with a foreign power, or engage in war, unless actually invaded, or in such imminent danger as will not admit of delay.

ARTICLE II

Section I

The executive power shall be vested in a President of the United States of America. He shall hold his office during the term of four years, and, together with the Vice-President, chosen for the same term, be elected as follows:

Each State shall appoint, in such manner as the legislature thereof may direct, a number of electors, equal to the whole number of Senators and Representatives to which the State may be entitled in the Congress; but no Senator or Representative, or person holding an office of trust or profit under the United States, shall be appointed an elector.

The electors shall meet in their respective States, and vote by ballot for two persons, of whom one at least shall not be an inhabitant of the same State with themselves. And they shall make a list of all the persons voted for, and of the number of votes for each; which list they shall sign and certify, and transmit sealed to the seat of government of the United States, directed to the President of the Senate. The President of the Senate shall, in the presence of the Senate and House of Representatives, open all the certificates, and the votes shall then be counted. The person having the greatest number of votes shall be the President, if such number be a majority of the whole number of electors appointed; and if there be more than one who have such majority, and have an equal number of votes, then the House of Representatives shall immediately choose by ballot one of them for President; and if no person have a majority, then from the five highest on the list said house shall in like manner choose the President. But in choosing the President the votes shall be taken by States, the representation from each State having one vote; a quorum for this purpose shall consist of a member or members from two-thirds of the States, and a majority of all the States shall be necessary to a choice. In every case, after the choice of the President, the person having the greatest number of votes of the electors shall be the Vice-President. But if there should remain two or more who have equal votes, the Senate shall choose from them by ballot the Vice-President.

The Congress may determine the time of choosing the electors and the day on which they shall give their votes; which day shall be the same throughout the United States.

No person except a natural-born citizen, *or a citizen of the United States at the time of the adoption of this Constitution,* shall be eligible to the office of President; neither shall any person be eligible to that office who shall not have attained to the age of thirty-five years, and been fourteen years a resident within the United States.

In case of the removal of the President from office or of his death, resignation, or inability to discharge the powers and duties of the said office, the same shall devolve on the Vice-President, and the Congress may by law provide for the case of removal, death, resignation, or inability, both of the President and Vice-President, declaring what officer shall then act as President, and such officer shall act accordingly, until the disability be removed, or a President shall be elected.

The President shall, at stated times, receive for his services a compensation, which shall neither be increased nor diminished during the period for which he shall have been elected, and he shall not receive within that period any other emolument from the United States, or any of them.

Before he enter on the execution of his office, he shall take the following oath or affirmation:—"I do solemnly swear (or affirm) that I will faithfully execute the office of the President of the United States, and will to the best of my ability preserve, protect and defend the Constitution of the United States."

Section II

The President shall be commander in chief of the army and navy of the United States, and of the militia of the several States, when called into the actual service of the United States; he may require the opinion, in writing, of the principal officer in each of the executive departments, upon any subject relating to the duties of their respective offices, and he shall have power to grant reprieves and pardons for offenses against the United States, except in cases of impeachment.

He shall have power, by and with the advice and consent of the Senate, to make treaties, provided two-thirds of the Senators present concur; and he shall nominate, and by and with the advice and consent of the Senate, shall appoint ambassadors, other public ministers and consuls, judges of the Supreme Court, and all other officers of the United States, whose appointments are not herein otherwise provided for, and which shall be established by law: but Congress may by law vest the appointment of such inferior officers, as they think proper, in the President alone, in the courts of law, or in the heads of departments.

The President shall have power to fill up all vacancies that may happen during the recess of the Senate, by granting commissions which shall expire at the end of their next session.

Section III

He shall from time to time give to the Congress information of the state of the Union, and recommend to their consideration such measures as he shall judge necessary and expedient; he may, on extraordinary occasions, convene both houses, or either of them, and in case of disagreement between them, with respect to the time of adjournment, he may adjourn them to such time as he shall think proper; he shall receive ambassadors and other public ministers; he shall take care that the laws be faithfully executed, and shall commission all the officers of the United States.

Section IV

The President, Vice-President and all civil officers of the United States shall be removed from office on impeachment for, and on conviction of, treason, bribery, or other high crimes and misdemeanors.

ARTICLE III

Section I

The judicial power of the United States shall be vested in one Supreme Court, and in such inferior courts as the Congress may from time to time ordain and establish. The judges, both of the Supreme and inferior courts, shall hold their offices during good behavior, and shall, at stated times, receive for their services a compensation which shall not be diminished during their continuance in office.

Section II

The judicial power shall extend to all cases, in law and equity, arising under this Constitution, the laws of the United States, and treaties made, or which shall be made, under their authority; — to all cases affecting ambassadors, other public ministers and consuls; — to all cases of admiralty and maritime jurisdiction; — to controversies to which the United States shall be a party; — to controversies between two or more States; — *between a State and citizens of another State;* — between citizens of different States; — between citizens of the same State claiming lands under grants of different States, and between a State, or the citizens thereof, and foreign states, citizens or subjects.

In all cases affecting ambassadors, other public ministers and consuls, and those in which a State shall be party, the Supreme Court shall have original jurisdiction. In all the other cases before mentioned, the Supreme Court shall have appellate jurisdiction, both as to law and fact, with such exceptions, and under such regulations, as the Congress shall make.

The trial of all crimes, except in cases of impeachment, shall be by jury; and such trial shall be held in the State where the said crimes shall have been committed; but when not committed within any State, the trial shall be at such place or places as the Congress may by law have directed.

Section III

Treason against the United States shall consist only in levying war against them, or in adhering to their enemies, giving them aid and comfort. No person shall be convicted of treason unless on the testimony of two witnesses to the same overt act, or on confession in open court.

The Congress shall have power to declare the punishment of treason, but no attainder of treason shall work corruption of blood, or forfeiture except during the life of the person attainted.

ARTICLE IV

Section I

Full faith and credit shall be given in each State to the public acts, records, and judicial proceedings of every other State. And the Congress may by general laws prescribe the manner in which such acts, records, and proceedings shall be proved, and the effect thereof.

Section II

The citizens of each State shall be entitled to all privileges and immunities of citizens in the several States.

A person charged in any State with treason, felony, or other crime, who shall flee from justice, and be found in another State, shall on demand of the executive authority of the State from which he fled, be delivered up, to be removed to the State having jurisdiction of the crime.

No person held to service or labor in one State, under the laws thereof, escaping into another, shall, in consequence of any law or regulation therein, be discharged from such service or labor, but shall be delivered up on claim of the party to whom such service or labor may be due.

Section III

New States may be admitted by the Congress into this Union; but no new State shall be formed or erected within the jurisdiction of any other State; nor any State be formed by the junction of two or more States, or parts of States, without the consent of the legislatures of the States concerned as well as of the Congress.

The Congress shall have power to dispose of and make all needful rules and regulations respecting the territory or other property belonging to the United States; and nothing in this Constitution shall be so construed as to prejudice any claims of the United States, or of any particular State.

Section IV

The United States shall guarantee to every State in this Union a republican form of government, and shall protect each of them against invasion; and on application of the legislature, or of the executive (when the legislature cannot be convened), against domestic violence.

ARTICLE V

The Congress, whenever two-thirds of both houses shall deem it necessary, shall propose amendments to this Constitution, or, on the application of the legislatures of two-thirds of the several States, shall call a convention for proposing amendments, which, in either case, shall be valid to all intents and purposes, as part of this Constitution, when ratified by the legislatures of three-fourths of the several States, or by conventions in three-fourths thereof, as the one or the other mode of ratification may be proposed by the Congress; provided *that no amendments which may be made prior to the year one thousand eight hundred and eight shall in any manner affect the first and fourth clauses in the ninth section of the first article;* and that no State, without its consent, shall be deprived of its equal suffrage in the Senate.

ARTICLE VI

All debts contracted and engagements entered into, before the adoption of this Constitution, shall be as valid against the United States under this Constitution, as under the Confederation.

This Constitution, and the laws of the United States which shall be made in pursuance thereof; and all treaties made, or which shall be made, under the authority of the United States, shall be the supreme law of the land; and the judges in every State shall be bound thereby, anything in the Constitution or laws of any State to the contrary notwithstanding.

The Senators and Representatives before mentioned, and the members of the several State legislatures, and all executive and judicial officers, both of the United States and of the several States, shall be bound by oath or affirmation to support this Constitution; but no religious test shall ever be required as a qualification to any office or public trust under the United States.

ARTICLE VII

The ratification of the conventions of nine States shall be sufficient for the establishment of this Constitution between the States so ratifying the same.

Done in Convention by the unanimous consent of the States present, the seventeenth day of September in the year of our Lord one thousand seven hundred and eighty-seven and of the Independence of the United States of America the twelfth. In witness whereof we have hereunto subscribed our names.

[Signed by]
G⁰ WASHINGTON
Presidt and Deputy from Virginia
[and thirty-eight others]

AMENDMENTS TO THE CONSTITUTION

ARTICLE I*

Congress shall make no law respecting an establishment of religion, or prohibiting the free exercise thereof; or abridging the freedom of speech, or of the press; or the right of the people peaceably to assemble, and to petition the government for a redress of grievances.

ARTICLE II

A well-regulated militia being necessary to the security of a free State, the right of the people to keep and bear arms shall not be infringed.

ARTICLE III

No soldier shall, in time of peace, be quartered in any house without the consent of the owner, nor in time of war, but in a manner to be prescribed by law.

ARTICLE IV

The right of the people to be secure in their persons, houses, papers, and effects, against unreasonable searches and seizures, shall not be violated, and no warrants shall issue but upon probable cause, supported by oath or affirmation, and particularly describing the place to be searched, and the persons or things to be seized.

ARTICLE V

No person shall be held to answer for a capital, or otherwise infamous crime, unless on a presentment or indictment of a grand jury, except in cases arising in the land or naval forces, or in the militia, when in actual service in time of war or public danger; nor shall any person be subject for the same offense to be twice put in jeopardy of life or limb; nor shall be compelled in any criminal case to be a witness against himself, nor be deprived of life, liberty, or property, without due process of law; nor shall private property be taken for public use without just compensation.

ARTICLE VI

In all criminal prosecutions, the accused shall enjoy the right to a speedy and public trial, by an impartial jury of the State and district wherein the crime shall have been committed, which district shall have been previously ascertained by law, and to be informed of the nature and cause of the accusation; to be confronted with the witnesses against him; to have compulsory process for obtaining witnesses in his favor, and to have the assistance of counsel for his defense.

ARTICLE VII

In suits at common law, where the value in controversy shall exceed twenty dollars, the right of trial by jury shall be preserved, and no fact tried by a jury shall be otherwise re-examined in any court of the United States, than according to the rules of the common law.

---

*The first ten Amendments (Bill of Rights) were adopted in 1791.

ARTICLE VIII

Excessive bail shall not be required, nor excessive fines imposed, nor cruel and unusual punishments inflicted.

ARTICLE IX

The enumeration in the Constitution, of certain rights, shall not be construed to deny or disparage others retained by the people.

ARTICLE X

The powers not delegated to the United States by the Constitution, nor prohibited by it to the States, are reserved to the States respectively, or to the people.

ARTICLE XI [Adopted 1798]

The judicial power of the United States shall not be construed to extend to any suit in law or equity, commenced or prosecuted against one of the United States by citizens of another State, or by citizens or subjects of any foreign state.

ARTICLE XII [Adopted 1804]

The electors shall meet in their respective States, and vote by ballot for President and Vice-President, one of whom, at least, shall not be an inhabitant of the same State with themselves; they shall name in their ballots the person voted for as President, and in distinct ballots the person voted for as Vice-President, and they shall make distinct lists of all persons voted for as President, and of all persons voted for as Vice-President, and of the number of votes for each, which lists they shall sign and certify, and transmit sealed to the seat of government of the United States, directed to the President of the Senate;—the President of the Senate shall, in the presence of the Senate and House of Representatives, open all the certificates and the votes shall then be counted;—the person having the greatest number of votes for President shall be the President, if such number be a majority of the whole number of electors appointed; and if no person have such majority, then from the persons having the highest numbers not exceeding three on the list of those voted for as President, the House of Representatives shall choose immediately, by ballot, the President. But in choosing the President, the votes shall be taken by States, the representation from each State having one vote; a quorum for this purpose shall consist of a member or member from two-thirds of the States, and a majority of all the States shall be necessary to a choice. And if the House of Representatives shall not choose a President whenever the right of choice shall devolve upon them, before *the fourth day of March* next following, then the Vice-President shall act as President, as in the case of the death or other constitutional disability of the President.

The person having the greatest number of votes as Vice-President shall be the Vice-President, if such number be a majority of the whole number of electors appointed; and if no person have a majority, then from the two highest numbers on the list the Senate shall choose the Vice-President; a quorum for the purpose shall consist of two-thirds of the whole number of Senators, and a majority of the whole number shall be necessary to a choice. But no person constitutionally ineligible to the office of President shall be eligible to that of Vice-President of the United States.

ARTICLE XIII [Adopted 1865]

1. Neither slavery nor involuntary servitude, except as a punishment for crime whereof the party shall have been duly convicted, shall exist within the United States, or any place subject to their jurisdiction.

2. Congress shall have power to enforce this article by appropriate legislation.

ARTICLE XIV [Adopted 1868]

1. All persons born or naturalized in the United States, and subject to the jurisdiction thereof, are citizens of the United States and of the State wherein they reside. No State shall make or enforce any law which shall abridge the privileges or immunities of citizens of the United States; nor shall any State deprive any person of life, liberty, or property, without due process of law; nor deny to any person within its jurisdiction the equal protection of the laws.

2. Representatives shall be apportioned among the several States according to their respective numbers, counting the whole number of persons in each State, excluding Indians not taxed. But when the right to vote at any election for the choice of Electors for President and Vice-President of the United States, Representatives in Congress, the executive and judicial officers of a State, or the members of the legislature thereof, is denied to any of the male inhabitants of such State, being twenty-one years of age and citizens of the United States, or in any way abridged, except for participation in rebellion, or other crime, the basis of representation therein shall be reduced in the proportion which the number of such male citizens shall bear to the whole number of male citizens twenty-one years of age in such State.

3. No person shall be a Senator or Representative in Congress, or Elector of President and Vice-President, or hold any office, civil or military, under the United States, or under any State, who, having previously taken an oath, as a member of Congress, or as an officer of the United States, or as a member of any State legislature, or as an executive or judicial officer of any State, to support the Constitution of the United States, shall have engaged in insurrection or rebellion against the same, or given aid or comfort to the enemies thereof. But Congress may, by a vote of two-thirds of each house, remove such disability.

4. The validity of the public debt of the United States, authorized by law, including debts incurred for payment of pensions and bounties for services in suppressing insurrection or rebellion, shall not be questioned. But neither the United States nor any State shall assume or pay any debt or obligation incurred in aid of insurrection or rebellion against the United States, or any claim for the loss or emancipation of any slave; but all such debts, obligations, and claims shall be held illegal and void.

5. The Congress shall have power to enforce, by appropriate legislation, the provisions of this article.

ARTICLE XV [Adopted 1870]

1. The right of citizens of the United States to vote shall not be denied or abridged by the United States or by any State on account of race, color, or previous condition of servitude.

2. The Congress shall have power to enforce this article by appropriate legislation.

ARTICLE XVI [Adopted 1913]

The Congress shall have power to lay and collect taxes on incomes, from whatever source derived, without apportionment among the several States, and without regard to any census or enumeration.

ARTICLE XVII [Adopted 1913]

1. The Senate of the United States shall be composed of two Senators from each State, elected by the people thereof, for six years; and each Senator shall have one vote. The electors in each State shall have the qualifications requisite for electors of [voters for] the most numerous branch of the State legislatures.

2. When vacancies happen in the representation of any State in the Senate, the executive authority of such State shall issue writs of election to fill such vacancies: Provided, that the Legislature of any State may empower the executive thereof to make temporary appointments until the people fill the vacancies by election as the Legislature may direct.

3. This amendment shall not be so construed as to affect the election or term of any Senator chosen before it becomes valid as part of the Constitution.

ARTICLE XVIII [Adopted 1919; Repealed 1933]

1. *After one year from the ratification of this article the manufacture, sale, or transportation of intoxicating liquors within, the importation thereof into, or the exportation thereof from the United States and all territory subject to the jurisdiction thereof, for beverage purposes, is hereby prohibited.*

2. *The Congress and the several States shall have concurrent power to enforce this article by appropriate legislation.*

3. *This article shall be inoperative unless it shall have been ratified as an amendment to the Constitution by the legislatures of the several States, as provided by the Constitution, within seven years from the date of the submission thereof to the States by the Congress.*

ARTICLE XIX [Adopted 1920]

1. The right of citizens of the United States to vote shall not be denied or abridged by the United States or by any State on account of sex.

2. The Congress shall have power to enforce this article by appropriate legislation.

ARTICLE XX [Adopted 1933]

1. The terms of the President and Vice-President shall end at noon on the 20th day of January, and the terms of Senators and Representatives at noon on the 3d day of January, of the years in which such terms would have ended if this article had not been ratified; and the terms of their successors shall then begin.

2. The Congress shall assemble at least once in every year, and such meeting shall begin at noon on the 3d day of January, unless they shall by law appoint a different day.

3. If, at the time fixed for the beginning of the term of the President, the President-elect

shall have died, the Vice-President-elect shall become President. If a President shall not have been chosen before the time fixed for the beginning of his term, or if the President-elect shall have failed to qualify, then the Vice-President-elect shall act as President until a President shall have qualified; and the Congress may by law provide for the case wherein neither a President-elect nor a Vice-President-elect shall have qualified, declaring who shall then act as President, or the manner in which one who is to act shall be selected, and such persons shall act accordingly until a President or Vice-President shall have qualified.

4. The Congress may by law provide for the case of the death of any of the persons from whom the House of Representatives may choose a President whenever the right of choice shall have devolved upon them, and for the case of the death of any of the persons from whom the Senate may choose a Vice-President whenever the right of choice shall have devolved upon them.

5. Sections 1 and 2 shall take effect on the 15th day of October following the ratification of this article.

6. This article shall be inoperative unless it shall have been ratified as an amendment to the Constitution by the Legislatures of three-fourths of the several States within seven years from the date of its submission.

ARTICLE XXI [Adopted 1933]

1. The eighteenth article of amendment to the Constitution of the United States is hereby repealed.

2. The transportation or importation into any State, Territory, or Possession of the United States for delivery or use therein of intoxicating liquors, in violation of the laws thereof, is hereby prohibited.

3. This article shall be inoperative unless it shall have been ratified as an amendment to the Constitution by conventions in the several States, as provided in the Constitution, within seven years from the date of submission thereof to the States by the Congress.

ARTICLE XXII [Adopted 1951]

1. No person shall be elected to the office of President more than twice, and no person who has held the office of President, or acted as President, for more than two years of a term to which some other person was elected President shall be elected to the office of President more than once. But this article shall not apply to any person holding the office of President when this article was proposed by the Congress, and shall not prevent any person who may be holding the office of President, or acting as President, during the term within which this article becomes operative from holding the office of President or acting as President during the remainder of such term.

2. This article shall be inoperative unless it shall have been ratified as an amendment to the Constitution by the legislatures of three-fourths of the several States within seven years from the date of its submission to the States by the Congress.

ARTICLE XXIII [Adopted 1961]

1. The District constituting the seat of Government of the United States shall appoint in such manner as the Congress may direct:
   A number of electors of President and Vice-President equal to the whole number of

Senators and Representatives in Congress to which the District would be entitled if it were a State, but in no event more than the least populous State; they shall be in addition to those appointed by the States, but they shall be considered for the purposes of the election of President and Vice-President, to be electors appointed by a State; and they shall meet in the District and perform such duties as provided by the twelfth article of amendment.

2. The Congress shall have the power to enforce this article by appropriate legislation.

ARTICLE XXIV [Adopted 1964]

1. The right of citizens of the United States to vote in any primary or other election for President or Vice-President, for electors for President or Vice-President, or for Senator or Representative in Congress, shall not be denied or abridged by the United States or any State by reason of failure to pay any poll tax or other tax.

2. The Congress shall have the power to enforce this article by appropriate legislation.

ARTICLE XXV [Adopted 1967]

1. In case of the removal of the President from office or of his death or resignation, the Vice President shall become President.

2. Whenever there is a vacancy in the office of the Vice President, the President shall nominate a Vice President who shall take office upon confirmation by a majority vote of both Houses of Congress.

3. Whenever the President transmits to the President pro tempore of the Senate and the Speaker of the House of Representatives his written declaration that he is unable to discharge the powers and duties of his office, and until he transmits to them a written declaration to the contrary, such powers and duties shall be discharged by the Vice President as Acting President.

4. Whenever the Vice President and a majority of either the principal officers of the executive departments or of such other body as Congress may by law provide, transmit to the President pro tempore of the Senate and the Speaker of the House of Representatives their written declaration that the President is unable to discharge the powers and duties of his office, the Vice President shall immediately assume the powers and duties of the office as Acting President.

Thereafter, when the President transmits to the President pro tempore of the Senate and the Speaker of the House of Representatives his written declaration that no inability exists, he shall resume the powers and duties of his office unless the Vice President and a majority of either the principal officers of the executive department[s] or of such other body as Congress may by law provide, transmit within four days to the President pro tempore of the Senate and the Speaker of the House of Representatives their written declaration that the President is unable to discharge the powers and duties of his office. Thereupon Congress shall decide the issue, assembling within forty-eight hours for that purpose if not in session. If the Congress, within twenty-one days after receipt of the latter written declaration, or, if Congress is not in session, within twenty-one days after Congress is required to assemble, determines by two-thirds vote of both Houses that the President is unable to discharge the powers and duties of his office, the Vice President shall continue to discharge the same as Acting President; otherwise, the President shall resume the powers and duties of his office.

ARTICLE XXVI [Adopted 1971]

1. The right of citizens of the United States, who are eighteen years of age or older, to vote shall not be denied or abridged by the United States or by any State on account of age.

2. The Congress shall have power to enforce this article by appropriate legislation.

ARTICLE XXVII [Sent to States, 1972]

1. Equality of rights under the law shall not be denied or abridged by the United States or by any State on account of sex.

2. The Congress shall have the power to enforce, by appropriate legislation, the provisions of this article.

3. This amendment shall take effect two years after the date of ratification.

Growth of U. S. Population and Area

CENSUS	POPULATION OF CONTIGUOUS U. S.	PERCENT OF INCREASE OVER PRECEDING CENSUS	LAND AREA, SQUARE MILES	POPULATION PER SQUARE MILE
1790	3,929,214		867,980	4.5
1800	5,308,483	35.1	867,980	6.1
1810	7,239,881	36.4	1,685,865	4.3
1820	9,638,453	33.1	1,753,588	5.5
1830	12,866,020	33.5	1,753,588	7.3
1840	17,069,453	32.7	1,753,588	9.7
1850	23,191,876	35.9	2,944,337	7.9
1860	31,443,321	35.6	2,973,965	10.6
1870	39,818,449	26.6	2,973,965	13.4
1880	50,155,783	26.0	2,973,965	16.9
1890	62,947,714	25.5	2,973,965	21.2
1900	75,994,575	20.7	2,974,159	25.6
1910	91,972,266	21.0	2,973,890	30.9
1920	105,710,620	14.9	2,973,776	35.5
1930	122,775,046	16.1	2,977,128	41.2
1940	131,669,275	7.2	2,977,128	44.2
1950	150,697,361	14.5	2,974,726*	50.7
†1960	178,464,236	18.4	2,974,726	59.9
1970	204,765,770 (including Alaska and Hawaii)			

*As remeasured in 1940.

†Not including Alaska (pop. 226,167) and Hawaii (632,772).

*Presidential Elections**

ELECTION	CANDIDATES	PARTIES	POPULAR VOTE	ELECTORAL VOTE
1789	**GEORGE WASHINGTON**	No party designations		69
	John Adams			34
	Minor Candidates			35
1792	**GEORGE WASHINGTON**	No party designations		132
	John Adams			77
	George Clinton			50
	Minor Candidates			5
1796	**JOHN ADAMS**	Federalist		71
	Thomas Jefferson	Democratic-Republican		68
	Thomas Pinckney	Federalist		59
	Aaron Burr	Democratic-Republican		30
	Minor Candidates			48
1800	**THOMAS JEFFERSON**	Democratic-Republican		73
	Aaron Burr	Democratic-Republican		73
	John Adams	Federalist		65
	Charles C. Pinckney	Federalist		64
	John Jay	Federalist		1
1804	**THOMAS JEFFERSON**	Democratic-Republican		162
	Charles C. Pinckney	Federalist		14
1808	**JAMES MADISON**	Democratic-Republican		122
	Charles C. Pinckney	Federalist		47
	George Clinton	Democratic-Republican		6
1812	**JAMES MADISON**	Democratic-Republican		128
	DeWitt Clinton	Federalist		89
1816	**JAMES MONROE**	Democratic-Republican		183
	Rufus King	Federalist		34
1820	**JAMES MONROE**	Democratic-Republican		231
	John Q. Adams	Independent Republican		1
1824	**JOHN Q. ADAMS** (Min.)†	Democratic-Republican	108,740	84
	Andrew Jackson	Democratic-Republican	153,544	99
	William H. Crawford	Democratic-Republican	46,618	41
	Henry Clay	Democratic-Republican	47,136	37
1828	**ANDREW JACKSON**	Democratic	647,286	178
	John Q Adams	National Republican	508,064	83
1832	**ANDREW JACKSON**	Democratic	687,502	219
	Henry Clay	National Republican	530,189	49
	William Wirt	Anti-Masonic	33,108	7
	John Floyd	National Republican		11
1836	**MARTIN VAN BUREN**	Democratic	762,678	170
	William H. Harrison	Whig		73
	Hugh L. White	Whig	736,656	26
	Daniel Webster	Whig		14
	W. P. Mangum	Whig		11

*Candidates receiving less than 1% of the popular vote are omitted. Before the 12th Amendment (1804) the Electoral College voted for two presidential candidates, and the runner-up became Vice-President. Basic figures are taken primarily from *Historical Statistics of the United States, 1789–1945* (1949), pp. 288–290; *Historical Statistics of the United States, Colonial Times to 1957* (1960), pp. 682–683; and *Statistical Abstract of the United States, 1969* (1969), pp. 355–357.

†"Min." indicates minority President—one receiving less than 50% of all popular votes.

Presidential Elections (Contd.)

ELECTION	CANDIDATES	PARTIES	POPULAR VOTE	ELECTORAL VOTE
1840	WILLIAM H. HARRISON	Whig	1,275,016	234
	Martin Van Buren	Democratic	1,129,102	60
1844	JAMES K. POLK (Min.)*	Democratic	1,337,243	170
	Henry Clay	Whig	1,299,062	105
	James G. Birney	Liberty	62,300	
1848	ZACHARY TAYLOR (Min.)*	Whig	1,360,099	163
	Lewis Cass	Democratic	1,220,544	127
	Martin Van Buren	Free Soil	291,263	
1852	FRANKLIN PIERCE	Democratic	1,601,274	254
	Winfield Scott	Whig	1,386,580	42
	John P. Hale	Free Soil	155,825	
1856	JAMES BUCHANAN (Min.)*	Democratic	1,838,169	174
	John C. Frémont	Republican	1,341,264	114
	Millard Fillmore	American	874,534	8
1860	ABRAHAM LINCOLN (Min.)*	Republican	1,866,452	180
	Stephen A Douglas	Democratic	1,375,157	12
	John C. Breckinridge	Democratic	847,953	72
	John Bell	Constitutional Union	590,631	39
1864	ABRAHAM LINCOLN	Union	2,213,665	212
	George B. McClellan	Democratic	1,802,237	21
1868	ULYSSES S. GRANT	Republican	3,012,833	214
	Horatio Seymour	Democratic	2,703,249	80
1872	ULYSSES S. GRANT	Republican	3,597,132	286
	Horace Greeley	Democratic and Liberal Republican	2,834,125	66
1876	RUTHERFORD B. HAYES (Min.)*	Republican	4,036,298	185
	Samuel J. Tilden	Democratic	4,300,590	184
1880	JAMES A. GARFIELD (Min.)*	Republican	4,454,416	214
	Winfield S. Hancock	Democratic	4,444,952	155
	James B. Weaver	Greenback-Labor	308,578	
1884	GROVER CLEVELAND (Min.)*	Democratic	4,874,986	219
	James G. Blaine	Republican	4,851,981	182
	Benjamin F. Butler	Greenback-Labor	175,370	
	John P. St. John	Prohibition	150,369	
1888	BENJAMIN HARRISON (Min.)*	Republican	5,439,853	233
	Grover Cleveland	Democratic	5,540,309	168
	Clinton B. Fisk	Prohibition	249,506	
	Anson J. Streeter	Union Labor	146,935	
1892	GROVER CLEVELAND (Min.)*	Democratic	5,556,918	277
	Benjamin Harrison	Republican	5,176,108	145
	James B. Weaver	People's	1,041,028	22
	John Bidwell	Prohibition	264,133	
1896	WILLIAM MCKINLEY	Republican	7,104,779	271
	William J. Bryan	Democratic	6,502,925	176
1900	WILLIAM MCKINLEY	Republican	7,207,923	292
	William J. Bryan	Democratic; Populist	6,358,133	155
	John C. Woolley	Prohibition	208,914	

*"Min." indicates minority President—one receiving less than 50% of all popular votes.

Presidential Elections (Contd.)

ELECTION	CANDIDATES	PARTIES	POPULAR VOTE	ELECTORAL VOTE
1904	THEODORE ROOSEVELT	Republican	7,623,486	336
	Alton B. Parker	Democratic	5,077,911	140
	Eugene V. Debs	Socialist	402,283	
	Silas C. Swallow	Prohibition	258,536	
1908	WILLIAM H. TAFT	Republican	7,678,908	321
	William J. Bryan	Democratic	6,409,104	162
	Eugene V. Debs	Socialist	420,793	
	Eugene W. Chafin	Prohibition	253,840	
1912	WOODROW WILSON (Min.)*	Democratic	6,293,454	435
	Theodore Roosevelt	Progressive	4,119,538	88
	William H. Taft	Republican	3,484,980	8
	Eugene V. Debs	Socialist	900,672	
	Eugene W. Chafin	Prohibition	206,275	
1916	WOODROW WILSON (Min.)*	Democratic	9,129,606	277
	Charles E. Hughes	Republican	8,538,221	254
	A. L. Benson	Socialist	585,113	
	J. F. Hanly	Prohibition	220,506	
1920	WARREN G. HARDING	Republican	16,152,200	404
	James M. Cox	Democratic	9,147,353	127
	Eugene V. Debs	Socialist	919,799	
	P. P. Christensen	Farmer-Labor	265,411	
1924	CALVIN COOLIDGE	Republican	15,725,016	382
	John W. Davis	Democratic	8,386,503	136
	Robert M. La Follette	Progressive	4,822,856	13
1928	HERBERT C. HOOVER	Republican	21,391,381	444
	Alfred E. Smith	Democratic	15,016,443	87
1932	FRANKLIN D. ROOSEVELT	Democratic	22,821,857	472
	Herbert C. Hoover	Republican	15,761,841	59
	Norman Thomas	Socialist	881,951	
1936	FRANKLIN D. ROOSEVELT	Democratic	27,751,597	523
	Alfred M. Landon	Republican	16,679,583	8
	William Lemke	Union, etc.	882,479	
1940	FRANKLIN D. ROOSEVELT	Democratic	27,244,160	449
	Wendell L. Wilkie	Republican	22,305,198	82
1944	FRANKLIN D. ROOSEVELT	Democratic	25,602,504	432
	Thomas E. Dewey	Republican	22,006,285	99
1948	HARRY S TRUMAN (Min.)*	Democratic	24,105,812	303
	Thomas E. Dewey	Republican	21,970,065	189
	J. Strom Thurmond	States' Rights Democratic	1,169,063	39
	Henry A. Wallace	Progressive	1,157,172	
1952	DWIGHT D. EISENHOWER	Republican	33,936,234	442
	Adlai E. Stevenson	Democratic	27,314,992	89
1956	DWIGHT D. EISENHOWER	Republican	35,590,472	457
	Adlai E. Stevenson	Democratic	26,022,752	73
1960	JOHN F. KENNEDY (Min.)*	Democratic	34,226,731	303
	Richard M. Nixon	Republican	34,108,157	219

*"Min." indicates minority President—one receiving less than 50% of all popular votes.

Presidential Elections (Contd.)

ELECTION	CANDIDATES	PARTIES	POPULAR VOTE	ELECTORAL VOTE
1964	LYNDON B. JOHNSON	Democratic	43,129,484	486
	Barry M. Goldwater	Republican	27,178,188	52
1968	RICHARD M. NIXON (Min.)*	Republican	31,785,480	301
	Hubert H. Humphrey, Jr.	Democratic	31,275,166	191
	George C. Wallace	American Independent	9,906,473	46
1972	RICHARD M. NIXON	Republican	45,767,218	520
	George S. McGovern	Democratic	28,357,668	17
1976**	JIMMY CARTER	Democratic	40,276,040	297
	Gerald Ford	Republican	38,532,630	241

*"Min." indicates minority President—one receiving less than 50% of all popular votes.
**Unofficial count from *The New York Times*, November 5, 1976.

Presidents and Vice-Presidents

TERM	PRESIDENT	VICE-PRESIDENT
1789–1793	George Washington	John Adams
1793–1797	George Washington	John Adams
1797–1801	John Adams	Thomas Jefferson
1801–1805	Thomas Jefferson	Aaron Burr
1805–1809	Thomas Jefferson	George Clinton
1809–1813	James Madison	George Clinton (d. 1812)
1813–1817	James Madison	Elbridge Gerry (d. 1814)
1817–1821	James Monroe	Daniel D. Tompkins
1821–1825	James Monroe	Daniel D. Tompkins
1825–1829	John Quincy Adams	John C. Calhoun
1829–1833	Andrew Jackson	John C. Calhoun (resigned 1832)
1833–1837	Andrew Jackson	Martin Van Buren
1837–1841	Martin Van Buren	Richard M. Johnson
1841–1845	William H. Harrison (d. 1841)	John Tyler
	John Tyler	
1845–1849	James K. Polk	George M. Dallas
1849–1853	Zachary Taylor (d. 1850)	Millard Fillmore
	Millard Fillmore	
1853–1857	Franklin Pierce	William R. D. King (d. 1853)
1857–1861	James Buchanan	John C. Breckinridge
1861–1865	Abraham Lincoln	Hannibal Hamlin
1865–1869	Abraham Lincoln (d. 1865)	Andrew Johnson
	Andrew Johnson	
1869–1873	Ulysses S. Grant	Schuyler Colfax
1873–1877	Ulysses S. Grant	Henry Wilson (d. 1875)
1877–1881	Rutherford B. Hayes	William A. Wheeler

Presidents and Vice-Presidents (Contd.)

TERM	PRESIDENT	VICE-PRESIDENT
1881–1885	James A. Garfield (d. 1881)	Chester A. Arthur
	Chester A. Arthur	
1885–1889	Grover Cleveland	Thomas A. Hendricks (d. 1885)
1889–1893	Benjamin Harrison	Levi P. Morton
1893–1897	Grover Cleveland	Adlai E. Stevenson
1897–1901	William McKinley	Garret A. Hobart (d. 1899)
1901–1905	William McKinley (d. 1901)	Theodore Roosevelt
	Theodore Roosevelt	
1905–1909	Theodore Roosevelt	Charles W. Fairbanks
1909–1913	William H. Taft	James S. Sherman (d. 1912)
1913–1917	Woodrow Wilson	Thomas R. Marshall
1917–1921	Woodrow Wilson	Thomas R. Marshall
1921–1925	Warren G. Harding (d. 1923)	Calvin Coolidge
	Calvin Coolidge	
1925–1929	Calvin Coolidge	Charles G. Dawes
1929–1933	Herbert C. Hoover	Charles Curtis
1933–1937	Franklin D. Roosevelt	John N. Garner
1937–1941	Franklin D. Roosevelt	John N. Garner
1941–1945	Franklin D. Roosevelt	Henry A. Wallace
1945–1949	Franklin D. Roosevelt (d. 1945)	Harry S Truman
	Harry S Truman	
1949–1953	Harry S Truman	Alben W. Barkley
1953–1957	Dwight D. Eisenhower	Richard M. Nixon
1957–1961	Dwight D. Eisenhower	Richard M. Nixon
1961–1965	John F. Kennedy (d. 1963)	Lyndon B. Johnson
	Lyndon B. Johnson	
1965–1969	Lyndon B Johnson	Hubert H. Humphrey, Jr.
1969–1974	Richard M. Nixon (resigned 1974)	Spiro T. Agnew (resigned 1973); Gerald R. Ford
1974–1976	Gerald R. Ford	Nelson Rockefeller
1976–	Jimmy Carter	Walter Mondale

Index